Mastering Aldus PhotoStyler

Sybil and Emil Ihrig

BANTAM BOOKS
NEW YORK • TORONTO • LONDON • SYDNEY • AUCKLAND

Mastering Aldus PhotoStyler

A Bantam Book/April 1992

Butterfly photo: Myron Dorf
Earth photo: Photori
Dunes photo: Masterfile
Cover art composed by Michael Johnson using Aldus PhotoStyler
Interior design by Emil Ihrig with Nancy Sugihara
Produced by Sybil Ihrig of VersaTech Associates, Escondido, California

ISBN 0-553-35453-1

Published simultaneously in the United States and Canada

Bantam Books are published by Bantam Books, a division of Bantam Doubleday Dell Publishing Group, Inc. Its trademark, consisting of the words "Bantam Books" and the portrayal of a rooster, is Registered in the U.S. Patent and Trademark Office and in other countries. Marca Registrada Bantam Books, 666 Fifth Avenue, New York, New York, 10103

PRINTED IN THE UNITED STATES OF AMERICA

0 9 8 7 6 5 4 3 2 1

For Richard Hinman, a memorable mentor

Foreword

Aldus PhotoStyler, simply put, empowers people who create printed or electronic materials to prepare and enhance photographic images on the desktop. Equipped with PhotoStyler and a relatively low-cost personal computer, you and millions of other PC users now have access to much of the power and sophistication that was once found only in high-cost prepress equipment or dedicated graphics computers.

Everything around us provides evidence that photographs can enrich any form of communication: publications and illustrations, training and analysis, advertising and multimedia—the list is endless. We've developed PhotoStyler so that you, too, can capture the power of photography for stand-alone images or as part of other materials. You can use it to enhance and retouch photographs for magazines; create images from scratch or composites for fine art and instructional materials; and modify images for presentations and informational kiosks. The more you work with Aldus PhotoStyler, the more uses you'll discover for it.

The book you hold is a complete, practical reference to using this exciting program. Sybil and Emil Ihrig do a fine job of explaining both the basic and advanced features of PhotoStyler. They show the new user how to get started in image processing and thoroughly explain how to use PhotoStyler in a professional environment. I can't think of better guides than they to help you get the most from this revolutionary technology.

If you're new to image processing on the PC, welcome to an exciting new world. If you're already an experienced PhotoStyler user, this book will aid you in applying those skills even more creatively.

Have fun! And be sure to send us samples of your best work!

Paul Brainerd
President, Aldus Corporation
Seattle, WA

Preface

All right, we admit it—we have an obsession with thoroughness. We'd like this book to be all things to all PhotoStyler users: a how-to for the uninitiated, a cookbook for intermediate and advanced users, a real-world guide for the practicing desktop publisher or graphics professional, and a source of creative inspiration for the artistically inclined. As a writer/digital artist team, we're accustomed to practicing what we preach, and we want current and prospective PhotoStyler users to benefit from our experience.

Whys and Wherefores

PhotoStyler first crossed our path in the winter of 1991, several months before its initial release by U-Lead Systems, Inc. We had been searching for years for a software application that would enable Emil Ihrig to enhance his color photography creatively on the PC and still permit professional-quality print output. And suddenly, here it was—bug-free, powerful, and easy to use. A revelation! From that moment on, we knew we had to write a book about this groundbreaking package.

We also knew that PhotoStyler users would come from a variety of professional backgrounds—desktop publishers, graphic designers, illustrators, photographers, and writers, to name a few—and that we'd need to provide information that each group could apply in the real world. The fact that desktop color was new on the PC added yet another challenging but enjoyable task to our goal of making PhotoStyler's unparalleled image creation and enhancement power accessible.

Last but not least, we had a large number of high-quality images at our disposal, thanks to Emil's twenty years of experience in editorial photography. We knew it would be easy to fill our book with attractive illustrations of image editing techniques that could provide graphic inspiration to PhotoStyler users at every level of expertise. If there's any inherent message in Aldus PhotoStyler, it's that no digitized image need ever be uninspiring again!

What's in It For You

We've organized this book in a way that will make it easy for users of all types to find the information they need quickly.

- Beginning and intermediate users will find the organization of chapters in tune with their usual working habits. We start by introducing PhotoStyler's user interface, go on to tackle scanning and input issues, and then delve into image correction, editing, special effects, and composition techniques. Output, whether to print, slide, or other media, comes at the end of the project; but we supply plenty of tips throughout the book on preparing your image for stunning output right from the start. We also include a number of hands-on exercises to try on your own.
- Advanced users will appreciate the numerous tips we supply for exploiting many not-so-obvious PhotoStyler editing and enhancement techniques. Practical information on input, output, and color will be welcome, too, as will the multitude of example illustrations we provide in both grayscale and color. The PhotoStyler Gallery includes samples of images by practicing PhotoStyler professionals who are using the package in many different applications. If you're interested in maximizing PhotoStyler's speed under Windows, Appendix A will provide helpful suggestions.
- And for those who would rather look at pictures than read, we've included workable illustrations for almost every technique mentioned. We also designed the book so you can find references to tools, hidden submenu and dialog box menu options, notes, tips, and cautionary remarks at a glance. PhotoStyler is icon-based, and so is our book.

Conventions Used in This Book

We've employed several typographical and visual conventions in this book that should shorten both your software learning curve and the amount of time you spend hunting for information. The most important of these conventions are the use of italics and of icons or other visual information.

Italics Italics are used when a technical term is used and explained in context for the first time in a chapter. Example: *Dot gain* is a condition in which halftone dots print larger than they should, resulting in a darker image, a muddying of ink colors, and reduced image contrast.

We also use italics to highlight keywords in some bulleted lists. For example:

- The *HSB Counterclockwise* color model generates a gradient fill transition by changing the hue, saturation and brightness (HSB) values that fall between the start and end colors.

Icons and Other Small Visuals In the white space to the left of the text, you'll occasionally see icons, submenus, or other small visuals. These visuals are elements of the PhotoStyler interface that are too small to include in a separate figure, yet too functionally important to describe in words only. You'll encounter three different types of visuals:

- Tool icons from the Paint or Select Palette, or small areas of the PhotoStyler application window that contain important information

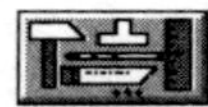

- Elements of dialog boxes that have important image editing functions, such as command buttons or the toolbox menu icon shown here; other small PhotoStyler interface elements

Expand... Ctrl+E
Border...
Soft Edge...
Export Mask...
Import Mask...
Hide Marquee Ctrl+H

- Submenus of main menu commands, or pop-up menus that are hidden inside tool palettes or dialog boxes

Our feeling is that your ability to see these items as they are mentioned will help reinforce their function and serve as a handy mnemonic aid.

We hope you'll find using this book enjoyable as well as instructive.

Acknowledgments

PhotoStyler is not an island unto itself. It links users to a rich new world of PC-based desktop color, including input devices, output devices, and software solutions. We're grateful to the many individuals and corporations who helped us bring together "the larger picture" and who provided technical and informational assistance for the production of the book.

First, we'd like to thank Michael Roney, our editor at Bantam, for his faith in and initial support of this project. His diplomacy, helpfulness in providing connections, and down-to-earth approach to bookmaking helped reduce the stress of completing an ambitious undertaking. Thanks also to Kenzi and Nancy Sugihara for their cooperation and support. Maureen Drexel deserves special commendation for her efficient coordination of the production process. And let's not forget Janice "Quality Control" Borzendowski, whose attention to often overlooked details rounded out many minor imperfections.

For technical information regarding PhotoStyler's features and their implications, we'd like to express our appreciation to Raymond Samson at Microtek, to LiMing Chen of U-Lead Systems and Mike Feng of Marstek, and to Sheldon Fisher and Russ DeVerniero at Aldus. Liaison to the developers and to Aldus would have been difficult to maintain without the ongoing coordination efforts of Rosemary Bach and Rod Bauer, both of whom went out of their way to smooth our path. Rod, you really went the extra mile!

Many thanks to Michelle Hammond at Microtek, to the Electronic Imaging Group at Nikon, and to STAC Electronics, Nisca, Inc., and TrueVision for loaning or donating equipment and software. For technical information regarding their technologies and products, we also want to thank Agfa Corporation, LaserMaster, QMS, Opta, MOST, Inc., Kodak, and Polaroid Corporation. Thanks also to Linotype-Hell, who kindly provided fonts for the production of the book.

For information on a wide range of technical, legal, and other subjects related to desktop color, input, and output, we're grateful to Greg Stone of STATS, Dan Caldwell, Jerry Anderson at Headline Graphics, the pros at SlideMasters, Agfa Corporation, Nisca, Inc., Peter Karlen, and Michael Kieran.

And very special thanks go to Jim Elder at Spring ACI and to Greg Stone at STATS for nursing our color pages and halftones so carefully.

Contents

2 The PhotoStyler Environment 13

3 Up and Running 29

6 Managing Image Display 115

Part III: ENHANCING, EDITING, AND RETOUCHING IMAGES

7 Working with Color and Grayscale Values 137

Appendixes

Part I:

DISCOVERING ALDUS PHOTOSTYLER

1

Image Processing Basics

Until recently, all graphics packages for IBM-compatible computers fell into one of two camps: drawing software or paint programs. If your job was to create "serious" artwork for print or other media, drawing software was your only credible choice. You could resize pictures created in a drawing program without distorting them, or transfer pictures between computers without worrying about how compatible the display resolutions might be. If your artwork was destined for print media, you could even use your drawing package to prepare professional-quality color separations. "Paint" programs, on the other hand, let you do none of these things. They were fun, yes, but awfully limiting, and not to be taken seriously.

The advent of Aldus PhotoStyler heralds a new level of sophistication in *image processing*, a type of software that you *can* take seriously for professional use in publishing, graphic design, and presentation work. Aldus PhotoStyler may have its roots in yesterday's paint packages, but it has transcended those roots to become something far more sophisticated and powerful. Never again will you have to discard a flawed scanned photograph, clip art sample, video capture image, or picture from a paint application. Using PhotoStyler's precise control over color, special effects, and image composition, you can rework any image and turn it into something more perfect or more imaginative than the original. If you prefer, you can create original artwork in the best "paintbox" tradition, but without having to worry about the hardware and output limitations of the past. Best of all, PhotoStyler gives you access to professional-quality color and grayscale printing that no paint software of yesteryear could ever match.

This book will help you discover PhotoStyler's versatile capabilities and make your latent creativity take flight. If you're new to this type of software, the next section will introduce you to the wonders of image processing. Later sections of this chapter suggest an image processing "game plan" that will result in consistently high quality for all the images with which you work.

What's Image Processing?

Data processing, forms processing, food processing: these terms sound like repetitive, dull assembly-line operations. Image processing, though, is highly creative and a great deal more fun than most of the other "processings" in human experience. Browse through the full-color Gallery section of this book for examples of just how creative image processing can be.

Briefly, *image processing* encompasses all the operations you can perform on a continuous-tone image to make it look its best at its final destination. A *continuous-tone* digital image is any bitmapped (pixel-based) graphic, whether it comes from a photograph, scanned artwork, paint program, clip art package, or screen or video capture. The most common operations you'll encounter in image processing are:

- *Input*—Where do you obtain your image, and how do you get it into the computer?
- *Image correction and enhancement*—It's often important to correct the colors or grays in the digital image so that they match the original. You can also create some exciting special effects by manipulating color or Grayscale values.
- *Selection and masking*—Usually, you'll want to mark specific areas of an image so that your editing operations won't affect the entire picture.
- *Retouching*—If you're working with photos, you may want to remove flaws or alter fine details to make images look more perfect than they do in reality. Some of the tools in PhotoStyler's Paint Palette perform traditional retouching functions such as smudging, lightening, or darkening. You can also "clone" parts of an image.

- *Painting*—Use the Airbrush, Paintbrush, Pencil, Line, Bucket Fill, or Gradient Fill tools in PhotoStyler's Paint Palette to paint portions of an image.
- *Editing image composition*—Alter the content of an image by merging elements of two or more images, defining unique patterns, or cutting and pasting within an image. Painting and image composition are among the most creative stages in image processing.
- *Output*—Print the image, export it to your page layout program, prepare color separations, or ready the digital image for a printer or slide service bureau.

You'll become proficient in each of these skills by the time you've completed this book.

PhotoStyler: A New Era in Image Processing

Think of PhotoStyler as a high-powered *electronic darkroom* that you can use not only with photographs, but with other types of bitmapped artwork as well. PhotoStyler's advanced features have earned it a position as the industry leader in PC-based image processing. Consider these capabilities:

- *Multiple-image display and editing*—As shown in Figure 1–1, you can display and edit more than one image at a time, with each image in a different magnification or view. Defining custom patterns or cutting and pasting between images is easier when multiple images are open.
- *Device-independent support for 24-bit color or 256 gray shades*—Store a file as a Grayscale (256 gray shades) or True Color (16 million colors) image, even if your display adapter allows you to see only 256 colors or just black and white. You'll be able to print or output high-quality color work, regardless of the limitations of your personal hardware. What you get is better than what you see!
- *Image correction power*—Remove noise and correct color inaccuracies introduced by a scanner or other input device. You can even specify precisely which colors or gray tones to include in the digital image. PhotoStyler's monitor calibration controls help you match the original undigitized image to the one you see on your computer screen.

Figure 1-1. Multiple document windows

- *Fully customizable Painting and Selection tools*—PhotoStyler's "floating palettes" contain many intuitive tools for selecting parts of an image and retouching or painting a picture. One or more customizable options for each tool let you define a personalized image editing style.
- *Advanced image composition techniques*—Cut and paste within a single image or between different images, define custom patterns and gradient fills, or "clone" areas of an image. The possibilities are endless.
- *Special-effects filters*—PhotoStyler includes many predefined "filters" that apply specific visual effects to an image or selected area. As an example, Figure 1–2 shows an original photo and the same photo after the Emboss filter has been applied to it. A built-in filter editor lets you (or third-party developers) supply a virtually limitless number of additional filters.
- *Process color separation*—Desktop color separation of bitmaps used to be an impossibility on the PC platform, which is one reason why professional designers preferred drawing software. But with PhotoStyler, not only can you separate color images into process color component channels; you can *edit* those channels as separate images, too. PhotoStyler gives you precise control over halftone generation and lets you customize settings to obtain best results for different printers, inks, and paper stocks.

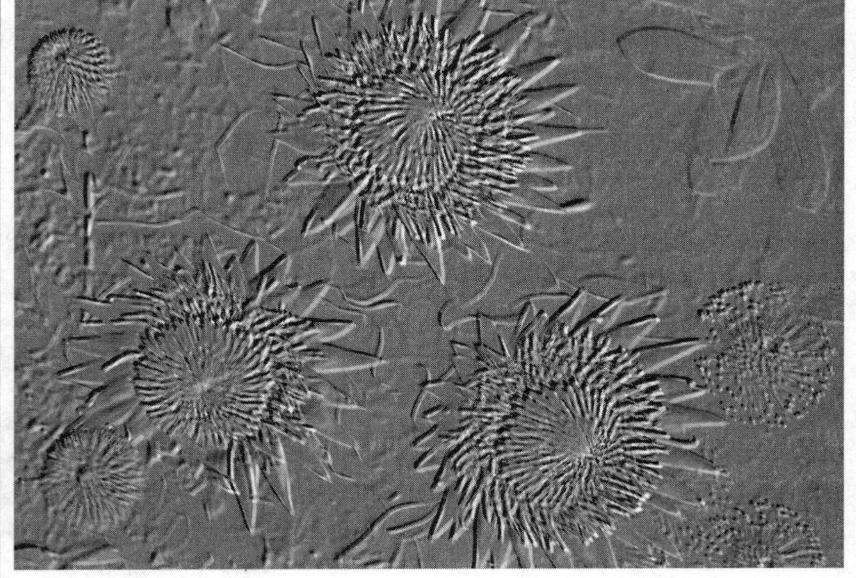

Figure 1-2.

An example of Emboss filter special effects

- *Modular program design*—The structure of PhotoStyler permits the addition of "plug-in" files by users and third-party developers. This means that you can add new scanner drivers, color and gradient fill palettes, custom brush shapes, fill patterns, special-effects filters, and printer calibration curves. The result is a package that you can tailor to your individual style and working methods.

With so much power at your fingertips, it's tempting to lose yourself in experimentation. That's why we've developed a basic PhotoStyler "game plan," a road map that will guide you to create successful final images without detours or unpleasant surprises.

A PhotoStyler Game Plan

The "process" of image processing is full of twists and turns. Many choices are available to you, but not all of them will enhance your image or result in pleasing output. To navigate the path successfully, it's important always to be mindful of the use to which you will put your image. Your goal will suggest important choices about input, editing, and output. For example, photographs for print media, fine art illustrations, and presentation graphics all require a different handling of images.

Until PhotoStyler becomes second nature to you, we suggest following a specific sequence of steps each time you edit an image. Figure 1–3 represents this sequence.

Obtaining a "Raw" Image (Chapter 4)

Before you can edit an image, you must bring it into your computer using an *input source*. Scanners, video capture boards, clip art packages,

Figure 1-3.

The image processing game plan

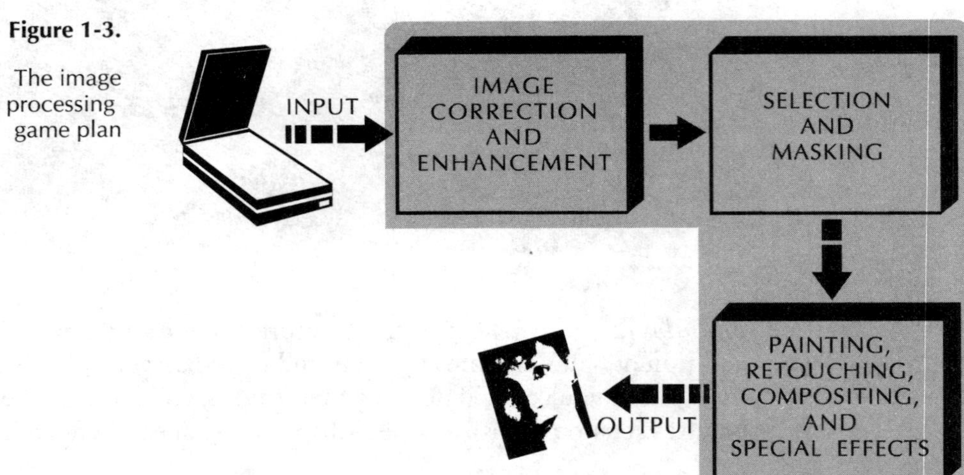

paint programs, and screen capture programs are all common input sources for images. Each type of input source has its own set of advantages and limitations. Some of these limitations depend on the eventual destination of the image (the output medium). Others stem from the nature of bitmaps, which, unlike object-oriented drawings, have fixed resolutions; changing the size or resolution of a bitmap always has the potential to degrade image quality.

PhotoStyler offers extensive controls for changing the size and/or resolution of images to minimize loss of quality. Still, it's best to bring your images into the computer at the size and resolution that matches your intended output. That way, you won't have to risk degrading the digital image later. You'll learn more about input source tricks and tips in Chapter 4.

Correcting and Enhancing the Image (Chapter 9)

When artwork reaches your computer through a scanner or video capture application, it's often necessary to adjust brightness, contrast, hue, or saturation to match the original. *Color correction* should therefore be the first step in image editing for most photographs, scanned artwork, or video stills.

Note *When you need to correct only a portion of an image, use PhotoStyler's masking and selection features, described in Chapter 8.*

PhotoStyler's color and Grayscale adjustment controls have creative as well as corrective applications. You can use them to generate special color or Grayscale effects. For example, you can *posterize* an image to reduce the total number of colors or gray shades it contains. Or, try experimenting with *Grayscale thresholding*, a process that can turn a Grayscale image into a stylized black-and-white image. Chapter 9 provides more hints about creative techniques for color and Grayscale enhancement.

Marking Selections and Creating Masks (Chapter 8)

You can edit an entire image in PhotoStyler at once, if you wish. In most cases, however, you'll first isolate portions of an image, marking *selections* so that your edits won't affect other areas. PhotoStyler provides a full palette of Selection tools that let you define a selection by color similarity, freehand tracing, or geometrical shape.

Even better, you can save the stencil of any selected area as a *mask* for later retrieval. If you've ever traced a complex selection by hand, you know how time-consuming (and frustrating) it can be to re-create that selection during a different session. By saving a selection as a mask file, you can "fit" it magically to the identical area of the original image later, without having to retrace the selection. Mask files also open up myriad possibilities for special effects, as you'll see in Chapter 8.

Painting, Retouching, Compositing, and Generating Special Effects (Chapters 10, 11, 12, 13, 14)

The bulk of your image editing work takes place in the retouching, painting and special-effects phase of image processing. This is where you select colors or gray tones and edit or create custom color palettes. It's where you smudge or blur images, apply fills and patterns, use airbrush techniques, add text and perspective, or clone portions of a picture. This is also the phase in which you can edit individual color *channels* or apply one of PhotoStyler's many special-effects *filters*.

The combination of tools and effects you use will depend on the application. If you're retouching a realistic photograph, you'll customize the tools for subtle results and won't need to work extensively with filters or channels. If, on the other hand, your projects include fine art or stylized commercial applications, you'll be more likely to use special effects and PhotoStyler's sophisticated image composition controls; create montages of two or more images; or copy, cut, and paste between images to generate original backgrounds and patterns. The possibilities are as unlimited as your imagination.

Output: The Final Destination (Chapters 15, 16)

Ah, yes, output. What you see on your monitor may not be what you get from a 300 dpi laser printer or high-resolution imagesetter. Yet, high-quality output is your ultimate goal. How can you assure yourself of predictable end results?

With Aldus PhotoStyler, the secret is to be mindful of your eventual output medium from the moment you first scan in or capture an image. You can refine PhotoStyler's user interface, image editing options, and color correction controls to compensate for possible output problems.

When it's time to print, PhotoStyler provides a broad range of user-definable controls that foster high-quality output. Crop marks and calibration bars can accompany each draft or final printout. Precise control over halftone settings is another PhotoStyler strength: you can specify halftone screen shape, frequency, and angles to match the capabilities of a particular printer or imagesetting device. To help you avoid moirés and other unpleasant color printing surprises, PhotoStyler provides controls for balancing the quantity and distribution of ink on the printing press.

In Conclusion. . .

Using PhotoStyler to its maximum potential is a little like riding a thoroughbred horse. There's more to horsemanship than learning how to ride. You also have to educate yourself about the history of the breed, the animal's personality, and the optimal environment for your horse. Similarly, with PhotoStyler you'll work to better advantage if you understand basic conventions of photography, color, and the printing industry. So that you can apply your skills successfully to real-world applications, we aim to provide you with as much background as possible in this book.

As for PhotoStyler, the power is there; it's up to you to harness it.

2

The PhotoStyler Environment

Aldus PhotoStyler's power stems only in part from its advanced features. The other equally important factor is PhotoStyler's intuitive user interface. It's easy to identify tools visually, locate controls, and understand options. As a result, you can become productive quickly with even the most advanced PhotoStyler features. Isn't that what true power is all about?

If you're already familiar with Aldus PhotoStyler, use this chapter to refresh your knowledge of PhotoStyler's user interface. If you're new to PhotoStyler, let this chapter acquaint you with the PhotoStyler application window before you begin working.

PhotoStyler and Microsoft Windows

You'll find that PhotoStyler's menu command structure, dialog box controls, and mouse conventions are similar to those of other applications running under Microsoft Windows 3.0 or later versions. These common interface standards help make PhotoStyler easy to learn and use.

But Microsoft Windows adds more than standard conventions and pretty tools to PhotoStyler's capabilities. Thanks to Windows' underlying support, you can cut, copy, and paste image data between PhotoStyler and other Windows graphics applications; run multiple applications at the same time; and work with 8-bit Grayscale or 24-bit color images regardless of your hardware setup.

Data Transfer and Exchange

PhotoStyler gives you access to two clipboards: its own private clipboard and the standard MS-Windows clipboard. Using the private PhotoStyler clipboard, you can copy, cut, and paste between PhotoStyler 8-bit Grayscale or 24-bit color images, with all edits and special effects intact. Using the Windows clipboard, you can transfer image data to and from other Windows applications, as long as those applications support the clipboard in the same way.

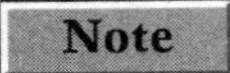

Certain limitations of the Windows clipboard cause color information from irregularly-shaped masks not to transfer properly. See Chapter 13 for more information on Windows' clipboard limitations.

Multitasking Ability

PhotoStyler runs in all three Windows memory modes: real, standard, and enhanced. If you run Windows in standard or enhanced modes, you can run multiple applications at the same time, switching between applications as necessary. You can mate PhotoStyler with your favorite word processing, desktop publishing, and graphics applications to complete a project more efficiently. We produced this book while running PhotoStyler, Ventura Publisher for Windows, Corel Draw, Tiffany Plus, and Word for Windows 2.0 all at one time. If your other Windows applications support Dynamic Data Exchange (DDE) and Object Linking and Embedding (OLE), you can even perform true multitasking.

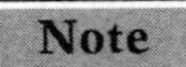

The number of applications you can run simultaneously depends on the amount of system memory you have and/or your use of a swap disk. Remember, too, that "real" multitasking (timeslicing) is possible only in 386 enhanced mode. In standard mode, only the currently active application continues to run, and other open applications remain frozen until you switch to them.

Device Independence

PhotoStyler works with any printer, display adapter, and monitor that MS-Windows supports. You'll achieve the most WYSIWYG screen results and have an easier time editing if your display adapter and monitor support super VGA standards (256 colors), 15- or 16-bit color (32,000-64,000 colors), or 24-bit color (16.7 million colors). Even if your system can't display at least 256 colors, you can still save your images in 24-bit True Color format, and they will print correctly. The same is true for 8-bit Grayscale images if you use a monochrome monitor.

PhotoStyler's modular *open architecture* permits third-party developers to supply plug-in drivers for scanners, image filters, or specialized output devices such as film recorders and continuous-tone color printers. This provides yet another level of device independence.

One level down from MS-Windows is the PhotoStyler application window, where all your image processing activities take place. This chapter familiarizes you with the elements of the application window so that in Chapter 3, you'll be prepared to experiment on your own.

The PhotoStyler Application Window

Figure 2–1 shows the elements that typically appear in the PhotoStyler application window: the main workspace, the standard MS-Windows title and menu bars, the status bar, one or more *document windows*,

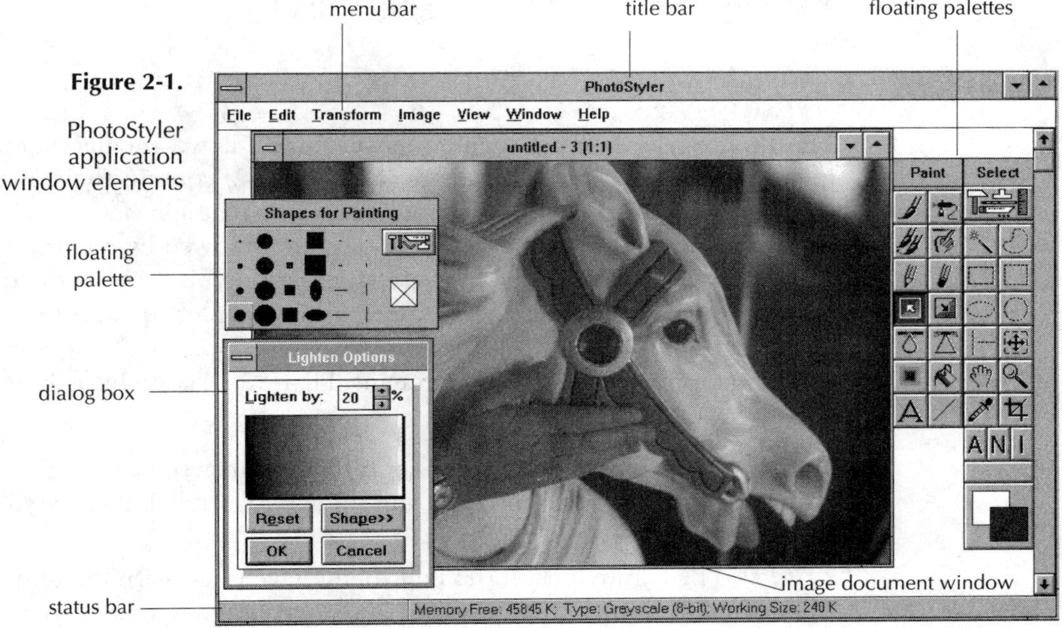

Figure 2-1.
PhotoStyler application window elements

a dialog box, and several *floating palettes*. Each of these elements has specific functions within PhotoStyler.

Let's first take a look at the elements that resemble those found in other Windows applications. The document windows, interactive dialog boxes, status bar, and floating palettes are unique to PhotoStyler, so we'll describe them separately.

Title Bar

As with all Windows applications, the color of PhotoStyler's title bar shows whether PhotoStyler is the currently active application or whether it is running in the background. You can move the entire application window by holding the mouse over the title bar and then dragging.

Within the title bar are three other standard MS-Windows elements. The *control menu box*, located at the upper left corner of the title bar, contains commands for moving, sizing, and closing the application window and for switching to another application. At the upper right corner of the title bar are the *minimize* and *maximize* buttons. Clicking on the minimize button causes the PhotoStyler application window to become a small icon at the lower left corner of your screen. (Double-clicking on an iconized image restores the PhotoStyler window to its normal size.) Clicking on the maximize button causes the application window to fill the entire screen.

Menu Bar

The PhotoStyler menu bar contains seven pull-down menus. Some menu commands, such as the one in Figure 2–2, contain their own *submenus*; you can identify these by the arrow that appears after the command name. Other menu commands are followed by an ellipsis (...). When you click on one of these commands, you access a dialog box and must supply additional information in order to execute the command.

Each of the seven PhotoStyler menus (Figure 2–3) contains a different set of command functions.

- *File*—The File menu contains commands that pertain to file manipulation, to image input or output, or to general PhotoStyler functions.
- *Edit*—The commands in the Edit menu have to do with PhotoStyler's image composition features. Look here when you need to cut,

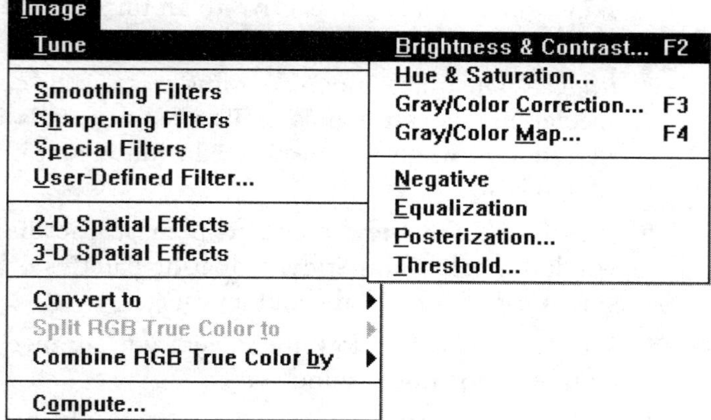

Figure 2-2. The Image/Tune menu command and its submenu

copy, and paste image data, work with fills and patterns, or merge two images.

- *Transform*—Use the Transform menu to perform the "acrobatics" of PhotoStyler. The Transform menu commands let you flip, rotate,

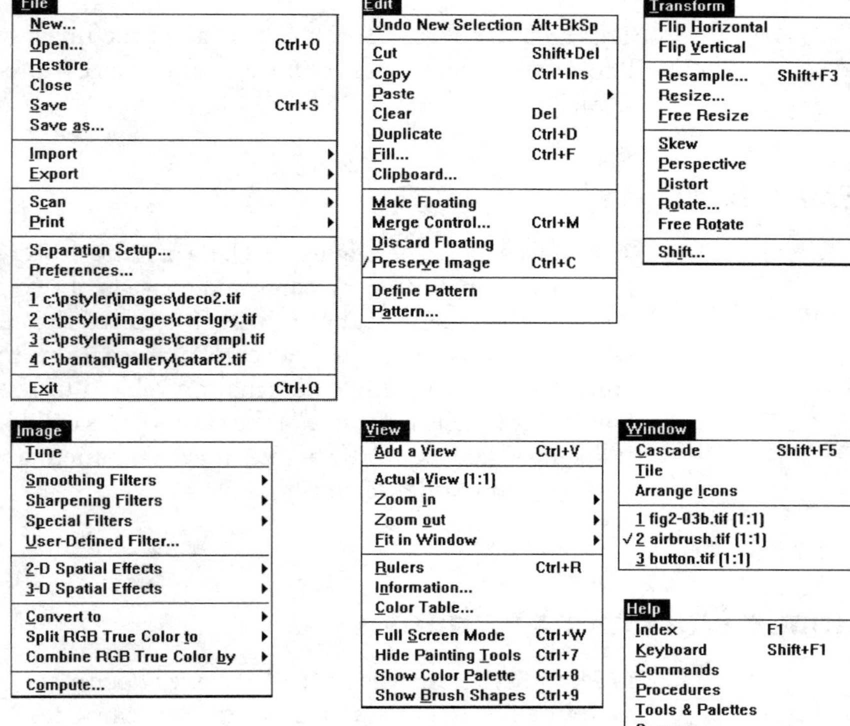

Figure 2-3. PhotoStyler's menus

skew, shift, or add perspective to an image, resize it, or change its resolution.

- *Image*—The Image menu contains most of the color correction and special-effects commands in PhotoStyler. This is also where you should look when you need to edit individual image channels (see Chapter 14).
- *View*—Use the View menu to manage the display of document windows, turn PhotoStyler's floating palettes on or off, and obtain statistical information about an image.
- *Window*—The Window menu lets you arrange and select image icons and document windows.
- *Help*—If you prefer to use menu commands instead of the mouse, the Help menu will direct you to PhotoStyler's extensive help files on almost every type of operation. If you installed a scanner driver with PhotoStyler, you'll also find a Scanner help file in this menu.

Main Workspace

This area (see Figure 2–1) contains all of the images you work with in PhotoStyler. You can't create or edit images directly in the main workspace.

Status Bar

The status bar (see Figure 2–1) forms the lower boundary of the PhotoStyler application window and consists of two parts. The smaller area at the left side of the status bar is called the *cursor area*. This is where you'll sometimes find color information, the current mouse cursor position, or other information related to the Paint and Select Palette tools. The right side of the status bar is called the *message area*. It displays data about the active image document and messages about current PhotoStyler operations.

Image Document Windows

In PhotoStyler, images are called *image documents* and are contained in framelike *document windows*. You can open and edit as many image documents as your system memory and available hard drive space will permit.

Each image appears in its own document window, and each document window contains a title bar, control menu box, and minimize and maximize buttons, just like application windows. You can move any image document within the application window by holding the mouse cursor over its title bar and dragging. Whenever you have multiple image documents open, you can remove clutter by minimizing all document windows in which you're not working at the moment (see Figure 1–1 in Chapter 1). You'll practice managing multiple document windows in Chapter 6.

Dialog Boxes

Dialog boxes in Aldus PhotoStyler contain a variety of controls, each one allowing you to specify information in a different way. Many of the controls are standard for most MS-Windows applications. In addition, some PhotoStyler dialog boxes are *interactive*, allowing you to preview some options before you exit the dialog box. Interactive dialog boxes contain special controls that are unique to PhotoStyler.

Standard MS-Windows Dialog Box Controls

Figures 2–4 and 2–5 show representative PhotoStyler dialog boxes containing standard MS-Windows controls. You can move forward or backward between options in a dialog box by pressing Shift or Shift-Tab, respectively. We'll review the functions of each type of control here. For detailed information on the keyboard and mouse techniques used with dialog box controls, consult your *Microsoft Windows User's Guide.*

- *Radio buttons* signify choices that are mutually exclusive. You can select only one radio button for a given option.
- *Check boxes* indicate options that are not mutually exclusive. Each check box you click with the mouse displays an "x" to show that it's active.
- *Numeric entry boxes* require that you type in a numeric value for a specific PhotoStyler function.
- *Command buttons* carry out common functions such as saving new settings, cancelling changes, or accessing a dialog box that's nested

Figure 2-4.

Standard dialog box controls

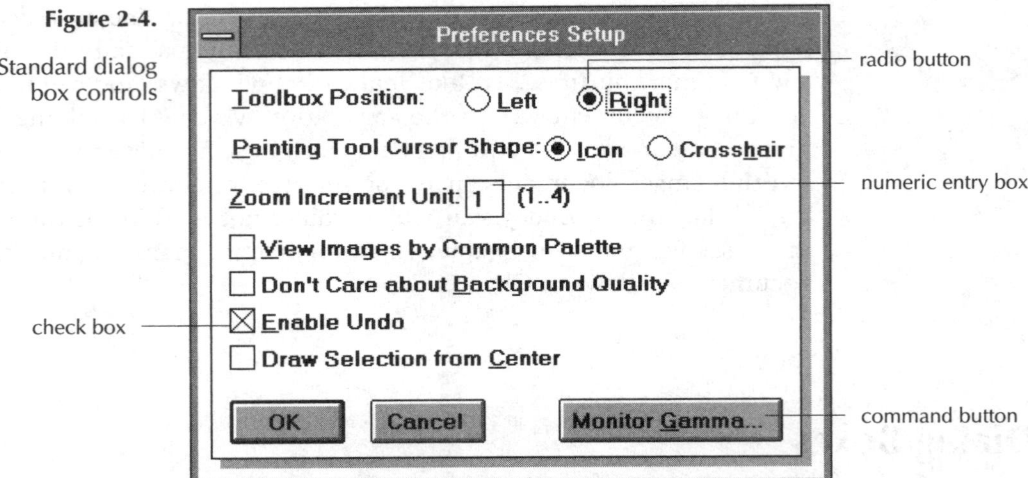

within the current one. All command buttons are rectangular and appear three-dimensional.

- *List boxes* like the ones in Figure 2–5 appear in dialog boxes that ask you to specify a filename, drive, or directory. If the list of available files is too long, the list box will display *scroll bars* that you can use to view additional choices. Clicking on a file, drive, or directory name selects it.

Figure 2-5.

More standard dialog box controls

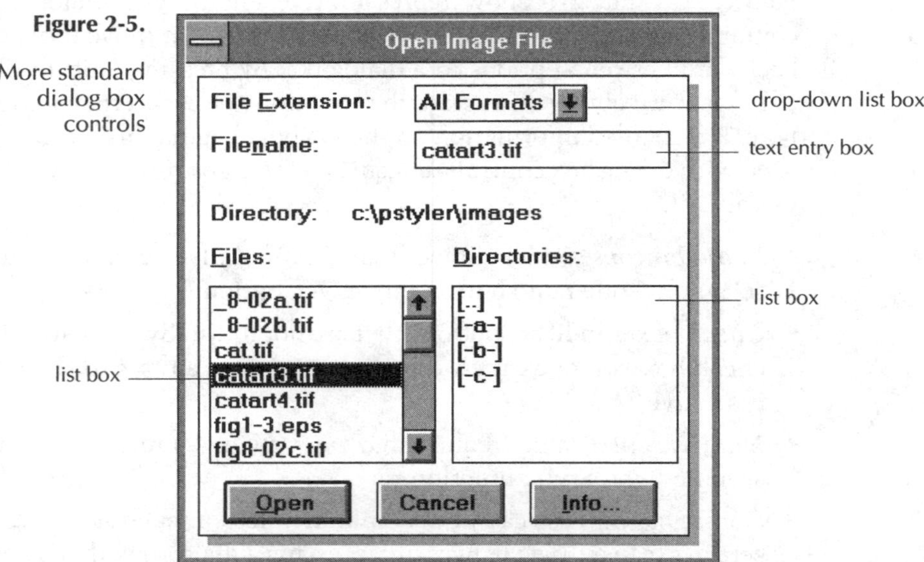

- *Text entry boxes* appear in the same dialog boxes as list boxes. Use these to type in a filename directly.
- *Drop-down list boxes* display the currently selected option in a rectangular window with a downward-pointing arrow beside it. Clicking on the arrow displays the other choices available to you.

PhotoStyler's Interactive Dialog Boxes

Many dialog boxes related to PhotoStyler's tools and color correction techniques are *interactive*; that is, they allow you to preview the results of your settings even before you exit the dialog box. The interactive dialog boxes require special types of controls not found elsewhere. Figures 2–6 and 2–7 show typical interactive dialog boxes and the controls that are unique to them.

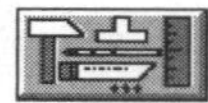

- *Dialog box menus* are identified by a rectangular toolbox icon. This icon conceals a menu of special functions related to the current dialog box. Click the icon to view the menu.
- *Display boxes* show information about an image through an abstract graphic. As you alter the settings in the dialog box (usually by moving a *slider arrow*), the contents of the display box change interactively. The associated image document changes, too.
- *Scratch pads* appear in dialog boxes that are associated with PhotoStyler's Painting tools. Like the one in Figure 2–7, they let you

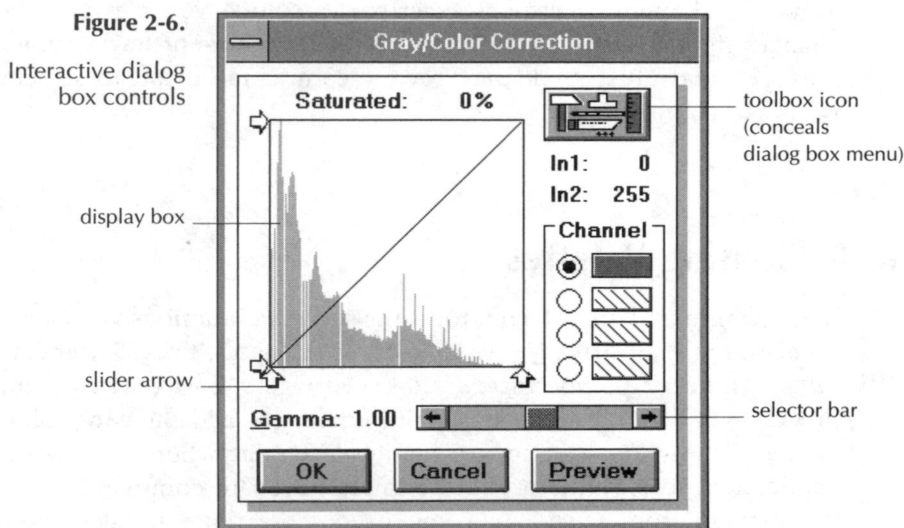

Figure 2-6. Interactive dialog box controls

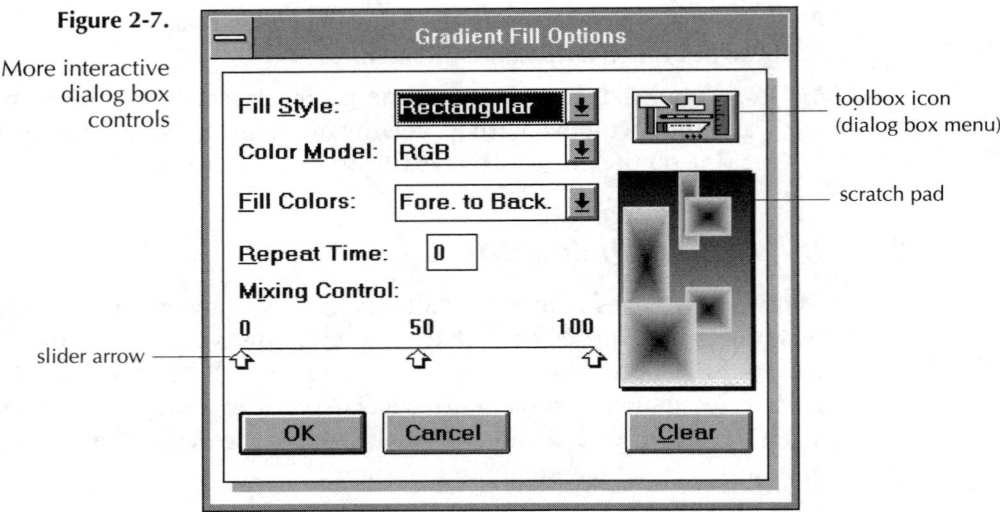

Figure 2-7. More interactive dialog box controls

experiment with tool settings without disturbing the image you're editing.

- *Selector bars* function like horizontal scroll bars, letting you select a value from a continuous range. As you move the scroll arrow or elevator inside the selector bar, the image will change interactively.

Unlike Painting tool dialog boxes, dialog boxes associated with color correction commands let you preview changes to the image you're currently editing—with one important caveat. If your display adapter and monitor display exactly 256 colors, you can preview changes in real time. If your monitor displays more or fewer colors, however, you must click the Preview command button to see the results of your settings.

PhotoStyler's Floating Palettes

Menu commands are fine, but for some software functions you need a quicker, more intuitive access to features and tools. PhotoStyler contains a number of *floating palettes* (see Figure 2–1) that ease the processes of defining selections, painting images, and choosing colors or gray tones. You can move these palettes anywhere within the application, display them with a simple keyboard command, or remove them from view when you need more room for document windows. Floating palettes build flexibility and improved productivity into the PhotoStyler interface.

The Select Palette

The Select Palette (see Figure 2–8, center) always remains visible in the PhotoStyler window, although you can move it about freely or change its default position. The tools in the Select Palette let you isolate and manipulate limited areas of an image that you wish to edit. Any editing operations you perform on a selected area affect only that area.

Some of the tools in the Select Palette help you define selection areas according to shape or color. Other tools let you move selections, crop, scroll, or magnify images, or choose colors or gray shades from an image that's currently open. The Select Palette also contains buttons that let you select an entire image, deselect everything in the image, or invert selected and unselected areas.

At the bottom of the Select Palette, the Current Color Indicators display the currently active foreground and background colors or gray shades. At the top of the Select Palette is a menu with options for expanding, adding a border to, or softening the edges of a selection, and for importing and exporting masks. Chapter 8 provides in-depth information and tips on using the Select Palette tools.

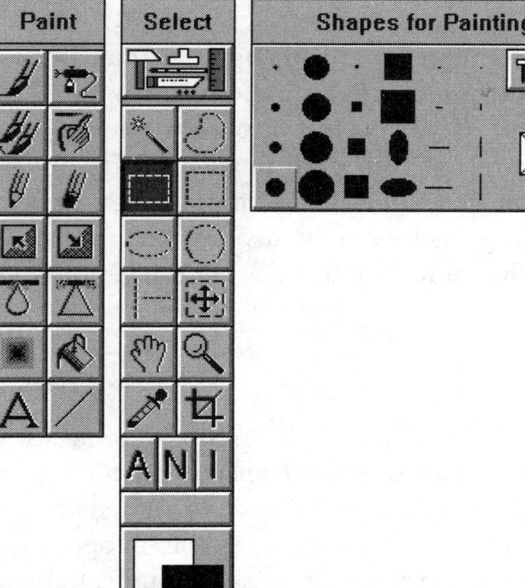

Figure 2-8.

The Paint, Select, and Brush Shapes Palettes

The Paint Palette

If you've ever used a paint package, you'll find some familiar tools in PhotoStyler's Paint Palette (Figure 2–8, left). However, the sophistication of PhotoStyler's Painting tools greatly exceeds that of ordinary paint programs. Double-click on any tool icon to bring up a dialog box that lets you customize the options for that tool. Chapter 10 delves into the imaginative uses of PhotoStyler's Painting tools.

The Paint Palette appears by default at the right side of the PhotoStyler application window, but you can move it freely or set it to appear at the left edge of the window. Double-clicking the title bar of the Paint Palette removes the palette from view.

The Brush Shapes Palette

The Brush Shapes Palette (Figure 2–8, right) lets you determine the size and shape of the brush you use with the Painting tools. You can use one of the 24 predefined brush shapes used with PhotoStyler or define your own. Unlike the Select and Paint Palettes, the Brush Shapes Palette is not automatically visible in the PhotoStyler application window, but you can display it by pressing F9. See Chapter 10 for more information about using the Brush Shapes Palette.

The Color Palette

You can select foreground and background colors quickly when painting by using the Color Palette shown in Figure 2–9 in the Color Section of this book. If you have a monochrome or grayscale monitor, the Color Palette on your screen will display only the available gray shades. You can choose one of the many predefined palettes that PhotoStyler provides or edit any palette to create your own. Chapter 7 describes the more intricate uses of the Color Palette.

The Color Picker

The Color Picker (Figure 2–10 in the Color Section of this book) offers you a more precise way of specifying foreground and background colors than the Color Palette. With the entire color spectrum available, you choose colors and gray shades by specifying exact component values. To access the Color Picker, simply click on one of the Current Color Indicators located at the bottom of the Select Palette.

Keyboard Shortcuts

For those who prefer typing to clicking mouse buttons, PhotoStyler offers timesaving keyboard shortcuts to many of its menu commands and interface controls. Table 2–1 contains a list of keyboard shortcuts organized alphabetically by function.

Now that you understand more about the elements that make getting around in PhotoStyler so easy, go on to Chapter 3. There, you'll gain hands-on experience with basic PhotoStyler operations and create an original image on your own.

Table 2-1. PhotoStyler Keyboard Shortcuts

Function	Keystroke(s)
File and Program Operations	
Close all open images, save no changes (ver. 1.1a)	Shift + Close
Exit PhotoStyler	Ctrl - Q
Exit PhotoStyler without saving any images (ver. 1.1a)	Shift + Exit, Shift + double-click on control menu
Open File	Ctrl - O
Open multiple files simultaneously (ver. 1.1A)	Ctrl + click filenames in Open Image File dialog box
Print	Ctrl - P
Resample Image	Shift - F3
Save File	Ctrl - S
Switch to Another Application	Ctrl - Esc
On-Line Help	
Help Index	F1
How to Use Help	Shift - F10
Keyboard Help	Shift - F1
Colors and Palettes	
Brightness & Contrast	F2

(continued next page)

Table 2-1. PhotoStyler Keyboard Shortcuts

Function	Keystroke(s)
Gray/Color Correction	F3
Gray/Color Map	F4
Select Background Color, Color Palette	F6
Choose Background Color (Fore Mode, Color Palette)	Shift - Click
Choose Foreground Color, Color Palette	F5
Select Foreground Color (Back Mode, Color Palette)	Shift-Click
Show/Hide Painting Tools	Ctrl - 7
Show Color Palette	Ctrl - 8
Show/Hide Brush Shapes Palette	Ctrl - 9
Image Display	
Add Rulers	Ctrl - R
Fit Document in Window	Ctrl + Magnification level (number)
Full Screen Mode/Normal Screen Mode	Ctrl - W
Tile Image Documents	Shift - F4
Cascade Image Documents	Shift - F5
Selection and Masking	
Add to Current Selection	Shift - Selection Tool + Drag/Click
Expand Selection	Ctrl - E
Hide Selection Marquee	Ctrl - H
Invert Selected and Unselected Areas	Ctrl - I
Select All	Ctrl - A
Select None (deselect all)	Ctrl-N
Subtract from Current Selection	Ctrl - Selection Tool + Drag/Click

(continued next page)

Table 2-1. PhotoStyler Keyboard Shortcuts

Function	Keystroke(s)
Image Composition and Editing	
Clear	Del
Copy	Ctrl - Ins
Cut	Shift - Del
Duplicate	Ctrl - D
Fill	Ctrl - F
Merge Control	Ctrl - M
Paste as Selection	Shift - Ins
Preserve Image Quality	Ctrl - C

3

Up and Running

In this chapter, you'll gain hands-on experience with Aldus PhotoStyler. You'll begin by adjusting certain elements of the MS-Windows interface so that PhotoStyler will perform smoothly for you. Next, you'll calibrate your monitor, a process that lets you maintain a consistent image display quality. You'll also create and save an original "paint" graphic and customize the PhotoStyler application window.

Optimizing the Windows Interface

It's important to adjust both the mouse speed and the color scheme under MS-Windows before you begin working with PhotoStyler. The color scheme you choose may affect your perception of colors and gray shades in PhotoStyler images. And if you ever edit sensitive areas of an image in high magnification, you'll want your mouse to respond in real time, not slower or faster than your hand movements.

Defining a Neutral Color Scheme

Yes, we know all about the wild bitmaps and psychedelic color schemes with which you can decorate MS-Windows. But if you plan to use PhotoStyler professionally and often, you should avoid vivid hues and distracting Desktop wallpaper patterns in favor of a neutral scheme of gray tones. That's because color perception is relative: colors adjacent to an object you're viewing can cause your perception of that object's colors to shift.

So, don't throw away that prize wallpaper bitmap of your wife, husband, lover, child, or pet; just tuck it safely out of sight and substitute the *gray.bmp* wallpaper when using PhotoStyler. We suggest a happy compromise for your color schemes, too: create a new Grayscale color scheme, name it Pstyler, and use it only when you'll be running PhotoStyler with color images during a Windows session. For other Windows sessions, you can safely trot out your craziest color schemes and Desktop wallpaper patterns.

There are two ways to create a new color scheme under MS-Windows. If you're content with copying the scheme we use, just try the following procedure. (Refer to your Microsoft Windows documentation if you need help in using Windows Notepad.)

1. Open the control.ini file under Windows Notepad and add the following line to the [color schemes] section, making sure that you don't leave any spaces:

   Pstyler=C0C0C0,FFFFFF,FFFFFF,0,FFFFFF,0,A4A0A0,C0C0C0,FFFFFF,A4A0A0,C0C0C0,0,C0C0C0

   Be sure to save the file and close Windows Notepad when you're done.

2. Double-click the Control Panel icon in the Windows Main Group window and then the Desktop icon. Change the Pattern to None and the Wallpaper file to gray.bmp, as shown in Figure 3–1. Select OK to activate your changes.

3. Finally, double-click the Color icon in the Control Panel. Change the Color Schemes to Pstyler and select OK, then close the Control Panel.

If you prefer to select your own gray shades for use with PhotoStyler, consult your Microsoft Windows User's Guide to learn how to modify existing color schemes with the Windows Control Panel.

Adjusting Mouse Speed

If you've worked with other paint or image processing packages, you may know the frustration of watching your mouse jerk along as you try to apply a tool smoothly. A fast mouse tracking speed may be fine for some applications, but for precise results in image editing, you may want to slow down your mouse. We recommend adjusting Mouse Tracking Speed (available through the Mouse icon of the Windows

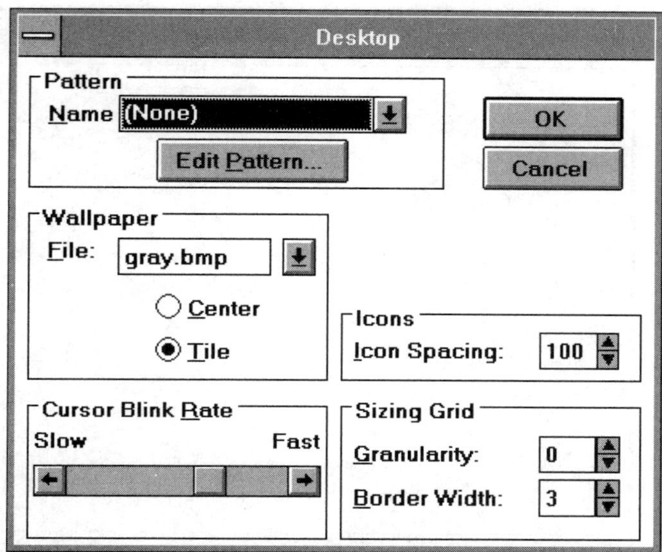

Figure 3-1.

The Windows Desktop dialog box

Control Panel) to somewhere between slow and medium, if you plan to retouch fine details of images. On the other hand, if you prefer quick, coarse strokes with less care for details, you may want a faster mouse tracking speed.

Starting PhotoStyler

To run Aldus PhotoStyler:

1. Run MS-Windows.

2. Go to the group window that contains the PhotoStyler application icon and double-click the icon. After a moment, the PhotoStyler application window appears, with the PhotoStyler logo in its center.
3. Click the left mouse button once to remove the PhotoStyler logo from the application window. If you haven't changed screen preferences, the Paint and Select Palettes will appear near the extreme right side of the application window, as shown in Figure 3–2.

4. If you like, click the maximize button at the upper right corner of the application window to make the PhotoStyler application window fill the screen.

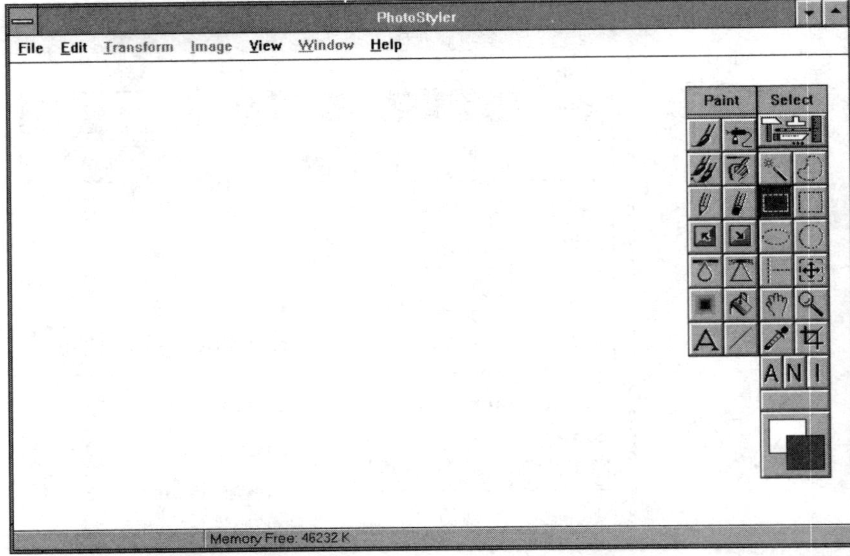

Figure 3-2. The blank PhotoStyler application window at startup

Opening an Image Document

The directory where you installed PhotoStyler also contains several sample image files that you installed with the program. In the following exercise, you'll open one of these files, *psgamma.tif*. This file is useful in calibrating color on your monitor.

To open a single image document:

1. Choose the Open command in the File menu, or press the keyboard shortcut, Ctrl-O. The dialog box in Figure 3–3 will appear. Unless you've changed directories, the Files list box will display the sample files in the directory where you installed PhotoStyler.
2. If necessary, use the Directories list box to change to the directory where you installed PhotoStyler.
3. Double-click the filename *psgamma.tif* to open the image document. If you have version 1.1a or later, the image begins to display immediately. The status bar at the lower left corner of the application window monitors the computer's progress in opening the file.

Once open, the complete image appears in its own document window as in Figure 3–4 in the Color Section of this book. The image contains solid color bands of red, green, blue, and gray, each with an inner and outer color segment. Leave this image on the screen; you'll

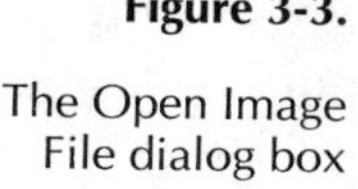

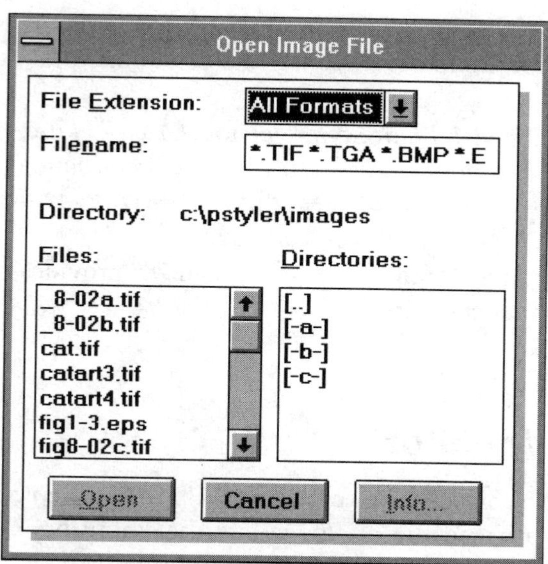

Figure 3-3.

The Open Image File dialog box

put it to good use in the "Calibrating Your Monitor" section of this chapter.

More about Opening Image Files

If you have PhotoStyler version 1.1a or later, you'll enjoy several enhancements related to the speed at which you can open image files and the way they display. Among these enhancements:

- All image filenames will display in each directory, regardless of the file format in which they've been saved.
- You can open multiple image files all at once by pressing Ctrl as you click on additional filenames in the Open Image File dialog box.
- To display information for multiple image files that you plan to open, select all desired filenames using the Ctrl key and then click the Info command button in the Open Image File dialog box.
- The names of the four most recently opened or saved image files appear at the bottom of the File menu. To reopen one of these files, just click the desired filename. This enhancement saves time by letting you bypass dialog boxes.

Info...

Tip

By default, the File menu in versions 1.1a or later displays the names of only the four most recently opened or saved image files. You can display up to sixteen filenames in the File menu by editing the pstyler.ini file in the directory where you installed PhotoStyler.

Note

Beginning with PhotoStyler version 1.1a and later, all images display in Fit in Window mode when you first open them. If an image is larger than your screen, you'll see it at a reduced viewing magnification.

Chapter 6, "Managing Image Display," provides more details about these enhancements.

Calibrating Your Monitor

There's a big difference between the *digital* colors that computers work with and the *analog* colors that monitors display. Computers represent colors by using consistent numerical data, but the monitors that receive the data are subject to mechanical and environmental variables. Many factors—monitor age, changes in contrast or brightness settings, ambient lighting—can cause subtle day-to-day shifts in a monitor's apparent colors. And if the colors on your monitor vary too much, you can't edit images with confidence.

To maintain consistent color display with PhotoStyler, you need to *calibrate* your monitor. Calibration is a process of matching the *output* (analog) colors on your display to the *input* (digital) colors as closely as possible. You should calibrate your monitor the first time you work with PhotoStyler. Once you've done so, colors will continue to display consistently unless one or more of the following takes place:

- You attach a different monitor to your computer.
- You install a different display adapter.
- The phosphor output of your monitor changes as the monitor ages.
- You change brightness or contrast settings.
- You alter the lighting in your workspace or move your workspace to another location where the lighting is different.

It's a good idea to recalibrate your monitor occasionally, just to ensure that one or more of these changes haven't altered the way colors appear to you.

To calibrate your monitor, you'll correct the gamma values for the red, green, and blue areas of the *psgamma.tif* file that you opened in the previous section. In *gamma correction*, you adjust the brightness and contrast of a color's midtones in order to compensate for the technological differences between input medium (color data) and output medium (here, monitor display).

Caution

If you're using PhotoStyler on a network, create a private PhotoStyler initialization file and add that filename to the command line every time you load PhotoStyler. For example, if your initialization file is called myfile.ini, always start PhotoStyler by typing:

win pstyler #c:\myfile.ini.

If you don't use a private initialization file, you'll change the color display on every monitor on the network—every time you calibrate your monitor! Tell your colleagues to do the same.

To calibrate your monitor:

1. If the *psgamma.tif* file isn't already open, open it now. Duplicate this file by pressing Ctrl-D and then close the original file.

Note

The use of a duplicate file for the calibration process protects you against accidentally altering the original file.

2. Choose the Preferences command in the File menu and click the Monitor Gamma command button in the Preferences Setup dialog box. The Monitor Gamma dialog box will appear.
3. Set the gamma values in the Red, Green, and Blue numeric entry fields to 1.00 as in Figure 3–5 and then click the OK command button. Then, click OK to exit the Preferences dialog box. The inner color blocks in the duplicate *psgamma.tif* file may darken.

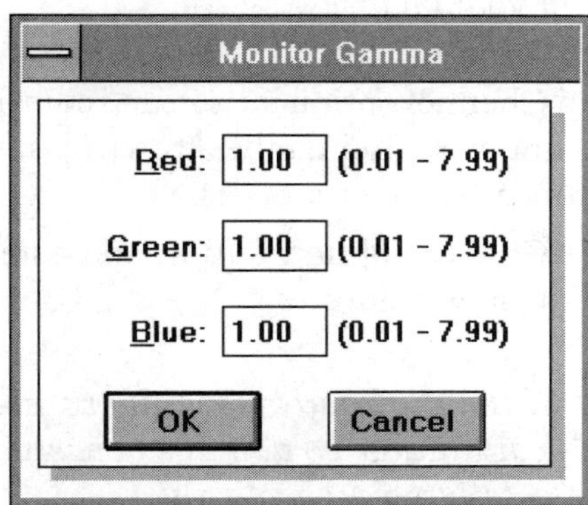

Figure 3-5.

The Monitor Gamma dialog box

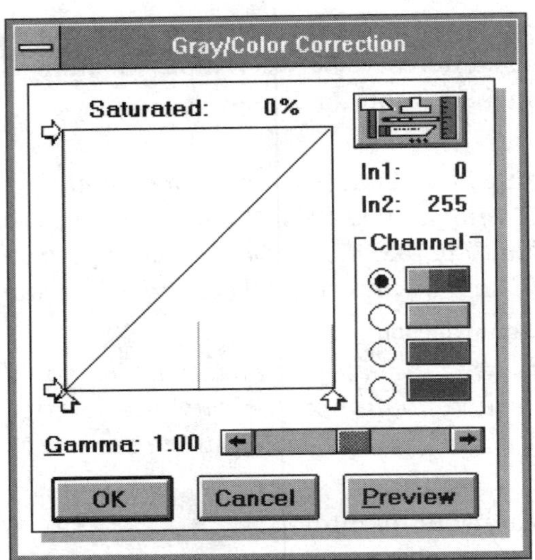

Figure 3-6.

The Gray/Color Correction dialog box

4. Choose the Tune:Gray/Color Correction command in the Image menu. The Gray/Color Correction dialog box will appear as in Figure 3–6.
5. Now, you're ready to adjust the red channel. Click the red Channel option button (the second button from the top). Drag the Gamma scroll bar thumb to the right or left, or click on the left or right Gamma scroll bar arrow. When the inner red block in the duplicate *psgamma.tif* file matches the outer red block, record the red gamma value on a piece of paper.

Note

If your monitor displays exactly 256 colors, you'll see a real-time color shift in the inner red block as the gamma value changes. If your monitor displays some other combination of colors, you'll have to click the Preview command button each time you want to see the results of your changes.

6. Click the green Channel option button and adjust the green gamma value in the same way. Remember to write down the new green gamma value once you have a match.
7. Click the blue Channel option button and adjust the blue value. Again, record the new value.

Note

The gray field in the duplicate psgamma.tif file has no practical function in this calibration, so don't be concerned if the inner and outer gray blocks fail to match exactly.

8. To exit the Gray/Color Correction dialog box, click the Cancel command button. Make sure you *don't* click OK, or you'll alter the duplicate *psgamma.tif* file and will have to reopen and duplicate the original file.
9. Choose the Preferences command in the File menu and click the Monitor Gamma command button once more.
10. Enter the new red, green, and blue gamma values in the respective numeric entry fields of the Monitor Gamma dialog box. To exit, click OK here and again in the Preferences dialog box.
11. Check the *psgamma.tif* document window. If you performed the calibration correctly, the red, green, and blue color bands should appear to be continuous tones. If you still can distinguish differences between the inner and outer segments of the color bands, carefully repeat the calibration process.
12. When you're done, close the duplicate *psgamma.tif* file by double-clicking the control menu box on the document window. Don't save the file.

Once you've calibrated your monitor, there are a few things you can do to maintain consistent color display. Avoid varying contrast and brightness levels; or, if you must vary them, mark the dials at the settings you use with PhotoStyler. Try to maintain constant lighting in your workspace throughout the day, too.

Keep in mind that even with a perfectly calibrated monitor, the colors of an image on your screen won't exactly match the colors of the same image when output to print media. Put simply, every medium has a different kind of color output technology. To learn more about the differences between printed output and the colors on your monitor, see Chapter 16.

Creating and Saving an Original Image

Most people don't realize it, but PhotoStyler is more than a retouching and image editing package. You can use it like a paint program to create original pixel-based artwork. So even if you have no scanner or clip art, you can illustrate with PhotoStyler—and the output quality of your images will be exceptionally high, because PhotoStyler can save the files in 24-bit (16 million colors) format.

In the following exercise, you'll design a simple Grayscale illustration for an imaginary service firm called Faxit! You'll try out quite a variety of PhotoStyler skills:

- Creating a new image document
- Defining objects with tools from the Select Palette
- Using the Color Palette to specify shades of gray
- Creating a simple gradient fill
- Adding text to an image
- Distorting text
- Saving a file

Creating a New Image Document

Let's begin by creating a new image document and specifying its resolution and image data type.

1. Choose the New command from the File menu. The Create New Image dialog box will appear.
2. Set the parameters for the new image as shown in Figure 3–7:

   Data Type: Grayscale, 8-bit per pixel
   Width: 3.75 inches
   Height: 2.75 inches
   Resolution: 133 pixels per inch
3. Click OK to create the image document. A new document window appears on the screen, bearing the name untitled-1 in its title bar. The background of this new image document will be white, unless you've changed the default foreground and background colors for PhotoStyler.

Using the Floating Palettes to Define and Color Objects

Once you've set up the new image, you can begin creating objects with tools from the Select Palette and filling them with tools from the Paint Palette (see Figure 2-8 in Chapter 2). You'll also practice selecting colors in this stage of the exercise.

1. First, you'll fill the entire new image with black. Display the Color Palette by pressing the keyboard shortcut, Ctrl-8. As in Figure 3–8, the palette is Grayscale because the active image document is a Grayscale type.

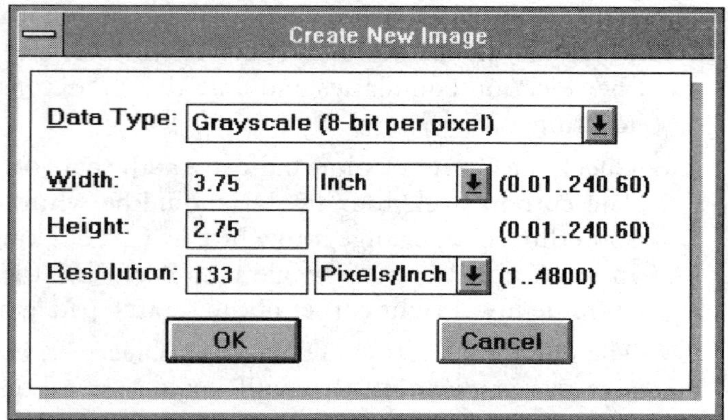

Figure 3-7.

The Create New Image dialog box

2. Move the mouse cursor into the scratch pad (the Grayscale area) of the Color Palette. Here, the cursor will take on the appearance of an eyedropper. Observing the cursor area of the status bar, move the Eyedropper to the extreme upper left corner of the scratch pad. When the status bar reads "gray=0" (black), click to make black the new foreground color.

3. To fill the image area with the new foreground color, click the Bucket tool icon in the Paint Palette and then click anywhere inside the selection marquee.

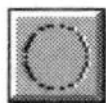

4. Next, you'll create a circle that partially fills the document window. Activate the Circle tool in the Select Palette by clicking once. Then, move the cursor into the untitled image document and drag diagonally upward and to the right to select a perfectly circular area. The circular selection should begin near the lower left corner of the image document and fill approximately the same area of the image as the example in Figure 3–9. To complete the selection area, release the mouse button.

5. If you didn't create a large enough circle, remove it by choosing the Undo command in the Edit menu. Then, begin with step 1 again.

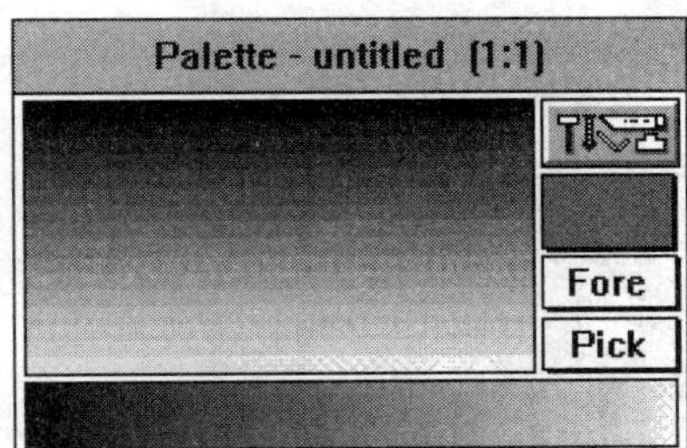

Figure 3-8.

The Color Palette displayed with Grayscale images

If you didn't place the circle exactly where you want it, activate the Move tool in the Select Palette. Then, position the cursor within the selection boundaries and drag the circular area to the desired location.

6. Check the Current Colors Indicator at the base of the Select Palette. The current background color should be white by default. If it's something else, change it to white by first clicking the Fore button in the Color Palette to toggle it to Back, and then clicking in the extreme lower right corner of the scratch pad (gray=255).

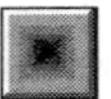

7. The circular selection area isn't an object yet, but you're about to give it a gradient fill that will make it stand out from the background as though it had three dimensions. Double-click the Gradient Fill tool icon in the Paint Palette to see the settings for this tool. If the settings match the ones in Figure 3–10 (Fill Style: Linear; Color Model: RGB; Fill Colors: Fore to Back; and Repeat Time: 0), click the OK command button. If you see other settings in the dialog box, change them to the ones just mentioned, and then click OK.
8. Move the mouse cursor back into the document window. Position the cursor just outside the circular marquee at the eight o'clock location and drag the mouse diagonally upward and to the right. A line follows the cursor, indicating the direction of the fill you're creating. Refer to Figure 3–11a and extend a similar line beyond the circular marquee at the two o'clock location.
9. When your line matches the line in Figure 3–11a, release the mouse button. A gradient fill from black to light gray will fill the circular area, just as in Figure 3–11b.

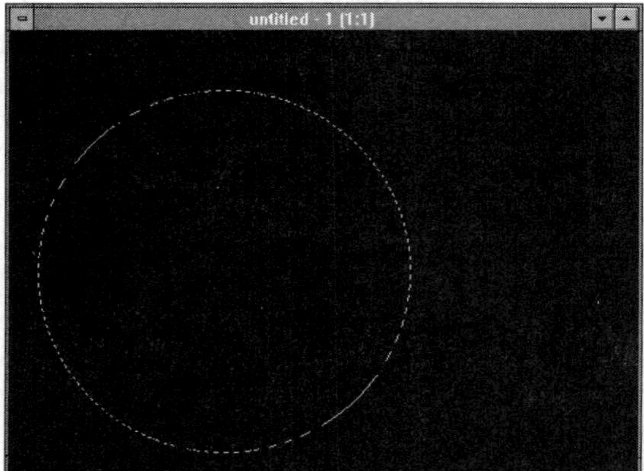

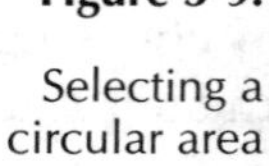

Figure 3-9.

Selecting a circular area

Figure 3-10.

The Gradient Fill Options dialog box

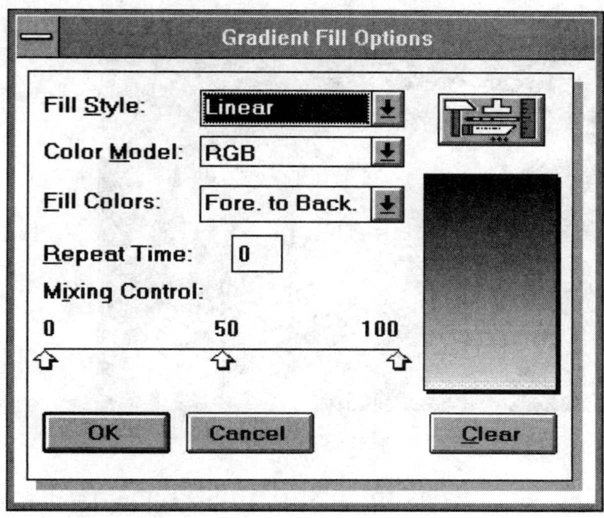

Note

If you had drawn the gradient fill line completely within the boundaries of the selection, the fill would have ranged from pure black to pure white. You didn't fill the circle in this way because the text you're about to add wouldn't be visible against a pure white background. See Chapter 10 for more information about defining gradient fills.

Adding and Positioning Text

PhotoStyler lets you add text to an image using any fonts available to you under MS-Windows. When you first create a text string, nothing exists but the outlines; you must fill them in order to make the text

Figure 3-11a.

Establishing a gradient fill within a circle

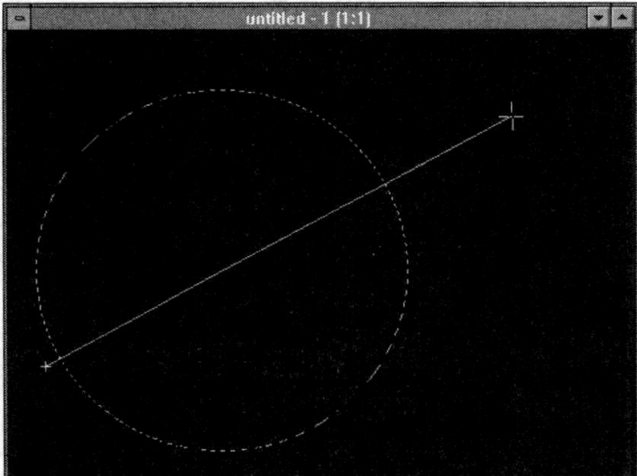

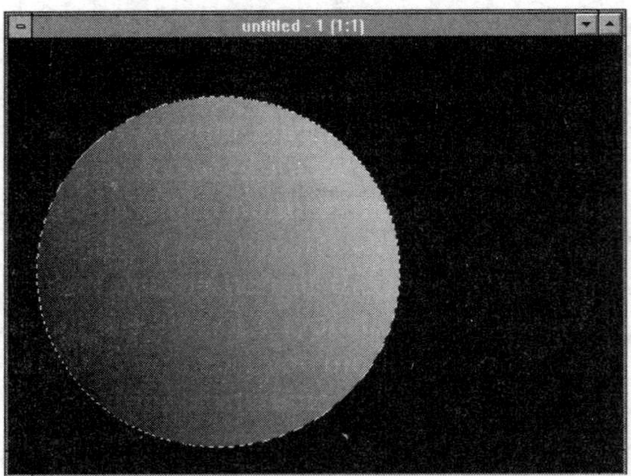

Figure 3-11b.

Gradient fill simulating a sphere

visible. As long as the text outlines remain selected, you can move them anywhere within the document window. Once you deselect the text, however, it becomes "frozen" within the image.

In this portion of the exercise, you'll create a text string, distort it to make a simple word picture, and then fill it.

1. Activate the Text tool in the Paint Palette by clicking on it once. Position the mouse cursor slightly above and to the right of the center of the globe and then click. The Font Settings Options dialog box will appear.
2. Using the drop-down list boxes, select Tms Rmn for the Font Face and 106 points for the Point Size. Click the Bold and Italic check boxes under Font Style. Then, click into the text box and type Faxit! in uppercase and lowercase letters, as shown in Figure 3–12.
3. Select OK to exit the Font Settings Options dialog box. Hollow text outlines will appear and extend outward from the globe.

Tip

If you use Adobe Type Manager, Bitstream FaceLift, or another font manager under Windows, you can use any screen font that's available. Be aware, however, that PhotoStyler uses bitmapped versions of these screen fonts. At small point sizes, text is likely to display "jaggies."

4. If necessary, move the text outlines so that the letter *x* extends beyond the rim of the globe. To reposition the text outlines, first activate the Move tool in the Select Palette. Then, position the

cursor inside the outlines of any letter and drag the text string to the new location.

Distorting and Filling Text

If you were to deselect the hollow text outlines at this point, nothing would be left behind. Fill them, though, and they become visible text. You'll distort and then fill the text outlines in this section of the exercise.

1. With the text outlines still selected, choose the Distort command from the Transform menu. A rectangular "envelope" with four corner handles will appear around the text as in Figure 3–13a.
2. Position the cursor over the upper right handle until the cursor becomes a two-headed arrow. Then, drag this handle diagonally upward to the right corner, as shown in Figure 3–13b. When you release the mouse button, the text outlines will conform to the shape of the envelope.

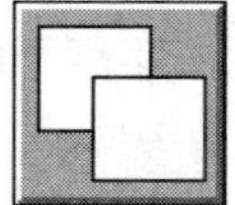

3. Using the Color Palette as in previous sections, change the current foreground color to white (gray=255 in the scratch pad).

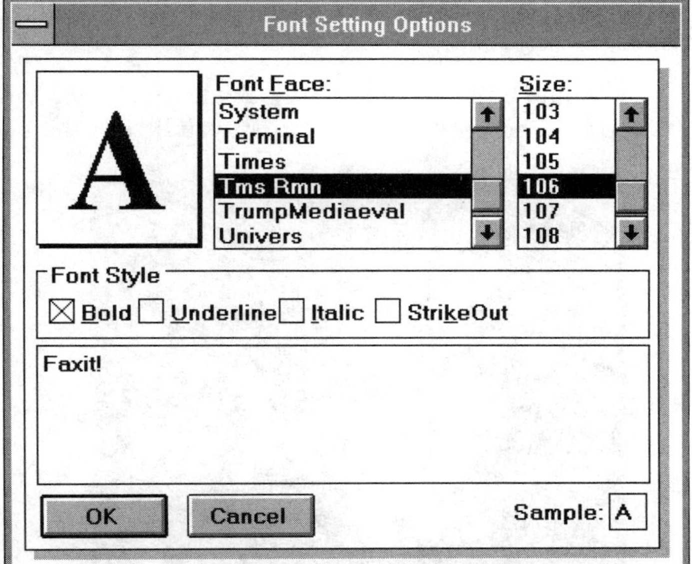

Figure 3-12.

The Font Setting Options dialog box

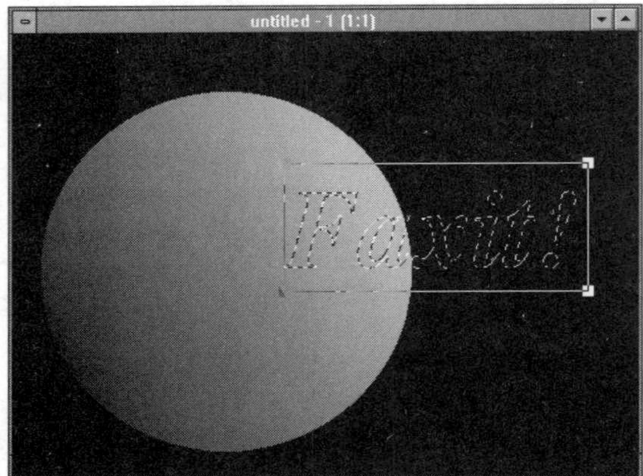

Figure 3-13a.

Text surrounded by distortion envelope

4. Double-click the Bucket Fill tool in the Paint Palette to see the current settings for this tool. When the dialog box in Figure 3–14 appears, change Color Similarity to 255. This setting ensures that the Bucket Fill tool will fill an *entire* selection area when you click anywhere inside the selection area boundaries. Click OK to exit the Bucket Fill Options dialog box.
5. With the Bucket Fill tool still active, click inside any of the text letter outlines. The entire text string will fill with white.

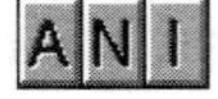

6. Click the "N" button in the Select Palette to deselect the text. Your basic illustration is complete and should resemble Figure 3–15.

Saving a File

It would be a shame to let the evidence of your hands-on expertise in Aldus PhotoStyler disappear, so you'll save the new image as a file.

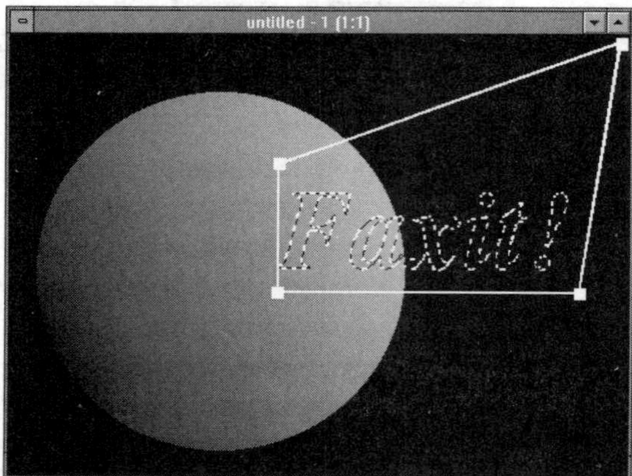

Figure 3-13b.

Dragging the distortion envelope handle

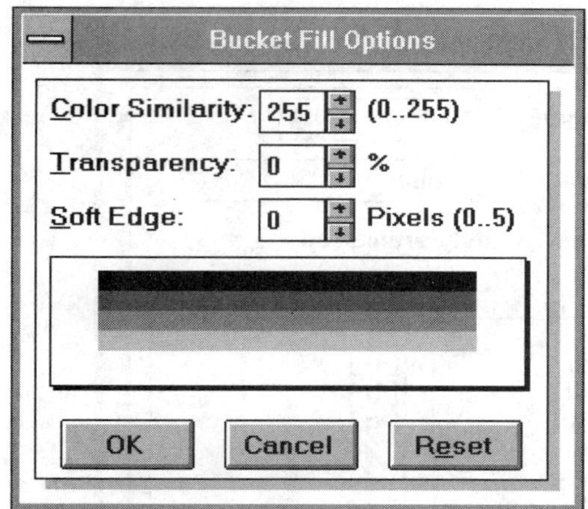

Figure 3-14.

The Bucket Fill Options dialog box

Saving an image in PhotoStyler requires that you specify the file format and any associated options, the filename, drive, and directory. To save the image you've just created:

1. Choose the Save As command from the File menu, or press the keyboard shortcut, Ctrl-S. The Save Image File dialog box will appear, with the cursor automatically at the Filename text entry box.
2. Type **faxillus** in the Filename text entry box; then, check the other options in the dialog box. Your settings should be the same as in Figure 3–16:

   File Format: *.TIF
   Filename: faxillus
   Directory: the directory where you installed PhotoStyler, or a subdirectory just for your images

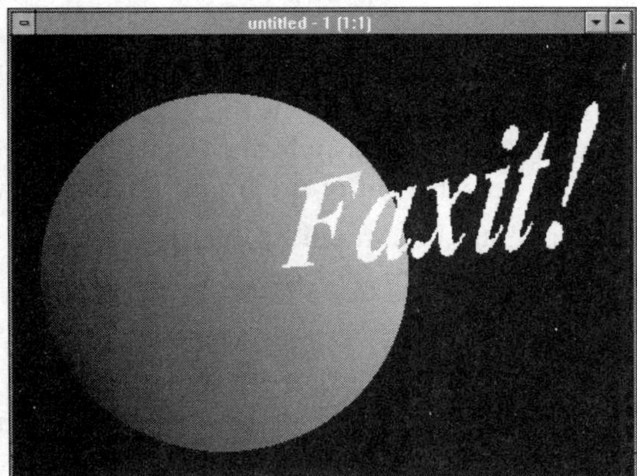

Figure 3-15.

The completed Faxit logo

Figure 3-16.

Saving the Faxillus.tif file

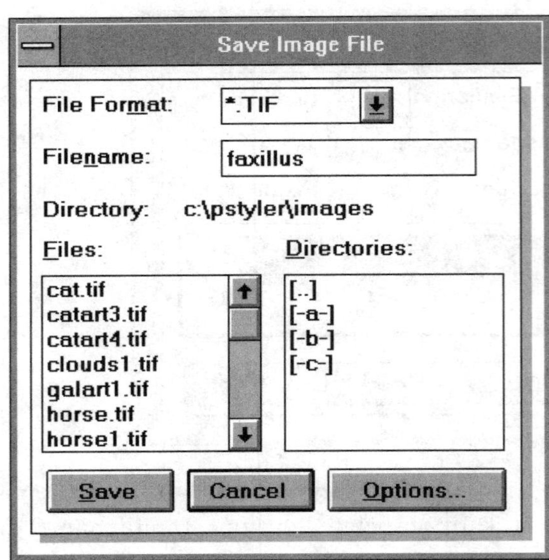

If the Save Image File dialog box shows other settings, use the drop-down list boxes and the Files and Directories list boxes to change them.

Tip

We recommend creating a subdirectory under your PhotoStyler directory for storing the images you create. That way, your images won't get lost amid the software and sample image files.

3. Click the Options command button in the Save Image File dialog box. When the TIFF Save Options dialog box appears, check the settings to ensure that they're the same as in Figure 3–17:

   Format: IBM PC
   Compression: Non-Compressed

4. Click OK twice to save the new file and exit the TIFF Save Options and the Save Image File dialog boxes. Now, the filename *faxillus.tif* appears in the title bar of the image document window.
5. Close the image document by double-clicking on the control menu box of the document window.

That's it! You've designed an original graphic illustration in PhotoStyler without so much as a pixel's worth of help from a scanner. Nonetheless, we know that most PhotoStyler users will be editing

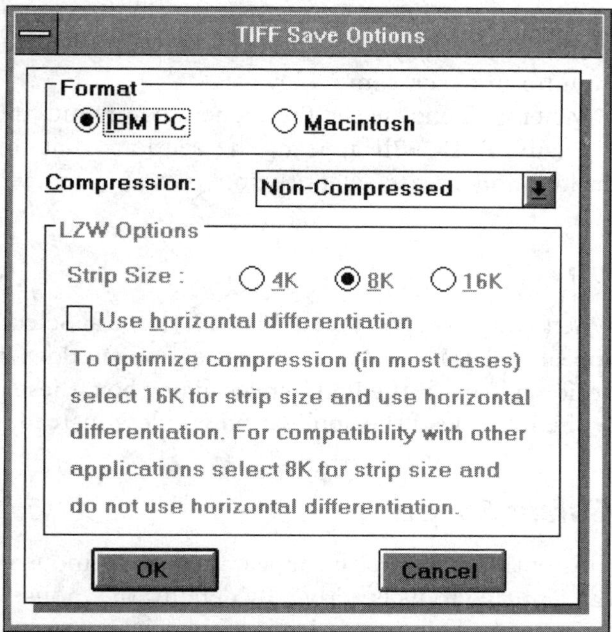

Figure 3-17. The TIFF Save Options dialog box

scanned photographs or existing clip art. If you belong to this majority, Chapter 4 is for you. Before moving on, take a moment to adjust the default screen preferences in PhotoStyler and customize the way you work.

Setting Screen Preferences

One key to PhotoStyler's flexibility is the number of choices you have for customizing the user interface. The Preferences command in the File menu lets you determine:

- Toolbox positions upon start-up
- Mouse cursor shapes when using the Paint tools
- Zoom increment units
- The content of the Color Palette when multiple images are on-screen
- Screen redraw speed and quality
- Use of the Undo command
- The initiation point for a selection area

As you already know, the Monitor Gamma command button in the Preferences dialog box is useful whenever you need to calibrate your monitor or check gamma levels.

When you choose the Preferences command, the dialog box shown in Figure 3–18 will appear. The sections that follow describe your options and how to select them.

Toolbox Position

When you first start Aldus PhotoStyler, the Select and Paint Palettes appear at the right side of the application window. If you select the Left option button in the Preferences dialog box, these palettes will appear at the left side of the application window instead.

Painting Tool Cursor Shape

This option refers to the appearance of the mouse cursor when one of the Painting tools is active. By default, the mouse cursor takes on the shape of the Painting tool you are using. However, some users feel that a crosshair-shaped cursor provides greater pixel-by-pixel accuracy when editing. Let your painting style dictate your choice.

Zoom Increment Unit

This option controls the behavior of the Zoom tool in the Select Palette. With the default setting of 1, you increase the magnification of the active image document by a factor of one each time you click.

Figure 3-18.

The Preferences Setup dialog box

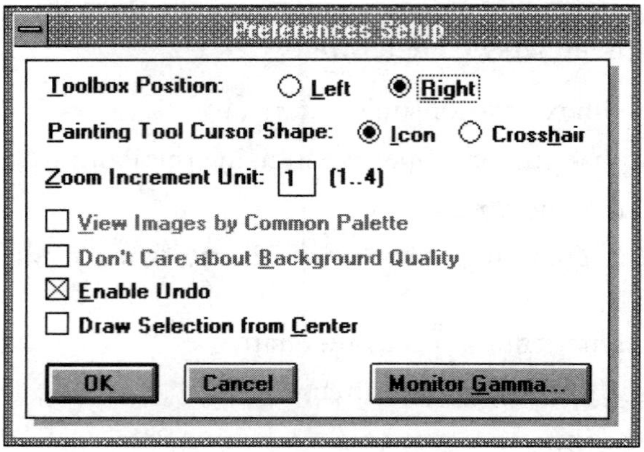

Preferences Setup

Toolbox Position: ○ Left ◉ Right

Painting Tool Cursor Shape: ◉ Icon ○ Crosshair

Zoom Increment Unit: 1 (1..4)

☐ View Images by Common Palette

☐ Don't Care about Background Quality

☒ Enable Undo

☐ Draw Selection from Center

OK | Cancel | Monitor Gamma...

You can vary this ratio to 2, 3, or 4 if it suits the needs of your application.

View Images by Common Palette

PhotoStyler supports the simultaneous display and editing of multiple images. Normally, the color makeup of the currently active image determines the appearance of the Color Palette. For instance, if you're working with a 24-bit True Color image, a 256-color Indexed Color image (Super VGA), and a 16-color Indexed Color image (EGA), the makeup of the Color Palette will change every time you activate a different image.

Under certain conditions, you might want to retain a single palette for all of the images that are currently open. Imagine, for example, that you're preparing a montage and want to see how well the colors match in each of the images you plan to merge. If you activate the View Images by Common Palette option in the Preferences dialog box, PhotoStyler will use a palette that includes every color contained in all of the images that are open. Having a common palette will help you adjust colors in one or more of the images so the final montage will seem more natural.

When this option is active, PhotoStyler will use the palette with the highest number of colors for all images that are open.

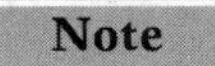

The View Images by Common Palette option is available only for display adapters that support 256 colors.

Don't Care about Background Quality

This option relates to the speed and quality of screen redraw when multiple images are open. By default, PhotoStyler redraws *every* image with equally high quality, even the ones that aren't currently active. As you can imagine, this can slow down program operation considerably and may not be useful to you. If you *don't* need to see high-quality representations of images other than the one you're currently working on, activate this option in the Preferences dialog box. PhotoStyler will then redraw background images quickly, but with less attention to color fidelity and high resolution.

Note

The Don't Care about Background Quality option is available only for display adapters that support 256 colors.

Enable Undo

Of *course* you want to be able to use the Edit menu's Undo command—unless you have very little memory to spare and want to conserve as much as possible. You've probably noticed that complex operations, such as creating the black background for your illustration in the previous exercise, require some time to execute because they're memory-intensive. When you undo a complex operation, PhotoStyler temporarily stores the image data in memory, which can sometimes take up hundreds of kilobytes. To avoid using up memory that you might not be able to spare, deactivate the Enable Undo option in the Preferences dialog box.

Undoing One or More Edits in PhotoStyler

While we're on the subject of clearing bloopers, Table 3–1 provides a handy summary of four different PhotoStyler techniques you can use to undo one or more edits. The first column lists each technique, while the second column describes the circumstances under which you can use it. You'll see other, more detailed references to these techniques scattered throughout this book.

Draw Selection from Center

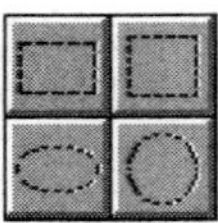

This option relates only to the geometrical selection tools—square, rectangle, circle, and ellipse—in the Select Palette. By default, you define these selections from the *corner* when you begin dragging the

Table 3-1. Undoing Edits in PhotoStyler

Command/Technique	Uses and Limitations
Undo/Edit menu	Restores only the most recent edit. This command doesn't apply to changes in magnification or view.
Eraser/Erase to Last Saved	Restores edits selectively
Restore/File menu	Reverts all edits since you last saved the image file. As with the Eraser tool method, you must have saved the image at least once.
Esc	Interrupts lengthy operations

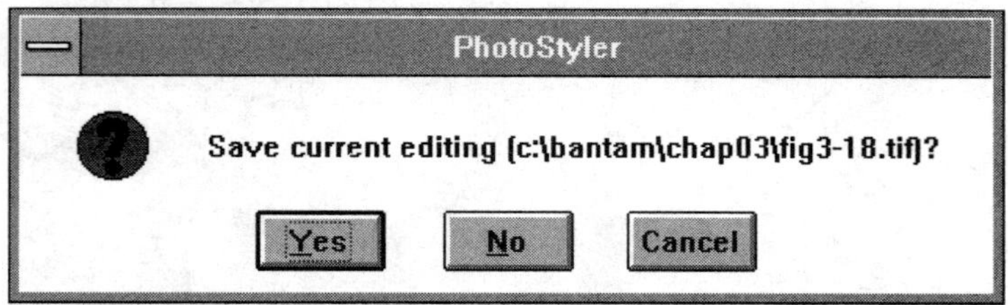

Figure 3-19.

The Save current editing message box

mouse. Some users feel that they can size and position a selection more accurately by defining it from the center outward; if you belong to this group, activate the Draw Selection from Center option.

Monitor Gamma

Click this command button when you are ready to begin calibrating or re-calibrating your monitor. See the "Calibrating Your Monitor" section of this chapter for more information.

Exiting PhotoStyler

You can quit PhotoStyler in one of several ways. The quickest method is to double-click the control menu box of the PhotoStyler application window. A second method, for those who prefer menu commands, is to choose the Exit command from the File menu.

If the application window contains any images that you've edited but haven't saved, a message box similar to the one in Figure 3–19 will appear when you attempt to quit PhotoStyler. This message will repeat for every unsaved image that's open. To save changes to an image before exiting, click Yes. To exit without saving, select No. And if you change your mind about exiting PhotoStyler, select Cancel.

In this chapter, you've tried your hand at a small sampling of PhotoStyler image editing techniques. In the next chapter, you'll find out how to bring images into your computer the right way, so you can avoid potential losses in image quality later in the editing process.

Part II:

MANAGING IMAGE DOCUMENTS

4

All About Input: Image Sources and Image Storage

Before you can edit an image in PhotoStyler, you first have to *digitize* it: translate that photograph, slide, printed or hand-drawn artwork, or still video frame into information that your computer can understand. Getting images into your computer involves a set of closely associated decisions:

- *Input device*—What kind of hardware will yield the highest image quality for your application?
- *Amount of image information*—How many pixels must a digitized image contain in order to look sharp in print or on a slide?
- *Input resolution*—How can you determine the optimum scanning resolution for an image that you will eventually output to print media? To slide format?
- *Storage requirements*—How much hard drive space do you need to store scanned images? Which storage media will best serve your needs?
- *Image sources*—Who created your source images and who holds the copyright? Which sources are legal, and which aren't?

We can't overemphasize the importance of making the *right* decisions at the outset. Digital images consist of a fixed number of pixels, so the act of scanning a source image immediately constrains the relationship between image size and sharpness. This means that the initial input or scanning resolution you choose will determine the quality of your final output, be it a printed advertisement, silk-screened T-shirt, or 35 mm slide.

Choices about input are inseparable from output issues. Arming yourself with knowledge about your application and eventual output medium is the best insurance against making bad input choices that you might rue later. In this chapter, we'll cover the do's and don'ts of input, with the aim of smoothing your path to successful output.

Your Source Image: How Good Is It?

As the computer industry saying goes, "Garbage In, Garbage Out." Yes, PhotoStyler boasts the most sophisticated color correction and image editing techniques available, but no electronic darkroom acrobatics can make up for an image that's inherently inferior. Whenever possible, make certain that your source image (or at least the part you want to cut and paste) is worth the time and trouble needed to enhance it.

What makes a source image worth the time and trouble? Choose an image that meets these criteria:

- *It's at least moderately sharp*—PhotoStyler's sharpening filters and tools can work wonders. But if your source image is fuzzy to start with, artificially increasing contrast between neighboring pixels won't help much.
- *The finish should be glossy rather than matte*—This rule applies if your source image is a photographic print rather than a slide. Textured papers degrade the inherent sharpness of prints and may show up as unwanted "noise" in scanned photos or artwork.
- *It should not originate from previously printed matter*—Images in published documents already contain many tiny halftone dots. If you scan or digitize such an image, you may end up with visual interference patterns known as moirés. You may be able to avoid moirés if you scan a published image at a very low resolution.

An image that meets these basic criteria has passed the first hurdle on the way to successful image processing. The next hurdle is the input device that brings the image into your computer.

Input Devices

An *input device* is the equipment and/or software that digitizes a source image and makes it available for work in PhotoStyler. Scanners, video capture boards, graphics tablets, and screen capture software are all examples of commonly used input devices. Each type of input device is best suited to specific applications, and each has corresponding limitations. We'll devote a large section of this chapter to scanners because they're the most commonly used input devices for PC users at this time.

A Short Course on Scanners

Scanners come in many different varieties, but most have some technological processes in common. Most scanner models illuminate an image one tiny area at a time, sending the altered light from each area to an array of optical sensing devices called CCD's (charge-coupled devices). The CCD's register electrical voltages from the light they sense. Finally, an analog-to-digital converter translates those voltages into numbers, which the computer then records. The cycle begins all over again as the scanner illuminates the next tiny area of the image.

Scanners vary according to the image resolution of which they are capable and the number of colors or gray levels they can reproduce.

- *Resolution*—The number of CCD's available per inch determines the upper limit of input resolution (measured in *ppi*, or pixels per inch) that a scanner can provide. The denser the arrangement of CCD's on the scanner head, the more information a scanner can capture—and the more expensive a scanning device is likely to be.
- *Number of colors/grays*—The number of colors or gray shades a scanner can reproduce depends on the number of levels into which its analog-to-digital converters can divide the voltage readings. There's a geometrical relationship between this number and the file size of a scanned image. Table 4–1 shows the relationship between

Table 4–1. Scanners: Number of Bits per Scan, Number of Colors, and Image File Size

Number of Bits (Levels)	Color or Gray Levels	Relative Image File Size
1 (2^1)	Black and White	1x (B/W is base)
2 (2^2)	4 gray levels	2x
4 (2^4)	16 gray levels	4x
8 (2^8)	256 colors/grays	8x (color requires more)
24 (2^{24})	16,777,216 colors	24x

the number of levels (expressed in bits), the number of colors or grays reproduced, and the size of the image files that a scanner generates.

The rest of this section describes the different types of scanners available, from the most to the least expensive. Each kind of scanner excels at certain types of images and has its own set of limitations, as summarized in Table 4–2.

High-end Rotary Drum Scanners

Traditionally the input device of choice for high-end advertising, the drum scanner offers superior image quality when color must be not just good, but perfect. The equipment requires trained operators and carries a high price tag. You'll find most of these scanners at prepress service bureaus and most of their clients at advertising agencies. Manufacturers of drum scanner systems include Scitex, Agfa Corporation, Crosfield, Dainippon, and Linotype-Hell. Figure 4–1 shows the DC-3000 rotary drum scanner from Linotype-Hell.

The drum scanning mechanism consists of a scanner proper and a long cylinder that extends outward from the scan head. During scanning, the cylinder rotates slowly, emitting a tiny point of light through a small hole above which the slide transparency or photographic print lies.

Drum scanners are usually part of a dedicated prepress system that includes "paintbox" software and a non-PostScript film output device. They scan transparencies at high resolutions, usually over 3000 dpi or ppi. Their superior color depth—as high as 12 bits per pixel—is one reason why images scanned by these devices often seem especially

Table 4-2. Advantages and Disadvantages of Scanning Devices

Scanning Device	Advantages	Disadvantages	Best applications
Drum scanner	Highest-quality scan, most information, best shadows and highlights	Expensive, requires large storage capcity	High-end advertising
Slide scanner	High resolution, WYSIWYG saturated colors	More expensive than flatbeds	Color print media
Flatbed scanner	Can scan 2-dimensional objects, all media except slides	Limited resolution, reflective color	Color and grayscale print media
Sheet-fed scanner	Good for tracing comps	Limited grayscale range, misalignment	Grayscale print media
Hand scanner	Portable, can trace some 3-D surfaces	Limited scan width, steady hand required for most models	Low-end color and grayscale media
Overhead scanner	Can scan 3-dimensional objects	Poor lighting control, no 2-D objects	Technical and manufacturing documents
Film scanner	Brighter colors for large transparencies	Limited to one medium	Presentations

lustrous in highlight and shadow areas. High color depth is also the reason why image files generated by drum scanners can easily fill 30, 40, or even 60 Mb of hard drive space. Transporting these huge files from the service bureau to your computer requires a removable hard drive such as the Syquest 44 or 88 Mb models.

An increasing number of drum scanner manufacturers now provide a software "link" to personal computer users whose final output will be a PostScript imagesetter. It's possible to convert proprietary-format drum scanner files to the TIFF or EPS format recognized by PhotoStyler.

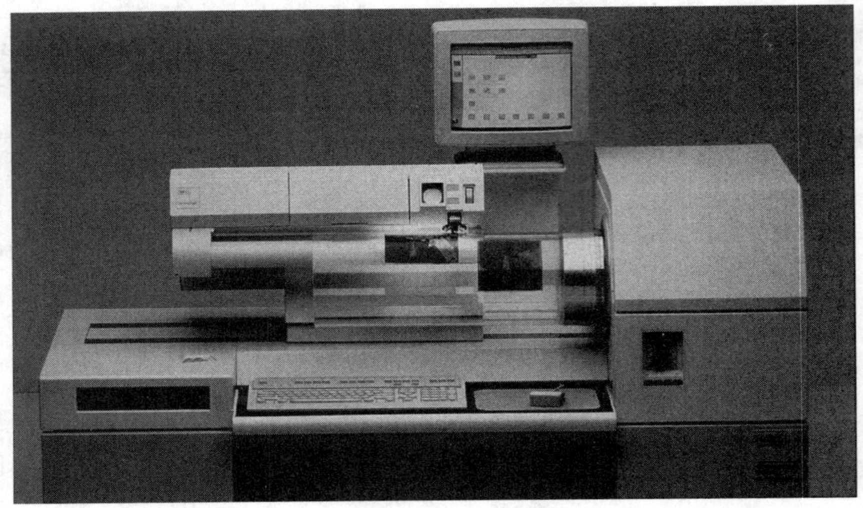

Figure 4-1.
The DC-3000 rotary drum scanner from Linotype-Hell

If you have Fortune 500 advertising clients and a Syquest removable hard drive, you can edit the high-quality scanned image in Aldus PhotoStyler and then set up color separations directly on your PC.

Note

Until recently, all software linking to high-end drum scanners was available for Macintosh users only. Check with your service bureau or color prepress house to see whether their equipment supports linking for PC customers, too.

Slide Scanners

If you work with images destined for full-color printing or presentations, but don't have the budget of a Fortune 500 corporation at your disposal, a desktop slide scanner may be the input device of choice. Slide scanners offer two advantages over flatbed scanners: better color quality and higher input resolutions. Those who know color understand that, when scanned, transparencies yield brighter, more saturated digital image colors than do photographic prints. That's because light passes directly through transparencies, but is *reflected* off the surface of a print. Slide scanners can also capture more visual information per inch than flatbed scanners. High-resolution slide scanners, such as the Nikon 3500AF series used by many service bureaus (Figure

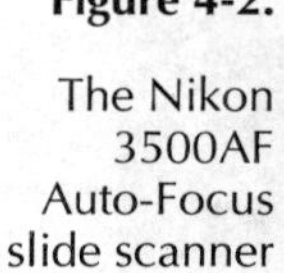

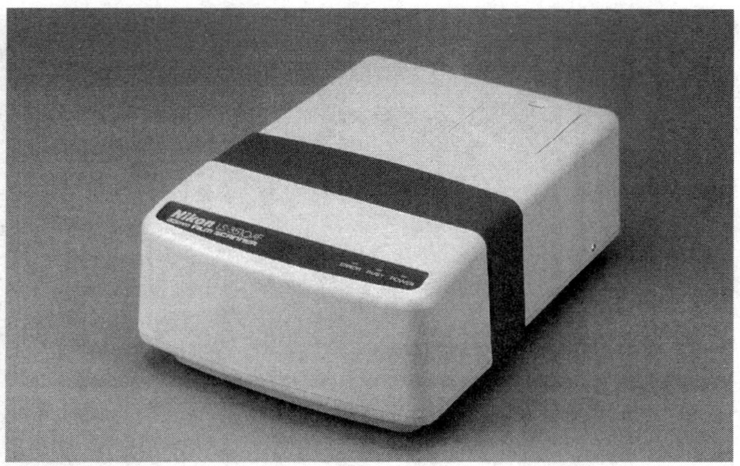

Figure 4-2. The Nikon 3500AF Auto-Focus slide scanner

4–2), can digitize up to 4000 pixels per inch. As you might expect, scanning at high resolutions generates large image files.

PhotoStyler supplies software drivers for Microtek and Nikon slide scanners. If you own one of these scanners, you can scan images directly from within PhotoStyler. If you own a different slide scanner, contact the manufacturer regarding the availability of a PhotoStyler driver.

Note

Slides, unlike photographic prints, are fixed in size. Horizontal-format 35 mm slides are 1.375 inches wide by .9375 inches high; vertical-format slides are .9375 inches wide by 1.375 inches high. If you scan a large 8" x 10" photographic print using a 600 dpi flatbed scanner, you may digitize just as much information as if you scanned a transparency of the same image at 4000 ppi or dpi. If you regularly scan in smaller *photographic prints, on the other hand, you can capture more information by scanning a slide of the same image.*

Until recently, slide scanners were several times as expensive as their flatbed counterparts, but the price gap is narrowing rapidly. New models aimed at the midrange color desktop publishing market, including the Microtek ScanMaker 1850 (Figure 4–3), feature competitive pricing and input resolutions of about 2000 dpi. As more and more desktop slide scanners become available, look for a continued decrease in prices coupled with an increase in maximum input resolution. By the time you read this, Microtek may already have released a desktop slide scanner capable of input at 4000 dpi.

Figure 4-3.

The Microtek ScanMaker 1850 slide scanner

If you don't need color, or if most of your source images are photographic prints or other printed matter, a slide scanner won't meet your needs. Look to flatbed scanners instead.

Flatbed Scanners

Flatbed scanners work a little like a photocopier. You place the image to be scanned face down on a glass plate and close the lid. When you start the scan, light reflects off the image as the scan head passes underneath. Flatbeds that can scan your choice of black-and-white line art, grayscale images, or 16,000,000 colors in the same unit are now common, with street prices well below $2,000. Dedicated grayscale flatbeds are also available for even less of an investment.

Beyond pricing, the main advantage of flatbeds is their versatility. You can scan almost any flat item and even (if you control lighting carefully) a single plane of small three-dimensional objects. The chief disadvantage of flatbed scanners is the low image resolution they offer relative to slide and drum scanners. Most popular models scan images at resolutions up to 300 or, in the case of the Microtek 600SZ (Figure 4–4), 600 dpi or ppi. Some scanners let you simulate higher resolutions by *interpolating* pixels between the ones its CCD's can physically register; but this isn't as good as adding more "real" visual information.

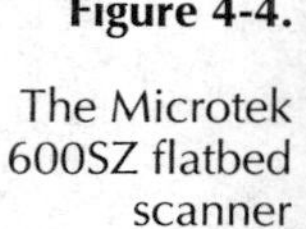

Figure 4-4.

The Microtek 600SZ flatbed scanner

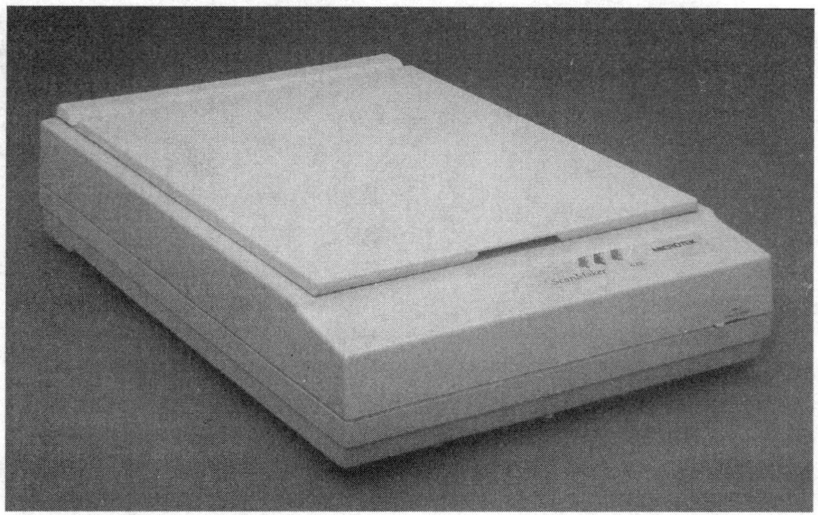

PhotoStyler supplies software drivers for Microtek, Hewlett-Packard, Epson, and Sharp flatbed scanner models. If you own one of these devices, you can scan images directly from within PhotoStyler.

For most grayscale and medium-budget color printing jobs, flatbed scanners can provide acceptable scanning quality. See the section entitled "Determining an Optimum Scanning (Input) Resolution" for detailed guidelines on achieving the right relationship between input resolution, final image size, and output resolution. Look ahead to Table 4–3, where you'll find handy formulas for calculating an ideal scanning resolution.

Sheet-fed Scanners

We don't recommend sheet-fed scanners for serious image processing. A lack of 8-bit grayscale and 24-bit color capabilities, low resolution, and the limitations of the physical scanning mechanism hamper their usefulness. Glossy papers or items that are other than standard paper size can shift as they pass through the mechanism, resulting in misaligned or skewed images. However, prices of sheet-fed scanners are extremely low. If you don't mind the limited number of gray shades available, a sheet-fed scanner can still be suitable for some low-end applications.

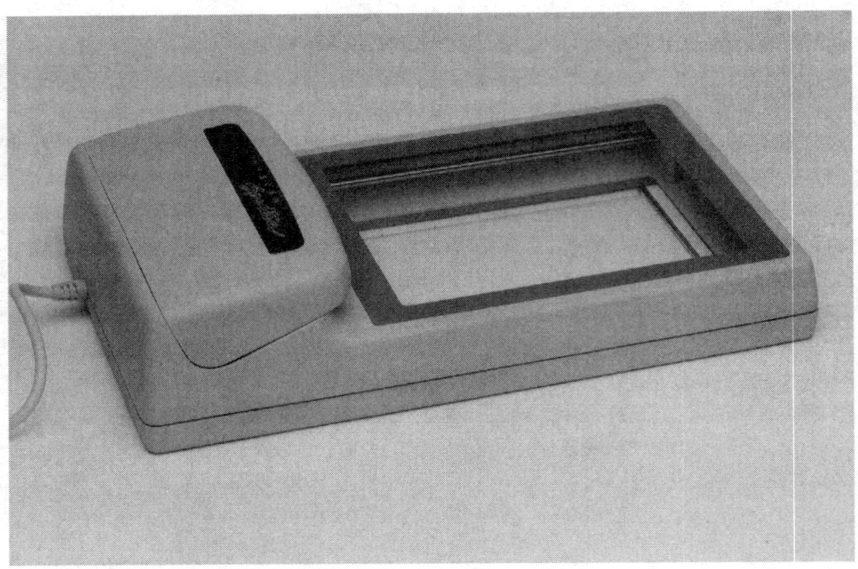

Figure 4-5.

The Niscan Spectra 24-bit color hand scanner

Hand Scanners

Once limited to grayscale models, hand scanners can now reproduce 256 or even (as in the case of the versatile Niscan Spectra in Figure 4–5) 16 million colors. Hand scanners are small, saving precious desktop space. They're inexpensive. They can do things that other scanners can't, such as record patterns on the flat surfaces of large three-dimensional objects. Some grayscale hand scanners even boast resolutions above 300 dpi.

The disadvantages of most hand scanners are twofold: they require a steady hand, and their image scanning area is limited to five inches wide or less. You can overcome the first limitation by mounting the hand scanner on a slide rail. The second disadvantage is not so easy to discount. Although many hand scanners provide software that lets you "sew" two halves of a large image together, the results aren't consistently reliable enough for professional-looking publications. If your chief image processing activity is editing small grayscale or color photos, hand scanners offer a perfectly adequate and inexpensive solution. For other applications, consider using a hand scanner for flexibility and a flatbed or slide scanner for large images or high input resolutions.

Tip

The Niscan Spectra (see Figure 4–5) is a notable exception to the disadvantages of conventional hand scanners. Its design features built-in rail mounts that allow the scan head to move across the source image automatically, eliminating misalignment problems. You can even scan slide transparencies with the Niscan Spectra: just place the slide on an illuminated light table and position the scanner on top of it.

Other Types of Scanners

Other scanners that have viable applications for PhotoStyler include film scanners and overhead (3-D) scanners.

- *Film scanners* are appropriate when your source images are large film transparencies (4 x 5 inches or 8 x 10 inches). Like 35 mm slide scanners, film scanners use mirrors to reflect light back to sensing devices at precise angles. Flatbed scanners use mirrors differently, so they can't reproduce large transparencies with the proper degree of sharpness or color fidelity.
- *Overhead scanners* involve cameras and/or lights above a flat table on which you place items you wish to scan. They're useful for scanning small three-dimensional objects such as medical devices or other corporate products. Since there's no shield to block out light, it's important to control lighting in order to obtain consistent results.

Determining an Optimum Scanning (Input) Resolution

Input and output issues in PhotoStyler are closely linked. In order to determine the optimum scanning (input) resolution for a given source image, you need to know as much as possible about your eventual output medium. Will your image end up as a printed advertisement? As a 35 mm presentation slide? As a silk-screened T-shirt? Quality output is the ultimate goal of all your work in PhotoStyler, after all. And output quality depends on an input resolution that will guarantee enough *information* in the digital image.

In the world of image processing, it's the amount of *information* (the number of pixels) in an image that counts. Never scan at an arbitrary resolution, or your images may contain more or fewer pixels than are necessary for good output. An image that contains too many pixels is not a problem; at worst, it will take up excess storage space on your hard drive and slow down the editing process on your computer. You can *resample* oversized images downward without degrading image quality (see Chapter 13). On the other hand, if you enlarge an already-digitized image that contains too *few* pixels, you'll sacrifice sharpness. The best strategy is to figure out exactly how much digital information you'll need before you even turn on your scanning device.

Determining the best possible scanning resolution is a two-step process. The first step is to calculate the amount of information you need to scan—the pixel width of the digital image. The final output medium you plan to use (print media, presentation slides, and so forth) will help you determine this figure.

The second step is to divide the desired amount of image information by the dimensions of the original source image. If storage space is at a premium for you, you may also want to calculate the size of the image file that you'll generate. Table 4–3 contains handy formulas that you can use to determine pixel width, input resolution, and image file size for various types of source images and output media.

Table 4-3. Image Scanning Formulas

To Determine . . .	Use This Formula . . . .
Optimum image width in pixels, print media output	Halftone screen frequency (lpi) x printed image width (inches) x 2
Optimum image width in pixels, slide media output	For horizontal-format slides: Film recorder resolution (lines) x 1*
	For vertical-format slides: Film recorder resolution (lines) x ⅔
Optimum input resolution (dpi)	Optimum pixel width ÷ source image width (inches)**
Image file size, 8-bit Grayscale input (bytes)	Horizontal scanning resolution x vertical scanning resolution x source image width x source image height
Image file size, 24-bit color input (bytes)	Horizontal scanning resolution x vertical scanning resolution x source image width x source image height x 3

*Typical output resolutions are 2000, 4000, or 8000 lines (pixels)

**35 mm slides have fixed dimensions: 1.375" x .9375" for landscape format, .9375 x 1.375" for vertical format

Note *Input and output terminology can sometimes be confusing. We measure source image dimensions in inches, scanning resolutions in dots per inch (dpi), pixels per inch (ppi) or lines per inch (lpi), professional print media output in lines per inch (lpi), and slide media output in lines (pixels). Don't let the lines of scanning resolutions and the lines of print media output bewilder you! They're not equivalent to one another.*

Calculating Input Resolution for Print Media Output

If a given image is slated for commercial offset printing, you'll probably be using a PostScript-based imagesetter to output the image to film or RC paper. You'll need to know the *halftone screen frequency*, measured in lines per inch (lpi), that you will specify for the imagesetting device (see Chapter 15). You'll also need to know the *width* of your final image on the printed page; the graphic designer for the project should be able to tell you this. Then, refer to Table 4–3 and derive the optimum amount of image information as follows:

1. Multiply the planned print width of the image by the halftone screen frequency you'll be specifying at the service bureau. This figure represents the *minimum* number of pixels the horizontal dimension of your image must contain. For example, if your halftone screen frequency will be 150 lines per inch (lpi) and the planned print width is four inches, you'll need a bare minimum of 600 pixels.
2. Next, double the minimum pixel width to obtain the *optimum* pixel width. For best PostScript output results, an image should contain about two pixels per halftone dot. In the example just given, a print width of four inches and a halftone screen frequency of 150 lpi would dictate a required pixel width of 1200 pixels (150 x 4 x 2).
3. Finally, divide the optimum pixel width by the width of the original hard copy print or transparency that you're going to scan. This tells you the scanning resolution you'll have to use if you want the final image to look as sharp as the original. In our example, a vertical format source image that's 8" wide by 10" high will require an input resolution of 125 ppi (1200 pixels / 8 inches = 125 pixels per inch). On the other hand, if the source image were a 35 mm slide

transparency in vertical format (0.9375" wide by 1.375" high), we'd require an input resolution of about 1280 ppi (1200 pixels / 0.9375 inches = 1280 ppi). Scan the photo at the required resolution, and you'll have exactly as much information as you need for good reproduction.

Tip

If PhotoStyler supports direct scanning from your flatbed or slide scanner, all you need to know is the horizontal pixel width you require (steps 1 and 2). The scanner interface will display the estimated pixel width of your image for a given input resolution, so you can adjust scanning resolution interactively until you get the right number of pixels.

Tip

If you plan to output a PhotoStyler image as a silk-screened product, calculate input resolution as though you were going to print the image commercially. The screen frequencies used in silk-screen work are usually coarser than those used for printing, but the principles are the same.

Calculating Input Resolution for Transparency Output

If a slide transparency is to be the final output of a PhotoStyler image, the dimensions of the source image and the output resolution of the film recorder will determine your optimum input resolution. Film recorders typically offer output resolutions of 2000, 4000, or 8000 *lines*, which refer to the horizontal pixel density of the slide. Both the horizontal and vertical pixel densities of a slide derive from the film recorder's output resolution. For example, 35 mm slides have a fixed width-to-height aspect ratio of three to two. At a film recorder resolution of 4000 lines, a 35 mm slide will be 4000 pixels wide and 2666 pixels high.

To determine the optimum input resolution for output to slide media:

1. Find out your eventual output resolution. This tells you how many pixels the horizontal dimension of a digitized source image should contain.
2. To derive the optimum scanning resolution for transparency output, simply divide the resolution of the film recorder by the *broadest* dimension of your source image. Let's use the example of the

8" x 10" source image again. If the film recorder output resolution will be 4000 lines (4000 pixels wide), we have: 4000 pixels / 10 inches = 400 ppi, the optimum scanning resolution. A film recorder output resolution of 2000 lines, on the other hand, would dictate a scanning resolution of only 200 ppi (2000 pixels / 10 inches).

If you're planning to output to slide format, but your source image has something other than a 3:2 aspect ratio, you may either have to crop the source image or leave blank space in the slide at output time.

Calculating Scanning Resolution: Video Output

A still frame of video, like a slide transparency, has a fixed aspect ratio. In the U.S., where the standard video format is NTSC, the ratio is 1.06:1 (525 pixels horizontally by 480 pixels vertically). In terms of the amount of visual information available, 525 by 480 pixels is a pretty poor resolution when compared with transparencies or print media. Still, we're so accustomed to viewing television that we don't often notice. One thing is sure: if your source image is a photographic print or slide, you won't need to use a very high scanning resolution to achieve final output quality.

Chances are that most of your source images for output to video will have been captured from a video source and will have the correct aspect ratio to begin with. But if your source images come from photographic prints or slide transparencies, here's how to determine the best scanning resolution:

1. Calculate the width and height of your source image in inches and determine the aspect ratio. If it's something other than 1.06:1, you'll have to crop the image to the proper aspect ratio before scanning.
2. Divide 525 pixels (the width of the video frame) by the cropped width of the source image. This is your best possible scanning resolution.

Preparing the Scan

As mentioned earlier in this chapter, Aldus PhotoStyler provides direct scan software modules for several popular slide and flatbed

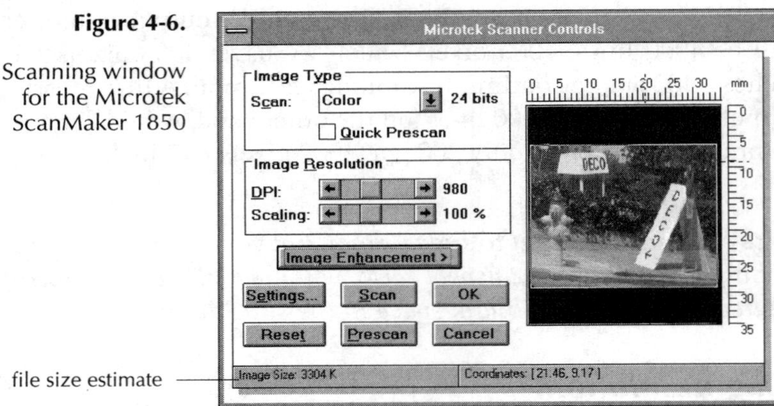

file size estimate

Figure 4-6.

Scanning window for the Microtek ScanMaker 1850

scanners. PhotoStyler's modular structure also allows third-party developers to supply plug-in scanning modules of their own. If PhotoStyler doesn't support direct scanning by your device, contact the scanner manufacturer to see if a driver is available.

The process of preparing a scan from within PhotoStyler varies, depending on the capabilities of your scanning device. Figure 4–6 shows the PhotoStyler scanning window for the Microtek ScanMaker 1850 slide scanner, but many elements of the user interface are similar for all scanner types. In most cases, you'll complete these steps to prepare a scan:

1. Make certain that your scanner is turned on and that the I/O address of your scanning device is correct. Choose the Scanner Setup command in the File/Scan submenu if you're not sure of the I/O address.
2. Choose the Scanner Controls command from the File/Scan submenu. A dialog box will appear.
3. Choose the image data type of the image to be scanned. This will be either 8bit Grayscale or, in the case of color scanners, 24-bit True Color.
4. Choose Prescan if you want to obtain a rough display of the source image. Such a display will aid you in positioning crop marks or precorrecting brightness and contrast.
5. Adjust gamma, brightness, and contrast, if necessary, and if your scanning module permits this. If you can't make these adjustments in the scanning module, don't worry; PhotoStyler's superb image correction controls will let you tweak the image later.

6. Crop the scanning area, if desired. Typically, cropping will involve drawing a rectangular box around the image or around the portion of the image that you want to scan.

Tip *If the image is smaller than the image display area of your scanner, be sure to crop before scanning. Otherwise, PhotoStyler will scan the entire image display area, creating a file that consumes far too much unnecessary disk space.*

7. If you want to scan the image at a size that's larger or smaller than the original, adjust the Scaling value. You may want to adjust the scaling factor in conjunction with the scanning resolution.
8. Select a scanning resolution from the available range. Keep the final output size of your image in mind and make sure the scanned image will contain a sufficient number of pixels.
9. Check the image storage space statistics in the scanner interface window to determine how much storage space the image will require. If you don't have enough storage space, scale down the scan size or reduce the resolution.
10. Click OK to begin the scan. If the Show Scan command in the File/Scan submenu has a check mark in front of it, you'll see a real-time visual simulation of the scanning process. As you scan, PhotoStyler will open a new document window called "Scanning a New Image." When the scan is complete, PhotoStyler will place the scanned image in this window as an untitled image document. You can then save the image, choosing one of the file formats described in Chapter 5.

Estimating Image File Size

If Aldus PhotoStyler supports your scanner directly, you won't need to guess how many Kb or Mb a source image will occupy once it's scanned. The scanning module will estimate storage space for you when you crop the representation of the image prior to scanning (see Figure 4–6).

If your scanner doesn't support direct scanning within PhotoStyler, there's a straightforward way to calculate approximately how many bytes a given scanned image will occupy (see Table 4–3). Three factors determine the size of an image file in bytes:

- The number of colors or grays your scanning device can reproduce, expressed in bits
- The dimensions of your source image
- The scanning resolution

Image File Size and Number of Bits

An 8-bit grayscale scanner provides 256 shades of gray, while a 24-bit color scanner can reproduce more than 16 million colors. The size of your image file increases in proportion to the number of bits (not colors) in your scan. A 24-bit scan requires about 24 times as much storage space as a black-and-white scan and about three times as much storage space as an 8-bit (256 colors or gray shades) scan of the same image. The number of *pixels* in the scanned image remains the same in each case, but the amount of *information* in each pixel increases with the number of bits in the scan. In 1-bit mode, a scanner records only on or off, black or white. In 8-bit mode, the scanner must pack eight times as much information into each pixel. And in 24-bit color mode, a scanner must record those eight bits of information three times for every pixel: once each for red, green, and blue.

Image Dimensions, File Size, and Input Resolution

The dimensions of your source image and your scanning resolution have a direct impact on file size, too. A scanner that can provide 300 dpi or ppi input resolution is actually producing 90,000 pixels per square inch (300 pixels wide by 300 pixels deep). For every square inch of a picture you scan, you're adding another 90,000 pixels to the digital image. Each time you double scanning resolution, therefore, you quadruple the size of the resulting image file.

Note

PhotoStyler characterizes image files not according to the number of bits in the scan, but according to their image data type, which is essentially the same thing. A PhotoStyler True Color image is the same as a 24-bit image; a Grayscale image and an 8-bit Grayscale image are also the same. Although PhotoStyler supports many different image data types, most Painting tools, filters, and other image editing functions apply only to 8-bit Grayscale and 24-bit True Color images. If you scan an image with a different number of color or gray levels, you'll need to convert it to Grayscale or True Color before you can do much work with it in PhotoStyler.

Calculating File Size: Grayscale and True Color Images

Most PhotoStyler users will be scanning images as either 8-bit Grayscale or 24-bit True Color. For 8-bit Grayscale images, the formula for calculating image file size is:

horizontal input resolution (ppi) x vertical input resolution (ppi) x source image width x source image height = image file size in bytes

For 24-bit color scans, just multiply the results of this formula by three to obtain the image file size.

Assume, for example, that you're going to scan a 5" x 7" color photo twice: once as a Grayscale image and once in 24-bit color. If your scanning resolution is 300 ppi, you'll end up with image files of the following sizes:

Grayscale: 300 ppi x 300 ppi x 5" x 7" = 3,150,000 bytes or 3.15 Mb

24-bit color: 300 ppi x 300 ppi x 5" x 7" x 3 = 9,450,000 bytes or 9.45 Mb

File sizes leap even more dramatically when you use the services of a high-end drum scanner at a service bureau. These devices feature not only extremely high input resolutions, but also color depth that exceeds 24 bits. Expect file sizes ranging from 30-60 Mb from these sources. For such large images, you'll require a large hard drive and removable hard drive storage. See "The Storage Issue" section of this chapter for information about the types of storage devices available to you.

Tips for Working with Large Image Files

One day, PhotoStyler may support a math coprocessor. Until then, editing and manipulating multimegabyte color image files can slow down your system and try your patience. We've assembled a number of technical tips for enhancing Windows and PhotoStyler performance in Appendix A. Here, though, we'd like to pass on some common sense suggestions for working smart rather than working hard with those mammoth image files.

Balancing RAM with the File Size of Typical Images

If you routinely edit image files that approach or exceed the amount of RAM in your computer system, consider increasing your system memory to speed image processing. Ideally, you should have at least twice as much memory as the file size of a typical image; 8 Mb, for example, if you usually work with 4 Mb image files. For those whose budget doesn't permit the ideal, your system memory should at least equal the size of a typical file. In the long run, scrimping on system memory will cost you more in terms of lost work time than you'd save on the price of memory chips. You might also benefit from some of the system enhancement tips we offer in Appendix A.

Using Grayscale Scans for Position Only in Your Page Layout Package

Formatting a document that contains many True Color (24-bit) images can really slow down the speed of your page layout software. If you publish catalogs or other documents that use lots of color images, here's a strategy that will speed your work: when you're finished editing the 24-bit color images in PhotoStyler, generate a Grayscale duplicate of each image as described in Chapter 5. Then, use the Resample command in the Transform menu (Chapter 13) to reduce both the resolution of each image and the number of pixels it contains. Place these low-resolution Grayscale images in the document for position-only proofing. When your layout is complete and approved and you're ready to generate final output, you can substitute the high-resolution True Color originals.

Designing Initial Comps Using Scaled-Down Image Files

Imagine yourself working on a True Color image for a large-format book cover or advertisement. Your image file is likely to fill up many megabytes. Even if you have 16 Mb or more of RAM and a substantial permanent swap file under Windows, most PhotoStyler operations will take quite some time to process because of the sheer number of pixels in the image. How can you be spontaneous and creative when you'll be spending so much time waiting?

One solution is to use low-resolution scans or resampled-down versions of images during the initial image planning stages. The use of a small image file lets you experiment playfully with your artwork and try out a variety of techniques, without being hampered by too much consciousness of the technology and its limitations. Save intermediate versions of your initial comps, and keep a detailed journal of the techniques you use. Then, when you're ready to substitute a multi-megabyte scan or image file, you can reproduce the final composition step-by-step without wasting time. If you have less memory or processing power than you'd like, this method of working will free you to be creative and save you time and money as well.

Obtaining Images from Other Input Sources

Although scanners are currently the most popular type of input device for PC users, various hardware devices and software utilities allow you to capture images from other sources. This section briefly describes those image sources and guidelines for using them as input devices with PhotoStyler.

Obtaining Images from Video Sources

A *video source* is any device or software utility that allows you to capture an image from a television, videotape, still video camera, or computer monitor. The number and types of these devices are proliferating rapidly due to advances in multimedia technology; we'll cover just the more familiar ones here.

Video Capture and Frame Grabber Boards

Many manufacturers now offer PC expansion boards and software that let you "grab" and digitize live images in video format. Some products also let you capture individual frames from a videotape. Due to North American video standards, the amount of information in images from these sources is low, never exceeding 640 x 480 pixels. For that reason, we don't recommend using video capture images in print publications unless you print the images at very small sizes. But if you want to edit a still video image and then output it to video again, PhotoStyler is an excellent tool—provided you can save the image in a format that PhotoStyler can read. The Targa (.TGA) format is an old standard in this field and one that most manufacturers continue to support.

The number of colors available in images you capture in this way depends on the hardware device. The current standards are 8-bit,

16-bit, 24-bit, and 32-bit boards, which yield 256, 32,000, 16.7 million, and 4.2 billion colors, respectively. Although PhotoStyler supports some editing of 256-color images, most of the tools and commands apply only to 8-bit Grayscale and 24-bit color images. If you capture images using 16- or 32-bit color hardware, the images will be read-only in PhotoStyler. Unless you can convert the captured image into a True Color (24-bit) image data type beforehand, you won't be able to edit it in PhotoStyler.

Still Video Cameras

Like flatbed and slide scanners, the new breed of still video cameras use CCD's to translate light into electronic signals. Still video cameras, such as the Sony ProMavica series, bypass film entirely by recording images directly onto two-inch floppy disks. Depending on the camera manufacturer, you can input these electronic images through an NTSC video cable or through a proprietary disk drive.

Although convenient, still video cameras are pricey, with the mid-range quality products costing from $2,000 to $4,000. In addition, the quality of the images they generate is much lower than that of images reproduced by traditional photography. The average still video camera can capture no more than 750 x 500 pixels. This may be enough information for small color images in low-end catalogs or newsletters, but it won't suffice for glossy high-end publications.

Standards among still video camera manufacturers vary. If you want to import a still video camera image into PhotoStyler, make sure it is the True Color (24-bit) data type, or convert it to True Color before you begin editing.

Screen Capture Software

Screen capture software lets you capture part or all of the contents of your computer display and save it as a bitmapped image file. These utilities are especially useful for people who have to produce manuals on commercial or industrial software. Hosts of screen capture programs are available, and most of them save images in at least one file format that is compatible with PhotoStyler. The program you use should also save images in 8-bit Grayscale or 24-bit color format for easier editing in PhotoStyler. Our own favorite is the Windows-based Tiffany Plus from Anderson Consulting & Software in North Bonneville, Washington.

Obtaining Images from Paint Programs

So, you're a computer artist who's created a series of bitmapped images in your favorite "paint" program, and you'd like to do some fancy stuff with these pictures in PhotoStyler. You can—with certain limitations.

Most PC-based paint programs can save images in one or more of the file formats that PhotoStyler supports. However, only the most recent crop of paint programs can save images in True Color format. Older-generation paint packages support only the number of colors or grays that your display adapter makes available: for example, 256 colors for SuperVGA. In order to edit a non-True Color paint image in PhotoStyler, you'll first have to convert it to the True Color or Grayscale image data type. Some loss of image quality may result from the conversion, especially if you have to resample the image to increase the amount of information it contains.

The Promise of CD-ROM

Late in 1990, Eastman Kodak announced the development of an integrated desktop color management system that would merge the strengths of high-quality photography with advances in digital imaging technology. The cornerstone of Kodak's system will be the *Photo CD* (Figure 4–7), scheduled to make its debut in the spring of 1992. With the Photo CD system, photographers, desktop publishing professionals, and the general public will be able to deliver film to photo finishing bureaus and receive a compact disc in addition to prints. If you have a standard CD-ROM XA player, you can download the images to your computer's hard drive. If you have a CD-I or proprietary Photo CD player, you can display the images on a television set as well.

Each Photo CD disk can contain up to 100 images, and each image is stored on the CD in five different resolutions ranging from 192 by 128 pixels to 3072 by 2048 pixels. To use an image with PhotoStyler, you'll download it at the resolution of your choice.

Major photo stock houses and clip art vendors are also making photographic images available in compact disk format. As a client of these services, you typically display the photos from the CD on your monitor, then receive a code to "unlock" the images you want.

The Storage Issue

You've seen how source image size, color depth, and input resolution can contribute to monster-sized image files that quickly eat up hard

Figure 4-7.

The Kodak Photo CD system will make it possible to download digital versions of photographs to the computer

disk space. If you work extensively with PhotoStyler, you'll need to come to grips with the issue of where to keep all those files. Of the many storage devices available, some are suitable for *primary storage* (storing the files as you edit them), while others are practical only for *secondary storage* (archiving the files once the project is over). Table 4–4 summarizes the advantages and disadvantages of each storage medium.

Floppy Disks

Floppy disks are never good primary storage choices. Even when images occupy less than an entire floppy, PhotoStyler needs additional space to manipulate the file as you edit. Floppy disks *can* provide adequate secondary storage, but only if most of your images are small grayscale pictures or if you use image compression software or hardware to reduce file size.

Hard Drives

Hard drives are the mainstay of primary storage, but we don't recommend them for long-term secondary storage. Even a one-gigabyte

Table 4-4. Storage Devices for PhotoStyler Images

Storage medium	Capacity	Advantages	Disadvantages	Primary storage/ Secondary storage?
Floppy disk	1.2 or 1.4 Mb	Convenient, portable	Most image files too large to store	No (color)/yes (small grayscale)
Hard drive	20 to 1200 Mb	Storage space, speed	Magnetically sensitive	Yes/no
Tape backup	40 to 256 Mb	Inexpensive, portable	Useful for backup only	No/yes
Removable hard drives	10 to 88 Mb	Portable for service bureau	Magnetically sensitive, limited long-term storage	No/yes
WORM optical drives	600-1200 Mb	Data safety, large capacity	Data cannot be overwritten	No/yes
Rewritable optical cartridges	128-256 Mb	Portable (service bureau), data safety, can store multiple large image files	Too slow for primary storage	Qualified yes/yes

wonder drive will fill up to capacity eventually if you stuff enough PhotoStyler images into it! That much aside, we have only this to say about choosing a hard drive for use with PhotoStyler: The bigger and faster, the better.

Hard Drive Size

In practical terms, it's the amount of *free* space on your hard drive that counts, not the total capacity of the drive. PhotoStyler uses the space on your hard drive for two different purposes:

- *Storing image files*—It's good practice to save multiple versions of a file as you edit, so you won't have to rescan and start from scratch if you decide you've made an error. Of course, multiplying the number of files on your hard drive also multiplies the amount of space they require.

- *Manipulating images*—As you edit images, PhotoStyler uses your RAM and your hard drive as a temporary workspace. The greater the number of operations you perform on an image without saving it, the more hard drive space PhotoStyler will use—often several times the amount of hard drive space that the image file itself occupies. A general rule of thumb is to determine how many Mb all the currently open image files occupy, and then make sure you have two to four times as much hard drive space available. For example, if three image files are open in your PhotoStyler application window and together they occupy 8 Mb, you should have between 16 and 32 Mb of space available on your hard drive. Saving images frequently will help reduce the drain on hard drive space, too.

Only you know how many images you'll typically work with at one time and how memory-intensive they are likely to be. In any event, an 80 Mb drive with 60 Mb free will serve you better than an equally fast 160 Mb drive with only 40 Mb free.

Hard Drive Speed

Hard drives vary in their *access time* (the amount of time it takes for the computer to begin communicating with the drive) and in the rate of data transfer. A hard drive with a fast access time will usually have a fast data transfer rate. Access times below 20 ms (milliseconds) are desirable; some newer drives feature access times as low as 9 ms.

Tape Backup

For long-term archival of your PhotoStyler images, magnetic tape backup drives and cartridges are among the most convenient and cost-effective storage media. Nominal storage capacities for popular tape cartridges range from 40 to 256 Mb, but many tape drives include built-in file compression options that can effectively double storage capacity. This means that you can store backups of even the largest color image files. Later, if the need arises, you can download them to your hard drive again for re-editing.

Removable Hard Drives

Multi-megabyte image and PostScript output files are the norm for many documents these days. As a result, sending floppy disks to service bureaus has become impractical. New types of removable storage media have arisen to solve this problem and accommodate the storage of large files. The most popular types of removable media are the *Bernoulli box* and the *Syquest* cartridge (see Figure 4–8). Cartridges for Bernoulli drives can contain between 10 and 45 Mb of data, while Syquest cartridges can hold either 44 or 88 Mb. If you plan to use removable drives when sending PhotoStyler output files to a service bureau, make sure your service bureau supports the hardware you've chosen. Make sure they support that hardware for the PC as well as the Mac, too! You'll find more information about using removable drives in Chapter 16.

Optical Drives and Cartridges

Optical storage devices, unlike magnetic media such as conventional hard drives and tape backup systems, provide high-quality data safety. They also support large quantities of image data in a more compact space than hard drives. They're much slower than hard drives and also more expensive, but for long-term archival of your images, they're ideal.

Rewritable Optical Drives

The most practical type of optical storage device is likely to be the new generation of fully rewritable optical cartridges now becoming available. Several manufacturers, including IBM, and Sony, offer rewritable

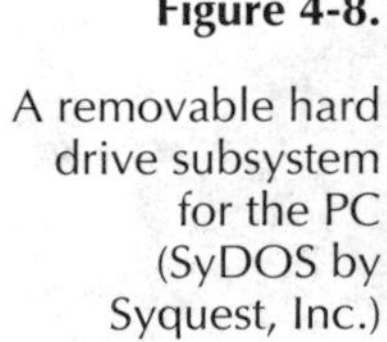

Figure 4-8.

A removable hard drive subsystem for the PC (SyDOS by Syquest, Inc.)

optical drive systems that will store 128 Mb worth of image data in a single 3.5" or 5.25" cartridge. The cartridge is similar in size and shape to a floppy disk and just as portable. MOST, Inc. of Cypress, California (see Figure 4–9) provides a 3.5" rewritable optical drive system that accommodates 256 Mb per 3.5" cartridge with fast data transfer rates.

Rewritable optical cartridges are sure to become the long-term storage medium of choice for multiple large image files. Once these systems become standard at service bureaus as well as among software end users, they'll be the ideal data transfer medium for big color separation files, too.

WORM Optical Drives

WORM (write once, read many times) drives are another species of optical device. They're more suited to long-term archival than to day-to-day backup, because the drives eventually fill up and old files cannot be overwritten.

Image and File Compression

For those who prefer conserving disk space to expanding it, a number of software- and hardware-based image compression solutions exist. Some were created specifically to compress bitmapped image files, while others compress all the data files on your hard drive. You can

Figure 4-9. The MOST 256/128 Mb rewritable optical drive subsystem

use these utilities not only to store images, but also to compress image files before modeming them to a service bureau (see Chapter 16). Keep in mind, though, that compressed files usually take longer to open than uncompressed ones.

PKZIP, LHARC Shareware Utilities

These two general-use compression utilities are available through a variety of sources including shareware catalogs and bulletin boards. They compress files by extracting specific characters, then replacing those characters when you expand the files again. The compression ratio varies, but you'll achieve greater compression ratios with Gray-scale images than with True Color ones. No loss of image quality occurs when you use these utilities.

General-Purpose Compression Boards

Stacker by STAC Electronics of Carlsbad, California "doubles" hard disk space by compressing every file on your hard drive and decompressing files as you need them. All compression is lossless and occurs at a ratio of approximately 2:1. Stacker comes in two versions: software-only and software with a coprocessor-assisted compression board. The hardware version compresses and decompresses even the largest files in real time. If you use the software-only version, you might notice slight reductions in speed when editing large image files with PhotoStyler.

JPEG Compression Solutions

As massive 24-bit color files began to proliferate, first on the Macintosh and then on the PC, a committee (Joint Photographic Expert Group, or JPEG) formed to develop a common standard for image file compression. Currently, several manufacturers produce software utilities and dedicated image compression boards based on this evolving standard. All are based on a sophisticated algorithm that can diminish the size of a True Color file dramatically, but with minimal loss of image quality. The user can control both the compression ratio and the amount of image degradation that occurs.

C-Cube JPEG Image Expand...

C-Cube JPEG Image Compress...

Versions 1.1a and later of PhotoStyler include plug-in modules for C-Cube JPEG compression and expansion solutions. These modules are available through the Import and Export commands in the File menu.

Caution *Some image degradation does occur with JPEG-based utilities; higher compression ratios result in more extreme losses in quality. With most images, you won't be able to see degradation with the naked eye at compression ratios of 10:1 or less. Keep compression ratios relatively low for images that you plan to publish.*

Copyright and Ethical Issues

Scanners, still video cameras, photo CDs, frame grabber boards: today's technologies present us with endless opportunities to take artwork from any source and bring it into the computer. Our newfound ability to digitize, alter, and then electronically reproduce *any* photographic or printed image opens a potential Pandora's box of legal and ethical problems. What legal obligations do you owe to the creators of your source images? Can you copy even a small part of some ad you see in a magazine? To what extent must you alter "borrowed" artwork in order to render it your own? At what point does pastiche become original? Under what circumstances can you copy even the *style* of another commercial artist's work?

According to the U.S. copyright law in effect since 1978, you'd better not "borrow" artwork from any copyrighted printed, published, or unpublished source unless you pay for its use or obtain express written permission. There are exceptions to this rule, but they don't apply if you plan to use all or part of the "borrowed" image for commercial purposes yourself. Theoretically, you're in violation of the law if you scan so much as an anonymous-looking cloud from a magazine advertisement. Even if you digitize a reproduction of a centuries-old artistic masterpiece from a book, beware—the publisher may hold the copyright to that reprint.

Frankly, though, the "real-world" answers to some of the questions we've just posed are unclear at the moment. The current confusion is due largely to the fact that the technologies involved are so new. We suspect that these technologies will eventually redefine the terms "copy," "creative," and "original," but right now there are vast gray areas.

Take the word "copy," for example. Does copying refer to *con*tent or *in*tent? If you digitize a copyrighted source image (content) and then alter it beyond recognition, does it become your "original" work? Maybe. On the other hand, if you digitize your own original photographs, but then edit their composition in a way that obviously imitates a work by another well-known artist, is your work still original? Maybe not. We know of one case in which an ad agency published an elegant, digitally composed ad for a corporate client, only to be chastized by the estate of a famous photographer for copying one of his more celebrated photos. The elements of the digitally composed ad were all "original," but that didn't stop the ad agency from settling out of court for an undisclosed sum of money. Pastiche, at least in this instance, was held to be in violation of copyright law. The verdict is still out on these and other issues.

Until the smoke begins to clear, let caution guide you when using existing images with PhotoStyler. We suggest following these guidelines:

- If you have a background in photography, use your own photographic work as source images whenever possible.
- If you require photographic images but aren't a photographer, obtain or have your clients obtain source images from reputable stock houses. Many stock houses are now digitizing their own images and providing electronic "catalogs" on CD.
- If you obtain images from other copyrighted sources, make sure the copyright holder(s) give you written permission to use them. The permission form should clearly state your rights, the copyright holder's rights, and the full extent of compensation for the images.
- If you obtain images from public domain sources, be aware that the heirs of the images' creators might still attempt—legally—to control the way you present or credit the works. Peter H. Karlen, a prominent copyright and arts attorney practicing in La Jolla, California, notes that artists, photographers, and their estates "can still control how the works are used through the law of moral rights and unfair competition," even if the works have passed into the public domain.
- Emulating the *style* of other artists or photographers may be permissible, but avoid consciously imitating their recognizable works.

Eventually, the new digital imaging technologies may fundamentally change society's understanding of copyright, creativity, and originality. In time, they'll probably impact the way copyright law is written, implemented, and enforced. When the powers that be finally sort out all the issues, perhaps they will conclude that images, like themes and ideas, can be eternally recurrent, and that *context*, not content, determines originality. In the meantime, tread carefully on the legal and ethical land mines of copyright.

In this chapter, we've looked at ways of bringing PhotoStyler images into your computer and keeping them there comfortably. The next chapter concerns itself with choosing the best file formats and image data types for your application.

5

Choosing File Formats and Image Data Types

So, you've scanned or imported an image into Aldus PhotoStyler. Before you begin editing, choose carefully the *file format* and *data type* in which you'll save and store the image. File formats and image data types are two different types of specification:

- File formats deal with the way a specific software package stores graphic information. When making decisions about which file format to use, you should take your cue from the other software, if any, you'll be using with PhotoStyler images.
- Image data types, on the other hand, have to do with the number of colors or gray shades an image can contain. When making decisions about data type, you should take into account the color needs of your application, the display capabilities of your computer, and the limitations of your input device. You can convert an image to a different data type to achieve special effects or compatibility with other applications.

The first section of this chapter reviews the uses of each file format in which you can import and save PhotoStyler images. In the second section, we describe the data types that PhotoStyler supports and show what happens when you convert images from one data type to another.

Image File Formats

Aldus PhotoStyler can open and save images in your choice of seven file formats:

- Tagged Image File Format, TIFF (.TIF)
- Targa (.TGA)
- Windows Bitmap (.BMP)
- Encapsulated PostScript (.EPS)
- PC Paintbrush (.PCX)
- CompuServe Graphics Interchange Format (.GIF)
- PhotoStyler's proprietary document format (.DCI)

Each file format has a niche in the world of publishing, film recording, or video. Not all file formats are equally desirable to use for all applications. Some file formats lack support for 24-bit color, while others generate larger-than-average files. Table 5–1 summarizes the uses of each file format. Table 5–2 shows the image data types that each PhotoStyler file format supports. Match your file format to the data type that your application requires.

Tagged Image File Format (.TIF)

Aldus Corporation introduced the TIFF file format (.TIF) several years ago when scanners began to assume importance among desktop publishers. Almost all scanners and most popular page layout packages support this format, which stores graphic information more compactly than .EPS, .BMP, and .TGA formats. TIFF is supported widely by software on both the Macintosh and IBM-compatible platforms and is therefore a good choice when you plan to use PhotoStyler images in workgroup publishing over a network. The TIFF format supports all PhotoStyler image data types.

Options...

Several variations of the "plain vanilla" TIFF format exist. You can save a TIFF image for the IBM platform, for the Mac platform, and in two different compression formats. Whenever you save an image as TIFF, click the Options button in the Save Image File dialog box and make sure the currently selected options in the TIFF Save Options dialog box (Figure 5–1) are correct.

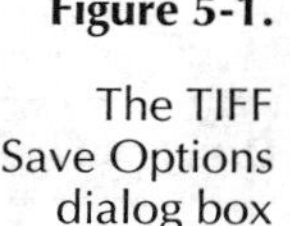

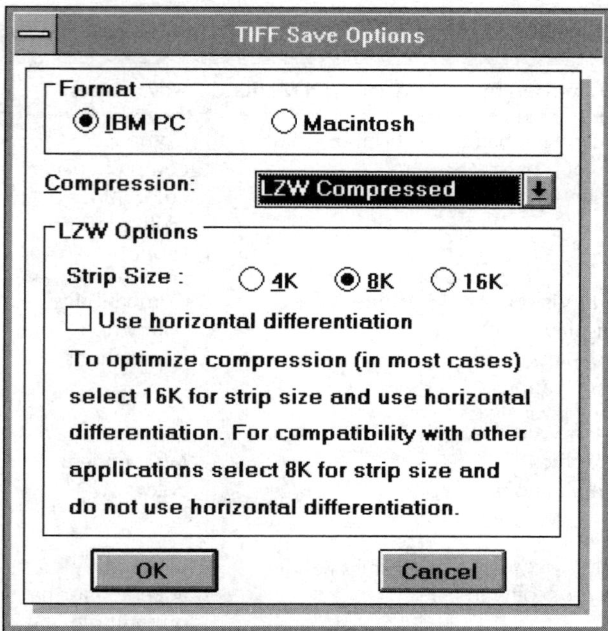

Figure 5-1.

The TIFF Save Options dialog box

IBM TIFF Format

Click the IBM PC radio button in the TIFF Save Options dialog box when you plan to use your TIFF image with other applications on the PC platform.

Macintosh TIFF Format

The TIFF format that Macintosh applications read differs slightly from the IBM PC format. If you plan to export your TIFF PhotoStyler image to Adobe PhotoShop, Aldus PageMaker, or Quark Express on the Macintosh, save it as a Macintosh TIFF file.

Compressed TIFF Formats

The Compression drop-down list box in the TIFF Save Options dialog box lets you save an image in uncompressed, LZW compressed, or PackBits compressed format. Both the LZW and PackBits compression algorithms reduce file size without loss of image data. The only disadvantage of a compressed file is that it takes longer to open in PhotoStyler.

Table 5–1. Uses of PhotoStyler-Supported File Formats

File Format	Supported by	Preferred Media	Advantages	Disadvantages
TIFF (.TIF)	Scanners, page layout, paint software	Print or slide	Compact, comprehensive color info, multi-platform support	Many variants of format exist
TARGA (.TGA)	TrueVision display adapters, video applications	Slide, video	Compatibility with video applications	Not widely supported for layout
Windows Bitmap (.BMP)	Many Windows graphics applications,	Print or display	Device-independent color	Limited support outside MS-Windows environment
Encapsulated PostScript (.EPS)	Most page layout software	Print or slide	Universally accepted format on multiple platforms	Large files
PaintBrush (.PCX)	Most paint software and page layout applications	Print or slide	Wide support among paint applications	Limited 24-bit color and cross-platform support
CompuServe (.GIF)	CompuServe, Macintosh, Amiga	Computer display	Support across multiple platforms	Not a good choice for print or slide media
PhotoStyler proprietary (.DCI)	PhotoStyler only	Monitor display	Saves files compactly with more information	Not supported outside of PhotoStyler

LZW Options LZW compression is available for RGB True Color, Indexed 256-Color, and Grayscale images. When you choose the LZW Compressed option, the Strip Size and Use horizontal differentiation options become available in the TIFF Save Options dialog box. The Strip Size options determine the size of the horizontal "strips" into which PhotoStyler divides the compressed image. Larger strip size values optimize compression, while smaller strip sizes optimize speed and performance. Choose the maximum 16K strip size if you plan to

Table 5–2. Image Data Types Supported by PhotoStyler File Formats

File Format	Data Types Supported				
	RGB True Color	Grayscale	Indexed 256-Color	Indexed 16-Color	Black & White
.TIF non-compressed	✓	✓	✓	✓	✓
.TIF LZW compressed	✓	✓	✓		
.TIF pack bits compressed					✓
.TGA	✓		✓		
.BMP	✓		✓	✓	✓
.EPS	✓	✓			✓
.GIF			✓	✓	✓
.PCX	✓	✓	✓	✓	✓
.DCI	✓	✓	✓	✓	✓

use the image in PhotoStyler only. If you plan to export a TIFF image to other applications, usually an 8K strip size is advisable.

The Use horizontal differentiation option, available for Grayscale and True Color images only, compresses an LZW TIFF file even more compactly. Files saved using this option may take longer to open than files saved with LZW Compression alone.

Note

Not all applications support LZW compression. If you import a PhotoStyler LZW Compressed TIFF image into an application that can't open it, save the image in PhotoStyler as a Non-Compressed TIFF image instead.

PackBits compression PackBits compression is available for Black & White image data types only.

Targa Format (.TGA)

The Targa (.TGA) file format was developed originally to support paintbox software running under TrueVision Targa display adapters. Since then, other paint packages, film recorders, and video applications have come to support this format as well. The .TGA format may be the best to use if video is your eventual output medium, and many slide service bureaus prefer this format, too. However, don't look for wide support of .TGA files among page layout software. The .TGA format doesn't retain information about the resolution of a file; so if resolution is important to you, resample the .TGA image (see Chapter 13) and then save it in another format.

Although you can open 32-bit color Targa images in PhotoStyler, you can't edit them. The .TGA format also lacks support for Black & White image data types. If you have PhotoStyler version 1.1a or later, however, you can both open and edit 16-bit grayscale .TGA images that were created in another application.

Windows Bitmap Format (.BMP)

Microsoft introduced the .BMP format specifically for the Paintbrush accessory that comes bundled with Windows 3.0 and later versions. Paintbrush files are device independent, meaning that the color information in them remains intact, regardless of how your display adapter and monitor represent colors or grays. A number of object-oriented graphics packages that run under Windows (Corel Draw, for example) now support the import of bitmaps in the .BMP format.

Encapsulated PostScript (.EPS)

The Encapsulated PostScript (.EPS) file format was developed as a common output standard for graphics files printed on PostScript printers and imagesetters. The .EPS format is universally accepted among page layout and graphics programs for both IBM and Macintosh platforms.

Caution

PhotoStyler won't open .EPS image files that were created in another application.

Options...

When you choose the .EPS file format in the Save Image File dialog box, the Options command button will become available. Always

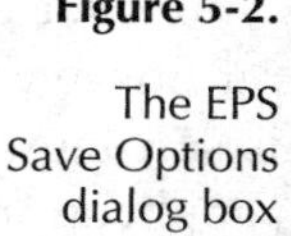

Figure 5-2.

The EPS Save Options dialog box

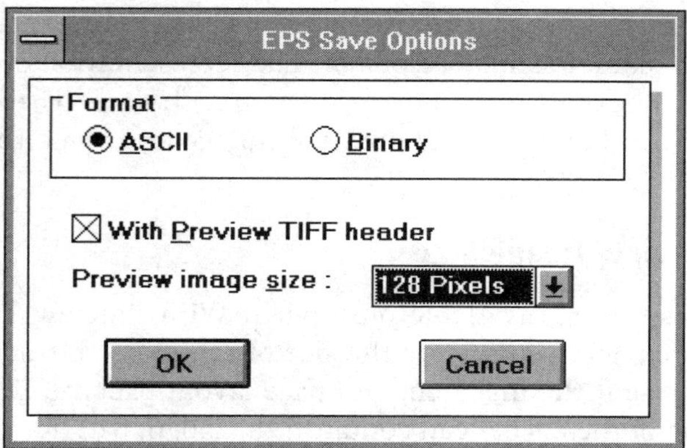

click this button and check the current settings in the .EPS Save Options dialog box (Figure 5–2) to make sure they're correct.

Format

You can save an .EPS file in either ASCII or Binary format. ASCII is an older, text-based format and more commonly accepted by page layout packages, but it generates extremely large files that print slowly. Choose ASCII whenever you're unsure about compatibility. Binary format generates smaller files that often print more quickly, but not all page layout packages support this format.

When saving a PhotoStyler .EPS file for use on the Macintosh, select Binary format and turn With Preview TIFF Header off.

With Preview TIFF Header

This option controls whether a bitmap header will accompany the file when you export it to a page layout package. On the IBM platform, TIFF headers are the only way to display an .EPS image; they're coarse and far from WYSIWYG, but their sole purpose is to help you proof pages for image position only. On the Macintosh, TIFF headers aren't necessary. Here's how to use this option:

- If you activate the With Preview TIFF Header option, the Preview Image Size options become available. The header you specify won't be visible as long as you edit the image in PhotoStyler. When you export the .EPS image to your page layout package, however, the bitmap header will represent the image position. Use this setting with images that you plan to use with PC page layout applications.

- If you leave With Preview TIFF Header unselected, you'll see only a blank box instead of a bitmap representation of your image when you export it to your page layout software. Use this setting when you plan to use a PhotoStyler image in a Macintosh application.

Preview Image Size

This option, available only when With Preview TIFF Header is selected, lets you specify the size of the coarse bitmap header that will represent the image in your page layout package. The longest dimension of the header can contain 128, 256, or 512 pixels. Since TIFF .EPS headers are coarse to begin with, we recommend using small headers to keep PostScript file sizes manageable.

PC Paintbrush (.PCX)

ZSoft Corporation originally developed the .PCX file format for its Paintbrush line of software. As one of the oldest bitmap formats on the IBM, .PCX has long been a standard among scanners, page layout packages, and almost every paint program ever invented. Only recently has the .PCX format come to support 24-bit color, though, so many applications that support .PCX may not have caught up. If you're not sure whether you can export a PhotoStyler True Color .PCX image to another software package, save the image in .TIF or .EPS format instead.

CompuServe Graphics Interchange Format (.GIF)

The .GIF file format evolved through the CompuServe information network, providing a graphics standard that many different computer platforms can use. Files in this format are transferable among IBM-compatible, Macintosh, and Amiga computers. The .GIF format is a poor choice for color print publishing, since it doesn't retain resolution information or allow you to save images in 24-bit color.

PhotoStyler's Proprietary File Format (.DCI)

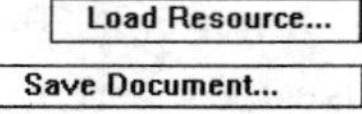

PhotoStyler's open architecture allows third-party developers to supply "plug-in" modules that support additional file formats, scanner and printer drivers, filters, palettes, and so on. The .DCI document format, developed by U-Lead Systems, Inc., is one such plug-in module. According to its developers, the .DCI format records image information more precisely and in a more compact way than other bitmap file formats.

To save an image in .DCI document format, choose the Export command in the File menu and then the Save Document command from the submenu that appears. When the Save Document Data to File dialog box in Figure 5–3 appears, change to the drive and directory where you want to store the file, and then type the desired filename in the Filename text entry box. Click Save to save the file.

To load a .DCI image into PhotoStyler, choose the Import command in the File menu and then the Load Resource command from the submenu that appears. When the Load Resource File dialog box in Figure 5–3 appears, choose .DCI Document File from the Resource drop-down list box and locate the desired file using the Files and Directories list boxes. Double-click the name of the file to load it.

About Image Data Types

Whatever the source of an image, Aldus PhotoStyler recognizes it as a collection of color or gray values. Image files vary, however, according to the maximum number of color or gray values they can contain. The factors that determine this number are:

- the number of bits needed to record color information about each pixel, and
- the number of color components (channels) that make up the image

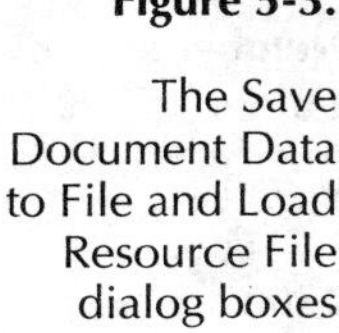

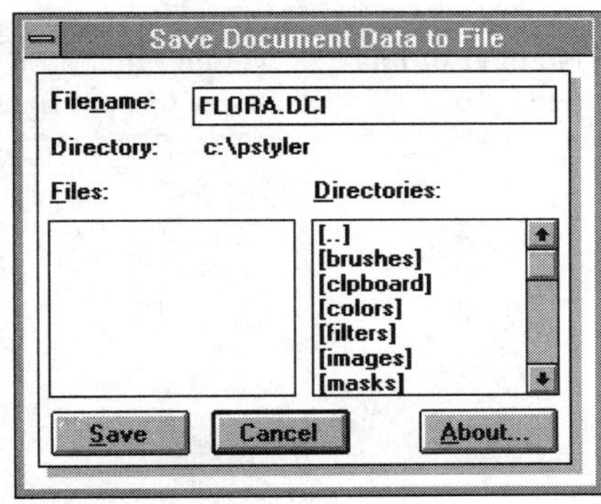

Figure 5-3.

The Save Document Data to File and Load Resource File dialog boxes

In PhotoStyler, we refer to these image characteristics collectively as the *data type*. Table 5–3 relates PhotoStyler's six image data types to the number of color or gray values assigned to each.

Most of PhotoStyler's Paint tools and editing commands work only with Grayscale (256 gray levels) and RGB True Color (16 million colors) images. If your input device supports something less than 8-bit grayscale or 24-bit color, don't worry. PhotoStyler lets you convert any image to the Grayscale or True Color data type once it's in PhotoStyler. Later, when you're ready to print or output the image to another medium, you can convert it back to a different data type.

Your application, the display capabilities of your computer, and the limitations of your input device all play a role in determining the best data type for a particular image. Here's the rundown on how PhotoStyler handles each data type.

24-Bit RGB True Color

Saving an image in the True Color data type lets you store and edit more than 16 million colors, even if your monitor and display adapter don't allow you to see that many. Each pixel in a True Color image has three separate color values—one each for the red, green, and blue image channels—and each of the three color values can range from zero (no color) to 255 (saturated color). Thanks to PhotoStyler's efficient screen dithering algorithms, the color on your monitor will seem fairly realistic if your system can display just 256 colors. If you plan to become a full-time color photo retoucher, however, you should invest in a 24-bit color display adapter for accuracy's sake.

Table 5–3. Color Characteristics of Supported Image Data Types

Data Type	Number of Bits per Byte	Number of Image Channels	Number of Colors
RGB True Color	24	3	16.7 million
Grayscale	8	1	256 grays
Indexed 256-Color	8	1	256 colors
Indexed 16-Color	4	1	16 colors
Black & White	1	1	2 gray shades

If you plan to output color images to print media, True Color will guarantee you the most realistic color reproduction. True Color images also let you use *all* of PhotoStyler's image editing features.

8-Bit Grayscale

Grayscale is the other data type that gives you maximum image editing power and flexibility in PhotoStyler. Unlike True Color images, Grayscale images contain only one data channel, but each pixel can contain any of 256 gray shades. Many color scanners can generate 8-bit grayscale images.

Indexed 16- and 256-Color

Images that contain only 16 or 256 colors out of a possible 16 million are called *indexed color* images. For each such image, PhotoStyler stores a *color table* that includes only the specific color values contained in that image. To see all the color values contained in an indexed color image, choose the Color Table command in the View menu. This command, unavailable for other image data types, will display the View Color Table dialog box shown in Figure 5–4.

Editing functions are limited for indexed color images, and you can't add any new color values to the color table, either. Get around these limitations by converting any indexed color image to the RGB True Color data type for editing in PhotoStyler. PhotoStyler will store 16 million colors worth of information even if your system can't display more than 16 or 256 colors. If you need to export an RGB True Color image to an application that supports only 16 or 256 colors, you can convert the image to one of the indexed color data types after editing. See the "Converting to Other Image Data Types" section of this chapter for more details.

Black and White

Some older scanners generate only black-and-white images; some clip art is available in this format as well. The single bit that controls each pixel in a black and white image can have only two values: zero (black) or one (white), off or on. In order to edit a Black & White image in PhotoStyler, you must first convert it to the Grayscale data type.

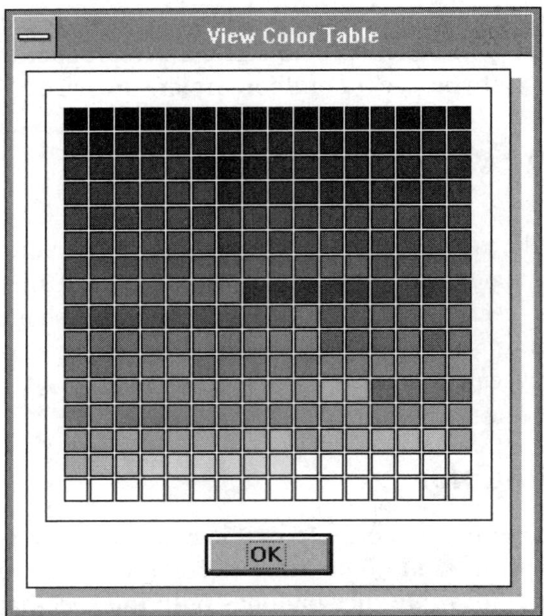

Figure 5-4.

The View Color Table dialog box for an Indexed 256-Color image

Converting to Other Data Types

You can convert any image in PhotoStyler to one of the other supported data types. There are several reasons why you might want to convert an image:

- *To obtain greater editing power and flexibility*. Most of PhotoStyler's tools and image editing commands work only on RGB True Color and Grayscale images. If your scanner supports a lesser number of color or gray values, you'll need to convert it before you can edit it effectively in PhotoStyler. Similarly, if you created the image in a software program that limits you to the number of colors your monitor can display, you can achieve device-independent grayscale or 24-bit color information by converting the image.
- *To generate special color effects*. You can sometimes generate special color effects by converting an RGB True Color image to an Indexed 16- or 256-Color data type, or by converting a Grayscale image to a Black & White halftone. If you're a fine artist or graphic designer, you might try colorizing a Grayscale image after first converting it to the RGB True Color data type.
- *To meet output requirements or ease image proofing*. Maybe you're exporting True Color PhotoStyler images to a page layout program,

and you want to generate position-only proof prints on a 300 dpi monochrome laser printer. By converting the color images to the Grayscale data type, you can reduce image file size and printing time for early drafts of your document.

- *To export a PhotoStyler image to an incompatible software application.* We'd like to think that PhotoStyler is the be-all and end-all of image editing applications, but we're realists, too. Perhaps you're just using PhotoStyler to clean up a scanned image, after which you plan to export the image to a drawing program, tracing utility, or presentation package. What if that other package doesn't support 16 million colors or 256 shades of gray? No problem—just convert the image to a compatible format after you edit it in PhotoStyler.

How PhotoStyler Manages Conversions

Whatever your reason for converting images between data types, you begin the process by making the desired image active and then choosing the Convert To command in the Image menu. This command has its own submenu containing the available data types. If a data type appears in gray rather than in black, you can't convert the active image to that data type. For example, you can't convert an indexed 16-color image directly to black and white; you have to first convert it to Grayscale and then from Grayscale to black and white.

Depending on the data types of the source image and target image, the conversion may take place automatically or may require you to set various options. In every case, PhotoStyler protects the safety of your image data by generating a separate document window for the converted image rather than overwriting your original image (Figure 5–5).

Note

A newly converted image document is a temporary file that has no file extension. PhotoStyler stores it in RAM or virtual memory as you work. If you want to retain the converted file, you must save it before you exit PhotoStyler.

Table 5–4 shows which conversions are direct and which are indirect.

Converting to RGB True Color

If you used an older scanner model or other input device to generate an image, chances are that the image doesn't contain 16 million colors.

Figure 5-5. PhotoStyler generates a separate document during image conversion

You can convert any image except Black & White images directly to the RGB True Color data type. The colors or gray shades in the original image won't change during the conversion process, but you can alter the color content of the converted image as you edit it. Conversion to RGB True Color is automatic, requiring no dialog boxes or options.

Note *To convert a Black & White image to an RGB True Color image, first convert the image to Grayscale and then to RGB True Color.*

Table 5–4. Direct and Indirect Conversions Between Image Data Types
(D = Direct; I = Indirect)

From	To			
	RGB True Color	**Grayscale**	**Indexed 256- and 16-Color**	**Black & White**
RGB True Color		D	D	I
Grayscale	D		D	D
Indexed 16- or 256-Color	D	D		I
Black & White	I	D	I	

Converting to Grayscale

Every image data type in PhotoStyler permits direct conversion to 8-bit Grayscale. When you convert any of the color image data types to Grayscale, the conversion proceeds automatically. When you convert a Black & White (line art) image to the Grayscale data type, however, PhotoStyler confronts you with several options. The rationale for these options has to do with fundamental differences between grayscale images and black-and-white ones.

Converting from Black and White to Grayscale

If you need to print a Black & White image and want it to look more photorealistic, first convert it to Grayscale. Then, use the Averaging filter in the Image/Smoothing Filters submenu (discussed in Chapter 12) to generate a larger number of gray shades.

Black & White images show "jaggies" because their pixels can be only one of two gray shades. Normal 8-bit Grayscale images, on the other hand, display smoother transitions in tone because they can contain up to 256 different shades of gray.

When you convert Black & White images to the Grayscale data type, PhotoStyler divides the image into square cells. The more pixels each cell contains, the larger the number of gray shades you can simulate, up to a maximum of 256. By adjusting options in the Convert to Grayscale dialog box (Figure 5-6), you define the number of pixels in each cell and thus the smoothness of the transitions between gray shades.

There's an inherent trade-off between the sharpness of the newly converted Grayscale image and the number of gray shades it contains. As

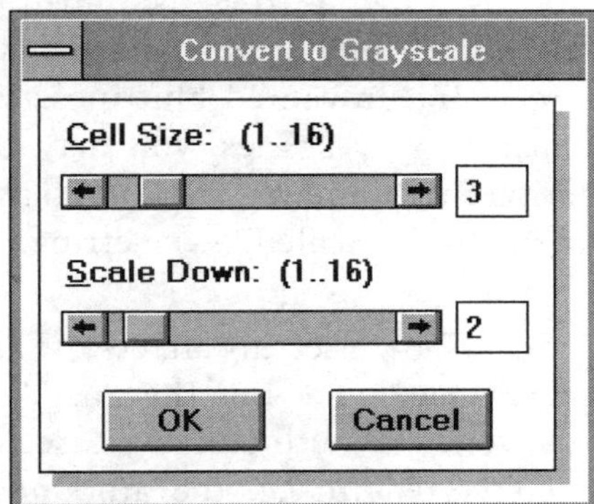

Figure 5-6. The Convert to Grayscale dialog box

you increase the number of gray shades in the converted image, the transitions become smoother—but the image loses some of its sharpness, too. That's because PhotoStyler can only modify existing information; it can't create new information that wasn't in the Black & White image to begin with.

The Convert to Grayscale dialog box contains two options that let you control both the smoothness of transitions between gray shades and the sharpness of the converted image. The Cell Size option lets you specify the size of each cell in the converted image, which determines the maximum number of gray shades possible in each cell. The Scale Down option lets you alter the amount of information (number of pixels) in the image to control image size, resolution, and sharpness. Let's take a look at some examples to clarify the way these options work.

Cell Size When you convert a Black & White image to the Grayscale data type, PhotoStyler arranges the pixels in square *halftone cells*. The principle is similar to the way monochrome laser printers and imagesetters simulate gray shades (see Chapters 14 and 15). The number of pixels within each halftone cell determines how many gray shades a single cell can contain and how smooth the transitions will be between gray shades. You control these characteristics using the Cell Size option in the Convert to Grayscale dialog box.

For example, if you set Cell Size to 3 as in Figure 5–7, PhotoStyler will generate halftone cells that are 3 pixels wide by 3 pixels deep (9 pixels altogether). These cells can contain up to nine different gray shades, a small number that will help the converted image retain the sharpness of the original. On the other hand, if you set Cell Size to the maximum value of 16, each cell will contain 16 by 16 pixels, or 256 pixels total. The number of possible gray shades will be 256, too. The important thing to remember is that as transitions between gray shades become smoother, the apparent sharpness of the converted image decreases. To avoid unwanted blurriness when generating a high number of apparent gray shades, you may need to reduce the amount of information in the image. You can do this by coordinating the Cell Size setting with the Scale Down setting.

Scale Down The Scale Down setting affects the amount of *information* in the converted image, and thus the image resolution, printed size, and file size as well. As you increase the Scale Down value, the resolution of the converted image, the amount of information it

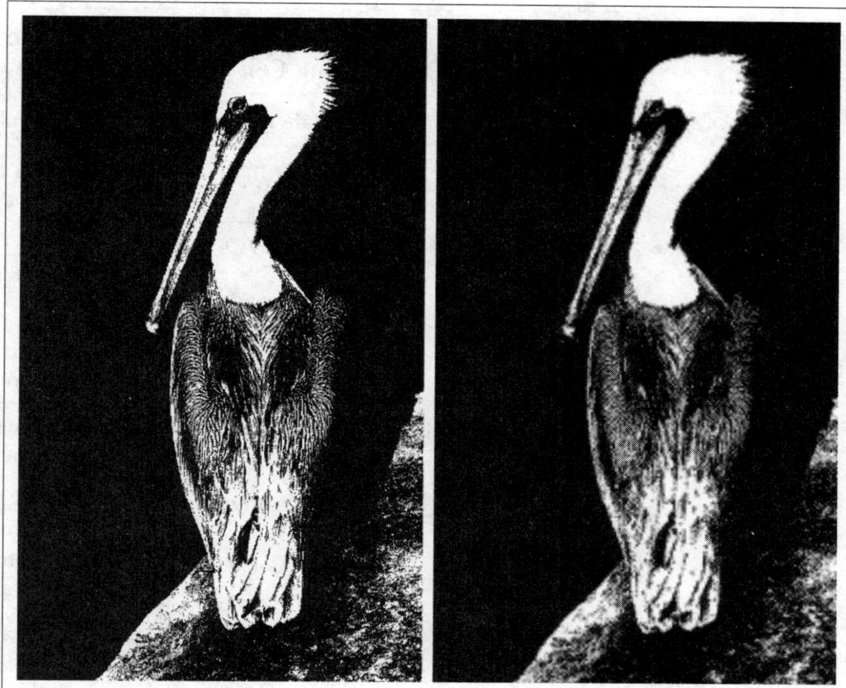

Figure 5-7.

A low cell size (here, 3) can add gray shades to a converted Black & White image without introducing unnecessary blurring

(l) original Black & White image

(r) image converted to Grayscale: Cell Size 3, Scale Down 1

contains, and the size of the image in print decrease proportionally. At the extreme setting of 16, you'll generate an image of very tiny proportions. If the Cell Size setting is low, too, the new image will be jagged as well as small.

In many cases, though, you won't be aiming for such an extreme effect. Assume, for example, that you're working with a 300 dpi Black & White line art image that's 600 pixels wide by 400 pixels high. If you set Scale Down to 4 when you convert this image to the Grayscale data type, the resulting image will be 150 pixels wide by 100 pixels high and have a resolution of 75 dpi. Meanwhile, the converted image will take up much less space on your disk than the original. If you print the image, it will be smaller on the page, too.

Some Black & White to Grayscale Guidelines Every Black & White image is different, so you'll need to experiment to achieve the best conversion to Grayscale. Still, we can offer some general guidelines to help you predict the results of adjusting the Cell Size and the Scale Down factor together. See Table 5–5 for brief descriptions of how these settings might combine.

Table 5–5. Converting from Black & White to Grayscale: Results of Combining Cell Size and Scale Down Settings

Cell Size	Scale Down factor	Result
Low (1-4)	Lower than Cell Size	The converted image remains fairly sharp
	Equal to Cell Size	The Grayscale version is still fairly sharp
	Higher than Cell Size	Grayscale transitions become more and more apparent
Moderate (5-10)	Lower than Cell Size	Grayscale image is rather blurry
	Near or Equal to Cell Size	The image looks like a fine-resolution geometrical mosaic pattern. Most details are still distinguishable
	Higher than Cell Size	Details are no longer distinguishable
High (11-16)	Much lower than Cell Size	The image is blurry overall
	High, approaching Cell Size	All that's left of the image is a highly stylized mosaic

Converting to Indexed 256- and 16-Color

If the final destination for your image will be a computer monitor or a film recorder that accepts a fixed number of colors, you might choose to convert to the Indexed 256- or 16-color format. Remember, though, that most editing options are available to you in Grayscale or RGB True Color format only. It's best to convert your images to the Indexed color formats only *after* you've completed the editing process.

You can convert Grayscale and RGB True Color images directly to one of the Indexed Color data types. Both of these conversions require that you specify options in a dialog box. If your source image is a Black & White image, you'll have to convert it to a Grayscale image first and then to one of the Indexed Color data types.

Converting from Grayscale to Indexed 256-Color

In PhotoStyler, both Grayscale and Indexed 256-Color images contain the same number of color or gray values. This type of conversion doesn't involve much of a loss in image quality; the important issue is *which* 256 colors out of a possible 16.7 million to include in the palette of the converted image.

PhotoStyler's solution to this issue is to offer you a choice of three different palettes when you convert a Grayscale image to the Indexed 256-Color data type. After you choose a palette, PhotoStyler generates a *color table* that includes all 256 of the colors available to the converted image. You can view this palette either by displaying the PhotoStyler Color Palette or by choosing the Color Table command in the View menu.

The three palettes PhotoStyler offers for this kind of conversion appear in the Indexed 256-Color dialog box in Figure 5–8. They are:

Gray Palette This palette contains 256 gray values ranging from black to white. PhotoStyler generates these gray values from equal values of red, green, and blue. When you convert to Indexed 256-Color using this palette, the appearance of the converted image doesn't change.

Firelight Palette When you convert a Grayscale image to Indexed 256-Color using this option, PhotoStyler assigns a Color Table derived from shades of red, yellow, and orange. This range of colors is quite narrow, so the transitions between colors in the converted image remain smooth (see Figure 5–9 in the Color Section of this book).

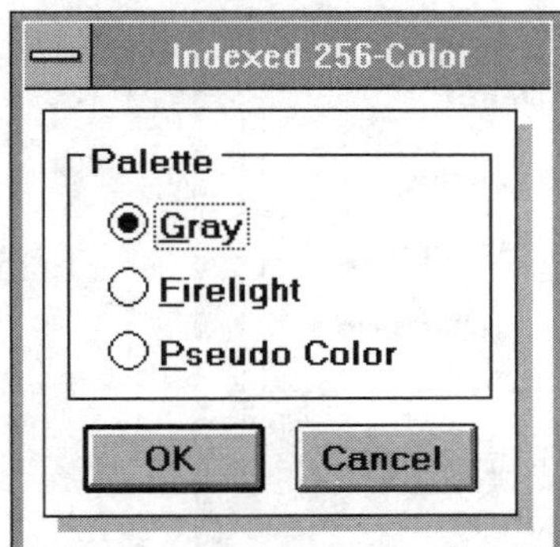

Figure 5-8.

The Indexed 256-Color dialog box for converting an image from Grayscale

Pseudo Color Palette The values that make up the Pseudo Color Palette derive from varying shades of blue, green, yellow, red, white, and black. This represents a much wider range of colors than the Firelight palette, with the result that transitions between colors in the converted image are more abrupt. You might choose Pseudo Color over Firelight when you prefer a more stylized, "contrasty" look to your output image, as in the example in Figure 5–10 in the Color Section of this book. Compare Figures 5-9 and 5-10 to see how PhotoStyler might convert the same image in two different ways.

Converting from Grayscale to Indexed 16-Color

PhotoStyler uses the same basic palettes for both Indexed 16-Color and Indexed 256-Color images. The main difference is that Indexed 16-Color images can contain no more than sixteen color values from the selected range of colors. To simulate the appearance of more colors, PhotoStyler uses one of several *dithering* options that you specify using the Convert to Indexed 16-Color dialog box (Figure 5–11).

None When you choose None, PhotoStyler applies sixteen colors or gray values without any dithering. Transitions between colors in the converted image will be abrupt.

Pattern Selecting the Pattern dither option causes PhotoStyler to arrange the sixteen colors in rectangular patterns that simulate color transitions. You probably won't see the differences between None and Pattern on your monitor unless you view the converted image(s) at high magnifications.

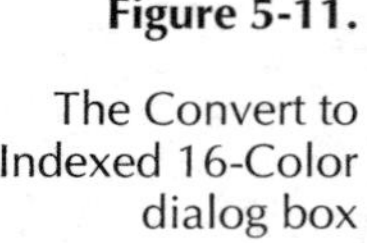

Figure 5-11.

The Convert to Indexed 16-Color dialog box

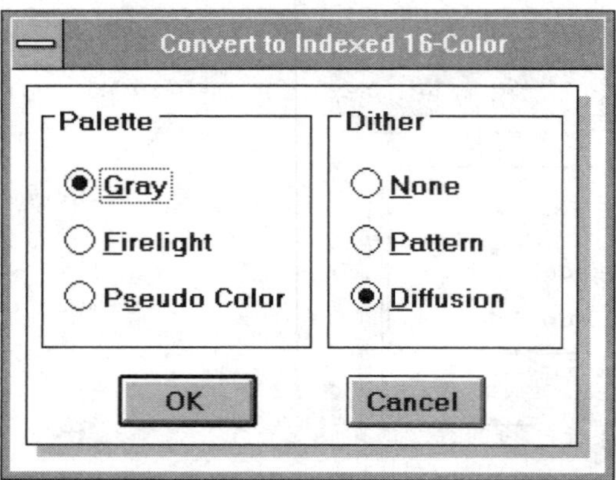

Diffusion Diffusion dither is a process by which PhotoStyler computes the color differences between adjacent pixels in the image, one pixel at a time. The result is a converted image that seems to have smooth color value transitions, even though only sixteen colors are represented.

Converting from RGB True Color to Indexed 256-Color

RGB True Color images can contain up to 16.7 million color values—more than 65,000 times as many colors as Indexed 256-Color images. The potential for abrupt color transitions is therefore much greater with this type of conversion than when you convert from a Grayscale image. If you're using a 256-color display adapter, you may not see many differences between the True Color original and its Indexed 256-Color conversion at a 1:1 viewing ratio. But if you view the same area of both images at a 16:1 magnification, the differences in color values will become apparent.

The dithering options for converting images from RGB True Color to Indexed 256-Color are the same as for conversions from the Grayscale data type. The Palette options, however, are different.

3-3-2 (bits) When you choose this option, PhotoStyler defines the color table for the converted image using three bits per pixel for red, three bits per pixel for green, and two bits per pixel for blue. The Color Palette for the converted image will contain eight shades of red, eight shades of green, and four shades of blue. PhotoStyler generates other color values using combinations of these.

6-7-6 (levels) This option indicates that the converted image will contain six shades of red, seven of green, six of blue, and combinations of these color values.

6-6-6 (levels) Choose this option to obtain a color table that includes six different values each of the colors red, blue, and green and combinations of these.

Note *PhotoStyler uses the 6-6-6 palette to display RGB True Color on 256-color computer systems. Because this palette is so well balanced, True Color images appear to display their full range of color values even on monitors that support only 8-bit color.*

Adaptive This is the most flexible palette option for conversions between True Color and Indexed 256-Color data types. The Adaptive palette is not a fixed set of color values like the other palettes. Instead, PhotoStyler determines which color values to include in the converted image based on the color values in the original True Color image.

Converting from RGB True Color to Indexed 16-Color

An Indexed 16-Color image can contain only a millionth of the color values available to a True Color image. It's no wonder, then, that conversions between these two data types result in visible transitions between colors in the converted image. PhotoStyler uses dither options to reduce the abruptness of these color transitions. These dither options are the same as for conversions from True Color to 256-color images.

You have a choice between two different palettes, System or Adaptive, when converting to the Indexed 16-Color data type.

System When you choose the System Palette option, PhotoStyler derives the color table of the converted image from your current MS-Windows display settings. To change those settings, use Windows Setup in the Main window.

Adaptive When you select the Adaptive Palette option, PhotoStyler derives the color table for the converted image from the most closely matched color values in the True Color image.

Converting to Black & White

The only direct conversion to the Black & White data type in PhotoStyler is from a Grayscale image. If you need to convert a different type of image to Black & White, convert it to Grayscale first.

The chief reason for converting a Grayscale image to Black & White is to simulate a halftone for output to a printer (such as a dot matrix printer) that can't generate its own halftones. (See Chapters 14 and 15 for more about halftoning.) You can also achieve some interesting image distortion effects by using this conversion.

Whereas a Grayscale image can contain up to 256 different shades of gray, a Black & White image can contain only two extreme shades: black and white. Converting from one data type to the other is a question of how to *simulate* gray tones in an image that can't reproduce the real thing. PhotoStyler's solution is to dither the Black & White image, grouping the pixels into *halftone cells*. The arrangement of black-and-white pixels in each halftone cell simulates a particular shade of gray. The number of shades of gray a given image can simulate depends on the size of the halftone cell and the image resolution, both of which you can specify during the conversion process.

When you choose the Convert To: Black & White command from the Image menu, the dialog box in Figure 5–12 appears. By varying the resolution and halftone screen settings in this dialog box, you can control the number of gray shades and the sharpness of the converted image. There is the potential for special effects here!

Resolution Options

PhotoStyler gives you several options for defining the resolution of the converted Black & White image. When choosing an option, ask yourself what the final output medium for the image will be (laser printer, monitor, imagesetter, and so forth).

- If you select *Current Image*, the converted image will have the same resolution and contain the same number of pixels as the original Grayscale image.
- The *Display* option yields a Black & White image at the same resolution as your monitor display (96 dpi for VGA, for example). This option is useful if you plan to use a monochrome monitor rather than a printer as your final output device.
- The *Printer* option causes PhotoStyler to generate an image at the same resolution as the printer that's currently selected under MS-Windows.

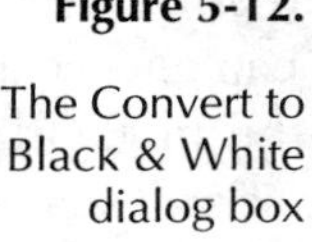

Figure 5-12.

The Convert to Black & White dialog box

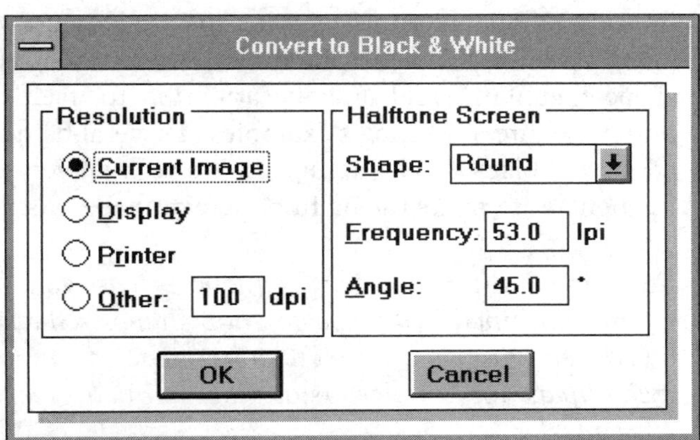

If you're set up for a laser printer, this resolution will most likely be 300 dpi. If you're set up for a high-resolution imagesetter, on the other hand, the resolution may be 1270 dpi or higher depending on the model.

Caution

As you increase image resolution, the file size will increase geometrically. For example, if you double the resolution from 100 dpi to 200 dpi, the file size will increase fourfold (four is the square of two). If you triple the resolution, the resulting file size will be nine times as large, and so on. Watch out for the enormous file sizes that a high-resolution Black & White image will generate.

- The *Other* setting lets you assign a custom resolution to the converted image. Use this setting if you aim to synchronize image resolution and halftone screen frequency in order to control the precise number of simulated gray shades in the converted image.

Halftone Screen Options

Here, we're getting into printing industry territory. If you're new to the concept of halftone screens, take a look at Chapters 14 and 15 before you start converting Grayscale images to black and white. For now, it's enough to know that the shape, angle, and frequency settings have a lot to do with how sharp or jagged an image looks when printed.

Halftone Screen Shape Basically, the *dot shape* you assign to a halftone determines the visual pattern of pixels that PhotoStyler uses to generate halftone cells. In many cases, you'll never be able to tell the difference between dot shapes with the naked eye. However, if you magnify an image several times, you can see the patterns created. If the image you're converting contains many elements with similar shapes (diagonal lines, rectangles, or circles, for example), you can choose a dot shape that will avoid drawing attention to itself in the final printed output. Figure 5–13 shows examples of several halftone screen shapes in converted Black & White images. We've used very low halftone screen frequencies to make the halftone screen shapes visible.

Tip

Very low halftone screen frequencies can generate special effects when combined with special dot shapes. Black & White images converted with such low screen frequencies can make excellent stylized clip art for newsletters or other publications. See Figure 5–13 for examples!

In addition to the traditional halftone screen shapes—round, elliptical, diamond, line, square, and cross—PhotoStyler also provides special dithering options that give converted Black & White images a unique look. Figure 5–14 shows examples of each of the three special dithering options: None, Diffusion, and Dispersion, respectively.

- The *None* option results in a high-contrast Black & White image with no intermediate gray shades. When you select this option, PhotoStyler converts all pixels with a grayscale value below 127 to black and all pixels above this value to white.
- Images converted using the *Diffusion* option look grainy but show less apparent contrast than images converted with the None option. PhotoStyler uses a mathematical process to simulate a higher number of apparent gray shades.
- If you choose the *Dispersion* option when converting to Black & White, the resulting image will show a more or less geometrical transition between apparent gray shades.

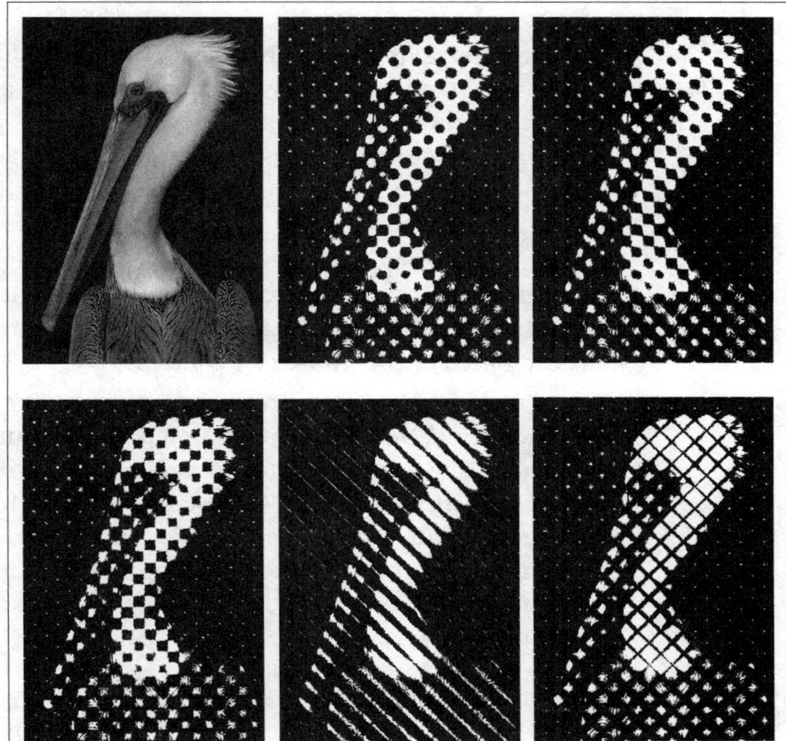

Figure 5-13.

Converted Black & White images with various halftone screen shapes at 10 dpi:

Above, l-r: original Grayscale, round, elliptical

Below, l-r: diamond, line, cross

Figure 5-14.

Converted Black & White images with halftone screen shapes of (l-r) None, Diffusion, and Dispersion

Note *If you choose None, Diffusion, or Dispersion as a halftone Shape, you cannot define a screen frequency or angle.*

Halftone Screen Frequency and Apparent Gray Shades As you'll see in Chapters 14 and 15, every printing device has a screen frequency, expressed as the number of lines per inch (lpi). A 300 dpi PostScript laser printer, for example, has a maximum effective screen frequency of 53-75 lpi, while imagesetters can output at screen frequencies as high as 133-200 lpi.

Screen frequencies chosen for image conversion behave like the screen frequencies you assign when printing. The screen frequency you assign to a converted Black & White image indicates how many cells each inch of the image can contain.

Here's where things get interesting: if you balance screen frequency with resolution, you can control precisely the number of simulated gray shades that a converted Black & White image contains. Let's say you're converting a 300 dpi Grayscale image to Black & White and want to simulate 32 shades of gray. To determine the screen frequency that will give you the desired number of apparent gray shades, divide the image resolution (here 300) by the *square root* of 32 (about 5.66). The result is 53 lpi.

Tip *If you know the image resolution and screen frequency, here's the formula for determining the maximum number of gray shades possible in an image conversion:*

(image resolution ÷ screen frequency)^2 = number of possible gray shades

If you know the image resolution and the number of gray shades, use this formula instead:

(image resolution ÷ square root of no. of gray shades = screen frequency

Experiment with converting a few images from Grayscale to Black & White. In most cases, you'll have to increase image resolution (and file size!) drastically in order to obtain a large number of simulated gray shades. In general, you'll generate a sharper, more well-defined Black & White conversion by simulating a small number of gray shades and defining very small halftone cells.

In this chapter, you've seen how PhotoStyler converts images between different data types. We hope we've given you creative stimulation as well as down-to-earth advice.

6

Managing Image Display

The range of techniques available for displaying images in a graphics program can enhance your creativity or hinder it. With PhotoStyler, every display technique is designed to foster speed, flexibility, and innovation.

PhotoStyler lets you open and edit multiple images (called *image documents*) within the application window. Each image document appears within its own *document window*, which surrounds the image like a frame. As Figure 6–1 shows, image document windows contain their own title bars and their own control menus, minimize buttons, and maximize buttons. You can move, resize, and arrange document windows, and add rulers for precise measurement when editing.

To make the editing process still more convenient, PhotoStyler provides intuitive controls for viewing specific areas of an image at your choice of magnification levels. And no matter how many image documents are open at one time, clutter need never be a problem: you can arrange images in a variety of ways to suit your style of working.

Opening and Closing One or More Image Documents

The initial release of Aldus PhotoStyler (version 1.1) allowed you to open only one image document at a time. Beginning with version 1.1a

Figure 6-1.

A PhotoStyler image document window

of PhotoStyler, however, you can open several images at once if you choose.

Opening and Displaying a Single Image Document

To open a single image document, choose the Open command in the File menu or use the keyboard shortcut, Ctrl-O. If you have PhotoStyler version 1.1a or later, "All Formats" will be the default setting for File Format in the Open Image File dialog box (Figure 3–3 in Chapter 3), and all of the filenames in the current directory will appear. If you have an earlier version of PhotoStyler, you may need to specify a file format before you can view available filenames. For all versions, double-clicking the desired filename will cause the image to open.

How PhotoStyler displays a newly opened image will depend on the version you are using:

- If you have version 1.1a or a later version, the image displays in Fit in Window mode. An image that is larger than your screen in terms of pixels will appear at a reduced magnification so you can view all of it at once. The current magnification ratio appears in the image document's title bar next to the filename.
- If you have a version of PhotoStyler prior to 1.1a, the image will initially display at a 1:1 viewing magnification (one pixel on your screen equals one pixel of the digital image). If the image doesn't fit

entirely within the application window, the document window will contain scroll bars to show you that more of the image is available.

An image that you've just opened becomes the active image document automatically. The active image document is the only one to which you can apply menu commands and palette tools.

Opening and Displaying Multiple Image Documents

If you have PhotoStyler version 1.1a or later, you can open multiple image documents at once. After accessing the Open Image File dialog box by choosing the Open command in the File menu, you can specify which files to open in one of the following ways:

- Click on the first filename, and then click on additional filenames while pressing and holding the Ctrl key. If the desired filenames are adjacent to one another in the list box, you can use the Shift key instead of the Ctrl key.
- Type multiple filenames (any format) in the text entry box, separating each filename with a space.

When you click OK, the image files will open one after another in Fit in Window mode. The image that opens last will become the active image document.

To prevent the next image in a series of images from opening, press Esc. To prevent all remaining images in a series of images from opening, press Shift-Esc.

Reopening Images (Version 1.1a and Later)

Beginning with PhotoStyler version 1.1a, the filenames of recently opened images appear at the bottom of the File menu. If you've recently closed an image, but want to reopen it again quickly, simply click on its filename in the File menu. By default, the File menu displays only the four most recently opened or saved images; you can increase this number to a maximum of 16 by editing the **FMS=** and **Num=** statements in the **[ROF]** section of your **pstyler.ini** file.

Closing One or More Image Documents

To close a single image document, first make sure it's the active image document (see "Working with Multiple Images" later in this chapter).

Then, either choose the Close command in the File menu or double-click the control-menu box at the upper left corner of the image document window. PhotoStyler will ask if you want to save any changes you've made to the image.

To close all image documents that are currently open (versions 1.1a and later), press and hold the Shift key and then choose the Close command in the File menu. Be careful when using this technique; PhotoStyler won't give you an opportunity to save changes to any of the images.

Working with Multiple Images

One of PhotoStyler's greatest boons is the freedom it gives you to open, display, and edit multiple images or even multiple views of a single image. It's so much easier to compare colors, cut and paste, create montages, and check painstakingly retouched details against an original when you don't have to close one image in order to open another.

You need to master only a few operations in order to work with multiple images in a way that will add convenience to your working habits. The most important operations are:

- activating one image document among several that are open
- adding a view of an image document
- arranging multiple images within the application window
- displaying images as minimized icons

Activating an Image Document Window

Only one image document window at a time can be active in PhotoStyler, no matter how many images are open. The image in the active document window is the only one you can edit. You can distinguish the active document window from inactive document windows by two visual clues: the coloring of its title bar and the presence of a control menu box and minimize/maximize buttons.

To activate an inactive image document window, simply click on its title bar. Make sure you don't click inside the image document itself, unless you want to apply the currently active tool to the image.

If the image document you want to activate is covered by another window, find the filename of the desired image document in the

Window menu and click on it. The selected document window will "jump" to the foreground.

Whenever you duplicate or add a view to the active image document, the window you just generated becomes the active document window automatically.

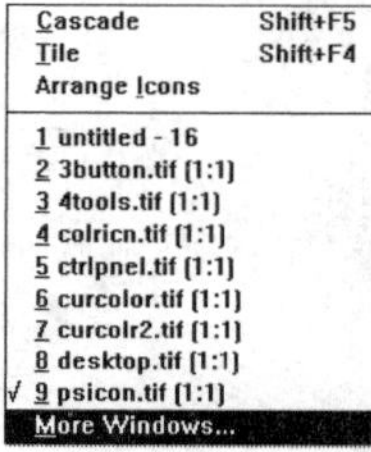

If you have a large number of image documents open at one time, the Window menu may not be able to display the full list. In this case, a More Windows command will appear at the bottom of the Windows menu. Click on this command, and a Select Window dialog box will appear on your screen (Figure 6–2). Use the scroll bar in the list box to find the document window you're seeking, and then double-click on its name to activate that window.

Adding a View of an Image Document

Imagine yourself retouching fine details of a multi-megabyte image at high magnification. Even if you have the world's largest high-resolution monitor, you probably won't be able to see more than a very small part of the total image. It's so easy to lose perspective. How can you see the effect of your edits on the image as a whole without tediously switching back and forth between different zoom levels?

With Aldus PhotoStyler, the answer is simple. Just add a view of the image document you're editing and then size that view so you can see the complete image. You can then obtain a real-time view of how your changes to a small area of the image affect the "big picture" (see Figure 6–3).

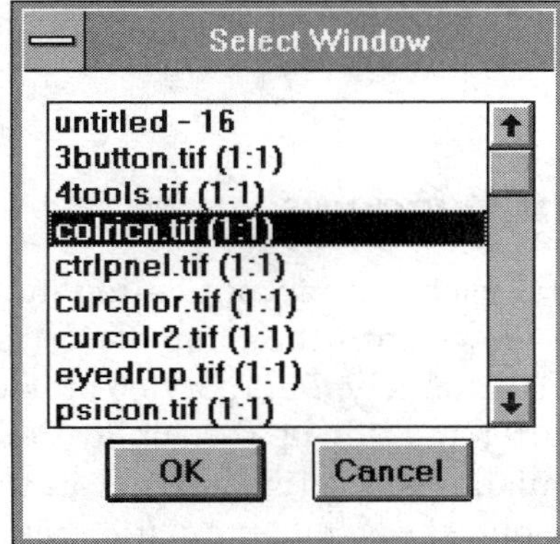

Figure 6-2. The Select Window dialog box

Figure 6-3.

Adding a view of an image document

To add a view of the active image document, choose the Add a View command from the View menu or press Ctrl-V. PhotoStyler always generates the new view at a 1:1 zoom level, but you can enlarge or reduce its document window using any of the techniques described earlier in this chapter. When you close one view of an image document, any other views of the same image remain open and you have to close them separately.

Tip

We can envision situations in which you might choose to generate several views, all at different magnifications. For example, you might edit a small area of an image in one window at an 8:1 zoom level, using as references a 2:1 magnified window of the same area and a 1:3 reduced window of the entire image. The flexibility you gain by adding views is enormous.

Arranging Multiple Document Windows

Some of us are digital pack rats, accumulating multiple image documents and multiple views until the PhotoStyler application window becomes cluttered. Fortunately, PhotoStyler provides techniques for you to minimize clutter and tidy up the application window. You can move windows manually as described earlier in this chapter, or you can arrange them by one of several automatic methods.

Tiling Windows

Choose the Tile command in the Window menu to arrange all open image document windows like tiles (Figure 6–4). PhotoStyler will adjust the window size of each image document at its current viewing magnification so that collectively, the document windows fill the application window. If any open image documents are minimized icons when you choose the Tile command, PhotoStyler will line up the icons at the bottom of the application window.

The Tile command is especially useful if you're creating and saving multiple versions of the same image document during the course of a project. Being able to compare various stages of the project at a glance can help you refine your image editing strategy.

Cascading Windows

Choose the Cascade command in the Windows menu to stack all open document windows diagonally as in Figure 6–5. The title bar of all document windows will remain visible so you can locate them easily. When you activate an image document window by clicking its title bar, that window will jump to the front of the stack.

Minimizing and Restoring Windows

You may not need to refer constantly to *all* of the image documents that are open at a given time. To free up space, you can *minimize* one

Figure 6-4.

Tiling multiple document windows

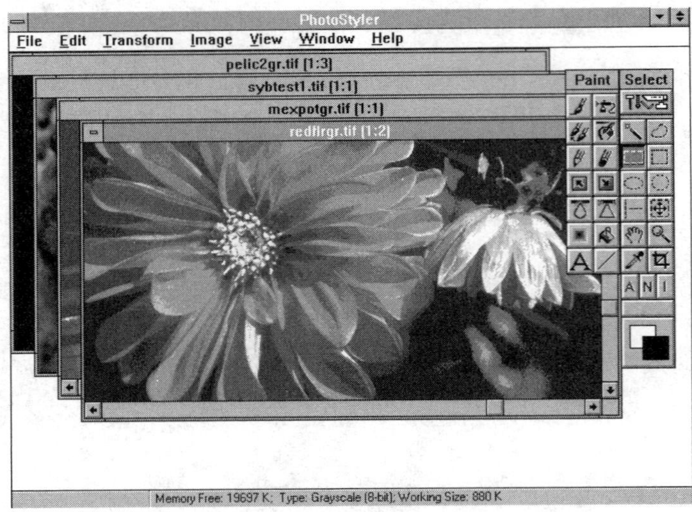

Figure 6-5. Cascading multiple document windows

or more document windows, turning them into miniature icons with the image document title beneath.

To minimize the active document window, click on the minimize button in the window's title bar, or choose the Minimize command in its control menu. To restore a minimized image document to its previous size, double-click the icon, or click once and choose the Restore command from the pop-up menu that appears.

Note *Minimizing icons can save memory if you're running Windows in standard mode. If you're running it in 386 enhanced mode, this advantage doesn't apply.*

Arranging Icons You can move any minimized document window to any position within the PhotoStyler application window. If you want to tidy up multiple document icons, simply choose the Arrange Icons command in the Windows menu. PhotoStyler will align all document icons from right to left at the bottom of the application window.

Duplicating an Image Document

It's a good idea to duplicate any image before you begin editing it. This practice lets you save multiple versions of an image and helps you avoid accidentally overwriting the original.

To duplicate an image, press Ctrl-D or choose the Duplicate command in the Edit menu. PhotoStyler will generate the duplicate image in Fit in Window mode, regardless of the magnification level of the original. The duplicate image, bearing the name *untitled-* plus a number in its title bar, will become the active image document. The duplicate image document may overlap the original, so you may want to move one of the windows as described in the next section.

Moving an Image Document Window

Sometimes you can't see a document window fully because a floating palette or another document window partially overlaps it. To move an image document window to another location within the PhotoStyler application window, position the cursor over the title bar of the document window and then drag it to the desired location.

If you move a document window past the edge of the PhotoStyler application window, the application window will display scroll bars. You can use these scroll bars to view the document windows that are outside the current viewing area.

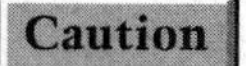

Make sure you drag the window by its title bar. If you click in the image document area itself, you may accidentally apply the currently active Paint or Selection tool.

Sizing an Image Document Window

If an image fits entirely within its document window, you'll rarely need to change the window's size. However, large images and magnified images may fit only partially within their windows. To make such document windows larger or smaller, you can resize them in the same way you size application windows under the MS-Windows operating environment.

1. Position the cursor along any border or corner of the active document window until the cursor changes to a double-headed arrow. The direction of the arrows (horizontal, vertical, or diagonal) shows the direction in which you can size the document window.

2. Drag the cursor inward or outward in the direction indicated by the arrows.
3. Release the mouse button when the document window has reached the desired size. Note that only the size of the document window changes. The viewing magnification of the image itself doesn't change.

Fitting an Image to Its Window

Perhaps you've changed the magnification of an image document so that only part of the image appears in the document window. Or, you may have resized the document window so that it extends beyond the image itself, as in the left image in Figure 6–6. PhotoStyler lets you fit the document window to the image document using one of several available reductions in image size.

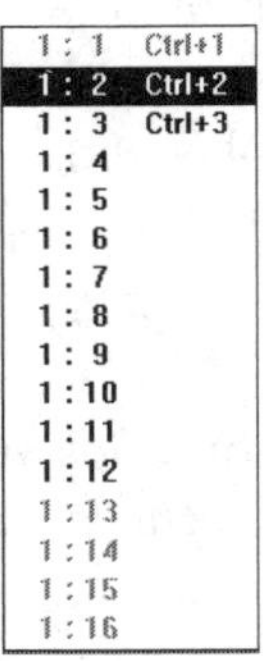

To fit the image to its document window, choose the Fit in Window command in the View menu. A submenu will pop up, displaying a list of viewing magnifications. Available magnifications will appear in black; other magnifications will be grayed out. The size of your image and the display resolution of your monitor will determine which ratios you can choose. Select the desired viewing magnification from the choices available. PhotoStyler will redraw the image at the selected size, shrinking the document window borders to fit the selected viewing magnification, as in the right image in Figure 6–6.

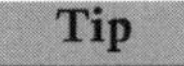

If the 1:1, 1:2, and 1:3 magnification ratios are available, you can bypass the Fit in Window command and use the keyboard shortcuts Ctrl-1, Ctrl-2, or Ctrl-3, respectively.

Figure 6-6.

Fitting an image document to its window

Tip

Some degradation in image display quality occurs when you reduce the viewing magnification of an image to a ratio below 1:1. Colors may shift slightly, the image may look brighter or darker, and less detail may be visible than at actual size. The original information remains in the image data, but at small viewing ratios, the image may not be completely WYSIWYG. We suggest that when editing color images for critical commercial applications, you always work at a 1:1 or magnified view rather than at a reduced view. Even if you see only part of the image at one time, it's better to play it safe and see exactly what you're doing than to risk introducing unexpected results. You can always add a small view of the image if you need to see the full picture. See "Adding a View of an Image Document" earlier in this chapter.

Zooming In And Out with the Zoom Tool

When the Zoom tool in the Select Palette is active, you magnify or reduce the view of an image document by a fixed increment each time you click in the image. Clicking while pressing the Shift key reduces the viewing magnification; clicking without the use of this key increases magnification. The point in the image at which you click the Zoom tool becomes the center of the document window after zooming.

The default zooming increment for each click is one, but you can change this value using the Preferences command in the File menu. To zoom in or out of an image with the Zoom tool:

1. Choose the Preferences command in the File menu. When the Preferences dialog box appears, enter a value between one and four in the Zoom Increment Unit numerical entry box. Press Enter or click OK to exit the dialog box and save the new setting.

2. Activate the Zoom tool by clicking on its icon once.
3. Move the cursor into the active image document where it takes the shape of the Zoom tool icon. Position the cursor over the point that should be in the center of the window after zooming.
4. To zoom *in* on the image, click the selected point. To zoom *out*, first press and hold the Shift key and then click. The magnification level of the image will change by the increment you selected in step 1, and the point you clicked will be at the center of the document window. The title bar of the image will indicate the new viewing

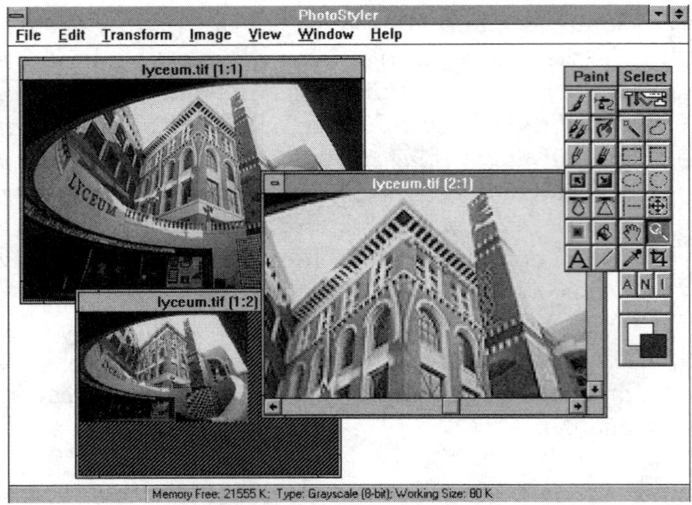

Figure 6-7. Zooming in and out: an image document at various magnification levels

magnification for your reference. Figure 6–7 shows three views of the same image document: a 1:1 magnification, a 2:1 zoomed view, and a 1:2 reduction.

5. If you want to magnify or reduce the image further, continue clicking (or pressing Shift and clicking). When you reach the maximum or minimum zoom level (16:1 or 1:16), you won't be able to zoom any further.

Note *When you press Shift to prepare for zooming out, the four arrows of the Zoom tool cursor reverse direction and point inward. This is a visual sign that you're ready to reduce rather than increase viewing magnification.*

Zooming In and Out Using Menu Commands

Another way to zoom in or out of an image document is to use the Zoom In or Zoom Out command in the View menu. If you know the exact viewing ratio you want to achieve, selecting the appropriate command will probably be faster than clicking several times with the Zoom tool.

To zoom in or out using a menu command:

1. Adjust the view of the active image document if you want a specific area of the image to appear at the center of the document window

after you change magnification. See "Controlling the Display of Large or Magnified Images" in this chapter.

2. Choose the Zoom In or Zoom Out command in the View menu and drag the cursor to the right until you see the submenu of options.
3. Click on the desired magnification level. The view of the active image document will change to match this level, and the image's title bar will reflect the new viewing magnification.

If rulers are attached to an image document when you change viewing magnification, the number of ruler increments may increase or decrease. Ruler increments are most accurate when an image is in a 1:1 viewing magnification.

Returning to a 1:1 View

Once you've changed the viewing magnification of an image, you can return to a 1:1 view at any time. PhotoStyler offers you a choice of four different techniques for returning to actual view:

- *Menu technique*—Choose the Actual View (1:1) command in the View menu.
- *Keyboard technique*—If your image is small enough to fit entirely within the application window, press Ctrl-1.
- *Zoom tool technique #1*—Double-click the Zoom tool icon in the Select Palette.
- *Zoom tool technique #2*—Activate the Zoom tool and move the cursor into the active image document. Click the right mouse button once to bring the image back to actual view.

Controlling the Display of Large or Magnified Images

Some images contain too many pixels to fit completely into the PhotoStyler application window at a 1:1 viewing magnification. Images viewed at a high level of magnification usually don't fit into the application window, either. PhotoStyler offers several types of image display controls that keep you from experiencing oversized images as an inconvenience. You can display selected areas of an image using scroll bars, keyboard shortcuts, or the Grabber tool. If you like to work with a single large image at a time, you can maximize the active image or use PhotoStyler's Full Screen Mode to fill the screen with as much of the image as your display resolution will allow.

Using Scroll Bars

Whenever an image is too highly magnified to fit within its document window, scroll bars appear along the bottom and right borders of the document window as inFigure 6–8. The horizontal scroll bar lets you view areas of the image that fall to the left or right of the current viewing area; the vertical scroll bar lets you see parts of the image that lie above or below the current viewing area. Unlike the Grabber tool, the scroll bar doesn't require that you deactivate a Paint or Select Palette tool in order to change the visible image area.

Scroll bars contain two types of controls that you can use to manipulate your view of the image:

- *Scroll arrows* let you scroll in one direction in small increments by clicking. If you press and hold the mouse button over the scroll arrow, you can scroll continuously.
- *Scroll thumbs* let you click to "jump" to another area of the image in large increments. To move more smoothly, you can drag the scroll thumb with your mouse.

Too much mouse movement can be time-consuming, so PhotoStyler lets you "scroll" using keyboard shortcuts, too. Table 6–1 lists the keyboard shortcuts you can use to scroll to areas of an image that aren't currently visible.

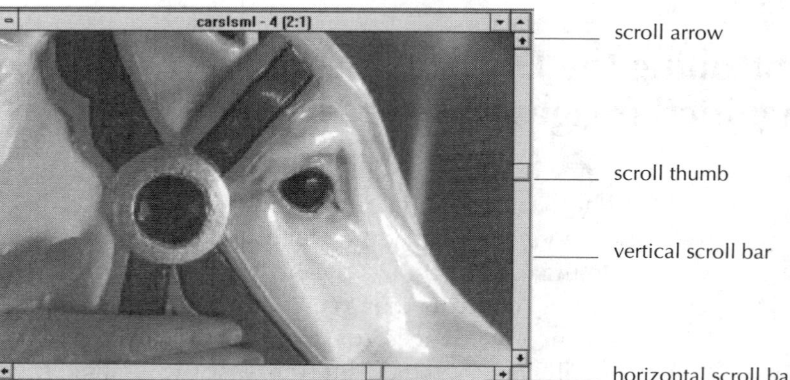

Figure 6-8.

A magnified image document with scroll bars

Table 6–1. Keyboard Shortcuts for Scrolling an Image Document

Key(s)	Effect
Home	Scrolls to the top of the image
End	Scrolls to the bottom of the image
Ctrl-Home	Scrolls to the extreme left of the image
Ctrl-End	Scrolls to the extreme right of the image
PgUp	Scrolls up half a window at a time
PgDn	Scrolls down half a window at a time
Ctrl-PgUp	Scrolls left
Ctrl-PgDn	Scrolls right

Using the Grabber

The Grabber tool in the Select Palette lets you scroll an image in any direction, including diagonally. For this reason, you may find the Grabber more handy to use than the scroll bars when an image is magnified or oversized. You'll temporarily have to deactivate any Paint or Select tool you've been using in order to activate the Grabber, but this is a minor inconvenience.

To change the viewing area of an image with the Grabber tool:

1. Click the Grabber tool icon in the Select Palette.
2. Move the cursor into the active document window.
3. Press and hold the mouse button and drag the cursor until the part of the image you want to see appears within the document window. Then, release the mouse button.

Viewing an Image in Full Screen Mode

A third way to manage the display of a large or magnified image is to work in Full Screen mode. In Full Screen mode, the menu and title bar of the PhotoStyler application window disappear, and the active image document expands to fill as much of the application window as it can at the current magnification level. The floating palettes remain visible, so you can continue to paint and make selections, but you can't apply menu commands in this mode.

To work in Full Screen mode, choose the Full Screen Mode command from the View menu, or press the keyboard shortcut Ctrl-W. Only the active image document remains visible on your monitor, as shown in Figure 6–9.

When you're ready to return to Normal Screen mode, press Ctrl-W or click the Select Palette menu and choose the Normal Screen Mode command. This command appears in the Select Palette only when you're working in Full Screen mode.

Tip

Full Screen mode is viable only when you're content to work on one image at a time. If you need to cut and paste between multiple image documents that you have open, you'll probably find using the scroll bars, the Maximize button, or the Grabber tool more convenient.

Maximizing an Image

If you want to fill the screen with a specific image but can't do without the menu bar, double-click the Maximize button at the upper right corner of the active image document window. This action will enlarge the image much like the Full Screen Mode command, except that the menu commands will remain available. The Maximize button will become a Restore button. To return to a normal viewing mode when

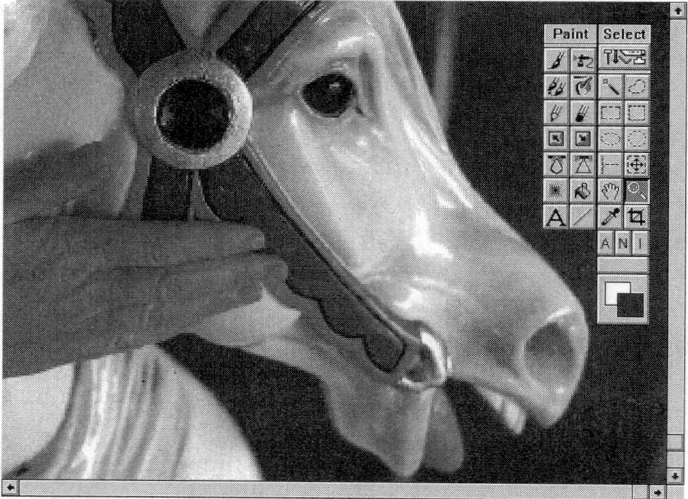

Figure 6-9.

Editing an image in Full Screen mode

you no longer need a maximized image, click the Maximize/Restore button again.

Identifying Precise Locations within a Document Window

PhotoStyler's user interface provides you with two ways to take precise measurements within an image document window. One way is to add rulers to a document window, using your choice of units of measure. The other way is to rely on PhotoStyler's status bar.

Adding Rulers to a Document Window

If your PhotoStyler projects require that you measure sections of an image precisely, you can add a horizontal and vertical ruler to any image document window. To add rulers as in the example in Figure 6–10, just choose the Ruler command in the View menu or use the keyboard shortcut, Ctrl-R. The rulers will adjust position automatically as you scroll the image.

Tip

After adding a Ruler to a small document window, you may find that the image document no longer fits entirely within the window. Re-apply the Fit in Window command in the View menu to adjust the image.

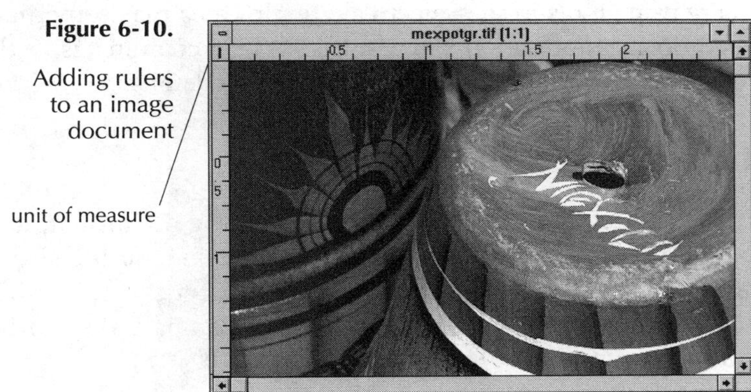

Figure 6-10. Adding rulers to an image document

Changing the Unit of Measure

By default, rulers that you add to an image document window display in inches, but you can display them in centimeters or pixels, too. At the point where the rulers meet is a small rectangle containing the capital letter "I" for inches (Figure 6–10). To change the current unit of measure, click on this rectangle to see a small drop-down menu. Drag the cursor until it highlights the unit of measure you want, and then release the mouse. The rulers will adjust, displaying the new unit of measure.

How Viewing Magnification Affects Rulers

The most accurate viewing magnification when you're using rulers is 1:1. Due to the intense calculations involved in measuring pixel locations in continuous-tone images, ruler increments are likely to change when you change the viewing magnification of an image document. Some slight inaccuracies are possible in viewing magnifications other than 1:1.

Identifying Pixel Locations with the Status Bar

As you saw in Chapter 2, PhotoStyler's status bar is a rich source of information about the active image document. Among other benefits, it can help you identify the exact pixel coordinates of your cursor so you can edit more precisely.

(325, 86) r=223, g=197, b=182

Whenever your cursor is within the active image document, the cursor area of the status bar (the left side) displays the current cursor location in parentheses. The first number represents the location of the mouse cursor relative to the *left* edge of the image. The second number represents the location of the cursor relative to the *top* edge of the image. When you're using tools in the Select Palette, this area may sometimes contain additional information about selection area coordinates or the color coordinates of pixels. See Chapter 8 for further details.

Viewing Information about an Image

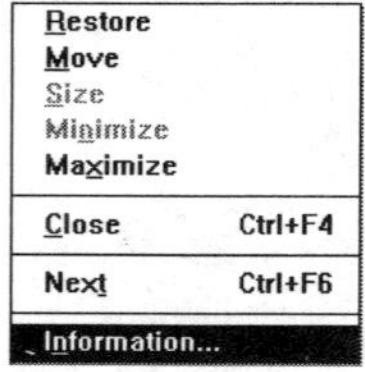

PhotoStyler maintains handy information about the file format, data type, pixel dimensions, print dimensions, resolution, and file size of every image. You may find this information useful, for example, when you need to recalculate output size or check file compatibility with a page layout program.

To access this information for an image that's already open, choose the Information command in the View menu. You'll see a dialog box similar to the one in Figure 6–11. This dialog box also tells you whether you have modified the active image document since the last time you saved it.

To get information about an image that you've minimized to an icon, click the document icon and then the Information command from the menu that pops up.

Info...

To access information for a file that's not open, choose the Open command in the File menu or press Ctrl-O. The Info button in the Open Image File dialog box will become available when you select a filename. Click this button to display the File Information dialog box. This dialog box differs from the Current File Information dialog box for images that are open in two respects:

- The Can be displayed? line indicates whether PhotoStyler is capable of opening the specified file.
- The Compressed line tells you whether the unopened image is in a compressed format.

Tip

To view information about multiple unopened images, choose the Open command from the File menu, select multiple filenames by clicking with the Ctrl key pressed, and then click the Info command button in the Open Image File dialog box.

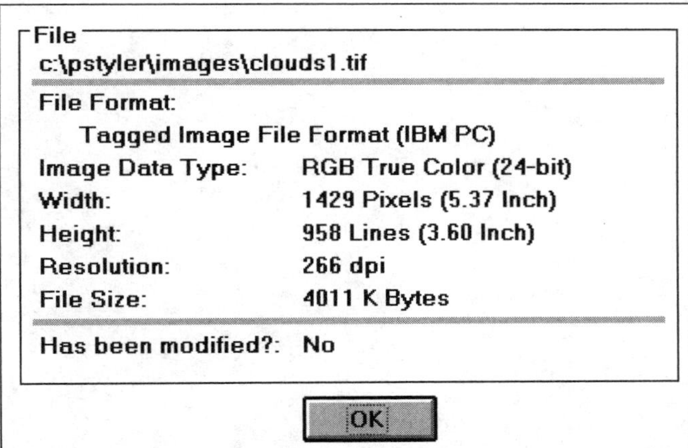

File
c:\pstyler\images\clouds1.tif
File Format:
Tagged Image File Format (IBM PC)
Image Data Type: RGB True Color (24-bit)
Width: 1429 Pixels (5.37 Inch)
Height: 958 Lines (3.60 Inch)
Resolution: 266 dpi
File Size: 4011 K Bytes
Has been modified?: No
OK

Figure 6-11.

The Current File Information dialog box

Viewing the Color Table (Indexed Color Images)

PhotoStyler attaches a *color lookup table* to all Indexed 16- and 256-color images. (See Chapter 5 for more about image data types.) When the active image is an Indexed 16- or 256-color image, you can see a visual representation of its color table by choosing the Color Table command in the View menu. This command is unavailable for other image data types.

The color lookup table (see a Grayscale version of it in Figure 5–4) consists of *cells* that represent all of the possible colors you can assign to the active image. You can view the color component values for any cell by clicking on that cell and looking at the status bar. When you're finished, click OK or press Enter to exit the color lookup table.

In this chapter, you've explored the many ways you can display image documents to promote a flexible working environment, enhance your editing powers, and stimulate your creativity. The next chapter delves into the mysteries of color—the heart of PhotoStyler's image editing power and the source of many special effects.

Part III:

ENHANCING, EDITING, AND RETOUCHING IMAGES

7

Working with Color and Grayscale Values

Understanding color is the most fundamental yet far-reaching skill you will ever master in Aldus PhotoStyler. Whether you work with True Color or Grayscale images, a basic knowledge of color will help you use the Paint tools, apply special-effects filters, define masks precisely, and exercise your creativity to the fullest.

Relax! You don't have to digest an engineer's course in Color Physics 101. We know that what you really want is to become *productive* with color and gray shades: to create dazzling images and then get them to show off in print, slide, or video form as elegantly as they did on your computer monitor. So we'll explore only as much color science as it takes to start your creative juices flowing. Then, we'll cover the basics of how to select and edit Grayscale and color values in PhotoStyler. To round out the chapter, we'll offer tips and example illustrations that will inspire you to make the most of the many tools, filters, and special effects that rely on the control of color.

How PhotoStyler Assigns Grayscale and Color Values

In most PhotoStyler operations, the numbers behind the colors or gray shades will be completely transparent to you. PhotoStyler's intuitive interface lets you concentrate on being creative with what you see. You'll have greater control over special effects, though, if you understand a little about how PhotoStyler turns numbers into colors.

The data type of a PhotoStyler image (Chapter 5) determines the maximum number of color values the image can contain. RGB True Color images have a *color depth* of 24 bits (16.7 million colors), while Grayscale images have a color depth of only 8 bits (256 shades of gray). Each pixel in a Grayscale image has a single value ranging from zero (black) to 255 (white). But it takes three values, not one, to describe the color of each pixel in a True Color image. The 16 million possible colors derive from combinations of these three values.

These numbers form the basis of the Color Palette, Color dialog box, and other color-related user interface aids you'll learn about in this chapter. They also are important for understanding the four *color spaces* that describe color values in PhotoStyler.

The Basics of Color Space

A desktop publisher acquaintance tells us that after his first session with PhotoStyler, his wife caught him muttering "RGB, HSB, hue only, 255, additive, subtractive" in his sleep. "What's the fuss?" he growled, throwing up his hands. "All I want to do is *paint*."

The "fuss" is about color: how to specify it, how to manipulate it, and how to transfer it from one medium to another. Basically, color (and that includes gray shades) results from the interaction between the surface of an object, a light source, and a human observer. If the object changes or is replaced with another object, light will interact with it in a different way. The observer will then perceive its color differently—perhaps seeing more colors, fewer colors, or a different range of colors entirely. So, for example, a "real" human face looks different to us from a digital photograph of the same face displayed on a computer monitor. And both of these look different from a printed photograph of the face.

That, in a nutshell, is the reason why there are multiple standards for reproducing color. The human eye *perceives* light, computer monitors *transmit* it, and printers' inks *reflect* it. Yet the need to describe color in a standardized way remains.

To meet this need, theoretical *color models* have evolved to describe and quantify color. Physicists envision these color models as three-dimensional geometrical spaces in which the distances between color values are measurable. In PhotoStyler, you'll encounter four commonly used color models: RGB, CMYK, HSB, and HLS. Figure 7–1 shows how color physics depicts the RGB and HLS color spaces; the CMYK and HSB color models are similar, as you'll see in the following sections.

Each of the four color models featured in PhotoStyler is designed for specific types of users and applications. The range of colors in one color model is never exactly equivalent to the colors in another. Transferring values between different color models is a little like translating to a foreign language: there's often no one-to-one correspondence, and sometimes subtle "shades" of meaning get lost.

Figure 7-1.

Visualizing the RGB/CMYK and HLS color spaces

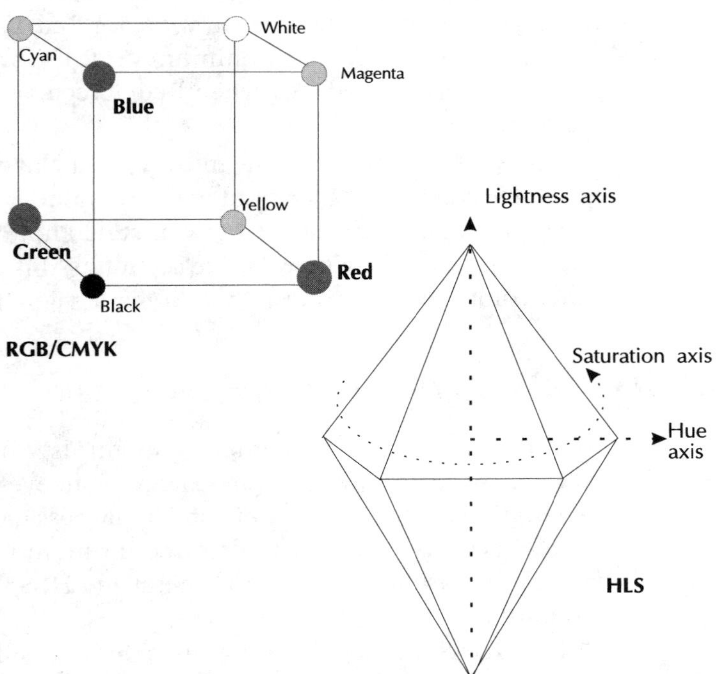

RGB: Color as the Computer Sees It

The RGB color model describes the color spectrum that the cathode ray tubes (CRT's) inside computer monitors can reproduce. RGB stands for Red, Green, and Blue, the colors of the phosphors that coat the inside of the CRT. When electron beams inside a computer monitor strike these phosphors, they transmit light in varying combinations, producing color. The key word is *transmit*: colors generated by computer monitors are strikingly luminous precisely because the CRT's phosphors transmit light rather than reflect it.

Computer monitors, even when supported by display adapters capable of generating 16.7 million different colors, can't reproduce as many colors as the human eye can perceive. However, they can reproduce a good many more color values than print media can. Monitor colors are also brighter than colors produced by printers' inks because of the *additive* light-transmitting technology involved.

As Figure 7–1 shows, the RGB color space is a cube. Red, green, and blue occupy three corners and lie diagonally opposite their complementary colors: cyan, magenta, and yellow. Red, Green, and Blue values can range from zero to 255. In this color model, a white pixel is one that contains the maximum value for Red, Green, and Blue (255). A black pixel contains the minimum value (0) for these three primary colors. Grays are produced when Red, Green, and Blue mix in equal amounts.

The RGB color model is the most natural "language" for computer-generated color. That's why Color Palette values for True Color images appear in RGB terms each time you start PhotoStyler. As you'll see when you reach the Color Palette section of this chapter, you can use other color models during a PhotoStyler session, too.

HSB and HLS: Color as the Eye Perceives It

RGB may be natural for computer monitors, but human beings see color in a different way. The physiology of our eyes leads us to see color as variations in hue, saturation, and brightness or lightness. The color spaces that have evolved to describe intuitive visual perception are HSB (Hue, Saturation, and Brightness) and HLS (Hue, Lightness, and Saturation).

The HLS color model is represented by a six-sided cone as in Figure 7–1. (The HLS model is a double hexcone and the HSB model is a single hexcone, but you needn't concern yourself with the details here.) The hue of a color (the H value) corresponds to its position in a circular color wheel and is expressed in terms of degrees. The six points around the base of the cone represent the six colors of the rainbow: red, orange, yellow, green, blue, and violet. Saturation (the S value in HSB and HLS) has to do with the purity of a light wave and is expressed in percentages. You'll find the most saturated and intense colors around the perimeter of the cone and the less intense or pastel colors closer to the core. Brightness or Lightness the B or L value) describes the intensity of light and is also expressed as a percentage, with white at the peak of the cone, black at the base, and grays running in a straight line down through the core.

HSB and HLS color spaces are intuitive for fine artists and photographers because they're based on visual perception. Color values in PhotoStyler also transfer well between HSB/HLS and RGB. Translating HSB, HLS, or RGB values to CMYK is another matter, though.

CMYK: Color as the Printing Industry Mixes It

CMYK, the color model used by printing professionals, takes its name from the cyan, magenta, yellow, and black inks used to reproduce color. Professional color separators and desktop publishers who regularly take color images to the printer are familiar with CMYK standards.

In theory, the CMYK model is a subset of the RGB model and, like it, takes the form of a cube. The maximum values of Cyan, Magenta, and Yellow mixed together in the CMYK model should produce black, just as the maximum values of Red, Green, and Blue in the RGB model produce white. In practice, however, the pigments used by commercial printers don't yield saturated blacks, so black is added as a fourth color. This presents special printing problems that we'll explore in Chapters 14, 15, and 16.

Whereas computer monitors transmit light, printers' inks absorb and reflect it. As a result, colors that you assign to an image on your CRT tend to appear darker once they're printed. Another consequence of this difference in technologies is that the spectrum of printable colors is much narrower than either the visual or the CRT spectrum.

"Yecch," we hear a few photo retouchers protest. "Let's avoid the whole CMYK mare's nest and just specify color in those vivid RGB terms." Not so fast. The truth is that the colors of images displayed on your monitor will *never* exactly match the colors of those same images when printed, no matter which color space you use. Some of the colors you can see on your screen just can't be reproduced on paper. So if any of your images is destined for print media, being an escapist about color systems won't help you (unless you can pass your work along to a color separation specialist after you're done being artistic). Monitor calibration won't solve the problem either, though it will stabilize your display. What *will* help you is getting a color proof from your service bureau, color samples from your commercial printer, or using a hard-copy color printing guide such as the Trumatch system. Take a closer look at Chapters 15 and 16 for practical information on how to overcome the CMYK hurdle successfully.

So much for the theory of color in PhotoStyler. In the next part of this chapter, you'll see how to select and edit colors and palettes in preparation for editing images.

Working with Foreground and Background Colors or Grays

At the base of the Select Palette, you'll find the Current Color Indicator: two small rectangular blocks inside a larger rectangle. The block in front displays the current foreground color, while the one in back shows the current background color. The current foreground and background colors also appear in the Color Palette whenever you display it by pressing Ctrl-8.

The use of foreground and background colors is vital to many painting and retouching operations in PhotoStyler. The following Paint tools and menu commands use the current foreground color to carry out their functions:

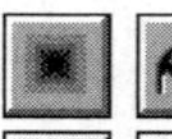

- the Gradient Fill tool
- the Bucket Fill tool
- the "traditional" Paint tools: Airbrush, Paintbrush, Pencil, and Line
- The Fill command (Edit menu)

Fill... Ctrl+F

The Eraser tool, Gradient Fill tool, and Fill command make creative use of the current background color.

PhotoStyler offers you four methods for specifying the current foreground and background colors or shades of gray. To select colors intuitively, you can use the Eyedropper tool in the Select Palette, a function key, or the scratch pad of the Color Palette. To specify colors precisely, you can use the Zoom mode of the Color Palette or the more exact Color dialog box. We'll describe the uses of the Color Palette and Color dialog box in their own sections later in this chapter.

Identifying and Selecting Color or Gray Values with the Eyedropper

The Eyedropper tool in the Select Palette has two functions. You can use it to:

- identify the precise color or gray values of any pixel in the active image document, or
- choose a new foreground or background color from the active image document

The second function is especially powerful for photo retouching and montaging operations.

Identifying Color or Gray Values

(325, 86) r=223, g=197, b=182

To see the color components or gray value of any pixel, activate the Eyedropper tool and move the cursor to the desired pixel in the active image document. The gray value or color components of the pixel will appear in the cursor area of the status bar.

Tip

Always magnify the active image document before you use the Eyedropper to obtain color information about a pixel. Otherwise, you won't be able to see which pixel the status bar is describing.

Tip

If you're viewing the CMYK color components of pixels (see "Working with the Color Palette" later in this chapter), first choose the Separation Setup command in the File menu and click the Default command button. This will adjust cyan, magenta, yellow, and black component values to something approximating desirable printing conditions. See Chapters 14, 15, and 16 for more about CMYK color values, image channels, and color separations.

Choosing Foreground or Background Colors from the Active Image Document

The Eyedropper tool also lets you choose the current foreground or background color from colors found in the active image document. In photo retouching, it's often necessary to blur, smudge, or fill areas with colors or grays from the photo itself. Montaging is another application where you should choose foreground and background colors directly from the images you're combining: You can then blend colors from one image into another so that the resulting composite looks more natural.

To choose a new foreground or background color from the active image document,

1. Open or activate an image document that contains the color or gray values you want to use.

2. Activate the Zoom tool in the Select Palette and magnify the area that contains the pixel whose color or shade of gray you want to select. Continue magnifying the area until you can distinguish the pixel clearly from its neighbors.

3. Activate the Eyedropper tool and move the cursor into the active document window. Here, the cursor takes on the shape of the Eyedropper.
4. To select a new *foreground* color, move the cursor to the pixel that contains the desired color and then click. The selected color or gray shade will appear in the Current Colors Indicator at the bottom of the Select Palette.
5. To select a new *background* color from the active image document, move the cursor to the desired pixel, press and hold the Shift key, and then click. The new background gray or color will appear in the Current Colors Indicator.

Using Function Keys to Select Foreground and Background Colors

Another way to change foreground and background colors in PhotoStyler is to use function key shortcuts. These shortcuts are even more versatile than the Eyedropper tool:

- You can use them with *either* the active image document or the Color Palette, and
- it doesn't matter which tool is active when you press the function key.

Press F5 to change the current *foreground* color to the color or gray shade of the pixel under the cursor. Pressing F6 causes the color of the pixel under the cursor to become the current *background* color.

When you need to use colors or gray values that you can't find in the active image document, the Eyedropper tool and function key shortcuts aren't enough. You'll need to use the Color Palette or the Color dialog box, which we describe in the next part of this chapter.

Working with the Color Palette

The Color Palette (Figure 7–2 in Grayscale version here and Figure 2–9 in the Color Section of this book) is among the most versatile and powerful of PhotoStyler's user interface tools. On the most basic level, you can use it to select foreground and background colors that aren't present in any of the images that are open. If you need to specify colors precisely, you can zoom in on the Color Palette or use color component scroll bars. Sophisticated users will appreciate the ability to use alternative color palettes, or to create and save custom palettes by cutting and pasting colors or even whole images.

Color Palette Basics

The Color Palette is available whenever one or more image documents are open in the PhotoStyler application window. To display the Color Palette, press Ctrl-8 or choose the Show Color Palette command in the View menu. The Color Palette will appear in the lower right area of the application window. To move the Color Palette to another location, drag it by its title bar. To hide the Color Palette when you no longer need it, press Ctrl-8 again or double-click its title bar. (The Color Palette will disappear automatically when you close the last open image document.)

The appearance of the Color Palette always matches the data type of the active image document. For example, when an RGB True Color image is active, the current Color Palette will appear in color. When a

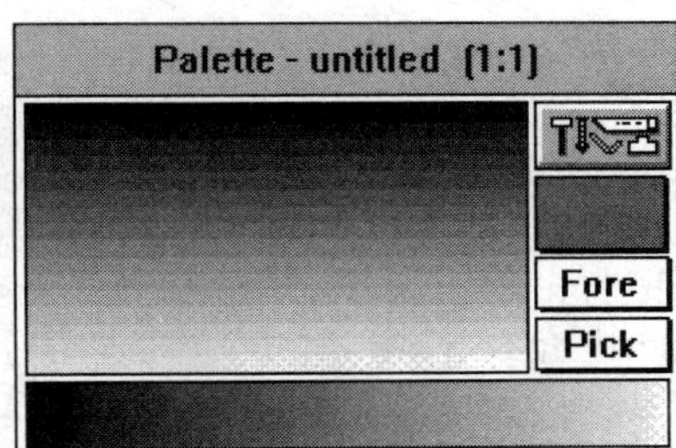

Figure 7-2.

The default Color Palette displayed with Grayscale images

Grayscale image document is active, the current Color Palette will show only Grayscale values. If another image data type is active, the Color Palette will change to match the spectrum available for that image.

Note *You can load alternative palettes or create custom palettes for RGB True Color and Grayscale images only.*

Figure 7–2 shows the elements of the Color Palette. The next few paragraphs describe briefly how each of these elements functions.

Title Bar

The title bar of the Color Palette displays the name of the current palette, as well as the current zoom level of the palette. You can move the Color Palette to another location by holding the mouse cursor over the title bar and dragging. Double-clicking the title bar hides the Color Palette from view.

Scratch Pad

The scratch pad has multiple functions. When the Color Palette is in Pick mode, the scratch pad displays all the colors or grays in the current palette and lets you choose a new foreground or background color by clicking. When the Color Palette is in Edit mode, you can use the Paint tools to edit the scratch pad, or zoom in on the scratch pad to see subtle differences between colors or gray levels.

Mini Color Bar

Available for RGB True Color or Grayscale images only, the mini color bar lets you select a foreground or background color from a compressed spectrum. Even if the range of colors in the current palette is limited, a fuller spectrum of grays or 24-bit color remains available to you through the mini color bar.

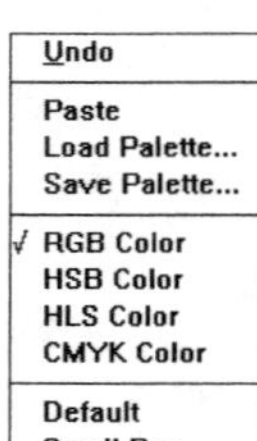

Color Palette Menu

The Toolbox menu icon in the Color Palette conceals a pop-up menu you can display by clicking. The commands in this menu give you options for using alternative palettes, creating custom palettes, and specifying color according to your choice of color models.

Mode Buttons

The two buttons to the right of the scratch pad function as a toggle: just click the button to switch back and forth between modes. The Fore/Back button lets you select a new foreground or background color using the Color Palette or the Color dialog box. The Pick/Edit button lets you alternate between selecting colors and editing the current palette.

When the Color Palette is in Edit mode, the only way you can change the current Foreground or Background color is to click the Current Color Indicator. This action brings up the Color dialog box described later in this chapter.

Current Color Indicator

When the Fore/Back button is in Fore mode, the Current Color Indicator displays the current foreground color. It displays the current background color when the Color Palette is in Back mode. Clicking once on the Current Color Indicator displays the Color dialog box so that you can specify a new color precisely.

Color Component Scroll Bars

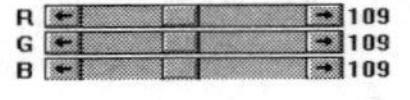

The Color Palette menu contains a Scroll Bar option. When you click this option, color component scroll bars will appear at the bottom of the Color Palette. If just clicking in the scratch pad isn't precise enough for you, try using the scroll bars after changing to the color space of your choice.

Selecting Color and Gray Values from the Color Palette

The Color Palette offers four different methods for choosing a new foreground or background color or shade of gray:

- Click in the mini color bar.
- Click in the scratch pad in Pick mode.
- Use the Zoom tool in Edit mode to choose a color from among a narrow range of colors.
- Specify colors precisely with color component scroll bars.

Choosing Colors from the Mini Color Bar

If the active image document is a Grayscale or RGB True Color image, the mini color bar (see Figure 7–2) will appear at the base of the Color Palette. You can always choose a new foreground or background color from the mini color bar, regardless of the current zoom level, the current Edit/Pick button mode, or currently loaded palette. To choose a new foreground or background color or gray from the mini color bar,

1. Toggle the Fore/Back button in the Color Palette according to whether you want to select a new foreground or background color.

2. Move the cursor into the mini color bar area. The cursor will take on the shape of the Eyedropper tool, no matter which tool is currently active.

(143, 60) grey=156

3. Watch the cursor area of the status bar (the left side) as you move the Eyedropper cursor along the mini color bar. The status bar will indicate the gray or color component values of each color over which the Eyedropper passes.

Fore Back

4. To choose a new *foreground* color in Fore mode or a new *background* color in Back mode, simply click on the desired color or gray, using the status bar as a guide. Both of the Current Color Indicators—the one in the Color Palette and the one at the base of the Select Palette—will change to reflect your new selection.

Tip *Press Shift and then click to select a new background color in Fore mode or a new foreground color in Back mode.*

Selecting Foreground and Background Colors from the Scratch Pad

Usually, you'll find the scratch pad more convenient than the mini color bar for selecting color or gray values. When you're using the default Untitled True Color or Grayscale palette, the spectrum in the mini color bar is just too compressed to let you see clearly what you're selecting. The scratch pad offers you a larger view and also lets you zoom in on available colors as if it were an image document. And if you've loaded an alternative or custom palette, the current palette colors will appear in the scratch pad.

Selecting Colors in Pick Mode If you don't need to zoom in on the scratch pad in order to select a color, the Color Palette must be in Pick mode. To choose a new foreground or background color using this basic scratch pad technique:

1. Toggle the Fore/Back button in the Color Palette according to whether you want to choose a new foreground or background color.

Pick

(325, 86) r=223, g=197, b=182

2. Toggle the Pick/Edit button to Pick mode and move the cursor into the scratch pad. No matter which tool is currently selected, the cursor will take on the appearance of the Eyedropper. The cursor area of the status bar will display the color or gray values of the pixels over which the cursor passes.
3. To select a *foreground* color in Fore mode or a *background* color in Back mode, click the desired color in the scratch pad. To select a background color in Fore mode or a foreground color in Back mode, press Shift as you click.

The color or gray shade you choose will appear in the Current Color Indicator of the Color Palette. It will also appear in the Current Colors Indicator at the base of the Select Palette.

Zooming in on the Color Palette in Edit mode You may sometimes want a close-up view of a narrow range of colors before you choose one from the scratch pad. To zoom in on the scratch pad and select a new foreground or background color:

1. Choose the Preferences command in the File menu and adjust the Zoom increment unit, if necessary. The scratch pad of the Color Palette will zoom by the same increment you've set for image documents. Select OK to exit the Preferences dialog box.

2. Display the Color Palette and activate the Zoom tool in the Select Palette.

Edit

3. Toggle the Pick/Edit button of the Color Palette to Edit mode.
4. Move the cursor into the scratch pad area, where it will take on the appearance of the Zoom tool.
5. Position the cursor over the color range that you want to be the center of the zoom and click once. The color or gray area you've selected will zoom by a factor of one, two, three, or four, depending

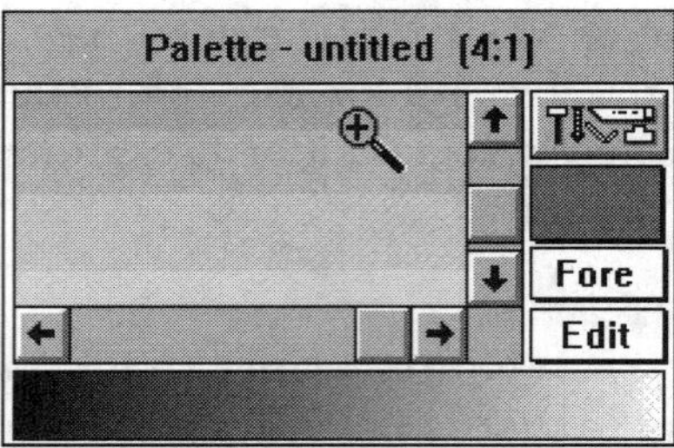

Figure 7-3. Zooming in on the default Color Palette for Grayscale images

on your Zoom increment unit setting in the Preferences dialog box. The title bar of the Color Palette will show you the current zoom level in parentheses, just as in Figure 7–3.

6. Continue clicking until you've reached a zoom level that shows you the narrow range of color or gray values you want to see clearly.
7. Toggle the Fore/Back button according to whether you want to select a new foreground or background value.

Pick

8. Click the Edit button to switch back to Pick mode.
9. Move the cursor to the color or gray value you want (observe the status bar for help) and click. The new color or gray shade will appear in the Current Color Indicators at the base of the Select Palette.
10. Switch back to Edit mode. To zoom back out to the default view of the scratch pad, click the right mouse button once.

The scratch pad appeals to users who like to choose colors or grays by sight. But the Color Palette can be useful to you even if you prefer to specify colors numerically. Just turn on the color component scroll bars and adjust them using your choice of color models.

Specifying Color Values Using Color Component Scroll Bars

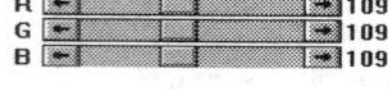

If you're editing a True Color image, you can specify foreground and background colors numerically with the help of the Scroll Bars command in the Color Palette menu. This command causes PhotoStyler to display *color component scroll bars* at the base of the Color Palette. The scroll bars display RGB color components by default, but you can adapt them to another color model by choosing the HLS, HSB, or CMYK option in the Color Palette menu. You can then use the scroll arrows or scroll thumbs to change color values precisely. Figure 7–4

Figure 7-4.

Specifying color with CMYK scroll bars

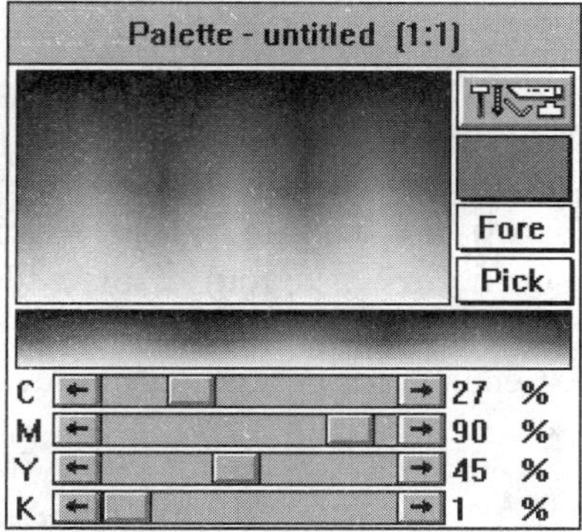

shows the Color Palette with CMYK scroll bars, which are useful for specifying color according to printing industry standards.

Caution

Don't assume that specifying colors in CMYK terms will cause those colors to print exactly as they appear on your monitor. Colors on your screen are brighter than printed colors, and some colors that you see can't even be reproduced on the printing press. Use a Trumatch or other process color printing guide as a reference when specifying in CMYK terms. And be sure to adjust the settings in the Separation Setup dialog box (Separation Setup command, File menu) before you begin specifying color in CMYK terms. See Chapter 14 for more about the Separation Setup command.

Note

In versions 1.1a and later, the color component scroll bars are merely viewing indicators when a Black & White, Grayscale, or Indexed Color image is active. You can specify only those colors that are available for the current image data type.

To specify foreground or background colors using color component scroll bars:

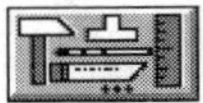

1. With the Color Palette displayed, click the Toolbox menu icon and select the Scroll Bars command from the Color Palette menu. Scroll bars for Red, Green, and Blue color components will appear at the base of the Color Palette.
2. To display the scroll bars according to a different color model, choose the desired color model from the options in the Color Palette menu.

Fore Back

3. Toggle the Fore/Back button according to whether you want to select a foreground or background color.
4. Adjust each component scroll bar one at a time. To change the value, you can type a numeric value in the entry box, click the scroll arrow, drag the scroll bar "thumb," or press and hold the mouse button over the scroll arrow. If your display adapter supports 256 colors, the color of the Current Color Indicator will change in real time as you adjust each color component value.

Tip

Do you want to specify shades of gray within a True Color image? Then use the intuitive HLS or HSB color space. Set the S color component to zero and adjust the B or L component to obtain various shades of gray from black to white.

For truly precision-minded retouchers, there's an even more accurate way to specify color: use the Color dialog box instead of the Color Palette. Even the default Untitled palette can't display the full range of colors available to a given color model, but the Color dialog box can. See "Specifying Color Precisely with the Color Dialog Box" later in this chapter.

Using Alternative Color Palettes

Aldus PhotoStyler supplies twenty-eight palettes in addition to the default palettes for RGB True Color and Grayscale images. Each palette is contained in a file in the \palettes subdirectory and has the extension .pal. Unlike the default palettes, these alternative palettes contain limited subsets of colors or shades of gray that you can use for special purposes. The 7balls.pal palette, for example, is useful for True Color images that require you to simulate three-dimensional lighting effects on rounded surfaces. And the metal1 palette provides easy access to a range of gold, silver, and brass tones. Table 7–1 lists the palettes provided with PhotoStyler, suggests applications for each palette, and indicates whether a palette is available for Grayscale as well as True Color images.

ASCII Palettes and Image-Based Palettes

The alternative palettes fall into two groups: ASCII palettes and image-based palettes. ASCII palette files begin with the _ character, such as _metal1.pal and _earth.pal. These palettes, like the _metal1.pal

Table 7–1. PhotoStyler Palettes and Their Uses

Palette filename	Data Types Supported	For images that require . . .
_clrbar.pal	RGB, GS	saturated hues and grays with high luminosity
_earth.pal	RGB, GS	naturalistic earth tones
_ega.pal	RGB, GS	the eight basic colors simulated by EGA display adapters
_hues1.pal	RGB, GS	saturated rainbow hues and shades of gray
_hues2.pal	RGB, GS	selected rainbow hues and shades of gray
_light.pal	RGB, GS	light shades of all colors
_metal1.pat	RGB, GS	metallic hues simulating silver
_pastel.pat	RGB, GS	pastel shades of all colors
_r2b2g2.pat	RGB, GS	a limited range of reds, greens, and blues generated from two shades of each color
_rainbo1.pal	RGB, GS	saturated rainbow colors (no shades of gray)
_rainbo2.pal	RGB, GS	light shades of rainbow colors (no shades of gray)
_rainbo3.pal	RGB, GS	deep shades of rainbow colors (no shades of gray)
_rgbcmyg.pal	RGB, GS	color and grayscale translation for print publishers who need to use both RGB and CMYK color spaces
_rgbg.pal	RGB, GS	pure red
_sepia.pal	RGB, GS	256 sepia tones for creating antique photo effects
_standa.pal	RGB, GS	saturated rainbow hues and grayscale with 50% lightness values
_standa1.pal	RGB, GS	saturated rainbow hues (no grayscale) with 50% lightness values
_standa2.pal	RGB, GS	saturated rainbow colors and grays for CMYK use
_standa3.pal	RGB, GS	RGB colors with graduated Blue values

(continued next page)

Table 7–1. PhotoStyler Palettes and Their Uses

Palette filename	Data Types Supported	For images that require . . .
_standa4.pal	RGB, GS	variations on metallic CMYK colors with one primary missing
_standa5.pal	RGB, GS	CMYK colors (and grayscale) with low graduated black values
_tones.pal	RGB	
_vga.pal	RGB, GS	standard 16 colors used on VGA displays
_vivid.pal	RGB, GS	vivid rainbow colors with slight variations in brightness
7balls.pal	RGB	spheres of 7 rainbow colors and graduated grayscale for simulating lighting effects on 3-dimensional rounded objects
buttons.pal	RGB	6 color "buttons" (including grayscale) for simulating lighting effects on 3-dimensional objects with flat surfaces
colorpad.pal	RGB	an example of how to customize a palette by "painting" images
space.pal	RGB	graduated rainbow colors (and grayscale) for selecting colors for continuous blending

palette in Figure 7–5, contain a fixed number of colors geometrically arranged in cells. You can edit these palettes in PhotoStyler or use a text editor such as the Windows Notepad. ASCII palettes will display in either a True Color or a Grayscale version, depending on the data type of the active image document.

Image-based palettes, like the buttons.pal palette shown in grayscale in Figure 7–5, contain graphic images instead of color cells. You can distinguish these palette files from their ASCII counterparts because

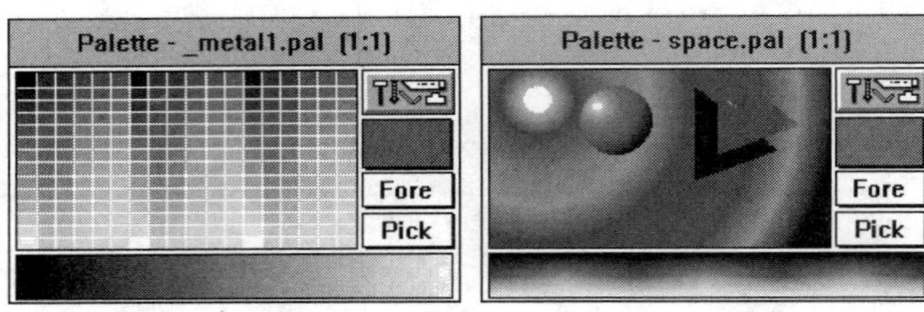

Figure 7-5. Examples of ASCII (l) and image-based (r) palettes

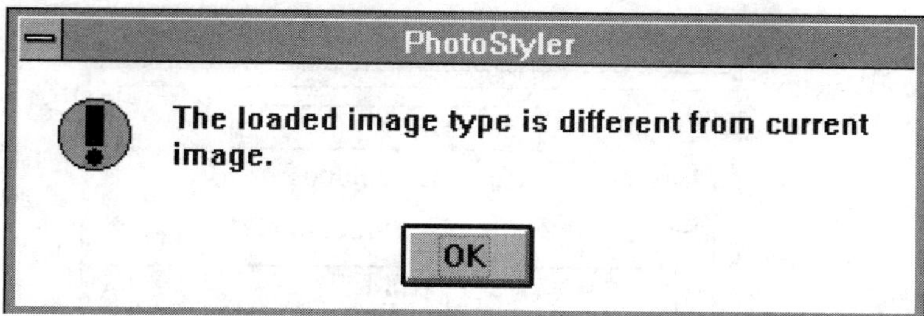

Figure 7-6.

Error message for image-based palette mismatch

they don't begin with the _ character. You can load image-based palettes only if the active image document is of the same data type. All the image-based palettes supplied with PhotoStyler were created for RGB True Color images; so if you try to load one for a Grayscale image, you'll see the error message that appears in Figure 7–6. However, you can create custom image-based palettes for Grayscale images, too. See "Creating and Saving Custom Color Palettes" in this chapter.

Loading Alternative Palettes

The first time you display the Color Palette during a PhotoStyler session, it contains the default RGB or Grayscale palette (depending on the data type of the active image document). You can load any predefined or custom alternative palette using the Load Palette command in the Color Palette menu.

To load a predefined alternative palette or one that you've created:

1. Make sure at least one image document is open and then display the Color Palette by pressing Ctrl-8.

2. Click the Color Palette menu icon and choose the Load Palette command. The Load Palette File dialog box shown in Figure 7–7 will appear.
3. If necessary, use the Directories list box to change to the \palettes subdirectory under the directory where you installed PhotoStyler. Scroll through the list of palette files until you find the one you want to load.
4. To load the new palette file, double-click on the desired filename. The scratch pad of the Color Palette will change to reflect the new palette colors or shades of gray.

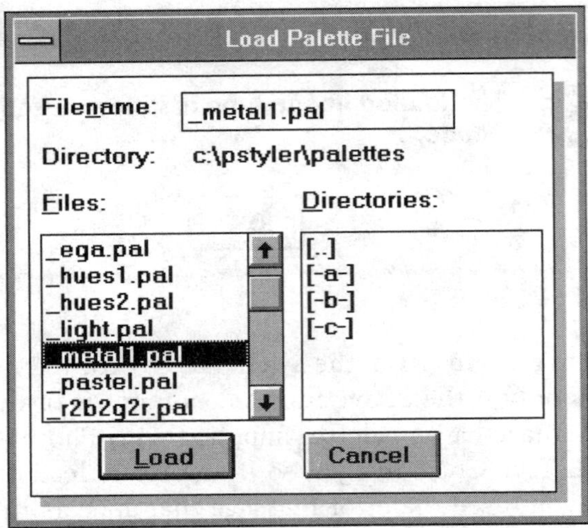

Figure 7-7. The Load Palette File dialog box

Creating and Saving Custom Color Palettes

PhotoStyler lets you edit any existing palette and save the customized palette as a new file for use with RGB True Color and Grayscale images. You can use one or more of these techniques to edit a palette:

- Replace existing color or gray values (ASCII palettes).
- Paint in the scratch pad.
- Paste images or selections from the clipboard.
- Load a palette file through the Import/Load Resource command (File menu) and then edit it as a normal image document.

We'll review each of these techniques and suggest interesting uses for them where applicable.

Replacing Existing Color Values (ASCII Palettes)

All the ASCII palette files arrange color values in discrete cells (see Figure 7–5). If you often work with the same types of images—people portraits, skyscapes, or still life scenes, for example—you may want to save frequently used color or gray values in custom cell arrangements. One way to create such custom arrangements is to edit an existing cell-based palette with one of the Paint tools and replace some of its color values. Here's how you might approach the task:

1. Open the image or images containing the color or gray values you'd like to save in a palette.
2. Load the cell-based palette you'd like to edit. PhotoStyler will assign it automatically to the active image document.
3. Set the Pick/Edit button on the scratch pad to the Edit mode.
4.  Activate the Eyedropper tool in the Select Palette. Using the technique described earlier in this chapter, assign a color value from the active image as the foreground color.
5.  Activate the Zoom tool in the Select Palette and zoom into the scratch pad so that you can "aim" accurately at a specific cell.
6.  Double-click the Bucket Fill tool icon in the Paint palette. When the Bucket Fill Options dialog box shown in Figure 7–8 appears, set Color Similarity to zero, and then select OK. This setting ensures that you'll fill only one cell at a time. (See Chapter 10 for more information about setting Bucket Fill tool options.)
7. Position the cursor in the center of the cell whose color or gray values you want to replace, and then click once. The current foreground color will replace the color value that was in the cell previously.

Edit other cell values in the same way, perhaps using multiple image documents as your sources.

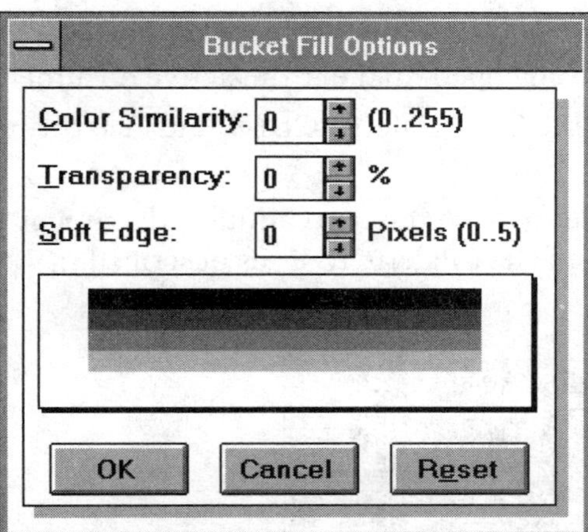

Figure 7-8.

Setting Color Similarity for the Bucket Fill tool to zero

Painting in the Scratch Pad

You can use any Paint tool except the Clone and Text tools to edit an ASCII or image-based palette file. For example, you might use the Smudge tool to smear colors in an existing palette or the Gradient Fill tool to fill a palette with smooth transitions between a limited range of colors. Figure 7–9 shows an edited Grayscale palette to which gradient fills have been applied.

To edit an existing color palette using the Paint Palette tools:

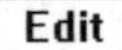

1. Toggle the Pick/Edit button in the Color Palette to Edit mode.
2. Zoom in on the part of the scratch pad you want to edit.
3. Activate one of the Paint Palette tools, adjust settings and Brush Shape as desired, and apply the tool to the scratch pad.

Pasting Images from the Clipboard into the Scratch Pad

In some cases, you might want to create palettes that contain whole or partial images. Maybe you've found a good example of common facial tones and want to save them for use with other images. Or, an image that reproduced colors well in print could come in handy if you save it as a "reference" image for use with the CMYK color space. Whatever your reasons, here's how to edit a palette by the cut-and-paste method:

1. Open the image document that contains an area you want to copy. If it's already open, make it the active document.
2. Display the Color Palette (Ctrl-8) and load the palette file you want to edit.
3. Select the part of the active image document you want to copy, using the Select Palette tools as described in Chapter 8.

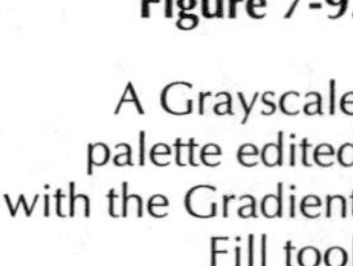

Figure 7-9.

A Grayscale palette edited with the Gradient Fill tool

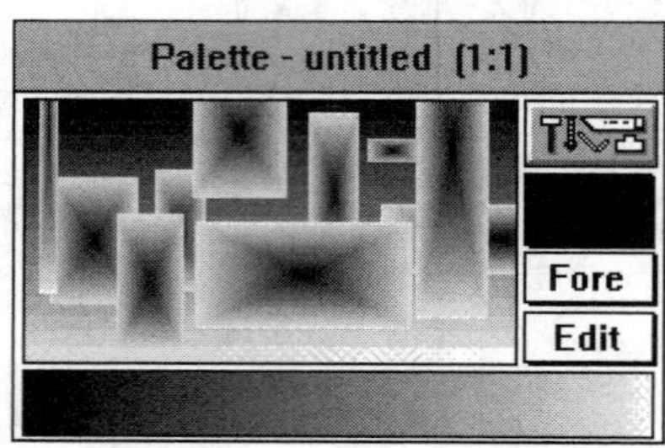

4. Use the Copy command in the Edit menu to copy the image or selection from the active document to the private PhotoStyler clipboard (see Chapter 13).

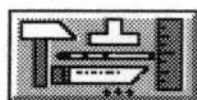

5. Choose the Paste command in the *Color Palette menu,* not the Paste command in the Edit menu of the application window. The image or selection will appear in the upper left corner of the scratch pad of the color palette. You won't be able to move the pasted image from this location.

Figure 7–10 shows a Grayscale scratch pad that was edited by pasting part of an image.

Note

If the image you paste into the Color Palette is too large, only the pixels that fit into the palette will be pasted.

Saving an Edited Palette

When you've finished editing a palette, you can save it as a new palette file or overwrite an existing palette file. Here's how:

1. Choose the Save Palette command in the Color Palette menu. The Save Palette Data to File dialog box in Figure 7–11 will appear.
2. Change to the \pstyler\palettes subdirectory if you're not there already.
3. Type the name of the new palette in the Filename text entry box. If your edited palette is an ASCII (cell-based) palette, begin the new filename with the _ character. If the new palette is an image-based one, you can omit this character.
4. Press Enter or click the Save command button to save the new palette.

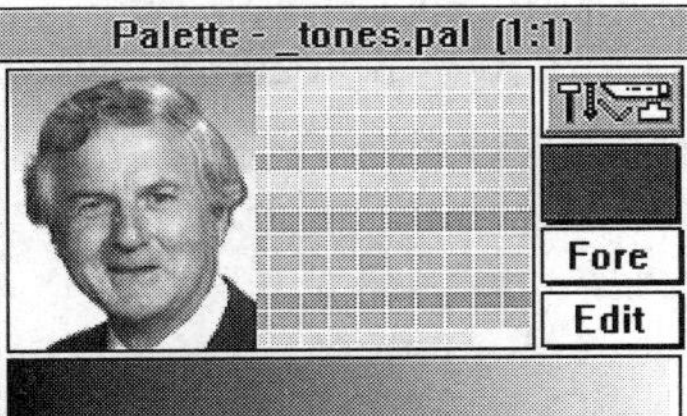

Figure 7-10.

A Grayscale palette edited by pasting portions of an image from the clipboard

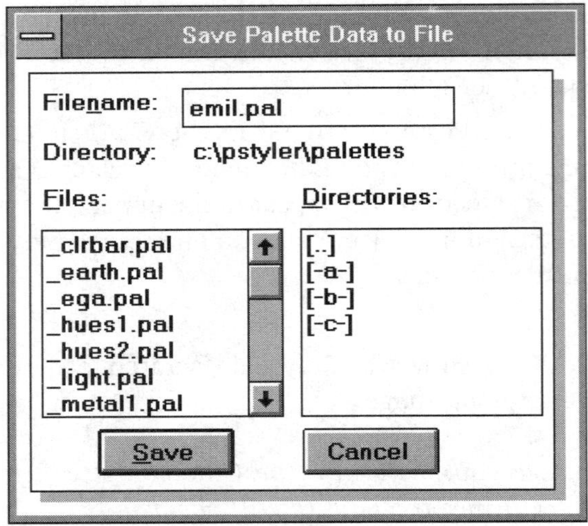

Figure 7-11.

The Save Palette Data to File dialog box

Tip

Each new True Color palette file contains a little more than 50K of memory; Grayscale palette files require less than 20K. If you're low on hard drive space, clean out unneeded palette files occasionally.

Load Resource...

Save Document...

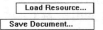

Editing and Saving a Palette File Using the Import/Load Resource and Export/Save Document Commands

If you edit an existing palette using any of the techniques just described, your options are more limited than when you edit an image document. For example, you can't select areas of the palette, use the Clone or Text tools, paste images anywhere other than the upper left corner of the scratch pad, or move pasted images around. But if you load a palette file using the Import/Load Resource command in the File menu, however, you can edit that palette as a normal image document. Every tool and command will be available to you. You can then save your edited palette using the Export/Save Document command in the File menu, described in Chapter 5. One tip: when you save the palette in the Save Document Data to File dialog box, be sure to save it in the \palettes subdirectory and give it the .pal extension rather than the default .dci file extension.

As we've seen in the foregoing sections, the Color Palette is a multipurpose tool. You can use it to select colors and gray values, to save custom collections of color values, or to specify color component values. You can edit the Color Palette as creatively as any image document. The Color dialog box, on the other hand, has one purpose only—but it fulfills that purpose better than the Color Palette can.

Specifying Color Precisely with the Color Dialog Box

The Color dialog box lets you specify foreground and background color and Grayscale values precisely using the RGB or HSB color model. Unlike the Color Palette, the Color dialog box gives you visual access to *all* the colors in the computer-generated color spectrum, even if your monitor can display only 256 colors. The Color dialog box also shows you the color you've selected in the context of colors with similar values.

Accessing the Color Dialog Box

To display the Color dialog box, use one of these techniques:

- Click one of the Current Color Indicators in the Select Palette. The indicator you choose will determine whether you are selecting a new foreground or background color.

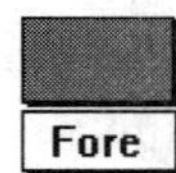

- Click the Current Color Indicator in the Color Palette.

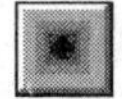

- If you've created a custom set of fill colors for the Gradient Fill tool (Chapter 10), click the color cell whose values you want to specify.

The Color dialog box (Figure 7–12 here and Figure 2–10 in the Color Section of this book) appears in the center of the PhotoStyler application window. You can move it elsewhere by dragging its title bar. To remove the Color dialog box from the screen, double-click the title bar, select the Cancel command button, or double-click the control menu box.

Color Dialog Box Controls

The controls in the Color dialog box let you specify color visually, by component values, or by comparison with similar colors. You can choose to distinguish colors by cells or to view them as a continuous spectrum.

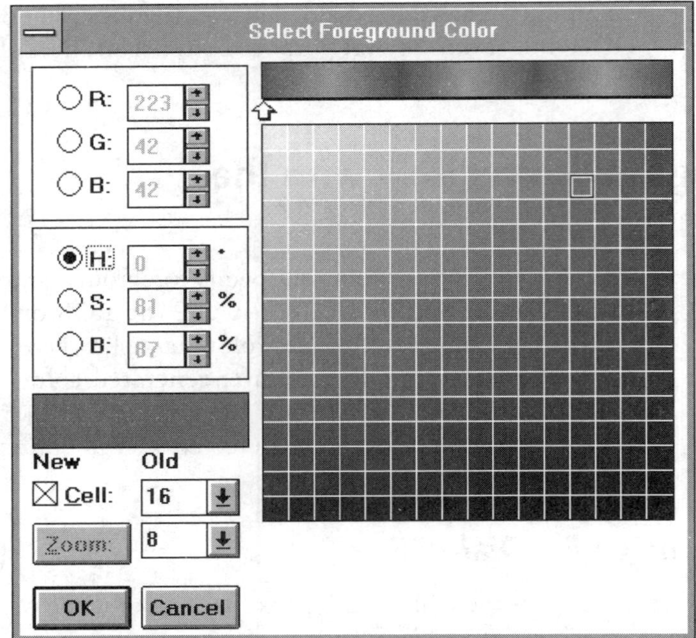

Figure 7-12. The Color dialog box

Title Bar

The title bar of the Color dialog box indicates whether you are specifying a foreground or a background color. You can also move the Color dialog box to another location on your screen by dragging its title bar.

Color Plane

The Color Plane is the visual display area of the Color dialog box, similar to the scratch pad of the Color Palette. The first time you call up the Color dialog box during a PhotoStyler session, the current foreground or background color appears in the context of neighboring colors in the Color Plane and is highlighted by a small outlined box within a grid (see Figure 7–12). This grid breaks down the continuous spectrum into discrete *color cells* so that you can distinguish and specify a single color value. You can turn the grid off by deselecting the Cell check box.

The Color Plane displays only a very small area of the color spectrum at a time: 65,536 colors out of a possible 16.7 million. The colors you see are the "next-door neighbors" to the current foreground or background color, the ones that have the same value as the active component. For example, if you specify a bright red according to the HSB color space, you can view it with colors that have the same Hue value, the same Saturation value, or the same Brightness value. The range of colors in the Color Plane changes dramatically each time you activate a different color component. But the highlighting box always remains as a placeholder for the current foreground or background color.

Color Plane Selector

The Color Plane shows only a minute portion of the color spectrum for the active color component, but the Color Plane Selector displays the full spectrum of values for that component. The position of the slider arrow beneath the Color Plane Selector indicates the part of the color spectrum that is currently visible in the Color Plane. To obtain a view of another part of the spectrum in the Color Plane, you need only drag the slider handle. The numerical color composition values for the new area of the spectrum will change as you do so.

Tip *Keep in mind that the Color Plane Selector shows the spectrum for only one color component at a time. For example, when the Hue component of the HSB color space is active, the Color Plane Selector displays all the hues of the rainbow. When the Saturation or Brightness component is active, on the other hand, the same Color Plane Selector shows a Grayscale gradient from dark to bright.*

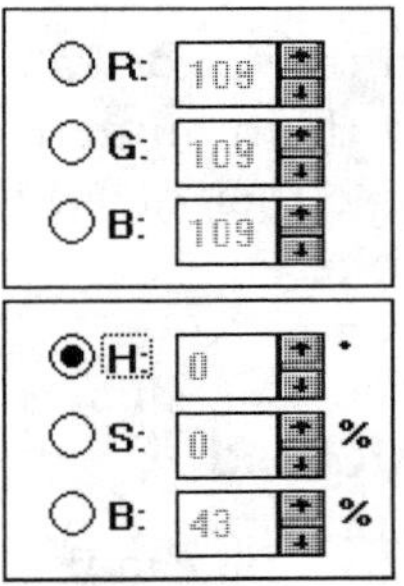

Color Component Options

The Color dialog box lets you specify color using one of two color models: RGB (Red, Green, Blue) or HSB (Hue, Saturation, Brightness). When you first call up the Color dialog box, the HSB color space is active; it's the more intuitive of the two from a visual standpoint. Only one component of the chosen color space can be active at a time. When the Cell check box is active, you must select a color with the mouse; when Cell is disabled, you can specify numeric values for the active color component.

Current Color Indicator

Both sides of this button display the current foreground or background color when you bring up the Color dialog box. If you choose a different color, that color will appear in the New section of the Current Color Indicator.

☒ Cell: 16

Cell Option, Cell Array List Box

When the Cell check box contains an x, a grid of cells overlays the Color Plane. You can zoom in or out of the Color Plane and change the number of cells by choosing a different number in the Cell Array list box. The default setting is 16, meaning that you can see 16 x 16 = 256 discrete colors in the Color Plane.

When you disable the Cell option, the grid disappears, and the Color Plane becomes a smooth spectrum of colors having the specified component value. Without a cell grid, you need to use the Zoom button to obtain a zoomed-in view of the Color Plane.

Zoom: 8

Zoom Button, Zoom Distance List Box

When the Cell option is disabled, you can use these controls to view just the immediate neighbors to the currently selected foreground or background color. The lower the Zoom distance value, the narrower the range of colors you display.

Specifying Color Values with the Color Dialog Box

The Color dialog box *is* more precision-oriented than the Color Palette. It allows you to select colors visually or specify them numerically. When you select colors visually, you can use either of two methods to zoom in on the area around the selected color.

The Color Plane Selector: The Intuitive Visual Method

To select a new foreground or background color visually, you can use the Color Plane and Color Plane Selector.

1. Bring up the Color dialog box by clicking on the foreground or background color indicator in the Select Palette or Color Palette. The Color dialog box window will appear with the title "Select Foreground Color" or "Select Background Color."

2. Click the option button for the color component you want to use when specifying a color. For example, if you want to fine-tune a color with respect to its brightness range only, click the B option button in the HSB color component section of the dialog box. The Color Plane will change, displaying all the colors that have the same brightness component value as the current foreground or background color. The Color Plane Selector will change, too, displaying the full spectrum for the color component you've selected.
3. To select a color within the visible range of the Color Plane, either click in the desired cell or drag the highlighting box to a new cell. (If you've turned the Cell option off, just click on or drag the highlighting box to the point that displays the color value you want.) The highlighting box will appear at the new location, and the New section of the Current Color Indicator will display the color you've selected.
4. If the color you want doesn't fall within the Color Plane, use the slider arrow under the Color Plane Selector to bring a different portion of the spectrum into view. Then, select a color as in the previous step.

Tip *To bring even greater precision to the selection process, turn the Cell option off and zoom in on the color you've selected. See "Refining Color Choices with the Cell and Zoom Features" in this chapter.*

5. If you want to fine-tune your color selection further, activate other color components and make your selections in the same way.
6. Click the OK command button when you're done. The new foreground or background color will appear in the Current Colors Indicator at the base of the Select Palette.

Refining Color Choices with the Cell and Zoom Features You've chosen a color value by clicking in the Color Plane. But what if one of the neighboring colors is just a little closer to the value you *really* want? You can refine your choice of colors in the Color dialog box using either of two different techniques for zooming in on the environment of a selected color. When the Cell option is turned on, you zoom in or out by varying the number of color cells in the cell array. When the Cell option is turned off, you can use the Zoom button and the Zoom distance list box to zoom in on a color's immediate environment.

To zoom in on or out of the Color Plane by varying the cell array:

1. Activate the Cell check box to turn on the cell grid. By default, PhotoStyler lets you see an array of 256 cells at a time in the Color Plane (16 horizontally x 16 vertically).
2. Click the scroll arrow on the list box next to the Cell check box. This is the cell array list box, and it lets you determine how many different color values the Color Plane can display at one time. You can choose an array of 64 (8 x 8), 256 (16 x 16), or 1024 (32 x 32) cells. As Figure 7–13 shows, it becomes more difficult to distinguish adjacent color values as the number of cells increases.
3. Click the desired array number. The appearance of the grid on the Color Plane will change accordingly.

Tip

Pressing the right or down cursor key on your keyboard increases the cell array number; pressing the left or up cursor key decreases it.

To obtain a zoomed-in view of the colors that immediately surround the currently selected color:

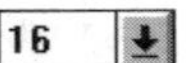

1. Deactivate the Cell check box. The cell grid overlaying the Color Plane will disappear, and the Zoom button will become active.

Zoom: 8

2. Adjust the Zoom factor, if necessary, by changing the value in the Zoom distance drop-down list box. You can set Zoom distance to 1, 2, 4, 8, or 16. A low Zoom distance number shows colors that are very similar to the selected color and is best for fine-tuning your selection.
3. To zoom in on the neighborhood of the currently selected foreground or background color, either double-click the current color highlighting box in the Color Plane or click the Zoom button once.

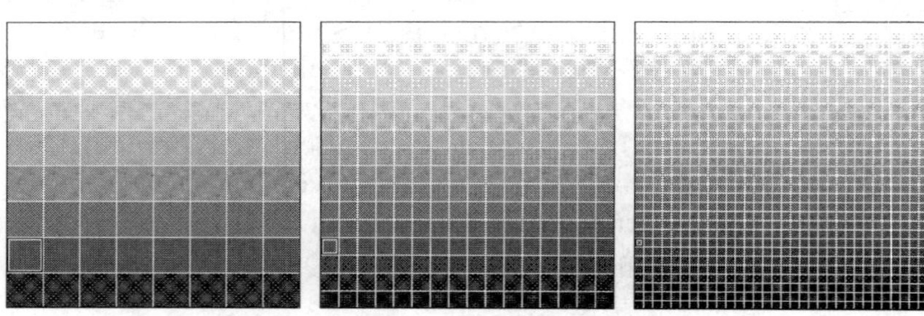

Figure 7-13.

The Color Plane with grids of 8 x 8, 16 x 16, and 32 x 32 cells

Figure 7-14.

The Pick a Color window

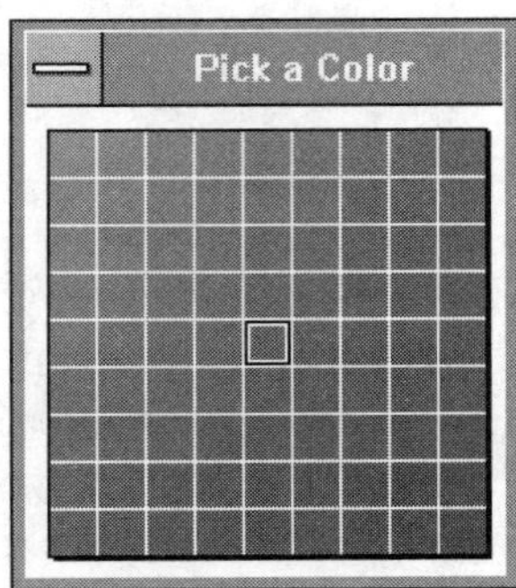

The Pick a Color window shown in Figure 7–14 will appear, with the currently selected color value marked. Depending on the Zoom distance factor you've chosen, there will be greater or lesser differences between color values in the 81 cells of this window.

4. Refine your color selection by clicking on the desired cell in the Pick a Color window. The Pick a Color window will disappear, and the current color highlighting box in the Color Plane will move to mark your new selection.

Specifying Color Values Numerically

When the Cell option is turned off, you can specify color values numerically as well as visually.

1. Access the Color dialog box. The current foreground or background color will appear in the Color Plane surrounded by a highlighting box.

2. If the Cell check box has an "x" in it, click to turn the option off. The numeric entry boxes for the color components will now become available.
3. Click the option button for the color component whose value you want to specify. To change the current value, you can type a different number in the numeric entry box or use the up or down scroll arrow next to the box. The appearances of the Color Plane and Color Plane Selector may also change, depending on the extent to which you vary the component value.
4. Specify color values for other components in the same way.
5. When you're done, click the OK command button to confirm the new foreground or background color.

Using Color and Grays Creatively in PhotoStyler

Quite frankly, there are few operations in PhotoStyler that *don't* involve the creative use of color or shades of gray. Practically every technique, from selecting image areas to fine-tuning special effects filters, builds upon a foundation of some color or grayscale building block. If you're aware of these building blocks, you can greatly enhance your creativity as you enhance your images.

Effects Based on Color Contrasts

Many of the most striking techniques in PhotoStyler are based on the effective manipulation of contrast among color and grayscale values. Among the Paint tools, for example, the Sharpen tool increases contrast in an image, while the Blur tool lessens it. The Soft Edge you can specify for many Paint tool operations lessens contrast between a selection and its background.

Color contrast forms the basis of many filters, too. The Trace Contour filter (see Figure 7-15) is one of the more dramatic examples, but the Emboss, Mosaic, and Motion Blur filters take color contrast as their foundation, too. That's to say nothing of the image correction control and special lighting effects made possible through the Tune: Brightness & Contrast and Gray/Color Correction commands.

Effects Based on Lightness or Darkness

Sophisticated image correction techniques in PhotoStyler let you enhance light or dark areas of an image without altering overall

Figure 7-15.

This striking line art was created by turning the original pelican image into a negative and then applying the Trace Contour filter

contrast, as you'll see in Chapter 9. You can use the Lighten and Darken tools in the Paint Palette to lighten or darken color or grayscale values in a selected area or throughout an image. And many Paint tools apply color or gray shades "intelligently," based on whether existing pixels are lighter or darker than the foreground color.

Effects Based on Hue, Color, Saturation, or Brightness

The HSB (Hue, Saturation, Brightness) color space is intuitive for graphics professionals because it's based on human visual perception. Not surprisingly, several PhotoStyler color correction and painting/retouching techniques build upon these color components. The Tune: Hue & Saturation command in the Image menu not only corrects scanning flaws; it can generate special color effects as well. The Fill and Merge Control commands in the Edit menu and many of the Painting tools let you apply just the hue, saturation, or brightness value of a color. You can use these techniques in countless ways—for example, to simulate a duotone in a Grayscale image that you've converted to True Color.

Effects Based on Color Models

A striking example of how color principles feed creativity in PhotoStyler is the Gradient Fill tool discussed in Chapter 10. The order of colors in a gradient fill depends on the color space you choose. Other Paint tools derive some of their effects from differences between the RGB color model, which is based on the way computer monitors transmit light, and the CMYK model, which is based on the technology of commercial printing inks. For instance, you can apply color in an additive way (brightening the color as a computer monitor does) or in a subtractive way (darkening color as with printers' inks).

Tip

Color creativity has its utilitarian side, too. You can create custom reference color palettes out of images that have printed well, and then, using the color model-switching commands in the Color Palette menu, display the color values of that image as HSB or RGB values. You'll achieve printing consistency for color publishing applications this way.

Effects Based on Color Similarity

A final (and highly sophisticated) use of color that you'll find vital to all your image editing work involves the notion of *color similarity*. Put simply, this has to do with painting and image selection techniques that intelligently measure the color or grayscale value differences between neighboring pixels in an image.

How does color similarity work? Each pixel in a Grayscale image has a single color value. Pixels in a True Color image, however, have three separate values (or four, if you specify color in CMYK). When you work with certain tools or commands, you can control exactly how much of an image to select or fill automatically, just by specifying a color similarity value. Commands and tools that use color similarity include the Bucket Fill tool in the Paint Palette, and the Magic Wand tool and the Expand command in the Select Palette. Chapters 8, 10, and 11 will cover the uses of color similarity in greater detail.

Color is one of the basic building blocks in PhotoStyler. An equally important building block is the concept of image selection, which is your gateway to creating montages, designing special effects, and performing flawless retouching. You'll learn all about the power of image selection techniques in the next chapter.

8

Selection and Masking Techniques

Half the battle of editing an image is controlling the effects of Paint tools, filters, and menu commands. In Aldus PhotoStyler, you achieve control by using tools and commands in the Select Palette to select and isolate limited areas of an image document. Seven tools let you define simple or complex selections in a variety of ways, and Select Palette menu commands augment your control with a number of creative techniques. Once you've selected part of an image, you can save the selected area as a *mask*, a separate Grayscale image document that helps you edit complex areas of images.

Follow along in this chapter and we'll show you not only how to define selections and masks, but also some of the uses to which you can put them in the real image editing world. We'll even provide an example exercise that you can try, using your own images. Flex your creative muscle!

Selection Basics

When you select an area in a PhotoStyler image document, an animated marker appears around the selected area as shown in Figure 8–1. This marker, called the *marquee*, shows you the boundaries of your selection. Any Paint tools, filters, or image processing commands that

Figure 8-1.

Marquees surround the selected areas of an image

you apply to the active image document while an area is selected will take effect within that area only.

Although an image document can contain only one selection at a time, you can add to an existing selection or make it more complex. You can also hide the selection marquee if it obstructs your view of the selected area.

When multiple image documents are open in PhotoStyler, each document can contain its own selected area. This convention makes it possible to create montages and to copy, cut, and paste between image documents. The only selection marquee that's visible, though, is the one in the active image document. Selection marquees in other image documents remain temporarily invisible until you activate those documents.

Selecting Areas with Similar Color or Gray Values

The Magic Wand is one of the most powerful tools in the Select Palette. It lets you select areas with complex shapes automatically, according to the similarity of their color or grayscale values. You can control the extent of the area you select by defining the degree of color similarity. For intricate parts of a picture such as wispy clouds or highlights in human hair, the Magic Wand eliminates the tedium (and sometimes the impossibility!) of tracing complex areas manually. Figure 8–1 shows the Magic Wand at work.

About Color Similarity

In Chapter 7, you saw how color can be thought of as a three-dimensional space, in which numbers express the location of a color within a spectrum. Comparing the color or gray values of two pixels is a matter of measuring their *color similarity*: a number that expresses the numerical distance between them as though it were a physical distance. The Magic Wand makes use of this number to determine just how many pixels to select when you click in an image document. The Color Similarity value you assign to the Magic Wand tells PhotoStyler to select only pixels whose values fall within a certain numerical range relative to the first pixel you select. As soon as PhotoStyler encounters pixels that fall outside the specified range, the selected area will stop expanding.

You can understand Color Similarity most easily if we use the Grayscale images in Figure 8–2 as an example. The image on the left shows what happened when we set Color Similarity for the Magic Wand to 64 and clicked on a pixel with a midtone value. PhotoStyler selected all neighboring pixels with gray values up to 64 values distant from (lighter or darker than) the value of this pixel. For the image on the right, we reduced Color Similarity to 23 and clicked on a light pixel on the recorder. PhotoStyler selected a much smaller area, including only the pixels with a narrower range of gray values.

Tip

For True Color images, the principle is the same, but the outcome is a little harder to predict visually because each colored pixel contains three separate color values. If any one of the three RGB values of a pixel falls outside the current Color Similarity range, that pixel won't be included in the selection area. We recommend that you magnify a True Color image document before you use the Magic Wand tool. Magnifying the image will let you see roughly how similar to one another the pixels in a given "neighborhood" seem to be. This knowledge will help you define a Color Similarity value that's appropriate for the level of contrast in that area of the image.

Selecting an Area with the Magic Wand

To select an area based on color similarity:

1. Double-click the Magic Wand tool icon in the Select Palette to bring up the Magic Wand dialog box shown in Figure 8–3.

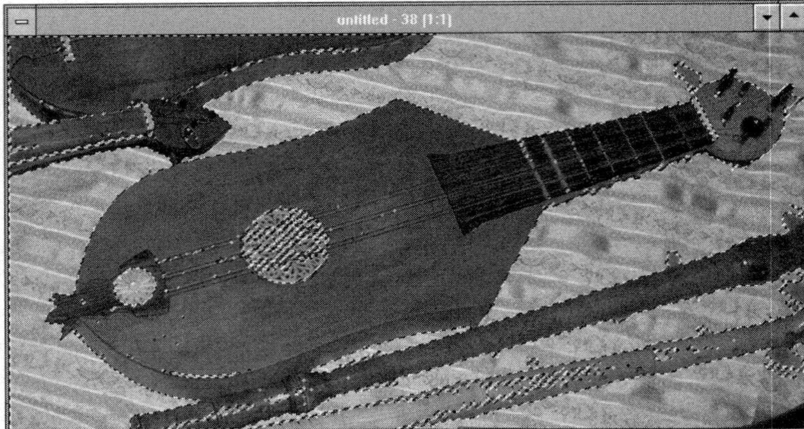

Figure 8-2.

Varying color similarity to select more (top) or less (bottom) of an image

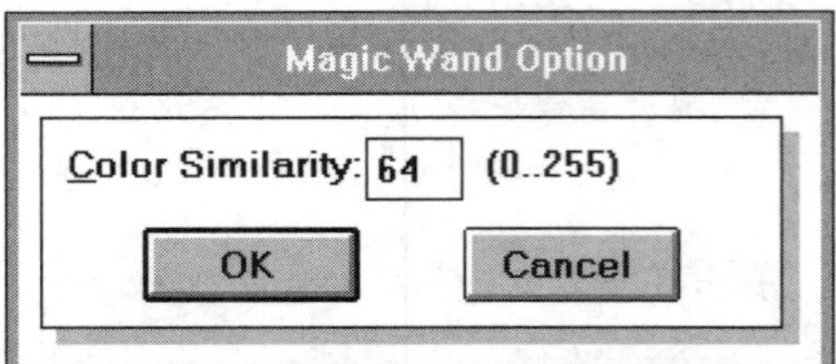

Figure 8-3.

The Magic Wand Option dialog box

2. Enter the Color Similarity value you want. The default value of 64 will let you select pixels that are fairly similar to one another. Keep in mind, though, that the level of contrast is always unique to a particular image or area of an image. You should adjust the setting to match the active image document.
3. Click OK to return to the active image document.

(325, 86) r=223, g=197, b=182

4. Move the mouse cursor to the area of the active image document that you want to select. Observe the status bar—it will show you the color or gray value of each pixel over which you move the mouse. Click to select the starting point pixel. After a moment, the selection marquee will appear around the area that you've defined.
5. If you don't like the results, press the right mouse button to cancel the selection and then try again. You might try changing the Color Similarity setting, clicking on a different pixel, or zooming in on the image. Remember, as soon as PhotoStyler encounters even one pixel that doesn't fall within the color similarity range you specify, the selection will stop expanding. So click carefully!

Tip

If you're viewing the active image at a 1:1 magnification, chances are you can't see just how many contrasting pixels are in the immediate area of the pixel you clicked. If the Magic Wand selects an area that's too small, zoom in on the desired area and click on a pixel that has fewer contrasts in its immediate neighborhood.

In some images that contain high color contrasts, you may have difficulty selecting the desired area with a single click. Later on in this chapter, you'll see how you can overcome this problem by adding to an existing selection.

Tracing an Irregular Selection Area

What if the area you want to select is both irregular in shape and high in color contrast? The Magic Wand won't do the job for you—try the Lasso tool instead.

The Lasso tool in the Select Palette lets you trace the border of a selection area using straight-line segments, curve segments, or a combination of both. To trace a selection area as a series of straight-line segments, you click the mouse button at each endpoint. To trace a curved segment, you press and hold the mouse button and *drag* the mouse instead of clicking. Unless you have an exceptionally steady hand, you'll probably be able to trace more precisely using the straight-line segment method and clicking at frequent intervals to maintain the smoothness of curves.

To trace an irregularly-shaped area:

1. Click the Lasso tool icon.

(181, 64)-(340, 256)

2. Position the cursor over the point in the active document window where the selection area should begin. Drag the mouse to trace an area freehand, or click to outline the area in straight-line segments. You can alternate between the two modes if you wish. The status bar will show the x and y coordinates of each pixel over which you pass. If the image extends beyond the edge of the document window and your mouse moves to the edge of the visible area, PhotoStyler will adjust the viewing area automatically so you can continue to trace.
3. When you're ready to close the selection area, double-click. A marquee will appear around the area.

You must fully enclose the selection area when using the Lasso tool. If you don't, PhotoStyler will close the area automatically with a straight-line segment running from the last point to the first point you traced.

Areas with extremely irregular shapes may require some time to trace accurately. If you have to trace the same area again later for further editing, chances are you won't be able to duplicate the area exactly. As you'll see further on in the chapter, PhotoStyler lets you save such complex selections as *mask documents* that you can retrieve later.

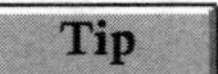

Another use for the Lasso tool is to deselect any current selection area. Double-click the Lasso tool icon in the Select Palette to deselect an area.

Selecting Geometrically Shaped Areas

Five of the tools in the Select Palette—the Rectangle, Square, Ellipse, Circle, and Linear tools—let you select geometrically shaped areas of an image. You can define a selected area freehand or (except for the Linear tool) by specifying an exact size.

While it's true that photographs and illustrations rarely contain regular shapes, you can use the geometrical selection tools in combination or with other selection tools to define more complex shapes. The "Adapting the Selection Area" portion of this chapter will demonstrate selection techniques for this purpose.

Selecting a Rectangular or Square Area

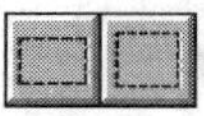

Rectangular and square selection areas are useful for defining and saving a pattern that you can use to fill other selection areas (see Chapter 10). You can also use them in conjunction with other selection tools to define a complex shape. Both tools let you define a selection freehand or by specifying the exact size of a selection area in a dialog box.

Defining a Selection Area Freehand

To define a rectangular or square selection by the freehand method:

1. Click the Rectangle or Square tool in the Select Palette, and then move the mouse cursor into the active document window.

(181, 64)-(340, 256)

2. If you're drawing the selection from a corner, click where you want to position the corner and then drag to define the selection area. If the Draw Selection from Center option in the Preferences dialog box is active, click at the desired center point and then drag outward. The status bar will display the current cursor coordinates as you drag.

Tip

If placing a selection area precisely is important to you, we suggest activating the Draw Selection from Center option in the Preferences dialog box (Preferences command, File menu).

3. Release the mouse button when the area is the desired size. If you've made an error, cancel the selection by pressing the right mouse button, and then try again.

Specifying the Size of the Selection Area

To define the exact size of a rectangular or square selection area in pixels:

1. Double-click the Rectangle or Square tool icon in the Select Palette. Depending on your choice of tools, one of the dialog boxes in Figure 8–4 will appear.

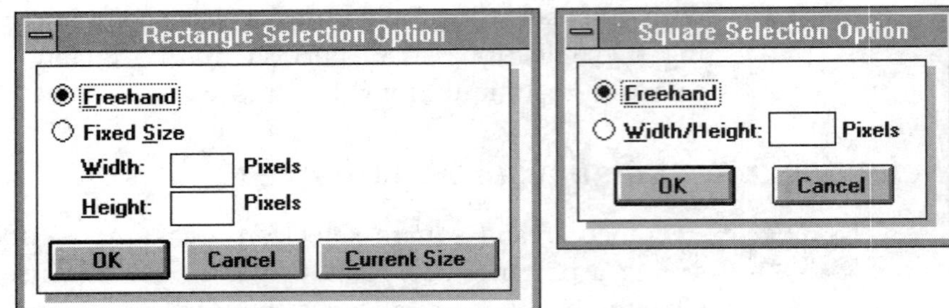

Figure 8-4. The Rectangle Selection Option and Square Selection Option dialog boxes

2. Click the Fixed Size option button and then type the dimensions of the selection area in pixels. If you're defining a rectangular area, you can specify a width that is different from the height.
3. Press Enter or click the OK command button to return to the application window.
4. If another selection is already in the active document window, deselect it by moving the cursor into the document window and clicking the right mouse button. Otherwise, you won't be able to select a new area unless the new area you select is completely outside the previous one.
5. If you're drawing the selection from a corner, click where you want to position the upper left corner. If the Draw Selection from Center option in the Preferences dialog box is active, click at the desired center point. PhotoStyler will draw the selection area automatically at the size you specified.

Note *If the visible area of the active image document is smaller than the size of the rectangle you specify, PhotoStyler will crop the selection area so that it fits into the document window.*

Tip *To define a pattern based on an area that you've already edited, use the Current Size option button in the Rectangle Selection Option dialog box. This option, available only when the active image document already contains a selected area, lets you define a rectangular selection of the same width and height as the current selection. It doesn't matter what tool you used to create the current selection. If it's irregular in shape, PhotoStyler will calculate the new rectangular selection so that it extends to the same width and height as the current selection.*

Selecting an Elliptical or Circular Area

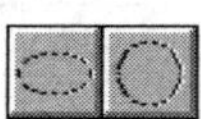

The Ellipse and Circle tools, like the Rectangle and Square tools, let you define a selection by dragging or by specifying the exact size of a selection area in a dialog box. You can combine these tools with other Select Palette tools to define an irregularly shaped selection area.

Defining a Selection Area Freehand

To define an elliptical or circular selection by the freehand method:

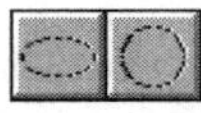

1. Click on the Ellipse or Circle tool in the Select Palette, and then move the mouse cursor into the active document window.

(181, 64)-(340, 256)

2. If you're drawing the selection from the rim inward, click where you want to position the rim and then drag to define the selection area. If the Draw Selection from Center option in the Preferences dialog box is active, click at the desired center point and then drag outward. The status bar will display the current pixel coordinates as you drag.

Tip

If placing a selection area precisely is important to you, we suggest activating the Draw Selection from Center option in the Preferences dialog box.

3. Release the mouse button when the area is the desired size. If you've made an error, cancel the selection by pressing the right mouse button, and then try again.

Specifying the Size of the Selection Area

To define the exact size of an elliptical or circular selection area in pixels:

1. Double-click the Ellipse or Circle tool icon in the Select Palette. Depending on your choice of tools, one of the dialog boxes in Figure 8–5 will appear.
2. Click the Fixed Size option button and then type the dimensions of the selection area in pixels.

Note

PhotoStyler uses an imaginary bounding box to calculate the size of an elliptical selection area. When you specify the dimensions of

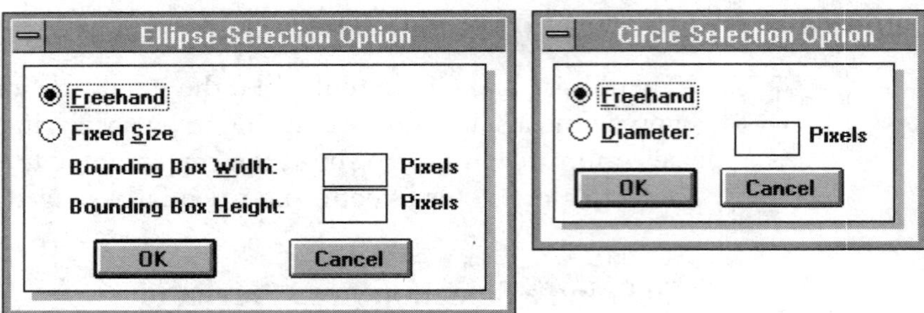

Figure 8-5. The Ellipse Selection Option and Circle Selection Option dialog boxes

an ellipse, you're actually defining the width and height of an imaginary rectangle.

3. Press Enter or click the OK command button to return to the application window.
4. If another selection is already in the active document window, deselect it by moving the cursor into the document window and clicking the right mouse button.
5. If you're drawing the selection from the rim inward, click where you want to position the upper left area of the rim. If the Draw Selection from Center option in the Preferences dialog box is active, click at the desired center point. PhotoStyler will draw the selection area automatically at the size you specified.
6. To move the selection area, drag it to the desired position without first changing to a different tool.

Selecting a Single Line of Pixels

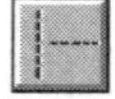

There may be times when you want to fill, delete, or otherwise edit a single line of pixels at the edge of an image document or elsewhere. The Linear tool in the Select Palette will let you select a line of pixels for editing. If the Draw Selection from Center option in the Preferences dialog is active, the line you draw will extend from the center point outward. Otherwise, you'll extend the line from one endpoint to the other.

Tip *Double-clicking the Linear tool icon deselects any current selection area in the active document window.*

The Selection Status Indicator

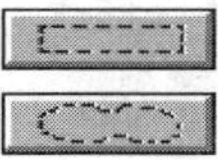

Just above the Current Colors Indicator in the Select Palette is a narrow bar, the Selection Status indicator. If the active image document contains no selection, the Selection Status indicator is blank. If a rectangular or square selection area is active, the indicator displays a rectangular dotted outline. For any other type of selection, the indicator displays an irregular dotted outline.

(181, 64)-(340, 256)

To see the pixel coordinates of a selection area, move the cursor over the Selection Status Indicator and then press and hold the mouse button. The pixel coordinates of the selection area's bounding box will appear in the message area of the status bar. If the current selection is rectangular or square, the status bar will also display the width and height of the selected area in pixels.

Moving a Selection or Just the Marquee

The animated marquee that surrounds a selected area may seem hollow, but it actually contains part of the underlying image. You can move the marquee with or without its contents, depending on the effect you want to achieve. Using the selection tools will move the marquee with its contents; using the Move tool will move the marquee alone.

Tip

The ifs, ands, or buts of moving marquees and selection areas in PhotoStyler can be pretty confusing. The tool you use to move selections is important. So is your timing: you'll obtain one result if you move a selection before you edit it and another if you move it afterward. Our best advice is—memorize the next few pages!

Moving the Marquee with its Contents

Before you move a selected area, always check the Edit menu and make sure that the Preserve Image command has a check mark in front of it. If it does, you can use any of the seven selection tools to move the marquee and its contents together. PhotoStyler will leave the "original" pixels in place and automatically create a copy of the pixels in the selected area. You can then edit or discard this copy, known as a *floating selection*, without displacing any pixels in the underlying image.

To move a marquee with its contents:

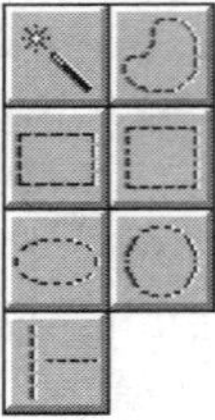

1. Activate any of the seven selection tools (Magic Wand, Lasso, Rectangle, Square, Ellipse, Circle, Linear), and move the cursor into the active image document.
2. Position the cursor somewhere inside the current selection marquee. A four-headed arrow will appear.
3. Press and hold the mouse button and drag the current selection to the new location. When you release the mouse button, a copy of the selection area will have moved to the new location, but the original area will remain whole. You can see an example of this principle at work in Figure 8–6, which uses the flower image from Figure 8–1.

You can edit a floating selection independently of the underlying image using any combination of tools and commands. See the "Editing Floating Selections" portion of this chapter for more about techniques of working with floating selections.

Moving the Marquee without its Contents

It's possible to move the selection marquee alone, as though it were a hollow outline containing no pixels. This technique has many potential applications. For example, you could use the Magic Wand or Lasso to outline a complex shape, move the marquee to another part of the

Figure 8-6.

Moving a selection marquee with its contents

Figure 8-7.

A custom pattern fill applied to a selection marquee that has been moved

image as though it were a stencil, and then paint in it or fill it. The image in Figure 8–7 illustrates a custom pattern fill applied to the selection area that we moved. Chapter 10 will explore this advanced feature.

To move a selection marquee without its contents:

1. Activate the Move tool in the Select Palette by clicking on its icon once.
2. Move the mouse cursor into the active image document and position it somewhere within the selection marquee. A four-headed arrow will appear.
3. Drag the selection borders to a new location. When you release the mouse button, the contents of the previous selection area will remain unchanged, but its borders will have moved.

Caution

Be careful about using the Move tool on a selection area that's already floating. Moving the marquee under these circumstances will deselect the floating pixels and cause them to replace the pixels in the underlying image. This may produce an unintended effect. Check the Edit menu before you use the Move tool on a selection area. If the Make Floating command isn't available, the selection is already floating.

Editing Floating Selections

A floating selection area behaves as though it were a separate layer of pixels above the underlying image. You can paint in it, color-correct it, transform it, or apply filters to it without disfiguring the "original" pixels underneath. You'll find floating selections useful in many situations. For example:

- "Testing" editing operations before committing changes to the underlying image
- Duplicating limited areas of an image for design effects
- Merging selections with other areas of an image to generate special color and grayscale effects (see Chapter 13)

We'll survey the basics of working with floating selections in this chapter. For a more in-depth treatment of how to use floating selections in montaging, see Chapter 13.

Making a Selection Float

As soon as you define a new selection area, it's a good idea to make it float as an "insurance policy" against inadvertent editing. If you edit a selection that's not floating, any changes you make will overwrite existing pixels in the image.

Here are all the techniques you can use to make a selected area float:

- Choose the Make Floating command from the Edit menu. This command is available only if the selected area isn't floating already.
- Move a new selection when the Rectangle, Square, Ellipse, Circle, Linear, Magic Wand, or Lasso tool is active.
- Paste the contents of the clipboard into the active Grayscale or True Color image document (see Chapter 13).
- Choose any command (except the Shift and Resample commands) from the Transform menu (see Chapter 13).

What happens to the underlying image when you float a selection depends on the status of the Preserve Image command in the Edit menu.

Preserving the Underlying Image

Normally, the Preserve Image command in the Edit menu has a check mark in front of it. When active, this command permits you to float a selected area without displacing pixels in the underlying image. However, if you deactivate Preserve Image and then move a floating selection, PhotoStyler will replace the "background" pixels with the current background color.

Discarding a Floating Selection

One of the advantages of floating a selected area is that you can easily get rid of both the selection and your edits to it. Just invoke the Discard Floating command in the Edit menu. The pixels in the underlying image will remain unaffected.

Merging a Floating Selection with the Underlying Image

If you decide to integrate a floating selection into the underlying image, two options are open to you. The first option is to deselect the floating selection by pressing the right mouse button, clicking the N button in the Select Palette, or pressing Ctrl-N. This method causes the pixels in the floating selection to replace the pixels "underneath" them.

The second option is to use the Merge Control command in the Edit menu. This option offers you much greater control over how the floating selection affects the underlying image. For example, you can generate special color effects, isolate image channels, and exclude a range of color or Grayscale values. Chapter 13 gives you a deeper understanding of how to use the Merge Control command.

Adapting the Selection Area

What if your first selection doesn't capture the exact area you want, no matter which tool you're using? Not to worry—PhotoStyler provides numerous options for selecting additional areas using any combination of selection tools. You can also subtract from an existing selection, invert selected and unselected areas, and deselect areas.

Adding to the Current Selection

PhotoStyler lets you enlarge an existing selection in one of two ways. The first way is to use the Shift key in combination with one or more selection tools. The second way is to expand the existing selection automatically according to color similarity values that you define.

Making Multiple Selections with the Shift Key

By pressing and holding the Shift key, you can continue to add areas to an existing selection using any combination of selection tools. Most likely, you'll use this technique when you want to refine an existing selection area or create an abstract design. To add to the current selection using the Shift key and one or more selection tools:

Figure 8-8.

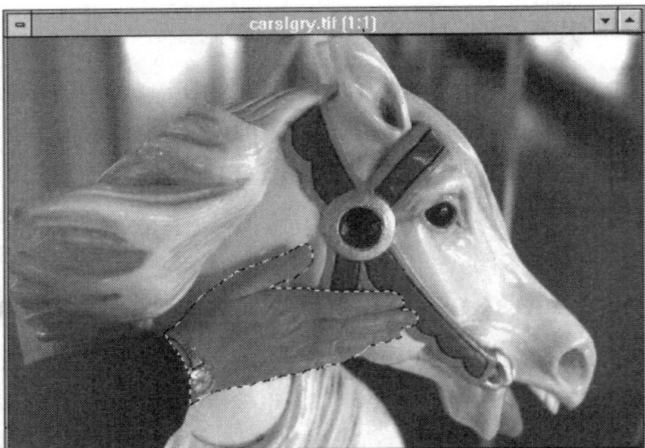

Top: Image containing an initial selection area. The hand was traced with the Lasso tool

Center: Non-overlapping selection areas, separate marquees: Harness medallion added to the initial selection area with the help of the Circle selection tool

Bottom: Overlapping selection areas, single combined marquee: Harness added to previous selection areas using the Magic Wand

1. Activate a selection tool and make an initial selection (see Figure 8–8, top).
2. Activate another selection tool. It can be the same or different from the one you used to make the initial selection.
3. Press and hold the Shift key. A plus sign (+) will appear inside the mouse cursor.

4. Use the selection tool normally. If the new selection area *doesn't* overlap the existing one, PhotoStyler will display the added selection as a separate marquee (see Figure 8–8, center). If the new selection area overlaps the existing one, PhotoStyler will combine them and display a single marquee (Figure 8–8, bottom).
5. Continue selecting additional areas with the tools of your choice until you've achieved the shape you want.

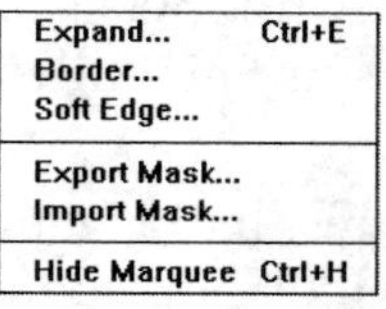

Expanding a Selection According to Color Similarity

The Select Palette contains a pop-up menu with several commands that enhance your selection options. The Expand command (keyboard shortcut: Ctrl-E) is useful when part of the area you want to select is similar in color to an existing selection area but separate from it. You control the degree of color similarity and the location of the pixels that PhotoStyler selects.

To add to an existing selection according to color similarity:

1. With an area already selected, choose the Expand command from the Select Palette menu. The Select Expand dialog box in Figure 8–9 will appear.
2. Enter a Color Similarity value between zero and 255 in the appropriate text entry box. Let two factors guide you:
   - the range of colors or grays in the current selection area and
   - the degree to which you want to expand the selection

   In most cases, you'll enter a very low value if the range of colors or grays in the current selection area is broad, and a higher value if the range is narrow.

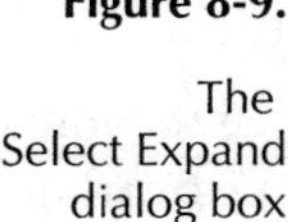

Figure 8-9. The Select Expand dialog box

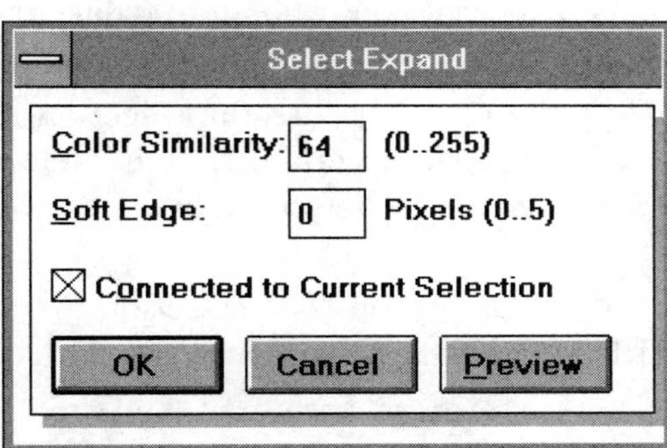

3. If you want to extend the selected area only to pixels that are "neighbors" to the current selection, make sure an "x" appears in the Connected to Current Selection check box. If you prefer to select colors or grays in the specified range throughout the image document, deactivate this check box.
4. Adjust the Soft Edge value, if desired. This setting lets you feather the edges of the selection so that any painting or editing you do will blend in seamlessly with the pixels outside the selection area. You may specify a value from zero (no feathering) to five (five pixels of feathering). See "Using a Soft Edge to Blend Selections Smoothly" later in this chapter.
5. Click the Preview command button to see the results of your settings without exiting the dialog box. If you don't like the results, change the settings and preview the new results.
6. When the settings produce an acceptable preview, click OK to exit the dialog box. The current selection area will expand according to your settings.

Subtracting from the Current Selection

PhotoStyler lets you subtract from the current selection area using the Ctrl key and any combination of selection tools. Use this technique to clean up untidy selection areas or to prepare special effects such as transparent clipping holes.

To subtract one or more areas from the current selection:

1. Activate the selection tool that you want to use and then move the cursor into the active image document. You can use the Magic Wand and Lasso as well as the geometrical selection tools.
2. Press and hold the Ctrl key. A minus sign (-) will appear inside the cursor to indicate that you're about to reduce the current selection area.
3. Still holding the Ctrl key, use the selection tool as if you were making an additional selection. If your "selection" overlaps the existing selection area, PhotoStyler will deselect only the overlapping part.
4. Release the mouse button. The selection marquee will disappear temporarily and then reappear with the deselected area excluded.
5. Deselect additional areas if required. You can use any combination of selection tools.

Selecting an Entire Image Document

Clicking the "A" button near the base of the Select Palette selects the entire active image document ("A" stands for "All"). If you want to apply most Transform menu commands to the full image document, or if you want to cut or copy the entire document to the clipboard, you'll first need to select the entire image this way. Pressing Ctrl-A achieves the same effect.

Deselecting All Current Selection Areas

There's more than one way to deselect everything in the active image document. The simplest way is to click on the "N" button at the base of the Select Palette ("N" stands for "None"), or to use the keyboard shortcut, Ctrl-N. If it's more convenient, you can choose instead to double-click the Move, Lasso, or Linear tool icon in the Select Palette.

Inverting Selected and Unselected Areas

Sometimes the hardest area of an image to select is the one you want to edit. For example, you might want to tint everything *except* the gray sky in a landscape or cityscape containing many complex objects. Your best bet in such cases is to select the "easy" areas using the Magic Wand or some combination of tools, and then to invert (switch) selected and unselected areas by clicking the "I" button at the base of the Select Palette ("I" stands for "Invert"). The keyboard shortcut for inverting selected and unselected areas is Ctrl-I.

Deleting a Selected Area

To delete an area that you've just selected, press the Delete key or choose the Clear command in the Edit menu. PhotoStyler will replace the deleted pixels with the current background color. The selection marquee will remain, however, until you deselect the area or make a new selection.

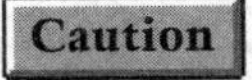

If you delete a floating selection, the deleted area continues to remain separate from the underlying image until you deselect it.

Special Selection Techniques

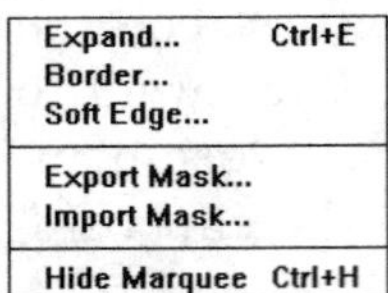

PhotoStyler's Select Palette menu and Edit menu contain commands that enhance your use of the selection tools. These commands let you:

- hide the selection marquee for an unobstructed view of the area you're editing
- create a variable-width border to outline the current selection area
- define a "soft edge" to feather the edges of a selection for smoother blending
- "float" a selection so that you can edit it without affecting the underlying image

We'll explore potential uses of these commands in this section.

Hiding the Selection Marquee

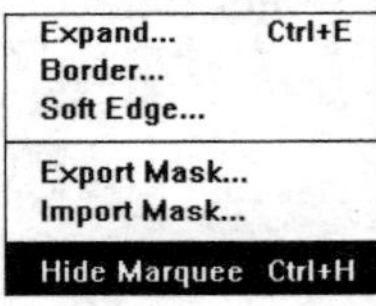

At times, the animated marquee around a selection area can obstruct your view of the image. The marquee can be especially annoying when you're painting in a selection area that's complex or narrow, or when you've assigned a Soft Edge to a selection and need a clearer view of its borders.

To make the editing process more convenient in these cases, you can hide the selection marquee using either the Hide Marquee command in the Select Palette menu or the keyboard shortcut, Ctrl-H. Paint tools and menu commands will still apply to the selected area only, even though the selection border won't be visible. To restore your view of the marquee, press Ctrl-H again, or choose the Show Marquee command in the Select Palette menu.

Creating a Border

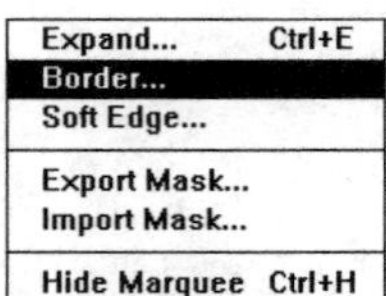

Using the Border command in the Select Palette menu, you can create (and immediately select) a variable-width border for any current selection area. Use this technique as the first step in creating outlines for geometric or complex shapes, generating "ghost" figures, or designing other special effects.

To create and select a border for the current selection area:

1. Select the desired area using any of the techniques described earlier in this chapter.
2. Choose the Border command in the Select Palette menu. The Select Border dialog box shown in Figure 8–10 will appear, with a default Border Width of one pixel.

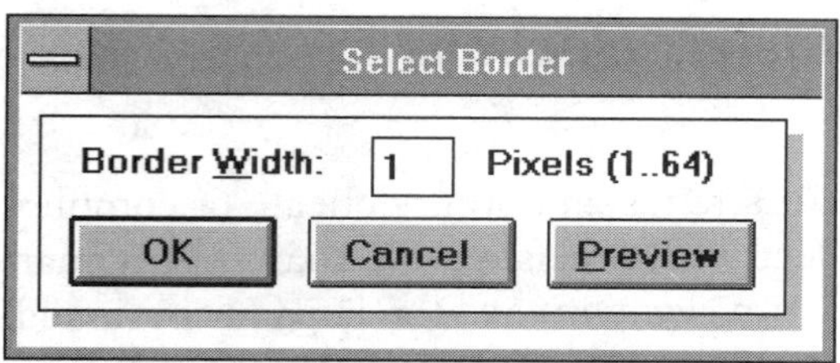

Figure 8-10.

The Select border dialog box

3. Specify the width of the border in the Border Width text entry box. A border can be anywhere from one to 64 pixels wide. Half of the border will fall inside and half outside the current selection area, so choose your width accordingly.
4. Click the Preview command button if you'd like to see in advance how your border will look. If you don't like the results, change the Border Width and preview it again.
5. Click the OK command button to create and select the border. PhotoStyler will deselect the previous selection area.

Figure 8–11 shows a selection border to which we then applied PhotoStyler's Trace Contour filter for an interesting outline effect.

If you select a border area and then assign a Soft Edge to it, you'll be able to create special effects such as luminous "auras" around figures. That's exactly what you'll do after the next section, which introduces you to the wonders of the Soft Edge.

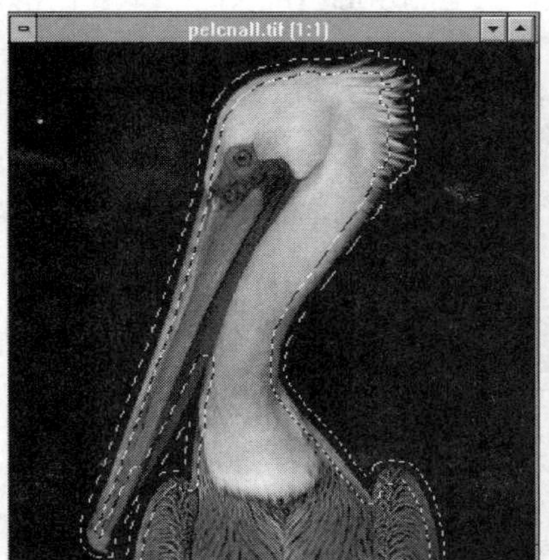

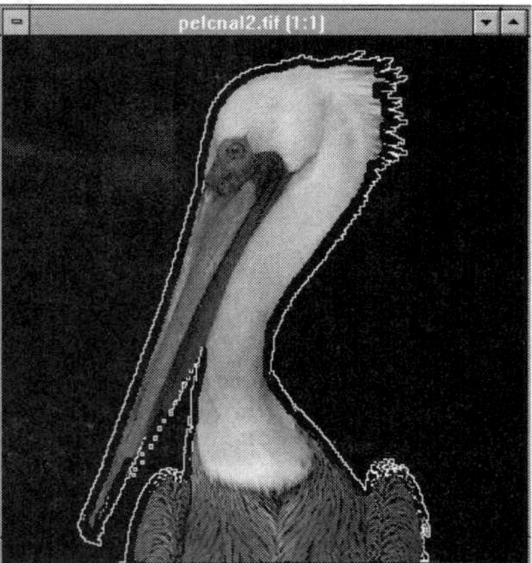

Figure 8-11.

A selection border (l) and an outline created from the border using the Trace Contour filter (r)

Using a Soft Edge to Blend Selections Smoothly

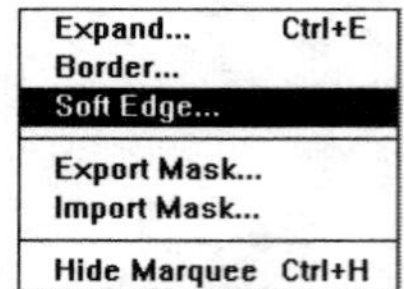

Human hair strands and other delicate or complex areas can be difficult to select with precision. No matter how many tools you use or how many times you invoke the Expand command, it seems there are always some tiny areas left over. Yet, photographic retouching requires that edited areas blend in smoothly with the rest of the image, even if they've been cut and pasted several times.

To help you select and edit complex areas while avoiding sharp, unnatural-looking color transitions, PhotoStyler has provided the Soft Edge command in the Select Palette menu. Use it to "feather" the edges of a selection area so that they blend smoothly into adjoining areas of the image. Soft edges aid in realistic retouching and can help you create an impressionistic effect in fine art images.

To define a soft edge for a selection:

1. Make the selection in the active image document.
2. Choose the Soft Edge command from the Select Palette menu. The Select Soft Edge dialog box in Figure 8–12 will appear.
3. Specify the width of the soft edge in pixels. You can enter a value between one and five. A wider soft edge will result in more feathering. If you require a wider soft edge than five pixels, you can apply the Soft Edge command again as many times as you want; the effect is cumulative.
4. Click the OK command button to create the soft edge.

When the selection marquee reappears, you may not see a visible adjustment of the selection edges unless you're in a magnified view. You'll really see the difference, though, when you begin copying and pasting the selected area, painting in it, or applying filters to it.

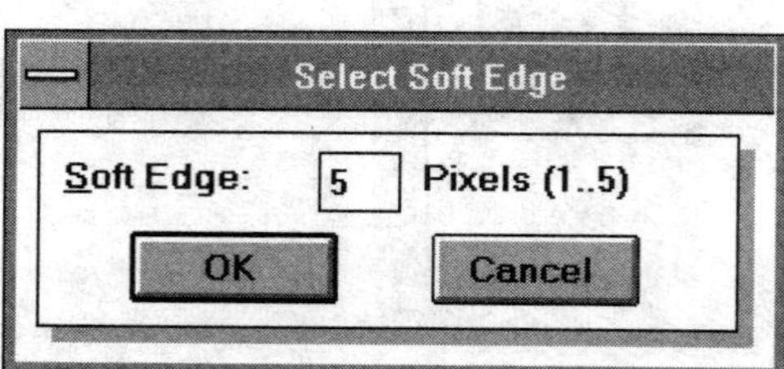

Figure 8-12.

The Select Soft Edge dialog box

The soft edge theme recurs in several places in PhotoStyler. For example, the Line, Bucket Fill, and Clone tools in the Paint Palette let you apply paint with a feathering effect, whether or not you've assigned a soft edge to a current selection. However, you achieve the most dramatic feathering using the Soft Edge command in the Select Palette menu.

Caution *If you apply a soft edge to a floating selection area, the floating image will become deselected and will merge with the background image.*

The next section gives you a chance to practice all the selection techniques we've discussed in this chapter, using your own photographic images. You'll make complex selections, define borders, and assign a soft edge to a selection in order to create a halo around a person's head.

Tip *To select delicate areas of an image so they'll blend smoothly into the background after editing, use the Magic Wand tool in conjunction with the Soft Edge command.*

Creating a Halo, Part 1

Almost everyone has a photographic portrait handy. How would you like to place a soft, saintly halo around your wife, husband, child, lover, pet, or (dare we suggest) boss? You can do so in just a few steps, using the selection techniques covered so far in this chapter.

1. Open a True Color or Grayscale image file that contains a close-up of a person. If you don't have such an image available, scan one in and save it using the Save As command in the File menu.

2. If necessary, magnify the image so that the subject's head fills most of the document window. If your image file is large, you may need to work in Full Screen Mode.

3. Activate the Lasso tool in the Select Palette and carefully trace the outline of the subject's head as in Figure 8–13. Begin at the chin and take your time to obtain the most accurate trace possible; try clicking once every few pixels to trace curves smoothly. The further in you zoom, the more likely you are to trace the outline without jaggies.

Figure 8-13.

Head shot for creating a "halo"

4. When you've traced the entire head and come back to where you started, double-click to close and complete the selection area. The animated marquee will appear.
5. Your selection outline may not follow the contours of the head exactly. If you need to tidy up the selection area, use the Lasso tool with the Ctrl key to subtract areas or with the Shift key to add areas.

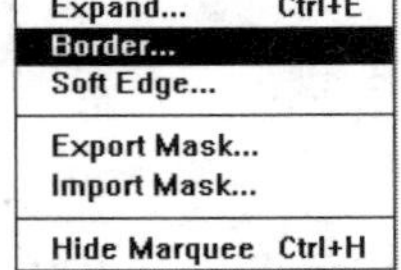

6. Click the Select Palette menu icon and choose the Border command. Enter a border width of 12 pixels in the Select Border dialog box, and then click OK. A border area surrounding the subject's head will replace the previous selection in your image document.
7. Choose the Soft Edge command in the Select Palette menu and set a Soft Edge of 5 pixels. Click OK to create the soft edge. You may or may not see a difference in the selection outlines.
8. Activate the Lasso tool and, using the Ctrl key, *subtract* the part of the border that surrounds the face rather than the hair.
9. Press Ctrl-8 to display the Color Palette. Set the Fore/Back button to Fore mode and the Pick/Edit button to Pick mode, if necessary.
10. If you're working with a Grayscale image, select a very light gray as the current foreground color. If you're working with a True Color image, select a soft, pale yellow.

11. Double-click the Bucket Fill tool icon in the Paint Palette. Set Color Similarity to 255 and then click OK. This, the broadest possible Color Similarity setting, will ensure that you fill every pixel of the selected area.
12. Hide the selection marquee by pressing Ctrl-H. This will give you a clearer view of the edges of the selection area as you paint.

13. Click anywhere within the border selection area. After a moment, the current foreground color fills the entire border area. The paint should fade out softly at the edges, as in Figure 8–14. Your subject has become an instant saint!
14. Redisplay the selection marquee by pressing Ctrl-H again. You won't want to lose track of future selections!

15. If you'd like to save the image with its new halo, click the N button in the Select Palette to deselect the border area, and then choose the Save As command from the File menu. Leave the original image unaltered; you might choose to use it again at the end of this chapter.

As you gain experience with PhotoStyler, you'll come to realize that many different paths can lead to the same image processing goal. Take the halo you've just created, for example. Near the end of the chapter, you'll create an even more refined halo using a different set of image selection and masking techniques.

Defining and Working with Masks

The use of masks may well be one of the hardest skills to master in PhotoStyler. It's also one of the most exciting, flexible, and creatively stimulating editing techniques you'll ever encounter. We hope to prod your imagination as well as satisfy your curiosity in the remaining pages of this chapter.

Figure 8-14.

Final head shot with halo added

Figure 8-15.

Above: Image containing a selection area

Below: Selection area exported as a mask document

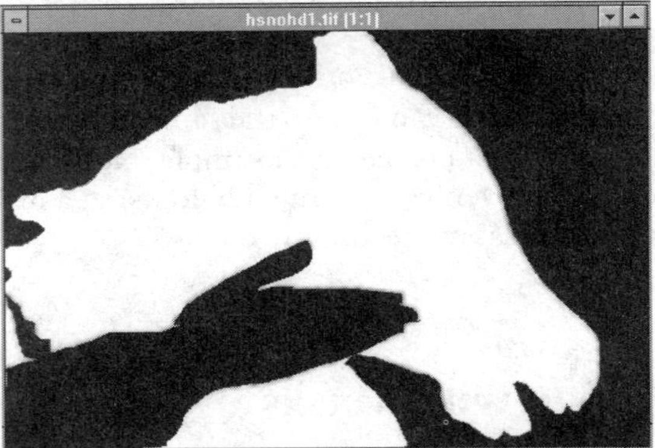

What's a Mask?

Imagine this: you've spent half an hour making a complex selection with several different selection tools, or painstakingly tracing the outlines of a model's windblown hair. Just when you start to edit the selection area, your alarm goes off. Horrors—you have to shut down your computer and rush off to a meeting or appointment. How can you save that marvelous selection area that you'll certainly never be able to duplicate again?

The answer: save the selection area as a Grayscale mask file (Figure 8–15) that you can drop into the original image document at any time to reselect the same area. Although masks are separate Grayscale image documents in their own right, you should always think of them as tools that help you edit other image documents.

Think of a mask as a sophisticated template, a convenient stencil that lets you refine selection areas and edit the same selection area repeatedly. White areas of the mask define the selection areas you've isolated in the original image document; these are the areas you can paint in when you re-import the mask later. Black areas, on the other hand, indicate all the protected, unselected areas in the original image document. Paint won't penetrate to these areas when you re-import the mask. If you've applied a soft edge to the selection area, that soft edge will show up in the mask as grayscale feathering. When you import a mask to its original image document, paint will apply to grayscale areas semitransparently. At its most basic, then, a mask is the perfect time saver, an automatic selection tool.

But a mask is even more powerful as a creative tool than as a convenience. Once you've created a mask, you can modify it just as you would any Grayscale image document. You can paint in it, apply filters to it, change its content, or alter the range of gray values it contains. The next time you import this mask back into the image document it came from, you'll be able to produce striking visual effects because of the way you've modified the selection areas. You'll have a chance to explore just a few of these effects in this chapter and in Chapters 13 and 14.

Exporting a Selected Area as a Mask

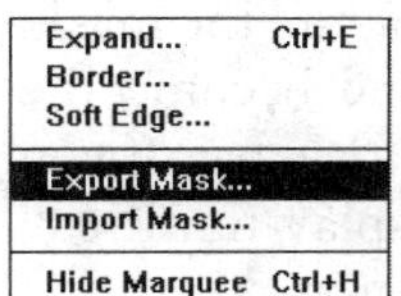

To generate a mask, you use the Export Mask command in the menu of the Select Palette. This command is available only if an area of the image document is already selected. PhotoStyler creates the mask as a separate Grayscale image document, in which selected areas are white, unselected (protected) areas are black, and soft edges show up as shades of gray.

To export a mask:

1. Select the area of the image that you want to retain as a mask. The selected area can be as simple or complex as you like.
2. Choose the Export Mask command in the Select Palette menu. The Export Mask dialog box shown in 8-16 will appear.
3. Enter a name for the mask in the Titled As text entry box. You don't have to name the mask, but if you create several of them during a PhotoStyler session, it helps to be able to tell them apart by their titles.
4. Activate the Minimize by Bounding box option *only* if you don't plan to use the mask in the same image document later. This option causes the mask document to be just large enough to contain the selected area(s). Figure 8–17 shows the difference between a minimized mask document and one that is the same size as the original image document.

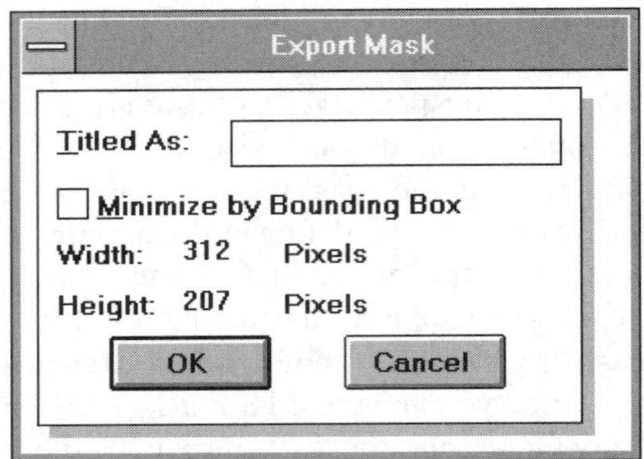

Figure 8-16.

The Export Mask dialog box

Tip

The Minimize by Bounding Box option is useful if you need to economize on file size, or if you plan to use the mask with an image document other than the one from which it came. However, if you want to use the mask as an automatic selection tool for the original image document, the mask and the original document must have the same dimensions. Otherwise, the mask won't overlay the original selection area properly when you re-import it.

5. Press Enter or click the OK command button to generate the mask. The mask document will overlay the original and become the active image document; its title will appear in the title bar. If you didn't name the mask document, its title bar will display "untitled" followed by a number.

Masks created in this way are good only for the current session of PhotoStyler. If you want to retain a mask across PhotoStyler sessions, you'll need to save it as a separate file. The next section shows you how.

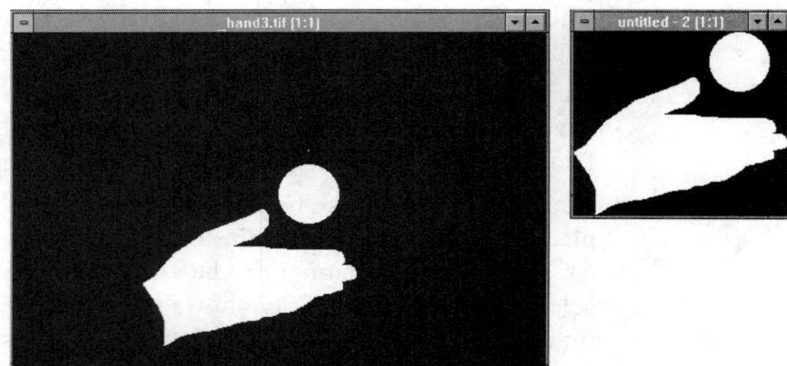

Figure 8-17.

Comparing a normal mask document with one that has been minimized

Saving, Naming, and Storing Mask Files

There's no limit to the number of mask documents you can create for a given image. This fact offers you enormous editing power and flexibility, but it also makes the process of storing and organizing masks more difficult.

Let's look at the storage issue first. Until and unless you save a mask document as a file, PhotoStyler stores it in system memory or in virtual memory. A large number of open, unsaved mask documents can slow down PhotoStyler's performance, especially if you have limited system memory (less than 4 Mb). To optimize performance, you should save as files any masks that you plan to use in future PhotoStyler sessions. Just use the Save As command in the File menu to save a mask document as a normal Grayscale image file.

And that brings us to the subject of organizing your mask files. PhotoStyler doesn't "know" which mask is associated with which image document. You have to help PhotoStyler along, either by organizing mask files in subdirectories or by naming them so that you'll recognize their link to a specific image file. Here are a few strategies you might find convenient:

- Store a single image file and its associated mask files together in one subdirectory.
- To distinguish mask files from the main image file, begin all mask filenames with the same character ($ or m, for example).
- Distinguish mask files from image files by storing them in a different file format. For example, you might store main image files as .tif files and mask files as .bmp files.
- Include characters in the mask filename that link it to another image document. For example, an RGB True Color image entitled stillife.tif might have several mask files, all beginning with the characters _st.

When it's time to archive your image files for long-term storage, it's a good idea to archive all the mask files you used together with the main image file. If you need to resurrect the completed image later for use on another project, you may well need some of the same masks again.

Editing and Enhancing Masks

The ultimate purpose of a mask is to help you edit the True Color or Grayscale image document from which it came (or another image document, if your masking techniques are advanced). A mask is itself a fully editable Grayscale image, but everything you do to enhance a mask is directed toward refining the selection area in another image document. Changes you make to the shading or composition of a mask will affect what happens after you import the mask to another image document later.

The key to editing masks productively is to know your goal. What effects do you want to achieve in the original image document? Some of the most common techniques used to enhance a mask include:

- cleaning up the outline of a selection area
- using filters, patterns, or the Airbrush tool to add texture effects within or outside the isolated area
- broadening the range of gray shades in the mask to permit semi-transparent painting in the original image
- adding illustration elements to the original mask, which will then become part of the source image when you import the mask and paint in it
- creating montages from multiple mask documents or Grayscale images

Chapters 10, 11, 12, 13, and 14 will touch upon some of the effects you can achieve with these and similar advanced masking techniques.

Tip

The relationship between gray shades in a mask and painting in the original image document after the mask is imported is like the relationship between the strainer in a faucet and the water that runs through the faucet. A faucet without a strainer, like the white areas of a mask after you re-import it, lets water (paint) flow through freely. At the other extreme, a capped faucet, like the black areas of a mask, permits no water (paint) to come through at all. Areas that were dark gray in the mask are like a strainer with very fine holes: they let very little water (paint) come through after you import the mask to another image document. And light gray areas, like strainers with larger holes, let paint flow through more readily.

Remember, editing a mask is only preparation for editing another image. The creative fireworks really begin after you import your enhanced mask back into another image document and continue editing.

Importing a Mask

PhotoStyler lets you import any Grayscale image into another image document as a mask. This means that you don't have to rely solely on the custom masks you create. All your Grayscale photographs are potential stencils that you can overlay onto any Grayscale or True Color image document! PhotoStyler has only two requirements for Grayscale images that you want to use as masks:

- The Grayscale image must contain at least one pixel with a gray value of 128 or higher. PhotoStyler won't recognize an image as a mask if it's too dark.
- Both the Grayscale image you want to use as a mask and the image into which you want to import it must be open at the same time.

To import a mask into an image document:

1. Open the image into which you want to import a mask and one or more Grayscale image documents. The Grayscale images may be mask documents that you've already exported, or simply Grayscale photographs or illustrations.
2. Activate the image document into which you want to import a mask.

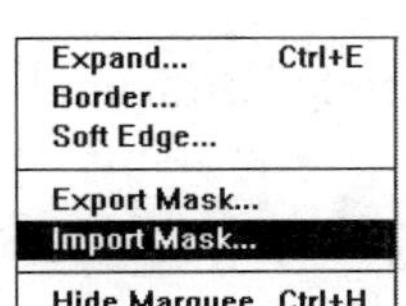

3. Choose the Import Mask command from the Select Palette menu. The dialog box in Figure 8–18 will appear. The Import Mask From list box will display all the Grayscale image files that are currently open.
4. Click on the filename of the Grayscale image document you want to use as a mask. Compare the pixel height and width of this image with the dimensions of the active image document.
5. If you want to change the dimensions of the selected Grayscale document before you import it as a mask, click the Cancel command button and then resize the image using the Resize or Resample command in the Edit menu (see Chapter 13).
6. If you don't need to change the mask's dimensions, click OK. After a moment, the mask will appear in the active image document as the outlines of a selection area. If the mask document is the same size as the active image document, the mask will overlay the active image exactly. If the mask document is smaller or minimized, PhotoStyler will position the selection outlines at the upper left corner of the active image document.

Figure 8-18.

The Import Mask dialog box

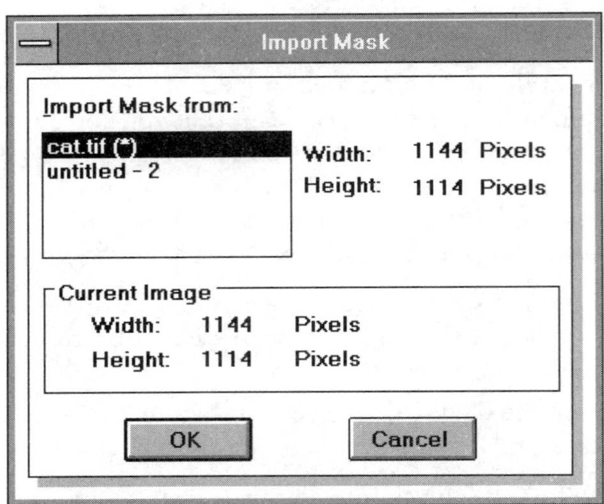

7. Move the new selection area as desired, and then paint in it or edit it as you would any other selection area.

So you've mastered selection and masking. Now what? Now you use the Paint tools (Chapter 10), apply filters (Chapter 12), edit the composition of the image (Chapter 13), and combine masks with other image channels (Chapter 14). Or, you could take a brief detour and experiment with our friend the halo once again—this time using a mask.

Creating a Halo, Part 2

Thinking creatively means thinking flexibly: coming up with several viable techniques for achieving the same goal. Dig out the portrait image you used in the "Creating a Halo, Part 1" section, and let's create a more refined halo with the help of a mask.

Tip

Selection areas are much easier to refine in a mask than in the original image document. This is due to the stark contrasts in most mask documents. Once you get used to editing selection contours in a mask, chances are you'll never want to do it any other way.

1. Open the True Color or Grayscale portrait image file you used in the earlier exercise in this chapter.

2. Magnify the image and then trace the outline of the subject's head as before, using the Lasso tool. Double-click to close the selection area.
3. Select the border of the current selection as before, using the Border command in the Select Palette menu.
4. This time, instead of tidying up the selection area immediately, choose the Export Mask command in the Select Palette menu. Title the new mask as halo-1 or something similar and click OK. Our unedited mask looks like the one in Figure 8–19 (left)—all black and white, with no soft edges.

5. You'll want to remove part of the white area of the mask so you won't end up with a halo around the chin (see Figure 8–19, right). Activate the Lasso tool and, using the Ctrl key, encircle the unnecessary white areas.
6. Display the Color Palette and make black the current foreground color.

7. Double-click the Bucket Fill tool icon and set Color Similarity for this tool to 255. Click OK and then click inside the currently selected area. The unwanted white area will turn to black (see Figure 8–19, right).
8. When you're finished editing the main contours of the selection area, press Ctrl-N to deselect all selection areas.

9. Activate the Smudge tool and blend the edges of the white area into the black area as in Figure 8–19, right. See Chapter 11 if you need to learn how the Smudge tool works. Remember, intermediate gray

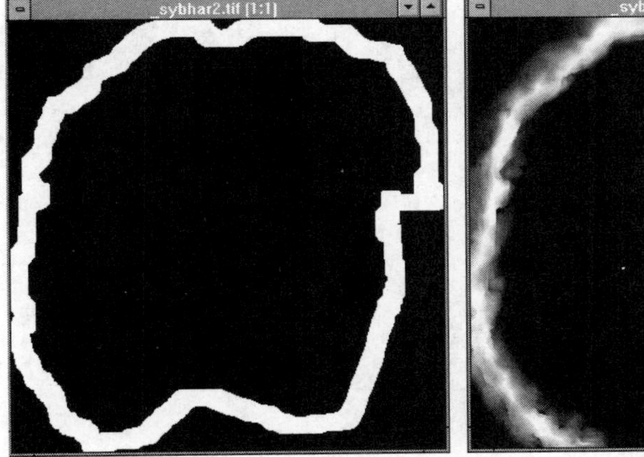

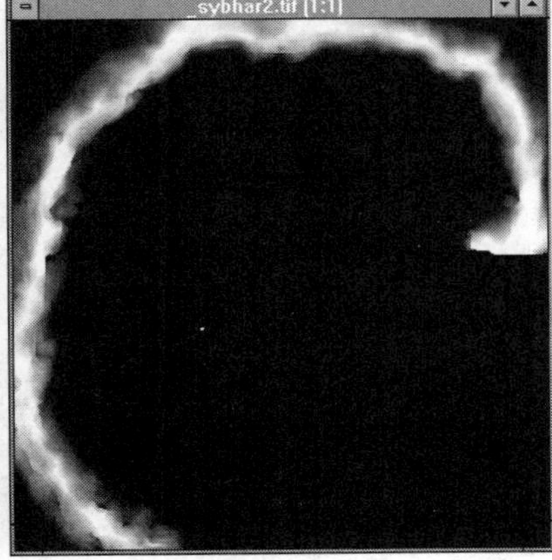

Figure 8-19.

Unedited mask (l) and edited mask containing "smudged" soft edge (r)

shades in a mask translate into semitransparent painting effects in the source image document.

10. When you're done refining the mask, make the original image document active again and then choose the Import Mask command from the Select Palette menu. Choose the mask document you've created and select OK. The mask will load and the selection area will have changed to reflect your enhancement of the mask. (Medium gray or darker areas of the mask won't show up on the marquee, but they'll still affect any painting you do.)
11. If the active image document is a Grayscale image, change the foreground color to a light gray. If it's a True Color image, change the foreground color to a soft yellow.

12. Double-click the Bucket Fill tool icon in the Paint Palette and set Color Similarity to 255 as before. Select OK to exit the Bucket Fill Options dialog box.
13. Click anywhere in the selection area. The entire area will fill with the foreground color. Due to the Smudge tool techniques you used, your halo will emit an even softer glow than the one you created using a Soft Edge earlier in this chapter.

This ability to control color transparency when painting is one of the most powerful advantages of using masks. You'll encounter this PhotoStyler theme again in Chapters 10, 11, 13, and 14. In the meantime, if one of your main activities in PhotoStyler is retouching scanned photographs or artwork, look at Chapter 9 to learn more about image enhancement and correction techniques.

9

Image Enhancement and Correction

Scanners, video capture boards, and most other input devices tend to reproduce color and gray values imperfectly. Before you begin editing any image in Aldus PhotoStyler, you should always adjust the digitized image so that it matches the source image as closely as possible. The photographic industry refers to this process as image correction. If the source image itself is weak, you may want to enhance the digitized image to make it look even better than the original.

Brightness & Contrast...	F2
Hue & Saturation...	
Gray/Color Correction...	F3
Gray/Color Map...	F4
Negative	
Equalization	
Posterization...	
Threshold...	

PhotoStyler's image correction and enhancement controls are grouped conveniently together in a submenu of the Tune command in the Image menu. If your main activity in PhotoStyler is retouching photographs, you can use these commands to adjust brightness, contrast, hue, saturation, highlights, shadows, and midtones as precisely or intuitively as you prefer. If your interest lies in fine art or graphic design instead, the Image/Tune commands will help you generate dazzling color or Grayscale effects such as silhouettes, posterization, or color inversion. Whatever the application, your ability to correct either complete images or limited selection areas greatly increases your editing power.

Fine-Tuning Scanned and Captured Images

Most of your images probably reach PhotoStyler by way of scanners, video capture boards, still video cameras, or other input devices. The technology behind a given input device places limits on the range of brightness levels, contrast levels, and colors that it can reproduce with fidelity. As a result, an image that arrives in your computer may not show the proper balance of details in the midtone, highlight, or shadow areas. Still other distortions can occur when you scan an image at a resolution higher than the scanner hardware is capable of handling efficiently. In these cases, scanners interpolate extra pixels, which may result in "noise" and a loss of image quality.

For these reasons, image correction and enhancement should always be an important first step in the image editing process. PhotoStyler's Image/Tune commands can adjust brightness and contrast, help reduce unwanted noise, and subtly correct deficiencies in hue or saturation. An invaluable aid in this process is your ability to see adjustments as you make them.

Real-Time Preview

Preview

As you correct or enhance images using the Image/Tune commands, PhotoStyler lets you see the tentative results of your changes without having to leave the dialog box. If your display adapter supports the Super VGA standard (256 colors), you'll see real-time color or Grayscale animation as you alter the settings. If you have a standard VGA, Hi-Color, 16-bit, or 24-bit adapter, you'll need to click a Preview command button in a dialog box in order to see your changes in advance. The Preview function lets you play "what if;" it doesn't really change the active image document. Only when you click OK and commit your settings do you alter the pixel information in the image document.

Tip

The Preview function is WYSIWYG—except when you're correcting or enhancing a selected area rather than the entire image document. Then, the entire image seems to change as you alter your settings. Don't be concerned; just concentrate on the effect your settings are having on the selected area. When you click OK and exit the dialog box, PhotoStyler will alter only the selected area of the image.

Precise Color Adjustments

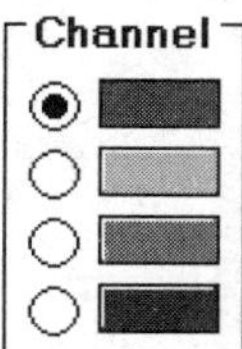

If you're enhancing or correcting a True Color image, PhotoStyler lets you adjust color values for the red, green, and blue image channels separately. Serious retouchers will find that this feature offers precise control over color, while graphic artists will appreciate the opportunity to introduce special color effects or shifts. In general, it's a good idea to adjust color for the integrated image first, and then refine individual color channels.

Developing Good Image Enhancement Habits

We all like to experiment with our images, and PhotoStyler makes experimentation all too easy. Keep in mind that, when altering brightness, contrast, hue, saturation, and midtones, you're often deleting color or grayscale information that you won't be able to recover later. So before we delve into the wonders of the eight Image/Tune commands, we'd like to offer some tips about good image enhancement habits. These good habits will minimize errors while letting you tweak pixels to your heart's content.

Print a Copy of an Image the First Time You Open It in PhotoStyler

Because computer monitors transmit light rather than reflect it (see Chapter 7), images are likely to look brighter on your screen than they will at the printer's. You don't want to reduce image brightness arbitrarily, only to find out too late that the printed image looks dull and dark. To avoid making this type of error, print a draft copy of each image as soon as you scan it or open it in PhotoStyler for the first time. Even if you end up printing a True Color image on a black-and-white laser printer, you'll obtain a rough idea of the relative brightness and contrast levels in the digitized image. Use this printed sample as your gauge when correcting the image in PhotoStyler.

Duplicate an Image Just before You Correct or Enhance It

It's a good idea to save multiple versions of an image, and the first place to start is when you prepare to correct it. Remember, if you accidentally delete certain gray levels or color values when tuning the image, you won't be able to get them back later. Having a duplicate handy provides insurance and saves rescanning time.

Adjusting Brightness and Contrast

PhotoStyler offers three different methods for adjusting brightness and contrast levels in an image or selected area. The Tune: Brightness & Contrast command is the most intuitive method. The straightforward controls in the Brightness & Contrast dialog box remind us of the remote control adjustments found on most television sets. For precise adjustments of brightness or contrast that give you greater control over detail in highlight, shadow, and midtone areas, use the Tune: Gray/Color Correction command described later in this chapter. And if you want to manipulate brightness and color values to obtain special effects, the Tune: Gray/Color Map command lets you draw freehand color or gray value "maps" for an image or selection.

To adjust brightness and contrast with the Brightness & Contrast command:

1. Activate the image document you want to adjust. To adjust brightness and contrast levels for one area of the image only, select that area now. Otherwise, PhotoStyler will adjust values throughout the image document.
2. Choose the Tune: Brightness & Contrast command from the Image menu, or press the keyboard shortcut, F2. The Brightness & Contrast dialog box shown in Figure 9–1 will appear. Both brightness and contrast will be at their default levels of zero percent. If you're working with a True Color image, four Channel option buttons will be available: one for the integrated image and one each for red,

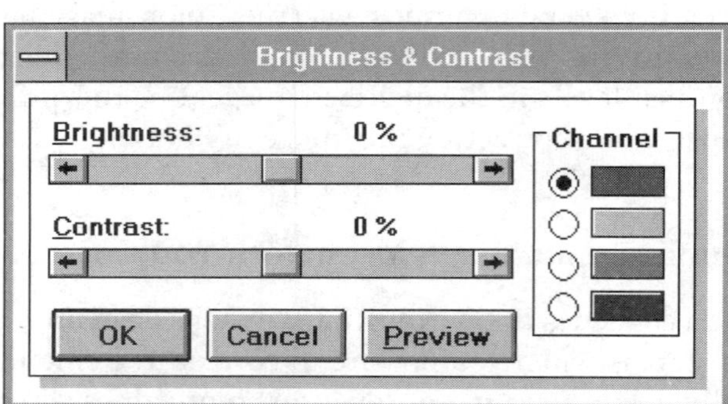

Figure 9-1.

The Brightness & Contrast dialog box

green, and blue. If your image is the Grayscale type, only the first channel will be available.

Tip *For color images, adjust the image as a whole first, and then fine-tune separate red, green, and blue channels if necessary. This method will assure you of a more evenly balanced image.*

3. Adjust brightness levels using the Brightness scroll bar. Clicking the right scroll arrow or dragging the scroll box to the right will increase brightness throughout the image or selection. Clicking the left scroll arrow or dragging the scroll box to the left will decrease brightness. If your monitor supports color animation, you'll see the effects of your changes as you make them. If you don't see any changes, click the Preview button to view them.

Note *Even if you've selected a limited area of the image, the preview function gives the impression that your changes will affect the entire image. Don't be concerned—when you exit the dialog box, the changes will take effect in the selected area only.*

4. Adjust contrast levels using the Contrast scroll bar. To increase contrast throughout the image or selection (a positive percentage value), click the right scroll arrow or drag the scroll bar to the right. To decrease contrast (a negative percentage value), click the left scroll arrow or drag the scroll box toward the left. If you don't see real-time changes to the active image document, click Preview.
5. If you're editing a True Color image and need more correction, click each channel option button and adjust brightness and contrast for the red, green, and blue channels separately. Preview your changes as before.
6. When you're pleased with your adjustments, press Enter or click the OK command button to commit your changes.

Remember that images look brighter on your monitor than they do in a publication, so avoid darkening the image as much as you think you ought. If you have doubts, print another copy of the image immediately after you adjust brightness and contrast, and use the Undo command if you've guessed wrong.

Tip *There may be times when you don't want to change brightness or contrast levels globally throughout an image or selection area. To* *adjust brightness levels manually using the mouse, use the Lighten and Darken tools in the Paint Palette. To adjust contrast levels manually, use the Blur and Sharpen tools. See Chapter 10 for more information.*

The next command in the Image/Tune menu lets you adjust hue and saturation in much the same intuitive way that you adjust brightness and contrast.

Adjusting Hue and Saturation

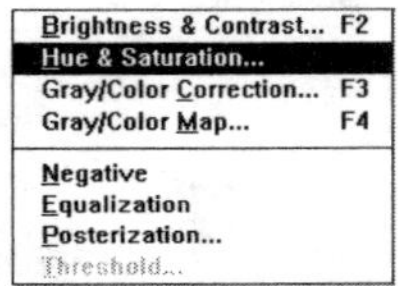

Scanners and other input devices often cause color shifts as well as shifts in brightness and contrast. As you may recall from Chapter 7, color as we perceive it has hue, saturation, and brightness components. When the hue component of a color changes, we see a shift from one color to another: red to orange, for example, or green to blue. When the saturation component changes, we see a shift in the intensity or depth of a color. The lower the saturation of a color, the more "washed-out" or gray it appears.

The Tune: Hue & Saturation command is available for True Color and Indexed Color images only. It lets you fine-tune hue and saturation levels intuitively throughout an image or selection area without affecting brightness. You adjust hues according to an imaginary 360-degree color wheel and saturation in terms of a percentage value. As Figure 9–2 in the Color Section of this book shows, you can also use the Hue & Saturation command to generate special color effects.

To adjust hue and saturation for a color image:

1. Activate the image document you want to adjust. If you want to adjust hue and saturation for one area of the image only, select that area now. Otherwise, PhotoStyler will adjust values throughout the image.
2. Choose the Tune: Hue & Saturation command from the Image menu. The Hue & Saturation dialog box shown in Figure 9–3 will appear. Hue and saturation will be at defaults of zero degrees and zero percent, respectively.
3. Adjust the hue using the Hue scroll bar. If you click the right scroll arrow or drag the scroll box to the right, you'll shift the hue counterclockwise around the imaginary hue wheel (see Figure 7–1).

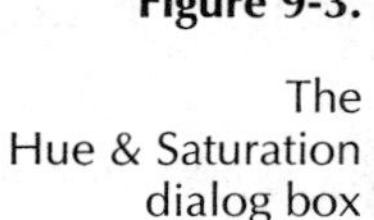

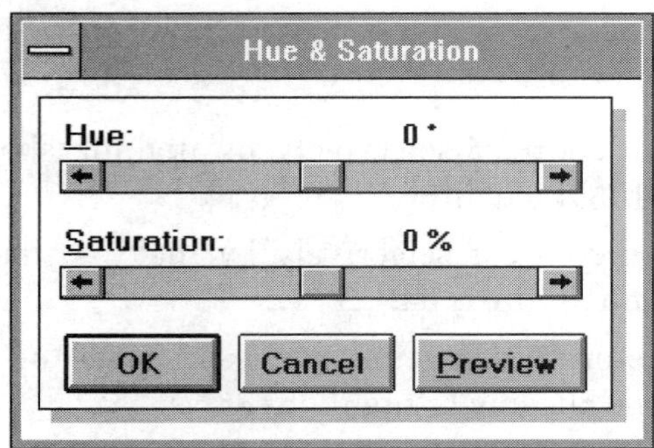

Figure 9-3. The Hue & Saturation dialog box

For example, if the predominant hues are red, moving the scroll box to the right will shift the tonalities in the order of red to orange to yellow to green. If you click the left scroll arrow or drag the scroll box to the left, you'll shift the hues clockwise around the hue wheel—from red to magenta to violet and blue. Remember, you're shifting the hue relative to the current tonality of the image or selection area. The specific hue you begin with will vary with each image, but the order of hues will remain constant. If your monitor supports color animation, you'll see the effects of your adjustments as you make them. If you don't see real-time changes, click the Preview button to view them.

4. Adjust saturation using the Saturation scroll bar. To intensify the colors throughout the image or selection (a positive percentage value), click the right scroll arrow or drag the scroll bar to the right. To make colors less intense (a negative percentage value), click the left scroll arrow or drag the scroll box toward the left. If you don't see real-time changes to the active image document, click Preview.
5. When you're pleased with your adjustments, press Enter or click the OK command button to commit your changes.

Precision Image Correction with the Gray/Color Correction Command

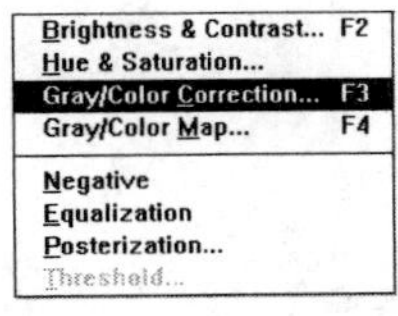

The Tune: Gray/Color Correction command gives you superior control over brightness and contrast in specific areas of an image or selection. This makes it more flexible than the Brightness & Contrast command, which merely adjusts brightness or contrast values evenly throughout the image. You can use Gray/Color Correction for three important functions:

- to increase contrast selectively by making shadow areas darker and/or highlights lighter
- to decrease contrast selectively by making shadow areas lighter and/or highlight areas darker
- to enhance or reduce detail in the midtones of an image without affecting the shadow or highlight areas

You achieve control over shadows, highlights, and midtones by defining exactly which color or grayscale brightness values to exclude from the enhanced image. The Gray/Color Correction dialog box lets you see a histogram, a graphic representation of these values. The histogram displays not only the range of color or gray values in the image, but also the relative number of pixels that correspond to each value.

The Gray/Color Correction Dialog Box

The Gray/Color Correction dialog box (Figure 9–4) may look forbiddingly "scientific" when compared to the straightforward scroll bars of the Brightness & Contrast dialog box. Actually, it's just as interactive. If you take a few moments to acquaint yourself with it, you'll find the payoff in image enhancement power more than worth the trouble.

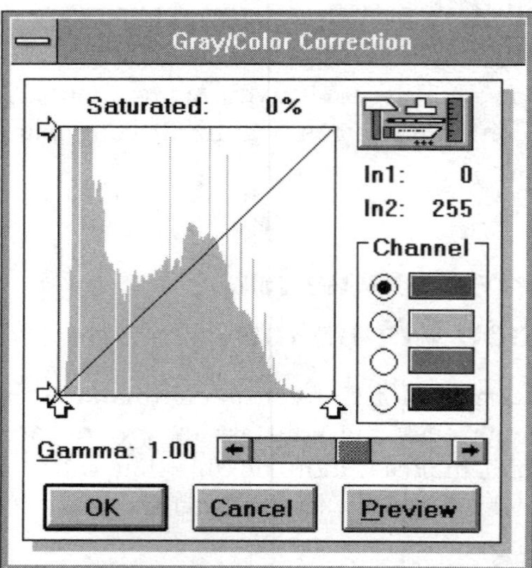

Figure 9-4. The Gray/Color Correction dialog box

To access the dialog box, simply choose the Tune: Gray/Color Correction command from the Image menu, or use the keyboard shortcut, F3.

Reading the Histogram and Mapping Curve

The graphic portion of the Gray/Color Correction dialog box consists of the histogram and the mapping curve. The histogram plots the brightness values in the active image as a graph. The horizontal axis of this graph describes the range of brightness values present, while the vertical axis shows how many pixels in the image correspond to each value. You can enlarge your view of the histogram by choosing the Enlarge Histogram command from the Gray/Color Correction menu.

Bisecting the graph is the mapping curve, the diagonal line or curve that gives you a quick overview of the range of brightness values in the image. The mapping curve summarizes three types of information:

- The angle of the mapping curve shows the upper and lower limits of the brightness values in the image.
- The curvature or straightness of the mapping curve shows how you've altered the midtones (gamma) in the image. A straight line indicates you've made no changes to the midtones. The steeper the curve, the more you've edited the midtone values.
- Flat areas of the mapping curve show brightness values that you've eliminated from the original image. PhotoStyler will map these pixels to black or white instead of their original values, thereby increasing image contrast.

Look at the mapping curve before and after you enhance an image; you'll gain a better understanding of how you've altered the brightness values. Figure 9–5 shows an example of how the shape of a mapping curve can change as you correct image values.

In1: 0
In2: 255

Input and Output Ranges, Saturation, and Slider Handles

To the right of the histogram is a set of two indicator numbers. When you first access the Gray/Color Correction dialog box, these numbers show the input range, which by default includes all possible brightness values (refer back to Figure 9–5, top). The Input indicator numbers correspond to the horizontal axis in the histogram and to the two slider handles along that axis. If you drag either of the two horizontal slider handles, you'll eliminate values at the lower or upper end of the input

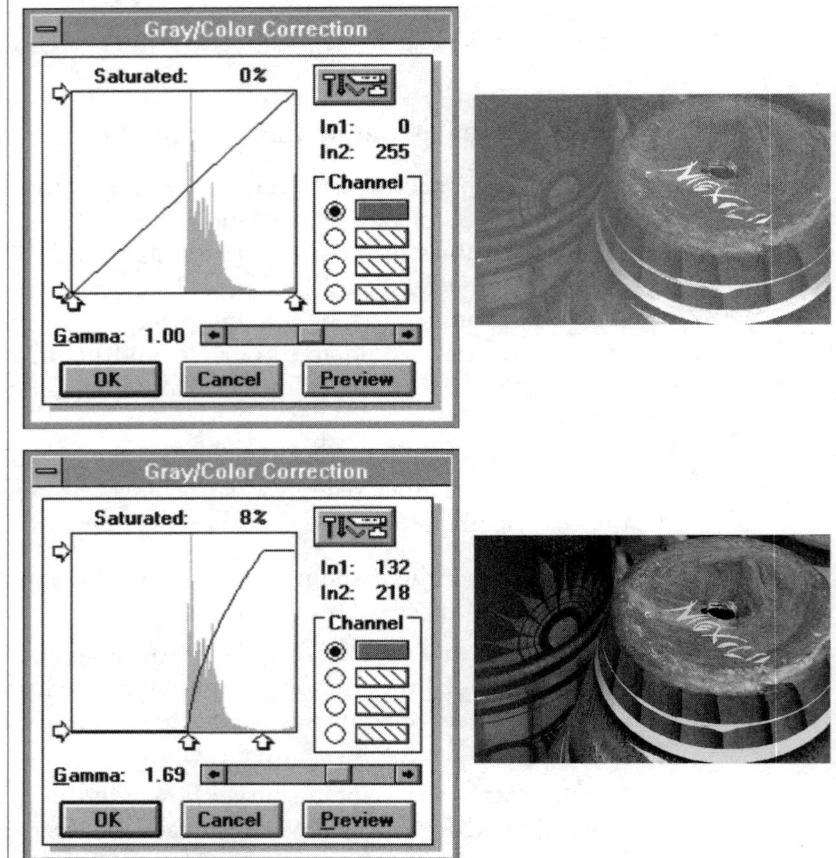

Figure 9-5.

Above: Default mapping curve for an imperfectly scanned image

Below: Mapping curve for same image after increasing, gamma, saturation, and contrast in highlights and shadows

range. The Input indicator numbers will change to reflect the new upper and lower limits for brightness values. PhotoStyler will remap the eliminated values to pure black or white, thereby increasing contrast in the image. As in Figure 9–5 (bottom), the percentage of pixels in the image that you've remapped to black or white will appear in the Saturated indicator just above the histogram.

The slider handles that lie along the vertical axis of the histogram, on the other hand, control the output range—the brightness values contained in the image after you've adjusted the input range. When you drag these vertical slider handles, you decrease contrast in the image, and the Input indicators turn into Output indicators. Adjusting the upper vertical slider handle decreases contrast by darkening the color or gray values in the shadow areas (see Figure 9–5, bottom). Adjusting the lower vertical slider handle, on the other hand, decreases contrast by lightening the color or gray values in the highlight areas.

Gamma

The gamma scroll bar beneath the histogram lets you increase contrast in the image by controlling the brightness of the midtones, those color or gray values that fall between the extremes of bright and dark. When you first access the Color/Gray Correction dialog box, the gamma value is always at 1.00 and the mapping curve is a straight line, as in the uppermost image in Figure 9–5. If you adjust gamma below 1.00, the image midtones will darken, overall contrast will increase, and the mapping curve will curve downward. If you adjust gamma above 1.00 (the limit is 8.0), the midtones will lighten, overall contrast will increase, and the mapping curve will curve upward. Refer to the lower image in Figure 9–5 for an example of how increasing the gamma changes the image and its mapping curve.

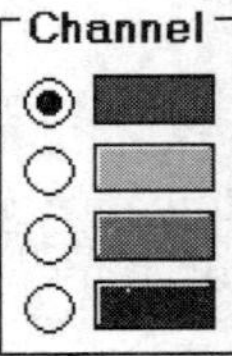

Image Channel Options

If the active image is an RGB True Color or Indexed Color image, four radio buttons will be available in the Channel area of the Gray/Color Correction dialog box. Activating the top radio button lets you adjust the integrated image. Activating one of the others lets you modify brightness values in the red, green, and blue image channels separately. Grayscale and Black & White images have only a single radio button available.

Auto Ranging
Reset
Enlarge Histogram
Reduce Histogram

Gray/Color Correction Menu

The toolbox icon in the Gray/Color Correction dialog box conceals a menu that gives you additional options for viewing the Gray/Color Map and for adjusting highlights and shadows. Just click the icon to access the menu.

Auto Ranging This command automatically optimizes brightness and contrast values. It matches the input range to the actual brightness and contrast values found in the unaltered image and extends the output range to its maximum (0 to 255). The Auto Ranging command is useful for routine processing of catalog or newsletter photographs, but it may not meet all your needs if you want to stylize images.

Reset The Reset command cancels any changes you've made in the Gray/Color Correction dialog box and restores all values to their previous levels.

Enlarge Histogram Some images contain an uneven distribution of brightness values—a large number of pixels within a small range of values and very few pixels in the rest of the range. To get a better look at the ranges that contain a relatively small number of pixels, you can choose the Enlarge Histogram command. Each time you invoke this command, your view of the histogram will enlarge by a factor of one, up to a maximum of 16x magnification. Figure 9–6 shows an unaltered histogram and one that has been enlarged by a factor of one.

Reduce Histogram The Reduce Histogram command is available only if you've already enlarged the histogram at least once. It reduces the viewing magnification of the histogram by a factor of one.

Increasing Contrast Selectively in Shadow and Highlight Areas

The first important function of the Gray/Color Correction dialog box is to help you increase contrast selectively in the shadow or highlight areas of an image. You do this by dragging the Input Range slider handles along the horizontal axis of the histogram.

When you drag the left Input Range slider handle to the right, you remap darker pixels in the image to pure black, thereby suppressing details in shadow areas and emphasizing them in lighter areas (see the transition between the top and center images in Figure 9–7). The image

Figure 9-6.

An unaltered histogram (l) and one that has been enlarged to show detail (r)

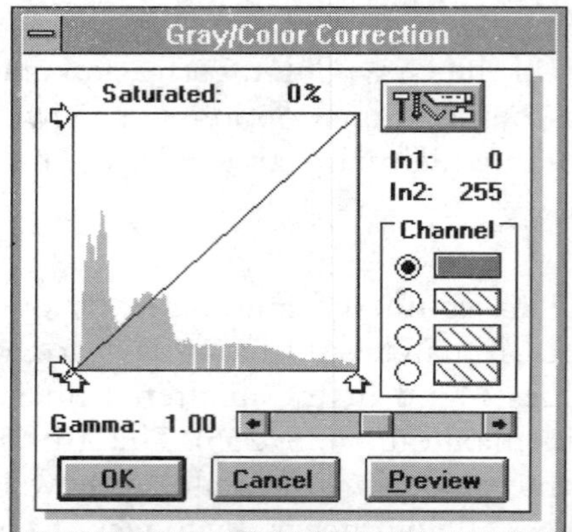

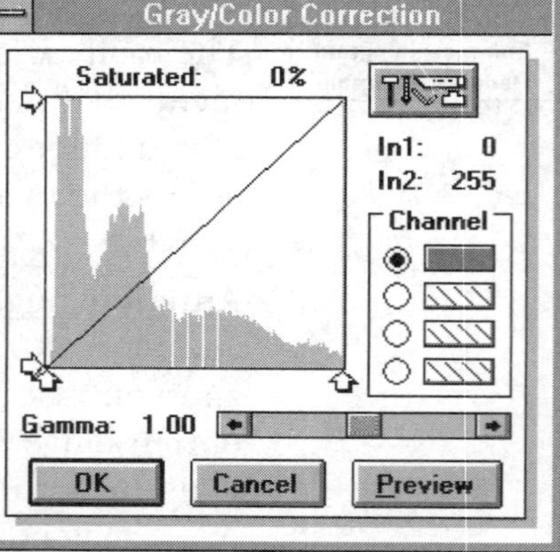

Figure 9-7.

Increasing contrast selectively in shadow and highlight areas:

Top: Mapping curve for uncorrected image

Center: Increasing contrast in shadow areas

Bottom: Increasing contrast in highlight areas

or selected area will become darker as a whole. Conversely, dragging the right Input Range slider handle to the left remaps lighter pixels in the image to pure white. This results in less detail in the highlight areas and emphasized detail in the shadow areas (see Figure 9–7, bottom). The image will become brighter as a whole. Overall contrast in the image will increase in both cases.

To increase contrast selectively in the highlight and shadow areas of an image:

1. Select a limited area of the image if you want to adjust contrast for a portion of the image. Otherwise, PhotoStyler will adjust values for the entire image.
2. Choose the Tune: Gray/Color Correction command from the Image menu, or use the keyboard shortcut, F3. The Gray/Color Correction dialog box will appear, showing a histogram that plots the distribution of brightness values in the image. If you need a more detailed view of pixel distribution, choose the Enlarge Histogram command from the Gray/Color Correction menu.
3. Move the Gray/Color Correction dialog box out of the way if it obstructs your view of the active image document.
4. To increase contrast so as to darken shadow areas and bring out detail in the highlight areas, drag the left Input Range slider handle to the right. PhotoStyler will remap all pixels that fall below the In1 value to black and show, through the Saturated indicator, the percentage of pixels that you've affected. The image will be darker as a whole, but detail in the lighter areas will be easier to see (Figure 9–7, center). You'll also suppress details in the dark areas.
5. To increase contrast so as to lighten highlight areas and bring out detail in the shadow areas, drag the right Input Range slider handle to the left. PhotoStyler will remap all pixels that fall above the In2 value to white, and the Saturation indicator will show the percentage of pixels that you've affected. The image will be lighter as a whole (especially in highlight areas, where details will be suppressed), but details in the shadow areas will be easier to see (Figure 9–7, bottom).

Tip

It's possible to move both of the Input Range slider handles for the same image document or selection. For example, if you want an extremely high-contrast image, you can limit brightness values at both ends of the spectrum, suppressing details in light and dark areas alike.

Preview

6. If your monitor doesn't support real-time animation, click the Preview command button to see how your changes will look. If you

don't like the results, you can start over again after choosing the Reset command in the Gray/Color Correction menu.

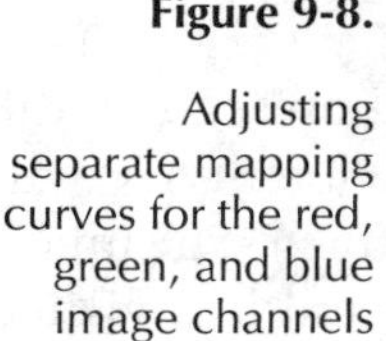

7. If you're working with a color image that needs additional correction or enhancement, now is the time to adjust each color channel separately. Click the desired red, green, or blue Channel option button to activate that channel and then drag the desired slider handle to the left or right. Figure 9–8 shows how your histogram might look if you adjust color values differently for each channel.
8. When you've achieved the results you want, click the OK command button to process your changes and return to the active image document.

Figure 9–9 in the Color Section of this book illustrates how you can predict the look of a color image when you edit individual color channels. The uppermost image in Figure 9–9 shows an unaltered True Color image with its default mapping curve. As you drag the left Input Range slider handle to the right, the deeper shades of the active channel drop out. The result is that the image begins to take on the tonality of the other image channels. For example, after activating the blue channel and moving the left Input Range slider handle to the right, an image will look progressively more golden yellow as in the center image in the figure. If you drag the right Input Range slider handle to the left, the more brilliant shades of the active channel (here, blue) begin to predominate as in the bottom image in Figure 9–9.

Figure 9-8.

Adjusting separate mapping curves for the red, green, and blue image channels

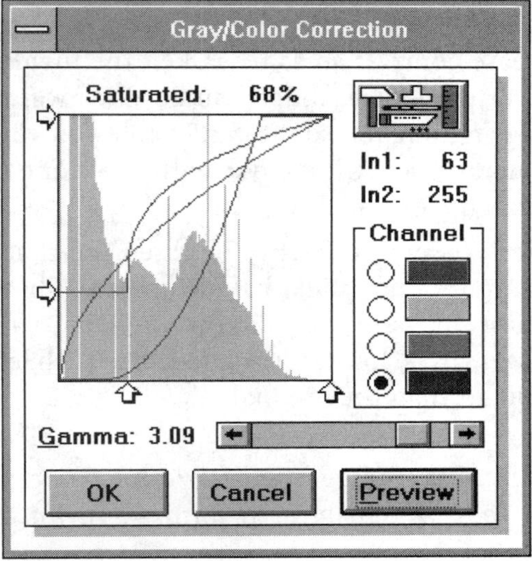

Decreasing Contrast Selectively in Shadow and Highlight Areas

A second function of the Gray/Color Correction dialog box is to help you decrease contrast selectively in the shadow or highlight areas of an image. You do this by dragging the Output Range slider handles upward or downward along the vertical axis of the histogram. When you drag the upper Output Range slider handle downward, you darken the highlight areas of the image by lowering the highest available brightness value. On the other hand, dragging the lower Input Range slider handle upward brightens the shadow areas of the image by raising the lowest available brightness value. Contrast in the image decreases in both cases.

To decrease contrast selectively in the highlight and shadow areas of an image:

1. Select a limited area of the image if you want to adjust brightness values for a portion of the image. Otherwise, PhotoStyler will adjust values for the entire image.
2. Choose the Tune: Gray/Color Correction command from the Image menu. The Gray/Color Correction dialog box will appear, showing a histogram that plots the distribution of brightness values in the image. If you need a more detailed view of pixel distribution, choose the Enlarge Histogram command from the Gray/Color Correction menu.
3. Move the dialog box out of the way if it obstructs your view of the active image document.
4. To decrease contrast so as to darken the highlight areas, drag the upper Output Range slider handle downward. PhotoStyler will remap all bright pixels to the Out2 value you've defined. The image will be darker as a whole, but with less contrast and less visible detail than the original.
5. To decrease contrast so as to brighten the shadow areas, drag the lower Output Range slider handle upward. PhotoStyler will remap the darkest pixels in the image to the Out1 value you've defined. The image will be lighter as a whole, but with less contrast and less visible detail than the original.

Caution

Keep in mind that images will always look brighter on your monitor than they will in printed form. Restrain the urge to darken accordingly!

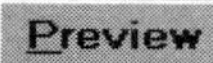

6. If your monitor doesn't support real-time animation, click the Preview command button to see how your changes will look. If you don't like the results, you can start over again after choosing the Reset command in the Gray/Color Correction menu.

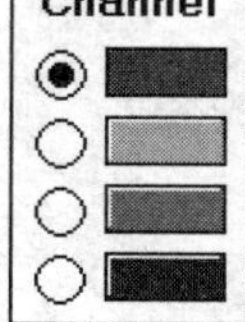

7. If you're working with a color image that needs additional correction or enhancement, now is the time to adjust each color channel separately. Click the desired red, green, or blue Channel option button to activate that channel and then drag the desired slider handle upward or downward.
8. When you've achieved the results you want, click the OK command button to process your changes and return to the active image document.

So far, you've seen how the Gray/Color Correction dialog box enhances your control over brightness, contrast, and detail in the shadow or highlight areas of an image. But what about the color or gray values between the extremes? Through the Gamma scroll bar, the Gray/Color Correction dialog box heightens your control over these midtone areas, too.

Adjusting the Midtones (Gamma)

In PhotoStyler, the term gamma refers to the way brightness values are distributed in the midtones of an image. Midtones are color or gray values that fall between the extremes of shadows and highlights. There are no fixed rules here, but you can safely consider color or gray values between about 75 and 200 as midtones.

Using the Gamma scroll bar in the Gray/Color Correction dialog box, you can adjust brightness and contrast in the midtones without distorting brightness information in the shadow and highlight areas. Increasing the gamma value enhances details in the shadow areas of an image while suppressing them in the lighter areas (see Figure 9–10). Conversely, reducing the gamma value enhances details in the lighter areas of an image at the expense of details in the shadow areas.

To enhance detail by adjusting the midtone values in an image:

1. Select a limited area of the image if you want to adjust gamma for a portion of the image. Otherwise, PhotoStyler will adjust gamma for the entire image.
2. Choose the Tune: Gray/Color Correction command from the Image menu, or press the keyboard shortcut, F3. When the Gray/Color

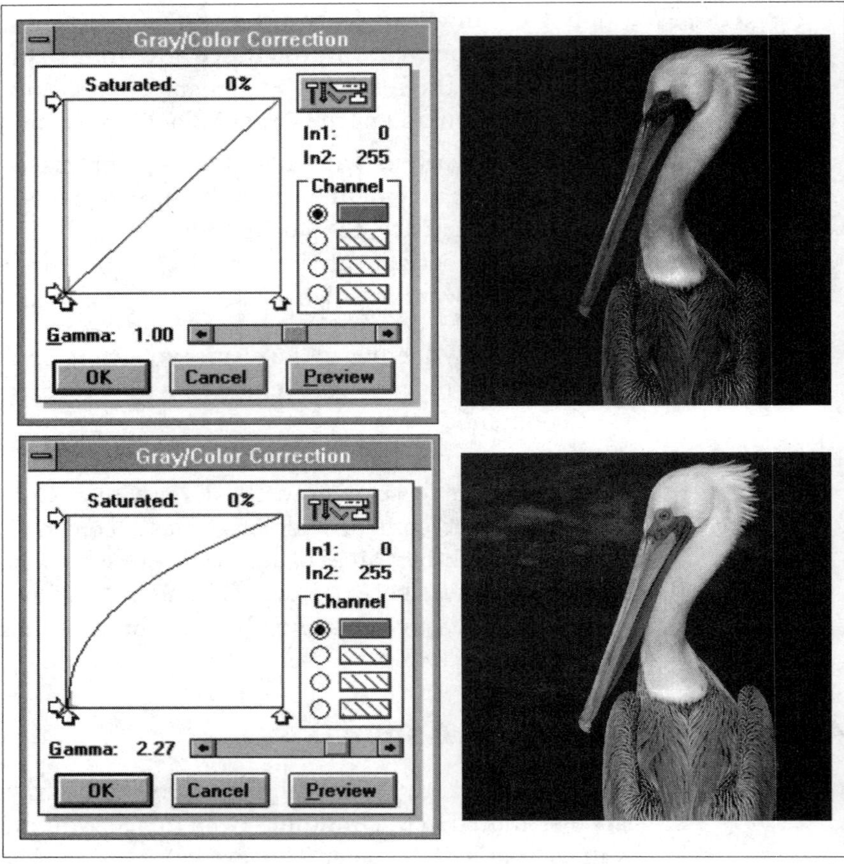

Figure 9-10. Increasing gamma to emphasize detail in midtones

Correction dialog box appears, the Gamma value will be set to 1.00 by default.

3. Move the dialog box out of the way if it obstructs your view of the active image document.
4. To enhance detail in the darker parts of the image, drag the Gamma scroll box to the right, or click the right scroll arrow on the scroll bar. You can adjust gamma as high as 7.99, but a value between 1.4 and 2.4 will probably meet your needs.
5. To enhance detail in the lighter parts of the image, drag the Gamma scroll box to the left, or click the left scroll arrow on the scroll bar.
6. If your monitor doesn't support real-time animation, click the Preview command button to preview the effects of your adjustment. Continue making adjustments if necessary.

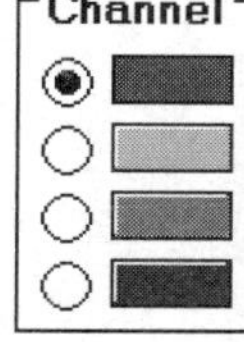

7. If you're editing a color image, adjust the gamma for individual color channels as desired. When you increase the gamma value for a particular color channel, the shadow areas will show more detail but will also look more saturated with the current channel color. When you decrease the gamma value for a particular color channel, the highlight areas will show more detail. At the same time, they'll also look more saturated with the other channel colors (blue-green for the red channel, for instance).
8. When you're pleased with your adjustment, click the OK command button to return to the active image document.

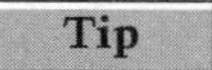

If your images are destined for print publishing, you should always increase gamma to compensate for dot gain at the printer's. See Chapters 15 and 16 for more tips on image output.

The Gray/Color Correction command suits precision-oriented photo retouchers and graphic artists. If you're the type of artist who likes to "play" with your images, however, you might prefer using the Gray/Color Map command instead.

Hands-on Image Enhancement with the Gray/Color Map Command

Think of the Tune: Gray/Color Map command as a more intuitive version of the Gray/Color Correction command. Instead of specifying numerical brightness values, you edit the mapping curve directly, dragging parts of the curve to "repaint" grayscale and color values. With the flexibility these techniques offer, you can obtain an infinite number of different mapping curves and a broad range of special color or Grayscale effects.

The Gray/Color Map Dialog Box

To access the Gray/Color Map dialog box (Figure 9–11), choose the Tune: Gray/Color Map command from the Image menu or press the keyboard shortcut, F4. This dialog box has many of the same features as the Gray/Color Correction dialog box: Input and Output value indicators, option buttons for color image channels, and a menu that contains additional functions. Where the Gray/Color Map differs is in

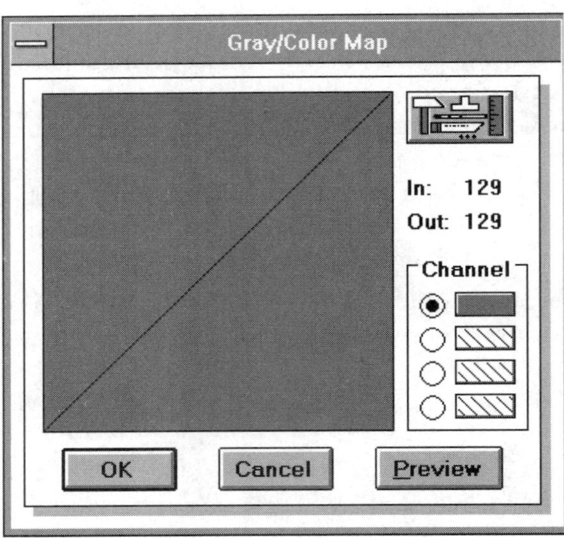

Figure 9-11.

The Gray/Color Map dialog box

its graphic presentation of information about brightness values in the image. Instead of a histogram, the Gray/Color Map presents a simple linear mapping curve on a gray background.

The mapping curve is your key to generating special Grayscale or color effects in the Gray/Color Map dialog box. You can edit this curve in one of two ways: directly by using the mouse, or by applying one of the commands in the Gray/Color Map menu. You can save mapping curves that yield your favorite effects and then apply them to other images later. What a great way to build a library of special effects!

Note

See the section entitled "The Gray/Color Correction Dialog Box" earlier in this chapter if you need to learn more about the elements of the Gray/Color Map dialog box.

Editing the Mapping Curve Directly

The most intuitive way to edit the mapping curve is to drag segments of the curve with the mouse, freehand-style. We can't tell you how to produce a specific effect, because each image is different and there is an almost infinite number of different ways to drag the curve. However, we can offer some guidelines that will help you get your bearings. Try each of the following techniques with one of your favorite images and see some of the exciting effects you can create.

- Dragging the upper part of the curve affects brightness and contrast in the highlight areas.
- Dragging the lower part of the curve affects brightness and contrast in the shadow areas of the image.
- Dragging the middle part of the curve affects brightness and contrast in the midtones of the image.
- Dragging the curve upward at a given point brightens the pixels that have the affected input value.
- Dragging the curve downward at a given point darkens the pixels that have the affected input value.
- Making a segment of the curve steeper heightens contrast in pixels of the affected range.
- Making a segment of the curve flatter decreases contrast in pixels of the affected range.
- Dragging the curve to the right at a given point decreases contrast while darkening the pixels within a range of output values.
- Dragging the curve to the left at a given point decreases contrast while lightening the pixels within a range of output values.

Caution *Whenever you change input values, you're deleting information from the image that you won't be able to recover later. Make a duplicate of the active image before you edit the Gray Map.*

To draw a freehand mapping curve for the active image or selection area:

1. Select a limited area of the image if you want to edit brightness and contrast for a portion of the image. Otherwise, PhotoStyler will edit values for the entire image.
2. Choose the Tune: Gray/Color Map command from the Image menu, or use the keyboard shortcut, F4. The Gray/Color Map dialog box will appear, with the mapping curve shown as a diagonal line. This diagonal shape indicates that you haven't remapped any brightness or contrast values: input values equal output values all along the curve.
3. Move the dialog box out of the way if it obstructs your view of the active image document.
4. Move the mouse cursor into and around the Gray Map area of the dialog box. The cursor will take on the shape of a pencil and the Input and Output values will change as you move the cursor.

Preview

5. Move the cursor to a part of the curve that you want to edit and drag in the desired direction. If your monitor supports animation, you'll see the results of your "drawing" immediately; if you don't, click the Preview command button.
6. Edit additional areas of the curve as desired. Feel free to play with the curve! If you don't like what you've done, you can always go back to the original mapping curve by choosing the Reset command in the Gray/Color Map menu.
7. If you're editing a color image, edit the mapping curve for individual color channels as desired.
8. When you're pleased with your adjustments, click the OK command button to return to the active image document.

Figure 9–12 in the Color Section of this book shows an example of special color effects achieved by creating custom mapping curves for the blue and red channels of an image. The resulting final image is a far cry from the grays, white, and dark blue-black that dominated the original photo of the pelican. Editing the Gray Map is one of our favorite techniques for turning a realistic photograph into a painterly image! Digital artist Emil Ihrig used this technique extensively to enhance several of his images in the PhotoStyler Gallery.

Using Gray/Color Map Menu Commands

Piecewise
Smooth
Gamma...
Logarithm
Equalize
Auto Ranging
Reset
Load...
Save...

A second way to edit the mapping curve in the Gray/Color Map dialog box is to use one or more of the commands in the Gray/Color Map menu. Some of the commands edit the curve automatically, while others start the job and let you finish with the mouse.

Piecewise

The Piecewise command works in combination with the mouse. When you choose Piecewise, PhotoStyler adds handles to the mapping curve as in Figure 9–13. These handles transform the mapping curve into a series of straight-line segments that you can edit by dragging them with the mouse. Shifts in brightness, contrast, and color tend to be dramatic because all changes to the mapping curve are angular.

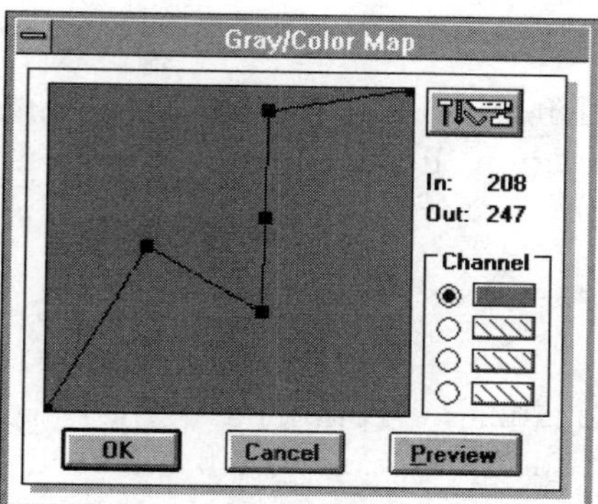

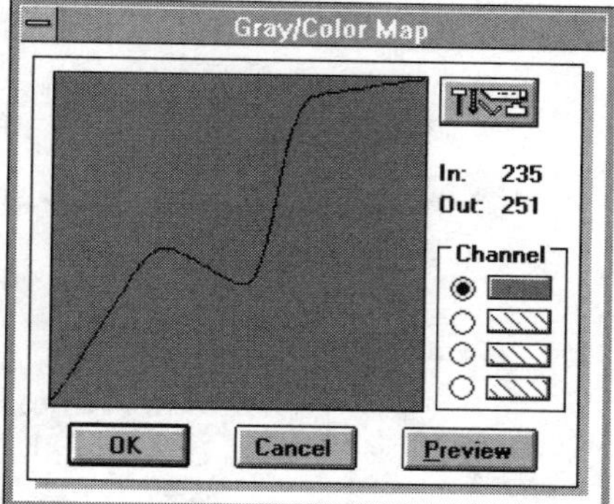

Figure 9-13.

Smoothing out a mapping curve after editing it with the Piecewise command

Smooth

A mapping curve that you've edited using the Piecewise command or the freehand method usually contains sharp angles and/or "jaggies." These jaggies translate into abrupt shifts in brightness, contrast, or color among pixels in a certain value range. To smooth the curve (and the color or Grayscale shifts), apply the Smooth command in the Gray/Color Map menu (Figure 9–13).

Gamma

The Gamma command adjusts the midtones in the image, much like the Gamma scroll bar in the Gray/Color Correction dialog box. When you choose this command, the dialog box in Figure 9–14 will appear, asking you to specify a gamma value. The range of acceptable gamma values is from 0.01 to 7.99. Gamma values below 1.0 will darken the midtones and enhance details in the lighter parts of the image. Gamma values above 1.0 will lighten midtones and enhance details in the darker parts of the image. When you exit the Gamma dialog box, the Gray Map in the Gray/Color Map dialog box will display the new mapping curve adjusted for the gamma value you specified. If your display adapter supports real-time preview, you'll see immediately how the gamma curve has affected the active image document.

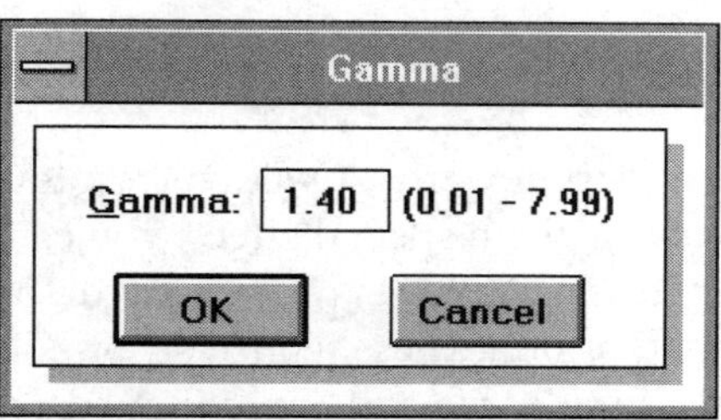

Figure 9-14.

The Gamma dialog box (Gamma command, Gray/Color Map dialog box)

Logarithm

This command changes the mapping curve according to a predefined mathematical function. Its effect is to brighten the midtones and shadow areas of the image in the extreme.

Equalize

Like the Tune: Equalization command in the Image menu, the Equalize command in the Gray/Color Map menu distributes brightness more evenly throughout the active image or selection.

Auto Ranging

This command, like its counterpart in the Gray/Color Correction dialog box menu, limits the input range to the brightness values actually found in the image. This command is the most automatic way to optimize brightness and contrast that we've found.

Reset

The Reset command cancels all changes you've made to the mapping curve and restores the image to its default appearance.

Load, Save

These commands let you save any mapping curve as a file and load it later for use with other images. The next section of this chapter tells you how.

We've found the commands in the Gray/Color Map menu to be an excellent starting point for editing brightness, contrast, and color in an image. After you apply the command of your choice, you can use the mouse to continue editing fine points of the mapping curve.

Saving and Loading Mapping Curves

Experimentation has its rewards. Once you've found the ideal mapping curve to achieve a given special effect, you can save that curve as a file with the extension .GMP. Later, when you open another image with a similar range of brightness, contrast, or color values, you can load your prize mapping curve and apply it automatically.

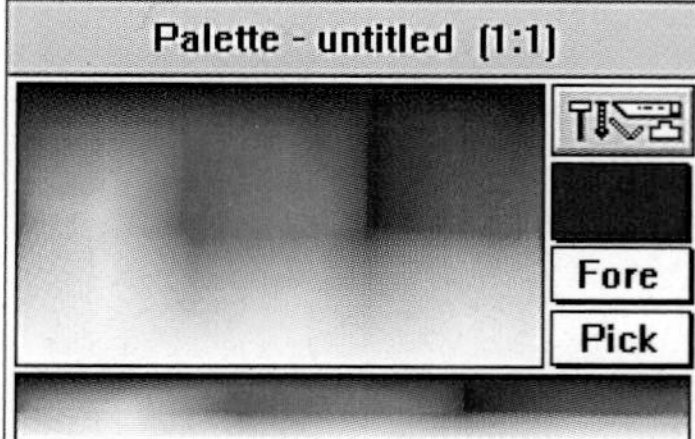

Figure 2–9.
The Color Palette

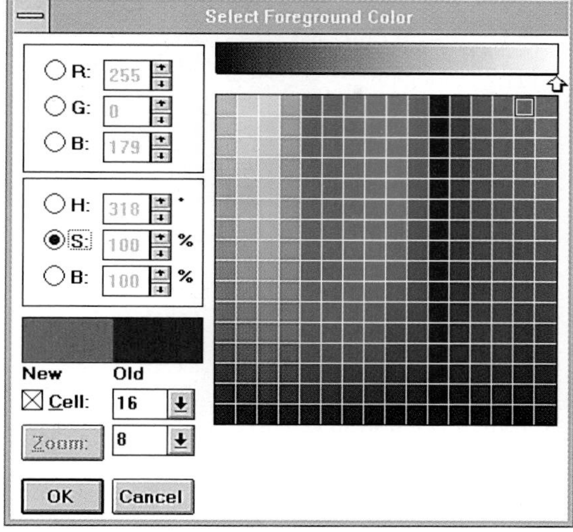

Figure 2–10.
The Color dialog box

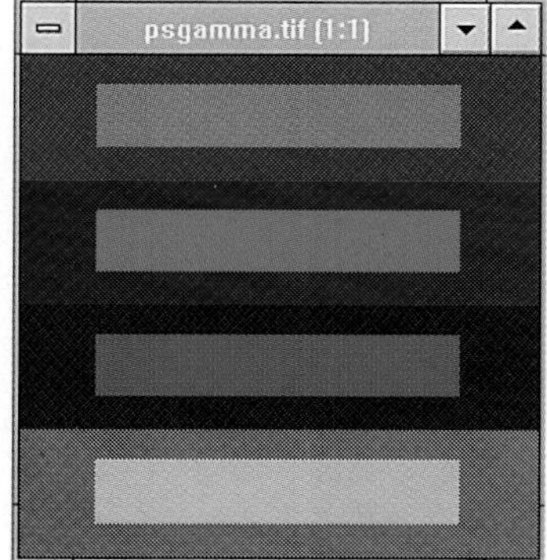

Figure 3–4.
The psgamma.tif file used for calibrating monitors

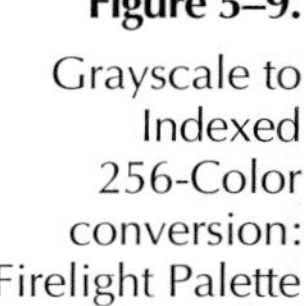

Figure 5–9.
Grayscale to Indexed 256-Color conversion: Firelight Palette

Figure 5–10.
Grayscale to Indexed 256-Color conversion: Pseudo Color Palette

Figure 9–2. An example of special-effects color shifts obtained with the Hue & Saturation dialog box

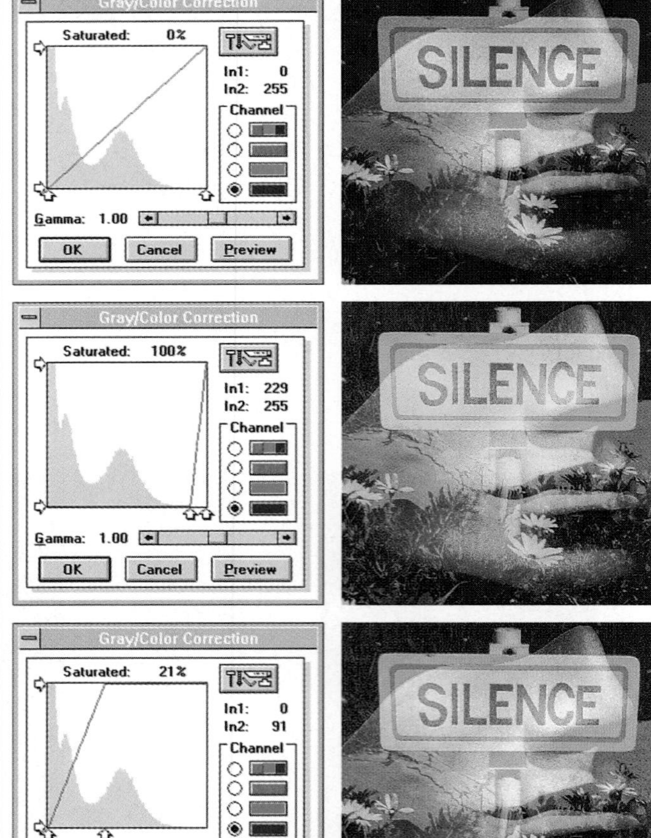

Figure 9–9. Adjusting input values for color channels:

Default mapping curve for the blue channel of an image

Increasing contrast in shadow areas of a color channel: shift toward the complementary color

Increasing contrast in the highlight areas of a color channel: the active channel color intensifies

Figure 9–12.

Painting stylized gray/color maps for special color channel effects

original photo with default Gray/Color Map

after editing the Gray/Color map for the Red and Blue channels

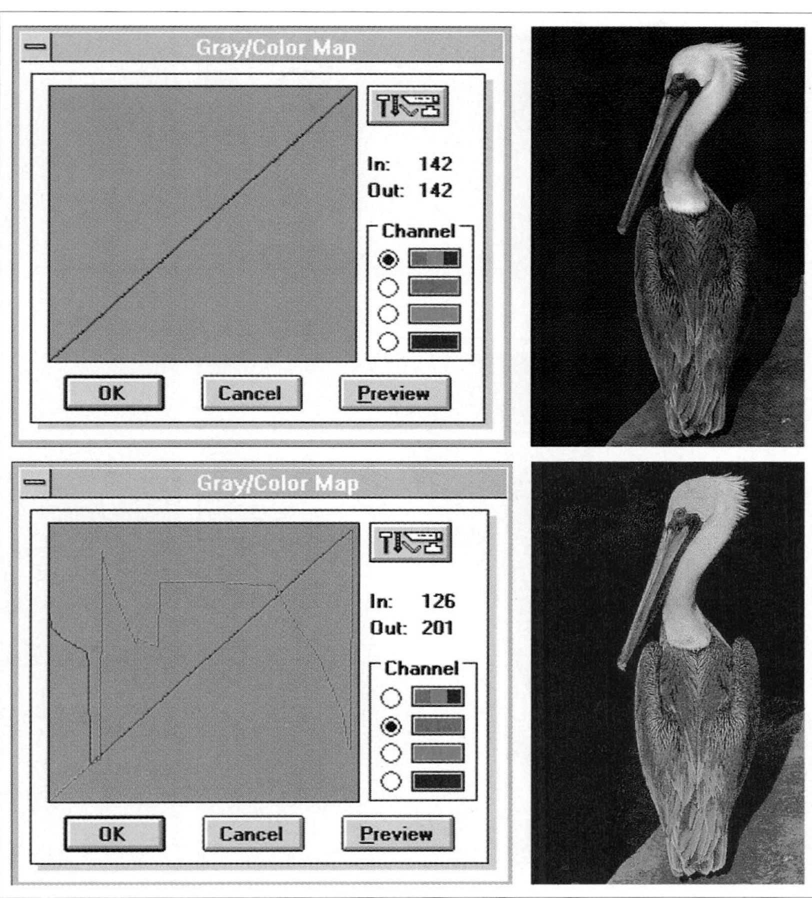

Figure 10–7.

Applying paint with various Use Foreground Color options

Top to bottom:

Always, If Darker, If Lighter, Hue Only, Color Only, Brightness Only, Additive, Subtractive

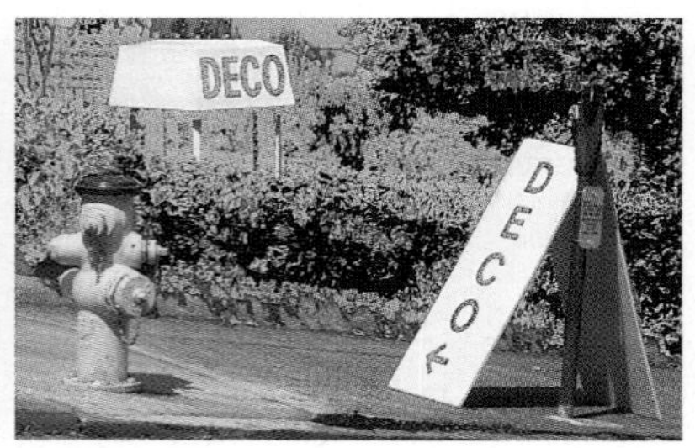

Figure 10–20.
Filling a selected area with the foreground color, Brightness Only (Brightness value 75%)

Figure 10–22.
Filling a selected area with a pattern:

(l) original image with target area selected

(r) Pattern non-aligned, Use Filled Color: Subtractive

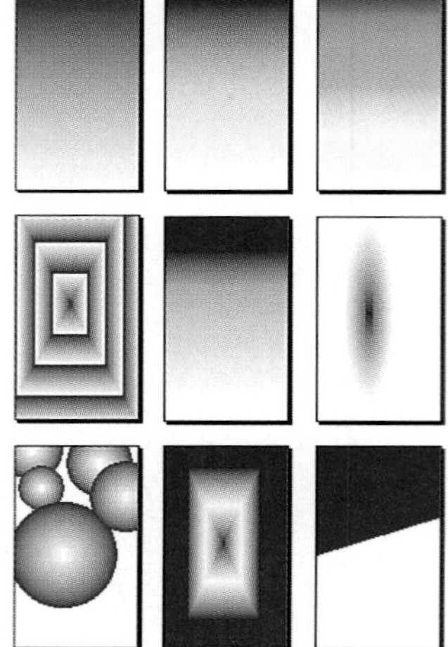

Figure 10–24.
Varying gradient fill settings: *Top, l-r:* RGB, HSB counterclockwise, HSB clockwise *Center, l-r:* repeat time 3, Mixing Control 16-33-88, Expand Ending Colors on *Bottom, l-r:* Expand Ending Colors off, Ping-Pong, Banding

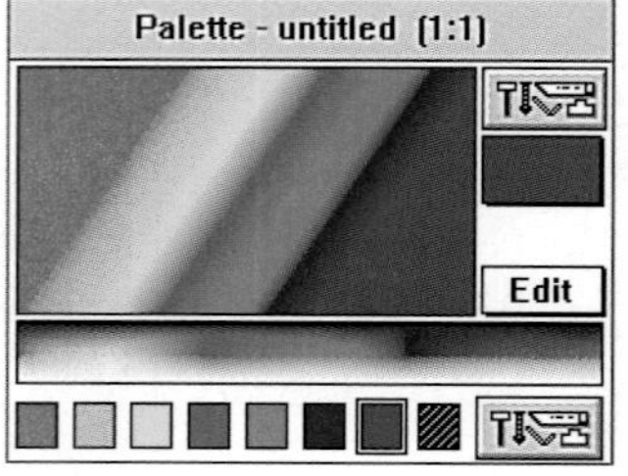

Figure 10–26.
The Custom Colors Palette showing a test gradient fill

Figure 10–29.
Applying Custom Colors gradient fills for painterly effects:

(l): original image

(r) hue190.clr applied to sky, rainbow fill applied to flower

Figure 10–30.
Custom Colors gradient fill effects with text: rainbow custom colors, elliptical fill style

Figure 12–4.
Adding glitter to an image with the Edge Enhancement filter

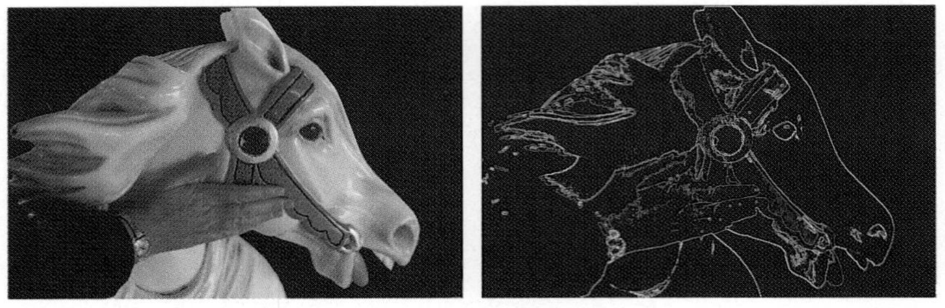

Figure 12–7.

Trace Contour filter effects:

(l) original image
(r) Trace Contour applied with settings of 75, Above, 8-neighbor

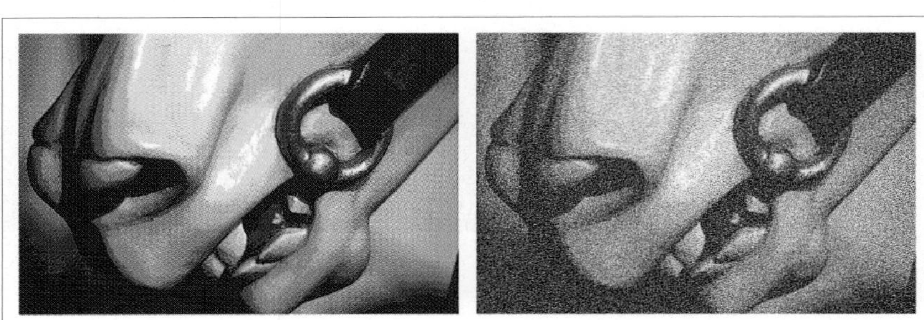

Figure 12–20.

Applying the Add Noise filter for pointillistic color effects:

Variance 150, Distribution Uniform

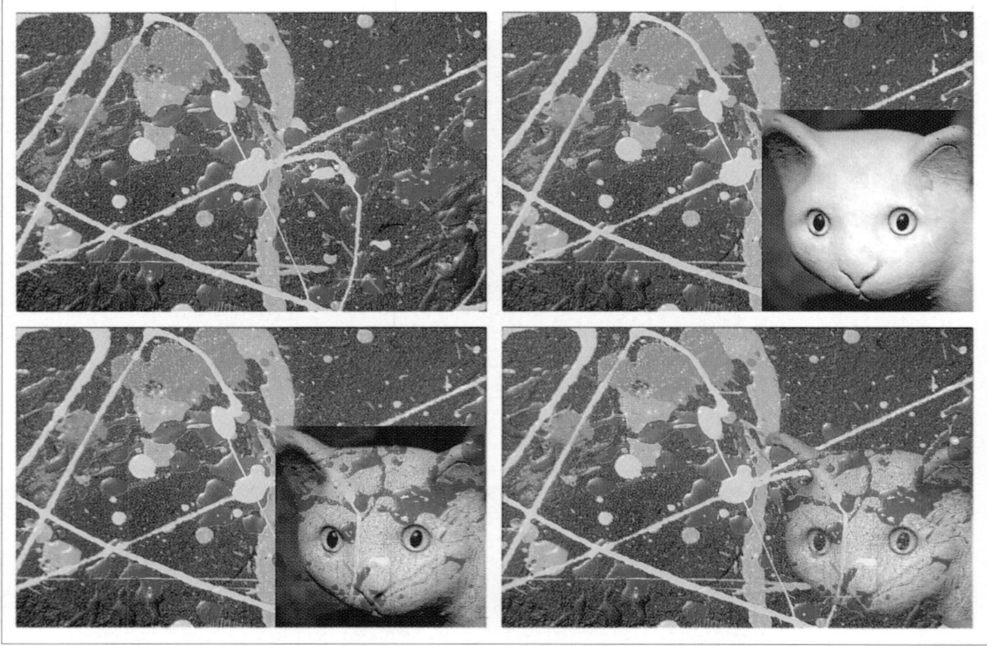

Figure 13–23.

Using the Merge Control command to montage a Grayscale and a True Color image:
Top, l-r: Original True Color image, pasting a Grayscale image
Bottom, l-r: Use Floating image: Brightness Only, removing dark floating image color values (0-44)

Figure 14–7.

Channel substitution:
(l) original, *(c)* RGB = blue, red, green, *(r)* RGB = red, green, red

Figure 14–11.

Substituting a mask for selected image channels:
(l-r): mask substituted for red RGB, blue RGB, and saturation HSB channels

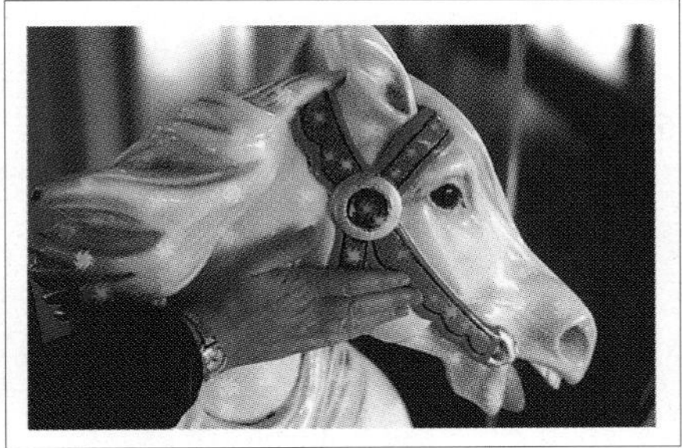

Figure 14–13.

Semitransparent "stars" created by painting in separate RGB channels

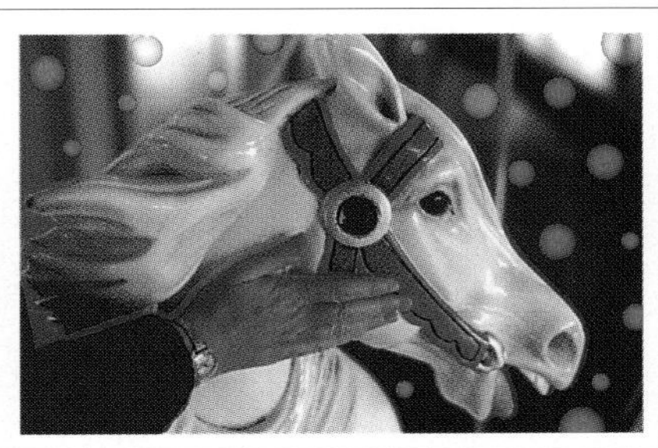

Figure 14–14.

"Neon horse" color effects created by editing red and blue RGB channels

Figure 14–16.

Using the Gaussian Blur filter in the red RGB channel to create drop shadows

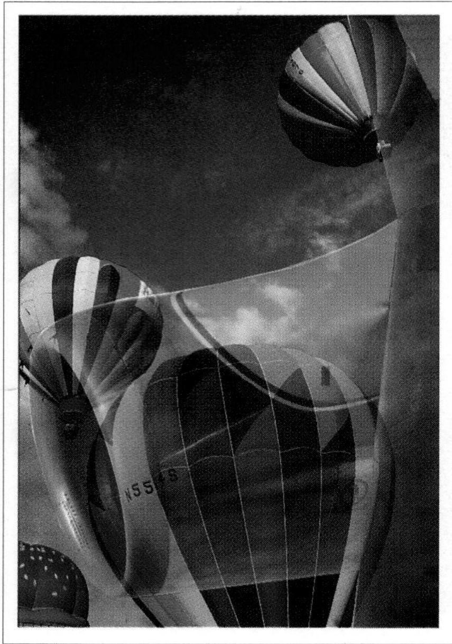

Figure 14–25.

Composite image generated with semitransparent effects (low-contrast mask)

Figure 14–26.

Composite image generated without semitransparent effects (high-contrast mask)

Figure 15–1.

The sizing and spacing of process color halftone dots create the illusion of many colors

halftone screen frequency 133 lpi

halftone screen frequency 65 lpi

cyan channel, 65 lpi

magenta channel, 65 lpi

yellow channel, 65 lpi

black channel, 65 lpi

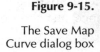

Tip *To keep your mapping curves in order, we suggest storing them in their own subdirectory (for example, MAPCURVE). You might also give them names that associate them with the image or image type to which you first applied them.*

To save a mapping curve as a file:

1. Draw the curve using any combination of commands and freehand techniques in the Gray/Color Map dialog box.
2. Choose Save from the Gray/Color Map menu. The Save Map Curve dialog box in Figure 9–15 will appear.
3. Use the Directories list box to locate the directory where you want to store the mapping curve, and then give it an appropriate name.
4. Click the Save command button. PhotoStyler will save the mapping curve as a file with the extension .GMP.

To load a mapping curved that you've saved and apply it to the active image document:

1. Open the image document to which you want to apply the mapping curve and choose the Tune: Gray/Color Map command from the Image menu.

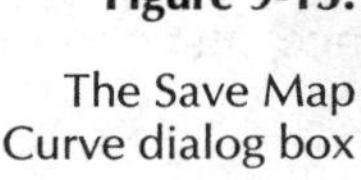

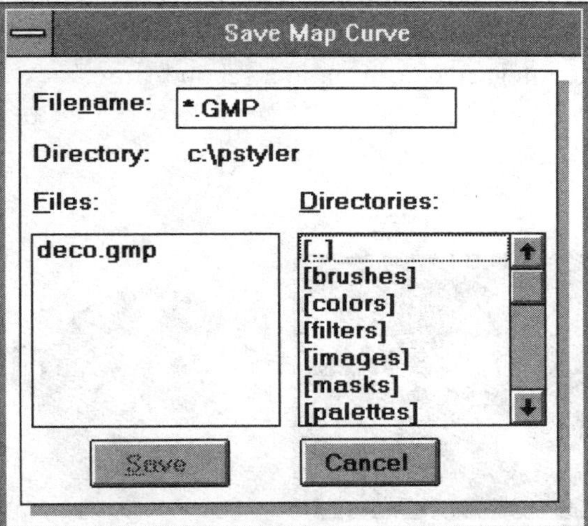

Figure 9-15. The Save Map Curve dialog box

2. Choose the Load command from the Gray/Color Map menu. The Load Map Curve dialog box, similar to the Save Map Curve dialog box, will appear.
3. Change to the directory where the mapping curve you want is located and double-click the desired filename. You will return to the Gray/Color Map dialog box, and the Gray Map will display the new curve. If your display adapter supports real-time animation, you will see the effects of the mapping curve immediately. If you don't see results, click the Preview command button.
4. Continue editing the curve if you wish, or click OK to apply the mapping curve to the active image document.

A custom mapping curve can have unpredictable results when you apply it to images other than the one you first used it with. We suggest using a mapping curve with images that have a similar range of brightness values or coloring.

The remaining sections of this chapter give you a brief tour of the last four commands in the Image/Tune submenu. These commands all let you apply special color or grayscale effects automatically.

Inverting Color or Gray Values

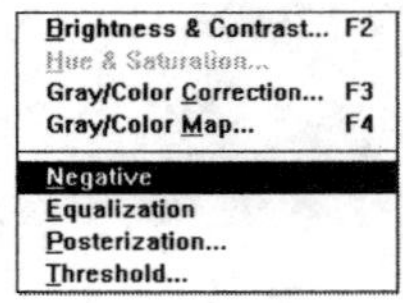

The Tune: Negative command in the Image menu inverts the color and brightness values of every pixel in an image document or selected area. Use this command when you need to create a film negative of an image or when you want to give an image the look of a negative, as in Figure 9–16. To restore an image to its original appearance, just choose the Tune: Negative command a second time.

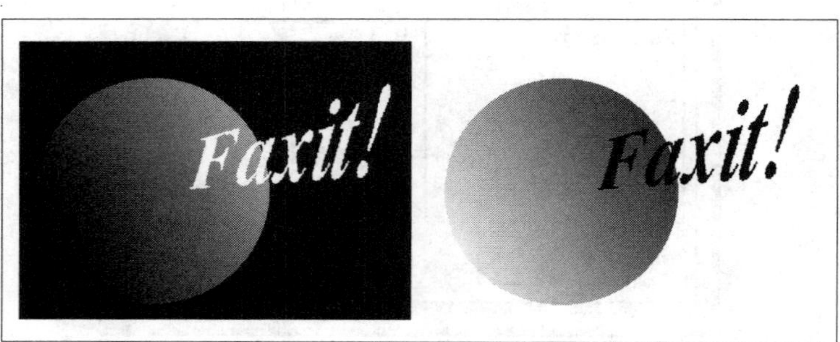

Figure 9-16. Creating a negative of an image

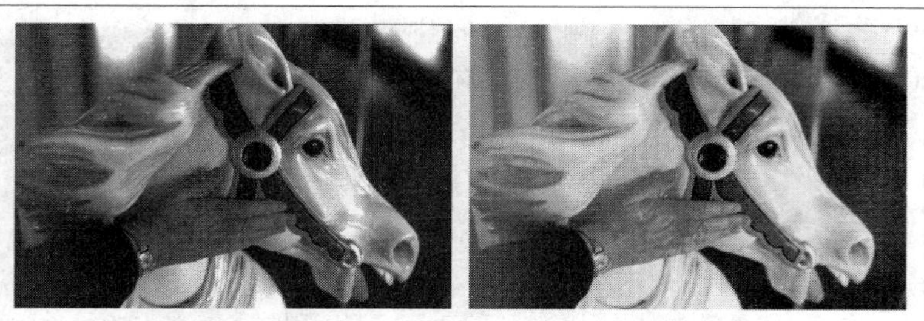

Figure 9-17.

Equalizing the brightness values in an image

Equalizing Color or Gray Values

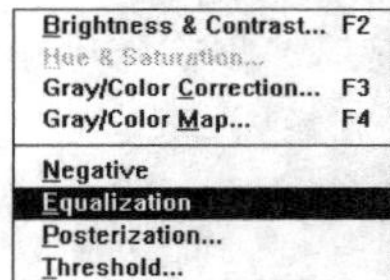

When you choose the Tune: Equalize command from the Image menu, PhotoStyler distributes color or grayscale values evenly throughout the active image document or selected area. The effect is usually to enhance detail in darker or midtone areas of the image (Figure 9–17). To gain a fuller understanding of the process, use the Tune: Gray/Color Correction command to view the histogram before you equalize the image, and then view it again afterward.

Posterizing Images

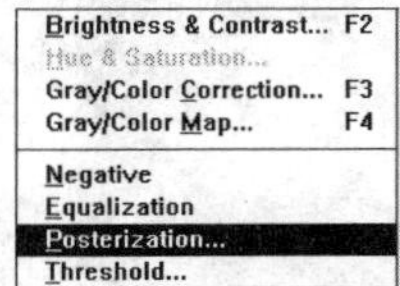

Using the Tune: Posterization command in the Image menu, you can reduce (or optionally, increase) the total number of color or gray levels in the active image document or selection. You do this by changing the number of color or gray values per image channel in the Posterization dialog box (Figure 9–18). Use this command to achieve dramatic high-contrast effects in True Color and Grayscale images.

Grayscale images normally have eight gray levels per channel, which translates to 256 shades of gray. If you reduce the number of

Figure 9-18.

The Posterization dialog box

Posterization

Levels per channel: (2..64)

8

OK | Cancel | Preview

Figure 9-19.

Posterizing a Grayscale image to four levels per channel (16 gray shades)

Above: Original Grayscale image

Below: Posterized image

gray levels to five per channel, for example, the image will contain only $2^5 = 32$ gray shades as in Figure 9–19. True Color images also have eight color levels per channel, but since there are three channels, the total number of colors is 2^{24} or 16.7 million. As you reduce the total number of color levels in a True Color image, you'll achieve increasingly dramatic color effects with higher and higher contrast.

Figure 9-20.

Varying threshold values for Grayscale images

(l) Original image
(c) Threshold 46, Black ratio 75%
(r) Threshold 73, Black ratio 88%

Creating Grayscale Silhouettes

Have you ever wanted to stylize a Grayscale photograph as a silhouette? Then use the Tune: Threshold command in the Image menu. This command, available for Grayscale images only, reduces the total number of gray shades from 256 to two—pure black and white. However, the dialog box associated with this command gives you complete control over the threshold value that determines which pixels become black and which white. Figure 9–20 shows the effects of choosing different threshold values when creating a silhouette from a Grayscale image.

Tip

Attention newsletter publishers! Using the Tune: Threshold command is a great way to stylize your Grayscale images.

The Threshold Dialog Box

Like the Gray/Color Correction dialog box, the Threshold dialog box (Figure 9–21) contains a histogram and a slider handle. The histogram

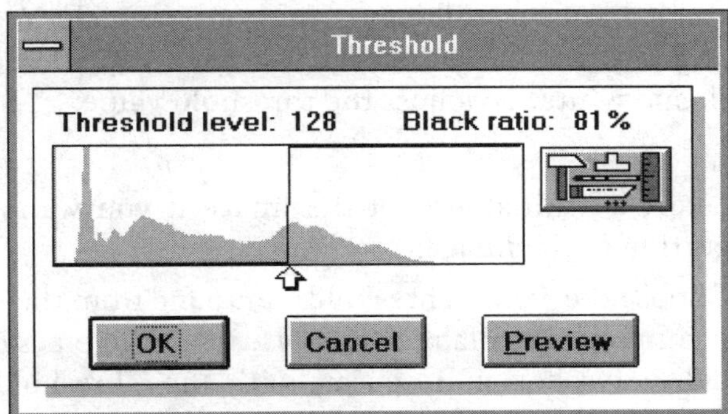

Figure 9-21.

The Threshold dialog box

plots the distribution of gray levels throughout the image or selection. The range of values in the histogram extend from zero (black) at the extreme left edge to 255 (white) at the extreme right edge. The position of the slider handle determines the Threshold level, the Grayscale value that will divide the active image document into black-and-white pixels. Dragging the slider handle changes the current threshold level, which appears in the dialog box just above the histogram. The Black ratio indicator always shows the percentage of pixels that will become black at the current threshold level.

Median
Reset
Enlarge Histogram
Reduce Histogram

The Threshold Menu

The Threshold dialog box also contains a menu with commands that help you adjust the threshold level.

Median The Median command seeks out the threshold level that will result in an image that is approximately 50% black and 50% white. The distribution of gray levels in a particular image determines the median gray level.

Reset Use this command to restore the threshold level to its default of 128.

Enlarge Histogram, Reduce Histogram These commands let you change the magnification level of the histogram in the Threshold dialog box. You can enlarge the histogram up to 16 times for a closer view of gray level distribution. The Reduce Histogram command is available after you've used the Enlarge Histogram command at least once.

Defining the Threshold Value

Creating a stylized silhouette from a Grayscale image is a matter of setting a threshold value that will give you the desired mixture of black and white. To adjust the threshold value:

1. Select a limited area of the image if you want to stylize only a portion of the image.
2. Choose the Tune: Threshold command from the Image menu. This command is available for Grayscale image types only. The Threshold dialog box will appear, with the Threshold level set at the default value of 128 (a medium gray).

3. Drag the slider handle to the left or right to specify the threshold value you want. If you drag the slider handle to the left, the resulting silhouette will contain more white pixels. If you drag the slider handle to the right, the silhouette will contain a higher percentage of black pixels. Watch the Black ratio value to keep track of the black levels in the silhouette.

Preview

4. If your monitor doesn't show real-time animation, click the Preview command button to see how the silhouette will look. Continue adjusting the threshold value if you don't like the results.
5. When you're pleased with the threshold value, click OK.

Many of the tools and concepts behind Aldus PhotoStyler have evolved from the "paint" programs of the past into something much more sophisticated. In the next two chapters, you'll see just how sophisticated and flexible the Paint tools have become, and how they can help you master the twin arts of photo retouching and fine art painting.

10

Painting Tools and Techniques

Painting and retouching operations in PhotoStyler involve many of the same tools and commands, but the philosophies behind them are very different. Painting techniques are the heart and soul of Aldus PhotoStyler's creative resources. When combined with a sound knowledge of filters, masking techniques, and image composition skills (Chapters 8, 12, 13), they let you turn realistic photographs into fine art illustrations. Even if you've never done anything "artistic" with images before, PhotoStyler gives you the power to transmute reality into the realm of the imagination.

Retouching, on the other hand, is a process of improving on reality: making a photograph look more believable, more real (if possible) than the original. Painting often involves high contrast, bright colors, broad brush strokes, and jarring juxtapositions; retouching usually requires painstaking detail work, photo-realism, subtle editing, and the addition of text. That's why we've split a discussion of PhotoStyler's painting and retouching powers into two chapters. This chapter deals with painting, the "creative" side of image editing. Chapter 11 covers retouching tools and techniques, which, though equally creative, are usually the province of commercial art, presentations, and photo-realistic applications.

The "tools" that make painting so powerful in PhotoStyler consist of the Brush Shapes Palette, several tools in the Paint Palette, and a number of commands in the Edit menu. Painting work consists of two distinct kinds of operations:

- *Painting*—Drawing and painting in an image with an emphasis on brush strokes, original (not scanned) images, and/or color
- *Fills*—Filling images and selection areas with solid colors, gradient color transitions, textures, and patterns

Some of these operations are suitable for both realistic photo retouching and graphic or fine art. In this chapter, though, we'll concentrate on their imaginative uses. We also hope to stimulate your imagination by providing examples of how and why you might use each tool or command in the "real world" of image editing and illustration.

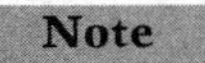

The compositing functions of painting and retouching overlap with Chapter 13. Turn to that chapter if montaging is a special interest of yours.

Paint Palette Basics

PhotoStyler has evolved from the digital "paint" programs of yesteryear to levels of power and sophistication that no mere paint package ever reached. This sophistication is due in part to the precision with which you can specify color values (Chapter 7), select image areas, and manipulate masks (Chapter 8). But another, equally important source of PhotoStyler's power is the number and breadth of options at your disposal for each tool in the Paint Palette.

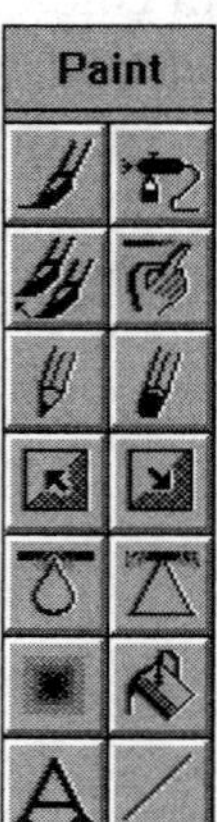

The floating Paint Palette appears at the right side of the application window when you start PhotoStyler. (You can cause it to appear at the left side automatically by using the Preferences command in the File menu.) To move the palette, drag it by its title bar to the desired location. If the application window becomes cluttered, you can remove the Paint Palette from the screen by double-clicking the Paint Palette title bar or choosing the Hide Painting Tools command from the View menu.

The tools in the Paint Palette have two distinct types of functions that sometimes overlap. The Airbrush, Paintbrush, Pencil, Line, Gradient Fill, Bucket Fill, and Text tools function somewhat like the tools in earlier generations of "paint" software, but more powerfully. The

Eraser, Smudge, Blur, Sharpen, Lighten, Darken, and Clone tools are most useful for retouching and restoring images.

Note *Some Paint Palette tools have multiple functions. The Eraser tool, for example, becomes a painting tool when you use it to apply the background color. The Clone tool, normally considered a retouching tool, can also be used to paint areas with patterns from the clipboard. We'll cover both the retouching and painting functions of the Eraser and Clone tools in Chapter 11.*

Activating, Customizing, and Applying the Paint Palette Tools

Most of the Paint Palette tools share common conventions for activating a tool, defining custom options, testing tool settings, and applying the tool in the active image document. We'll review these conventions before we explore the uses of individual tools.

Activating and Customizing a Paint Palette Tool

To activate a Paint Palette tool *without customizing any options*, click its icon once. The icon will darken.

To activate a Paint Palette tool and customize the way it works, *double-click* its icon. A dialog box containing one or more options will appear. After selecting your options, click OK to activate the new settings.

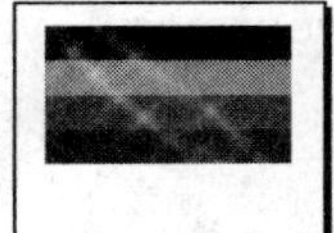

Reset

Scratch Pads

In the world outside your computer, you use a scratch pad to jot down ideas and test sketches before you commit yourself more formally. The scratch pads in many Paint tool dialog boxes serve the same function. Each scratch pad looks different, depending on the function of the tool. After you adjust settings for the tool, you can test their effects in the scratch pad without ever leaving the dialog box. To remove your test painting from the scratch pad, just click the Reset command button in the dialog box.

Applying a Paint Palette Tool

To apply the currently active Paint Palette tool, move the mouse cursor into the active image document. Here, the cursor will take on the shape of either the tool or a crosshair, depending on your settings in the Preferences dialog box. If no part of the image document is selected, you can use the tool anywhere. If the active image document contains a selection area, the tool will work inside the selection marquee *only*. You'll hear a beep tone if you try to apply it elsewhere in the image.

You can apply most of the Paint tools in one of two ways. If you *click* in the image or selected area, you'll change the color or gray values of just a few pixels under the cursor. If you *drag* the mouse, you'll alter pixel values more or less continuously throughout a given area. Some tools, including the Bucket Fill, Gradient Fill, and Text tools, perform their actions by clicking only.

Most dialog boxes associated with the Paint Palette tools share some common elements, too. *Scratch pads* enhance the speed and convenience of your work, while *brush shapes* let you control the way a tool spreads paint.

Working with Brush Shapes

A painter working in traditional media requires a brush in order to move color from the palette to the canvas. The same is true in PhotoStyler. Except for the Gradient Fill and Text tools, every tool in the Paint Palette depends partly for its effect on the *brush shape* with which you apply it. This dependence is most noticeable with the true "painting" tools—the Airbrush, Paintbrush, Pencil, and Line tools—but it applies to other tools as well.

PhotoStyler provides you with a large number of predefined brush shapes from which to choose. If these don't meet all your needs, you can devise and save custom brush shapes.

The Brush Shapes Palette

The Brush Shapes Palette (Figure 10–1) is the tool you use to select, edit, and define brush shapes. You can display this palette in two different ways:

- To display it as a freestanding floating palette, press Ctrl-9 or choose the Show Brush Shapes command from the View menu. The palette will appear and display "Shapes for Painting" in its title bar. To remove the floating Brush Shapes Palette from the screen, press Ctrl-9 again, choose the Hide Brush Shapes command from the View menu, or double-click the palette's title bar.

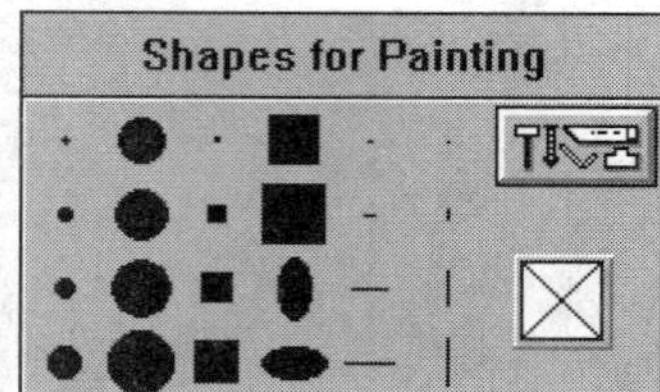

Figure 10-1. The Brush Shapes Palette

- You can also display the Brush Shapes Palette from within any Paint tool dialog box except the Gradient Fill and Text tool dialog box. Just click the Shapes command button in the dialog box, and the Brush Shapes Palette will pop out to the right of the dialog box as in Figure 10–2.

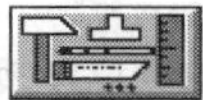

The floating Brush Shapes Palette consists of a title bar, 24 predefined brush shapes, one predefined custom brush shape that you can edit, and a menu (accessed through the toolbox menu icon shown here) with options to help you edit, save, and load custom brush shapes. To move the Brush Shapes Palette to another location, just drag it by its title bar as you would do with any image document.

Selecting a Predefined Brush Shape

The 24 predefined shapes in the Brush Shapes Palette include circular, elliptical, rectangular, square, and linear brush shapes, with the smallest shape being a single pixel. Selecting one of the predefined brush shapes is as easy as clicking on the desired shape with the mouse. A brush shape remains in force from the time you choose it until you select a different one, even if you use multiple Paint tools in the interim.

Brush shapes determine the way a given Paint tool applies paint, though the exact effect will depend on the tool. Figure 10–3 shows examples of using multiple brush shapes with the Paintbrush, Pencil, and Line tools.

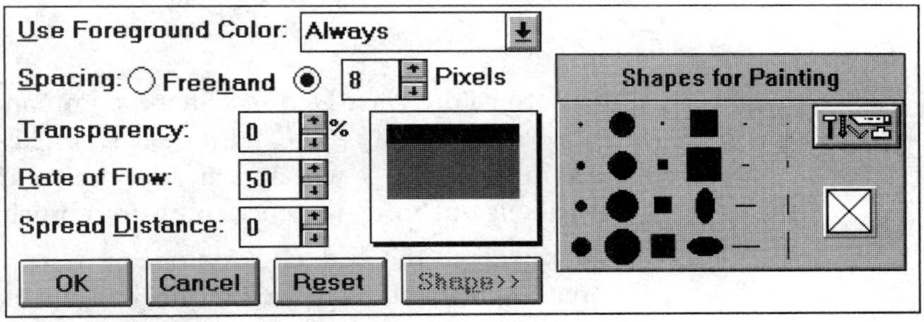

Figure 10-2. Accessing the Brush Shapes Palette from a painting tool dialog box

Figure 10-3.

Three brush shapes applied with the Paintbrush, Pencil, and Line tools

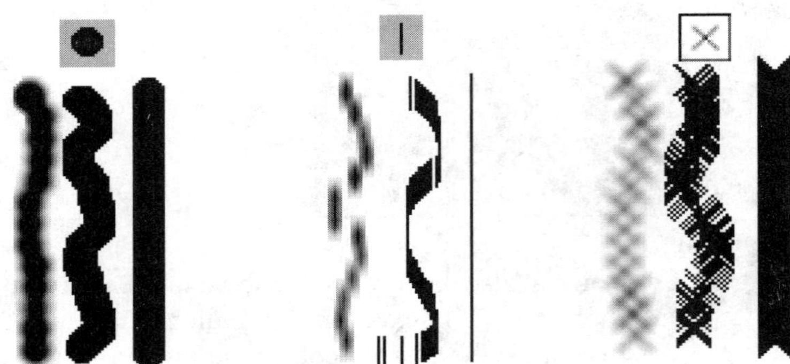

Tip

Use small brush shapes for most realistic photo retouching operations. This kind of retouching requires attention to detail at high viewing magnifications, and a slip of a couple of pixels could mean the difference between perfection and carelessness. Graphic design and fine art, on the other hand, generally allow greater leeway for larger brush shapes and custom brush shape effects.

Editing and Defining Custom Brush Shapes

You don't have to be contented with PhotoStyler's assortment of predefined brush shapes. If your application calls for some special "stroke" effects, you can create and save any number of original brush shapes. You can edit the single custom brush shape provided, design a new one pixel by pixel, or define a brush shape from part of an image.

Editing the Current Custom Brush Shape To the right of the 24 predefined brush shapes is a space for the current custom brush shape. PhotoStyler provides one predefined custom brush shape, but you can create an infinite number of others up to a maximum size of 24 pixels wide by 24 pixels high.

To modify the current Custom brush shape:

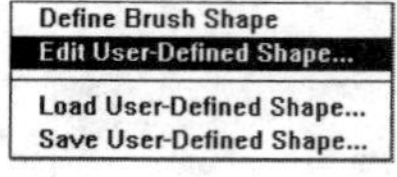

1. Choose the Edit User-Defined Shape command from the Brush Shapes Palette menu. The Edit User-Defined Shape dialog box shown in Figure 10–4 will appear. It contains a grid of black-and-white pixels outlining the current custom brush shape.
2. To add pixels to the grid, click on one or more "blank" white grid squares. Each square you click will fill with a black pixel.

Figure 10-4.

The Edit User-Defined Shape dialog box

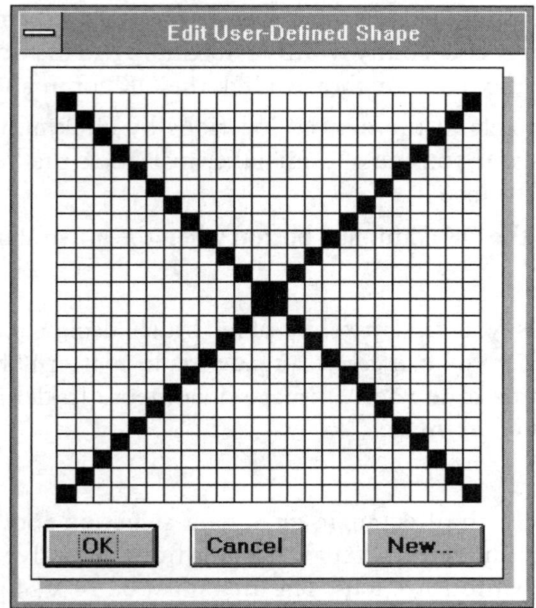

3. To erase pixels from the current custom brush shape, click on the desired black pixels. Each black grid square you click will turn white.
4. To use the new brush shape immediately, click OK and then click on the Custom Brush Shape.

Later, you may wish to save the edited brush shape. See the section, "Saving and Loading Custom Brush Shapes" for details.

Defining a New Custom Brush Shape You may decide you want to design a completely original custom brush shape instead of modifying the current one. There are two ways to do so:

- "Paint" a new brush shape pixel by pixel, or
- Define a brush shape from a selected area of the active image document.

To design an original brush shape pixel by pixel:

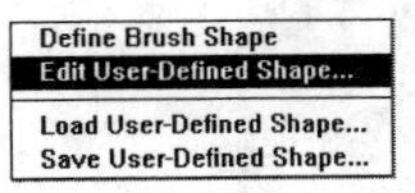

1. Choose the Edit User-Defined Brush Shape command from the Brush Shapes Palette menu.
2. When the Edit User-Defined Brush Shape appears, click the New command button. The New User-Defined Brush Shape dialog box

will appear, asking you to specify the size of the new brush shape. You may choose any width or height up to a maximum of 24 pixels. After making your choice, click the OK command button.

3. Add pixels in the desired locations by clicking in the white grid squares. If you make a mistake, just click the "erroneous" black pixel to erase it.
4. Click the OK command button when the brush shape is satisfactory.

Perhaps you find pixel-by-pixel brush design tedious. The good news is that you can create a ready-made "pattern" brush shape from a small area of the active image document. To define a brush shape from part of an image:

1. Activate the Rectangle or Square selection tool from the Select Palette and select a very small area from the active image document as in Figure 10–5 (left). The area must be 24 x 24 pixels or smaller.

Tip

You'll find it easier to define a small selection area precisely if the Draw Selection from Center option in the Preferences dialog box is active.

2. Display the Brush Shapes Palette, either by pressing Ctrl-9 or double-clicking the selection tool icon and then clicking the Shapes command button.

Define Brush Shape
Edit User-Defined Shape...
Load User-Defined Shape...
Save User-Defined Shape...

3. Choose the Define Brush Shapes command from the Brush Shapes Palette menu. If the current selection area is larger than 24 x 24 pixels, a warning message will appear. If the selection area fits within the required size range, a black-and-white version of the selection area will appear in the custom brush shape space as in Figure 10–5 (center).
4. To use the new custom brush shape immediately, activate the Paint Palette tool that you want to use and then click the Custom Brush

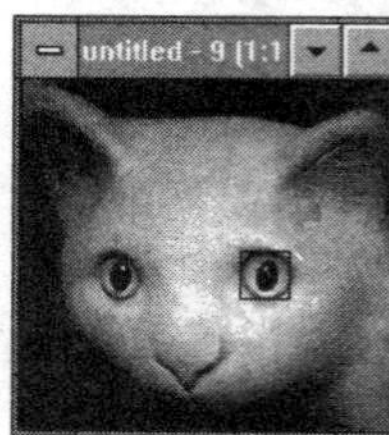

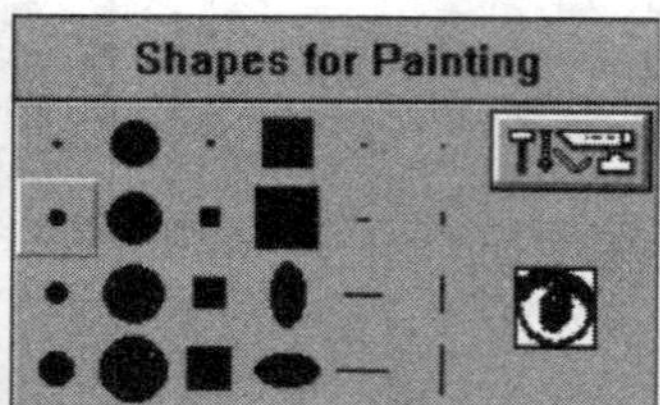

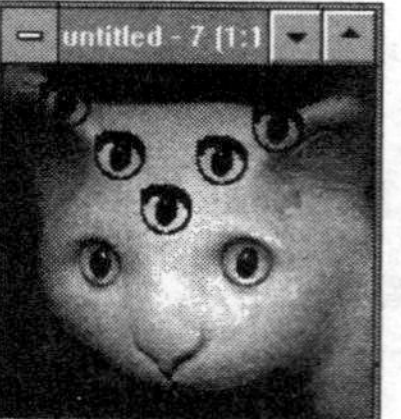

Figure 10-5. Defining a custom brush shape from an image area

Shape in the Brush Shapes Palette. Figure 10–5 (right) shows an example of using the Pencil tool to paint with a pattern brush shape.

Tip

The best candidates for defining brush shapes are high-contrast areas of an image. Remember, PhotoStyler converts all color or gray values in the selection area to black and white when defining a custom brush shape. Subtle gradations, such as the stripes in a low-contrast tie, are likely to be lost, and you'll end up with a blob of black instead of a pattern. When you need to duplicate color or gray values as well as shapes, use the Clone tool discussed in Chapter 11.

Saving and Loading Custom Brush Shapes

PhotoStyler lets you save an infinite number of custom brush shapes. In order to retain a custom brush shape that you've edited, you must save it to a file. Otherwise, you'll lose it when you exit PhotoStyler or edit the custom brush shape again.

To save the current custom brush shape:

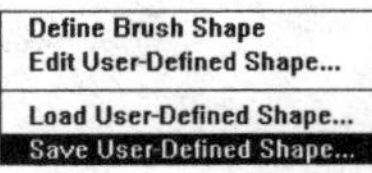

1. Display the Brush Shapes Palette and choose the Save User-Defined Shape command from the Brush Shape Palette menu.
2. In the Save User-Defined Shape dialog box (Figure 10–6), type the name of the new brush shape in the Filename text entry box. Give the brush shape a name that will remind you of its shape or function later. The example brush shapes shown here have the names pinwheel, thikstar, and cinroll.
3. If necessary, use the Directories list box to change to the drive and directory where you want to store the brush shape. We suggest storing all brush shape files in a separate subdirectory named **BRUSHES** or something similar.
4. Click the Save command button. PhotoStyler will save the new brush shape and add the file extension **.SHP** automatically.

To load a custom brush shape that you've saved to a file:

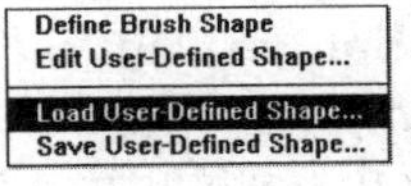

1. Display the Brush Shapes Palette and choose the Load User-Defined Shape command from the Brush Shapes Palette menu.
2. When the Load User-Defined Shape dialog box appears, use the Directories list box to locate the directory where the brush shape is stored.

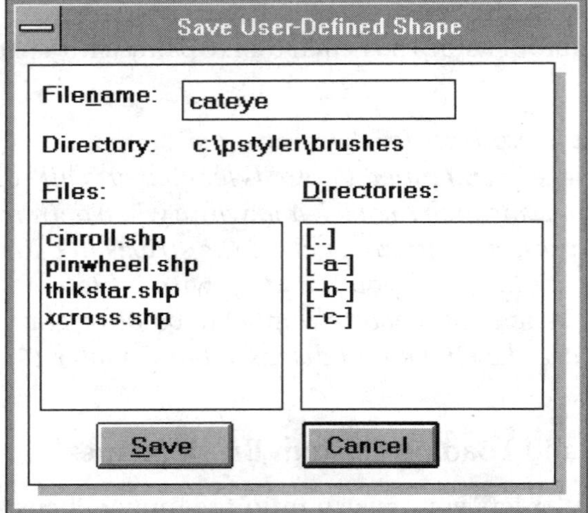

Figure 10-6.

The Save User-Defined Shape dialog box

3. To load the selected brush shape, double-click on its filename, or highlight the desired brush shape filename with the mouse and then click the Load command button. The selected brush shape will appear in the Brush Shapes Palette, displacing the previous custom brush shape.

Now that you're acquainted with the logistics of Paint Palette tools and their dialog boxes, let's explore the tools themselves. We'll look first at the "painting" tools that derive from past generations of paint software. Then, we'll review retouching tools, image composition aids both inside and outside the Paint Palette, and tools and commands that you can use to fill areas with colors or patterns.

Painting with the Airbrush, Paintbrush, Pencil, and Line Tools

The Paint Palette tools that most closely resemble their counterparts in familiar "paint" packages are the Airbrush, Paintbrush, Pencil, and Line tools. (The Bucket Fill tool is an old friend, too, but we want to explore fills in a separate section.) The Airbrush "sprays" paint, the Paintbrush lays it down in a soft-edged path, the Pencil draws it in a hard-edged path, and the Line tool creates a solid line with or without a soft edge (refer back to Figure 10–3).

Tip

In its Erase to Background Color mode, the Eraser is more like a painting tool than a retouching tool. This mode lets you paint with the background color rather than with the foreground color that most other Paint Palette tools use.

Tool Options and Color Effects

The Airbrush, Paintbrush, Pencil, and Line tools share several options in common. These options give you full control over the flow, transparency, spacing, and color or grayscale values of the paint you apply. Here, we'll review just those options that appear in several of the painting tool dialog boxes.

If Darker
If Lighter
Always
Hue only
Color only
Brightness only
Additive
Subtractive

Use Foreground Color

The "paint" that these four tools apply is always the current foreground color or shade of gray. With the help of the Use Foreground Color option, you can control which pixels absorb the color, how evenly the color applies, and which components of the color "soak into" the pixels. Depending on your settings, the Use Foreground Color option can enhance realistic lighting and shadow effects, create impressions of depth or transparency, and make a single foreground color look like multiple colors. Figure 10–7 in the Color Section of this book shows lines painted with each of the eight Use Foreground Color options.

Note

The Always, If Darker, and If Lighter options are available for both True Color and Grayscale images, but all other options are available for True Color images only.

Always When this option is active, the foreground color simply *replaces* the colors or gray shades of the pixels over which the tool passes (see Figure 10–7). Other settings in the tool's dialog box may determine *which* pixels receive the foreground color.

If Darker When you choose this option, the tool will apply paint wherever the foreground color or gray shade is darker than the existing pixels (Figure 10–7). Where the foreground color is lighter than the existing pixels in the image, no paint will appear.

If Lighter When you choose this option, the tool will apply paint wherever the foreground color or gray shade is lighter than the existing pixels in the image (Figure 10–7). Wherever the foreground color is darker than the existing pixels, no paint will appear.

Hue Only (True Color Images) Remember the hue, saturation, and brightness components of color in the HSB color space (Chapter 7)? When you select the Hue Only option, the active tool paints the *hue* of the current foreground color, without changing the current brightness or saturation values of pixels in the image. Choose this option when you want to achieve a luminous look, retaining the current highlighting and shadow effects in the active image document or selection (Figure 10–7).

Color Only (True Color Images) When you select this option, the active tool paints both the *hue* and *saturation* of the current foreground color, without changing the brightness levels of existing pixels in the image. The effect is more opaque than when you use the Hue Only option (Figure 10–7).

Brightness Only (True Color Images) When you paint with Brightness Only selected, the active tool replaces the brightness values of existing pixels with the brightness value of the current foreground color. However, the hue and saturation (the colors) of existing pixels remain unchanged. The effect of using this option is most dramatic when you pass the Paint tool across areas that vary in color, especially if you're using a striking brush shape (Figure 10–7).

Additive (True Color Images) The foreground color looks lighter than it really is when you paint it with the Additive option selected (Figure 10–7). That's because you're *adding* light to the image. PhotoStyler adds the RGB values of the foreground color to the pixels over which the tool passes.

Subtractive The foreground color looks darker than it really is when you paint it with the Subtractive option selected (Figure 10–7). That's because you're *subtracting* light from the image. PhotoStyler subtracts the RGB values of the foreground color from the pixels over which the tool passes.

Spacing

The Spacing option lets you determine *which* pixels will absorb paint as you drag the tool across an image or selected area. This option is unavailable for the Line tool, which automatically paints a continuous line.

- When you set Spacing to Freehand or to a value of zero, paint "drops" according to the speed with which you move your mouse. If you move the mouse quickly across a large area, paint will appear at wide intervals. If you move the mouse slowly, the paint will form an almost continuous line. Only these settings permit variable spacing of paint.

- When you set Spacing to a value between one and 100, paint "drops" at fixed intervals, no matter how quickly or slowly you move the mouse. For example, a setting of 18 would cause a brush stroke to appear regularly at every 18th pixel. You can generate special effects by combining fixed-interval spacing with a custom brush.

Transparency

The Transparency setting appears in the dialog boxes of all four painting tools. It lets you determine how much of the paint "shows through" the colors or gray shades of the existing pixels in the image. The range of transparency is from 0% (opaque) to 99% (almost invisible).

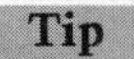

A high degree of transparency is useful for creating impressionistic effects. You can achieve special effects by experimenting with combinations of Transparency and Use Foreground Color settings.

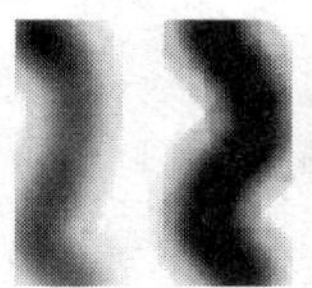

Rate of Flow

The Rate of Flow option is available for the Airbrush and Paintbrush tools only. It lets you control how paint "behaves" when you move your mouse slowly or hold it still. When you set Rate of Flow to zero, no paint buildup occurs, no matter how long your hold the mouse in one place. As you increase the value up to a maximum of 100, paint builds up more and more quickly. A high value causes paint to spread out and saturate neighboring pixels in the image.

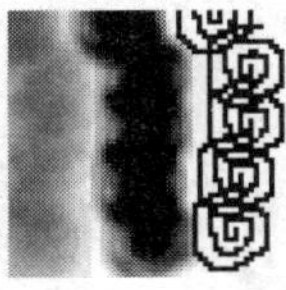

A Note on Brush Shapes

Each of the four "traditional" painting tools applies paint in a unique way. A given brush shape will have one effect when used with the Airbrush, another when wielded by the Paintbrush, and still another when applied by the Pencil or Line tool (see Figure 10–3). Make a habit of experimenting with several different painting tools for each brush stroke that you use.

Airbrush Tool Tips

The Airbrush tool "sprays" paint with a soft-edged effect. Paint is denser and more opaque at the center of the brush "stroke" and begins to blend with the background pixels as it approaches the outer edge. This fade-out effect occurs because the Airbrush always uses an enlarged version of the current brush shape.

Because of its soft edge, the Airbrush is ideal for image areas that require an impressionistic treatment of color or a dispersed handling of light and shadow. You can vary the spacing, transparency, rate of flow, and use of color in the Airbrush Options dialog box (Figure 10–8) to achieve softer or more dramatic effects.

Tip

To create the special "starry night" effect in Figure 10–9, we used a custom brush shape and set the Airbrush for a high rate of flow and a moderate degree of transparency. To create the stars in the foreground, we held the mouse in a stationary position for some time. The high rate of flow caused these foreground stars to appear thicker, brighter, and nearer. To create the stars in the background, we held the mouse stationary for shorter periods of time.

Tip

The Airbrush can also be useful for retouching applications. Spray an area with the Airbrush and then use the Smudge tool to blend in the color you applied. The effect will be softer than if you used a different painting tool.

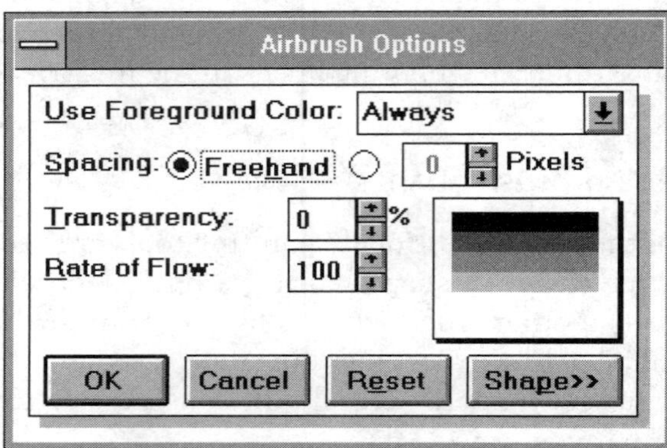

Figure 10-8. The Airbrush Options dialog box

Figure 10-9.

Creating a starry night effect with the Airbrush at a high rate of flow

Paintbrush Tool Tips

Both the Paintbrush and the Airbrush apply paint with a soft edge. However, color applied with the Paintbrush seems thicker or heavier because fade-out from the center to the edge of the brush stroke is less dramatic.

Actually, the Paintbrush tool has its *own* kind of fade-out, thanks to the Spread Distance option in its dialog box (see Figure 10–10). This option lets you simulate various levels of manual pressure and differing amounts of paint on the brush. If you set Spread Distance to zero (infinite) or 100 (the maximum value), you can apply paint for what seems like forever and it will never trail off. If you set Spread Distance to a very low value, you'll seem to "run out of" paint after dragging the mouse only a short distance. As you increase the Spread Distance value, the distance you can drag the mouse before running out of paint will increase.

The other options in the Paintbrush Options dialog box are similar to Airbrush tool options.

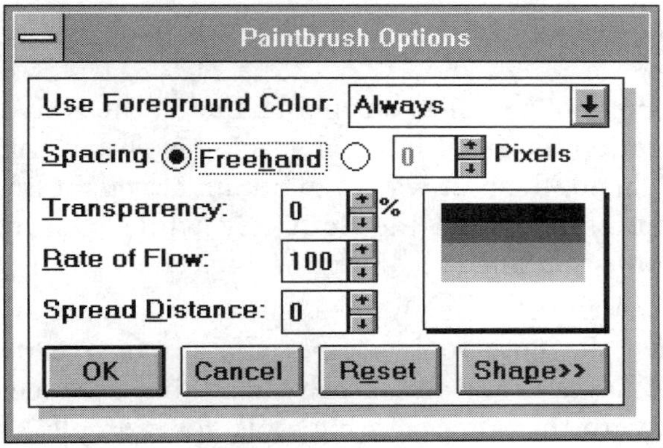

Figure 10-10.

The Paintbrush Options dialog box

Paintbrush Options

Use Foreground Color: Always

Spacing: Freehand 0 Pixels

Transparency: 0 %

Rate of Flow: 100

Spread Distance: 0

OK Cancel Reset Shape>>

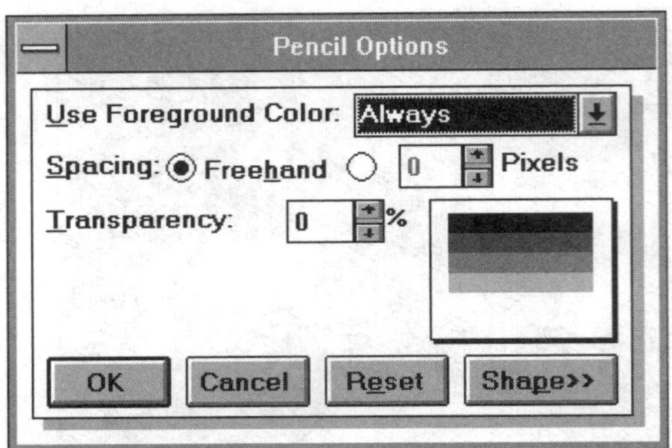

Figure 10-11.

The Pencil Options dialog box

Pencil Tool Tips

Unlike the Airbrush and Paintbrush tools, the Pencil applies paint with a hard edge. This hard edge makes the Pencil well suited for drawing and painting well-defined objects or brush strokes. Figure 10–3 illustrates the difference between the tool "strokes" clearly. The same brush shape creates stars when used with the Airbrush, snowflakes when used with the Paintbrush, and crisp geometrical design with the Pencil. The Pencil Options dialog box in Figure 10–11 contains no Rate of Flow option: you can't thicken or spread paint by holding the mouse stationary or moving it slowly.

Precisely because of its hard edge, the Pencil tool can be used to create "clones" of a small image area. First, define a custom brush shape from a small image area and make that the current brush shape. Then, set Spacing for the Pencil tool to a fixed interval of pixels, and "paint" the tiny clone in the current image document or selection.

Line Tool Tips

The Line tool paints a *continuous* line in the active image document or selection; no fixed-interval spacing is possible. Unless you have a steady hand, the best way to maintain a straight line free of "jaggies" is to press and hold the Shift key while painting. The Shift key constrains the line to a 45-degree angle.

Although the Line Options dialog box (Figure 10–12) contains few options, the Line tool is especially responsive to unusual custom brush shapes. The same brush shape that produced stars and snowflakes with the other painting tools, for example, creates some inter-

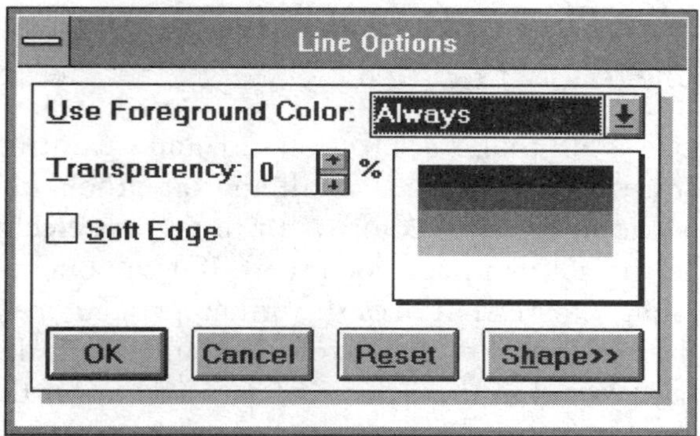

Figure 10-12. The Line Options dialog box

esting geometry with the Line tool. Add a feathery Soft Edge to such a line, and you can improvise further.

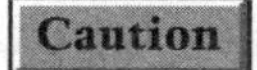

Lines drawn at a low image output resolution or at angles other than zero, 45, or 90 degrees may show visible "stair-stepping" jaggies. To reduce their visibility, specify a soft edge for the line.

The traditional "painting" tools we've seen so far in this chapter generate their effects by applying color and brush strokes to a few pixels at a time. Let's turn our attention to the way PhotoStyler handles fills and patterns—a particularly rich area for creative exploration, and one that lets you alter large areas of an image with a single click of the mouse.

Using Patterns and Fills in PhotoStyler

PhotoStyler gives you a multitude of choices for filling areas of an image with a color or pattern. Three Paint Palette tools and several Edit menu commands provide you with many flexible, creatively stimulating options:

- The Bucket Fill tool uses the current foreground color, filling areas selectively according to color similarity.

- The Clone tool (Chapter 11) lets you fill areas selectively with any predefined or custom pattern.
- The Fill command lets you fill areas with a broad variety of colors or patterns.

- With the Gradient Fill tool, you can fill areas with smooth transitions between sets of up to eight custom colors.

The Bucket Fill Tool: Filling Areas Selectively with the Current Foreground Color

The Bucket Fill tool is a selection tool and a painting tool in one. Like the Airbrush, Paintbrush, Pencil, and Line tools, the Bucket Fill tool applies the foreground color to an image or selected area when you click in the active image document. But the Bucket Fill tool uses no brush shape. Instead, it uses the principle of *color similarity* to determine automatically which pixels it should fill. In this respect, it's like the Magic Wand in the Select Palette. The lower the color similarity value you define, the more limited the fill area will be. The higher the color similarity value, the further the fill area will extend.

Bucket Fill Options

When you double-click the Bucket Fill icon, you access the Bucket Fill Options dialog box (Figure 10–13). The options in this dialog box give you complete control over the extent, opacity, and softness of the fill color.

Color Similarity The Color Similarity value works with the placement of your mouse cursor to define the extent of a fill. Valid values range from zero to 255. With a low value, PhotoStyler will fill only those pixels that hardly deviate in color from the pixel on which you click. As the color similarity value increases, the filled area will extend further and further from the click point. A maximum Color Similarity value of 255 will cause PhotoStyler to fill the entire selected

Figure 10-13.

The Bucket Fill Options dialog box

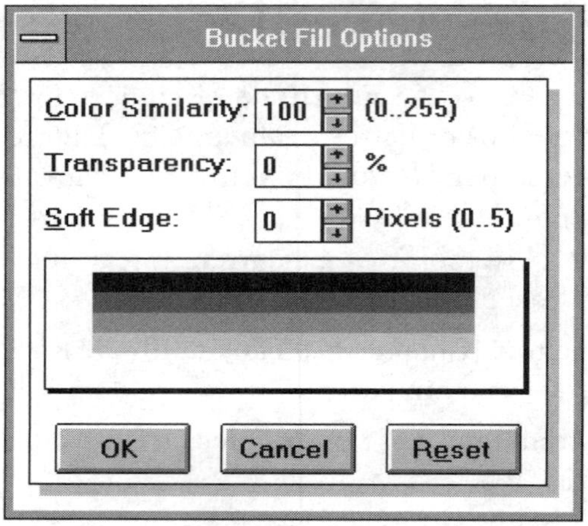

Figure 10-14. Painting in a selected area with the Bucket Fill tool

(l) Color Similarity 100: paint applies to only part of the selected area; *(r)* Color Similarity 255: paint applies to the entire selected area

area. Figure 10–14 shows how varying the Color Similarity value will change the extent of a fill.

Transparency You can define a Transparency value from zero (opaque) to 99 (almost totally transparent). As the Transparency value increases, the foreground color used as a fill will become more transparent, and more of the existing pixel colors will show through.

Soft Edge This is an anti-aliasing setting that lets you control how smoothly the edges of a fill will blend with neighboring pixel colors. At the default setting of zero, the fill color will end abruptly. As you increase the Soft Edge value to a maximum of five pixels, the edges of the fill will fade out more and more softly.

Bucket Fill Tips and Color Effects

Variations in Color Similarity, Transparency, and Soft Edge settings can produce an almost infinite variety of Bucket Fill effects. Here are just a few tips that may enhance your mastery of the Bucket Fill tool.

Filling Text Strings or Varicolored Selection Areas A text string contains multiple selection areas, one for each letter. If the text outlines overlay an area of an image that contains multiple color or grayscale transitions, set Color Similarity for the Bucket Fill tool to

255. This setting ensures that PhotoStyler will fill the entire text string on the first click. Use the same setting when you want to fill any selection area that extends over multiple color transitions.

Tinting Areas Selectively You can combine Color Similarity, Transparency, and Soft Edge settings to apply soft *tints* of a color selectively within an image. This technique is especially effective for highlighting minor variations in color and lighting, such as we see in a person's hair. If you use a low Color Similarity setting, the fill will stop automatically as soon as PhotoStyler encounters a significant change in color or grayscale values.

Defining, Loading, and Saving Patterns

Both the Fill command and the Clone tool let you fill areas with patterns as well as with solid colors or grays. PhotoStyler provides nine predefined pattern textures with your software. If these aren't enough, you can always define custom patterns from any image document and build your own library of pattern files.

Note *Pattern fills are available for RGB True Color and Grayscale images only.*

Defining a Pattern

Using the Define Pattern command in the Edit menu, you can turn any rectangular selection area of a True Color or Grayscale image document into a custom pattern. PhotoStyler stores the current custom pattern temporarily in a special clipboard. Unless you save it as a file, however, a custom pattern will be lost when you define another one or exit PhotoStyler. See the "Viewing, Loading, and Saving Patterns" section immediately following this one for information on how to save a custom pattern for later use.

To define a custom pattern for use during the current session:

1. Activate the image document that contains the area you want to define as a pattern.
2. Activate the Rectangle or Square selection tool in the Select Palette.

3. Move the cursor into the active image document and select the rectangular or square area that contains the pattern.
4. Here's an optional step if the selection area is too "busy" and you need to streamline its contents before making a pattern out of it. Choose the Make Floating command from the Edit menu and then edit the selection area using any combination of tools and commands. Since you're working with a floating selection, the changes you make won't affect the underlying image. Figure 10–15 shows a rectangular selection area and the same selection area after applying the Make Floating command, resizing the selection area, and editing the dark cherry out of it. Note that the underlying image hasn't changed.
5. Choose the Define Pattern command from the Edit menu. PhotoStyler will transfer the image data immediately into the PhotoStyler Pattern clipboard.
6. If you've edited the selection area in order to prepare the pattern (step 4), choose the Discard Floating command from the Edit menu.

Now, you're ready to use the new custom pattern with the Fill command or Clone tool. If you want to view the pattern before using it, you'll need to choose the Pattern command in the Edit menu.

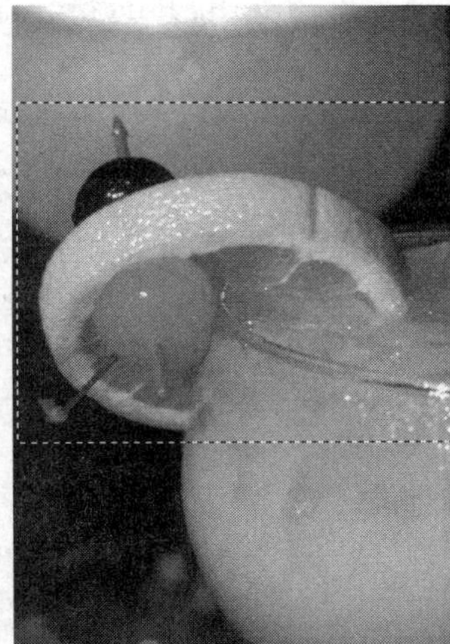

Figure 10-15.

Defining a pattern from a rectangular selection area: *(l)* the unedited selection area; *(r)* selection area floating, resized, and streamlined

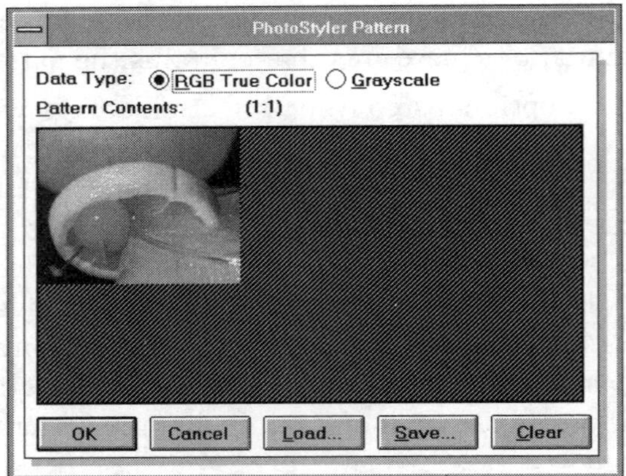

Figure 10-16.

The PhotoStyler Pattern dialog box

Viewing, Loading, and Saving Patterns

The Pattern command in the Edit menu serves several functions. It lets you:

- View a custom pattern that you've created using the Define Pattern command
- Save a custom pattern to a file for later use
- Load a predefined pattern or a custom pattern that you've already saved

When you choose the Pattern command, the PhotoStyler Pattern dialog box shown in Figure 10–16 will appear. If you've defined or loaded a pattern at least once during the current session, that pattern will appear in the viewing area. If no pattern appears here, you'll need to load one before you can use it with the Fill command or Clone tool.

Loading a Pattern To load a predefined pattern or one you've already saved:

1. Choose the Pattern command from the Edit menu. When the PhotoStyler Pattern dialog box appears, click the RGB True Color or Grayscale button according to the way you want pattern data to display.
2. Click the Load command button in the PhotoStyler Pattern dialog box. The Load Pattern File dialog box shown in Figure 10–17 will appear.
3. Change to the directory where the pattern file you need is located. The nine predefined pattern files are in the \patterns subdirectory and have the extension .PAT.

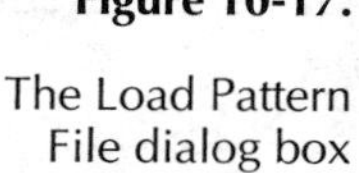

Figure 10-17.

The Load Pattern File dialog box

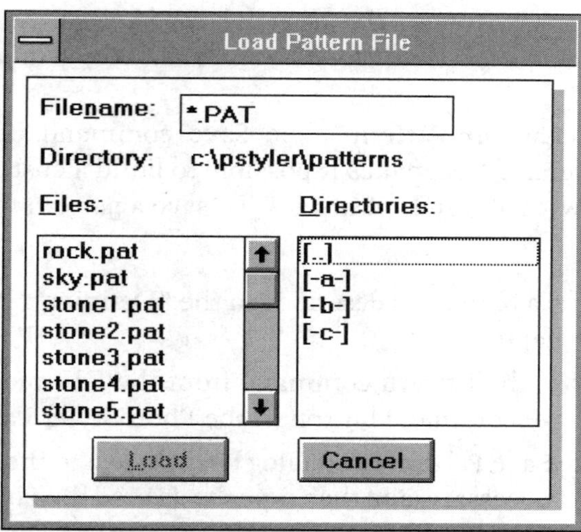

4. To select and load a pattern file, double-click its filename. The pattern will appear in the viewing area of the PhotoStyler Pattern dialog box, aligned with the top left corner of the image area. It will appear in color or grayscale according to the radio button you chose in step 1.

Viewing a Pattern Patterns are always at a 1:1 viewing magnification when you first load them. Before applying a pattern, you may wish to see it at a different viewing magnification or change its data type to match the active image document.

To change the viewing magnification of the pattern, move the cursor over the image itself. Here, it takes on the appearance of the Zoom tool cursor.

- Clicking the left mouse button *increases* the magnification by a factor of one. The maximum view is 16:1.
- Pressing Shift as you click the left mouse button *decreases* the viewing magnification by a factor of one. The minimum view is 1:16.
- To change back to a 1:1 viewing magnification instantly, click the *right* mouse button once.

The Pattern Contents indicator just above the viewing area always shows the current viewing magnification.

Tip

A pattern takes up system memory when it's being stored in the PhotoStyler Pattern dialog box. When you no longer need the current pattern, choose the Pattern command and then select the Clear command button in the dialog box. This action will remove the pattern and make additional system memory available.

Saving a Custom Pattern The Save command in the PhotoStyler Pattern dialog box makes it possible to build a custom pattern library for use with all kinds of images. To save a pattern to a file:

1. Define a pattern as described in the "Defining a Pattern" section of this chapter.
2. Choose the Pattern command from the Edit menu and then click the Save command button in the PhotoStyler Pattern dialog box.
3. In the Save Pattern File dialog box, change to the \pattern subdirectory if necessary, and then type the desired filename in the Filename text entry box. PhotoStyler will add the .PAT extension automatically when you save the file.
4. Click the OK command button to save the pattern as a file. You'll return to the PhotoStyler Pattern dialog box. Click OK again to exit the dialog box.

Patterns are only one fill option available for the Fill command. In the next few sections, you'll find out how to make the most of *all* the Fill command options.

Using the Fill Command

The Fill command in the Edit menu gives you the broadest range of fill options in all of PhotoStyler. For Black & White, Indexed Color, and RGB 8-Color images, it's also the *only* command or tool you can use to fill image areas. The greatest range of options is available for RGB True Color and Grayscale image data types. Table 10–1 shows the options available to each image data type through the Fill command.

Choosing Fill Dialog Box Options

When you choose the Fill command, the Fill dialog box in Figure 10–18 will appear. The options available to you depend on three factors:

- The data type of the active image document—Table 10–1 gives an overview of how the data type of the active image document influences the available options.

Table 10–1. Fill Command Options Available for Each Image Data Type

Fill Options	Data Type			
	B/W	Grayscale	Indexed Color	RGB True Color
Use Filled Color		✓		✓
Foreground Color	✓	✓	✓	✓
Background Color	✓	✓	✓	✓
Black	✓	✓	✓	✓
White	✓	✓	✓	✓
Gray		✓		
RGB Color				✓
Indexed Color			✓	
Pattern (Aligned)		✓		✓
Pattern (Non-Aligned)		✓		✓

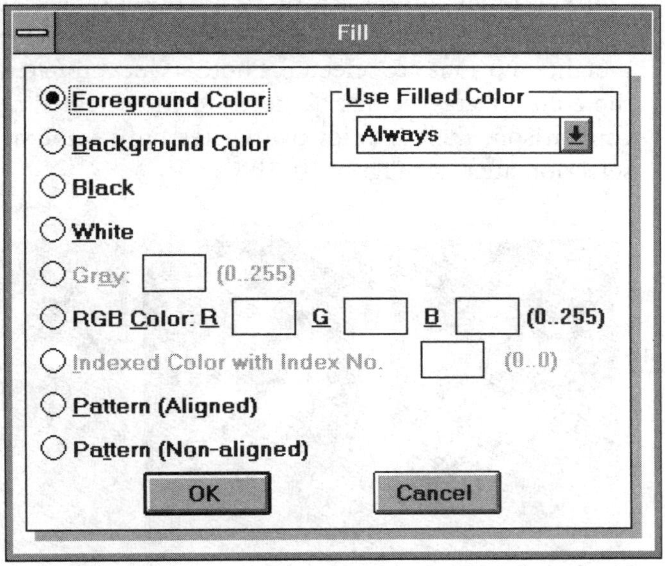

Figure 10-18.
The Fill dialog box

Fill
Foreground Color
Use Filled Color
Always
Background Color
Black
White
Gray: (0..255)
RGB Color: R G B (0..255)
Indexed Color with Index No. (0..0)
Pattern (Aligned)
Pattern (Non-aligned)
OK
Cancel

- The presence of a pattern in the PhotoStyler Pattern dialog box—The Pattern (Aligned) and Pattern (Non-Aligned) options are available only when you've loaded a pattern into the PhotoStyler Pattern dialog box or defined a pattern during the current session.
- Whether you're applying the fill to a selection area or to an entire image document—Oops! If you haven't defined a selection within the active image document, the fill color or pattern you choose will overwrite every pixel in the image. The Use Foreground Color option, which makes special color effects and semi-transparent patterns possible, is available *only* if you've defined a selection. If you want to apply one of these special effects throughout an image, select the entire image using the A button at the base of the Select Palette.

The Foreground Color, Background Color, Black, White, Gray, RGB Color, and Indexed Color options are self-explanatory. We'll devote special attention to the Use Filled Color and Pattern options, which let you enhance an image with special color or transparency effects.

If Darker
If Lighter
Always
Hue only
Color only
Brightness only
Additive
Subtractive

Special Effects with the Use Filled Color List Box

The Use Filled Color drop-down list box is available for True Color and Grayscale images only, and only when these images contain a selection area. This option works like the Use Foreground Color option in the painting tool dialog boxes; you may want to review the section on those tools.

If you're applying a fill to an area of a Grayscale image, you can choose from Always, If Darker, and If Lighter. When the If Darker or If Lighter options are selected, PhotoStyler compares the fill color with the color or gray values of pixels in the selected area. Based on that comparison, the fill color overwrites only some of the pixels in the selection area (see Figure 10–19).

Figure 10-19.

Use Foreground Color settings, Fill command

(l) Background of hydrant selected
(c) If Darker
(r) If Lighter

If you're working with a True Color image, you have an even richer array of choices at your disposal. The Hue Only, Color Only, and Brightness Only options isolate components of the selected fill color, which you can then apply semi-transparently to the selection area. The Additive and Subtractive options apply the selected fill color brighter or darker than it was originally. Figure 10–20 in the Color Section of this book shows an example of special color effects created with the help of the Use Foreground Color: Brightness Only setting. Initially, we selected the foliage and other elements in the original image using the Magic Wand tool (see Chapter 8) and then generated the mask shown in Figure 10–21. Finally, we imported the mask and applied the Fill command.

Special Effects with Pattern Fills

The two pattern options in the Fill dialog box are available only when you've defined a pattern during the current session or loaded one into the PhotoStyler Pattern dialog box using the Pattern command. When you choose the Pattern (Aligned) option, the fill pattern aligns itself with the upper left corner of the image document, no matter where the selection area lies. On the other hand, the Pattern (Non-Aligned) command aligns the pattern tiles with the upper left corner of the current selection area.

Both the Fill command and the Clone tool let you apply any predefined or custom pattern as a fill, but they work in different ways. The Fill command applies the pattern throughout the image or selected area. The Clone tool (Chapter 11) lets you apply the pattern

Figure 10-21. A mask used to select an area for Brightness Only fill (see Figure 10-20, Color Section)

selectively, controlling the location and frequency of the pattern by the movement of your mouse.

The Fill command definitely has the advantage over the Clone tool when it comes to special color effects. If you use the two pattern options in the Fill dialog box *in conjunction with* the Use Fill Color options, an almost infinite number of different effects becomes possible. The Hue Only, Color Only, Brightness Only, Additive, and Subtractive options often generate the most subtle or dramatic pattern effects for use in True Color images. These options usually result in a semi-transparent application of the pattern fill, unless the pattern image is high in contrast. For Grayscale images, the If Darker and If Lighter options can yield interesting pattern fills.

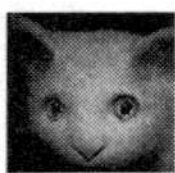

Figure 10–22 in the Color Section shows an example of applying a pattern fill with the Pattern (Non-Aligned) and Use Fill Color: Subtractive settings. To generate the fill, we began with the grayscale cat's head shown here, converted the cat's head to True Color, and used the Fill command to fill the image with a bright yellow foreground color at the Color Only setting. Next, we chose the Define Pattern command to generate a pattern from the cat's head. We then selected the white area of the "Deco" sign (Figure 10–22, left) and applied the pattern fill in a subtractive way (Figure 10–22, right).

Tip

Experiment with using patterns to fill the white areas of a mask. The pattern will introduce intermediate grayscale values to the mask. When you re-import the edited mask into the original image document and then paint in the selected area, the grayscale values in the mask will allow some (but not all) of the paint to flow through to the original image. The transparency of the paint colors will vary according to the grayscale values from the mask. See Chapter 8 if you want to review the theory and practice of using and editing masks.

You can also use the Clone tool to fill areas of an image with patterns. Unlike the Fill command, the Clone tool lets you fill areas *selectively* according to the movement of your mouse. To find out more, see the sections on the Clone tool in Chapter 11.

Creating Gradient Fills

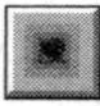

PhotoStyler's Gradient Fill tool has such rich and varied options that it almost deserves a floating palette to itself. It's an understatement to say merely that the Gradient Fill tool lets you fill selected areas of an image with smooth transitions between multiple colors or shades of gray. This tool is a hidden treasure trove of color effects for presentations, photorealistic retouching, and fine art applications. By coordinating mouse movement with options in the Gradient Fill Options dialog box, you can control:

- the shape of the fill
- the extent of the color transition(s)
- the direction of the transition
- the color model used
- the number and order of colors in the transition
- the beginning, middle, and end points of each color or grayscale transition
- the number of times the transition repeats itself
- special color effects

You can also specify *and save* custom gradient fill palettes that can include up to eight color or gray values each. If you regularly retouch photos or images that have many visual similarities, you'll find this feature to be a real time saver.

Note *Like most of the other Paint Palette tools, the Gradient Fill tool is available for True Color and Grayscale images only.*

Gradient Fill Options

If you click the Gradient Fill tool icon only once, any gradient fill you create will reflect the default settings: a linear fill from the current foreground to the current background color using the RGB color model. To customize your fill options, double-click the Gradient Fill tool icon, and the Gradient Fill Options dialog box (Figure 10–23) will appear.

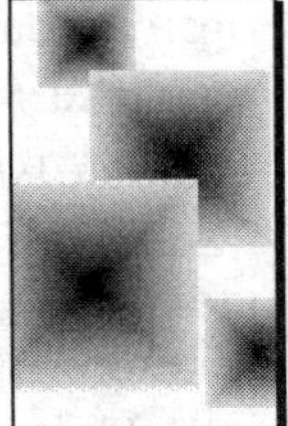

Scratch Pad Like most of the other dialog boxes in the Paint Palette, this one contains a scratch pad that you can use to try out your settings. With the Gradient Fill tool, though, both mouse movement and choice of options have a tremendous influence on the extent and direction of the transitions. Changing just one of them can alter the look of a gradient fill drastically! Be sure to use the scratch pad every time you change even a single setting. Throughout these sections, we'll be using the Gradient Fill scratch pad to show examples of each setting.

Figure 10-23.

The Gradient Fill Options dialog box

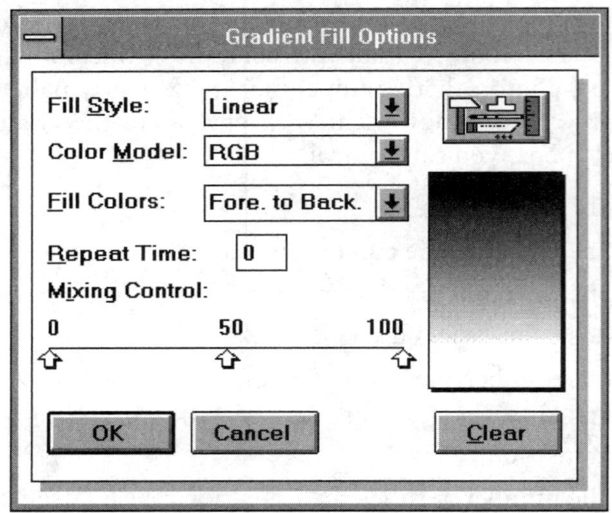

Linear
Circular
Elliptical
Square
Rectangular

Fill Style and the Shape and Extent of the Fill The options in this drop-down list box control the *shape* of the fill.

- *Linear* fills follow a straight or diagonal line, according to the way you drag the mouse. Mouse movement also determines the extent of a linear fill and the position of the start and end colors.
- *Circular* and *elliptical* fills extend outward from the center of their respective shapes. You define the center point when you click and begin to drag the mouse. At the point where you release the mouse, the circular and elliptical shapes end and the end color continues.
- *Square* and *rectangular* fills also extend outward from the center. The point where you click and begin to drag the mouse defines the center of the shape. If you use only two colors or grays, the resulting gradient fill will look like a three-dimensional pyramid.

RGB
HSB ⟲
HSB ⟳

Color Model and the Order of Fill Colors This set of options determines how PhotoStyler generates the transition between the foreground and background colors in the gradient fill. As you may recall from Chapter 7, each color space has its origin in a three-dimensional mathematical model. The color model you choose will determine the order in which colors appear in the gradient fill. It will also determine whether intermediate colors appear in the fill. Figure 10-24 in the Color Section illustrates nine of the options in the Gradient Fill Options dialog box.

Note

The Color Model option has little effect on gradient fills applied to Grayscale images.

- The *RGB* color space creates a transition by changing the Red, Green, and Blue components of the start and end colors. Only the foreground and background colors are visible (see Figure 10–24 in the Color Section of this book).
- The *HSB Counterclockwise* color model generates a transition by changing the hue, saturation and brightness (HSB) values that fall between the start and end colors. The number of colors visible in the transition depends on the relative position of the start and end colors in the HSB rainbow color wheel. It also depends on whether you choose Fore to Back or Back to Fore in the Fill Colors drop-down list box. For example, a transition from blue (foreground) to white (background) will produce blue, magenta, and white (see Figure 10–24 in the Color Section). On the other hand, a transition from white (foreground) to blue (background) will produce white, yellow, green, aqua, and blue.

Tip

By choosing your colors and a Fill Colors option carefully, you can use the HSB Counterclockwise and HSB Clockwise color models to control the warmth or coolness of colors in the transition.

- The *HSB Clockwise* color model is similar to the HSB Counterclockwise model, except that the color transition moves in the opposite direction on the color wheel. For example, a transition from blue (foreground) to white (background) will produce white, yellow, green, aqua, and blue. A transition from white (foreground) to blue (background) will produce blue, magenta, and white.

Fore. to Back.
Back. to Fore.
Custom Colors

Fill Colors and the Order of Color Transition The Fill Colors option works with the Color Model option and the action of your mouse to determine the order and number of colors in a gradient fill. When you choose Fore to Back, the foreground color appears at the point where you click and begin to drag, and the background color appears where you release the mouse button. The colors appear in the reverse order when you choose Back to Fore. When Custom Colors is selected, only the RGB option in the Color Model list box is available. See the section "Defining Custom Color Gradient Fills" for more information about working with sets of custom fill colors.

Repeat Time The Repeat Time option controls the number of times the gradient fill pattern repeats itself. You can set this option to any value from zero (no repetitions) to 99. However, the number of repetitions that are *visible* in the fill area will depend on the size of the area and the size of the fill pattern. Here and in Figure 10–24 in the Color Section, we see a rectangular fill repeated three times.

Mixing Control When you let mouse movement determine the rate of color transition in a gradient fill, the start color begins where you click the mouse, the end color appears where you stop dragging, and the halfway transition is—you guessed it—halfway in between. You can change the rate of transition, though, by dragging the slider handles under the Mixing Control slider. The first slider handle represents the start point for the start color, the second stands for the halfway transition mark, and the third represents the end point for the end color. The first example in Figure 10–24 in the Color Section shows a gradient fill at the default Mixing Control settings of 0, 50, and 99; the fifth example shows the same fill with Mixing Control settings of 16, 33, and 88. Experiment with these settings to obtain interesting graphic design effects.

√Expand Ending Color(s)
Ping-Pong
Banding

Menu Options The Gradient Fill menu contains several additional options that foster stimulating graphic effects. A check mark appears in front of any option that is currently selected. To turn any option on or off, click the command name once.

- When the *Expand Ending Colors* option is active (the default setting), a gradient fill will always extend to the edges of the area you're filling. Even if the movement of your mouse causes the color transitions to occur within a narrower range of the fill area, the end color will continue to the edges of the fill area as in in the sixth example in Figure 10–24 in the Color Section. You can create only one gradient fill at a time in a selection area when Expand Ending Colors is active.

  There may be times, though, when you don't want *anything* to fill the areas beyond where you drag the mouse. For example, you may want to create multiple gradient fills within the same selection area. In these cases, deselect the Expand Ending Colors option. The seventh example in Figure 10–24 in the Color Section shows multiple circular fills within a single area when Expand Ending Colors is turned off.

- The *Ping-Pong* option causes the gradient fill to "bounce" from the start color to the end color and back again. This option can create an interesting "sandwich" gradient fill effect as in the eighth example in Figure 10–24 (Color Section).

Note

When you activate Ping-Pong while defining a gradient fill with custom colors, PhotoStyler repeats only the start color.

- When the *Banding* option is active, the transition between the start and end colors is sharp and sudden, as in the final example in Figure 10–24 in the Color Section. No intermediate colors appear, regardless of which Color Model setting you've chosen.

Clear

Clearing the Scratch Pad Normally, any test fills you create in the scratch pad will remain there until you create another one. If you want to erase all test fills, click the Clear command button.

Defining a Gradient Fill with the Foreground and Background Colors

The range and number of options in the Gradient Fill Options dialog box can be bewildering until you get the hang of them. Here's a brief rundown of the steps involved in defining a gradient fill with the current foreground and background colors. If you plan to use sets of custom colors, see the "Defining Custom Gradient Fills" section following this one.

1. Select an area in the active Grayscale or True Color image document. If you don't make a selection, the gradient fill will replace every pixel in the image.
2. Change the current foreground and background colors, if necessary. (This doesn't apply if you're planning to use a set of custom colors.)
3. Double-click the Gradient Fill tool icon to access the Gradient Fill Options dialog box.
4. Select the shape of the fill pattern using the Fill Style drop-down list box. Test the results in the scratch pad.
5. Select a color model based on the order and number of colors that you want the fill to contain. (This step is less important for Grayscale images.) Test your results in the scratch pad again.

6. Select the desired Fill Colors option (Fore to Back or Back to Fore only), depending on the direction in which you want the fill to extend. If you want to use custom colors, see the section entitled, "Defining Custom Color Gradient Fills."
7. Set the repeat time according to the number of times you want the fill pattern to repeat. Test your setting in the scratch pad!
8. If you want a custom rate of transition, experiment with the Mixing Control slider, testing your settings in the scratch pad each time you make a change.
9. Check the Gradient Fill menu to see if you want to change any of the options there for special effects. Drag the cursor through the scratch pad again to test your settings.
10. Keep changing your settings until you're satisfied. Then, exit the dialog box by clicking the OK command button.
11. Move the cursor into the active document window and into the selection area. At the desired starting point for the start color, click and drag the mouse. Depending on the Fill Style setting you've chosen, a line or shape outline will follow the cursor.

Tip

To constrain the angle of a Linear fill to zero, 45, or 90 degrees, press Shift as you drag the mouse.

12. To define the end point for the end fill color, release the mouse button. After a moment, PhotoStyler will paint the selection area with the fill. If the Expand Ending Color(s) option in the Gradient Fill menu is active, the fill will extend all the way to the edges of the selection area. Otherwise, the fill will appear only in the area where you dragged the mouse.

Defining Custom Gradient Fills

You don't have to be satisfied with the current foreground and background colors when defining a gradient fill. When you select the Fill Colors: Custom Colors option in the Gradient Fill Options dialog box, you can access four subdirectories full of predefined custom color palettes. Each of these predefined palettes contains between two and eight colors and can be used for specific purposes. Imagine a gradient fill with not one, but multiple color transitions!

If the sixty-odd sets of custom colors supplied with your software don't satisfy all your needs, you can define your own sets of up to eight custom colors and save them to a file for later use.

The Custom Colors Palette With Fill Colors: Custom Colors selected, the Custom Colors Palette (Figure 10–25 here and Figure 10–26 in the Color Section) will appear after you exit the Gradient Fill Options dialog box. Although it's similar to the regular Color Palette, the Custom Colors Palette contains a few additional functions specifically designed for use with gradient fills. We'll review these differences briefly here.

- *Scratch pad, Pick/Edit button*—You can load any palette file into the scratch pad area, just as with the normal Color Palette. When the scratch pad is in Pick mode, you choose the colors for your gradient fill from this area. When the scratch pad is in Edit mode, you can create test gradient fills in it, as shown in Figure 10–26 in the Color Section.
- *Color Slots*—At the base of the Custom Colors Palette are eight "slots" representing the colors in the current custom color set. To change one of these colors, double-click on the desired slot. The Color dialog box will appear as in Figure 10–27, bearing the title, "Select Current Custom Color." (See Chapter 7 for more on defining colors with the Color dialog box.) To delete a color from a slot and make that slot empty, click the slot using the right mouse button.
- *Current Color Indicator*—In the Custom Colors Palette, this indicator displays the color in the currently selected color *slot*. To access the Color dialog box and change the color represented by the current color slot, click the Current Colors Indicator.

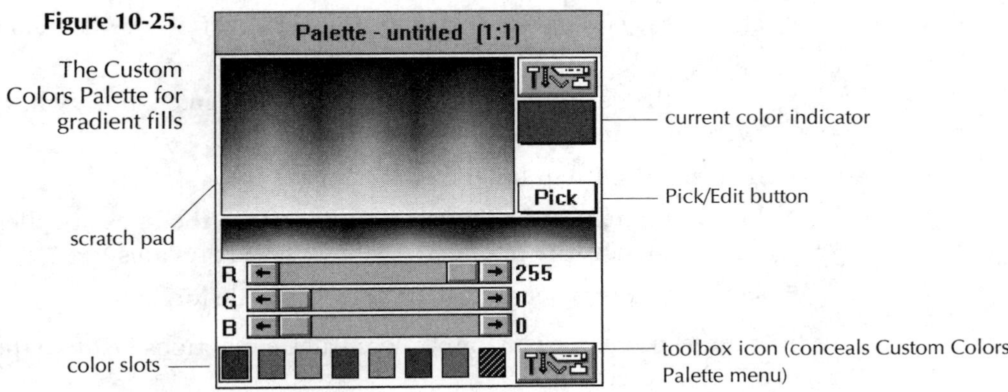

Figure 10-25. The Custom Colors Palette for gradient fills

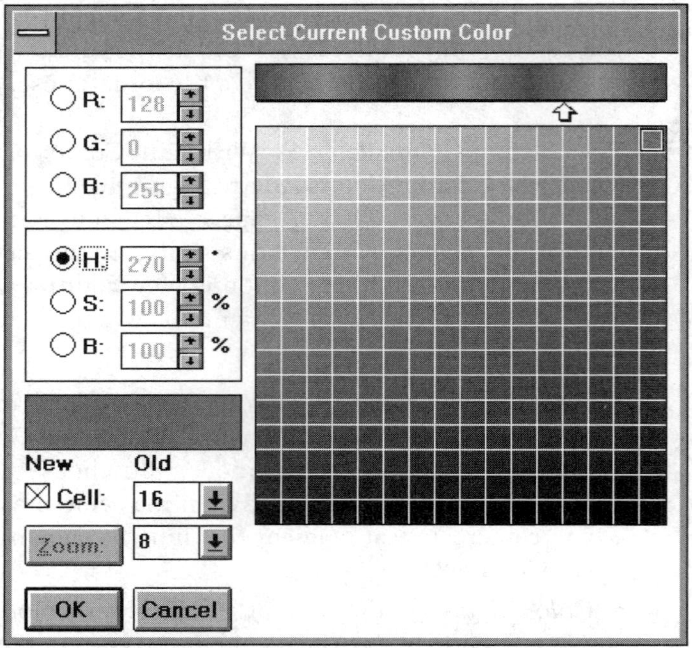

Figure 10-27.

Using the Color dialog box to select a current custom color for gradient fills

√Expand Ending Color(s)
Ping-Pong
Banding

- The *Custom Colors Palette Menu* pops up when you click the toolbox icon at the *base* of the Custom Colors Palette. The options in this menu give you lots of flexibility in selecting slots and arranging the order of colors. You can use these commands to:
  - undo other commands
  - add a color when one or more slots are currently empty
  - delete the color in the currently selected slot
  - delete all colors except the currently selected one
  - change the current set of custom colors to a set of seven rainbow hues
  - restore the default set of custom colors (red, green, blue, white, cyan, magenta, yellow, and black)
  - reverse the current order of colors in the color slots
  - load a different set of custom colors, either the ones supplied with your software or one that you've saved previously
  - save the current set of custom colors to a file for later use.

In other respects, the Custom Colors Palette functions just like the regular Color Palette.

Loading and Using a Predefined Set of Custom Colors PhotoStyler supplies you with more than 60 sets of custom colors for use with the Gradient Fill tool. The custom color files all have the extension **.clr** and are contained in four subdirectories of the \pstyler\colors directory. Each group of custom color sets has specific uses:

- The **hue** subdirectory (Figure 10–28) contains 36 sets of custom colors based on 10-degree increments of a hue wheel. Each set of custom colors in this directory contains eight different shades in the same color range. The hue wheel on which these files are based derives from the HSB color model (see Chapter 7), so the order of colors represented proceeds from shades of red through orange, yellow, green, cyan, blue, purple, and magenta (see Chapter 7).
- The **rainbow** subdirectory (Figure 10–28) contains five sets of custom colors based on different combinations of rainbow colors. The letters in each filename indicate which colors are included in a specific set and the order in which they appear. For example, the **cgyormb.clr** file contains cyan, green, yellow, orange, red, magenta, and blue.

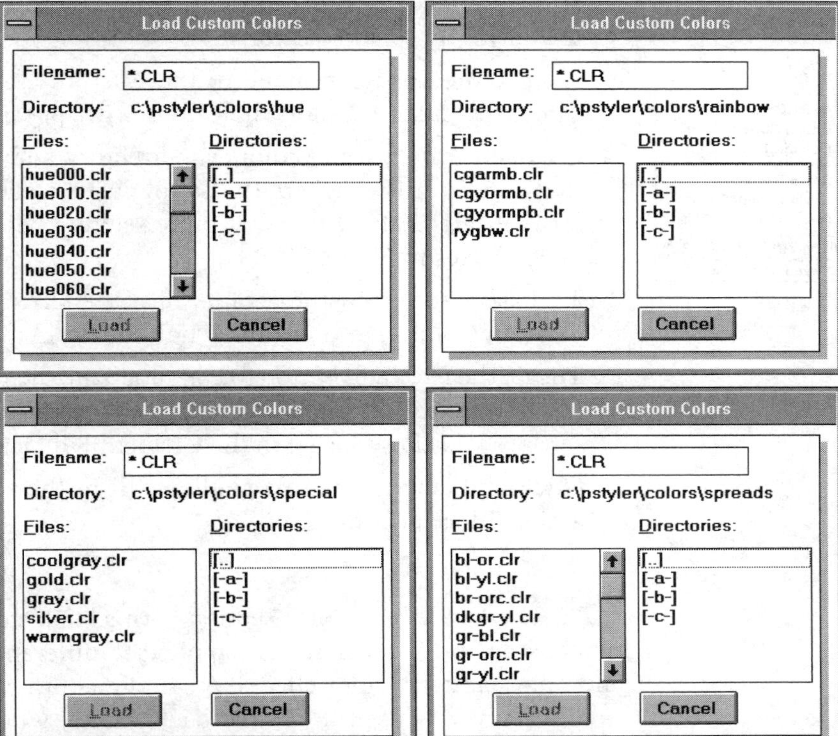

Figure 10-28.

Four varieties of custom color gradient fill palettes

- The **special** subdirectory (Figure 10–28) contains five custom color sets based on shades of gold, silver, and gray.
- The **spreads** subdirectory (Figure 10–28) contains 20 sets of two colors each. The letters in each filename indicate which two colors the file represents. For example, the **pr-pk.clr** file generates a transition from purple to pink. The files in this subdirectory are especially useful for creating backgrounds in slide presentations.

To define a gradient fill based on one of the custom color sets supplied with your software:

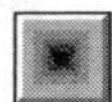

1. Double-click the Gradient Fill tool in the Paint Palette. Whatever other settings you choose, set Fill Colors to Custom Colors.
2. Click OK when you're satisfied with all your settings in the dialog box. The Custom Colors Palette will appear. If you've worked with this palette at least once during the current session, it will contain the most recently saved set of gradient fill colors. If this is the first time you've used it, it will display default custom colors in seven of the eight color slots. The slot marked with a white highlight is the currently selected color slot.

Undo
Add a Color
Delete Current Color
Delete Other Colors
Set to Rainbow
Set to Default Colors
Reverse
Load Custom Colors...
Save Custom Colors...

3. Choose the Load command in the Custom Colors Palette menu. The Load Custom Colors dialog box will appear.
4. Change to the \pstyler\colors subdirectory and then to one of the four subdirectories where the set of custom colors you're looking for is located. The directory you're seeking will match one of the dialog boxes in Figure 10–28.
5. To load a set of custom colors into the slots at the base of the Custom Color Palette, double-click the desired filename.
6. Toggle the Pick/Edit button to Edit mode and then try out one or more test gradient fills in the scratch pad. The test fills will reflect all the settings you chose earlier in the Gradient Fill Options dialog box.
7. Click and drag to create a gradient fill in the selected area of the active image document.

Figure 10–29 in the Color Section of this book shows an example of two custom color gradient fills applied to different areas of a nature photo for painterly color effects. A set of custom colors from the **hue** subdirectory was used to fill the background, while a set of custom colors from the **rainbow** subdirectory was applied to the flower itself.

Editing, Creating, and Saving a Set of Custom Colors If you like, you can use a set of predefined custom colors as a basis for creating your own sets. To edit and save a set of custom colors for a gradient fill:

1. Double-click the Gradient Fill tool in the Paint Palette. Whatever other settings you choose, set Fill Colors to Custom Colors.
2. Click OK when you're satisfied with all your settings in the dialog box. The Custom Colors Palette will appear.
3. If you want to load a predefined custom color set or one that you've saved previously, choose the Load command in the Custom Colors Palette menu. Select the color set you want in the Load Custom Colors dialog box and then click OK.
4. To begin editing one or more of the colors in the set, click the desired slot once. You can edit the color in this slot using one of the following techniques:
   - Double-click on the slot to display the Color Picker and specify a new color there.
   - Click a color in the mini color bar.
   - Set the scratch pad to Pick mode using the Pick/Edit button, and load any predefined color palette file you want to use (see Figure 10–28). Click on a color in the scratch pad to select it.
   - Choose the Scroll Bar command in the upper Color Palette menu and specify colors numerically using the color component scroll bars.
5. To delete a color from a slot, click on the slot while pressing the right mouse button.
6. Continue editing colors in the slots until your set is complete.
7. Toggle the Pick/Edit button to Edit mode and then try out one or more test gradient fills in the scratch pad. The test fills will reflect all the settings you chose earlier in the Gradient Fill Options dialog box.
8. Click and drag to generate a custom gradient fill in the selected area of the active image document.
9. To save an edited set of custom colors, choose the Save command in the Custom Colors Palette menu and type the desired filename in the Save Custom Colors dialog box. Click the Save command button; PhotoStyler will save all custom color palette files with the extension .CLR.

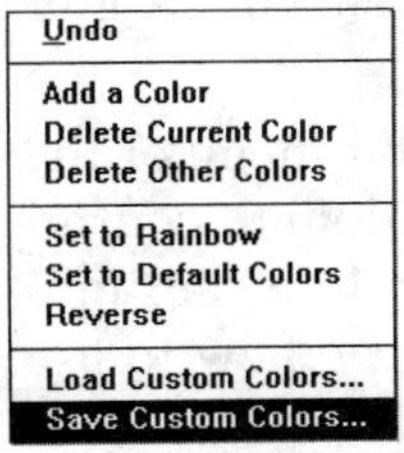

Undo
Add a Color
Delete Current Color
Delete Other Colors
Set to Rainbow
Set to Default Colors
Reverse
Load Custom Colors...
Save Custom Colors...

If you plan on developing several custom colors palettes, we recommend saving them in a separate subdirectory.

Gradient Fill Tips and Tricks

Gradient fills have so many applications in both Grayscale and True Color images that it's difficult to cover them all. We'll pass on a few ideas here to stimulate your creative juices.

Gradient Fills and Text Gradient fills can be especially exciting when used with text. Try varying the shape, direction and extent of the fill to see what settings and techniques yield the best results for a given application. Text that contains transitions between eight colors can be stunning! See Figure 10–30 in the Color Section of this book.

Realism vs. Graphic Design For realistic photo retouching applications, choose custom colors that are close in value to create subtle blends. The files in the \colors\hue subdirectory may meet your needs best. For graphic design applications that don't require realistic color transitions, contrasting fill colors or gray values might be eye-catching. Try the sets of custom colors contained in the \colors\spreads and \colors\rainbow subdirectories.

Merging Gradient Fills into an Existing Image Normally, a gradient fill will overwrite an entire image when that image contains no selection areas. However, it's possible to blend a gradient fill with another image document using either the Merge Control command in the Edit menu (see Chapter 13) or the Compute command in the Image menu (Chapter 14). Here's how:

1. First, create a new image document having the same pixel dimensions as the one with which you want to merge the gradient fill.
2. Fill the new document with a gradient fill of your choice.

3. Select the entire image document (Ctrl-A) and then copy it to the PhotoStyler clipboard using the Copy command in the Edit menu.
4. Activate the existing image document and paste the contents of the clipboard into it using the Paste: As Selection command in the Edit menu.
5. Finally, use the Merge Control command in the Edit menu or the Compute command in the Image menu (Blend option) to control the degree of transparency with which the gradient fill blends into the existing image. See Chapters 13 and 14 to review how to use these commands.

Enhancing Masks with Gradient Fills As you saw in Chapter 8, the purpose of editing a mask is to enhance the image document from which the mask originated. If you select the white areas of a mask, apply a gradient fill to them, and then re-import the mask into the original image document, any solid color or pattern fills you apply to the original image will show gradations in brightness because of the gradient fill in the mask. Some especially beautiful and subtle effects can be achieved through experimenting with the Use Fill Color option in the Fill Options dialog box (Fill command, Edit menu). Try this technique to give your images a little extra pizazz.

We've given a few brief hints in this chapter about Paint tool techniques that help you edit the content or composition of an image. Image composition is a vast subject in its own right, as you'll see in Chapter 13. First, though, take a look at Chapter 11 to unlock the secrets of seamless photo-realistic retouching with PhotoStyler.

11

Retouching Tools and Techniques

We admit it: photo retouchers and fine artists often inhabit the same body. Newsletter and catalog editors, photo restorers, and commercial artists—the respectably successful Dr. Jekylls of the daytime—have been known to turn into wildly imaginative Mr. Hydes during off hours. We think that PhotoStyler and other new digital imaging technologies will soon begin to blur the distinctions between art and reality, even in commercial applications. Until then, personalities remain split—and so do our chapters on painting and retouching with PhotoStyler.

Retouching with the Smudge, Blur, Sharpen, Lighten, Darken, Eraser, Clone, and Text Tools

The Smudge, Blur, Sharpen, Lighten, Darken, Eraser, and Clone tools in the Paint Palette have one thing in common that distinguishes them from the traditional "painting" tools covered in Chapter 10. Instead of adding original graphics to an image, they edit what's already there, helping you to retouch and restore images. Each of these tools accomplishes that purpose in a unique way.

- The Smudge tool is an *anti-aliasing* aid that helps you blend neighboring colors or shades of gray selectively. Depending on your settings, you can use the Smudge tool either to smooth or heighten the distinctions between neighboring colors.

- The Blur and Sharpen tools let you soften and sharpen areas of an image, respectively, by decreasing or increasing the contrast among neighboring colors or shades of gray.

- The Lighten and Darken tools lighten or darken the color or gray values of pixels over which the cursor passes. You define the percentage of lightening or darkening that occurs.

- The Eraser tool lets you *restore* areas of an image that you've painted over or replaced through cutting and pasting operations.

- With the Clone tool, you can duplicate areas of an image to round out a composition or create the illusion of additional elements. This tool adds something *new* to the content of an image; it doesn't just remove flaws or restore something that was there previously.

- The Text tool may not be a retouching tool in any literal sense; after all, it *does* add original graphics to an image. But we'll include it with the retouching tools because you're likely to use it for similar types of newsletter, catalog, and advertising applications.

We'll devote this chapter to an exploration of each of the retouching and restoring tools and the options that let you maximize their power. We also hope to stimulate your imagination by providing examples of how and why you might use each tool in the "real world" of photo-realistic retouching.

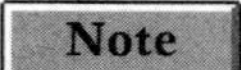

Some Paint tools have multiple functions. The Eraser tool, for example, behaves like a painting tool when you use it to apply the background color, but as a retouching tool when you use it to restore previously saved areas of an image. The Clone tool can act both as a retouching tool and (in its pattern fill mode) as a paint tool, too.

Activating, Customizing, and Applying the Retouching Tools

The retouching tools share common conventions for activating a tool, defining options, testing tool settings, and applying the tool in the active image document. To activate a tool without customizing any options, click its icon in the Paint Palette once. To apply an active retouching tool, move the mouse cursor into the active image document, click, and drag. If you prefer to edit just a few pixels at a time, you can click repeatedly rather than drag the tool icon. The effect will depend on the tool and on your current brush shape.

Retouching Tool Options

Like the painting tools, most of the retouching and restoring tools share common controls. Except for the Eraser, they all include scratch pads in their dialog boxes so you can test your settings without making blunders in the actual image document. They allow you a choice of brush shapes, too. The Smudge, Blur, Sharpen, and Clone tools also let you control the use of color and the spacing of the pixels that you affect by retouching.

Tip

For most realistic retouching work, it's best to keep brush shapes conservative and small. Accuracy is vitally important in retouching, which means that you'll be working at higher viewing magnifications and shouldn't alter too many pixels at a time. Large or custom brush shapes can introduce errors or distortions. They're acceptable if special effects are your goal, however.

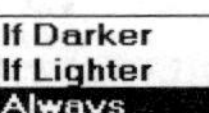

Use Foreground Color

Don't let appearances deceive you. Although the Use Foreground Color option appears in the dialog boxes of both retouching and painting tools, the term "foreground color" has a very different meaning for each type of tool. For painting tools, "foreground color" refers to the *current* foreground color, which is the color or shade of gray that the tool will use as paint. But for the retouching tools, "foreground color" refers simply to the *existing* color or gray values of all the pixels over which the tool passes. The retouching tools edit what already exists in the image; they don't add anything new.

Three choices are available for the Use Foreground Color option that appears in the dialog boxes of the retouching tools. These choices let you control the degree to which a specific retouching tool alters color or gray values.

Always When Always is selected, the tool affects *all* pixels over which it passes, regardless of whether they're dark or light.

If Darker When you select If Darker, PhotoStyler compares the color or gray values of pixels under the cursor to the values of neighboring pixels. As you drag the mouse, the retouching tool will affect only pixels that are *lighter* than the pixels over which the cursor has just passed. The end result will be to darken the lighter areas of the image.

If Lighter When you select If Lighter, PhotoStyler compares the color or gray values of pixels under the cursor to the values of neighboring pixels. As you drag the mouse, the retouching tool will affect only pixels that are *darker* than the pixels over which the cursor has just passed. The end result will be to lighten the darker areas of the image.

Spacing

Whereas the Use Foreground Color option constrains retouching according to color or gray values, the Spacing option limits it according to an arbitrary distance between pixels.

- When you set Spacing to Freehand or to a value of zero, the speed with which you move your mouse determines which pixels PhotoStyler edits. If you move the mouse quickly across a large area, retouching will occur at wide intervals. If you move the mouse slowly, the retouching will affect almost all the pixels over which the cursor passes. And if you vary the speed at which you move the mouse, the distance between affected pixels will vary, too.
- When you set Spacing to a value between one and 100, retouching affects pixels at fixed intervals, no matter how quickly or slowly you move the mouse.

Smudge Tool Tips

As the extended finger of its icon suggests, the Smudge tool simulates finger painting techniques. When the Smudge tool is active, the colors of pixels over which you drag the mouse "smear" and blend together.

The Smudge tool is a favorite among retouchers because it's so versatile. You can use it alone, of course, to remove flecks or other small imperfections from a photographic image. When you use it in combination with other tools, though, it becomes even more powerful.

Take the example of a portrait of someone who has dark circles or visible lines under the eyes (Figure 11–1, left). You might derive a new foreground color from lighter areas under the eye and spray that color

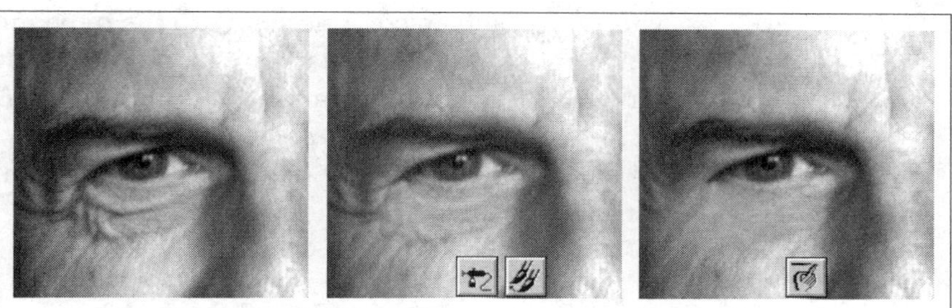

Figure 11-1.

Removing lines under the eye with the Airbrush, Clone, and Smudge tools

onto the dark areas with the Airbrush. At this stage, you might also use the Clone tool to duplicate areas under the eye that show skin pores (Figure 11–1, center). Then, you could use the Smudge tool to blend in the lighter "paint" with the existing tones (Figure 11–1, right).

By varying settings for the options in the Smudge Options dialog box (Figure 11–2), you can control:

- the direction of the smudge (Use Foreground Color)
- the spacing between affected pixels (Spacing)
- the intensity of the smudging effect (Smudge Amount)

Controlling the Path of the Smudge

The Use Foreground Color option determines which pixels smudge which other pixels. When you select Always, any pixel can blend into the colors or shades of gray next to it. When you select If Darker, darker pixels under the cursor will smudge lighter ones, and the overall effect will be to darken the image. When you select If Lighter, lighter pixels under the cursor will smear over darker ones, and the end effect will be to lighten the image.

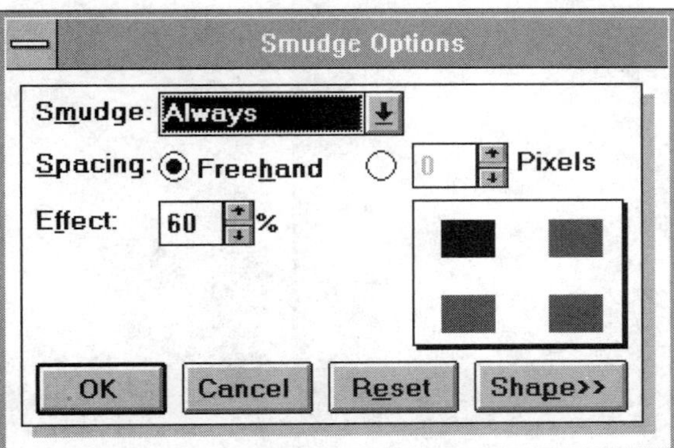

Figure 11-2.

The Smudge Options dialog box

This option acts in conjunction with the movement of your hand to determine just how much darkening or lightening takes place. When If Darker is selected, for example, you'll get a darker, thicker smear if you drag from dark to light areas than if you drag from light to dark areas. The direction of your hand movement becomes especially important when you're smudging in a selected area.

Controlling the Smudge in a Selected Area

When an image document contains a selection, PhotoStyler's tools limit their effects to the selected area only. The Smudge tool is no exception. However, you *can* introduce colors from outside the marquee into the smudge, simply by controlling the direction in which you move the cursor.

- If you confine the cursor within the selection marquee, only the colors or gray shades that fall within the selected area will participate in the smudge.
- If you drag the mouse back and forth between selected and unselected areas, the colors or gray shades of pixels outside the marquee can affect the shading of pixels inside the marquee. The reverse doesn't hold true, however. When the If Lighter option is active, the net effect will be to lighten the selected area. When the If Darker option is active, the net effect will be to darken the selected area (see Figure 11–3). And if you choose the Always option, *all* the colors of pixels outside the marquee can bleed into the selected area.

Tip *To get a better view of how smudging is affecting a selected area, hide the selection marquee temporarily (Ctrl-H).*

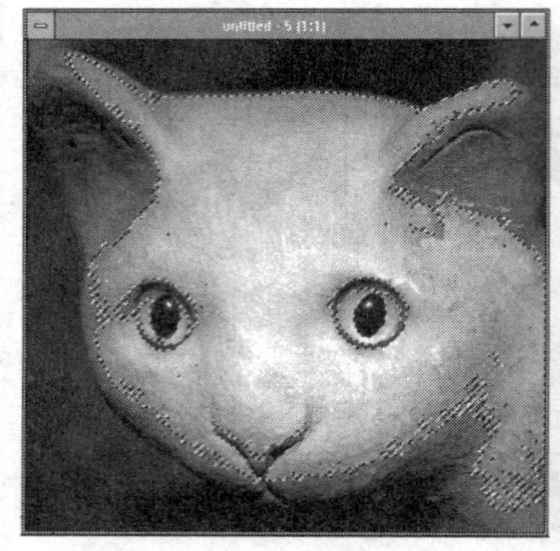

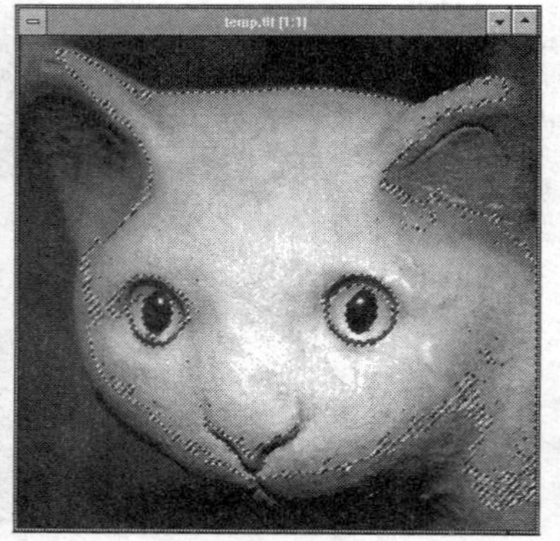

Figure 11-3. Enhancing contours with the Smudge tool: Dark pixels smudged from cat's unselected right ear into lighter pixels of selected area (one-way smudge)

Varying the Intensity of the Smudge

You've seen how the movement of your hand works with the Use Foreground Color setting to determine the direction of a smudge. To control the *intensity* of a smudge, you can vary the Smudge Amount setting and the brush shape. Low Smudge Amount values (the range is from 1% to 100%) result in a less dramatic smudge; high values result in an intense smudge. Similarly, a small brush shape will yield a more subtle effect than a large or custom brush shape.

Blur and Sharpen Tool Tips

The Blur tool softens details in an image by reducing contrast between neighboring pixels over which the mouse cursor passes. Its counterpart, the Sharpen tool, *increases* contrast among neighboring pixels, making details in an image stand out more. The effects are similar to those produced by the blurring and sharpening filters in the Image menu, except that the Blur and Sharpen tools let you edit pixels selectively.

The options in the Blur Options and Sharpen Options dialog boxes (Figures 11-4 and 11-5) let you control the use of color or gray values, the spacing of affected pixels, and the degree of blurring or sharpening.

Controlling the Use of Color

When the If Darker option is selected, the area you blur or sharpen will darken somewhat. When you select the If Lighter option, the net effect of retouching will be to lighten the area you blur or sharpen. If you drag the mouse back and forth repeatedly over the same areas, the degree of darkening or lightening will increase.

Figure 11-4.

The Blur Options dialog box

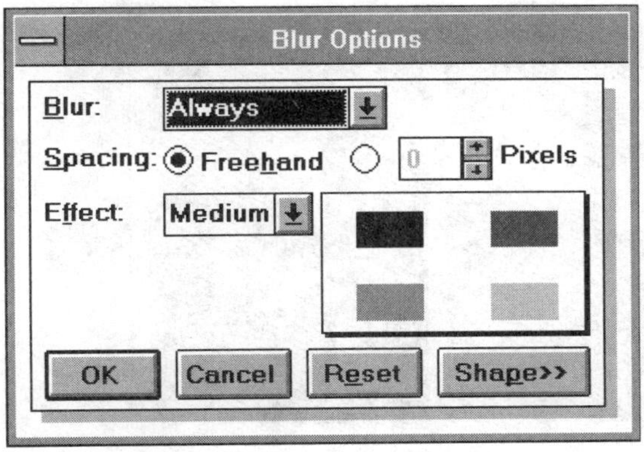

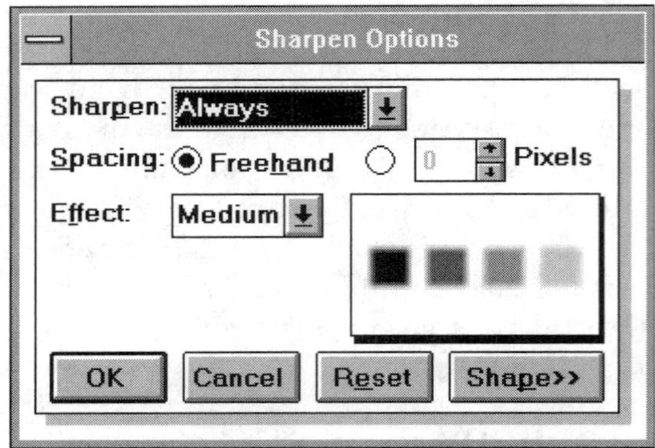

Figure 11-5.

The Sharpen Options dialog box

Controlling the Degree of Blurring or Sharpening

There are two ways to control the intensity of the effects you obtain with the Blur and Sharpen tools. The first way is to adjust the Blur or Sharpen option in their respective dialog boxes. The options are Light, Medium, and Heavy. You may not notice the difference between these options unless you work at a magnification level higher than 1:1.

Another way to control the intensity of the blurring or sharpening effect is to drag the cursor *repeatedly* over the area you want to adjust. The fruit and rim of the glass in Figure 11–6 (left) look rather dull, but after several passes of the Sharpen tool at the Sharpen: Heavy setting, glistening highlights appear (11-6, right).

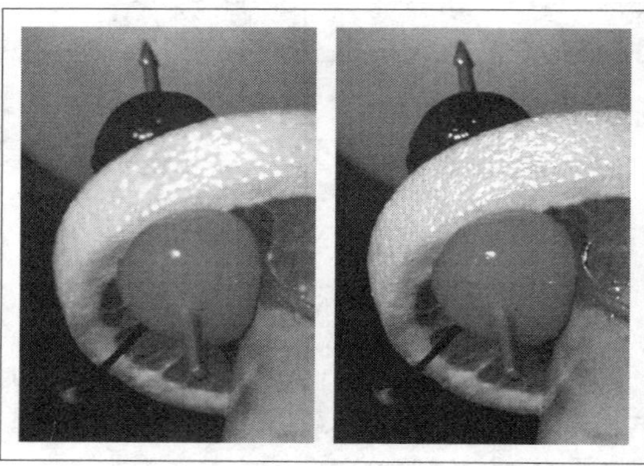

Figure 11-6.

Bringing out highlights with the Sharpen tool *(l)* original image *(r)* after applying the Sharpen tool to increase contrast in the highlight areas

Controlling Contrast between Selected and Unselected Areas

When you apply the Blur or Sharpen tool to a selected area, the dividing line between selected and unselected areas can become annoyingly visible. To avoid obvious "demarcation" lines, assign a Soft Edge several pixels wide to the selected area *before* you use the Blur or Sharpen tool. If the Soft Edge doesn't do the trick, deselect the area after you're finished with the tool and then blur or sharpen the area near the former selection boundaries.

Darken and Lighten Tool Options

The Darken and Lighten tools work like the Brightness scroll bar in the Brightness & Contrast dialog box (see Chapter 9). However, the tools let you lighten or darken pixels selectively, simply by dragging the mouse cursor over them. No Spacing option is available in the Lighten Options and Darken Options dialog boxes (Figure 11–7), so *every* pixel over which the mouse passes will change its color or gray values.

You control the degree of lightening or darkening by specifying a percentage in the dialog box. Valid values are from 1% to 100%.

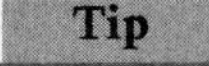

As long as the mouse button remains depressed, pixels change their value only once, even if you drag the cursor over them several times. If you need to lighten or darken the same pixels again, first release the mouse button temporarily, then begin dragging the mouse once more.

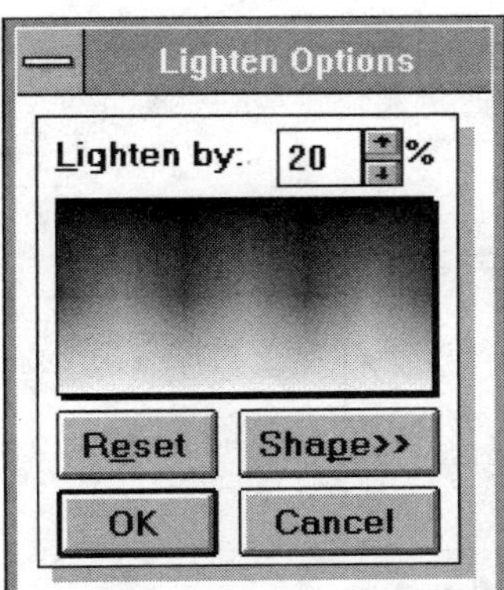

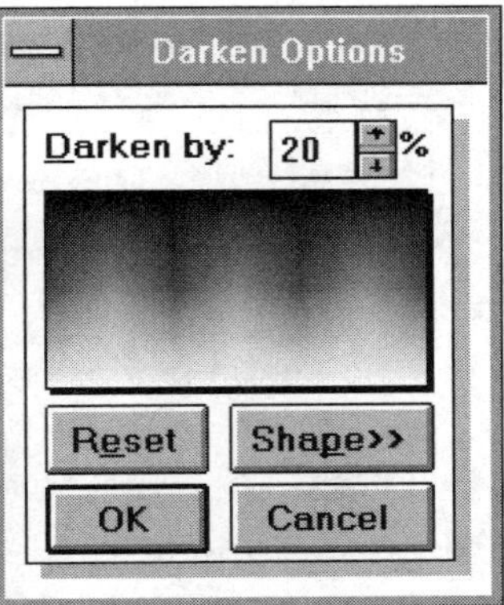

Figure 11-7. The Lighten Options and Darken Options dialog boxes

Controlling Contrast between Selected and Unselected Areas

After you lighten or darken a selected area, you may sometimes notice unsightly contrast between the selected area and surrounding areas. In some cases this may be intentional. But, if you want to reduce this contrast, deselect the retouched area and then use the Blur tool to smooth the area around the selection's former borders.

Eraser Tool Tips and Techniques

The Eraser tool plays two roles, as you can tell from the options in its dialog box (Figure 11–8). In its "painting" mode, you can use the Eraser to paint areas with the current background color rather than the foreground color. In its "Magic Eraser" mode, this tool selectively erases changes you have made to an image since the last time you saved it. In both modes, you determine how transparently the tool paints or erases.

Erasing to the Background Color

When you select the Erase to: Background Color option, the Eraser works like an inverted Pencil tool, painting the current background color with a hard edge. If you leave the Transparency at its default value of 0% (opaque), the areas you paint will look like "holes" of a single color. But if you introduce a degree of transparency, you can use the Eraser tool to tint a selected area subtly, letting the existing pixels show through. When you're finished, you can use the Soft Edge

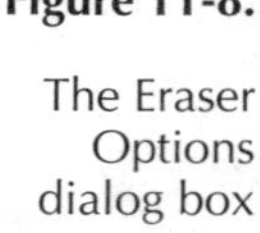

Figure 11-8.

The Eraser Options dialog box

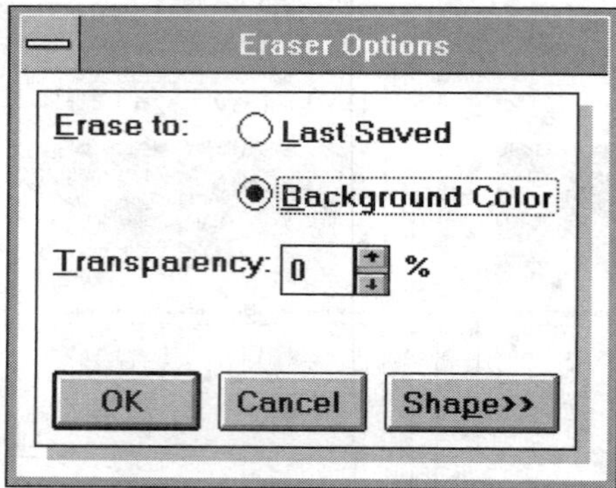

command in the Select Palette menu to blend colors or gray shades at the edges of the selection.

Tip *In its "painting" mode, the Eraser tool can help you clean up and fine-tune a mask. If black is the background color, the Eraser will subtract areas from the mask, so that the total selection area will be smaller when you import the mask into another image document. If white is the background color, the Eraser will add to the mask, making the total selection area larger. If the background color is an intermediate shade of gray, the Eraser tool will add to the mask, but the effects will be semitransparent when you fill or paint in the selection area later.*

Restoring in "Magic Eraser" Mode

If you've saved the image you're working on at least once, the Erase To: Last Saved option in the Eraser Options dialog box will be available. Selecting this option turns the Eraser into a retouching and restoration tool *par excellence*. Unlike the Restore command, which reverts all changes globally throughout an image, the Eraser tool lets you restore areas selectively according to the way you control the mouse.

In its "Magic Eraser" mode, the Eraser tool is invaluable for merging and montaging images realistically. After pasting an object into the active image document, you can use the Eraser tool to restore areas that you don't want the pasted image to cover up (see Figure 11-9). This technique can enhance the illusion of three-dimensional depth. See Chapter 13 for more tips on using the Eraser and other retouching tools to create montages.

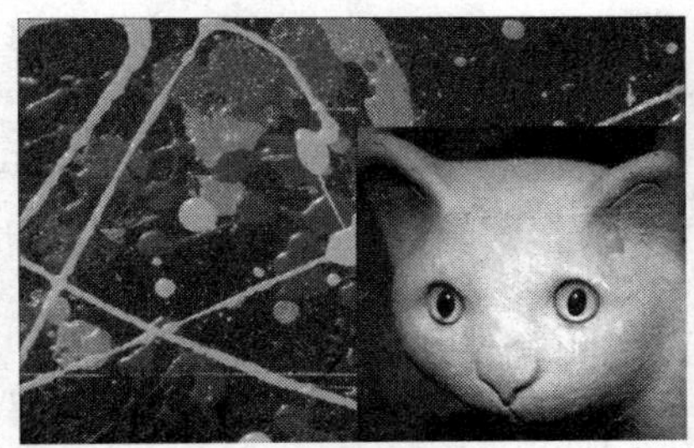

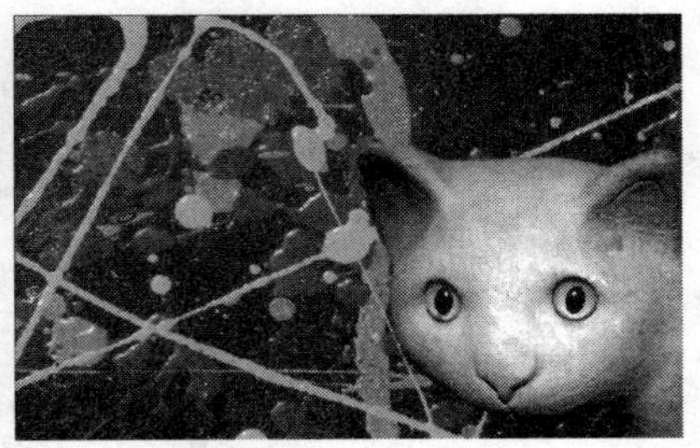

Figure 11-9.

The Eraser as an aid in montaging: *(l)* cat's head pasted into another image *(r)* after using Eraser in Last Saved mode

Duplicating Areas of an Image with the Clone Tool

For the four painting tools, "paint" is the current foreground color. For most of the retouching tools, the color and gray values of existing pixels in the image are themselves the "paint." The Clone tool, however, can use the actual content of an image or pattern as its paint. By making it possible to duplicate parts of an image or apply a pattern, the Clone lets you alter the *composition* of an image document.

The Clone tool has two basic functions:

- You can use it to clone part of an image and then paint that part elsewhere in the same image document. The part that you clone is called the *source image.*
- You can paint an image or selection with a pattern that you've defined or loaded into the Pattern dialog box.

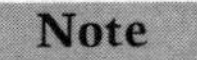

As an image composition tool, the Clone has more in common with the Edit and Transform menu commands than with the other tools in the Paint Palette. We'll explore the basic uses of the Clone in this chapter. You can also experiment with the Clone tool on your own after reading Chapter 13, "Editing Image Composition."

Clone Tool Options

To make the most of the Clone tool, you should customize its options every time you use it. Double-click the Clone tool icon in the Paint Palette to access the Clone Options dialog box (Figure 11–10). The most important issues you need to consider are these:

- *Paint*—Will the source image be a clipboard pattern, or part of the active image document?
- *Transparency*—How ghostly should the cloned image or pattern look? How much should the existing pixel colors bleed through?
- *Coloration*—Should the cloned image or pattern overwrite all the existing pixels? Or should the Clone tool paint over only the dark (or light) areas of the image?
- *Selective Spacing*—Should the tool paint the image (or pattern) continuously? Or should the "paint" appear at fixed intervals, merely *suggesting* a cohesive image or pattern?

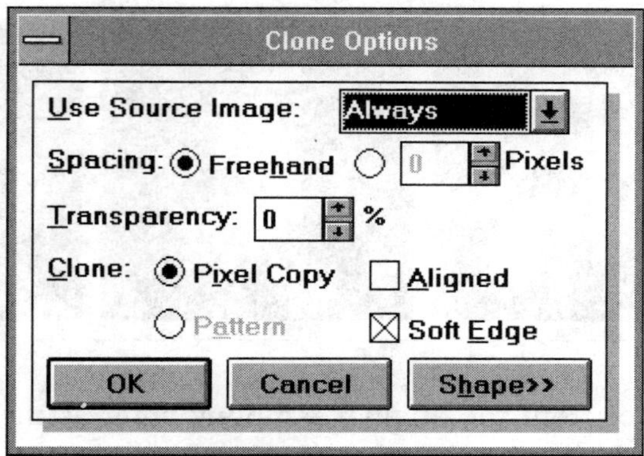

Figure 11-10. The Clone Options dialog box

- *Source Image Alignment*—Do you want to clone the same area over and over again every time you click the mouse? Or would you rather paint contiguous areas even if you click and drag in another part of the image?

  Each choice makes specific types of special effects possible.

Clone: Pixel Copy or Pattern?

Your choice for this option is the most critical one in the entire dialog box. If you choose Pixel Copy, you're electing to clone part of the active image document and paint it onto another part. If you choose Pattern, you'll be applying the current clipboard pattern instead. The Pattern option is unavailable whenever the clipboard is empty.

Clone: Aligned

After you exit the Clone Options dialog box, you define the starting point for a clone (the central sampling point) by pressing Shift and clicking once. The status of the Aligned option determines what will happen when you click or drag the mouse thereafter.

- When the Aligned option is *not* selected, you'll paint the central sampling point and the pixels that immediately surround it every time you click and/or drag the mouse (Figure 11–11, center).
- When Aligned is selected, you'll be able to paint contiguous areas of the cloned area without dragging the mouse continuously. The first time you click and drag the mouse, you'll paint the central sampling point and the area that surrounds it. Each succeeding time you click and drag, you'll paint a part of the image that's the same

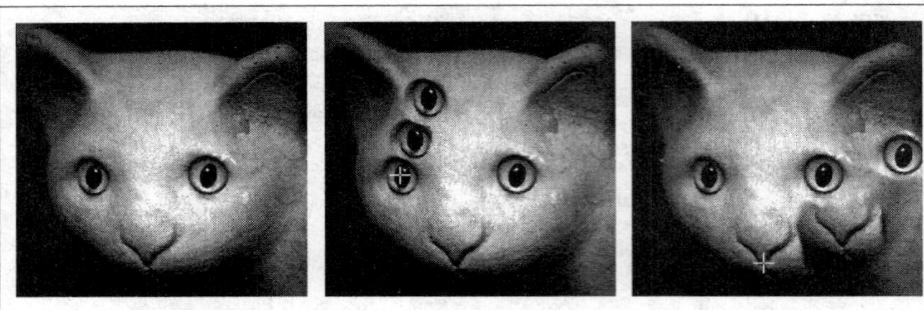

Figure 11-11.

Cloning and the Aligned option: *(l)* original image; *(c)* eye as sampling point, unaligned; *(r)* nose as sampling point, Aligned selected

distance from the original sampling point as the cursor is (Figure 11–11, right).

Clone: Soft Edge

When Soft Edge is selected, the edges of the cloned area will blend softly with the existing pixels in the image. Be sure to activate Soft Edge whenever you use the Clone tool for photo-realistic retouching; you'll want to avoid the visible "jaggies" that can occur during copying, cutting and pasting operations.

Tip

Combining Soft Edge with some degree of transparency will heighten the impressionistic effects you can achieve.

If Darker
If Lighter
Always

Use Source Image

This option determines which areas of the image (or pattern) will replace pixels in the underlying image. Select Always to overwrite all the existing pixels with the cloned area wherever you drag the mouse. Select If Darker to paint only the areas of the cloned image that are darker than the existing pixels. Select If Lighter to paint only those areas of the cloned image that are lighter than the existing pixels. The color or Grayscale makeup of both the cloned area and the existing pixels will determine the exact results.

Spacing

When you set Spacing to Freehand or zero pixels, the speed at which you move the mouse will determine just how continuously the cloned image will be painted. Move the mouse slowly if you want to paint continuous areas. If you're impatient with slow mouse movement, try setting Spacing to 1 pixel. The cloning may take a while to catch up to your hand movements, but at least you won't skip over any pixels. A fixed Spacing value will cause the tool to skip a specified number of pixels when painting the cloned image.

Tip

If you set Spacing to a large number of pixels, the brush shape you use will be very apparent.

Transparency

At the default setting of 0%, you'll paint an opaque copy of the area you want to clone. As you increase the level of transparency, more and more of the background pixels will show through as you paint.

Yes, the Clone tool does present you with a lot of choices. Most of the time, though, you'll use it for one of two "cloning" purposes: to retouch small areas of an image, or to copy objects from one part of an image document to another. In the next pair of sections, we streamline the steps involved in each of these two cases.

Cloning a Small Area Repeatedly

The Clone tool can be extremely useful for retouching small areas of an image. Imagine, for example, that you need to remove unsightly facial blemishes. In order to "erase" these, you would need to "graft" healthy skin tones from other areas of the face. If the skin tones in the surrounding area change, you might need to define several different sampling points to achieve seamless, realistic results.

Here's a summary of the best settings to choose and the best way to handle the mouse for this type of cloning:

1. With the desired image document active, double-click the Clone tool icon in the Paint Palette. The Clone Options dialog box will appear.
2. Select the Pixel Copy and Soft Edge options in the Clone section of the dialog box. Make sure that the Aligned option is *not* selected.
3. Set Spacing to Freehand.
4. Adjust the other settings as necessary. If you plan to retouch an area like the example we described, set Use Source Image to Always and Transparency to 0%. These settings may not apply to all applications, however. Make sure you've chosen an appropriate brush shape for the size and shape of the area you need to clone.

5. Click OK to exit the dialog box, and then move the cursor into the active image document.
6. Position the cursor exactly over the pixels you want to duplicate, then press Shift and click once. A flashing crosshair will mark this area as the central sampling point.
7. Now, move the cursor to the point where you want to begin painting the cloned area. *Click*, rather than drag, the mouse once here. You will paint a brush-sized clone of the pixels at the central sampling point.
8. Continue *clicking* along the entire area in which you want to substitute the cloned pixels. Each time you click, you'll paint the same small brush-sized clone area. If you need to clone another small area along the way to make the substitution look seamless, just press Shift and click over the pixels that have the desired color or Grayscale values.

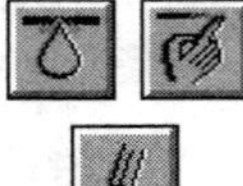

9. When you're finished substituting pixels, use one of the other retouching tools to help "clean up" the job if necessary. For example, you might use the Blur tool to soften any rough edges or sharp contrasts between the cloned areas and the original pixels. The Smudge tool could help you blend pixel tones within the cloned area. Or, you might use the Eraser in Last Saved mode to restore pixels that you overpainted by mistake.

Cloning Large Areas of an Image

A second use for the Clone tool is in duplicating larger objects or background areas in an image. For example, you might need to copy one or more flowers in order to round out a skimpy background. In situations like these, you need to match Clone tool options and mouse movement to the requirements of cloning larger, continuous areas of an image.

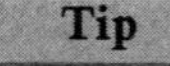

If you're using the Clone tool alone, the object or area you clone must originate in the same image document into which you plan to paint it. If you want to clone part of a different image document and paint it into the active image, you need the help of the Define Pattern command in the Edit menu. See the "Using Patterns and Fills in PhotoStyler" section of Chapter 10 for details.

To clone and paint large areas of an image:

1. With the desired image document active, double-click the Clone tool icon in the Paint Palette. The Clone Options dialog box will appear.
2. Select the Pixel Copy and Soft Edge options in the Clone section of the dialog box. If the area you're cloning is quite large relative to the rest of the image, select the Aligned option, too. Otherwise—especially if you plan to paint more than one clone of the same image area—leave Aligned unselected.
3. Set Spacing to 1 pixel. This will ensure that you paint the cloned area continuously, without skipping over any pixels.
4. Adjust the other settings as necessary. If you plan to copy part of an image in a photo-realistic style, set Use Source Image to Always and Transparency to 0%. You might vary these settings for more impressionistic applications, however.
5. Click OK to exit the dialog box, and then move the cursor into the active image document.
6. Position the cursor over the pixels that should be at the center of the area you want to duplicate, and then press Shift and click once. A flashing crosshair will mark this area as the central sampling point.
7. Now, move the cursor to the point where you want to begin painting the cloned area. It helps to magnify your view of this area so that you don't overpaint more pixels than necessary.
8. Click and then begin to drag the mouse slowly back and forth where you want the cloned image to appear. You will paint not only the central sampling point, but also the pixels that surround it. As you drag, a square icon will move around the central sampling point to show you which areas you're using as paint.
9. What you do next depends on whether you activated the Aligned option in the Clone options dialog box.
   - *Aligned not selected*—If you're cloning a small object that you plan to paint repeatedly, continue dragging the mouse until you've painted the entire object. Then, release the mouse button and move the cursor to the next point where you want to begin painting the same object again. Click and drag here as before.
   - *Aligned selected*—If you're painting a single large cloned area of the image, you can release the mouse button temporarily. When you begin to drag again, you'll continue to paint more and more of the image aligned to the sampling point.

10. When you're finished painting the cloned image area, use one of the other Paint tools to help "clean up" the job if necessary. For this type of cloning, we recommend using the Eraser in Last Saved mode to restore pixels that you overpainted by mistake. For the sake of exactness, be sure to use a small brush shape and to work at a high viewing magnification.

Creating Pattern Fills with the Clone Tool

Like the Fill command in the Edit menu, the Clone tool lets you apply a pattern to an image or selected area. Unlike the Fill command, the Clone tool makes it possible to apply patterns selectively, controlling the location and frequency of the pattern by the movement of your mouse.

Creating a pattern fill with the Clone tool is very similar to painting a clone. Only the source of the image is different. A cloned image must come from the same image document into which you paint it, but a pattern fill can originate from a predefined pattern file or any image document that's open.

To apply a pattern fill with the Clone tool:

1. Define a pattern from any image document using the Rectangle or Square selection tools and the Define Pattern command in the Edit menu. Figure 11–12 (left) shows a rectangular pattern defined from a small flower.

2. Double-click the Clone tool icon in the Paint Palette to access the Clone Options dialog box (refer back to Figure 11–10).
3. Select the Pattern option button in the Clone section of the dialog box.
4. Adjust other parameters as desired, and then select OK.
5. Click and drag at the point in the active image document or selection area where you want to begin painting the pattern. If you selected the Aligned option, you'll paint the pattern tiles contiguously no matter how many times you release the mouse button while painting. If you left the Aligned option unselected, you'll begin painting the pattern from its center every time you click and drag. Figure 11–12 (right) shows a custom pattern that has been painted several times into an image.

With the Clone tool, you apply a pattern selectively rather than automatically throughout an image or selection as with the Fill command.

Figure 11-12.

Painting a custom pattern with the Clone tool: *(l)* Defining the pattern *(r)* Pattern painted multiple times with Clone tool

This means that the brush shape used and the action of your mouse will have a great deal to do with the final appearance of the pattern.

Adding Text to an Image

The Text tool lets you add text strings of up to 250 characters each to an image document, using any fonts and point sizes available to you under Microsoft Windows. If you're running Adobe Type Manager, Bitstream FaceLift, or another font manager, you'll be able to use all the fonts you've installed.

When you first place text in an image document, it's no more than a floating selection area. You can move it, fill it, paint in it, or otherwise edit it like any other selection area. Once you deselect the text, however, it becomes fixed in the active image document and will no longer be easy to manipulate. So be sure to finish editing a text string as soon as you create it!

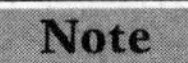

The Text tool is the only Paint Palette tool that works with all image data types.

Placing Text and Defining Options

To insert text into the active image document:

1. Click the Text tool once to activate it, then click at the point in the active image document where you want to position the text. The Font Setting Options dialog box shown in Figure 11–13 will appear, with the cursor blinking in the text entry box.

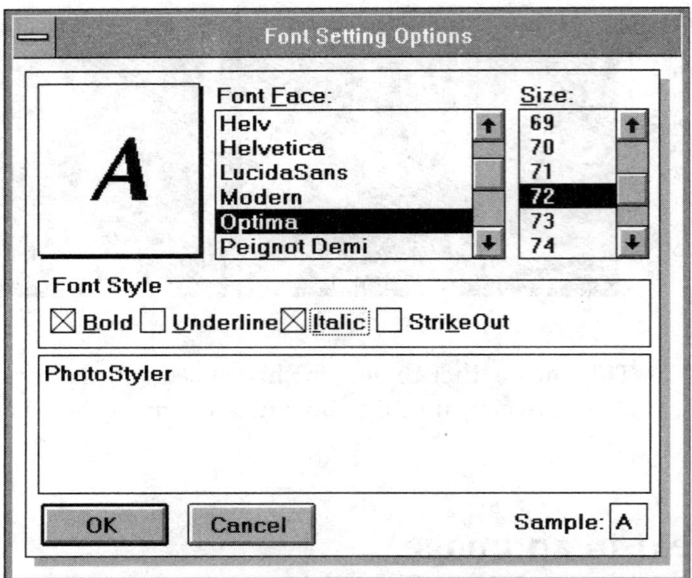

Figure 11-13.

The Font Setting Options dialog box

2. Type your message in the text entry box. You can type a maximum of 250 characters per text string. Text will wrap automatically if it exceeds the length of a line, but you can press Ctrl-M or Ctrl-Enter to begin a new line at a given point. You can also use the mouse and the standard Windows editing keys (Shift-Del, Ctrl-Ins, Shift-Ins) to cut, copy, and paste text within the entry box.

Note

There's no limit to the number of separate text strings you can create in a single image document.

3. Select a typeface and a point size using the Font Face and Size list boxes. The sample character in the Text Preview window will show a letter in the chosen typeface and point size. (To change the sample character, simply type a different letter or ASCII code in the Sample text entry box at the lower right corner of the dialog box.)
4. If you want your text to have special attributes such as bold, italic, or underline, activate the appropriate check box under Font Style.
5. When you've specified all your options, click OK. The text will appear as a floating selection area just to the right of the point where you clicked. The characters will be aligned just as they were in the dialog box.
6. Fill or paint in the text selection area as desired. You may also choose to move the text to another location.

7. When you're finished editing the text string, deselect it to fix it within the image document.

Note *If the active image document is anything other than a Grayscale or RGB True Color image, your only painting option will be to use the Fill command in the Edit menu.*

Text Tips and Techniques

There are quite a few things you can do to enhance the appearance of text in PhotoStyler and give it the pizazz of graphic design. We'll cover a few tips and techniques here; no doubt you'll develop your own with experience.

Avoiding the Jaggies

Text that you create in PhotoStyler isn't as smooth-looking as text generated in a drawing program such as Corel Draw. It's bitmapped, so there will be some stair-stepping "jaggies." The severity of the jaggies will depend on the font you use, the size of the text relative to the complete image, and the total *output* size of the image. In some cases, stair-stepping won't even be visible to the naked eye, but in others it might be quite annoying.

Perhaps a future release of PhotoStyler will provide automatic anti-aliasing for text. Until then, you can use several techniques to smooth the jaggies on your own:

- Create text at large point sizes. Stair-stepping is definitely less noticeable at sizes above 36 points. At smaller point sizes, letters may even run together if the chosen font has a broad character width. If the maximum font size for your system is limited and you want to increase text size even further, use the Resize command in the Transform menu after you place the text outlines in the image. (See Chapter 13 for more about using the Resize command.)
- Add a small (one pixel) soft edge to the text selection area using the Soft Edge command in the Select Palette menu. But beware: There's always a trade-off between sharpness and smooth blending. If you specify a thicker soft edge, you might clog up the internal spaces in letters like a, o, and p. If text is too small, even a one-pixel soft edge might cause letters to run together.

- Add a border to the text string and then specify a one-pixel Soft Edge for the border. Don't combine this technique with a soft edge for the text string itself, though.
- Avoid using text in low-resolution image documents or images having small output dimensions.

Enhancing Text with a Border

We can't even begin to explore the many techniques you can use to add "pizazz" to text in PhotoStyler. You can fill it, paint in it, transform it, break it down into channels, apply filters to it—the list goes on and on. To whet your appetite, we provide a simple example of enhancing text with a border.

1. Open an existing image document, or create a new one. The image document should have a fairly high output resolution (say, 200 dpi or better) and be several inches in width.

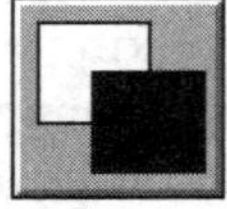

2. Check the current background color. If it's something other than white, display the Color Palette (Ctrl-8) and make white the background color.

3. Click once on the Text tool icon in the Paint Palette and then at the point in the active image document where you want to place the text. The Font Setting Options dialog box will appear.
4. Type *Pizazz!* in the text entry box. Choose a font to your liking and set the point size as high as your system or font manager software will allow. Activate the Bold attribute, and then click OK. The text outlines will appear in the active image document, as shown in Figure 11–14.
5. Most likely, your text doesn't fill the image document. To make your text even larger, choose the Resize command in the Transform menu and specify a pixel width that nearly matches the width of the image. Make sure Aspect Ratio is set to Fixed, and then click OK.

6. Activate the Eyedropper tool in the Select Palette and then press Ctrl-8 to display the Color Palette. If you're working with a True Color image document, select a bright red as the current foreground color. If the active image document is Grayscale, select black as the current foreground color.

Figure 11-14. Placing text outlines in an image document

7. Double-click the Pencil tool icon. When the Paintbrush Options dialog box appears, set Use Foreground Color to Always, Spacing to a fairly high number—say, between 10 and 20 pixels. Set Transparency to 0%. Click the Shape command button and select the default custom brush shape, or load another custom brush shape that you've created. Click OK when your settings match these.
8. Move the cursor within the text outlines and begin painting. As you drag the mouse, paint will appear in the custom brush shape at intervals of the specified number of pixels. Keep painting until you've filled areas of each letter with the brush shape, as shown in Figure 11–15. We used a custom brush shape of our own design for this exercise.
9. If you were to deselect the text string now, it wouldn't be very legible because of the incomplete filling by the Pencil. To remedy that defect and add contrast, you'll add a border. Begin by choosing the Border command from the Select Palette menu. The larger your image and the higher your image resolution, the larger your border should be. We specified a border width of four pixels. When you click OK, the text string will be deselected and the border will become the new selection area.

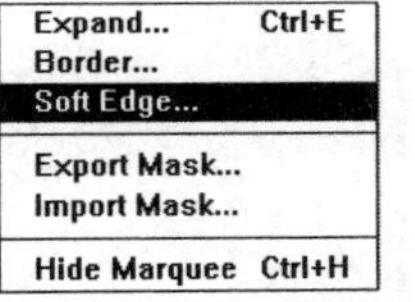

10. You'll want the border to look smooth after you fill it, so choose the Soft Edge command from the Select Palette menu and specify a soft edge several pixels thick. We set Soft Edge at 5 pixels (one pixel larger than the border width) to simulate a large amount of anti-aliasing. Let the size of your image, the size of your text string, and the resolution of your image guide you in choosing a Soft Edge width.

Figure 11-15.

Filling a text string with a custom brush shape (Pencil tool)

11. If you're working with a Grayscale image, change the current foreground color to a medium gray. If your image is True Color, access the Color dialog box and choose a less saturated shade of red.

12. To fill the outline, double-click the Bucket Fill tool and set Color Similarity to 255. As you'll see in the section on using fills, this setting will ensure that you'll fill the entire border with a single click. Click the OK command button to exit the dialog box.
13. Move the cursor inside the text outline borders and click once. The border will fill with a soft-edge solid color, as in Figure 11–16. If you want a better view of the border, hide the marquee temporarily with the keyboard shortcut Ctrl-H.

14. Deselect the border by clicking the N button near the base of the Select Palette. Both text string and border are now "frozen" in the active image document.

Figure 11-16.

The finished text string with a soft-edged, solid color border

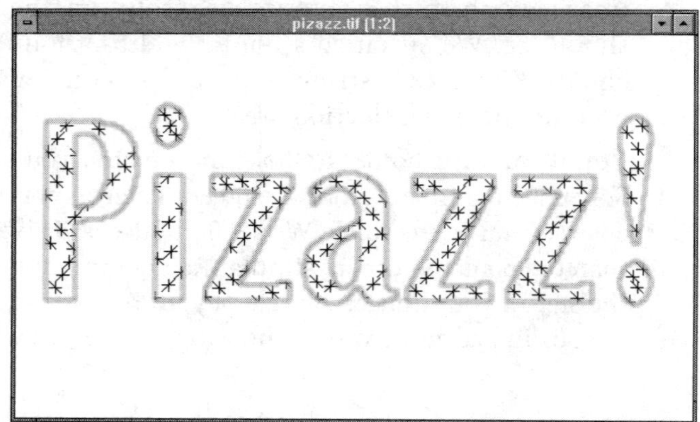

There's no built-in anti-aliasing for text in PhotoStyler, so a soft edge or border is usually advisable, especially if your text is large and your image resolution high. If you want to decrease "jaggies" even further, you can perform manual anti-aliasing with the help of the Smudge tool. Magnify the image and apply the Smudge tool around the edges of the text border, using a very small brush shape.

Note *If your images are destined for high-end advertising in print media, you may find the use of bitmapped text inconvenient. Try overlaying text from your page layout program instead.*

To the extent that the retouching tools in the Paint Palette help you edit and merge parts of multiple images, they can also be considered image composition tools. You'll have the opportunity to explore the finer points of image composition techniques in Chapter 13. In the meantime, browse through Chapter 12 to discover the special-effects magic of PhotoStyler's versatile image filters.

12

Editing Images with Filters

Traditional photographers place *filters* on their camera lenses to add special effects to the subjects they photograph. Each type of lens filter alters a photographic image in a specific way. Lens filters have a few limitations, though. For one thing, their effects are rendered permanent on the film; there's no easy way to "undo" a traditional filter if you change your mind about the results. Lens filters also don't allow photographers to create multiple special effects in a single exposure. And if the photographer wants to add effects to a restricted area of an image, it's necessary to spend time in the darkroom with lots of toxic chemicals.

PhotoStyler provides twenty-seven predefined *digital* filters that are much more flexible than their analog counterparts. Located in the Image menu, these filters let you blur or sharpen images, produce a variety of painterly special effects, and add two- and three-dimensional effects. You can introduce more than one type of effect to the same image, or even to different areas of an image. Best of all, you'll never run out of filters that suit your needs. If PhotoStyler or a third-party developer doesn't supply what you want, you can easily create custom filters of your own.

Note *Filters in PhotoStyler are available for Grayscale and True Color images only. If you want to use a filter on another image data type, first convert the image to Grayscale or RGB True Color.*

What Are Digital Filters?

Digital filters achieve special effects by modifying color or Grayscale values in an image automatically. PhotoStyler's filters do their magic by calculating new values for a whole "neighborhood" of pixels at a time. In some cases, you can define the number of pixels that make up each neighborhood or *matrix*. Other filters work with matrices of a set number of pixels.

Just because a given filter uses the same mathematical formula over and over doesn't mean it always produces the same visual results. The predominant color or gray values in an image or selection area help determine how a filter will affect it. So do the distribution of colors and the degree of image sharpness.

Applying a PhotoStyler Filter

All of PhotoStyler's filters are located in six commands or submenus of the Image menu: Smoothing Filters, Sharpening Filters, Special Filters, User-Defined Filters, 2-D Spatial Effects, and 3-D Spatial Effects. To apply any of PhotoStyler's filters to an image or selected area:

1. Activate the Grayscale or RGB True Color image document to which you want to apply the filter. If you want to apply a filter to a specific area of the image, select that area first. Otherwise, the filter will affect the entire image document.
2. Choose the appropriate command from its submenu in the Image menu. Some filters don't require that you specify any options; these filters will perform their actions immediately.
3. If a dialog box appears, specify settings for each option and then click the OK command button. The filter will carry out its function.

A Note on the Speed of Filters

No matter how much memory your system contains, filters work more slowly than other PhotoStyler features. This is because filters require an enormous number of calculations, several for each pixel in the image. And a four- or five-megabyte file can easily contain a couple of million pixels! If you have PhotoStyler version 1.1a or later, however, you may notice increased speed in the execution of filters.

Using the Smoothing Filters

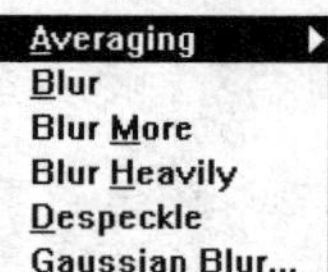

Several PhotoStyler filters act to soften the contrast between neighboring pixels in an image document or selection area. These filters are grouped together in the Smoothing Filters submenu of the Image menu. Each of the Smoothing Filters—Averaging, Blur, Blur More, Blur Heavily, Despeckle, and Gaussian Blur—has specific uses and affects an image in a unique way. Table 12-1 should help you decide when to use one Smoothing Filter instead of another.

The Averaging Filter

When you convert a Black & White or Indexed 16- or 256-Color image document to Grayscale or RGB True Color, PhotoStyler uses a dither pattern to simulate a higher number of colors or gray shades than the original image actually contained. These dither patterns result in sharp, unsightly transitions between colors or grays, as shown

Table 12–1. A Comparison of PhotoStyler's Smoothing Filters

Filter	Effect
Averaging	Smooths dither patterns in images that have been converted from B/W or Indexed Color to Grayscale or True Color
	Blurs images and retains very little contrast between neighboring pixels
Blur	Reduces contrast slightly throughout an image document or selected area
Blur More	Reduces contrast moderately throughout an image document or selected area
Blur Heavily	Reduces contrast greatly throughout an image document or selected area
Despeckle	Removes noise from poorly scanned images
	Reduces contrast and softens edges in high-contrast areas of an image only
Gaussian Blur	Blurs images with precise control over cell size and contrast

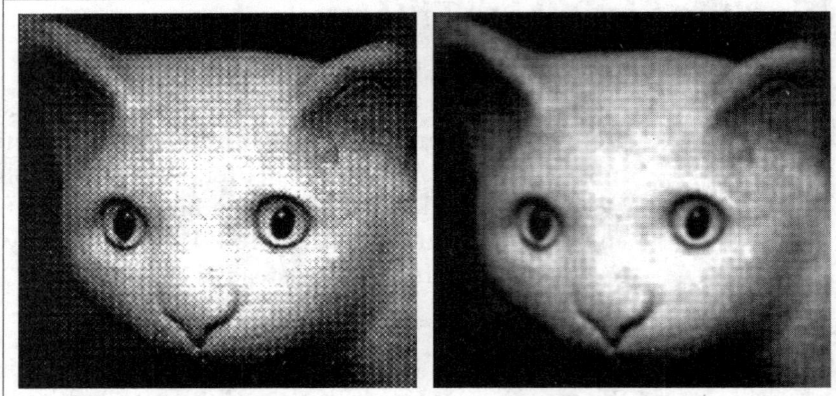

Figure 12-1.

Using the Average filter to increase the number of gray shades in an image converted from Black & White
(l) converted image
(r) after averaging in 8 x 8 cells

by the first image in Figure 12–1. To smooth the transitions, use the Averaging filter.

The Averaging Filter command in the Image: Smoothing Filters submenu smooths color or Grayscale transitions while increasing the number of actual color or gray values that the image or selection area contains. It does so by averaging the color or gray value of each pixel with the color or gray values of its neighbors and then assigning the averaged value to all the pixels in an imaginary matrix cell.

You can control how much smoothing takes place by using the Averaging submenu options to specify the number of pixels in each matrix cell. The larger the cell, the smoother the transitions will be, and the more color or gray values the resulting image document will contain. Figure 12–1 (right) shows the converted image after applying the Average filter in smoothing cells of 8 x 8 (64) pixels. If we had used a cell of 2 x 2 pixels, there would have been fewer gray shades in the resulting image and thus less realistic transitions.

Caution

There's always a trade-off between smoothness and sharpness when you use the Averaging filter. An image document averaged with the highest number of pixels per cell (8 x 8, or 64) may contain realistic transitions between colors or gray shades, but it may also look out of focus. Using one of the Sharpening filters won't correct the problem, either.

When you use the Averaging filter on an image document that *hasn't* been converted from some other data type, its effect is simply to blur the image. The larger the cell size you specify, the greater the blurring effect. The main advantage of using the Averaging filter over the Blur, Blur More, and Blur Heavily filters is that you can control the size of the matrix cell that PhotoStyler uses to calculate new color or gray values.

The Blur, Blur More, and Blur Heavily Filters

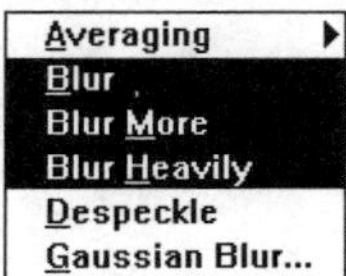

Like the Averaging filter, the three Blur filters reduce contrast between neighboring pixels in an image or selection area. Unlike the Averaging filter, though, each Blur filter uses a fixed matrix cell size. The size of each matrix cell used to average color or gray values together is 3 x 3 (9) for the Blur and Blur More filters and 5 x 5 (25) for the Blur Heavily filter.

Each Blur filter also uses a weighting function that retains varying degrees of contrast between neighboring pixels. Compare the effects of the Blur filters with the Averaging filters on the same image area. You'll see that the Blur filters retain more contrast between neighboring pixels than the Averaging filter.

If you're not sure how much blurring an image needs, be conservative and use the Blur filter. You can apply the same filter repeatedly to continue blurring the image bit by bit.

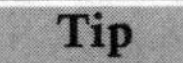

To control blurring selectively in an image document or selected area, use the Blur tool instead of the Blur filters. The Blur tool reduces contrast only in the pixels over which the cursor passes (Chapter 11).

The Despeckle Filter

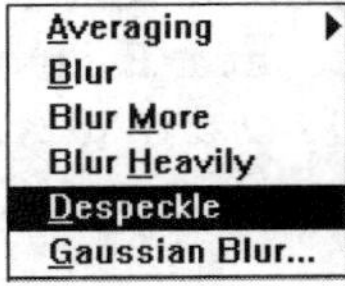

The Despeckle filter reduces contrast more selectively than the other filters in the Smoothing Filters submenu. It smooths transitions only in areas of an image that already contain high contrast or hard edges. As a result, its effects are more subtle than those of its sister filters. In fact, the action of the Despeckle filter is more aptly described as a *toning down* than as a blurring. If you use the Despeckle filter on an image document that doesn't contain much contrast, you may not even see a noticeable "before and after" difference.

Use the Despeckle filter to eliminate "noise" produced by poor scanning, to tone down glitter or harsh lighting effects, and to reduce detail in less attractive areas of an image.

The Gaussian Blur Filter

The Gaussian Blur filter gives you more control over the degree of blurring than any of the Smoothing Filters. The Variance scroll bar in the Gaussian Blur dialog box (Figure 12–2) lets you vary the size of the matrix cell that PhotoStyler uses to average color or gray values from 1 to 100 pixels. Smaller cells produce more subtle blurring, but even at low Variance values the Gaussian Blur reduces sharpness to a

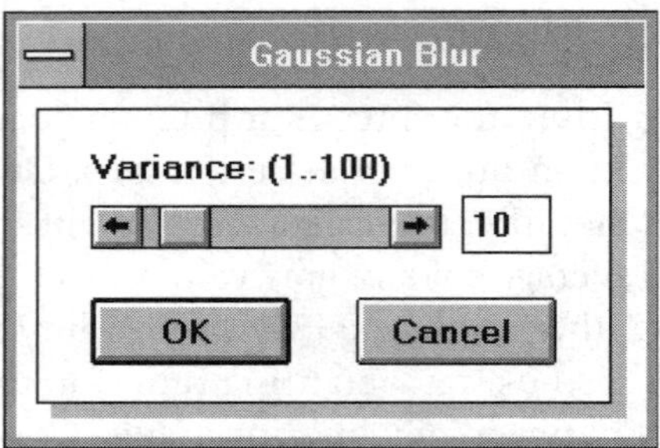

Figure 12-2. The Gaussian Blur dialog box with Variance scroll bar

greater degree than the Blur filter. At the upper Variance limit where cells are huge, the blurring effect is so extreme that the image or selected area looks as though you were viewing it underwater.

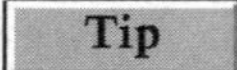

You can use the Gaussian blur filter on individual image channels to create drop shadows for text. See Chapter 14 for a hands-on exercise that will let you try out this technique.

Sharpening Filters

Edge Enhancement
Find Edge
Find Edge & Invert
Sharpen
Sharpen More
Sharpen Heavily
Trace Contour...

The Image: Sharpening Filters submenu contains seven filters that act to sharpen and increase contrast in an image or selected area. Each of the seven filters affects images in a unique way. Table 12–2 provides a quick reference that will help you decide when to use one sharpening filter instead of another.

The Edge Enhancement Filter

Edge Enhancement
Find Edge
Find Edge & Invert
Sharpen
Sharpen More
Sharpen Heavily
Trace Contour...

An *edge* is any area in an image where abrupt changes in brightness and contrast occur between neighboring pixels. The Edge Enhancement filter increases contrast along edge pixels throughout an image or selection, but leaves pixels in low-contrast or smooth areas of the image unchanged.

The effect of using the Edge Enhancement Filter depends on the makeup of a particular image. In images where most brightness transitions are smooth or occur along well-defined lines, such as the fax illustration in Figure 12–3, Edge Enhancement will create continuous outlines around objects. In images where contrast is diffused throughout the image, such as the carousel horse in Figure 12–4 in the Color Section, Edge Enhancement will add texture and glitter as it sharpens.

Table 12–2. A Comparison of PhotoStyler's Sharpening Filters

Filter	Effect
Edge Enhancement	Increases contrast in areas where noticeable changes in brightness or contrast occur
	Adds texture, glitter, or outlines
Find Edge	Reduces images to colored or Grayscale outline strokes against a dark background
Find Edge & Invert	Reduces images to colored or Grayscale outline strokes against a light background
Sharpen	Increases contrast slightly throughout an image or selected area
	Heightens focus of blurry areas
Sharpen More	Increases contrast moderately throughout an image or selected area
Sharpen Heavily	Increases contrast strongly throughout an image or selected area
Trace Contour	Reduces Grayscale images to white outline strokes on a black background
	Reduces True Color images to up to eight colors of outline strokes on a dark background, with precise control over color values and the number and location of outlines

Tip

When applied to text, the Edge Enhancement filter will reduce "jaggies" and outline the letters automatically.

The Find Edge Filter

The Find Edge filter is truly a special-effects filter. Two things happen when you apply this filter to an image or selected area:

- It inverts the colors or gray shades in the image, which usually results in a dark background (black for Grayscale images).

Figure 12-3.

Adding outlines to high-contrast images with the Edge Enhancement filter

- It seeks out the pixels where significant brightness transitions occur and connects them, forming fine, bright outline strokes.

The original color or gray values of pixels on either side of the edge pixels will determine the colors of the outline strokes. In any case, the outlines will be bright, producing a hand-sketched look (Figure 12–5).

Tip

For best results, images to which you apply the Find Edge filter should be fairly high in contrast.

The Find Edge & Invert Filter

Edge Enhancement
Find Edge
Find Edge & Invert
Sharpen
Sharpen More
Sharpen Heavily
Trace Contour...

This filter works just like the Find Edge filter, with one important difference: it inverts all the color or gray values in the outlined image. The result is a series of dark or colored outline strokes on a white or light-colored background (Figure 12–6).

Note

Keep in mind that the Find Edge and Find Edge & Invert commands tend to "flatten" an image, giving it a distinctly two-dimensional look with no depth.

Figure 12-5.

Turning a high-contrast image into an etching with the Find Edge filter

Figure 12-6. Creating an inverted "etching" with the Find Edge & Invert filter

The Sharpen, Sharpen More, and Sharpen Heavily Filters

Edge Enhancement
Find Edge
Find Edge & Invert
Sharpen
Sharpen More
Sharpen Heavily
Trace Contour...

These three filters sharpen an image or selection by heightening contrast among neighboring pixels in varying degrees. They work according to the same principles as the Blur, Blur More, and Blur Heavily filters in the Smoothing Filters submenu. Each Sharpen filter uses a fixed matrix cell size: 3 x 3 (9) pixels for the Sharpen and Sharpen More filters and 5 x 5 (25) pixels for the Sharpen Heavily filter. Each Sharpen filter also uses a weighting function that heightens contrast between neighboring pixels to varying degrees.

The three Sharpen filters are appropriate for realistic photo retouching because their effects are fairly subtle. In some cases, you may need to apply the same filter more than once to obtain the desired effect. If you're looking for intense, special-effects sharpening, try the Edge Enhancement filter instead.

Tip

To sharpen pixels selectively instead of throughout an image document or selected area, use the Sharpen tool in the Paint Palette.

The Trace Contour Filter

Edge Enhancement
Find Edge
Find Edge & Invert
Sharpen
Sharpen More
Sharpen Heavily
Trace Contour...

Think of the Trace Contour filter as a sophisticated version of the Find Edge filter. Like Find Edge, it reduces an image or selected area to outline strokes against a dark background, but with purer and more extreme contrasts between color and gray values:

- Grayscale images turn into white outlines on a black background.
- RGB True Color images are reduced to outlines of up to seven brilliant colors (white, red, green, blue, cyan, magenta, and yellow)

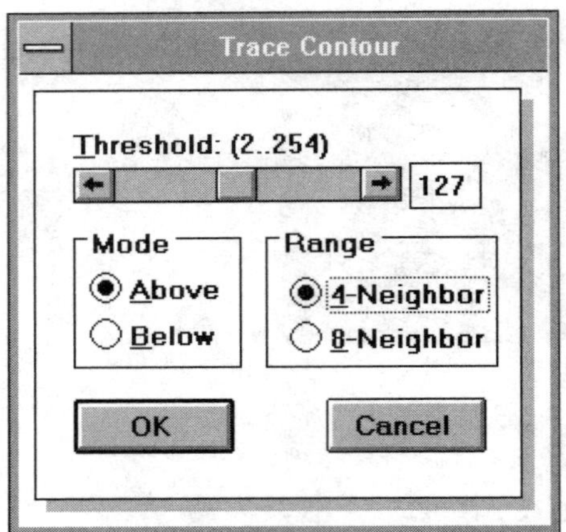

Figure 12-8. The Trace Contour dialog box

against a black background (see Figure 12–7 in the Color Section of this book).

Unlike the Find Edge filter, Trace Contour gives you precise control over:

- the relative proportion of black and colored/white areas
- the location of black and colored/white areas
- the continuity of the outlines

You control these factors through the Threshold, Mode, and Range options in the Trace Contour dialog box (see Figure 12–8).

The Threshold Option: Controlling the Location and Relative Proportion of Black and Colored/White areas

The Threshold option in the Trace Contour dialog box tells PhotoStyler what color or gray value to use as a guide when tracing an edge or *contour*. Let's say you use the default value of 127—halfway between black (0) and white (255). PhotoStyler will seek out all the instances where a pixel with at least one value *below* 127 falls next to a pixel with at least one value *above* that threshold. Wherever it finds two such pixels, PhotoStyler will trace an edge—in white for a Grayscale image or in one of seven brilliant colors for a True Color image. The pixels that surround the contour will become black. By varying the Threshold value, you're changing the placement of contours and the amount of detail in the filtered image. If you're working with a True Color image, adjusting the Threshold value can alter the color makeup of the contours, too.

Take the image of the horse in Figure 12–7 in the Color Section, for example. A threshold setting of 75 gave us the most colorful outlines and the greatest amount of detail. Had we chosen a much higher threshold value, the filter would have produced an image with fewer outlines and either fewer or different color combinations. The best Threshold setting to use will depend on the relative brightness and contrast levels in a given image. Experiment with various settings to find the one that's right for you.

A Note about Tracing Grayscale vs. True Color Image Contours
The Threshold setting affects Grayscale and True Color images differently. As you'll recall from Chapter 7, pixels in a Grayscale image have a single value, so the process of seeking out and tracing contours is pretty straightforward. With True Color images, the process becomes slightly more complex, because each pixel has three separate values. By comparing the color values of each pair of neighboring pixels along a contour, PhotoStyler determines which of the seven colors will appear as the contour color.

The Mode Option: Controlling the Placement of Contours

If the Threshold option determines where PhotoStyler draws the contour outlines, the Mode option determines which of each pair of threshold pixels PhotoStyler will highlight in color or white. Selecting Above tells PhotoStyler to highlight the *darker* of each two pixels that meet the Threshold value criterion. Selecting Below tells PhotoStyler to highlight the *lighter* of each pair of contour pixels.

The Mode option rarely has much effect on the appearance of contours in Grayscale images. When you're working with a True Color image, on the other hand, Mode can be important. If a given pair of contour pixels has distinctly different colorations, your choice of Mode will change the color of the contour at that point.

The Range Option: Controlling the Continuity of Contours

The Range option determines the size of the matrix cell that PhotoStyler uses when calculating the placement of contours and black areas. A larger cell will produce more continuous contour outlines than a smaller cell.

- When you choose 4-Neighbor, PhotoStyler uses a cell of five pixels. Contour outlines will tend to be somewhat fragmented with this setting. For a hand-sketched look, 4-Neighbor may be just what you want.

- When you choose 8-Neighbor, PhotoStyler calculates contours using a cell of nine pixels. Since more color or gray values are being calculated at a time, contour outlines will be more continuous—a little like neon tubing if you're tracing contours for a True Color image. We used the 8-Neighbor setting for Figure 12–7 in the Color Section of this book.

Using 2-D Filters

The filters contained in the Image: 2-D Spatial Effects submenu produce specialized two-dimensional distortion patterns. Both of these filters—2-D Ripple and 2-D Whirlpool—simulate effects related to water.

The 2-D Ripple Filter

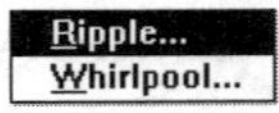

The 2-D Ripple filter in the Image: 2-D Spatial Effects submenu distorts an image or selection area in a way that simulates a breeze blowing over the surface of water. This filter yields more subtle effects than the 2-D Whirlpool filter.

When you choose this filter command, the 2-D Ripple dialog box shown in Figure 12–9 will appear. The options in this dialog box let you vary both the height and the frequency of the ripples.

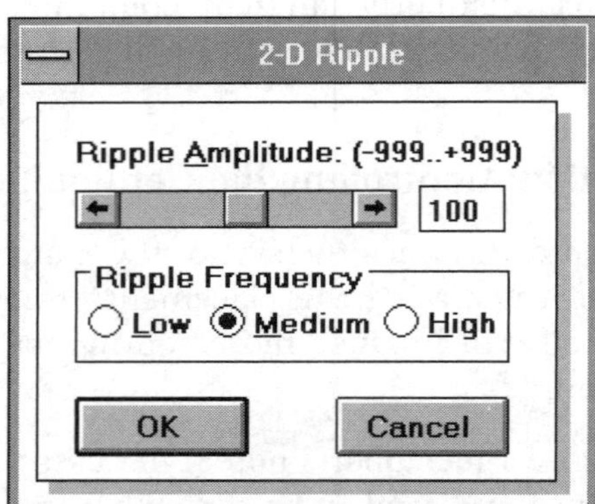

Figure 12-9.

The 2-D Ripple dialog box

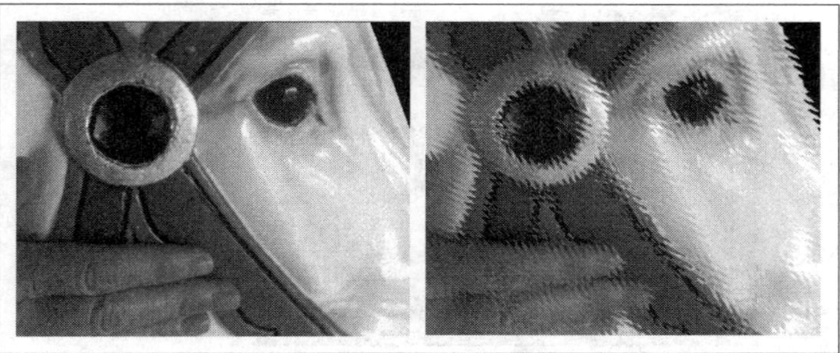

Figure 12-10.

Applying the 2-D Ripple filter: Amplitude 999, Ripple frequency medium

Ripple Amplitude

The Ripple Amplitude scroll bar lets you determine both the height and the direction of the ripples used to distort an image area. The range of values available is from -999 to +999. If you select a positive value, ripples created by the filter will begin with the crest. If you select a negative value, the ripples will begin with the trough.

At the default value of 100, distortion will be subtle. The higher the numerical value in either direction, the more extreme the distortion and the height of the ripples will be. Figure 12–10 shows a close-up of an image before and after applying the 2-D Ripple filter at an Amplitude of 999.

Ripple Frequency

The Ripple Frequency radio buttons control the spacing of the ripples in the image document or selected area. A setting of low results in ripples spaced far apart—very subtle, especially if the Ripple Amplitude setting is near zero in either direction. A setting of Medium yields a moderate frequency (see Figure 12–10), and a setting of High results in ripples spaced very close together. For maximum distortion, you'd set Ripple Amplitude to a high numerical value and Ripple Frequency to High.

The 2-D Whirlpool Filter

The 2-D Whirlpool filter creates a spiral effect in an image document or selected area. The greatest amount of twisting occurs at the center of the image, with the effects lessening toward the edges.

When you choose the 2-D Whirlpool filter command in the Image: 2-D Spatial Effects submenu, the dialog box in Figure 12–11 will appear. There's only one option for this filter: you control the intensity of the twisting effect by the angle you set here. The higher the angle,

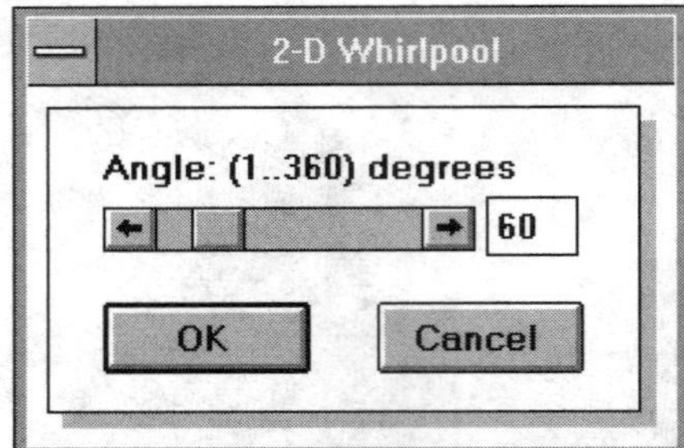

Figure 12-11. The 2-D Whirlpool dialog box

the more obvious the spiral effect will be, and the further out from the center the twisting will extend (see Figure 12–12). At a low angle, the twisting effect may disappear entirely before it reaches the border of the image or selection area. The filter "twists" the image in a counterclockwise direction.

Tip *The 2-D Whirlpool filter is most effective on areas of an image that already contain rounded or oval contours.*

Using 3-D Filters

It's no simple task to simulate the depth of three dimensions in a flat, two-dimensional image. The five filters in the Image/3-D Spatial Effects submenu do just that, though. When you apply one of these filters to an image document or selected area, PhotoStyler creates three-dimensional effects by expanding and compressing areas of pixels. The names of the four predefined filters in the 3-D Spatial Effects

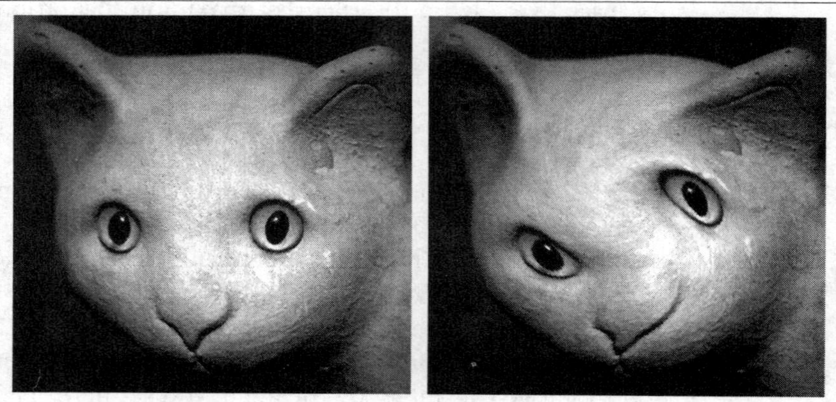

Figure 12-12. Applying the 2-D Whirlpool filter at an angle of 100 degrees

submenu—Cylinder, Pinch, Punch, and Sphere—describe the "geometry" they impose on the image or selection to which you apply them.

The distortion effect for all 3-D filters is always most intense at the center of the image or selected area and decreases toward its outer edges. If you apply a 3-D filter to a square image document or to a square or circular selection area, the distortion will seem to follow a circular pattern. If you apply such a filter to a rectangular image document or to a rectangular or elliptical area, the distortion will follow an elliptical pattern. And if you use a 3-D filter on an irregular selection area, PhotoStyler will apply the filter based on the shape of the bounding box that surrounds the area.

A fifth option in the 3-D Spatial Effects submenu, Custom, lets you create 3-D effects of your own and save them for later use. We'll look at the method for creating custom 3-D and other filters in the "Creating User-Defined Filters" section of this chapter.

The 3-D Cylinder Filter

Use the 3-D Cylinder filter when you want an image or selected area to protrude outward in the center and inward along its horizontal edges. The effect is like wrapping an image around a cylinder or pole (Figure 12–13). Unlike the 3-D Sphere filter, 3-D Cylinder doesn't compress the *vertical* edges of the image or selected area. The distortion is most intense near the center of the image, so define the selection area carefully.

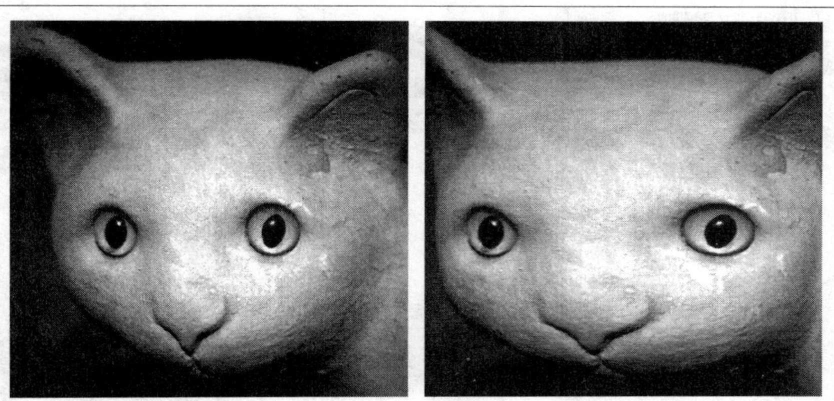

Figure 12-13.

Applying the 3-D Cylinder filter

Figure 12-14.

The 3-D Pinch dialog box

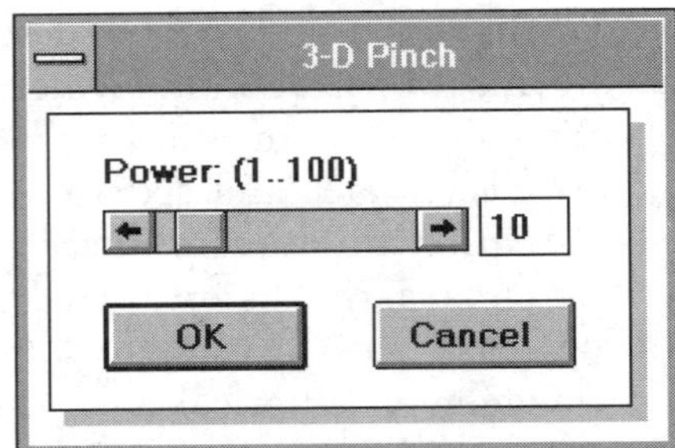

The Pinch Filter

When you choose the 3-D Pinch filter, PhotoStyler compresses pixels in the center of the image document or selected area, giving the image a squeezed or concave look. The Power scroll bar in the 3-D Pinch dialog box (Figure 12–14) lets you determine just how intense the pinching effect will be. The default value for a fairly subtle distortion is 10, but you can specify any value from one (very subtle) to 100 (very intense). Figure 12–15 shows the effects of applying the 3-D Pinch filter at a power of 50.

The Punch Filter

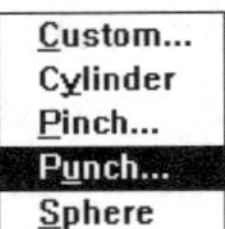

Instead of compressing pixels at the center of an image as the Pinch filter does, the 3-D Punch filter expands them, giving the central part of an image or selected area a "flattened" look. When you choose the 3-D Punch command, the dialog box in Figure 12–16 will appear, letting you determine the intensity of the flattening effect by specifying a power. The higher the numerical value you choose, the more intense the punch distortion will be. Figure 12–17 shows an image to which the 3-D Punch filter was applied at a power of 75.

Figure 12-15.

Applying the 3-D Pinch filter at a power of 50

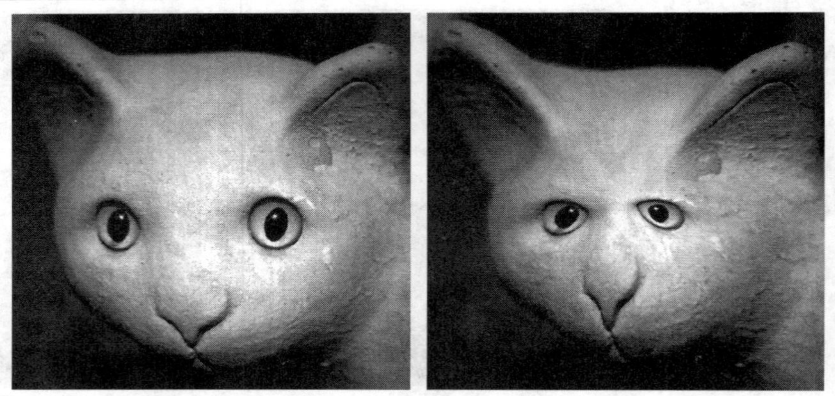

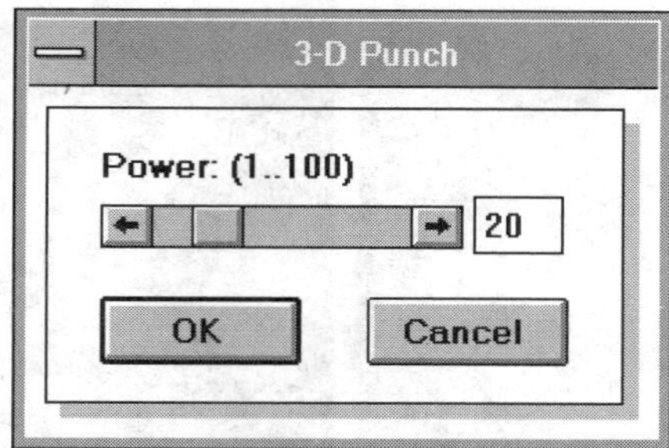

Figure 12-16.

The 3-D Punch dialog box

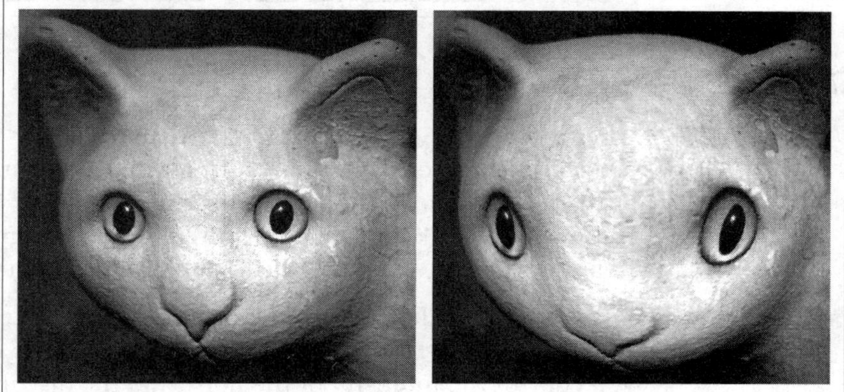

Figure 12-17.

Applying the 3-D Punch filter at a power of 75

The Sphere Filter

Custom...
Cylinder
Pinch...
Punch...
Sphere

The 3-D Sphere filter expands an image or selection area at the center and compresses it along *all* its edges—not just along the horizontal ones like the 3-D Cylinder filter does. The result is an image that seems to be wrapped around a globe or ball. The shape of this filter is most obvious when you apply it to an area that contains circular shapes (see Figure 12–18).

Using Other Special-Effects Filters

Add Noise...
Emboss...
Maximum...
Median...
Minimum...
Motion Blur...
Mosaic...

The Special Filters submenu under the Image menu houses a number of filters that have nothing to do with blurring, sharpening, or adding two- or three-dimensional effects. For want of a better term, we'll call them special-effects filters.

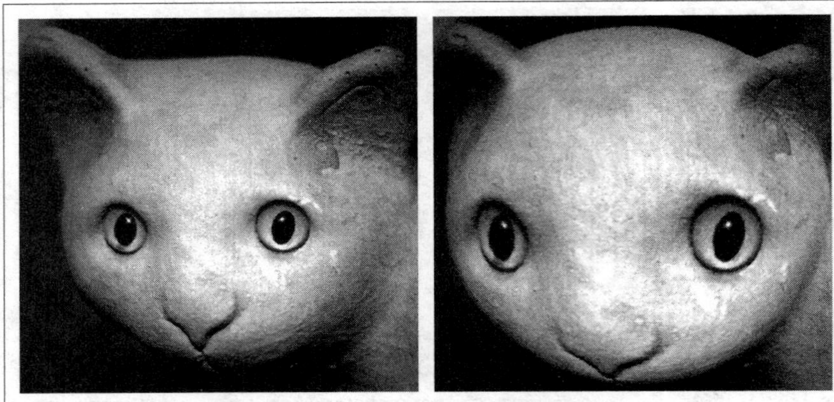

Figure 12-18.

Applying the 3-D Sphere filter

The Add Noise Filter

Choose the Add Noise filter command to add "snow" (random changes in gray or color values) to an image document or selection area. In a Grayscale image document, the noise effect is like the "snow" patterns on black-and-white TV sets. In an RGB True Color image document, the Add Noise filter produces multicolored glitter.

When you click on the Add Noise command, the Add Noise dialog box in Figure 12–19 will appear. By defining options in this dialog box, you control the intensity of the noise and the distribution of its color or Grayscale values.

- The Variance scroll bar determines how much "snow" or noise the filter will generate and how far pixels may stray from their original color or gray values. At the default value of 100, the effect will be

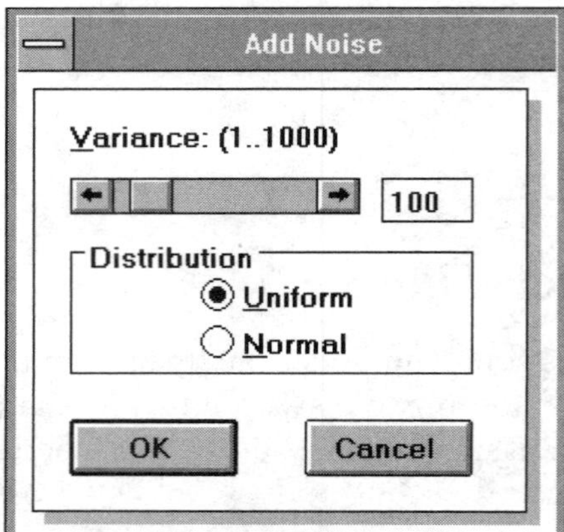

Figure 12-19.

The Add Noise dialog box

mild. As the value increases to its maximum of 1000, the noise will increase. Figure 12–20 in the Color Section shows the effect of a Variance setting of 150.

- The option buttons in the Distribution section of the dialog box determine how evenly the noise or snow is distributed throughout an image. If you select Uniform, the distribution of pixel changes will be regular. If you select Normal, random changes in pixel values will intensify as you increase the Variance value.

We've found by experimentation that at a given Variance value, the Normal distribution setting yields a "noise" pattern that follows the contours of objects within the image document or selected area. The Uniform setting, on the other hand, tends to obscure the contents of an image or selected area.

The Emboss Filter

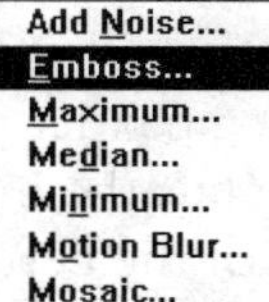

Some filters produce dazzling effects with color images but don't do justice to Grayscale ones. That's not true of the Emboss filter, though. This filter causes a bare "sketch" of an image or selected area to stand out in relief against a solid-color image background as in Figure 12–21. The effect is like the embossing seen on elegant stationery or business cards.

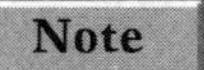

The Emboss filter, like the Find Edge filter, locates the "edges" or contours of an image along the highlight and shadow area. These mark the contours that will appear in relief in the image or selected area.

When you choose the Emboss command, the dialog box in Figure 12–22 will appear. The options in the Emboss dialog box let you specify whether the embossing will be concave or convex, the depth of the embossing, and the color or gray value used to "coat" all but the highlights of the image.

Figure 12-21.

Emboss filter: Depth 3 pixels, Midtone coating

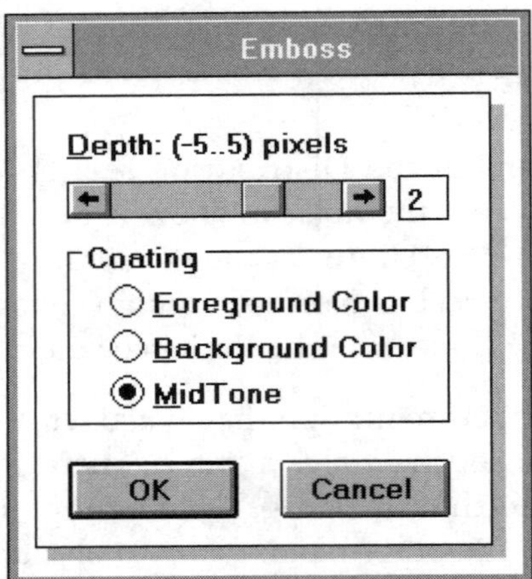

Figure 12-22.

The Emboss dialog box

- The Depth scroll bar has a range of -5 to +5 pixels. A negative value will cause the embossing to seem concave, while a positive value will make it seem to stand out from the rest of the image. At a value of zero, the image will look absolutely flat.
- The option buttons in the Coating section of the dialog box let you control the color or gray value used to coat everything but the highlighted areas of the image. You can coat the image with the current foreground or background color, or with a gray midtone value. Naturally, you can use the Color Palette to change the current foreground and background colors if you're aiming for a special effect.

The Maximum, Median, and Minimum Filters

These three filters all reduce the number of color or gray values in an image or selected area, resulting in a more streamlined look. All the dialog boxes for these three filter commands have controls similar to

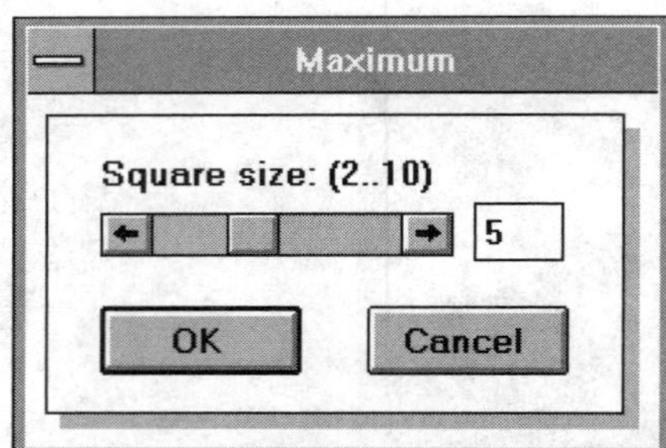

Figure 12-23.

The Maximum filter dialog box

the one in Figure 12–23. You control both the type and the extent of changes to pixel values:

- The filter you choose will determine whether the image area becomes brighter (Maximum) or darker (Minimum) or merely evens out the highlights and shadows (Median).
- By defining the size of the matrix cell or *square* that PhotoStyler uses to calculate new pixel values, you determine how much streamlining takes place. The larger the cell size you choose, the more extreme the color or Grayscale reduction will be.

The Maximum Filter

The Maximum filter brightens color or gray values in an image as it reduces the total number of colors. To achieve this overall brightening effect, it recalculates pixel values based on the *lightest* pixel in each matrix cell or square. Square sizes can vary from two to ten pixels. Smaller square sizes yield a subtle brightening effect, moderate reduction of colors, and little or no blurring. Larger square sizes result in more extreme brightening, fewer color or gray values, and increased blurring.

The Median Filter

The Median filter homogenizes highlight and shadow areas in an image as it reduces the total number of color or gray values. To achieve this "toning down" effect, the filter recalculates color or gray values based on the values of the *median* pixel in each matrix cell or square. Smaller square sizes yield a subtle toning down of highlights and shadows and little or no blurring. Larger square sizes result in more extreme flattening of highlights and shadows and increased blurring.

The Minimum Filter

The Minimum filter darkens color or gray values in an image as it reduces the total number of colors. To achieve this overall darkening effect, it recalculates pixel values based on the *darkest* pixel in each matrix cell or square. Square sizes can vary from two to ten pixels. Smaller square sizes yield a subtle darkening effect, moderate reduction of colors, and little or no blurring. Larger square sizes result in more extreme darkening, fewer color or gray values, and increased blurring.

The Motion Blur Filter

The Motion Blur filter is useful for enhancing sports photos and other images that emphasize speed and motion. This filter simulates motion by dragging pixels at a distance and angle that you specify, while leaving a residual image behind.

When you choose the Motion Blur command in the Image/Special Filters submenu, the Motion Blur dialog box in Figure 12–24 will appear. The two scroll bars in this dialog box let you control the distance and angle at which PhotoStyler drags the image or selected area.

Length

The Length scrollbar controls the distance over which motion seems to occur. The available range is from two to fifty pixels. As the distance increases, so will be the degree of blurring.

Angle

The Angle scroll bar determines the direction in which motion seems to occur. At the default value of zero degrees, the image or selected area seems to move directly to the right. At 45 degrees, the image moves diagonally upward and to the right.

Figure 12–25 illustrates a carousel horse in motion at an angle of 45 degrees. Since the hand was *deselected* when we applied the Motion Blur filter, it appears to be stationary as the horse begins to gallop away from it. Take a close look at the harness above the horse's eye. It seems sharper than the rest of the "moving" horse because its contours are at the same 45-degree angle at which the rest of the horse is moving.

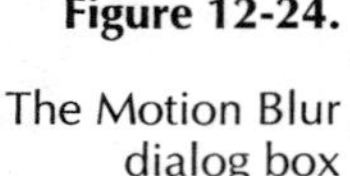

Figure 12-24.

The Motion Blur dialog box

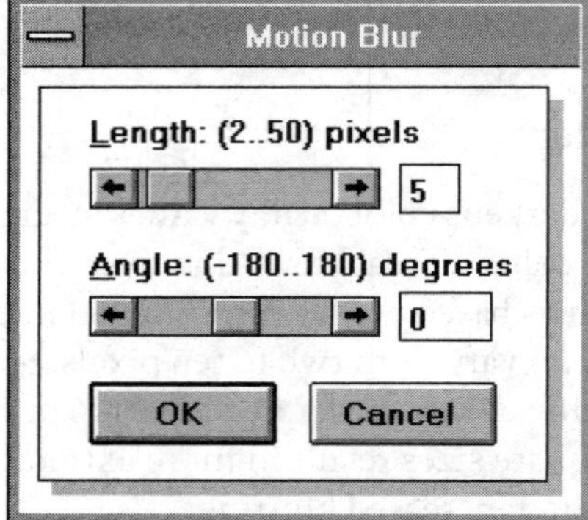

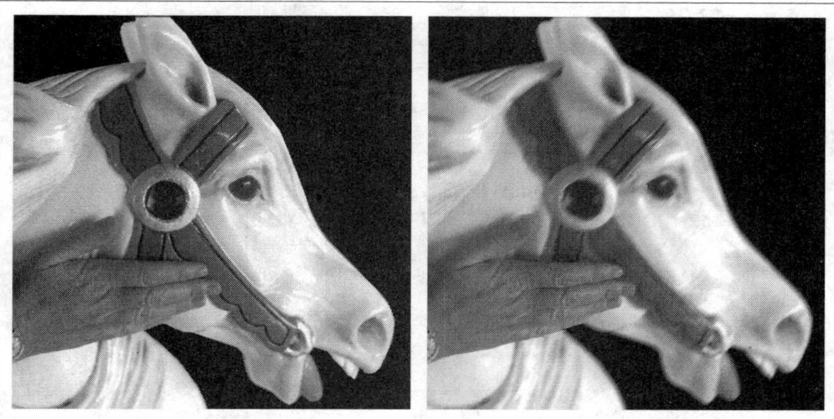

Figure 12-25.

Applying the Motion Blur filter to the horse, excluding the hand: Length 15 pixels, Angle 45 degrees

Tips for Obtaining a Natural-Looking Motion Blur

If your specialty is fine art rather than photo retouching, realism may not always be crucial to your application. But if you need to ensure the most natural-looking motion blur effect possible, here are some things you can do:

- Match the angle of motion to other elements in the image. For example, if most objects in the image tend to move the eye upward and to the right, a motion blur that emphasizes movement upward and to the left could create a jarring effect.
- Don't increase the distance of the motion blur beyond what's necessary. As you increase the length of the filter effect, you also increase the blurriness.
- If you're applying the Motion Blur filter to a selected area of an image only, extend the selection area by a few pixels in the intended direction of motion. If you don't extend the selection area, you may end up with what seems like lots of blur and no motion—PhotoStyler won't be able to drag the object past the "wall" formed by the edges of the selection area.

The Mosaic Filter

Add Noise...
Emboss...
Maximum...
Median...
Minimum...
Motion Blur...
Mosaic...

Television and video programs sometimes use mosaic patterns for special effects or to disguise people's identity. With the Mosaic filter, you can achieve the same effects, breaking up an image into rectangular cells. PhotoStyler averages the current pixel values in each cell and reduces them to a single color or gray value.

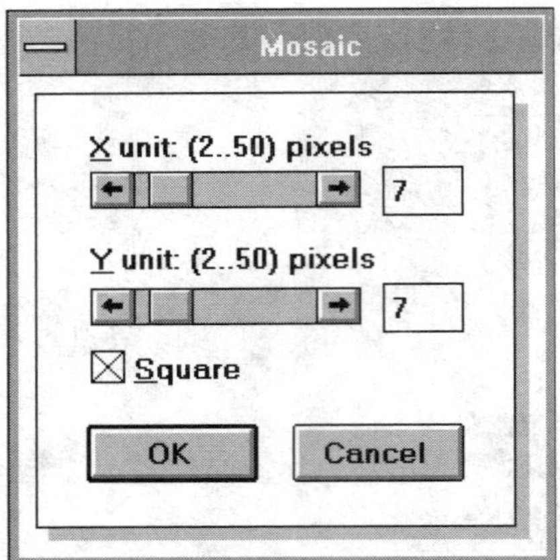

Figure 12-26.

The Mosaic dialog box

The Mosaic dialog box that appears when you choose the Mosaic command (Figure 12–26) lets you define the size of the mosaic cells that the filter will generate. The X unit defines the width of each cell, while the Y unit controls the length. As you increase the size of the mosaic cell, you further reduce the number of overall colors or grays in the image. If you activate the Square check box, any changes you make to the length or width of the mosaic cell will be mirrored in the other dimension.

We applied the Mosaic filter with a 15 x 15 pixel cell to the "face" of the scarecrow in Figure 12–27.

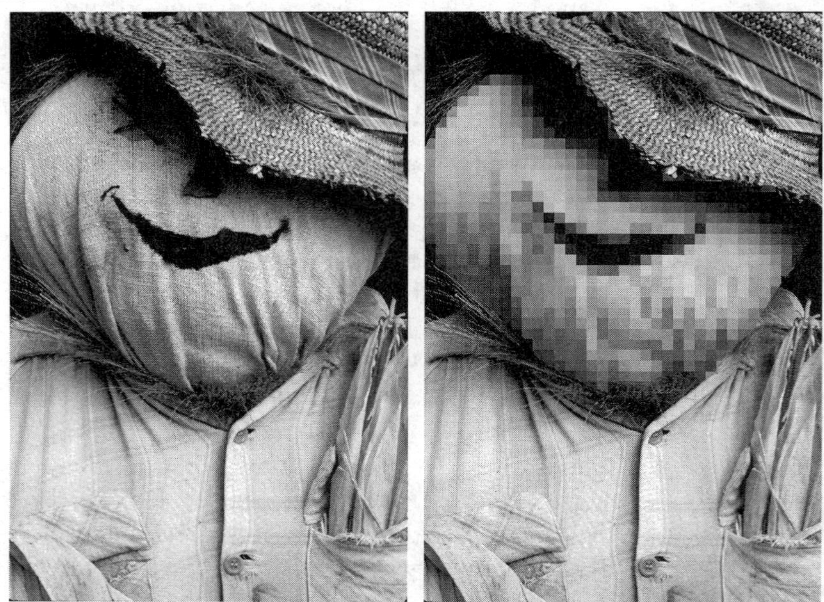

Figure 12-27.

Applying the Mosaic filter to a selected area

Creating and Saving Custom Filters

You don't have to be contented with the predefined filters that PhotoStyler provides. Two commands—the User-Defined Filter command in the Image menu and the Custom command in the Image/3-D Spatial Effects submenu—let you create and save custom special-effects filters of your own. It's possible to build an entire library of custom filters for special retouching or fine-art purposes.

Creating User-Defined Filters (Non-3D)

Except for 3-D effects filters, most of PhotoStyler's predefined filters work by recalculating pixel values within a matrix cell. In many cases, you can influence the effects that the filter produces by specifying the number of pixels in each cell.

The principle behind designing custom filters with the User-Defined Filter command is the same, but you exercise even greater control over the way PhotoStyler manipulates color or Grayscale values. Not only do you specify the number of pixels in each matrix cell; you also tell PhotoStyler how to multiply or average the brightness values of each pixel in order to arrive at new values. The tool you use to design and automate a new filter is the User-Defined Filter dialog box that appears when you choose the User-Defined Filter command.

The User-Defined Filter Dialog Box

The User-Defined Filter dialog box (Figure 12–28) provides five types of controls that determine how a custom filter will affect an image document or selected area. These controls and their functions are:

Matrix Field Custom filter calculations are always based on an imaginary matrix cell containing up to 25 pixels (5 x 5 pixels square). Each matrix entry field in the dialog box represents one pixel in the matrix cell. The number of pixels that the filter actually uses for each set of calculations depends on the values you enter (or don't enter) into each of the 25 matrix entry fields. The way PhotoStyler changes pixel values also depends on the values in these matrix fields.

- If a value of zero (the default) appears in a matrix field, the pixel that the matrix field represents won't enter into the calculations and its brightness value won't change.

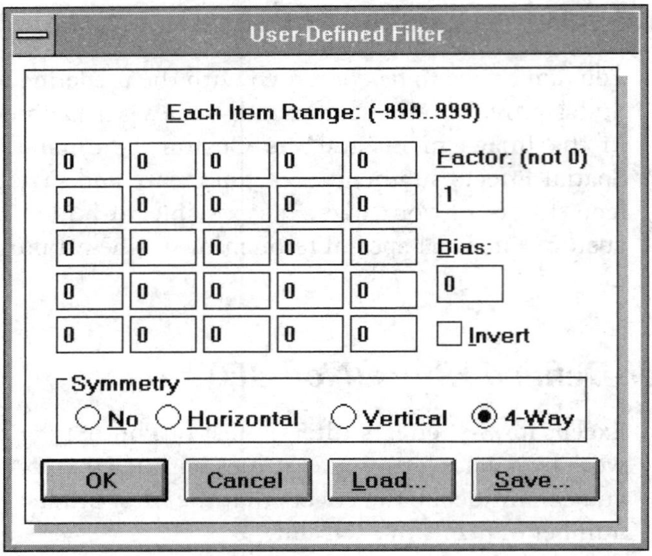

Figure 12-28.

The User-Defined Filter dialog box

- If a matrix field contains a positive or negative number, the filter will multiply that number by the brightness value of the pixel that the field represents. The range of allowable numbers is from -999 to 999.

Symmetry The four radio buttons in the Symmetry section of the dialog box determine how automatically you'll choose the numbers for the matrix entry fields.

- Select No if you want to be able to enter any number in any matrix field.
- When you select Horizontal, any number you enter in a given matrix field will appear in the horizontally opposite field as well.
- Selecting Vertical causes any number that you enter in a given matrix field to appear in the vertically opposite field, too.
- When you select 4-way, a value that you enter in one matrix field will appear in the diagonally, horizontally, and vertically opposite fields as well. This setting generates filters in the most "automatic" way.

There are no set rules for choosing matrix values; your results will depend on the color or grayscale makeup of a particular image. Experiment until you find settings that work for you.

Factor If you multiply the existing brightness values of pixels by a high matrix field number, many of the pixels will turn white (255 is the upper brightness limit). To compensate for this situation, PhotoStyler divides the "new" brightness values by the number you've entered into the Factor entry box. So if some of the recalculated pixel values are higher than the allowable limit of 255 (white), division by the Factor value may bring them back within the normal color range. The Factor value can be any integer between -999 and 999, except zero.

Bias After a filter divides the brightness values in each cell by the Factor value, it derives the final brightness values by adding the current Bias value to each pixel. The Bias value can be any number between -999 and 999, including zero.

Invert When you activate this check box, PhotoStyler will invert the color or gray values of all pixels in the cell after all the other calculations have been performed.

Creating a New User-Defined Filter

To design a new custom filter with the help of the User-Defined Filter command in the Image menu, you don't have to be a mathematician. Just experiment with the following steps a few times. Eventually, you'll come up with a filter you really like, one which yields consistent results with many different types of images.

1. Activate the image document you want to experiment with. If you want to apply the new filter to a selected area only, make the selection now.
2. Choose the User-Defined Filter command from the Image menu to access the User-Defined Filter dialog box.
3. Select the Symmetry option that best matches the degree to which you want to automate the process of defining a filter. If you select No, you'll be able to enter any allowable value into any matrix field. Selecting one of the other three radio buttons will automate the data entry process to a certain extent.
4. Enter values into the matrix entry fields, beginning with the target field at the center of the matrix. You don't have to alter values in all of the fields. To create a filter that changes brightness values only minimally, leave all the matrix field values at zero except the fields that immediately surround the center (target) pixel.

5. Enter a value other than zero into the Factor field. PhotoStyler will divide this number into the values of pixels that have been multiplied by the matrix entry field numbers.
6. Enter a value into the Bias field. PhotoStyler will add this value to each pixel in the cell.
7. If you want PhotoStyler to invert the brightness values of each pixel in the cell after all other values have been calculated, activate the Invert check box.
8. Click the OK command button to cause the new filter to take effect in the active image document or selection area.
9. If you don't like the results, choose the Undo command in the Edit menu and try again. If you do like the results and want to save this filter for later use, see the next section.

Figure 12–29 shows the numerical settings for a custom filter that we designed. We nicknamed it the "Earthquake" filter because its mixture of blurring, sharpening, and contrast-heightening effects produces the impression that the subjects in an image are bouncing up and down uncontrollably. Take a look at what happened when we applied our "Earthquake" filter to the image in Figure 12–30 and you'll see what we mean! Apply this filter when you want to evoke jarring movement or tension in areas of an image.

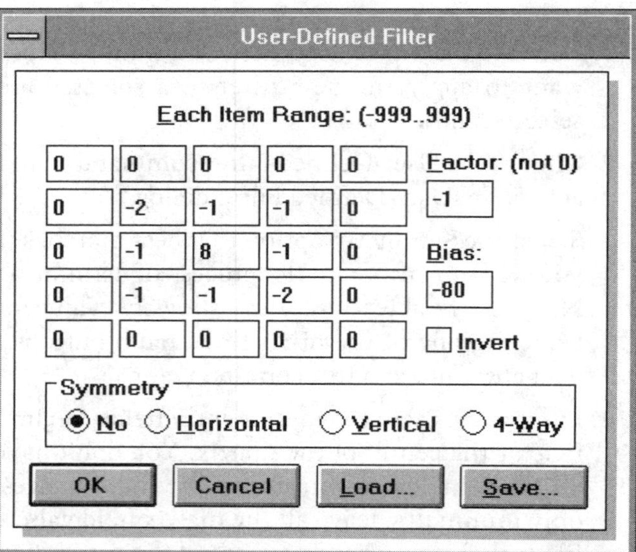

Figure 12-29.

Settings for a custom "Earthquake" filter featuring mixed blurring, sharpening, and contrast-heightening effects

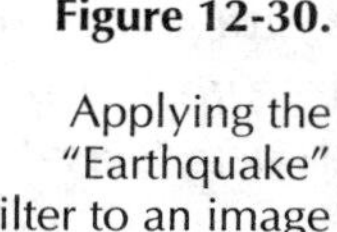

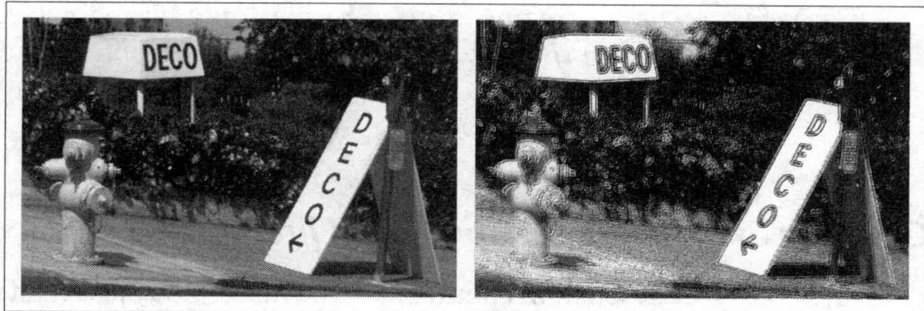

Figure 12-30. Applying the "Earthquake" filter to an image

Saving and Loading User-Defined Filters

Once you design a filter that works well with many images, you can save it to a file and load it later. To save the custom filter that's currently in the User-Defined Filter dialog box, click the Save command button in the User-Defined Filter dialog box. When the dialog box in Figure 12–31 appears, change directories if necessary, then enter a filename for the filter and click OK. PhotoStyler will add the .UDF extension to the new filter file automatically. We recommend saving all custom filters in the \filters subdirectory under your PhotoStyler directory.

To load a filter that has already been saved, click the Load command button in the User-Defined Filter dialog box. When the Load User Defined Data from File dialog box appears, change to the drive and directory where the filter file is located, and then click OK. The filter you've chosen is now ready for use with the active image document.

Figure 12-31. The Save User Defined Data to File dialog box for saving custom filters

Save User Defined Data to File

Filename: *.UDF

Directory: c:\pstyler\filters

Files:
average.udf
blur.udf
earthquk.udf
emboss.udf
sharpen.udf

Directories:
[..]
[-a-]
[-b-]
[-c-]

Save Cancel

Tip *The Averaging, Blur, Sharpen, and Emboss filters are available through the Load command button. To obtain a clearer idea of how these filters were created, load them one at a time into the User-Defined Filter dialog box.*

Creating and Saving Custom 3-D Filters

The Custom command in the Image/3-D Spatial Effects menu lets you define new filters that produce three-dimensional effects. Just as with the predefined 3-D filters, the effect of a custom 3-D filter will always be strongest at the center of an image or selected area and will dissipate outward toward the edges in a circular or elliptical fashion.

To begin creating a custom 3-D filter, choose the Custom command in the Image/3-D Spatial Effects submenu and repaint the mapping curve in the 3-D Custom dialog box.

The 3-D Custom Dialog Box

The 3-D Custom dialog box shown in Figure 12–32 has a lot in common with the Color/Gray Map dialog box (see Chapter 9). In fact, you work with the 3-D mapping curve and the Gray Map in the same way: repainting the curve with the mouse or applying a predefined menu function to it. Instead of altering color and gray values, however,

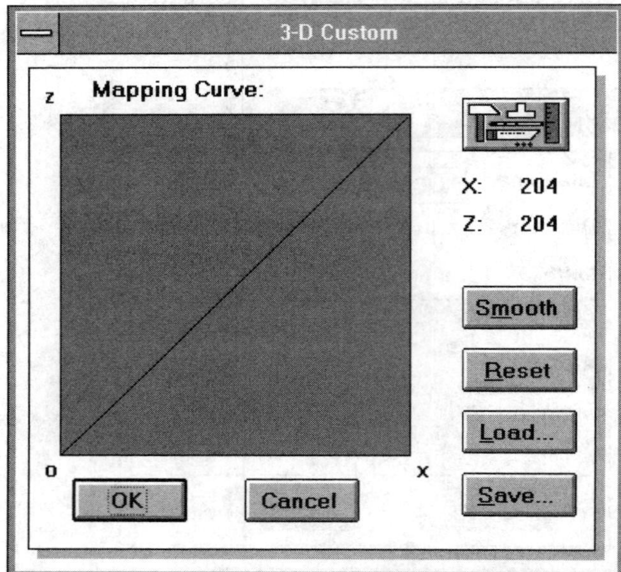

Figure 12-32. The 3-D Custom dialog box

the 3-D mapping curve compresses or expands areas of pixels, letting you determine the origin, intensity, and radius of a 3-D distortion effect. The menu functions and command buttons in the dialog box all serve this same purpose.

Understanding the 3-D Mapping Curve The 3-D Mapping Curve is at the heart of the process of defining a custom 3-D filter. Instead of Input and Output axes that define color values, the 3-D Mapping Curve contains an o-point, an x-axis, and a z-axis.

- The o-point indicates the origin of the 3-D effect, the point where distortion is always greatest.
- The x-axis describes the location(s) of the 3-D effect along a radius that extends from the origin point to the edges of an image document or selected area. Higher values indicate pixels that are farther away in all directions from the center of the image.
- The z-axis describes the intensity of the 3-D distortion. The greater the z-axis value, the stronger the three-dimensional depth of the custom effect will be.

In repainting or defining the 3-D Mapping Curve, then, you're determining the intensity of a distortion effect at every point between the center of an image or selected area and its edge.

When you first access the 3-D Custom dialog box, the 3-D Mapping Curve is a straight line at a 45-degree angle. To create a visible 3-D effect, you have to turn this straight line into a curve or group of curve segments; straight-line segments neither compress nor expand the areas of the image that they represent. If you're painting the 3-D mapping curve freehand, use these guidelines:

- Increase the steepness of the curve wherever you want pixels to be expanded.
- Decrease the slope of the curve wherever you want pixels to be compressed.
- To keep the distortion effect mild, move the beginning of the curve away from the o-point (the point of origin).
- For a strong distortion effect, draw the steepest slopes and inclines closest to the point of origin.

Smooth

Smooth The Smooth command button smooths the "jaggies" out of any mapping curve you've drawn freehand. Remember, straight-line segments have no 3-D effect on an image, so it's to your advantage to use the Smooth command button frequently.

Reset

Reset Use the Reset command button to cancel any editing to the curve and return it to its straight-line default state.

Load...

Load The Load command button lets you load custom 3-D mapping curves that you've saved previously to a file.

Save...

Save Use this command button to save the current custom 3-D mapping curve to a file. You can retrieve such curves later and use them with other images.

Piecewise
Circle
Logarithm
Sine
Square
Square Root

3-D Custom menu When you click on the toolbox icon in the 3-D Custom dialog box, a pop-up menu appears. The options in this menu apply predefined effects to the 3-D mapping curve.

Tip

Always start with the default diagonal line when you're ready to apply a predefined mapping curve. If you don't, the predefined curve will simply add its effect to the existing mapping curve, and the final effect may not be "pure." However, you can use any predefined 3-D curve as a starting point from which to continue freehand editing of the mapping curve.

- The *Piecewise* command adds control points to the 3-D mapping curve, letting you manipulate the curve as a series of straight-line segments. When you're done editing these segments, you can use the Smooth command button to transform them into curves.
- The *Circle* command loads a curve that re-creates the effect of the 3-D Sphere filter. You can edit this curve further in the 3-D Custom dialog box.
- The *Logarithm* command loads a curve that re-creates the effect of the 3-D Pinch filter. Load and edit this curve if you wish to modify the basic Pinch effect.
- The *Sine* command loads a curve that re-creates the effect of the 3-D Punch filter. Load and edit this curve to modify the Punch effect.
- The *Square* command loads a curve that produces a partly flattened 3-D oval effect.
- The *Square root* command loads a curve that produces a softer 3-D pinching effect than the Logarithm command.

Custom...
Cylinder
Pinch...
Punch...
Sphere

Creating a Custom 3-D Filter

Although you can produce an infinite number of 3-D mapping curves, there are only a few basic effects possible. Many custom effects will seem like subtle variations on a theme. To create a custom 3-D filter:

1. Activate the image document to which you want to apply the custom effect. If you want to confine the effect to certain areas of the image, select those areas now.
2. Choose the Custom command from the Image/3-D Spatial Effects submenu to access the 3-D Custom dialog box.
3. If you prefer to apply a predefined 3-D effect, choose one of the commands from the 3-D Custom menu. You may wish to use one of these commands as a starting point for further editing.

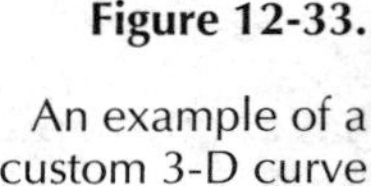

4. If desired, edit the curve freehand by placing the cursor in the 3-D Map and then dragging the mouse in the desired direction. Don't worry about "jaggies"; you can smooth those out afterward.

Note *To restore the 3-D mapping curve to its default diagonal format at any time, just click the Reset command button.*

5. When you're finished editing, click the Smooth command button to remove the rough angles and straight-line segments from the 3-D mapping curve.
6. Click the OK command button to apply the new custom mapping curve to the active image document.

Figure 12–33 shows an example of a custom 3-D filter mapping curve that elongates an image from background to foreground while

Figure 12-33.

An example of a custom 3-D curve

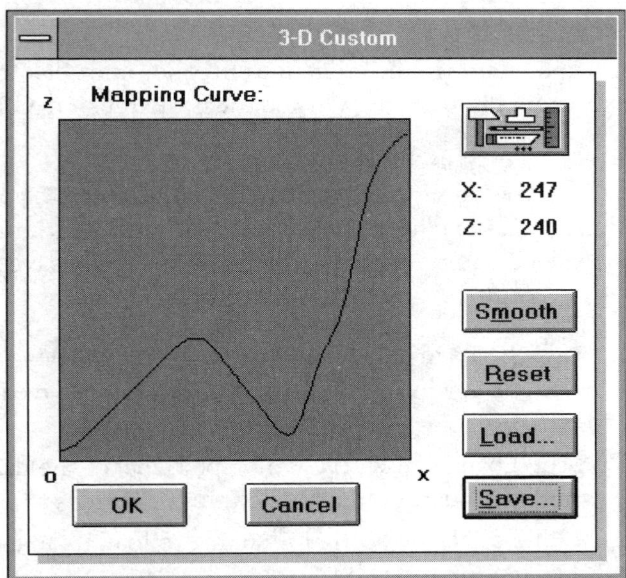

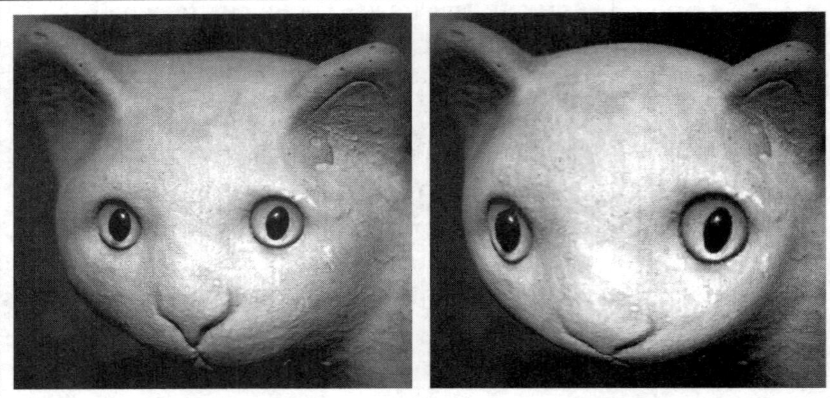

Figure 12-34. Applying a custom 3-D "Bug-eye" filter: upper regions expanded, middle areas pulled forward and elongated, lower regions compressed and pulled downward

expanding upper areas and compressing lower areas of the image. We applied this custom 3-D curve to the image in Figure 12–34.

Saving and Loading Custom 3-D Curves

The 3-D Custom dialog box also lets you save 3-D mapping curves and load them for later use. To save the current 3-D mapping curve as a file:

Save...

1. Click the Save command button.
2. In the Save Map Curve dialog box shown in Figure 12–35, locate the desired drive and directory.
3. Type a name in the Filename entry box and click the Save command button. PhotoStyler will add the file extension .CRV automatically.

Once you've saved a custom 3-D curve to disk, you can use it with other images or edit it as a basis for defining additional custom curves. To load a custom 3-D filter that you've already saved:

Load...

1. Click the Load command button. The Load Map Curve dialog box will appear. This dialog box is similar to the Save Map Curve dialog box.
2. In the Load Map Curve dialog box, locate the drive and directory where the custom mapping curve file resides.
3. Double-click the desired filename to load its mapping curve in the 3-D Custom dialog box.

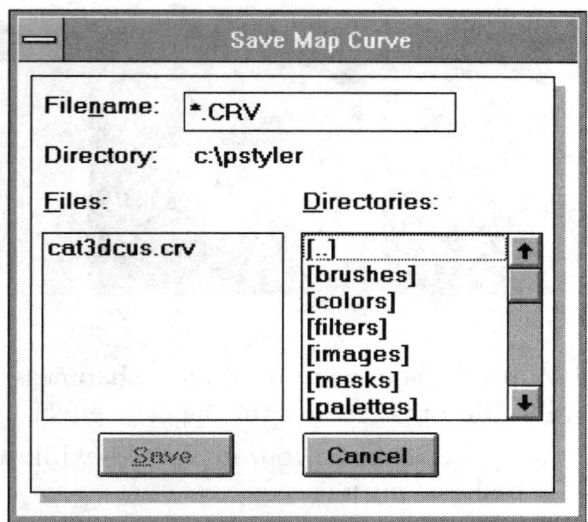

Figure 12-35. The Save Map Curve dialog box for custom 3-D curves

4. To apply the curve immediately, click the OK command button in the 3-D Custom dialog box. If you wish, you can continue editing the curve before applying it.

Filters from Third-Party Developers

PhotoStyler's open architecture permits third-party developers to supply additional filters beyond the ones supplied with your software. As we went to press, Silicon Beach Software had announced plans to make its Gallery Effects line of filters (previously created for Digital Darkroom) available for Windows image editing applications. Check with companies that already offer digital filters for Macintosh-based imaging applications; they're likely to develop filters for Windows software packages, too.

Filter Tips

Filters offer one of the most powerful ways to enhance an image with a minimum of effort. To save you even more effort and help you get the best results with filters, here are a few tips:

- Avoid applying both smoothing and sharpening filters to the same image document or selected area. Once you've changed the brightness

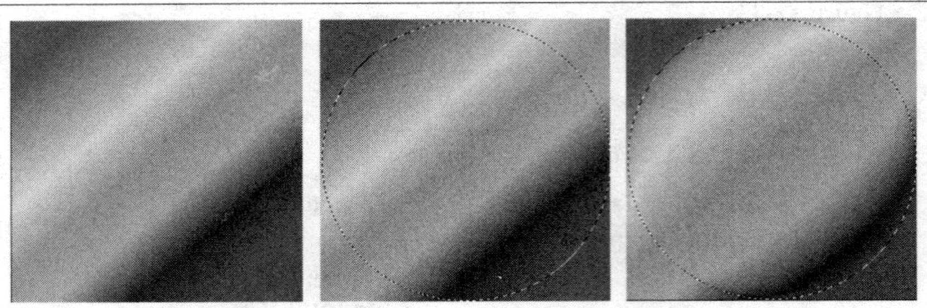

Figure 12-36. Creating a multicolored 3-D "crystal ball" for pasting into another image document

values of pixels, you won't regain lost sharpness or smoothness by applying a filter that creates the opposite effect.

- Save multiple versions of your image files while applying filters, in case you make an error.
- To create a multicolored ball that you can copy and paste into another image document (see Figure 12–36), first create a new image document and fill it with a Custom Color gradient fill as described in Chapter 10. Then, select a circular area of the new document and apply the 3-D Sphere Filter from the Image/3-D Filters submenu to turn this circular area into a globe. The gradient fill inside the selection area will simulate 3-D highlights. Copy this selection area to the clipboard and paste it into the document of your choice. If you're into surrealistic space art, you can have a field day with this technique. Of course, you're not limited to using gradient fills. You can turn the contents of *any* circular selection area into the inside of a paperweight or crystal ball!
- Split a True Color image document into component channels and apply filters to one or more of the separate channels. Then recombine the channels to experiment with a variety of special effects. Emil Ihrig developed his "Homage to Andy" image in the PhotoStyler Gallery using this type of technique. You'll have the opportunity to try out some of these effects in Chapter 14.

13

Editing Image Composition

In PhotoStyler, it's possible to paint and enhance an image to your heart's content without altering the elements that determine its *composition*. Yet, for a real mastery of PhotoStyler, it's important to acquaint yourself with the powerful features that can help you alter image composition. You can flex PhotoStyler's most powerful image composition muscles by combining the selection and masking techniques from Chapter 8 with the commands in the Edit and Transform menus discussed in this chapter.

Tip

The Transform menu commands are available for use with any selection area within an image, not just with selections that have been pasted from the clipboard.

Creating Composite Images

One key to PhotoStyler's creative power is the variety of methods you can use to achieve a single goal. That's especially obvious when it comes to merging multiple images. You can create composites by using any combination of the following techniques:

- using the clipboard to copy, cut, and paste selections (this chapter)
- transforming the content of pasted or unpasted selection areas (this chapter)

- merging images using the Merge Control command (this chapter)
- creating, moving, editing, and deselecting floating selection areas within an image document (Chapter 8)
- importing and exporting masks (Chapter 8)
- filling selection areas with patterns (Chapters 10, 11)
- splitting and combining image channels (Chapter 14)

We'll spend the next few sections exploring the use of the clipboard, which you haven't worked with previously in this book. Along the way, we'll provide plenty of visual examples to guide your own experiments in montaging and compositing images.

Copying, Cutting, and Pasting Image Selections

Your greatest allies in combining multiple images are the Select Palette tools and the temporary storage area known as the clipboard. After selecting any simple or complex area, you can copy or cut it to the clipboard, then paste the selection back into the same or another image document in a variety of ways. PhotoStyler supports two different types of clipboards for this purpose: its own "private" clipboard and a more limited Windows clipboard.

Note *If you have PhotoStyler version 1.1a or later, you'll notice a dramatic improvement in speed and performance when working with both the private PhotoStyler and the Windows clipboards.*

PhotoStyler's Two Clipboards

PhotoStyler supports not one, but two clipboards. The default clipboard is the private PhotoStyler clipboard, which supports all of PhotoStyler's features. PhotoStyler also supports the Windows clipboard used by other applications. You can switch between these clipboards using the Clipboard command in the Edit menu, which we'll discuss shortly.

The private PhotoStyler clipboard is the best one to use when you're merging images within PhotoStyler. It lets you transfer data between Grayscale and RGB True Color images, leaving the shapes and color values of complex selection areas intact. During a work session, the

PhotoStyler clipboard saves data to a temporary file on your hard drive, so your system memory doesn't limit the amount of clipboard data you can store. You can also save cut or copied data to a clipboard file (extension .CLI) and load clipboard files that you've already saved. The downside: you can't paste images from the private PhotoStyler clipboard to any other Windows application.

The Windows clipboard, on the other hand, can accept only rectangular selection areas and can absorb only as much data as your system memory will permit. However, the Windows clipboard can accept data from every image data type, not just from Grayscale and 24-bit color images. You can also transfer data from the Windows clipboard to other applications that run under Windows.

Note *Image data from PhotoStyler doesn't always transfer to other applications with the colors you'd expect. To understand why, see the section entitled "Pasting to or from Another Windows Application" later in this chapter.*

Table 13–1 summarizes the benefits, drawbacks, and uses of the private PhotoStyler and Windows clipboards.

Switching Between Clipboards

Only one of the two PhotoStyler clipboards can be active at one time. Whenever you begin a PhotoStyler work session, the private PhotoStyler clipboard is the active clipboard. To switch back and forth between the PhotoStyler and Windows clipboards:

1. Choose the Clipboard command in the Edit menu. The PhotoStyler Image Clipboard dialog box (Figure 13–1) will appear. If you've already cut or copied a selection during the current session, the Clipboard Contents area will contain image data; otherwise, it will be blank.
2. Click the radio button that represents the clipboard you want to make active. If that clipboard already contains image data, the data will appear in the Clipboard Contents area.
3. Click the OK command button to activate the selected clipboard. The next time you cut or copy a selection, PhotoStyler will store it in this clipboard.

Table 13–1. PhotoStyler's Two Clipboards: A Comparison		
Feature	**PhotoStyler private clipboard**	**Windows DIB clipboard**
Storage method	stores data to temporary file on hard drive optional permanent storage to .CLI file	stores data temporarily in system RAM; no permanent storage
Storage memory limits	none (limited only by hard drive space)	available system memory
Memory usage	minimal; image data written to disk	determined by file size of clipboard contents
Mask shapes supported	supports all complex selection and mask shapes	supports rectangular selection areas only; irregular areas replaced by current background color
Uses within PhotoStyler	seamless transfer of image data among True Color and Grayscale images	transfer of data to and from B/W and Indexed Color images
Uses with other applications	clipboard data not available outside of PhotoStyler	available to all Windows applications, but multiple clipboard standards may result in unexpected color shifts and loss of irregular shapes

Note *If the active clipboard already contains image data when you make the switch, that data won't be lost. It will simply remain dormant until you switch back to the clipboard that stores it.*

Cutting or Copying a Selection

The first step in combining two image documents is to cut or copy a selection to the clipboard. Afterward, you can paste the selection into the same image or into another image that's open.

When the private PhotoStyler clipboard is active, you can copy, cut, and paste selections of any type to and from Grayscale or RGB True

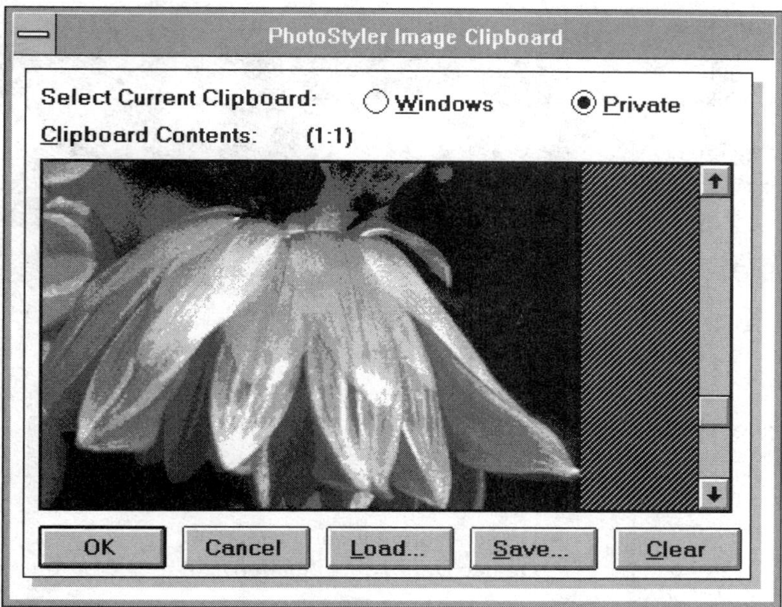

Figure 13-1.

The PhotoStyler Image Clipboard dialog box

Color images. The private clipboard is the best one to use if you're concerned about the accurate transfer of color and irregularly shaped selection areas. When the Windows clipboard is active, you can copy, cut, and paste rectangular selections to and from *any* image data type. The Windows clipboard is preferable only if one of the images you're combining is an Indexed Color or Black & White data type.

To cut or copy a selection to the active clipboard:

1. Activate the image document from which you want to cut or copy an area. If it's a Grayscale or True Color image, you can use either the private PhotoStyler clipboard or the Windows clipboard. If it's any other image data type, you must use the Windows clipboard.
2. Choose the Clipboard command and make sure the active clipboard is the one you want to use. If it isn't, click the desired radio button in the PhotoStyler Image Clipboard dialog box and then select OK.
3. Select the area you want to cut or copy. If the private PhotoStyler clipboard is active, you can use any combination of selection tools and select irregularly shaped areas. If the Windows clipboard is active, you should use only the rectangular or square selection tool.
4. Choose the Cut or Copy command from the Edit menu. If you choose Cut, PhotoStyler will *remove* the selection area from the active image document, replacing the pixels with the current

Figure 13-2.

Cutting a selection replaces image data with the current background color

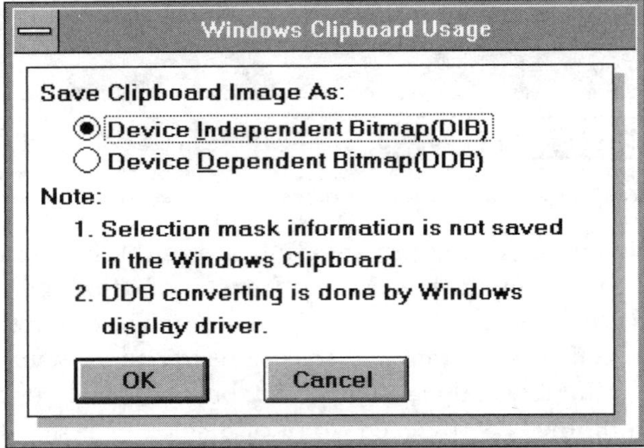

Figure 13-3.

The Windows Clipboard Usage dialog box

background color as in Figure 13–2. If you choose Copy, PhotoStyler will send a copy of the selection area to the clipboard, but the appearance of the active image document won't change.

Note

When the Windows clipboard is active, PhotoStyler displays the dialog box shown in Figure 13–3. If you send data from an irregularly shaped selection area to the DIB clipboard, Windows will store it in a rectangular area of the current background color. If you choose the DDB clipboard, the results will depend on the capabilities of your display adapter. Generally, it's best to use the DIB clipboard unless you plan to transfer the data to an application that supports only the DDB clipboard.

Once a selection area is in the clipboard, you can use the Clipboard command to view it before pasting it into another image document.

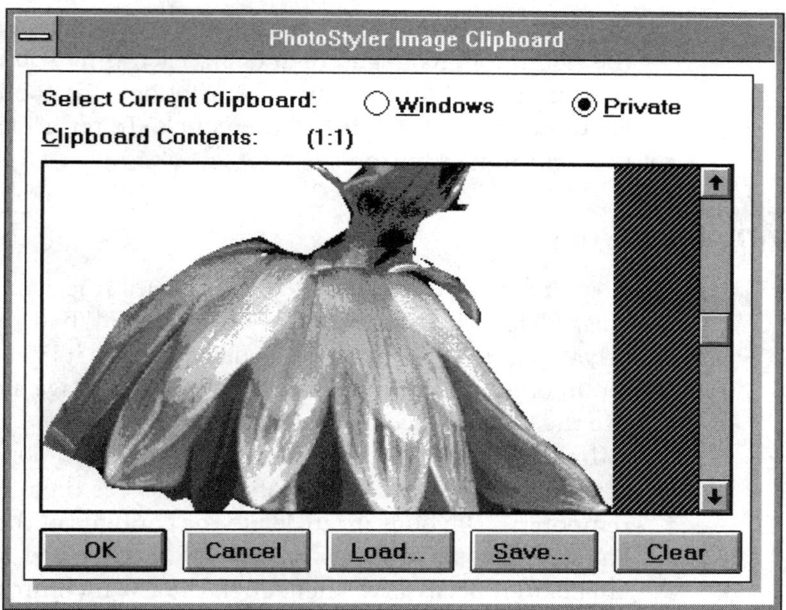

Figure 13-4. Irregularly shaped clipboard images appear against a background of the current background color

Viewing the Contents of the Clipboard

To view the contents of the clipboard after you've cut or copied a selection to it, choose the Clipboard command from the Edit menu. The most recent item that you cut or copied to the active clipboard will appear in the Clipboard Contents area as in Figure 13–4. If the image is larger than will fit in the clipboard, scroll bars will appear. Irregularly shaped image areas always appear with a rectangular background of the background color, regardless of which clipboard you used to cut or copy them.

Note *When you paste an irregular image area from the Windows clipboard into an image document, the background color will be pasted along with it. This doesn't happen when the irregular image area comes from the private PhotoStyler clipboard, though.*

The inactive clipboard may contain image data, too. You can view any such data simply by clicking the radio button that will activate the other clipboard.

Zooming In and Out of the Clipboard

You may want to see a close-up of the image in the clipboard before pasting it into an image document. To zoom in on the clipboard image, move the cursor into the image (where it takes on the appearance of the Zoom tool icon) and then click. Each time you click, the viewing magnification increases by a factor of one. To zoom out on the clipboard image, press Shift and then click. To return to a 1:1 view, press the right mouse button.

Clearing the Clipboard

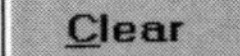

If you're sure you won't need a clipboard image any longer, you can clear (delete) it from the active clipboard. When the image is in the private PhotoStyler clipboard, you can delete it from within PhotoStyler. In order to delete a Windows clipboard image, however, you must use the Clipboard application under MS-Windows.

Images in the private PhotoStyler clipboard don't consume much system memory, because PhotoStyler stores them on your hard drive temporarily. If you want to delete the contents of the private clipboard anyway, choose Clipboard from the Edit menu and activate the Private clipboard if necessary. Then, click the Clear command button.

On the other hand, images in the Windows clipboard remain in system memory and can slow down PhotoStyler's performance if they're very big. To clear the contents of the Windows clipboard:

1. Press Ctrl-Esc and switch to the Windows Program Manager.
2. Double-click the Clipboard icon in the Main window.
3. Choose the Delete command from the Edit menu.

Saving and Loading Clipboard Files

Both the Windows and the private PhotoStyler clipboard can contain only one image at a time. As soon as you copy or cut another selection to the clipboard, the new image replaces the previous one. However, with the private PhotoStyler clipboard you have the option of saving the clipboard contents to a file (extension .CLI). You can build a library of clipboard selections and reload them into the clipboard for later use.

Saving the Contents of the Clipboard

To save the current contents of the private PhotoStyler clipboard:

1. Choose the Clipboard command from the Edit menu to access the PhotoStyler Image Clipboard dialog box.

2. If necessary, click the Private radio button to activate the private PhotoStyler clipboard and display its contents.

Save...

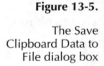

3. Click the Save command button. When the Save Clipboard Data to File dialog box appears as in Figure 13–5, type a name for the file and locate the drive and directory where you want to store the file. If you plan to build a library of clipboard files, we recommend saving them in a separate subdirectory under your PhotoStyler directory.
4. Click the Save command button. PhotoStyler will save the clipboard contents to your hard drive, adding the .CLI file extension automatically. You'll return to the PhotoStyler Image Clipboard dialog box.

The image you've just saved still appears in the Clipboard Contents area of the dialog box. Now, though, you can safely replace the clipboard contents without losing this image forever.

Loading a Clipboard File

The advantage of having a library of clipboard files is that you can load an image into the clipboard at any time and then paste it into the image document of your choice. To load a previously saved file into the private PhotoStyler clipboard:

1. Choose the Clipboard command from the Edit menu to access the PhotoStyler Image Clipboard dialog box.

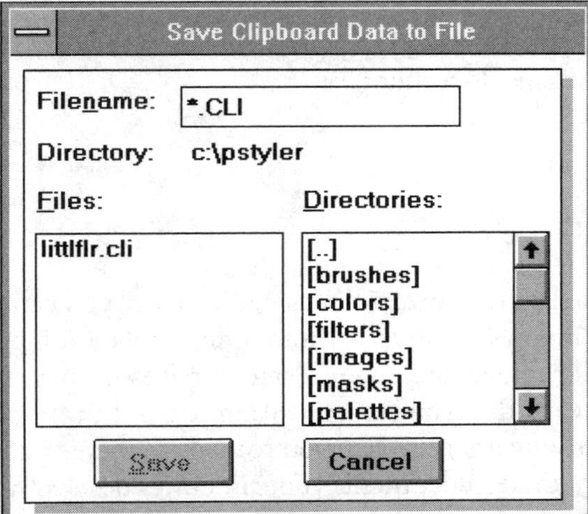

Figure 13-5. The Save Clipboard Data to File dialog box

Figure 13-6.

The Load Clipboard File dialog box

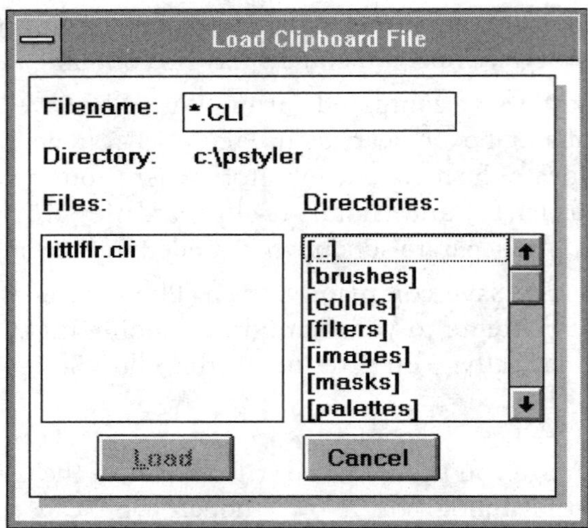

2. If necessary, click the Private radio button to activate the private PhotoStyler clipboard.

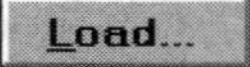

3. Click the Load command button. When the Load Clipboard File dialog box appears (Figure 13–6), use the Directories list box to locate the clipboard file you want.
4. In the Files list box, double-click the filename you want, or click the filename once and then select Load. You'll return to the Photo-Styler Image Clipboard dialog box, where the contents of the selected file will appear.
5. Click OK to exit the PhotoStyler Image Clipboard dialog box.

Now, you're ready to paste the contents of the clipboard into another image document.

Pasting a Selection

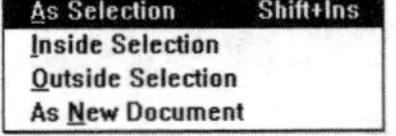

Using the Paste command in the Edit menu, you can paste the contents of the Windows or private PhotoStyler clipboard into any Grayscale or True Color image document. Pasted images become floating selections, which means that you can reposition or paint in them without affecting the underlying image. When you're ready to merge a pasted selection into the active image document, you can either deselect it or use the Merge Control command described later in this chapter.

Note

You can't paste the contents of either clipboard into Indexed Color or Black & White image documents. Clipboard images that originated in Indexed Color or Black & White image documents will retain their original colors when you paste them into a True Color document. If you paste these images into a Grayscale document, PhotoStyler will translate their colors into shades of gray.

Caution

If you paste a selection into an image document that's too small for it, PhotoStyler will crop the pasted image. To avoid this problem, always check the pixel dimensions of the source and target images before you copy a selection to the clipboard. If it looks as though the source image won't fit into the target document, resize the selection area before you copy it to the clipboard.

The Paste command contains a submenu with four options: As Selection, Inside Selection, Outside Selection, and As New Document. Each option has special uses and is available only under certain conditions.

As Selection Shift+Ins
Inside Selection
Outside Selection
As New Document

Pasting the Clipboard Contents as a Separate Selection (As Selection)

The Paste: As Selection option is always available when you paste a clipboard image into a Grayscale or RGB True Color image document. What happens when you choose Paste As Selection depends on whether the active image document already contains a selection area.

- If the active image document contains no selection, the pasted image will appear as a floating selection in the upper left corner of the image document (Figure 13–7, left).
- If the active image document already contains a selection (Figure 13–7, center), PhotoStyler will deselect it and position the pasted image as a floating selection where the previous selection area was located (Figure 13–7, right).

Note

PhotoStyler always adapts the resolution of a clipboard image to the image document into which you paste it. For example, if the image in the clipboard originally came from a document at 1000 dpi and you paste it into a document at 1400 dpi, the pasted selection will take on a 1400 dpi resolution, with no data loss.

Figure 13-7. Pasting a clipboard image as a separate selection: *(l)* no previous selection area *(c)* existing selection area *(r)* pasted image replaces previous selection

As Selection Shift+Ins
Inside Selection
Outside Selection
As New Document

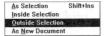

Pasting the Clipboard Contents Inside the Current Selection

The Paste: Inside Selection option is available only when the active image document already contains a selection area (see Figure 13–8, top). When you choose this option, PhotoStyler "remembers" the location of the previous selection area and treats it like a "window" through which you can display all or part of the newly pasted image (Figure 13–8, center). If you move the pasted image around, only those parts that overlap the previous selection area will be visible inside the marquee (see Figure 13–8, bottom). Deselect the floating pasted selection when it's in the position you want.

The Paste: Inside Selection command has useful applications for montaging images. For example, you could use it to create a custom pattern in the shape of an existing part of the image. You might also use it to place one image in *front* of another, adding to the perception of depth. If you're a fine artist, you might use this command to create a surrealistic landscape inside an eye or a window.

As Selection Shift+Ins
Inside Selection
Outside Selection
As New Document

Pasting the Clipboard Contents Outside the Current Selection

An even better name for this option would be Paste: *Behind* Selection, because that's really what it allows you to do. Like the Paste: Inside Selection command, Paste: Outside Selection is available only when the active image document already contains a selection area (see Figure 13–9, top). When you choose this option, PhotoStyler "remembers" the location of the previous selection area and blocks any part of the newly pasted image from showing through it (Figure 13–9, center). In effect, you're placing the pasted image *behind* the previously

Figure 13-8.

Pasting a clipboard image "inside" a previous selection area

image with previous selection area

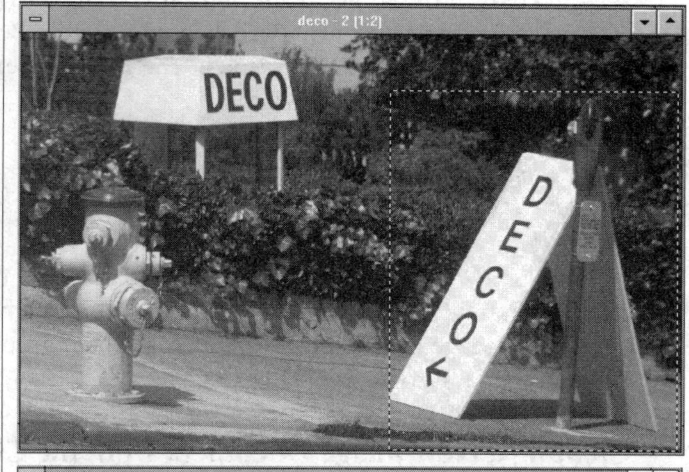

pasted image overlaying previous selection area

pasted image becomes "invisible" when moved outside previous selection area

selected part of the image document. If you move the pasted selection around, different parts of it will become visible behind the blocked area (Figure 13–9, bottom). Deselect the floating selection area when just the right parts of it are visible.

Tip

If the pasted image doesn't fit quite as you expected, you may need to resize it. Try the Resize command described later in this chapter.

The Paste Outside Selection command also has many applications for montaging images. Use it, for example, to heighten depth perception in an image or to replace the existing background behind human subjects in a photograph.

As Selection Shift+Ins
Inside Selection
Outside Selection
As New Document

Creating a New Image Document from the Clipboard Contents (As New Document)

When you choose the Paste: As New Document command, PhotoStyler places the contents of the clipboard in a new image document that's sized to fit the pasted image exactly. If the shape of the clipboard image is irregular, PhotoStyler will paste its background color along with it.

Pasting to or from Another Windows Application

If you've cut or copied a selection to the Windows clipboard, you can paste it into another Windows application. Be prepared, however: in some applications, you may experience color shifts, banding instead of gradient fills, and other unexpected changes in the pasted image. The reasons for this have to do with the fact that there are multiple clipboard standards in the MS-Windows environment. Aldus PhotoStyler supports the DIB (Device Independent Bitmap) standard, which maintains the integrity of digital colors across hardware platforms. Some graphics applications support the DDB (Device Dependent Bitmap) standard, which interprets color information according to the capabilities of your display adapter. When you paste a PhotoStyler image into one of these applications, some colors may change to fit the capabilities of your hardware. The same may occur when you paste an image from another Windows application into PhotoStyler.

Moving a Pasted Selection Area

A newly pasted area becomes a floating selection automatically, as we've mentioned. To move it to another location within the active

Figure 13-9.

Pasting an image "outside" (behind) a previous selection area

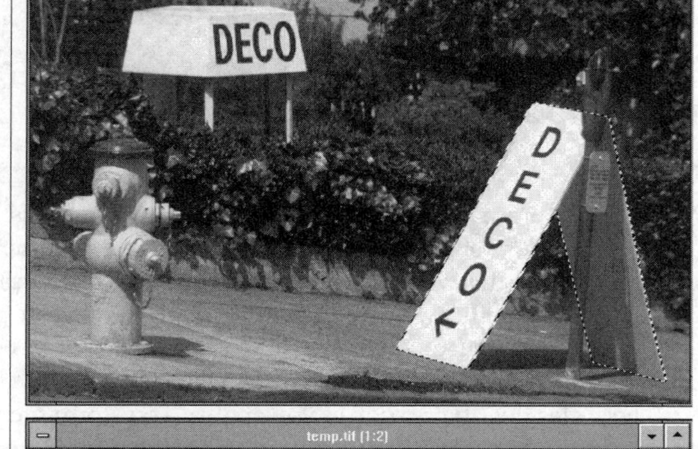

previous selection area

pasted image visible only where no overlap with previous selection area occurs

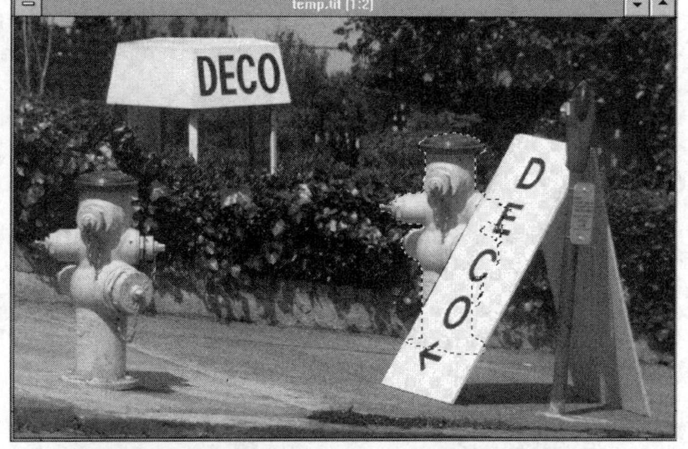

pasted image "peeks out" from behind previous selection area when moved

image document, simply position the mouse cursor within the selection marquee and drag to the desired location.

Editing the Composition of a Selected Area

Using commands in the Transform and Edit menus, you can edit the composition of any selected area of an image document. If the selected area is one that you've pasted from the clipboard, these commands will help you finalize changes to its content before you merge it with the underlying image. You can also use these commands on a selected area that is "native" to the active image document. Any selection area becomes floating as soon as you apply a Transform menu command to it.

Some of the Transform menu commands apply to an entire image document rather than just a selected area. We'll save a discussion of those for last.

Deleting (Clearing) a Selection Area

To delete the content of a selected area of an image document, choose the Clear command in the Edit menu. The current background color will replace the content of the selected area, just as when you cut a selected area to the clipboard (refer back to Figure 13–2). PhotoStyler doesn't send the deleted data to the clipboard, so unless you choose the Undo command immediately, you won't be able to recover the lost content later.

Caution *An area that you've deleted is no longer floating. If you move the selection area after deleting it, you'll leave behind a duplicate area filled with the background color.*

A Word about Using the Transform Menu Commands

How the Transform menu commands affect an image depends on whether you're working with a newly pasted image selection or one that was already part of the active image document. If the selected area is already part of the active image document, PhotoStyler leaves the original pixels fixed in place, and the Transform menu command edits a floating duplicate of the original. If your intent is to *replace* the original area with the transformed selection, you'll have to edit out the original pixels after you deselect the floating selection area.

If the selected area is a newly pasted one, on the other hand, it's already floating. The Transform menu commands won't leave any duplicates behind.

Resizing a Selected Area

Often, you may find yourself copying and pasting data between images that differ greatly in pixel size. When this happens, you may need to make a selected or pasted area larger or smaller so that it will fit the proportions of the target image document.

Three of the commands in the Transform menu—Resample, Resize, and Free Resize—affect the size of an image or selected area. The Resample command always affects an entire image document, so we'll cover that at the end of the chapter. The Resize and Free Resize commands, on the other hand, are available for selected image areas only. The Resize command offers a precise way to change the size or number of pixels in a selected area. The Free Resize command lets you resize a selection area interactively.

A Word about Resizing

Be conservative when resizing selected areas with the Resize and Free Resize commands. These commands change the amount of information in an image area without changing its output resolution. If you *increase* the size of a selected area, PhotoStyler will interpolate new pixels, guessing at the best color or gray values for each. As a result, you'll usually suffer some loss of image quality. If you *decrease* the size of a selected area, on the other hand, you'll eliminate details by trying to cram the same visual information into a smaller number of pixels. The selected area may look just as sharp—as long as you don't increase its size again afterwards! Avoid "see-saw" experimentation with resizing by planning your moves in advance.

Resizing Selected Areas Precisely

If you want to control the size of a selection area numerically, choose the Resize command in the Transform menu. This command will bring up a dialog box (Figure 13–10) that lets you specify a new size for the selected area in terms of pixels, dimensions, or percentage increase or decrease.

To resize a selected area precisely:

1. Select an area of the image, or paste an image from the clipboard.
2. Choose the Resize command in the Transform menu to access the Resize dialog box. This dialog box will display the current width, height, and resolution of the selected image area.
3. Use the drop-down list box in the New Image Information area to specify the unit of measure you want to use when resizing. You can specify a new size according to the number of pixels, the dimensions in inches or centimeters, or a percentage change.
4. Check the Aspect Ratio area of the dialog box and select a different option, if desired. If you click the *Arbitrary* radio button, you can change the width and height of the selected area separately, but the resulting image area may be distorted. If you choose *Fixed*, the selected area will maintain its current aspect ratio (proportions) when you resize it.

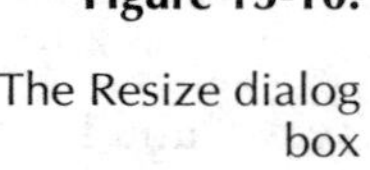

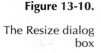

Figure 13-10.

The Resize dialog box

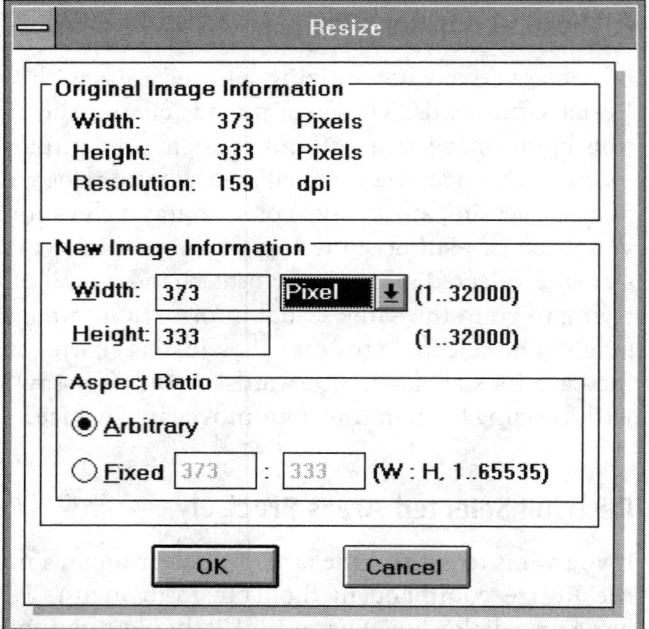

5. In the Width and Height fields, enter the new sizing values for the selected area. If the Fixed option is selected, changing the width will change the height automatically and vice versa.
6. Click the OK command button to exit the dialog box and resize the selected area.

Resizing Images Interactively

To change the size of a selected area by sight rather than numerically, use the Free Resize command in the Transform menu. When you choose this command, a bounding box with eight square handles will appear around the selected area as in Figure 13–11 (left). Dragging the mouse diagonally from one of the *corner* handles will resize the area proportionally (see Figure 13–11, center). If you drag one of the *middle* handles, on the other hand, you'll distort the aspect ratio of the selected area (Figure 13–11, right).

Tip

If you're using the Clone tool to clone the same object several times, you probably don't want the duplicates to look monotonously alike. You can avoid too artificial a look by using the Resize or Free Resize command along with the Clone tool. After cloning the object once, select the painted area and invoke the Resize or Free Resize command in the Transform menu to create a floating duplicate. Make the floating duplicate larger or smaller as desired. To place the resized duplicate in another part of the image, drag it to the desired location and then deselect it.

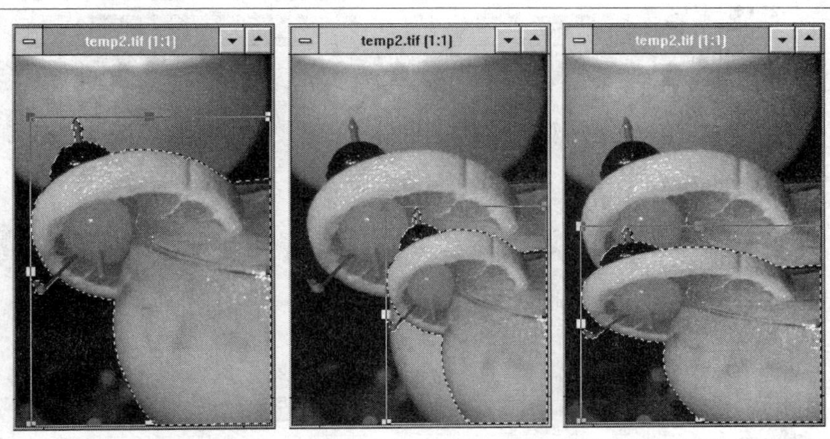

Figure 13-11. Resizing a selection area freehand

(l) selected area with resizing "handles"
(c) area resized proportionally (corner handles)
(r) area resized with distorted aspect ratio (middle handles)

Flipping an Image or Selection Area

Flip Horizontal and Flip Vertical are among the few commands in the Transform menu that work with both selected areas and entire image documents. Use the Flip Horizontal command when you want an object to face in the opposite direction (Figure 13–12, left and center); use the Flip Vertical command when you want to turn all or part of an image upside down (Figure 13–12, right). When you apply these commands to a selected area, the selection becomes a floating duplicate and you can continue to edit it without affecting the underlying image.

Rotating an Image or Selection Area

The Rotate and Free Rotate commands in the Transform menu offer you two ways to rotate an image or selected area. The Rotate command, which can apply to an entire image as well as to a selected area, lets you specify an angle of rotation numerically. The Free Rotate command, on the other hand, lets you rotate a selected area freehand.

Specifying a Precise Degree of Rotation

When you've scanned an image into PhotoStyler sideways, use the Rotate command in the Transform menu to turn it in the proper orientation. You can also use the Rotate command to rotate any selected area at an exact angle that you specify. To rotate an image or selected area using the Rotate command:

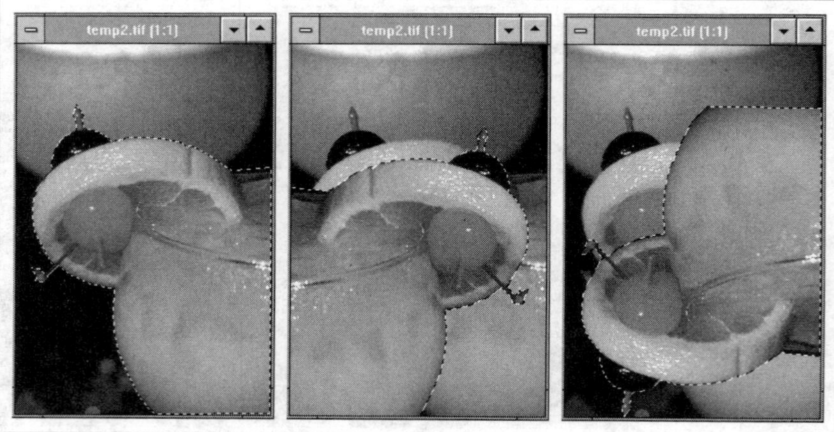

Figure 13-12. Flipping a selected area of an image (*l*) the selected area (*c*) flipped horizontally and moved (*r*) flipped vertically

1. Select the area(s) you want to rotate, or paste it into the active image document. If you don't select an area, PhotoStyler will rotate the entire image.
2. Choose the Rotate command in the Transform menu to access the Rotate dialog box (Figure 13–13).
3. Click on the clockwise or counterclockwise radio button to define the direction of rotation.
4. Enter the degree of rotation in the Degree text entry box. The default is 90 degrees.
5. Click the OK command button to rotate the image document or selected area. You may need to wait briefly while PhotoStyler calculates where to reposition the pixels.

Rotating a Selected Area Interactively

To rotate a selected area by sight rather than numerically:

1. Select the area you want to rotate, or paste it into the active image document.
2. Choose the Free Rotate command in the Transform menu. A rectangular bounding box with four corner handles will appear around the selected area, as in Figure 13–14 (left).
3. To rotate the selection, drag the handle of your choice in the desired direction. As you drag, the left side of the status bar will display the degree of rotation relative to the original starting point.

Note

If the selected area was part of the original image document and not pasted into it, PhotoStyler will rotate a copy of the original pixels. The original object will remain fixed in the image document.

Figure 13-13.

The Rotate dialog box

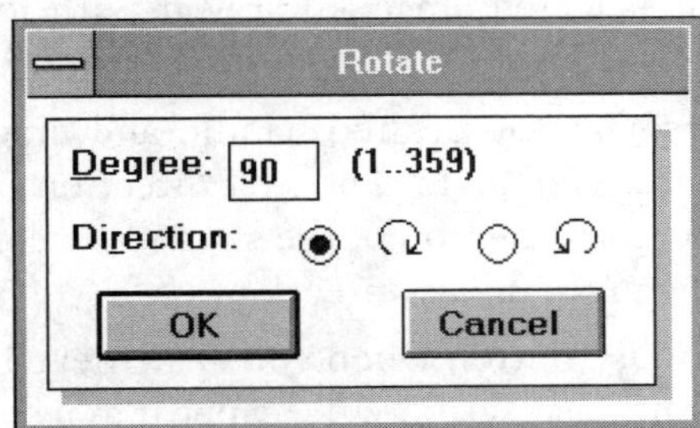

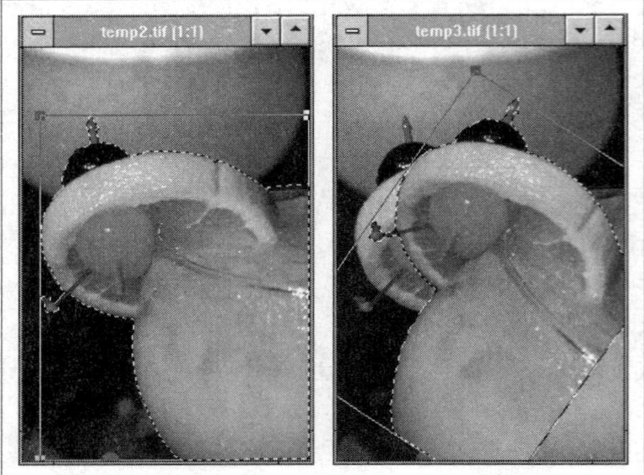

Figure 13-14.

Rotating an image interactively (Free Rotate)

4. When you've rotated the selection to the desired angle, release the mouse button. The rotated image will reappear at the new angle (Figure 13–14, right).

Skewing a Selected Area

Some graphic designers and digital photographers like to experiment with planes, trying to give the illusion of depth to flat photographic images. One way to introduce planes into an image document is to *skew* a selected area. In skewing, you distort a selection at a horizontal or vertical angle, in such a way that opposite sides of the bounding box move parallel to one another (Figure 13–15).

To skew a selected or pasted area:

1. Paste an image into the active image document, or select an area of the document.
2. Choose the Skew command from the Transform menu. The bounding box of the selected area will appear with four handles at its corners.
3. Place the cursor at the desired handle and drag the mouse at a vertical or horizontal angle. The first direction in which you drag will determine the direction of the skew. You can skew a selected area up to 75 degrees in any direction.
4. Release the mouse button when you've achieved the desired skew angle. The floating selection will reappear at a slant.

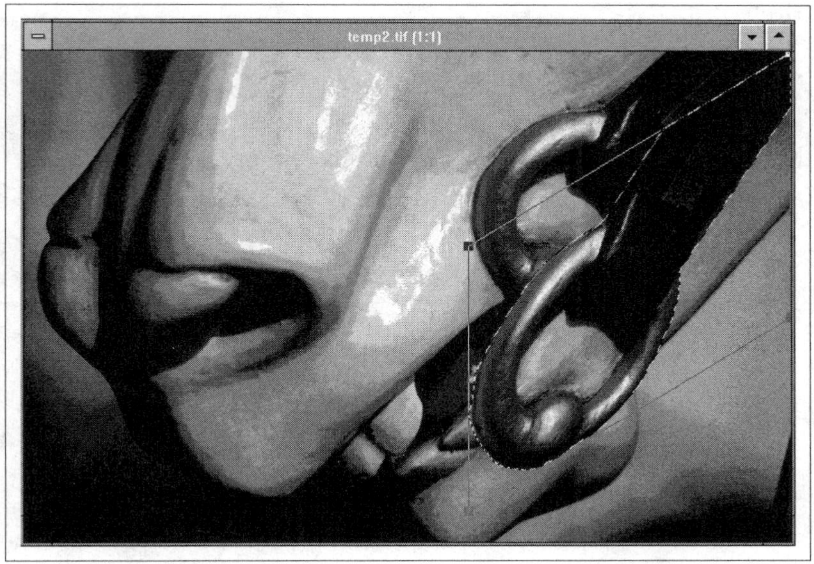

Figure 13-15. Skewing a selected area

Tip

If you press and hold the Shift key while skewing, you'll force only one handle to move at a time. Use this keyboard shortcut to create interesting distortions like the distorted bit ring in Figure 13–16. You can generate other shapes, too, depending on where you place the handles of the selected area.

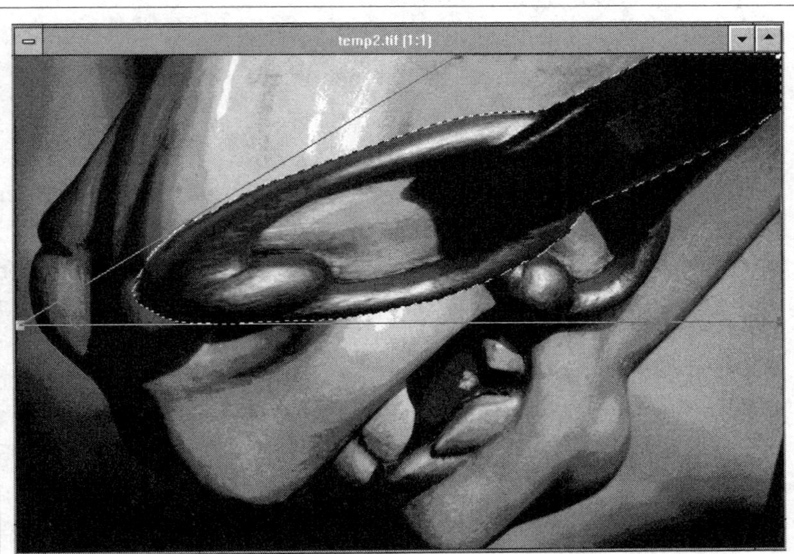

Figure 13-16. Skewing with the Shift key depressed

Figure 13-17.

Creating perspective: pulling the sign "handlles" upward and outward

Changing the Perspective of a Selected Area

When you choose the Perspective command, the two sides of a selected area's bounding box move toward or away from one another, not parallel to one another as with the Skew command. This apparent movement creates the illusion of three-dimensional perspective (Figure 13–17). The *vanishing point*, the point toward which the two sides of the bounding box narrow and recede, seems further away, while the broadened areas of the image look closer.

Tip

The Perspective command is especially effective with text. When adding perspective to selected text, though, you may want to add a one-pixel soft edge to prevent stair-stepping and "jaggies" from becoming apparent.

To change the perspective of a selected area:

1. Select an area or paste an image from the clipboard. If the selected area was already part of the active image document, you'll be adding perspective to a *copy* of its contents.
2. Choose the Perspective command from the Transform menu. A bounding box with four corner handles will appear around the selected area.
3. Move the mouse cursor to a corner and drag in the desired direction. You won't be able to change direction once you start dragging. The direction you choose will determine which sides of the selected area recede toward an imaginary vanishing point.
4. Release the mouse button when you've achieved the perspective you want.

Tip

If you press and hold the Shift key while dragging, you'll force the handles of the bounding box to move in a horizontal direction. If you press and hold the Ctrl key, you'll force the handles to move in a vertical direction.

Distorting a Selected Area

The Distort command differs from the Perspective and Skew commands in that it lets you reshape a selected area freehand. You can distort a *single* side of the selected area's bounding box at a time and distort as many sides as you like (Figure 13–18).

To reshape a selected area using the Distort command:

1. Select an area of the active image document, or paste an image from the clipboard.
2. Choose Distort from the Transform menu. A bounding box with four corner handles will appear around the selected area.
3. Position the cursor at one of the handles and drag the mouse in the desired direction. If you change your mind in midstream, you can alter the direction in which you distort the image.
4. If desired, stretch or pull one of the other handles to continue reshaping the selected area.

Tip

Normally, PhotoStyler redraws the selected image area every time you release the mouse button after dragging a handle. If you want PhotoStyler to redraw the image only after you're completely finished reshaping it, press and hold the Shift key as you drag. You'll see the bounding box move, but the original selected area will seem to remain unchanged. When your reshaping job is over, release the Shift key and click on any handle; PhotoStyler will then redraw the selected area.

Figure 13-18. Distorting a selected area of an image

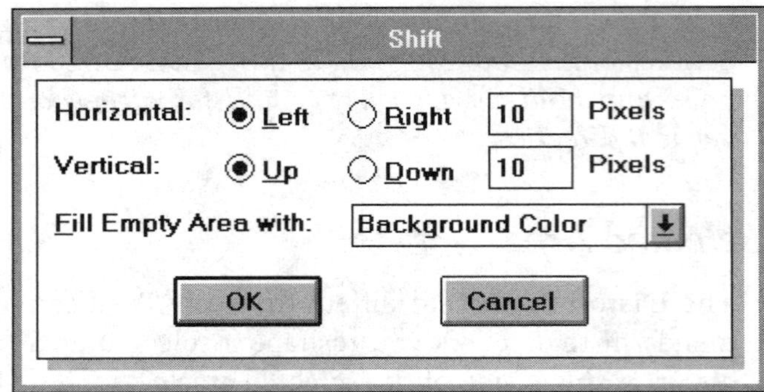

Figure 13-19.

The Shift dialog box

Shifting an Image or Selected Area

Using the Shift command in the Transform menu, you can scroll the content of a selected image area horizontally and/or vertically by a specified number of pixels. Of course, when the contents of a selection shift sideways, up, or down, they leave an empty area behind within the marquee. The Fill Empty Area with option in the Shift dialog box (Figure 13–19) lets you control what PhotoStyler uses to replace the shifted-out pixels.

Replacing Empty Areas with the Background or Foreground Color

When you select Background Color or Foreground Color, the areas that would have been empty after shifting now fill with the current background or foreground color. If you shift a selected area by a small number of pixels, you can use these options to create subtle drop shadows or haloes as in Figure 13–20 (left). If you shift a selected area by a large number of pixels, you can create surrealistic three-dimensional effects like the one in Figure 13–20 (right), in which the horse appears to be pulling back and away.

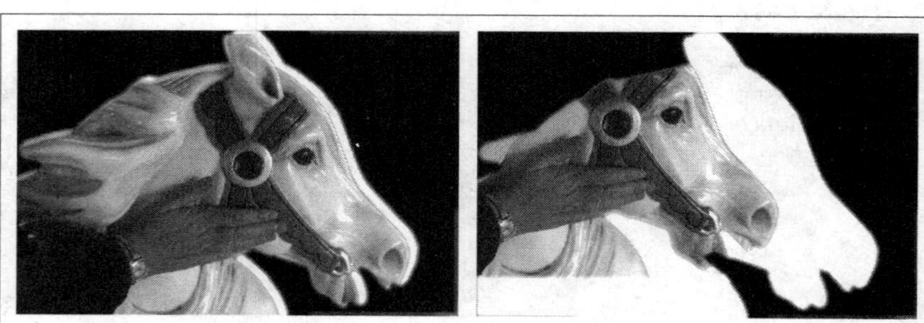

Figure 13-20.

Using the Shift command
(l) Subtle shifts: creating a halo effect
(r) Extreme shifts: surrealistic 3-D effects

The Background Color and Foreground Color options are available for both rectangular and irregular selection areas.

Replacing Empty Areas with Old Boundary Pixels

The Old Boundary Pixels option, available only for rectangular selection areas or an entire image, is useful for making a solid-color object look larger than it really is (Figure 13–21). This option fills the "empty" areas with the pixels that were formerly at the boundaries of the selection area or image. The effect is similar to cloning a single line of pixels (or two lines, if you shift the image in two directions) over and over again.

Replacing Empty Areas with the Shifted-Out Image

The Shifted-Out Image option, like the Old Boundary Pixels option, is available only for rectangular selection areas or an entire image. Its effect is to fill emptied areas of a selection with the pixels that have been shifted out from the opposite side(s) (Figure 13–22). Use this option to simulate a film image that's out of synchronization.

Controlling Montage Effects with the Merge Control Command

When you simply deselect a selected image area after editing it, you have no control over the way it merges with the active image document. The pixels in the selected area simply replace whatever was

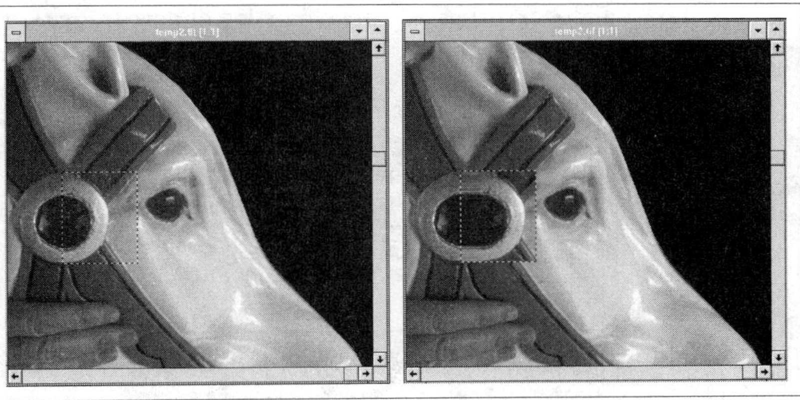

Figure 13-21.

Expanding a solid color area with the Shift command: Shifting a selected area to the right while substituting old boundary pixels

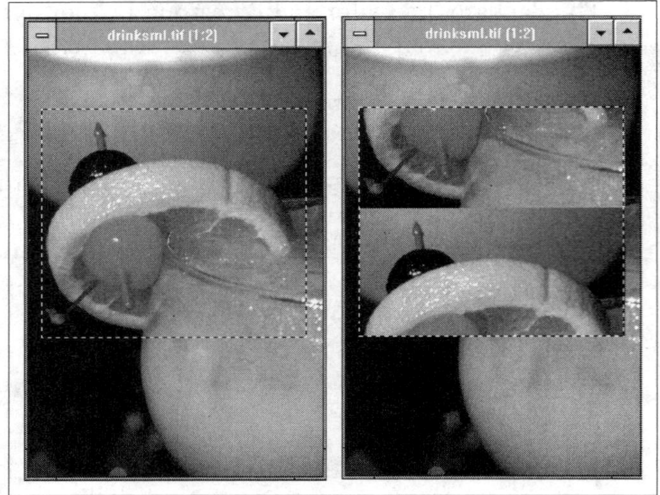

Figure 13-22.

Replacing empty areas with shifted-out pixels for an out-of-sync effect

there previously. However, if a pasted image or other selected area is *floating* (Chapter 8), you can use the Merge Control command in the Edit menu to customize the way the selected area will combine with the underlying image document. Merge Control gives you the ultimate in precise control over color values, degree of transparency, and image channels. As shown in the four "stages" of Figure 13–23 in the Color Section, we used the Merge Control command to montage a Grayscale photo of a cat's head with a True Color image containing brightly colored splashes of paint on a pavement.

The Merge Control Dialog Box

Few tools or commands in PhotoStyler let you customize your image composition work as thoroughly as the Merge Control command. The dialog box that appears when you choose Merge Control (Figure 13–24)

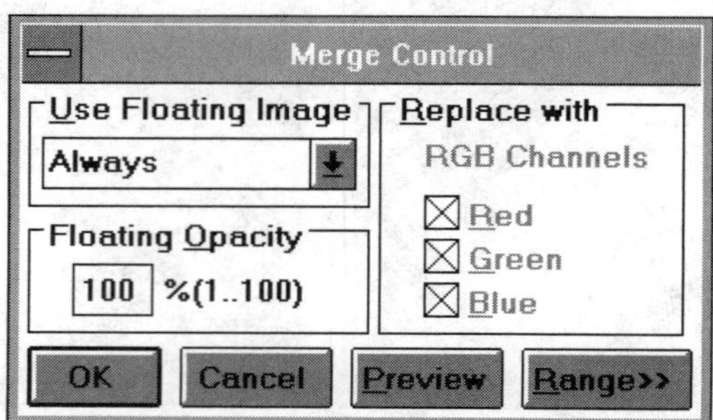

Figure 13-24.

The Merge Control dialog box

contains a large number of options, each of which can influence the effects of the others.

If Darker
If Lighter
Always
Hue only
Color only
Brightness only
Additive
Subtractive

Use Floating Image

Your setting for this option determines when and to what extent the color values in the floating selection will overwrite the pixels in the underlying image. These settings are similar to the Use Foreground Color settings found in the dialog boxes of many Paint Palette tools. Refer back to Chapter 10 if you need to review these color effects.

Always This is the default setting. It ensures that all the pixels in the floating image will overwrite all the pixels in the underlying image. If the active image document is an RGB True Color type, selecting Always makes the Replace with options available so that you can isolate and merge just one or two RGB color channels from the floating image.

If Darker, If Lighter These settings, available for both Grayscale and True Color image documents, cause PhotoStyler to compare the color or gray values of the floating image with the values in the underlying image document. Pixels in the floating selection area will replace existing pixels in the image based on whether they are darker or lighter than those pixels.

Hue Only, Color Only, Brightness Only These settings, available for True Color image documents, have their basis in the intuitive HSB (Hue, Saturation, Brightness) color space described in Chapter 7. Depending on which setting you choose, PhotoStyler will use just the hue component, the hue and saturation components, or the brightness component of the pixels in the floating selection area. The other color components of the pixels in the underlying image document will be preserved. We chose the Use Floating Image: Brightness Only option to obtain the special color merge effects in the lower left image in Figure 13–23 (Color Section).

Additive, Subtractive These settings derive from the differences between the RGB colors displayed by your monitor and the CMYK color space used by the printing industry. When you select Additive, PhotoStyler will merge the floating and underlying images in such a way that the final colors will be brighter than in either of the two source images. When you select Subtractive, colors in the merged area will be darker than in either the floating or the underlying image.

Replace with
RGB Channels
☒ Red
☒ Green
☒ Blue

Replace with

The options in the Replace with section of the dialog box are available *only* with True Color images and only when Always is selected as the Use Floating Image option. By clicking and placing an "x" in one or more check boxes, you control which color channels of the floating image (Red, Green, and Blue) will appear in the underlying image document after merging takes place. See Chapter 14 for more about isolating and editing individual channels of a color image.

Floating Opacity

Use this option to control how transparent the floating image pixels will be after you merge them with the underlying image document. A low value will result in more of the underlying image showing through; a high value will cause the floating image to be more opaque.

Preview Command Button

Unlike the dialog boxes of PhotoStyler's color correction commands, the Merge Control dialog box doesn't let you preview the results of your settings automatically. To see how settings will affect the merge, you need to click the Preview command button each time you make a change.

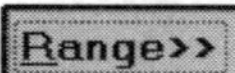

Range Command Button

This button works as a toggle. To make the Floating and Target range section of the Merge Control dialog box appear as in Figure 13–25, click the Range command button. To hide this section, click the Range button again.

Floating and Target Range Sliders

A floating selection area in an RGB True Color image may contain objects that you'd like to eliminate, like the area around the cat's head in the upper right image of Figure 13–23 in the Color Section. If these "objects" consist of pixels with similar color values, you can use the Range section of the Merge Control dialog box to isolate and then

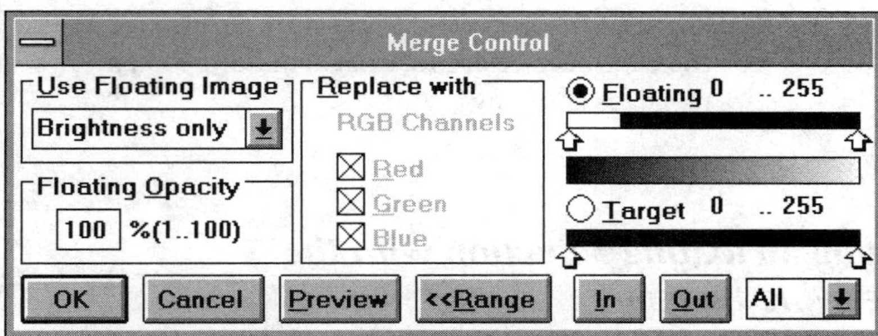

Figure 13-25. The Merge Control dialog box with Range controls visible

exclude those values from the merged image document. Conversely, you can *emphasize* specific color ranges in a floating selection area by eliminating other color values in the area.

Tip

To determine which color values you want to eliminate from a floating image, use the Eyedropper tool before you use the Merge Control command. Sweep the Eyedropper cursor slowly over the floating image to get an idea of the range of color values present.

When you want to isolate and then merge *specific ranges* of color values in either the floating selection or the underlying image, use the Floating and Target range sliders, In and Out buttons, and image channel drop-down list box. The range sliders represent the full range of RGB color values for the floating and target (underlying) images, from dark (0) to bright (255).

All
R
G
B

Image Channel Drop-Down List Box

The image channel drop-down list box at the lower right edge of the dialog box lets you specify which color values to include in and exclude from the integrated image, or from the Red, Green, and Blue image channels separately. To eliminate color values you *don't* want to appear in the merged image, adjust the slider handles for the floating or target image until the area between the handles represents the values you want to *remove*. Then, click the Out (output) button to eliminate those values.

To refine your color merge effects, you can repeat this process for each color channel separately. See Chapter 14 for in-depth information about working with color channels.

To finalize the montage of the two images in Figure 13–23, we used the Floating range slider to eliminate all values between zero and 44

(Figure 13–23, right). This setting eliminated the darker values around the edge of the floating image, making for a more seamless merge with no edges showing.

Merging a Floating Selection with the Underlying Image

Describing all the possible effects you can achieve with the Merge Control command would take up half a book by itself. The range of options at your disposal can produce many different results, depending on the color makeup of the images you're merging. The basic steps that follow will guide you through choices you'll always make about the opacity of the floating image, the use of individual color channels, and special color effects. Refer to Figure 13–23 in the Color Section to see one example of the Merge Control process at work.

Tip

If a semitransparent floating selection is all you're after, there are other ways to achieve your goal than using the Merge Control command. For example, you could import the superimposed image as a Grayscale mask document, make it floating, and then fill it using the Fill command in the Edit menu. Since the floating mask image presumably contains a range of Grayscale values already, the color or pattern you use to fill it with will be semitransparent. See Chapter 8 to review the uses of masks.

To merge a floating selection area with the underlying image document:

1. Make sure a selected area is floating *before* you edit it. As you'll recall from Chapter 8, any editing you do in a floating selection area won't affect the underlying image. You can generate a floating selection by:
   - pasting a selection from the clipboard
   - applying one of the Transform menu commands to a selection area
   - selecting an area normally and then moving it
   - selecting an area normally and then choosing the Make Floating command

- importing a mask and then immediately moving it or choosing the Make Floating command.

2. Do all your editing in the selected area while it's floating.
3. When you're ready to combine the floating selection with the underlying image, choose the Merge Control command in the Edit menu. The Merge Control dialog box shown in Figure 13–24 will appear.

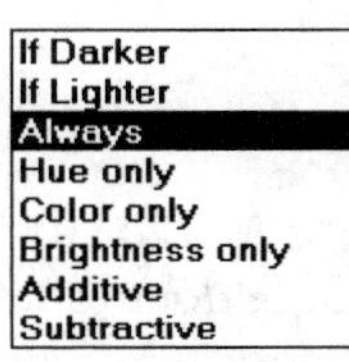

4. Click the scroll arrow in the Use Floating Image drop-down list box and select one of the options available. (If you're working with a Grayscale image, only the Always, If Darker, and If Lighter options will be available.) Your choice determines which pixels in the floating selection will show through in the underlying image document and which color components PhotoStyler will extract from those pixels. Click Preview to try out your choices. The lower left image in Figure 13–23 in the Color Section shows the results of choosing the Brightness Only option.

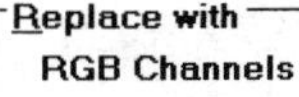

5. If you chose Always in step 4, review the "Replace with" area of the dialog box. Deselect the color channel(s) of the floating image that you *don't* want to merge into the underlying image document. Click Preview again to see the results of your choices in advance.
6. Vary the degree of transparency of the floating image by entering a number between zero and 100 in the Floating Opacity entry box. The default value of 100% will result in a completely opaque selection area. Click Preview once more to test your results.

Range>>

7. If you want to isolate specific objects or color ranges within the floating image or underlying image, click the Range command button.
8. To remove color values from the floating image, adjust the Floating range sliders until the values you want to eliminate lie between the slider handles. Then, click the Out button followed by the Preview button to see the tentative results. If you want to remove color values from the target (underlying) image as well, adjust the Target range sliders in the same way. The lower right image in Figure 13–23 (Color Section) shows a seamless merge obtained by removing darker color values from the floating image.

Caution

Once you remove a range of values with the Range sliders, you won't be able to put them back in the image, even if you re-adjust the Range sliders and click the Preview button. You'll need to click Cancel and then begin the Merge Control process all over again.

9. When you're finished making adjustments and have previewed the tentative results, click OK. The floating selection area will have changed in appearance according to your settings. You won't be able to undo the results of using the Merge Control dialog box.

10. Merge the floating image area with the underlying image by clicking the N button (select None) at the base of the Select Palette. The pixels now in the floating selection will replace the underlying pixels.

Tip *Here's a relatively painless application that will put the Merge Control command to good use. Create a new True Color image document of the same size and resolution as another image document you have open. Fill the new image document with a multicolor gradient fill or a pattern, then copy its entire contents to the clipboard. Paste the contents of the clipboard to the other image document, then use the Merge Control command to vary the transparency, color effects, and color channels used in the overlay.*

If the Merge Control command doesn't eliminate all the pixels you hoped it would, remember that PhotoStyler has other tools and commands to help you. For example, you might use the Eraser tool in its Erase to: Last Saved mode to finish the job.

Controlling Merge Effects with the Compute Command

The Compute command in the Image menu provides an even more sophisticated set of merge options than the Merge Control command. You can add, subtract, or multiply the values in two Grayscale or True Color images, blend two images together, compare the differences in their color or gray values in several ways, or create a composite. The Image Compute dialog box that appears when you choose this command (Figure 13–26) may seem daunting at first, but don't let the mathematical formulas frighten you off! The real purpose of this command is to let you "play" with images and experiment to your heart's content.

A favorite use of the Compute command is to compare and merge individual *channels* of an image in preparation for creating a new True Color image document. Look ahead to Chapter 14, "Image Channels

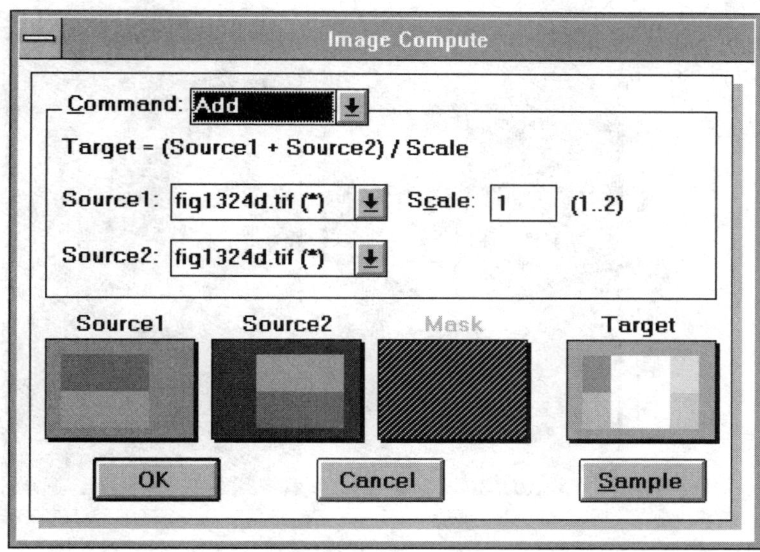

Figure 13-26. The Image Compute dialog box: an alternative way to montage images

and Special Color Effects," for in-depth information on using the Compute command to merge images.

Cropping an Image

After combining two images, you may well decide that some areas of the image are unnecessary. To crop an image document:

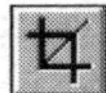

1. Activate the Crop tool in the Select Palette and then move the cursor into the active image document.
2. Position the cursor where you want one of the outer boundaries of the cropped image to be and begin dragging. As you drag, a rectangular outline will follow the cursor.
3. Release the cursor when you've surrounded the image area you want to preserve. A rectangular bounding box with eight handles will appear as in Figure 13–27 (left).
4. If you need to adjust the crop area, drag any side of the bounding box as desired.
5. To crop the image document, eliminating pixels outside the bounding box, double-click anywhere along the outline of the bounding box. The image will redraw with a reduced image area as in Figure 13–27 (right).

Figure 13-27.

Cropping an image

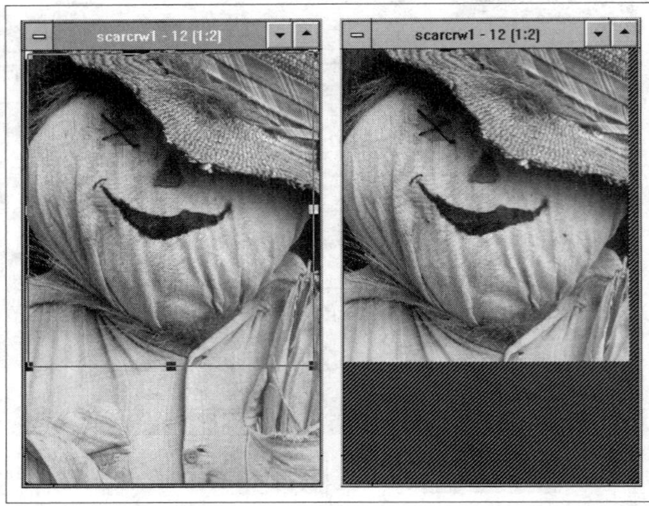

The Resample Command: Resizing an Image for Output

Three commands in the Transform menu allow you to resize images: Resize, Free Resize, and Resample. The Resample command (keyboard shortcut: Shift-F3) always affects an entire image, while the Resize and Free Resize commands are available only when the current image contains a selected area.

There are other, more important distinctions between these commands. When you use the Resize or Free Resize command to change the size of a selected area, there's always a loss in image quality. You're simply adding or deleting pixels, with no way to adjust output resolution. The Resample command, on the other hand, can change the amount of information in an image, its output size for print media, or both. Use the Resample command to retain precise control over the resolution, size, and sharpness of an image.

Usually, you'll use the Resample command to optimize the size and resolution of an entire image document—*after* you've finished editing its composition but *before* you output it to print or film. Ideally, you should never *have* to resample an image if you scanned the source image at the correct resolution for your output medium in the first place (see Chapter 4). We don't always have control over our image sources, though, and sometimes our output requirements change in midstream. For these frustrating occasions, the Resample command saves the day.

When to Resample an Image

The Resample command lets you change the dimensions, output resolution, and aspect ratio of an image document. You'll want to do one or more of these things when:

- You need to increase or decrease the size of an image without sacrificing image quality.
- Your image contains more information than an imagesetter can use efficiently, and you want to reduce file size for faster processing.
- You need to fit an image into a larger or smaller space than you originally planned for.

Table 13–2 provides a quick reference to the use of the Resample command. It shows each reason for using the command, the image parameters you'll need to change to achieve your ends, and how changes to dimensions and/or resolution will affect the sharpness, printed size, and amount of information in an image document.

The Resample Dialog Box

The Resample dialog box (Figure 13–28), which appears when you choose the Resample command or press Shift-F3, lets you determine exactly how you'll change an image: by changing its dimensions, the amount of information it contains, its resolution, or all of these at once.

Original Image Information

The Original Image Information section of the dialog box displays the current dimensions of the image in pixels and the resolution in dots per inch. If you change only the resolution of an image, PhotoStyler will give you the option of making the changes in the original image document. If you change only the dimensions of an image, or both the dimensions and the resolution, PhotoStyler will automatically generate a new image document, letting you preserve the original unaltered.

Aspect Ratio

The aspect ratio of an image document is the proportion of its width to its height. Most of the time, you'll want to select Fixed, which is the default option in PhotoStyler 1.1a and later versions. With this option selected, the height value for an image will change automat-

Table 13–2. Changing Image Parameters with the Resampling Command

To achieve this goal. . .	Changing these parameters . . .	. . . causes these effects
Reduce output size without changing amount of image information	Increase resolution only	Image becomes smaller and looks sharper
Increase output size without changing amount of image information	Decrease resolution only	Image becomes larger and looks less sharp
Increase output size while adding image data	Increase dimensions only	Image increases in size, but may look blurrier and less realistic; new pixels interpolated without adding new details
Reduce output size while deleting image data	Decrease dimensions only	Image becomes smaller but also loses detail; may introduce jaggies
Vary both output size and amount of image data	Vary both dimensions and resolution	Result depends on how the ratio of dimensions to resolution changes; risks include artifacts, loss of detail, or blurriness

ically whenever you change the width.If you choose an Aspect Ratio setting of Arbitrary (the default setting for versions prior to 1.1a), you can distort the image, changing its width and height values separately.

Changing Resolution Only (No-Loss Resizing)

As we mentioned back in Chapter 4, the main factor in determining the quality of an image is the amount of *information* (the number of pixels) it contains. When you change only the Resolution value in the Resample dialog box, you affect only its printed size. You resize the image automatically without any loss of information. Increasing the resolution causes the printed size of the image to decrease; decreasing

Figure 13-28.

The Resample dialog box

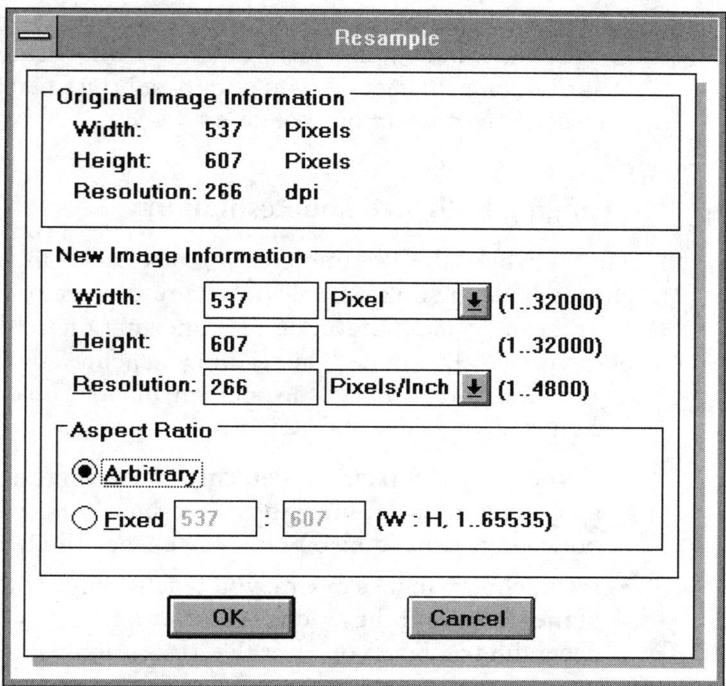

the resolution causes it to increase. Naturally, the image will *look* sharper if you increase the resolution and less sharp if you decrease it. But the number of pixels and the file size remain the same in both cases. See Table 13–2 for a better understanding of how a change to the resolution of an image affects image size.

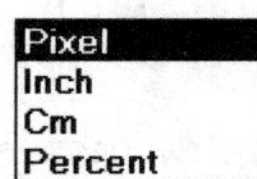

Changing Dimensions Only

PhotoStyler lets you specify the new dimensions of an image in pixels, inches, centimeters, or as a percentage change. When you change the dimensions without changing image resolution, you're telling PhotoStyler to add pixels to the image or delete pixels from it (see Table 13–2).

There's always some loss of image quality when you add or delete information from an image. When you increase image dimensions, PhotoStyler *interpolates* new pixels between existing ones, calculating the differences in the color or gray values of neighboring pixels so that transitions in the new image will remain fairly smooth. When you decrease image dimensions, PhotoStyler *averages* information, calculating which pixels to eliminate so that transitions don't become too jagged. Keep in mind, though, that if you simply add pixels to an image, you're not adding "real" detail and may risk blurring the image or introducing artifacts. If you simply subtract pixels from an image, you sacrifice some amount of detail.

Changing Both Size and Resolution

This is where the Resample dialog box gets a bit tricky. When you change both the dimensions and the resolution of an image, you can increase or decrease the amount of information in, sharpness, and size of the image all at once. The results you achieve will depend not only on the direction of change (up or down) but also on the unit of measure you choose for Width and Height.

- If you choose Pixels or Percent, you'll increase or decrease the amount of information in the image, but the output size may or may not change depending on how you change the Resolution value.
- If you choose Inches or Cm, you'll definitely change the output size of the image, but the amount of information may or may not change depending on how you alter the Resolution value.

Resampling Do's and Don'ts

There's only one way to resample an image without loss of quality, and that's to change the resolution only. Any other adjustments you make may compromise sharpness or detail for the sake of proper sizing or resolution. Of course, if an image contains more information than you need for a given print width, you can reduce its dimensions without a problem.

The challenge with the Resample command is to balance loss with the urgent requirements of your project. Fortunately, that's a challenge that PhotoStyler meets with great sophistication. Here are a few tips to help you make the right resampling decisions.

Reducing the Size of an Image is Usually Preferable to Increasing It

If you have a choice between reducing image size and increasing it, choose reduction whenever possible to retain image quality. If two images contain the same amount of pixel information, the smaller image will always look sharper than the larger one.

Adding Pixels Never Adds "Real" Information

If you must increase the amount of information in and/or the size of an image document, by all means increase the resolution, too. But do so in moderation. Interpolating pixels never adds real information to an image; it just simulates it. If you didn't capture enough information in your original scan (see Chapter 4), the "new" information is pseudo-detail. This is not a problem as long as you increase the size or number of pixels just a little. But if the change is too great, you may see a visible loss of sharpness.

Eliminating Pixels Always Results in a Loss of Detail

Avoid reducing the total number of pixels when resampling an image, unless you plan to reduce image size as well. You'll want to retain as much information as possible. Fewer pixels means less "real" information and less detail, with the accompanying risk of "jaggies." If you can choose between reducing number of pixels (reducing dimensions) and reducing size (resolution), you're usually better off reducing size.

Resampling Upward is a Better Choice for Painterly Images than for Photo-Realistic Ones

As we've mentioned, resampling an image upward won't add "real" information to an image. If you increase the amount of information in a photograph, there's an inherent risk of generating an image with a grainy, artificial, or mottled appearance. But if an image is intended as fine art, one of these effects may be just what you intended. Let your application be your guide.

Avoid Resampling the Same Image More than Once

PhotoStyler creates a new image document each time you change the dimensions (or the dimensions and resolution) of an image. Remember, there's a loss, however slight, each time you make these kinds of changes. If you resample an image, don't overwrite the original version; instead, save the resampled version as a separate file. That way, you can use the original image if you need to resample a second time. Resampling the same image more than once is courting second- and third-generation disaster, unless you change only the resolution.

Tip

True Color (24-bit) images can really slow down the speed of your page layout software, especially if you publish catalogs or other documents that use lots of them. Here's a strategy that will speed the process of formatting your document. When you're finished editing all the 24-bit color images in PhotoStyler, generate a Grayscale duplicate of each image as described in Chapter 5. Then, use the Resample command in the Transform menu to reduce both the resolution of each image and the number of pixels it contains. Place these low-resolution Grayscale images in the document for position-only proofing. When your layout is complete and approved and you're ready to generate final output, you can substitute the high-resolution True Color originals.

As you've seen in this chapter, editing the composition of an image draws on a wide variety of techniques. There's often more than one way to achieve a certain visual goal. In the next chapter, we'll introduce the many uses of splitting a True Color image into its component color channels. On a basic level, you can use channels to improve your color separation output. If you're artistically inclined, you can combine channels with filters, image composition, and retouching techniques to create special color effects within an image.

14

Image Channels and Special Color Effects

Whether you're a photo retoucher, a desktop publisher, or a graphic artist, you're about to discover yet another level of PhotoStyler's image editing power in this chapter. You may ask, "How many *more* ways to tweak a pixel can there be?" The answer lies with three commands in the Image menu: Split RGB True Color to, Combine RGB True Color by, and Compute.

The Split RGB True Color to command is the digital equivalent of splitting the atom. Using this command, you can split a True Color document into its color component image channels and then edit each channel as a separate Grayscale document. When you're done editing channels, you can use the Combine RGB True Color by command to merge them into a new True Color image. Finally, the Compute command lets you merge any two same-size True Color images, Grayscale images, or image channel documents to produce a wide range of special effects.

What Are Channels?

As you'll recall from Chapter 7, it takes three separate values—one each for red, green, and blue—to define the color of every pixel in a True Color image. Because of this phenomenon, we speak of a True Color image document as containing three *image channels*. On the other hand, Grayscale images contain only one value per pixel and thus only one channel: gray.

If you split a True Color image into its component channels, each channel becomes a Grayscale image document representing the values of a particular color component. For example, the gray values in a document that represents the red channel of a True Color image will match the R values of those same pixels in the original color image. The difference is that the red channel image document has only one value per pixel, and so all the pixels look gray.

The beauty of working with image channels is that they give you unparalleled control when refining and editing True Color images. You can enhance image channels just as you would any normal Grayscale image document. Paint in them, change brightness and gamma, alter their content by cutting and pasting, apply filters—the list goes on and on. When you recombine the separate image channels, the resulting new True Color image document may look entirely different from the original source image.

Splitting a True Color Image into Component Channels

RGB Channels
HSB Channels
HLS Channels
CMYK Channels

To split the active True Color image document into channels, you choose the Split RGB True Color to command in the Image menu. A submenu will pop up, letting you decide which set of color components to use when splitting the image. These sets of color components—RGB, HSB, HLS, and CMYK—are based on the four color spaces described in Chapter 7.

Depending on which color space you choose, PhotoStyler will generate three or four new Grayscale image documents. These are temporary files, much like newly created mask documents are (see Chapter 8). As shown in Figure 14–1, the title bar of each channel document displays the name of the original True Color image document, followed by a dash and an initial that identifies the channel. You can save these documents as normal image files if you plan to work with them beyond the current PhotoStyler session.

Splitting an Image into RGB Channels

For most applications, you'll want to split a True Color image into RGB channels as shown in Figure 14–1. This is the "native" color space for the computer, so there's no need to translate color values from one model to another or lose color data in doing so.

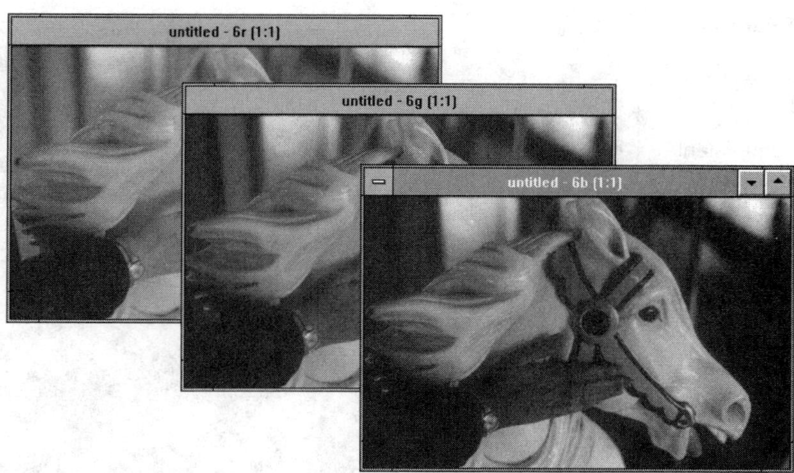

Figure 14-1. Splitting a True Color image into RGB image channels, each with an identifying title bar

Understanding the makeup of each channel will help you choose which channel to edit to achieve specific effects. As you prepare to edit one or more of the RGB channels you've created, keep this information in mind:

- The red (r) channel is usually the brightest of the three. It contains the highest proportion of brighter Grayscale values.
- The green (g) channel contains the broadest range of Grayscale values and thus shows more contrast than the other channels.
- The blue (b) channel is generally the darkest of the three channels and contains the highest proportion of darker gray values.

Splitting an Image into HSB or HLS Channels

Strictly speaking, HSB and HLS channels aren't really *color* channels at all. The channels generated when you split a True Color image into HSB components (Figure 14–2) represent the hue, saturation, and brightness values in the image. The channels you generate when you choose HLS components represent the hue, lightness, and saturation values in the image. Base your choice of components on the attributes you want to adjust during editing.

Note

Translating RGB data into HSB channels requires some fiddling with color values. The translation isn't direct in every case, so after you recombine HSB channels into a new True Color image, some colors may not match the original exactly.

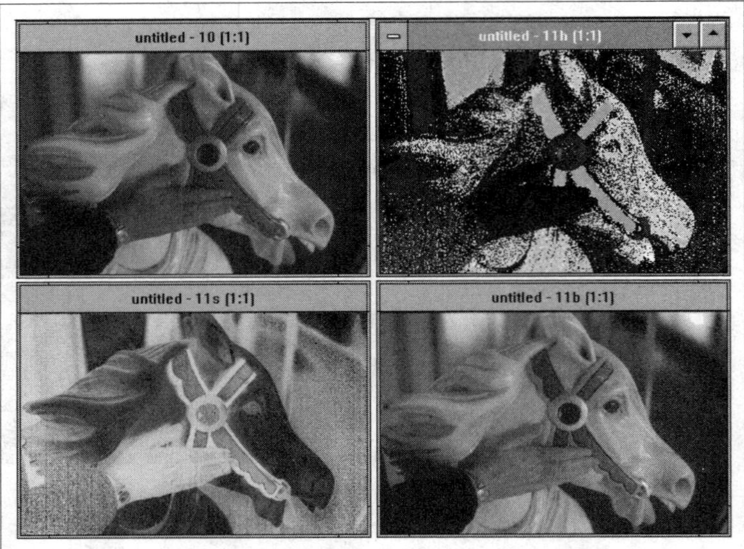

Figure 14-2. A True Color image (here in Grayscale equivalent, top left) split into its Hue, Saturation, and Brightness channels

- The Hue (h) channel represents the colors of pixels as seen in a rainbow spectrum. In the HSB color space, the spectrum begins and ends with red; in the HLS color space, the spectrum begins and ends with violet. This channel is the most grainy in both the HSB and HLS component sets, since hue values in many images change from one pixel to the next.
- The Saturation (s) channel in both the HSB and HLS color spaces resembles a film negative. Darker areas represent little color, while brighter areas represent more saturated colors.
- The HSB Brightness (b) and HLS Lightness (l) channels are the most realistic-looking in their respective channel sets. Edit these channels when you want to adjust brightness values for the original color image.

Splitting an Image into CMYK Channels

RGB Channels
HSB Channels
HLS Channels
CMYK Channels

When you want to edit a color image with a view toward refining commercial printing results, choose the Split to CMYK Channels command. PhotoStyler will generate four image channels as in Figure 14–3, one each for the cyan (c), magenta (m), yellow (y), and black (k) inks used in standard four-color printing. This is the same process that PhotoStyler uses to generate color separations; you'll learn more about this process in Chapters 15 and 16.

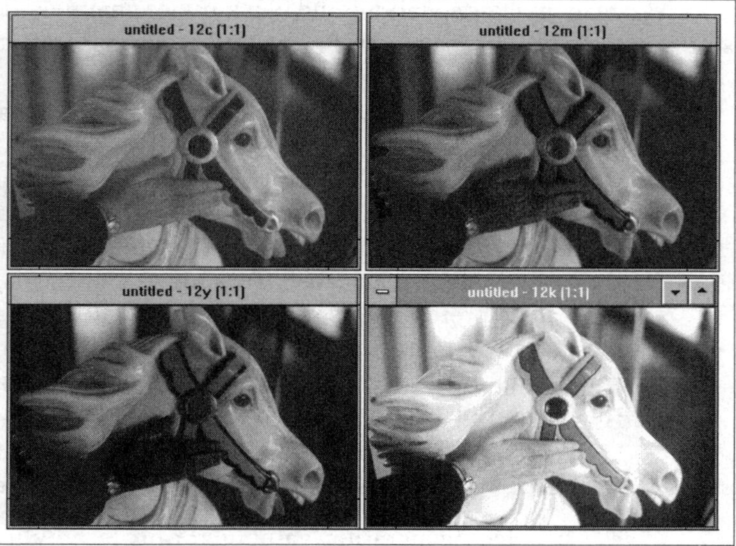

Figure 14-3. CMYK channels of a True Color image, generated at default Separation Setup settings (Black Generation 3.0, Under color removal 10%, Total ink limit 350%)

There are no exact CMYK equivalents for many RGB color values. The reason for this has to do with the gap between the theory of color and the practice of commercial printing. On your computer monitor, white appears wherever red, green, and blue are at their maximum values (255), and black appears wherever red, green, and blue values are all zero. Theoretically, cyan, magenta, and yellow should produce black when mixed at high percentages, because they're the complementary colors of red, green, and blue. In practice, however, maximum mixtures of CMY inks produce a muddy brown. That's why commercial printers add black ink as a fourth color—and why PhotoStyler must add a fourth (black) channel after converting RGB values directly to CMY ones.

But the addition of the black channel throws a wrench in the color works, making it necessary to adjust CMYK channel values to obtain the best color saturation possible. The time to make these adjustments is *before* you split a color image into CMYK channels. And the tool you use for this purpose is the Separation Setup command in the File menu.

Adjusting CMYK Channel Values with the Separation Setup Command

The Separation Setup command in the File menu lets you adjust the way PhotoStyler distributes color values when splitting an image into cyan, magenta, yellow, and black image channels. This command also tells PhotoStyler how to generate color separations for commercial process color printing (Chapters 15 and 16).

Why would you want to redistribute gray values in the first place? Well, if you're editing CMYK channels, you're probably planning to use commercial four-color print methods to output the final image. And it's in your best interest to see that the component values in each channel promote color saturation while minimizing the muddiness that too much ink can cause. To achieve these goals, commercial color separation professionals use a technique called Gray Component Replacement. This technique is the basis for the controls in the Separation Setup dialog box (Figure 14–4), which appears when you choose the Separation Setup command in the File menu.

The three options in this dialog box let you determine how and when to replace CMY values with black when image channels are generated:

- The Black generation value determines *how much* black a given pixel may contain. This setting influences the range of contrast in the black image channel.
- The Under color removal value determines the extent to which PhotoStyler will reduce color in the cyan, magenta, and yellow image channels to compensate for the black added. Usually, Under color removal affects darker areas of an image most strongly.
- The Total ink limit value determines the total amount of ink coverage for any pixel in the image. It affects the brightness and contrast ranges of all four CMYK channels.

Note

Use this command before *you split a color image into CMYK channels. Altering the parameters in the Separation Setup dialog box will have no effect on channels that you've already generated.*

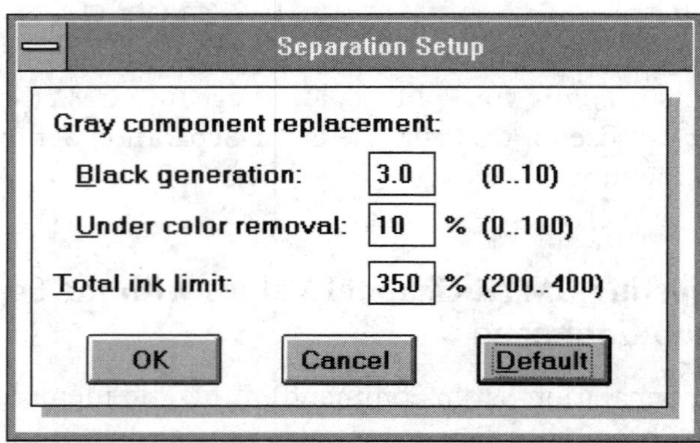

Figure 14-4.

The Separation Setup dialog box showing default settings

Black generation The Black generation setting determines the maximum amount of black that PhotoStyler can add to the image. As you increase the value (the acceptable range is from 0 to 10.0), the amount of black and the range of gray shades in the black channel will increase. The default value of 3.0 tends to intensify color saturation when you recombine image channels to form a new True Color image.

Under color removal When pixels in a CMYK image contain values for *all three* CMY components, the addition of black can lead to muddying of inks during printing. To prevent this, the Under color removal (UCR) option in the Separation Setup dialog box lets you reduce color in the cyan, magenta, and yellow image channels to compensate for the added black channel.

As you increase the UCR percentage, PhotoStyler replaces more and more CMY color with black. The effect on the four split channels is as follows:

- The CMY channels brighten and the range of contrast in each of these three channels decreases.
- The K channel increases in contrast and becomes darker.

The effects of UCR will be most noticeable in darker areas of an image, but it can affect any pixel in the image that contains black.

This juggling act, if you handle it deftly, has the effect of enhancing color saturation in the combined CMYK image document. Keep the UCR setting low, though, or your colors in the combined image may end up looking washed-out instead of richer.

Caution Always *consult with both your service bureau and your print vendor about the Separation Setup options they'd like you to use when splitting a True Color image into CMYK channels. Most professionals have their own preferences, and they won't take responsibility for printing jobs that have been botched by arbitrary software settings.*

Tip *When you apply the Under color removal principle to the four-color printing process, the effect is to reduce the total amount of ink used in the shadow areas.* *See Chapters 15 and 16 for more details.*

Total ink limit Both the Under color removal and the Total ink limit options affect the brightness and contrast ranges of the CMY channels. But while Under color removal primarily affects brightness and contrast in the shadow areas, Total ink limit shifts brightness and contrast throughout each image channel. As you decrease the Total

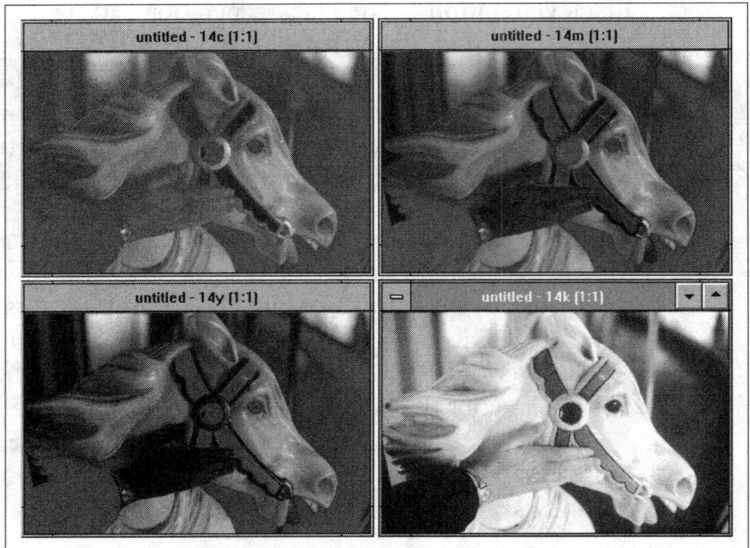

Figure 14-5.

CMYK channels generated at Separation Setup settings of Black generation 3.0, Under color removal 20%, Total ink limit 280%

ink limit percentage, PhotoStyler will brighten the gray values in each of the three CMY channels while reducing contrast within each channel. When you recombine image channels, the result of decreasing the total ink limit will be to intensify colors. If you were printing the image channels as color separations, you'd improve color saturation while using less ink.

Figure 14–3 shows CMYK channels generated at default settings of 3.0 Black generation, 10% Under color removal, and 350% Total ink limit. Figure 14–5 shows the same channels generated at settings of 3.0 Black generation, 20% Under color removal, and 280% Total ink limit. Comparing these two groups of figures will give you an idea of how these settings alter image channels and affect process color printing.

Tip *The characteristics of the paper stock, inks, and printing press to be used in your print run have an important bearing on the Total ink limit value you should choose. See Chapters 15 and 16 for more information.*

Combining Image Channels into a True Color Image Document

In two important respects, image channels are like masks: they're Grayscale documents, and they exist to help you edit something that you've isolated in an image. But whereas masks isolate entire groups of pixels, channels isolate color values, brightness, saturation, or other *attributes* of pixels.

Once you've edited the channels that you generated, you can recombine them (or any other Grayscale image documents of the same size) to form a new True Color image document. To combine Grayscale channels:

1. Make certain that all the channels you want to combine are open and in the PhotoStyler application window. If you want to combine these channels with one or more *other* Grayscale documents of the same pixel height and width, open those other documents now.
2. Activate any of the channel documents that you want to combine.

RGB Channels...
HSB Channels...
HLS Channels...
CMYK Channels...

3. Choose the Combine RGB True Color by command in the Image menu and select the desired set of channels from the submenu that appears. You can choose from RGB, HSB, HLS, or CMYK channels. A dialog box corresponding to the set of channels you chose will appear. Figure 14–6 shows the dialog boxes for combining RGB and CMYK channels.
4. Review the Grayscale document names that appear in the drop-down list boxes next to the names of each channel. If the only Grayscale documents open are the ones into which you split the original True Color image, then these channel names will appear automatically in the appropriate list boxes. Click the scroll arrow beside each drop-down list box to view the names of all the Grayscale documents that are open.
5. If you want to change the order of channels or substitute another open Grayscale document of the same size, use the drop-down list boxes to select the desired documents. Changing the order of channels will alter the color balance in the image, as you'll see in the next section.
6. When you're satisfied with your choices, click the OK command button. After a moment, a new untitled True Color document formed from the channels you selected will appear.

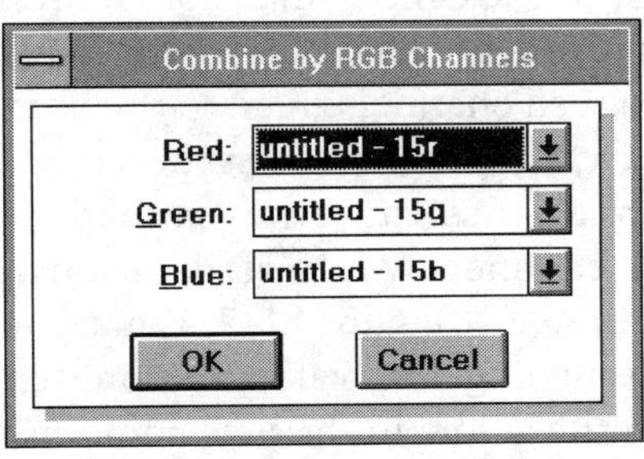

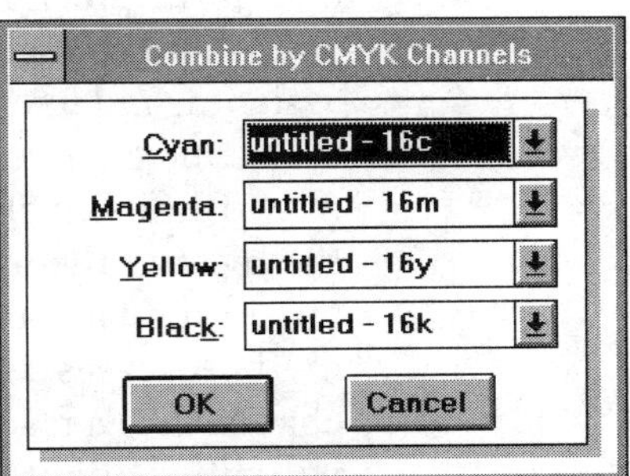

Figure 14-6.

The Combine by RGB Channels and Combine by CMYK Channels dialog boxes

The new True Color image document is untitled and bears a number after its name, just like the Grayscale channel documents. You can save this document to a file if you wish. The Grayscale channel documents remain open, too. If you no longer need them, close them one at a time by making each one the active image document and then double-clicking its control menu box.

Combining Channels for Special Effects

There are two basic ways to alter a True Color image once you've split it into component channels. The first way to alter a True Color image through its channels is to edit one or more channels separately and *then* recombine the channels. In the "Editing Image Channels" section, we'll look at techniques for editing individual channels.

The second way to edit an image using channels is to be choosy about which channels you combine. In this part of the chapter, we'll explore unusual ways to combine channels and show you how channel combinations by themselves can create interesting visual effects.

Switching Channels or Substituting One Image Channel for Another

As we've already mentioned, each channel in a given set of channels has predictable characteristics. In the RGB set, for example, the red channel is brightest, the green channel shows the broadest range of contrasts, and the blue channel is the darkest. An awareness of each channel's characteristics will help you choose which channels to substitute in order to produce special visual effects such as tints and color shifts.

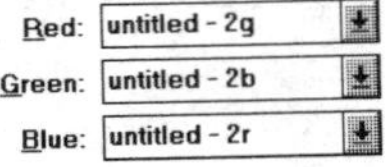

This game of switching channels can take various forms, as shown by the examples in Figure 14–7 in the Color Section of this book. To obtain the green tint in the center image of Figure 14–7, for instance, you would change the order of channels in the Combine by dialog box, assigning red to the green channel, green to the blue channel, and blue to the red channel. Or, you might assign the same channel document to two different channels. Assigning the red channel document to both the red and the blue channels would produce a magenta tint like the one in the far right image of Figure 14–7. What you're actually doing in these cases is assigning the values of one channel to another channel. As a result, the colors in the new combined image document will differ from the colors in the original.

Splitting and Recombining Channels According to Different Color Models

Another way to obtain interesting effects is to split a True Color image according to one set of channels and then combine them according to another. For instance, you might split an image by RGB channels, then choose the Combine True Color by HLS command and recombine these channels *as if they were* HLS channels as shown by the dialog box in Figure 14–8. You don't have to be content with the default order of channels as PhotoStyler presents them in the dialog box, either.

The color makeup of a particular image will determine what happens when you switch channel sets. Experiment until you find the combination and order of channels that yields the most pleasing results. Viewing the channels of different color models side by side can also help you imagine what the end results of various channel combinations might be. For comparison's sake, Figure 14-9 juxtaposes the RGB channels of a True Color image with the HSB channels of the same image.

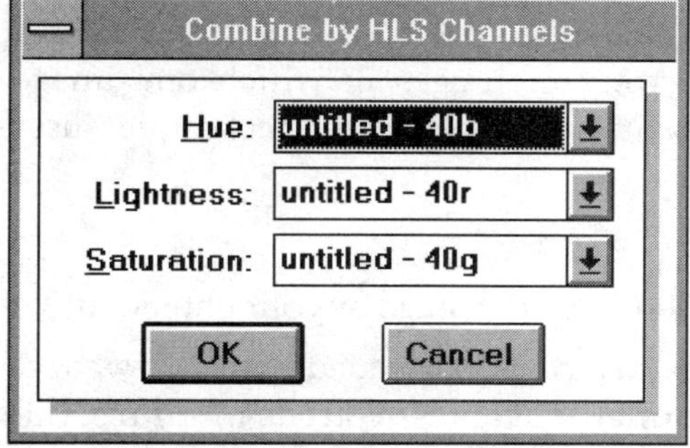

Figure 14-8. Combining RGB channels as though they were HLS channels

Figure 14-9. Comparing channels of different color models can help you choose which channels to recombine *Above, l-r*: RGB channels; *Below, l-r*: HSB channels

Caution *Avoid recombining RGB channels according to the CMYK color model. It can be done, of course: since CMYK requires four channels and you have only three to start with, you can use one of the channels twice. But in most cases, any RGB channel substituted for the black channel will result in a very dark image. You'll achieve better results if you recombine HSB or HLS channels according to the CMYK model, especially if you brighten the resulting True Color image afterward.*

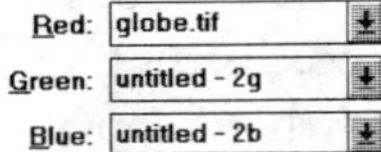

Combining Grayscale Images as Channels

Any Grayscale image document that's open is a potential channel. The creative implications of this statement are enormous. If a Grayscale image has the same pixel width and height as a color image that you've split into channels, you can substitute it for one of the "normal" image channels when you recombine them.

If you regularly use a slide scanner, many of your digital images will have the same standard pixel width and height to begin with. If your images come from a variety of sources, you may need to resize or resample an independent Grayscale image before you can substitute it for a "normal" image channel.

Combining channels from different images is a marvelous technique for creating montages in which one image overlays another semitransparently. To try out this technique, just follow these basic steps:

1. Split the True Color image of your choice into channels.
2. Open the Grayscale image document you want to substitute for one of the "normal" channels. You can minimize this document to save space in the application window.
3. Using the Information command in the View menu, compare the size of the independent Grayscale image with that of the True Color image that you've split into channels. If there's a mismatch, you'll need to resize the independent Grayscale image document; otherwise, it won't appear as a channel option in the Combine by dialog box. We recommend using the Resample command in the Transform menu to resize the Grayscale document (see Chapter 13). In some cases, you'll have to distort the image in order to fit it to the correct pixel width and height.
4. Choose the Combine RGB True Color by command in the Image menu and select the option that fits the set of channels you're using. When the Combine by dialog box appears, use the appropriate

drop-down list box to substitute the independent Grayscale document for one of the channels. Then, click the OK command button.

The channel for which you substitute the independent Grayscale document will determine the color makeup of the combined True Color image and the appearance of the independent image overlay. Have fun experimenting!

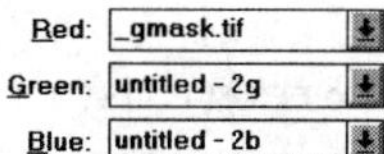

Substituting a Mask for One of the Channels

One more way to produce exciting color effects when you combine image channels is to substitute a mask document for one of the channels. If you've created a mask for the original True Color image or one of its Grayscale channels, the rest is easy. Just combine that mask with other channels to create a new True Color image document with high-contrast special color effects. Figure 14–10 shows a Grayscale channel and a mask exported from a selection area of that channel. Figure 14–11 in the Color Section of this book shows a few examples of the results you can achieve. The image on the left shows the result when the red RGB channel is used as a mask. The center image shows what happens when the blue RGB channel is used as a mask. And the far right image, created by recombining channels according to the HSB model, is the result of substituting the mask for the saturation channel.

Let's review how and why this technique works. As you may recall from Chapter 8, a mask is a Grayscale document that helps you refine a selection area in another image document. Most unedited mask documents are stark black and white, like the example in Figure 14–10. Black areas of a mask represent all the *unselected* areas in an image document, while white areas represent the selected areas. White areas of a mask are equivalent to values of 255 in a "normal" image channel, and black areas are equivalent to channel values of zero. The results of substituting a mask document for an image

Figure 14-10.

A Red channel document and a mask extracted from it

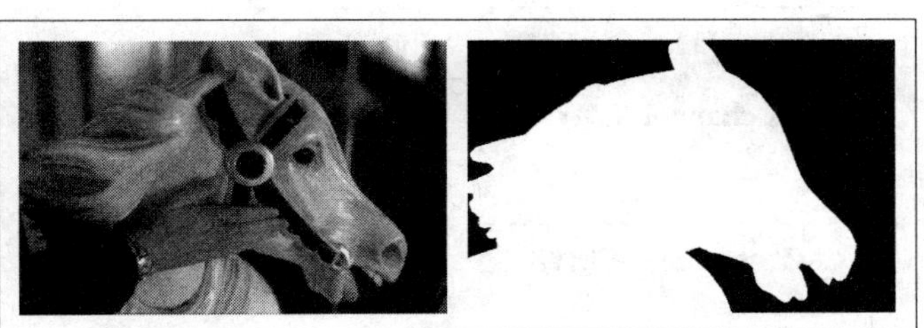

channel are therefore predictable. No matter which channel set you're working with or which channel you substitute a mask for, you're going to create a True Color image with high contrast.

But which channels should you substitute? Each set of channels and each channel within a set make specific color effects possible. Table 14–1 provides a "cookbook" reference to help you make that decision.

Editing Image Channels

In one important respect, image channels are like masks: they exist to help you edit something that you've isolated in an image. But whereas masks let you isolate *areas* of an image, channels let you isolate color values, brightness, saturation, or other components of pixel color. In this part of the chapter, we'll concentrate on techniques for editing individual channels.

Table 14–1. Combining Image Channels: Effects of Substituting High-Contrast Masks for Specific Image Channels

Mask substituted for . .	Color effects in bright mask areas	Color effects in dark mask areas
RGB channels	Surrealistic neon red, green, or blue tints	Tints in the complementary color
Hue channel, HSB	Soft reddish tint	Warm reddish tint
Saturation channel, HSB or HLS	Intense color	Shades of gray
Brightness channel, HSB	Bright, light colors	Pure black
Hue channel, HLS	Soft blue-violet tint	Intense blue-violet tint
Lightness channel, HLS	White	Black
Black channel, CMYK	Pastel colors (may vary according to Separation Setup options)	Black
CMY channels, CMYK	Tints in the channel color	Tints in the complementary color

Painting in a Single Image Channel

An image channel is a normal Grayscale image document to which you can apply any fill color, pattern, or Paint Palette tool. Changes you make to a single channel will produce a subtle or semitransparent effect in any new True Color image document that you create by recombining channels later. The exact effect of your changes will depend on:

- the set of channels into which you've split the original color image (RGB, HSB, HLS, CMYK)
- the channel you choose to edit
- the tool, fill effect, or pattern you've applied to the channel
- the way you've isolated specific areas of the image channel through selections and masks

Table 14–2 is a useful guide that lets you choose a channel or set of channels to edit based on the effects you want to produce.

For example, we decided to add a soft, starry effect in multiple colors to the carousel horse in Figure 14–12 (left). If we had simply painted the colors into the True Color image document, the effect would have been less subtle, even with a moderate transparency setting. Instead, we proceeded like this:

1. Starting with a True Color image of a carousel horse, we created and refined a mask that excluded everything but the body of the horse. We used the Lasso tool to outline the desired selection area and then applied a three-pixel soft edge before exporting the selection area as a mask (Figure 14–12, center).
2. We split the True Color image into RGB channels and made the red channel the active image document.
3. Next, we imported the mask (Figure 14–12, center) into the red channel document in preparation for painting in a selected area.

Figure 14-12.

Editing Grayscale RGB channels and a mask to produce special color effects

Table 14–2. Editing Image Channels: Matching Desired Effects to Specific Channels

To produce this effect . . .	Edit this channel or set of channels. . .
Semitransparent effects	Any single channel of any channel set
Single-color effects	RGB or CMYK channels
Multicolored or targeted single-color effects	The H channel in the HSB or HLS channel set
Brightness and contrast effects	The B or L channel in the HSB or HLS channel set
Color intensity effects	The S channel in the HSB or HLS channel set

4. We chose a gray value of 255 (white) as the current Foreground color. With RGB channels, this would translate into a bright value of whatever color channel we worked in.

5. We activated the Paintbrush tool at its default settings and chose a custom pinwheel brush shape.
6. Next, we imported the horse mask into the red channel document and applied the Paintbrush tool freehand throughout the selected area, creating the stars that appear in Figure 14–12 (right).
7. We activated the green channel, imported the same mask document, and painted the "stars" in the selection area in the same manner.
8. We repeated step 7 with the blue channel.
9. Finally, we chose the Combine RGB True Color by RGB Channels command in the Image menu and combined the edited red, green, and blue channel documents. The resulting True Color image (Figure 14–13 in the Color Section) displays a multicolored "sparkly" effect throughout the body of the carousel horse.

Adjusting Highlights, Shadows, and Midtones Separately for Each Channel

Another useful application for image channels is to help you refine your adjustment of highlights, shadows, and midtones. As Tables 14-1 and 14-2 show, each set of channels has specific uses, and so does each channel within a specific set.

To alter contrast throughout a color image, for example, you might split the image into RGB channels and then edit brightness and contrast for the green channel using the Tune: Gray/Color Correction command in the Image menu (see Chapter 9). This channel already contains the broadest range of brightness values, so your editing would be more effective here than in the red or blue channels.

You could achieve the same goal by splitting the color image into HSB channels and then editing brightness and contrast in the Brightness channel. If, on the other hand, you wanted to adjust the *intensity* of colors in the original image, you would edit the Saturation channel instead.

Editing the Composition of One or More Image Channels

The image composition techniques we described in Chapter 13 —pasting from the clipboard, using Transform menu commands on selected areas or masks, filling selected areas with patterns—can produce dazzling results in any image document. But when you use them on one or more image channels that you intend to recombine later, the possibilities are truly magical. That's because any changes you make to the content of one channel will appear semitransparent once you recombine all channels into a new True Color image document. The *kinds* of effects you produce will depend both on the set of channels you're using and on the specific channel you choose to edit (see Tables 14-1 and 14-2).

The "Neon Horse" image in Figure 14–14 in the Color Section is an example of semitransparent single-color effects generated by editing the composition of two RGB channels. To evoke the magic of childhood through the neon horse and the shimmering playthings cascading downward, we stylized the carousel horse as follows:

1. We split the original True Color image (refer to the Grayscale version in Figure 14–12, left) into RGB channels.
2. Our next task was to prepare a child's ball with a three-dimensional look. We created a new image document, filled it with a Custom Color gradient fill, selected a circular area of this image document, and then applied the 3-D Sphere filter to it. The gradient fill and 3-D filter (Chapters 10 and 12, respectively) provided the three-dimensional look that turned the circle into a globe.
3. We copied the multicolored ball to the clipboard.

4. Next, we made the red channel the active image document and pasted the ball into it several times, each time resizing and repositioning the floating selection (figure 14–15, left). Since the channel was a Grayscale document, the gradient fill in each ball simulated changes in lighting and brightness rather than color.
5. We then made the blue channel the active image document and imported the mask shown in the center image of Figure 14–12. The mask excluded everything from the selection area except the carousel horse itself.
6. We applied the Border command in the Select Palette menu and specified a border 3 pixels in width. The border area "outlined" the previous mask area.
7. Using the Color Palette, we made white (gray = 255) the current Foreground color and filled the selected border area with it as shown in Figure 14–15 (right). We knew that white in a Grayscale image would translate into the brightest value of blue once we recombined the three RGB image channels.
8. Finally, we chose the Combine RGB True Color by RGB Channels command in the Image menu. The result was the carousel horse shown in Figure 14–14 in the Color Section, with an outline of neon blue and a background filled with a cascade of semitransparent bouncing red balls.

Tip

When editing image channels, always think in terms of the color or feature that a particular channel represents. In creating the sphere, for example, we knew that the original hues of the custom color gradient fill would be lost when we pasted it into the Grayscale red channel. But we also knew that the gradient-filled spheres would translate into reds of varying brightness levels once we recombined image channels, helping to create a shimmering look. In the same vein, we knew that applying a white fill to the border area in the blue channel would be like applying

Figure 14-15.

Editing the red and blue RGB image channels separately to produce special color effects

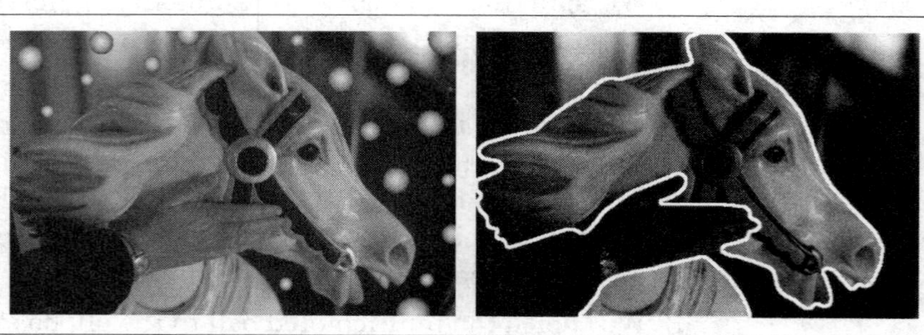

a bright blue hue-only fill to the same area in the combined True Color image.

Applying Filters to Individual Image Channels

A wisely chosen filter applied to an image channel can generate enhanced color or brightness effects in the recombined True Color image document. We say enhanced, because the color or component that a Grayscale image channel represents will modify a filter's effect on the recombined True Color image.

You can use every PhotoStyler filter on an image channel, but not every filter will introduce noticeable effects to the recombined image document. Table 14–3 lists the filters which, in our experience, are most likely to produce dramatic results in a recombined color image. When photographic realism is your goal, you may find that other filters that produce more subtle effects are equally useful.

Your choice of channels will help determine the intensity of the effect, too. When you want dramatic results, always apply a filter to the channel that contains the brightest values or the greatest range of contrasts in the set.

Creating Drop Shadows for Text: Using the Gaussian Blur Filter on an Image Channel One simple but effective way to edit an image channel using filters is to apply the Gaussian blur filter to selected areas in the RGB channel. This technique can create glowing drop shadows for text, as shown in Figure 14–16 in the Color Section of this book. Here's how to do it:

1. Display the Color Palette (Ctrl-8) and change the current background color to black.
2. Create a new True Color image using the New command in the File menu. Let your system memory and hard drive space guide you in choosing dimensions and resolution for the new image.

3. Activate the Text tool in the Paint Palette and add a short text string to the image. Remember to make the text large enough to keep adjacent letters or spaces within letters from running together.
4. Using the Color Palette, make a bright yellow the new foreground color.

5. Double-click the Bucket Fill tool icon and set Color Similarity to 255, then click the OK command button. Click anywhere inside the text outlines to fill the text string.

Table 14–3. Effects of Editing Image Channels with Selected Filters

Filter	Channel	Effect
Gaussian blur	Red RGB channel, Cyan CMYK channel	Adds a warm, grainy look that simulates immediacy; good for photojournalism
	Hue HSB or HLS channel	Causes a shift in colors and makes image grainier
Edge Enhancement	Red RGB channel, Cyan CMYK channel	Adds contrast throughout an image and a warm glow to the edges of objects
	Saturation HSB channel	Causes dramatic color shifts in selected areas, with enhanced contrasts
Find Edges	RGB channels, CMYK channels	Tints an image in the color that's complementary to the channel, while adding outlines in the channel color
Trace Contour	RGB channels, CMYK channels	Adds a textured effect while tinting the image in the color complementary to the channel
	Hue HSB or HLS channel	Applies a uniform shift of color
Add Noise	All channels	Adds a glow and grainy texture to an image
Maximum	RGB, CMYK channels	Adds stunning highlighting and glitter effects in the color or complementary color of the channel edited
Mosaic	RGB, CMYK channels; Hue HSB or HLS channel	Adds subtle geometrical undertones to an image in a particular color or set of colors
3-D Filters	RGB, CMYK channels	Creates semitransparent "ghost" images in the chosen channel color or complementary color

6. Choose the Split RGB True Color to command in the Image menu and select RGB Channels.
7. Activate the red channel that you've just generated.

8. Double-click the Magic Wand in the Select Palette and set Color Similarity to 64. Press Enter to save this setting, and then click anywhere inside the text outlines to select one of the letters.
9. To select the remaining letters of the text string, choose the Expand command in the Select Palette menu. Set Color Similarity to 64 and make sure the Connected to Current Selection is *not* active. When you click the OK command button, PhotoStyler will outline the rest of the text string in the red channel.
10. Choose the Border command in the Select Palette menu. Set a border 2 pixels wide and then click the OK command button. This border area will form the basis for the glow or shadow effect you're about to create.

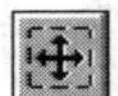

11. Activate the Move tool in the Select Palette and drag the text border area just slightly below and to the right of its original position.
12. Use the Color Palette to change the current foreground color to gray=255 (white). Let the status bar help you choose this shade accurately.

13. Activate the Bucket Fill tool and click once anywhere inside the border selection outlines to fill the border area around the text string. (If you can't see the area inside the border, magnify the image using the Zoom tool.) Remember, what's white in this Grayscale image channel will become bright red once you recombine all channels to form a new True Color image. But this red is a little harsh, so we'll soften it and make it more subtle with the Gaussian Blur filter.
14. Choose the Smoothing Filters/Gaussian Blur command in the Image menu and set Variance to 50 in the Gaussian Blur dialog box. Click OK to begin filtering the text border area.
15. When the filter has done its work, choose the Combine RGB True Color by RGB Channels command in the Image menu. The result will be a soft red drop shadow slightly below and to the right of the text string, similar to Figure 14–16 in the Color Section of this book.

You could just as easily have chosen to edit the green or blue channel in the foregoing steps. The results would have been similar, except that the drop shadow in the recombined image would have appeared in the color of the channel you edited.

We've only scratched the surface of the creative possibilities open to you when you begin to edit individual image channels. Take some time to experiment on your own—through play, you'll discover a host of ways to make your images more dazzling.

Using the Compute Command for Special Effects

The Compute command in the Image menu provides a sophisticated set of options for comparing two True Color or two Grayscale image documents and merging them to form a third document. In some respects, it's similar to the Merge Control command in the Edit menu, but your range of options is much broader.

This command has an almost infinite number of potential applications—so many, in fact, that we can't even imagine them all. Here are just a few of the uses to which you can put the Compute command:

- Edit Grayscale image channels before you combine channels to form a new True Color image document.
- Tint a Grayscale image that you've converted to True Color.
- Combine two True Color images to enhance color values.

One thing's certain: It's a great tool for creating special color effects.

The Image Compute Dialog Box

When you choose the Compute command, the Image Compute dialog box shown in Figure 14–17 will appear. Don't let the mathematical formulas and multiple options intimidate you! Think of this dialog box as a flexible tool for exploring and experimenting with special effects. There are few rules and even fewer guidelines: the results of changing a single option will vary with every pair of images, and no two images are alike.

Once you understand the functions of each element in the Image Compute dialog box, you'll be able to wield the powerful tools that it provides.

Figure 14-17.
The Image Compute dialog box

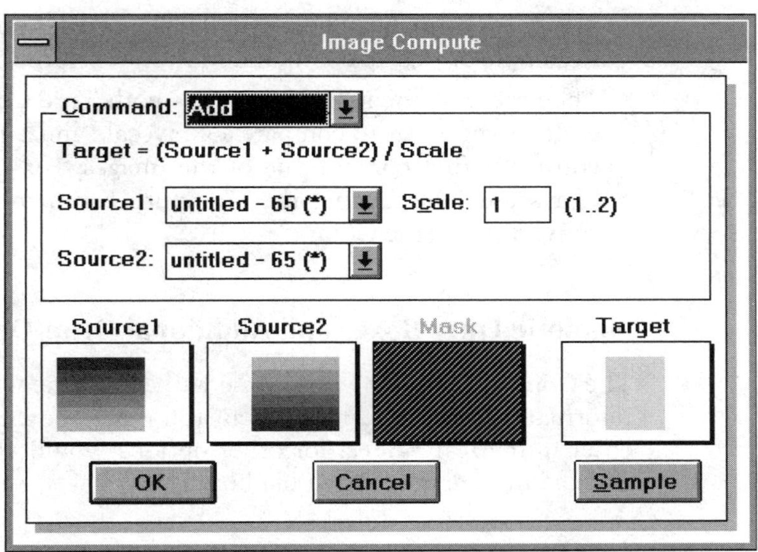

Add
Subtract
Shift
Multiply
Difference
Blend
Composite
Lighter
Darker
Extract

Command Drop-Down List Box

The options in this list box define ten ways to compare and combine images. Whenever you choose an option, the dialog box will reset, and some of the other controls in the dialog box may change. The ten Command options are: Add, Subtract, Shift, Multiply, Difference, Blend, Composite, Lighter, Darker, and Extract. We'll devote a section to each option and its uses.

Target Image Formula

Each Command option is associated with a mathematical formula, called the *target formula*. This formula describes how PhotoStyler derives a new target image from the two source images you've selected. Typically, the formula involves adding, multiplying, subtracting, and/or dividing the color or gray values in the source images.

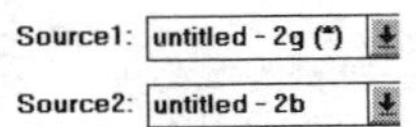

Source 1 and 2 Drop-Down List Boxes

Depending on which Command option you choose, you can specify one, two, or even three source images from which to derive a new image. The source images must meet two requirements:

- Their width and height in pixels must be identical. If there is a disparity between them, one of the images won't appear in the

Source drop-down list box. You'll have to resize one image using the Resample or Resize command in the Transform menu.

- They must be the same data type—both True Color or both Grayscale. If you want to compare a Grayscale and a True Color image, you must first convert one of the images. For example, to tint a Grayscale image using the Compute command, you must first convert it to True Color.

Numeric Entry Boxes and Additional Drop-Down List Boxes

The Command option you choose will determine what other kinds of information you have to enter in the dialog box. Sometimes you'll enter numerical values; for other options, you'll choose parameters from additional drop-down list boxes.

Display Boxes, Sample Button

The display boxes at the bottom of the dialog box show how PhotoStyler uses default values for the current Command option to merge the source images. Each time you choose a new Command option, the content of the display boxes will change. If you change the default values for the current Command option, click the Sample command button to see how your changes will affect the way the source images merge.

Adding Channels or Images

Add
Subtract
Shift
Multiply
Difference
Blend
Composite
Lighter
Darker
Extract

The Add command option in the Image Compute dialog box (see Figure 14–17) is fairly straightforward. When you choose this command option, PhotoStyler compares the two source images you specify in this way:

1. It adds the color or gray values of all the pixels in the two source images. The resulting pixel values could range anywhere from zero to 510. (Anything over 255 will be white.)
2. It then divides each of the resulting pixel values by the number you specify in the Scale entry box. This number can be either one or two. If the Scale value is 1, all the resulting pixel values will be brighter than in either of the original source images. If the Scale value is 2, PhotoStyler will average the combined pixel values of the source images.

Application Examples

Among the many applications possible with the Add command are three that you may frequently find useful.

Tinting a Grayscale Image To tint a Grayscale image or a Grayscale channel document with a single color:

1. Begin by making a Grayscale image the active image document. If you prefer, split a True Color image document into its component RGB channels.
2. Using the Convert to command in the Image menu, convert the Grayscale image (or the green channel, if you've split a color image) into a True Color image document.
3. Using the Color dialog box, change the current background color to the color you want to use as a tint. The tint color *must* have a green component value that's in the midtone range (110-140). If the tint color has a more extreme green component value, you run the risk of obscuring detail in the True Color image. A midtone green value will ensure that the tint color will blend evenly throughout the converted Grayscale image, yielding the maximum color saturation.
4. Duplicate the new True Color image document, and then choose the Clear command in the Edit menu. The duplicated document will now be filled with the current background color.
5. Choose the Compute command from the Image menu and then select the Add command option.
6. In the Source1 drop-down list box, select the image that you converted from Grayscale to True color. In the Source2 list box, select the tint color document.
7. Set Scale to 1 and then click OK. PhotoStyler will generate a new image tinted with the color of one of your source images.

Lightening a Dark Image Another use for the Add command option is to lighten a very dark image. Select the same dark image document for *both* Source list boxes and apply the Add command with a Scale factor of one. In effect, you're adding the image to itself, doubling (and therefore lightening) the gray or color values in the image.

Combining Two Grayscale Image Channels A third use for the Add command option is to combine two Grayscale image channels from the same True Color image document. Afterward, you can substitute this "hybrid" channel for one of the regular channels when creating a new True Color image.

Subtracting Channels or Images

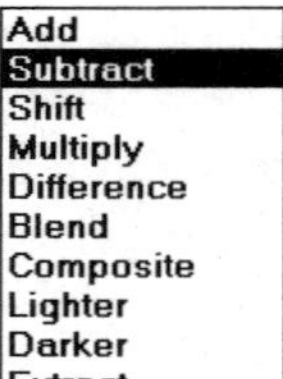

When you choose the Subtract command option in the Image Compute dialog box (Figure 14–18), PhotoStyler compares the two source images you specify in this way:

1. It subtracts the color or gray values of all the pixels in the Source2 image from the values of the corresponding pixels in the Source1 image. Choose the order of your images carefully! The resulting values can range from -128 to +128.
2. It then divides each of the resulting pixel values by the number you specify in the Scale entry box. This number can be either one or two. Either value will result in a darker image than either of the source images, but a value of 2 will darken the target image further.

Application Examples

You can use the Subtract command to merge two different True Color or Grayscale images with one another, provided they have the same

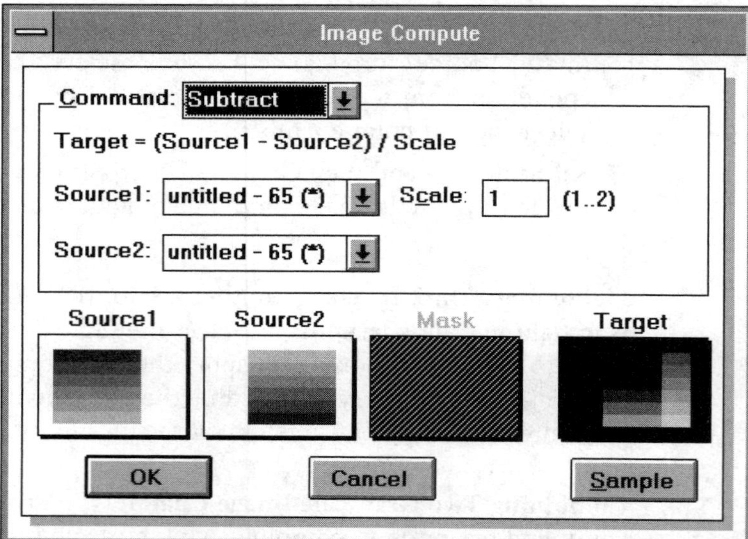

Figure 14-18.

Options for subtracting image channels

pixel dimensions. If you leave the Shift setting at its default value of 1, the target image will contain a negative of the Source2 image superimposed on the normal color values of the Source1 image. Keep in mind that if you use two separate images, they both must have the same pixel dimensions.

You can also use this command to subtract an overly bright Grayscale or True Color image from itself. The result will be a darker image than the original.

Shifting Channels or Images

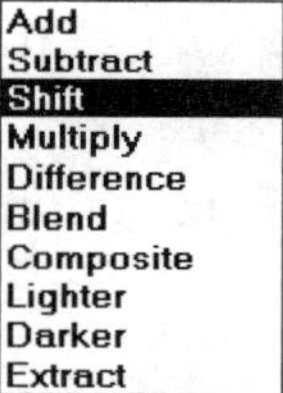

When you choose the Shift option in the Image Compute dialog box (Figure 14–19), PhotoStyler generates a new target image by adding a fixed value to every pixel in the Source1 image. This value can range from -255 to +255. Negative values will result in an image with decreased brightness, while positive values will result in an image with increased brightness.

Application Examples

The simplest use for the Shift option is to brighten or darken every pixel in an image by an equal amount. You can also apply this option *after* you tint a Grayscale image using the Add command as described earlier in this section. If the tint color you selected has a bright or dark

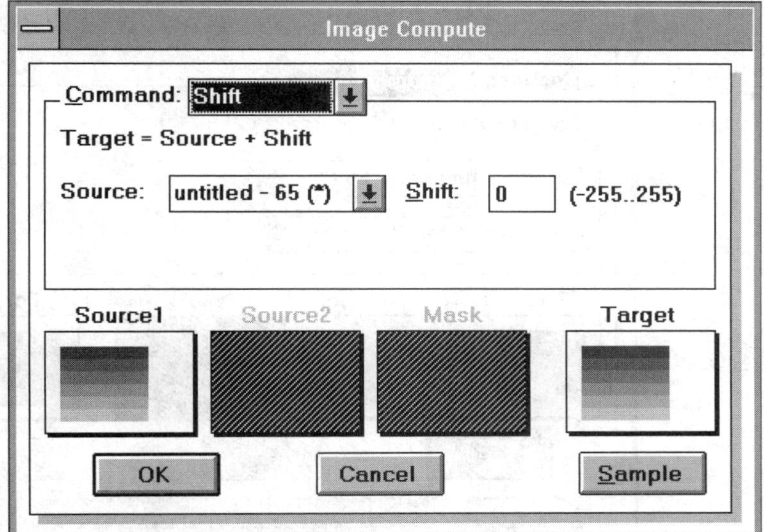

Figure 14-19.

Options for Shifting image channel values

green component value, the converted Grayscale image will look "washed out." You can remedy this situation by choosing the Shift option and setting the Shift value to the *negative* of the tint color's green component value. This step will ensure that the tint color will blend evenly throughout the converted Grayscale image.

Multiplying Channels or Images

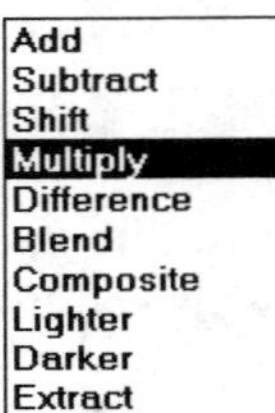

When you choose the Multiply option in the Image Compute dialog box (Figure 14–20), PhotoStyler generates a new image in this way:

1. It multiplies all pixel values in the Source1 document by all the pixel values in the Source2 document.
2. It then divides the resulting pixel values by 255. The target image will be less bright than the source images.

Application Examples

The Multiply command is useful for toning down a bright image that has too much glare. Simply select the same image document as both Source1 and Source2. The new image that you generate will show enhanced detail and increased overall contrast.

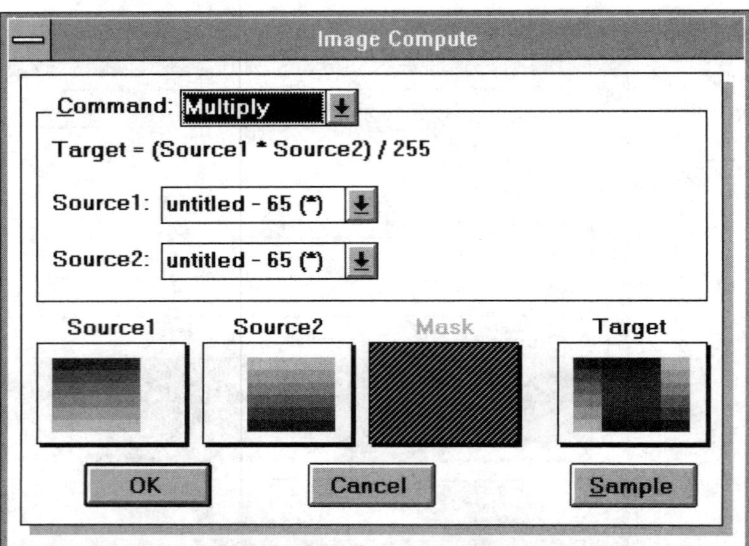

Figure 14-20. Options for multiplying images or channels

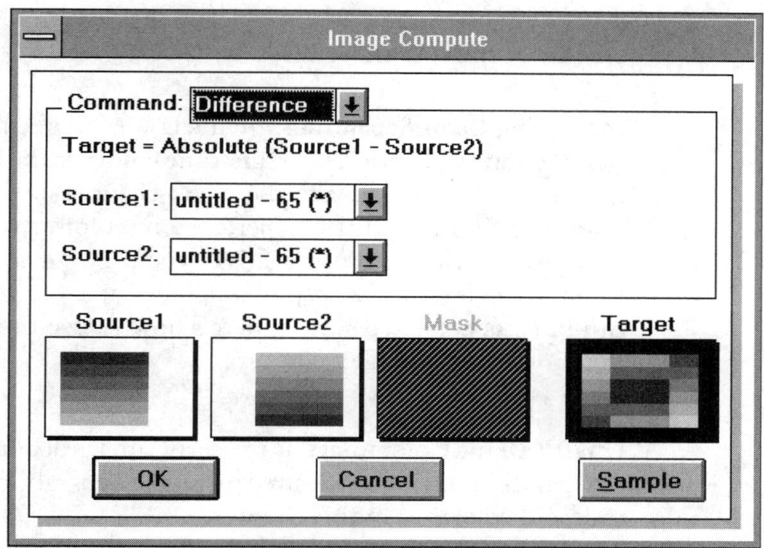

Figure 14-21. Options for computing the difference between images or channels

Comparing the Difference between Channels or Images

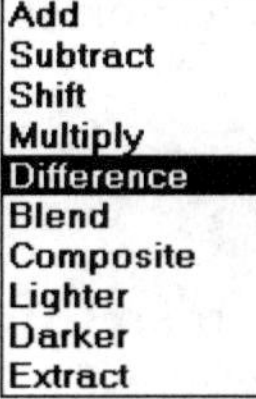

When you choose the Difference command in the Image Compute dialog box (Figure 14–21), PhotoStyler subtracts the pixel values of the Source2 image from the pixel values of the Source1 image. The image generated from this process will show how the color or Grayscale values of the two source images differ. If you select the same image document as both Source1 and Source2, PhotoStyler will generate a black image, indicating that there are no differences.

Application Examples

You can use the Difference command option to merge two same-size images with some degree of transparency. This option can also help you refine a set of color separations.

Merging Two Same-Size Images with Partial Transparency It's possible to use the Difference command option to merge two unrelated images of the same size. The results will depend on which source image you subtract the color or gray values from. Part of one image will show through the other image. If any color values from the Source2 image turn out negative after they are subtracted from the

Source1 image values, PhotoStyler makes them positive. You'll see some color shifts in these cases.

Fine-tuning Color Separation Channels A practical use for the Difference command option is to fine-tune color separations, using a True Color image as Source1 and the black channel of the same image as Source2. If you have little experience in color separation and aren't sure how to read a color negative, you'd best leave this command option to a color separation professional. But if you're used to working with process color separation, here's how to use the Difference command to best advantage:

1. With a True Color image as the active image document, adjust color separation settings as desired using the Separation Setup command described earlier in this chapter.
2. Split the True Color image into its component CMYK channels.
3. Convert the black channel to a True Color document for purposes of comparison, using the Convert to command in the Image menu. If you don't convert it, you won't be able to compare it to the original True Color document from which it was generated.
4. Choose the Compute command in the Image menu and select the Difference command option.
5. Select the original True Color image document as Source1 and the converted black channel as Source2.
6. Click the OK command button. After a moment, PhotoStyler will generate a document that will be like a film negative of the CMY channels put together.

If the generated image is too bright, you may need to reduce the amount of black in your black channel or risk washing out the colors in the other three channels. If the generated image is too dark, your black channel may not be saturated enough—and colors in the printed image may not be, either.

Color separation is an art, not a science, and it takes an experienced eye to know what the ideal combination will be. If you don't like the looks of the generated image, go back and readjust the Separation Setup command settings. Then, try using the Difference command option again. Keep adjusting the Separation Setup settings and using the Difference command option until you feel the balance between CMYK channels is right.

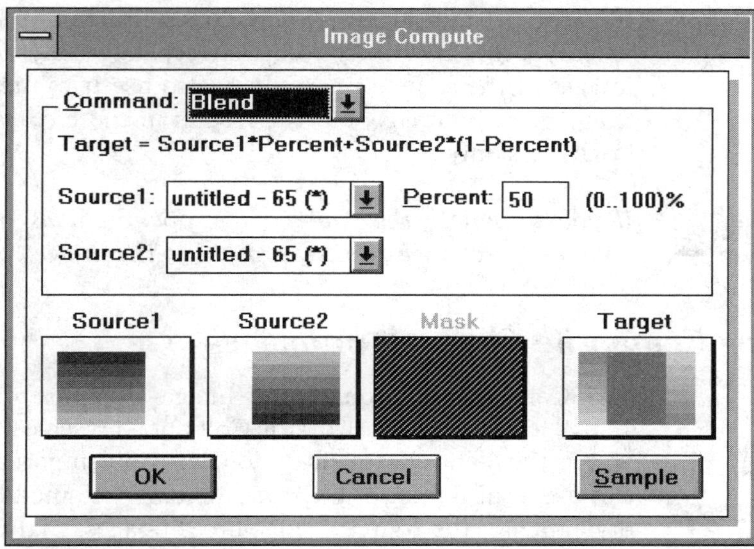

Figure 14-22.

Options for blending images or channels

Blending Channels or Images

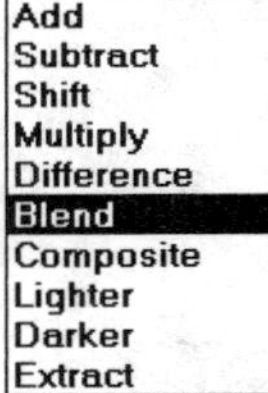

The Blend command option merges two separate images with varying degrees of transparency. When you choose this option (see Figure 14–22), PhotoStyler generates a third image in the following way:

1. It multiplies the color or gray values of each pixel in the Source1 image by the percentage you specify in the Percent numeric entry box. This percentage must be 100 or less.
2. To the values obtained in step 1, PhotoStyler adds a percentage of the color or gray values of each pixel in the Source2 image. The percentage used here is 100 minus whatever value you specified in the Percent numeric entry box. If you specify 75%, for example, PhotoStyler will generate an image that contains 75% of the color values from the Source1 image and only 25% of the color values from the Source2 image.

Application Examples

Using the Blend command option is similar to invoking the Merge Control command in the Edit menu. It lets you determine how much of each source image will show through and how much will be transparent in the blended image. You'll find this option most effective when you use it with two entirely separate Grayscale or True Color images of the same size. You can also use it to merge two channels from the same image, but the results in these cases will affect pixel brightness only.

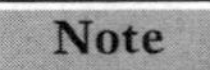

If you designate the same image document as both Source1 and Source2, no change at all will occur to the image.

Creating Composite Channels or Images

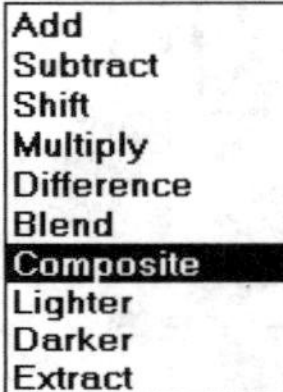

The Composite option in the Image Compute dialog box (Figure 14–23) lets you merge two True Color or Grayscale images in the same way as the Blend command option, with one important exception. You can use a third image—a Grayscale mask—to modify the way PhotoStyler blends the Source1 and Source2 images. In the target image, the Source1 image will be more visible in areas that correspond to lighter pixels in the mask; the Source2 image will be more visible in areas that correspond to darker pixels in the mask. The range of gray values in the mask image you use will determine what kind of target image you'll generate with the Composite option.

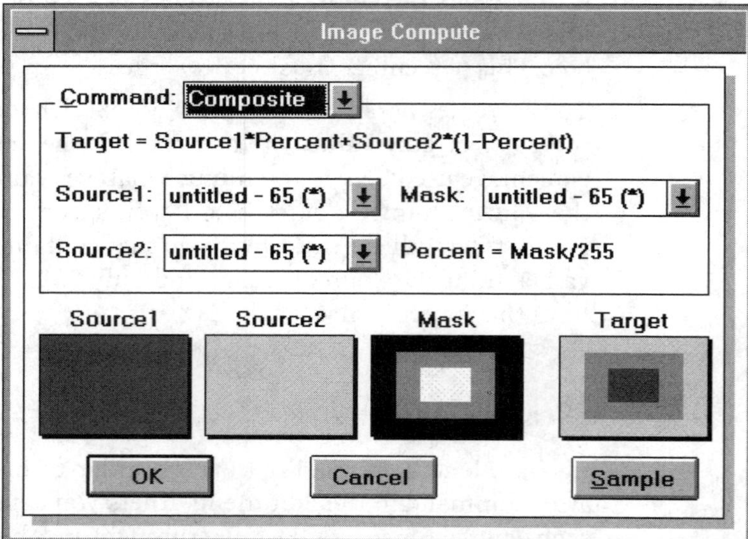

Figure 14-23. Options for creating composite images or channels

Application Examples

The Composite option has many applications. Among the most practical are:

- merging two separate images with precise control over opaqueness and transparency, and
- merging multiple versions of the *same* image or channel in order to combine the enhancements made to each version

We'll provide an example of each application in this section.

Merging Two Separate Images with Control over Opaqueness and Transparency We used the Composite option in the Image Compute dialog box to merge a True Color photo of a balloon race with a color shot of an airplane in flight (Figure 14–24 here and Figure 14–25 in the Color Section). Our goal was to let the balloon image show through the engine and wing of the airplane semitransparently. Here's how we proceeded:

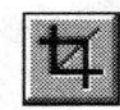

1. We cropped and resampled both images (see the Grayscale versions in Figure 14–24, top) to a standard pixel width and height.

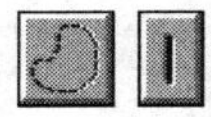

2. Using the Lasso tool, we outlined the contours of the airplane (Figure 14–24, top right) and then used the I button at the base of the Select Palette to invert the selection area. We also added a Soft Edge of one pixel to the inverted selection area.
3. Next, we exported the mask of the airplane image (Figure 14–24, bottom left).
4. After exporting the mask, we changed the current foreground color to a gray value of 95 and filled the black area of the mask with it (Figure 14–24, bottom right).

Note

Since we wanted our montage to be semitransparent, we had to edit the mask image in this way. If we had generated a composite immediately without editing the mask, the body of the airplane would have remained opaque; no part of the balloon image would have shown through. Refer to Chapter 8 if you need to review masking techniques.

5. Next, we chose the Compute command in the Image menu and the Composite option in the Image Compute dialog box. We specified the balloon image as Source1, the airplane photo as Source2, and the modified Grayscale mask as the Mask image. When we clicked the OK command button, PhotoStyler generated the composite

Figure 14-24.

Using the Composite option to merge two images

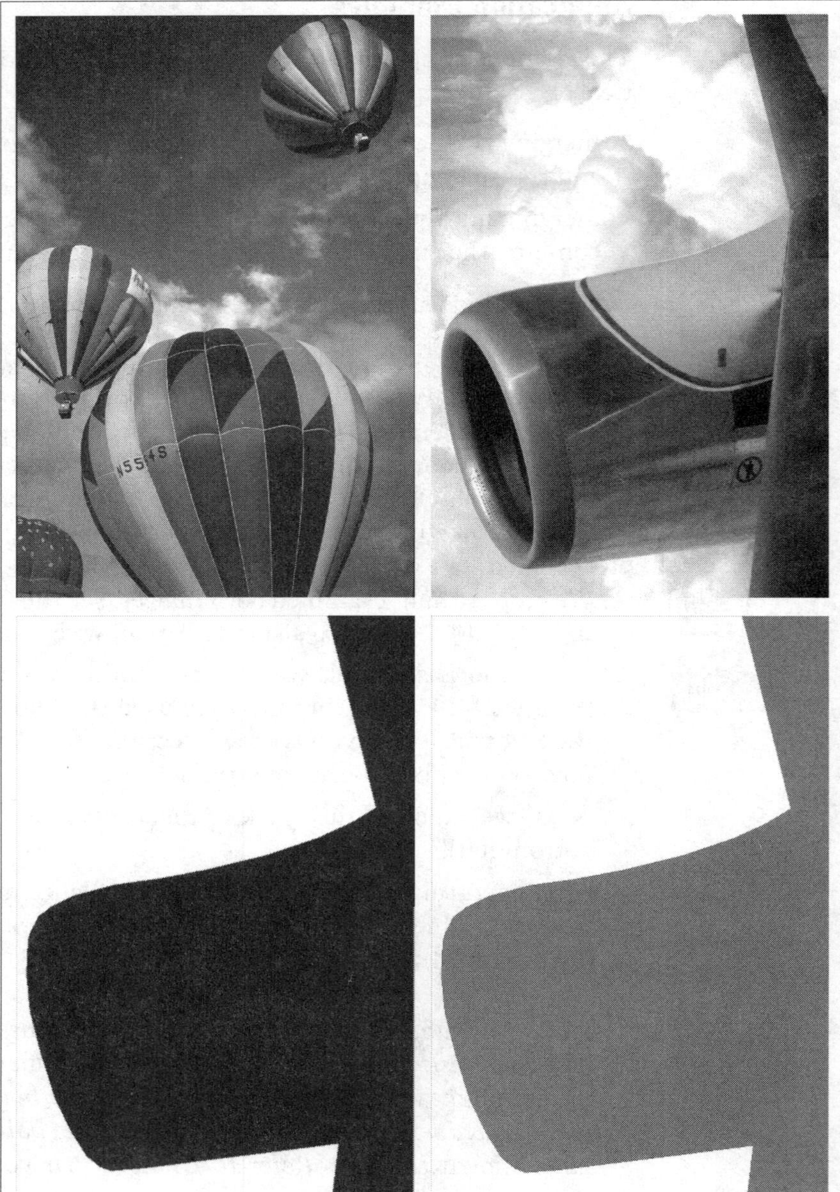

l-r: Source1 and Source2 images

l-r: inverted high-contrast mask made from Source2 image, mask edited to generate semitransparent montage effects

image that appears as Figure 14–25 in the Color Section. The intermediate gray shade in the mask permitted the balloon image to show through the engine and wing of the airplane semitransparently.

This example shows only one way to apply the Composite option. We could just as easily have used the unedited black-and-white mask, in which case we would have generated a simple composite like the one in Figure 14–26 in the Color Section. When you use a black-and-white mask with the Composite option, PhotoStyler will generate a montage in the following way:

- The colors or gray values of the Source2 image will be opaque in areas of the composite image that correspond to black areas of the mask.
- The colors or gray values of the Source1 image will be opaque in areas of the composite image that correspond to white areas of the mask.

Choose the order of your Source1 and Source2 images carefully!

Merging Multiple Versions of the Same Image Using a Continuous-Tone Grayscale Mask Have you ever looked at two working versions of the same image and thought, "Now, if only I could merge the effects of the filter in *this* version with the color enhancements in *that* one"? The Composite option in the Image Compute dialog box has the power to make your "if onlys" a reality. If you use a continuous-tone Grayscale image as the mask document, the resulting composite will blend pixel values from the Source1 and Source2 images subtly and smoothly. Emil Ihrig followed the steps in the following example to create the "Sky Race" image in the PhotoStyler Gallery.

To merge enhancements from two different versions of the same True Color or Grayscale image:

1. Start with an unedited True Color image and convert it to Grayscale using the Convert to command in the Image menu. PhotoStyler will generate a separate Grayscale image document, which becomes the active document (see Figure 14–27, left). Minimize this document for now; you'll use it as the mask later.
2. Activate the True Color image again and duplicate it by pressing Ctrl-D. The duplicate color image will become the active document.
3. Apply a filter of your choice to the duplicate True Color image. Emil Ihrig used the Trace Contour filter in the Image/Sharpening Filters submenu at a Threshold value of 75. The center image in Figure 14–27 shows a Grayscale version of the result.

Figure 14-27. Using a continuous-tone Grayscale mask to merge two versions of the same image: *(l)* the Grayscale mask *(c)* Source1 image, Trace Contour filter *(r)* Source2 image, posterized to 5 bits/channel

4. Activate the original True Color image document once more, and then use the Tune: Posterize command in the Image menu to posterize it at 5 bits per channel. Figure 14–27 (right) displays a Grayscale version of the posterized True Color image we used.
5. Choose the Compute command in the Image menu and select the Composite command option. Make the posterized True Color document the Source1 image, the filtered document the Source2 image, and the converted Grayscale document the mask, then click OK. In the new document that PhotoStyler generates ("Sky Race," in our case), the blend will be fairly smooth throughout.

Creating Lighter or Darker Image or Channel Combinations

Add
Subtract
Shift
Multiply
Difference
Blend
Composite
Lighter
Darker
Extract

When you choose the Lighter or Darker command option in the Image Compute dialog box (Figure 14–28), PhotoStyler compares the color or Grayscale values in each pixel of the two source images. If you choose the Lighter option, the target image will contain only the lighter pixels. If you choose the Darker option, the target image will contain only the darker pixels.

Application Examples

Use these two commands to combine two different Grayscale image channels in preparation for creating a new True Color image. For example, you might use the Lighter option to combine the red channel of a True Color image (the brightest channel) with a high-contrast

Figure 14-28.

Options for lightening images or channels

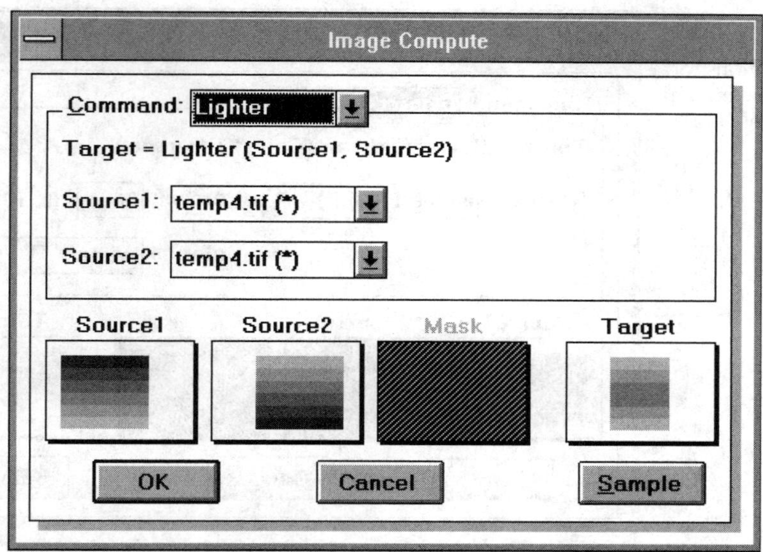

mask. The result would be a new mask document containing a broad range of gray shades. Later, you could substitute this hybrid mask document for the original red channel when combining channels to form a new True Color image.

Extracting Color or Gray Values from Image Channels

Add
Subtract
Shift
Multiply
Difference
Blend
Composite
Lighter
Darker
Extract

When you choose the Extract command option in the Image Compute dialog box (Figure 14–29), you can select only one source image. PhotoStyler blends this source image with the current foreground color, the current background color, white, black, or a shade of gray, according to a percentage that you specify. At percentages below 50%, more of the solid color or gray shows through in the target image. At higher percentages, more of the source image shows through in the target image.

Application Examples

The Extract command option is most useful for:

- tinting a True Color image using the current foreground or background color, or
- making a True Color or Grayscale image lighter or darker by blending it with black, white, or a shade of gray

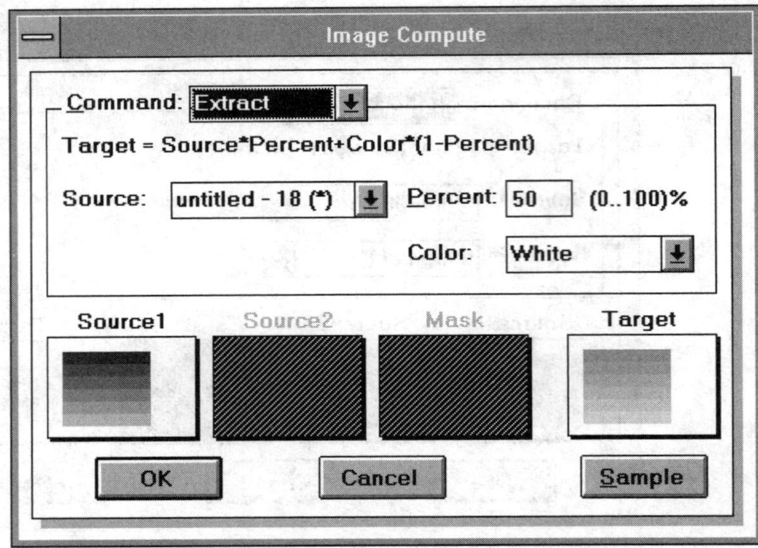

Figure 14-29.

Options for extracting image or channel values

In the past several chapters, we've concentrated on techniques for enhancing your photographs and artwork. The next chapter introduces you to the ultimate challenge: how to get your artwork out of the computer and into the world intact.

Part IV:

OUTPUT: THE FINAL DESTINATION

15

PhotoStyler's Printing Tools

No matter how dazzling a PhotoStyler image may look on your monitor, the acid test of quality is whether you can extract it from the computer with its dazzle intact. This journey to a "final destination"—a newspaper, a brochure or product catalog, a magazine advertisement, a slide presentation, or a fine art poster on the wall —is what *output* is all about.

As multimedia comes of age on the PC, digital and analog video applications for PhotoStyler images are likely to become popular. Until then, the final output destination for most PhotoStyler users will be print or slide media. This chapter will acquaint you with basic issues related to printing continuous-tone images of any data type from PhotoStyler. We'll also review PhotoStyler's extensive controls to help you achieve quality printed output. Chapter 16, "Prepress and Imaging Issues," moves beyond the world of PhotoStyler to "real-world" issues related to color print and slide output. If you work with True Color images, interact with desktop publishing or color service bureaus and print vendors, or output your images to slide or silk-screen media, you'll want to continue with Chapter 16 after you finish this chapter.

Printing from PhotoStyler: The Wider View

Some PhotoStyler users will choose to import their images into a page layout program and print them from there. However, you can print images of any data type and generate color separations for even the most demanding True Color images directly from PhotoStyler. PhotoStyler also lets you customize the way an image prints to a given output device. If your page layout package doesn't offer you an equivalent degree of printing sophistication or doesn't let you output color separations for 24-bit color images, printing directly from PhotoStyler may well be the safest, most reliable option.

Yet, printing PhotoStyler images involves much more than knowing which commands to choose. Preparing printed output for continuous-tone images has always been a much more demanding process than preparing output for text-only documents. There are so many more variables to be considered, especially if you're working with color. For most applications, you'll need to inform yourself about four interrelated processes:

- *Getting to know PhotoStyler's print-related commands*— Becoming familiar with the options in the Print, Page Setup, Printer Setup, and Separation Setup commands covered in this chapter.
- *Initial proofing*—Checking the preliminary results of your image editing work on some kind of printing device. Most black-and-white and color laser printers used by corporations and consultants are suitable for draft output only; they can't provide satisfactory camera-ready artwork for continuous-tone images.
- *Prepress*—Preparing output files for a service bureau, adjusting calibration curves for the output device you'll be using, and generating camera-ready artwork (RC paper or film) with the help of a service bureau's imagesetter or high-end proprietary color system. If you're preparing output for color images, prepress work may include setting up color separations and obtaining one or more color proofs from the service bureau for color matching purposes. This stage of the output cycle, covered in greater detail in Chapter 16, gives you the best opportunities for avoiding errors that might result in poor print quality later.
- *Printing*—Choosing a commercial print vendor and specifying the hardware, inks, and paper stock to be used. You and the print vendor interact closely in order to avoid errors involving registra-

tion, dot gain, and muddy colors. You assume final responsibility for avoiding many of these errors.

As you've probably guessed from the foregoing information, the output process for continuous-tone images can be quite complex, with little room for carelessness. If you're planning to output Grayscale images, there's a lot to learn. If you're working with True Color images, there's a lot more to learn. In fact, if you're new to the world of full-color publishing, you may feel that you've just entered a land mine zone with your eyes blindfolded. The range of choices you have to make can seem daunting at times. But if you constantly keep the following questions in mind as you prepare for output, you'll stand a good chance of reaching your destination safely and with pride in your work:

- What kind of document are you producing and for what purpose?
- Are your images in color or are they Grayscale?
- What kind of input device did you use to bring the original image into PhotoStyler?
- What's the resolution of the image? What's the image width in pixels?
- What constitutes "acceptable" quality for your application? How much quality can you afford?
- What kind of output device(s) can you use for proofing? What device will prepare camera-ready output?
- What kind of commercial printing press will run your job—silk-screen, newsprint, web, sheetfed?
- Are you working closely with a service bureau and printer whose expertise you can trust?

Let's take a look at the mechanics of output for digital images and the hardware that can provide printed output at the draft stage. Then, we'll survey the software-related steps you'll need to perform in order to obtain quality draft and final output for your PhotoStyler images.

Continuous-Tone Images, Halftones, and Output Quality

The device you use to output your PhotoStyler images places very real limits on the level of print quality you can obtain. Most of the printing devices within reach of the average corporate or consultant's budget are fine for proofing continuous-tone images, but not for producing final output. To understand why this is so, you need some background information about the *halftoning* process that translates photographs into printable information.

The Halftoning Process

PhotoStyler artwork consists of continuous-tone images: bitmapped photographs or digital "paintings" that contain up to 256 shades of gray or as many as 16.7 million different colors. Whereas artwork from drawing programs such as Aldus Freehand or Corel Draw consists of objects that can be described mathematically, bitmapped artwork must be described one pixel at a time. Translating a photo's continuous tones into some kind of digital pattern for the printing press involves a process called *halftoning*.

Conventional Halftone Basics

Photographic prints are produced by a chemical process that allows colors or gray tones to blend smoothly into one another. Photos in commercially printed documents, on the other hand, consist of black or colored dots against a background; the spacing and sizing of the dots produce the illusion of continuous tones. Hold a printed black-and-white photograph under a magnifying glass to see for yourself: you'll find only black dots of varying sizes, spaced at even intervals. Light grays are simulated by tiny dots, medium grays by slightly larger ones, and darker grays or black by still larger ones.

In a printed *color* photo, there are only four different dot colors: cyan, magenta, yellow, and black. The illusion of a much larger number of colors blending smoothly together results from the sizing and spacing of the dots and the angles at which dots of a certain color appear (see Figure 15–1 in the Color Section of this book). We'll devote more attention to screen angles in later parts of this chapter and in Chapter 16.

This process of converting photographs into dots that simulate gray shades or colors is known as *halftoning* when it applies to Grayscale images and as *color separation* when it applies to True Color images. Halftoning is the basis of all commercial image reproduction. Before personal computers invaded the publishing world, commercial printers produced halftones by photographing images through a screen of fine lines. The *screen frequency*, measured in lines per inch, determined how sharp the resulting printed image would look and how smooth the transitions between gray shades or colors would be. Fine screens yielded smaller dots, tighter dot spacing, and sharper printed images, while coarser screens resulted in larger dots, looser spacing, and grainier-looking images. The decision as to which screen frequency to use depended then, as it does now, on the purpose of the document being printed and the types of press equipment and paper stocks that will be used (see Table 15–1).

Digital Halftoning and Printer Resolution

Desktop publishing hasn't changed the principles of halftoning, but it *has* changed the way halftones are generated. Digital output devices—including laser printers, imagesetters, and high-end systems—are more limited than conventional prepress methods in two important ways:

- they can't vary the sizes of the dots they produce, and
- they operate at fixed printing resolutions.

Table 15-1. Recommended Output Parameters for Digital Image Publishing Applications

Application	Paper Stock	Press Equipment	Recommended Screen Frequencies
T-shirts, mugs, commercial imprint products	Various materials	Silk-screen	45-65 lpi
Newspapers	Newsprint	Open web	65-85 lpi
Low-end catalogs & magazines	Various stocks	Open web	85-120 lpi
Newsletters, trade books	Book stock	Open web	90-133 lpi
Commercial magazines, catalogs, brochures	Glossy stock	Heat-set web	120-150 lpi
High-end advertising, magazines, annual reports, art books	Glossy stock	Sheet-fed	150-200 lpi

These devices use a special method to overcome the first obstacle, but the second is more difficult to surmount.

Note

The new breed of continuous-tone color printers from Kodak, Fuji, and other manufacturers doesn't suffer from the limitations of PostScript and other laser devices. These devices can print color images at near-photographic quality because of the subliminal dye inks they use. A driver for the Kodak XL7700 is included with PhotoStyler and you can install it by running Setup. When you're ready to output an image to the Kodak XL 7700, choose the Export command from the File menu.

To simulate the look of variable-sized dots, digital output devices group their fixed-size dots together in *halftone cells*. Each halftone cell contains a fixed number of same-size dots (also called "spots"), and each spot within a cell is either "on" (black) or "off" (white). The apparent size of the dot within each halftone cell depends on how many tiny spots in the cell are dark. If very few spots are dark, the cell appears light gray (or a lighter color, in the case of a color laser printer). If many of the spots in the cell are dark, the cell appears dark gray or more saturated in color. This process, called *dithering*, lets laser printers and imagesetters simulate multiple shades of gray or a large number of colors.

But here's the clincher: the resolution of an output device fixes a stiff ceiling on the number of gray shades that the device can reproduce with any degree of sharpness. Dithering technology itself forces a trade-off between screen frequency and the number of gray shades (or colors) that a device can simulate. Larger halftone cells reproduce more gray shades, but they also limit the *number* of halftone cells within a given space and thus the screen frequency and sharpness of the printed image. Conversely, a higher screen frequency limits the size of the halftone cells and thus the number of gray shades that the output device can reproduce.

The upshot of it all is that 300 dpi laser printers may be fine for some text-only documents, but they just can't deliver an acceptable halftone for continuous-tone images that contain 256 shades of gray or 256 tones per color channel. That goes for 300 dpi color printers, too. Even 600 dpi printers can't generate enough gray shades to reproduce images sharply. As Table 15–2 indicates, it takes a printer resolution of at least 1000 dpi to generate halftones decent enough for a newspaper. Acceptable output for higher-quality Grayscale images requires an imagesetter capable of 1270 or, in some cases, 2400 dpi. And

Table 15–2. PostScript Output Devices: Balancing Resolution with Screen Frequency
(PostScript maximum: 256 gray shades or tones per channel)

Output device and maximum output resolution	Number of tones per channel @ screen frequency
300 dpi b/w laser printer	16 gray shades @ 75 lpi
	32 gray shades @ 53 lpi
300 dpi color laser printer	16 colors per ink, dithered to simulate 4,096 colors @ 75 lpi
600 dpi b/w laser printer	64 gray shades @ 75 lpi
	100 gray shades @ 60 lpi
1000 dpi plain-paper typesetter	100 gray shades @ 100 lpi
	120 gray shades @ 90 lpi
1200 dpi plain-paper typesetter	144 gray shades @ 100 lpi
	225 gray shades @ 80 lpi
	256 gray shades @ 75 lpi
1270 dpi imagesetter	128 gray shades @ 100 lpi
	256 gray shades @ 80 lpi or lower
2400 dpi imagesetter	256 gray shades @ 150 lpi or lower
2540 dpi imagesetter	256 gray shades @ 160 lpi or lower
3386 dpi imagesetter	256 gray shades @ 200 lpi or lower

color separations usually demand output resolutions or 2400 dpi or greater.

Tip

Newer-model Agfa and Linotype-Hell imagesetters that feature improved screen angle technologies can reproduce a full 256 shades of gray at 1270 dpi ("medium") output resolution. If you plan to output Grayscale images or color separations at screen frequencies of 133 or lower, and if your service bureau has one of these imagesetters, you may be able to save money and output time by specifying medium output resolution.

Tip

To calculate the maximum number of gray shades or color tones per channel that a given output device will reproduce at a desired screen frequency, use this formula:

$\{\text{Device resolution} \div \text{screen frequency}\}^2$ = max. no. of gray shades or tones per channel

At a screen frequency of 53 lpi, for example, a 300 dpi laser printer will reproduce only 32 shades of gray ($\{300 \div 53\}^2$ = approximately 32). If the screen frequency is unknown, but you know the output resolution of the printing device and the number of gray shades you want to reproduce, use this formula instead:

Device resolution ÷ square root of desired no. of gray shades = maximum screen frequency

Printing Devices: Draft and Final Output

By now, you've probably guessed that you'll need to strike up the acquaintance of a few service bureaus if you plan to output PhotoStyler images to print media. You're right! To do justice to continuous-tone images, you'll need the assistance of an imagesetter, a high-end color output system, or (for small in-house print runs) a continuous-tone color printer such as the Kodak XL7700. You don't have to abandon your trusty black-and-white or color laser printer—just don't expect it to provide camera-ready output for anything but Grayscale images destined for undemanding documents.

Here's a brief rundown of common types of printing devices that are suitable for proofing PhotoStyler images during the initial phases of the output cycle. Dot-matrix printers are conspicuously absent from this listing: their resolution is too poor even for image proofing purposes.

Low-Resolution B/W Laser Printers

In the desktop publishing community, PostScript and LaserJet-compatible laser printers with a resolution of 300 dpi have long been the standard output devices for proofing purposes. For limited-circulation documents that contain text and line art only, they can sometimes provide acceptable final output. But, as we've just seen, 300 dpi is not an adequate resolution for reproducing continuous-tone images created in PhotoStyler. Effective screen frequencies for these printers are limited to the 53 to 75 lpi range, which yield only 32 or 16 shades of gray, respectively (see Table 15–2). At these screen frequencies, portraits look grainy, other images lack detail, and gradient fills show obvious banding.

Standard laser printers do have several useful proofing functions. Among them:

Proofing for Brightness and Contrast As soon as you scan a new image into PhotoStyler, print a sample of it on your 300 dpi black-and-white laser printer. A 300 dpi print sample will give you a rough—and we do want to emphasize the word *rough*—idea of the brightness and contrast ranges in an image. Remember, even with a correctly calibrated monitor, you can't be sure that you'll get in print exactly what you see on the screen. An image that looks glaringly bright on your monitor might look balanced on paper. So before you apply any image correction commands from the Image/Tune submenu, get a printed sample to make sure you're not altering something that doesn't need changing.

Proofing for Image Position Only Magazines, catalogs, and some other documents can contain a large number of continuous-tone images. If you include high-resolution, multi-megabyte scans of every image in the document, you're likely to slow down the performance of your page layout program. A more efficient strategy is to use two different files for each image: a high-resolution file that contains enough pixels to generate a good halftone at your desired screen frequency (see Chapter 4), and a low-resolution counterpart with the same output dimensions that you've resampled downward. Use the unedited low-resolution scans in the document while proofing your page layout, and do all your editing, retouching, and special effects operations in the high-resolution originals. When you're ready to generate color separations for the document or output to film, substitute the retouched high-resolution scans for the unedited low-resolution ones. This strategy can save hours of work as well as money—as long as you remember to replace all the images!

If your page layout software doesn't support the linking of different versions of images, you can leave the high-resolution images in your document, but print them at a low screen frequency (53-75 lpi) during the layout phase of production. Using a higher frequency would increase print time unnecessarily without improving real output quality. Just remember to increase the screen frequency for each image when it's time to generate final output.

Tip

If your images are destined for a high-budget catalog or magazine, you may obtain your initial image scans from a proprietary drum scanning system at a specialized color prepress service bureau (see Chap-

ter 16). Image files like these can sometimes run to file sizes of 30-40 Mb. If you don't want to or can't resample these multi-megabyte files yourself, most color service bureaus can provide you with low-resolution, for-position-only versions of scans upon request. When it's time to output to film, the service bureau then substitutes the high-resolution color images, placing them in your document before producing color separation files.

Whichever method you choose, having draft versions of all your images in place will provide you with a much clearer idea of how the final document will look than if you just leave keylines in your page layout document and have images stripped in later.

Proofing Color Separations Color separations, like image channels, are Grayscale documents. Each separation contains all the values for one of the four colors—cyan, magenta, yellow, and black—used in commercial printing. Although most black-and-white laser printers can't print color separations directly from PhotoStyler, there's an easy workaround. Just split a True Color image into its component CMYK channels, save each component channel as a separate Grayscale image document, and print each Grayscale document one at a time. Draft color separations will give you a rough idea of the brightness and contrast ranges for each ink color. If you suspect there's an imbalance, you can correct it before generating final film separations through a high-resolution imagesetter or dedicated color system.

Plain-Paper Typesetters

Black-and-white laser printers with resolutions of 600, 1000, or even 1200 dpi are now becoming common. Sometimes referred to as "plain-paper typesetters," these printers, such as the ones in the LaserMaster series, offer much higher-quality draft output than their 300 dpi counterparts. If you use them to proof brightness and contrast or proof image positions within documents, you'll obtain a fairly faithful notion of the tonal ranges you can eventually expect from an imagesetter or dedicated color system.

For many types of images, though, these printers still aren't adequate to provide camera-ready output. For example, at a screen frequency of 75 lpi (newspaper quality), only the 1200 dpi printers can produce a sharp halftone with the full range of 256 shades of gray (see Table 15–2). If you're producing Grayscale images for newspapers or for low-budget newsletters or catalogs, a 1200 dpi printer can probably provide camera-ready output. However, True Color images require film rather than paper output, for reasons we'll go into in Chapter 16.

Caution

Some 1200 dpi laser devices actually print at a "pseudo" 1200 x 800 resolution. The higher horizontal resolution successfully fools the eye into seeing 256 shades of gray, even though the actual number produced is smaller owing to the lower vertical resolution. When printing an image on such a device, make sure that the image is at a 1:1 aspect ratio in PhotoStyler.

Tip

If you frequently posterize Grayscale images, reducing the number of gray shades they contain, you might be able to use a 600- or 1000-dpi laser printer for camera-ready output.

Low-Resolution Color Laser Printers

Many service bureaus, corporations, and graphic designers use 300 dpi-resolution color PostScript printers for proofing composites ("comps") of True Color images. Based on thermal wax transfer technology, these printers (including the QMS ColorScript 100 shown in Figure 15–2) simulate a large number of colors by melting three colors of ink and dithering them to generate halftone dots. The actual number of colors that these printers can reproduce depends on the screen frequency you request for a given image. At the recommended maximum screen

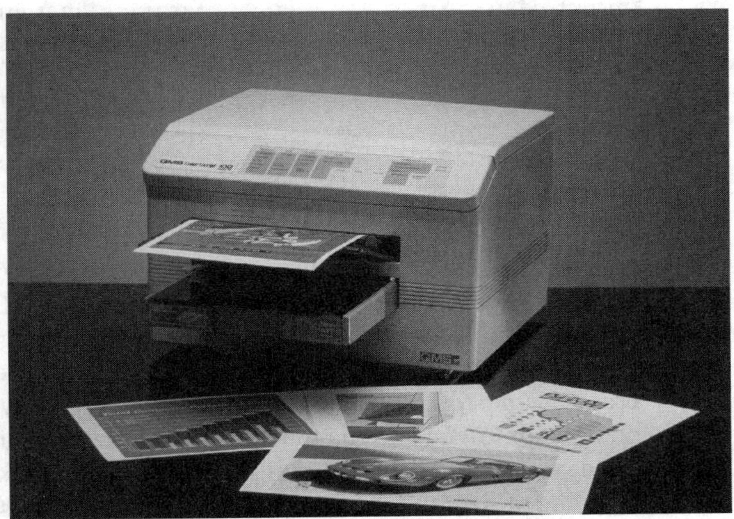

Figure 15-2.

The QMS ColorScript 100 thermal wax transfer printer

frequency of 75 lpi, for example (see Table 15-2), you can simulate up to 4,096 colors: 16 tones each for cyan, magenta, and yellow.

Still, even 4,096 colors are a far cry from the 16 million that a True Color image can contain. That's one reason why low-resolution color printers are good for proofing but not for final output. Another reason has to do with the inks used by these printers. There are only three inks, not four as required for conventional process color printing, and their composition, consistency, and color makeup are different from commercial printers' inks. As a result, colors from the laser printer are not likely to match colors printed on an offset press.

Tip

The latest generation of thermal wax transfer printers operate at a 400 dpi resolution and can reproduce 15,625 colors at a screen frequency of 80 lpi. While that's still not good enough for production quality images, it's a significant improvement over the capabilities of the 300 dpi models and permits somewhat more realistic proofing.

Imagesetters, Continuous-Tone Color Printers, and Dedicated Color Prepress Systems

Most PhotoStyler users will need to work with a service bureau to generate high-quality camera-ready artwork for the printing press. Service bureaus typically use imagesetters, high-end color prepress systems, or both types of equipment as output devices. For in-house corporate applications or images that require only a small number of copies, you might choose a continuous-tone color printer as your final output device. Since you'll encounter the higher-end output devices during the prepress phase of your work, we'll cover these types of devices in Chapter 16.

Using PhotoStyler's Print Commands

Four commands in the File menu—Separation Setup and the Print, Page Setup, and Printer Setup commands in the Print submenu—let you customize parameters for printing your images directly from PhotoStyler Each of these commands plays a different role in the preparation of draft or final output. In this chapter, we'll cover the use of each command and the meanings of the settings in their respective dialog boxes. Turn to Chapter 16 for a more comprehensive understanding of the color and prepress issues behind those settings.

Printing draft images, color comps, draft color separations, or output files for a service bureau directly from PhotoStyler is a three- or four-step process that involves:

1. checking your MS-Windows printer configuration
2. customizing print parameters such as crop marks, calibration bar, halftone screen settings (optional), and the calibration curve of your printer (optional)
3. setting up color separation parameters (True Color images)
4. specifying print sizing, page position, and the number of copies

It's important to review each of these steps every time you print an image.

Checking Your Printer Configuration

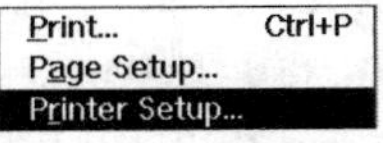

If you always use the same printer, never change the paper size or orientation, and never create an output file for a service bureau, you may not have to concern yourself with the Printer Setup command in the File/Print submenu. But if you do one or more of these things from time to time, you should always choose this command before any print operation to make sure the current printer configuration is correct.

The Print/Printer Setup command gives you access to the Windows Control Panel without making you switch applications or leave PhotoStyler. The Printer Setup dialog box (Figure 15–3) will show all printers currently installed under Windows, with the active printer highlighted. To select a different printer from the available list, click on the desired printer name. If you need to specify additional setup

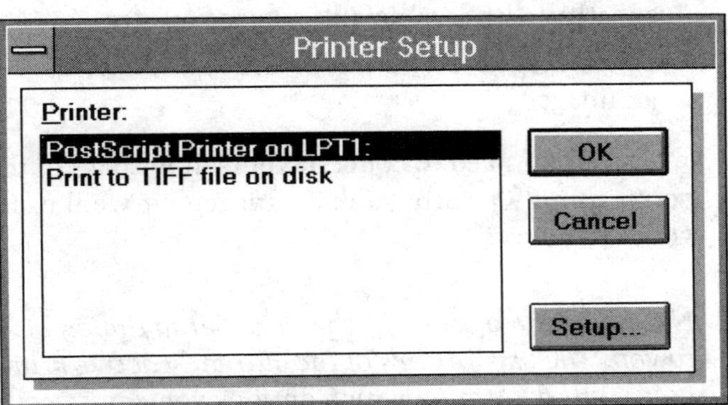

Figure 15-3.

The Printer Setup dialog box (PostScript example)

options for the active printer, click the Setup command button to see a dialog box of additional options specific to your printer. See your Microsoft Windows documentation if you need more information on how to change the printer configuration.

Note

If the Setup button in the Printer Setup dialog box doesn't respond when you click on it, you haven't selected a Default Printer under Microsoft Windows. To do so, switch to the Windows Program Manager, double-click the Control Panel icon in the Main window and the Printers icon in the Control Panel window, and then double-click the name of the printer that you want to use as the default printer. Select OK to save the new default printer selection.

Customizing Printer Settings with the Page Setup Command

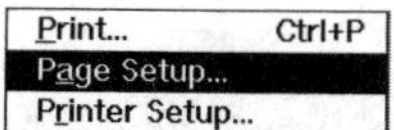

The Page Setup command in the File/Printer Setup submenu is the "Grand Central Station" of all printer settings in PhotoStyler. You should choose this command and review all the current settings (including the ones in nested dialog boxes) every time you prepare to print. If you neglect to do so, you could inadvertently apply settings that you had intended for a different image or output device. The options that appear in the Page Setup dialog box (Figure 15–4) let you:

- title your printouts for handy cataloging and reference
- add crop marks (all PhotoStyler versions) and registration marks (versions 1.1a and later) to a printout
- include a calibration bar for checking the Grayscale or color fidelity of your draft or final output device
- adjust the current halftone screen settings or have the active printer substitute its own default screen settings
- adjust the way an output device reproduces the brightness values in an image

You won't need to concern yourself with all of these settings when you're simply printing a draft image, but we'll explain them here for your reference.

Note

Not all of the options in the Page Setup dialog box will be available to you. The capabilities of the currently active printer under MS-Windows will determine which options you can select.

Figure 15-4.

The Page Setup dialog box with default settings for a monochrome PostScript printer

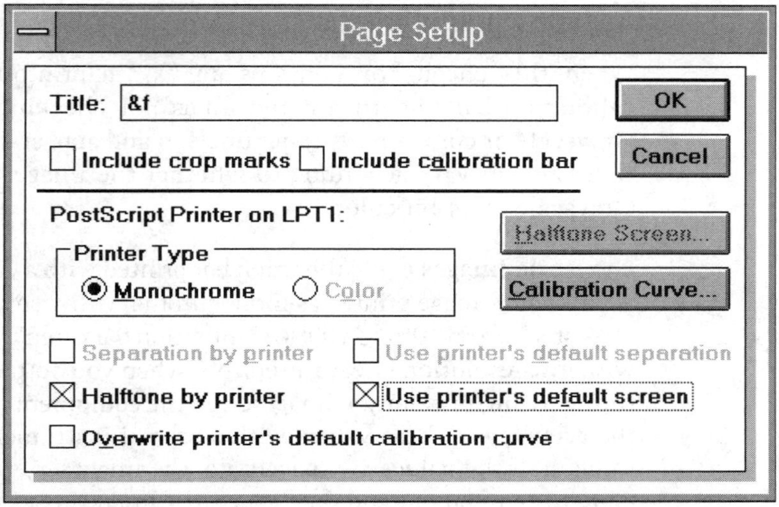

A Note on the PSD (Printer Description) File

PhotoStyler saves your most recent settings for the Page Setup command in the Printer Description File (extension .PSD). This ASCII file, located in the directory where you installed PhotoStyler, retains its settings even between PhotoStyler sessions. You can change the settings either by using the controls in the Page Setup dialog box, or by editing the .PSD file using Windows Notepad or another ASCII text editor.

Title

With the default setting of *&f*, PhotoStyler will print the filename of the active image document above the draft image. If you change the characters in the Title entry box to *&t*, PhotoStyler will print the current date and time instead. To print any message of your choice above the image, delete the current entry and type the desired characters in the Title entry box. The Title option offers a great way to catalog draft printouts or to make notes to yourself about an image in progress.

Include Crop Marks ("Include Printer Marks" in Versions 1.1a and Later)

When this check box contains an "x," a printout will include crop marks at each corner of the image for pasteup purposes.

Include Calibration Bar

When this check box contains an "x," a printout will include a calibration bar underneath the image for checking the accuracy of Grayscale or color values. The function and appearance of the calibration bar will vary according to whether the image you're printing is Grayscale or 24-bit color.

Grayscale Images A calibration bar printed with a Grayscale image (or with a color image printed as monochrome) will display tints of black in 10% steps, from 10% to 100%. Calibration bars aren't particularly useful with low-resolution laser printers, but when you output an image to film through a high-resolution imagesetter, the equipment operator can check the accuracy of these values with a special instrument, called a densitometer. If the values are inaccurate, the imagesetter operator can calibrate the equipment and then generate film again.

Color Comps When you print a color comp on a color printer and the Include calibration bar setting is active, the printout will include both a calibration bar beneath the image and a color bar to the left of the image. The calibration bar will show the same range of gray shades as when you print a Grayscale image, but they are composed of equal percentages of the process colors cyan, magenta, and yellow. The color bar to the left of the image will display cyan; magenta; yellow; red; green; blue; black composed of 100% cyan, 100% magenta, and 100% yellow; and pure black.

Color Separations If you choose to include a calibration bar when printing color separations to a file or directly to an imagesetter, PhotoStyler will add both a color bar and a calibration bar. The color bar will show only eight shades of gray on each separation. However, when a commercial print vendor prints all four separations together, the ink colors cyan, magenta, yellow, red, green, blue, composite black, and solid black will appear in the color bar.

Note *If you include a calibration bar when printing individual image channels as draft color separations on a black-and-white laser printer, no color bar will print.*

Printer Type Area

Just above the Printer Type option, PhotoStyler displays the name of the current printer driver and the port to which it is connected. If either of these is incorrect, cancel out of the Page Setup dialog box and select another printer or port using the Printer Setup command in the File/Printer Setup submenu.

In the Printer Type group box are two radio buttons: Monochrome and Color. The availability of one or both buttons depends on the capabilities of the active printer installed under MS-Windows.

Monochrome If the active printer is a black-and-white or Grayscale laser printer or imagesetter, the Monochrome button will be selected, and the Color button will be unavailable. The active printer will output all images as Grayscale or black-and-white, no matter what the data type. To output color separations from a Monochrome printer, you'll need to split a True Color image into its component CMYK channels (see Chapter 14) and then print each Grayscale image channel separately.

If the active image is a True Color image and you want to print a draft to a monochrome laser printer for proofing purposes, we recommend converting the image to Grayscale first. Outputting the image as a color image will take unnecessarily large amounts of time, and the image will still print as a monochrome image. Use the Convert to Grayscale command in the Image menu and then print the Grayscale version instead of the True Color version.

Color If the active printer is the Color type, both the Color and Monochrome buttons will be available. When you select the Color radio button, you can print composite color images to a color laser printer or continuous-tone color printer. You can also print color separations to printers that are capable of generating color separations. When you select the Monochrome button for a color printer, you can print any image as a Grayscale image, or output individual color channels as Grayscale documents.

Separation by Printer, Use Printer's Default Separation (Color Printers Only)

The Separation by printer and Use printer's default separation options are available only for color printers when the Color option is active. Their intended use is to let a color printer generate color separations without any software instructions from PhotoStyler. Not all color printers can do this, so check the documentation that came with your printer. Three choices are possible for these settings:

- When both the Separation by printer and Use printer's default separation options are selected, the printer will generate color separations internally when you send a color image to it. PhotoStyler won't send software instructions for generating the separations.
- When only the Separation by printer option is active, the printer and your current Halftone Screen and Separation Setup settings in PhotoStyler will share control of the process of generating color separations.
- When the Separation by printer option is deselected, the Use Printer's default separation option will become unavailable, too. PhotoStyler will assume full control of the generation of color separations based on your settings for the Separation Setup command in the File menu and in the Halftone Screen dialog box.

Halftone by Printer, Use Printer's Default Screen

These two options relate to the way PhotoStyler generates a halftone screen when you print an image (see "The Halftoning Process" section near the beginning of this chapter). By default, both options are selected for all Color and most Monochrome printer types. Three combinations of options are possible:

- When both Halftone by printer and Use printer's default screen are selected, the active printer will generate halftones using its own default screen shape, frequency, and angle, without software input from PhotoStyler.

Halftone Screen...

- When you select the Halftone by printer option only, the Halftone Screen command button will become available so that you can specify a custom halftone screen shape, frequency, and angle. Both the output device and your software settings will share control of the process of generating a halftone screen.
- If you deselect the Halftone by printer option, the Use printer's default screen option will become unavailable, too. Your settings in the Halftone Screen dialog box (accessed by clicking the Halftone Screen command button) will assume full control of generating the halftone screen during printing.

Overwrite Printer's Default Calibration Curve

This option, available only when you've selected the Halftone by printer check box, determines whether PhotoStyler will adjust the way the current printing device "interprets" brightness and contrast values in an image. Two choices are possible:

- When you activate Overwrite printer's default calibration curve, PhotoStyler will ignore the output device's built-in method of handling image brightness and contrast during printing. Instead, it will send the information you've set up in the Calibration Curve dialog box, which you access by clicking the Calibration Curve command button (see "Defining a Custom Calibration Curve").
- When OverWrite printer's default calibration curve is deselected, the output device will control the output brightness and contrast values of an image during printing. If you've defined a custom calibration curve, the output device and your custom information will share control of the calibration curve.

Caution

The Overwrite printer's default calibration option is intended chiefly for expert users, such as imagesetter operators at service bureaus. Most end users will never need to overwrite the default calibration curve of their output devices.

Halftone Screen and Calibration Curve

Halftone Screen...

Calibration Curve...

When you click either of these command buttons in the Page Setup dialog box, another dialog box will appear. The Halftone Screen dialog box (see "Defining a Halftone Screen") lets you customize the shape, frequency, and angle of the halftone generated when you print a Grayscale or True Color image. The Calibration Curve dialog box (see "Defining a Custom Calibration Curve") lets you determine the way your printer will adjust brightness and contrast values of an image during printing.

Defining a Halftone Screen

Halftone Screen...

Halftoning determines just how a printer will generate the dots that simulate continuous tones in an image (see "The Halftoning Process" in the early pages of this chapter). The pattern of halftone dots in a particular image is called the *halftone screen*, and it has three components: a dot shape, a frequency, and an angle. You can adjust each of these components in the Halftone Screen dialog box (Figure 15–5) that appears when you click the Halftone Screen command button in the Page Setup dialog box.

Halftone screen patterns usually serve a utilitarian purpose: to ensure the smoothest-looking printed image possible, given the limits imposed by the resolution of your output device. Screen patterns can also have a design-oriented purpose. For example, if you vary the screen shape at extremely low frequencies (10 lpi to 30 lpi), you can create special pattern effects in which the shapes in an image are barely suggested. See Figure 5-13 in Chapter 5.

Note

You don't have to adjust halftone screen settings. If you select the Halftone by printer and Use printer's default screen options in the Page Setup dialog box, the current printing device will use its own default settings. Whenever the Use printer's default screen option is selected, the Halftone Screen command button will be unavailable.

The options for halftone dot shape appear in the Shape drop-down list box of the Halftone Screen dialog box. To define halftone frequency and angle, you must specify numeric values using the entry boxes next to the Frequency and Angle options. There are four columns of entry boxes: one each for the cyan, magenta, yellow, and black channels of a True Color image. The number of entry boxes available will depend not on the data type of the active image, but on the Printer Type you selected in the Page Setup dialog box. If you selected Color as the current Printer Type, all four columns of numeric entry boxes will be available. If you selected Monochrome as the current Printer Type, only the numeric entry boxes under the Black column will be available.

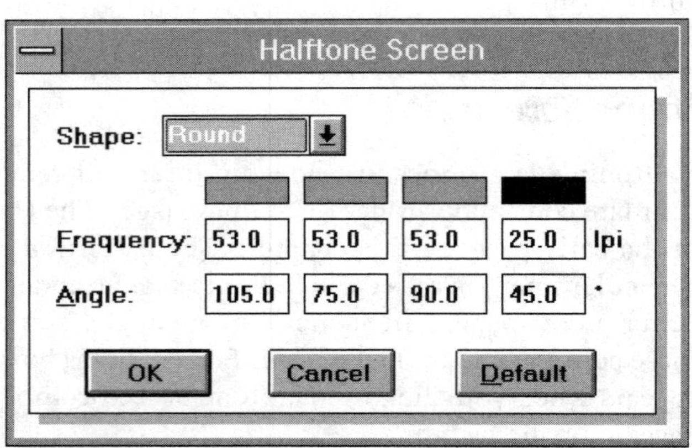

Figure 15-5.

The Halftone Screen dialog box with default settings for a 300 dpi color PostScript laser printer

Defining a Screen Shape

As you've already seen, digital output devices simulate a conventional halftone dot by arranging small spots in halftone cell patterns. Every halftone dot in a given Grayscale or color image has the same basic shape, which you determine by selecting an option from the Shape drop-down list box. Round is the default shape, but there are five others available: Elliptical, Diamond, Line, Square, and Cross. These shapes are self-explanatory and in common use in the printing industry.

In most cases, your choice of a halftone dot shape should be guided by the content of an image and the arrangement of lines, curves, and other shapes within it. Your main goal, unless you're interested in special visual effects, should be to make sure that viewers see the image, not the halftone dots that make it up. Round halftone dots usually produce good results with Grayscale images, and elliptical shapes have been known to work well for color images when you output the final separations to film. However, some images require special shapes so that the halftone pattern won't interfere with the way viewers see the lines and curves in the image. Consult your clients, your service bureau, and your commercial print vendor about the best shape to use for a given image.

Defining Screen Frequency

The frequency of a halftone screen determines the amount of detail and the level of contrast in a printed image. Halftone dots in a printed image are always equidistant from one another, and it's the screen frequency that determines that mutual distance. With a low screen frequency, halftone dots are further apart, yielding less overall detail. As the screen frequency increases, halftone dots are spaced closer together, resulting in greater sharpness and detail.

However, a high screen frequency can compromise the number of gray shades reproduced in an image or channel unless your target output device is capable of a high output resolution or you'll be using an imagesetter with Balanced Screen Angles or HQS screening technology. That's because the maximum resolution of a printer determines the size of a halftone dot; the lower the resolution, the larger the dot, and the higher the resolution, the smaller the dot. If you stretch the screen frequency beyond the limits of your output device, you'll end up with an overly dark image that lacks both contrast and detail. So set a low screen frequency when you're proofing an image on a laser printer, and a higher frequency when you're ready to send a final output file to an imagesetter. Refer back to Table 15-2 for a rough guide to screen frequencies, and consult with your client/boss, your service bureau, and your print vendor about the best screen frequency for your application.

When the Monochrome Printer Type radio button is selected, you can specify only one frequency: the one for the black channel. This applies whether you're printing Grayscale images, True Color images, or image channels to be output as draft color separations. When you're printing draft color separations from a Color printer type, on the other hand, you must specify a frequency for four channels: one each for cyan, magenta, yellow, and black. Make certain that you specify the same frequency for all channels.

In Chapter 16, we'll return to the subject of halftone screen frequencies and their relationship to other factors that impact print quality.

Defining Screen Angle

The angle of a halftone screen, like its shape, should be chosen so as to avoid disturbing visual patterns that interfere with the image itself. A case in point is the 45° angle most often assigned to Grayscale images: 0° or 90° angles tend to conflict with horizontal and vertical orientations of objects within those images, but diagonal angles usually don't.

The problem of undesirable ink patterns becomes much trickier when the images are in color. As you'll recall from Chapter 14, commercial printing for a color image involves the generation of four Grayscale separations: one each for cyan, magenta, yellow, and black. When the plates made from each separation are printed on an offset press, the inks for each color need to be arranged in a pattern that looks as though the colors were mixing physically to form additional colors. If the registration or alignment of any of the four printing plates is off, or if the angles between color plates aren't properly spaced, the final printed image will have disturbing *moiré* patterns that are the telltale signs of poor quality color reproduction.

Through experimentation, printing industry professionals have established standard screen angles that minimize moiré patterns. If the halftone screen angles for each color are about 30° apart, the human eye will perceive the ink colors as blending smoothly in a *rosette*. The default angles that you see in the Halftone Screen dialog box when preparing color separations derive from these industry standards: cyan, 105°; magenta, 75°; yellow, 90°; and black, 45°. The angle for the yellow separation is halfway between cyan and magenta because it's a light color and its halftone dots are therefore less likely to attract attention to themselves in a four-color printed image.

Caution

Some newer-model imagesetters (particularly the Agfa and Linotype-Hell line) feature advanced screening technologies that require you to output color separation files at special screen angles. These angles are sometimes different from the ones traditionally used in process color printing. If your service bureau uses one of these imagesetters, it's important to use the halftone screen angles that are recommended for best results.

Tip

If you're printing separate Grayscale CMYK channels to a black-and-white printer, remember to set the halftone screen angle for each channel as though it were a color separation document.

Beware—don't regard these angles as sacrosanct. Software developers throughout the graphics industry are still working the kinks out of digitally produced halftone screen angles. Moirés are still a problem at the exact angles that PhotoStyler and other programs use as defaults. The latest generation of imagesetters, as well as printing devices that use PostScript Level 2, adjusts angles automatically to eliminate the problem. Consult with your service bureau and your print vendor regarding the best way to obtain the most exact angles for your color application. We'll have more to say on the subject of screen angles in Chapter 16.

Defining a Custom Calibration Curve

Calibration Curve...

If you click the Calibration Curve command button in the Page Setup dialog box, the Calibration Curve dialog box shown in Figure 15–6 will appear. This dialog box lets you adjust the calibration curve that tells your output device how to "see" the color and brightness values in an image document. You can create any number of different calibration curves, save them as files, and load them for use with a particular image or output device. Calibration curves don't change the actual digital color or grayscale values in an image file; they simply change the way the output device interprets those values. But a different "interpretation" of these values will certainly affect the balance of colors or grays in the printed image.

When to Use a Custom Calibration Curve

Calibration curves are intended for use with your own printer or your own imagesetter, if you have one. Service bureaus usually have

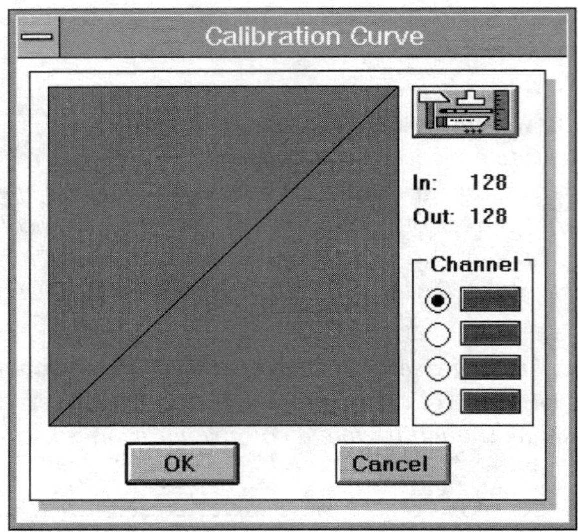

Figure 15-6.

The Calibration Curve dialog box showing a default printer calibration curve

specialized software for calibrating film output and may not want or be able to use your curves. If you like to "tweak" the output of your own printing device, however, you can use calibration curves to adapt an image to a particular printing device or a printing device to a particular image. Here are some real-world uses for custom calibration curves:

- *Proof an image for brightness and/or contrast*—If an image seems too dark or too bright the first time you print it, adjust the calibration curve accordingly and then print another proof. Once you find a curve that gives you satisfactory output, you can either save the new curve to a file or use the Tune: Gray/Color Correction command in the Image menu to change the actual color or gray values in the image file.
- *Adapt image data to the characteristics of a particular output device*—If you have more than one output device, you can adjust the calibration curve differently for each one.
- *Adapt output for images that have certain characteristics in common*—You may find that certain classes of images (portraits, for example) don't print out well on your output device. If you adjust the calibration curve so that these images will yield predictably good results, you can save that curve and use it with every image that has similar characteristics.
- *Create special color or grayscale effects for printing purposes only*—Apply a custom calibration curve to an image to shift colors or gray

values in a specific way during printing. Once you know the effects that a certain curve generates, you can save it and apply it to many different images—without altering the images themselves.

- *Adjust output brightness to compensate for ink spreading (dot gain) on low-grade paper stock*—If the document that will contain your images is printed on highly porous paper, the printing ink used is likely to spread, causing loss of contrast and detail. But if your printing device can generate acceptable camera-ready output, you can apply a custom calibration curve that will brighten image values during printing and minimize the dot gain phenomenon.

Note *Most PhotoStyler users will find the default calibration curves for their output devices satisfactory. Unless you're an expert user who likes to tweak controls for the best trial and error results, you may never need to design custom calibration curves.*

The Calibration Curve Dialog Box

The "look and feel" of the Calibration Curve dialog box is similar to that of the Gray/Color Map dialog box. Many of the controls are similar, too. But unlike the Gray/Color Map dialog box, the Calibration Curve dialog box doesn't change the actual color values in the image. Instead, it changes only the way your output device interprets those values for output onto paper or film.

The Calibration Curve The Calibration Curve maps the relationships between the actual color values in the image (the input values) and the color values that the output device uses during printing (the output values). The horizontal axis corresponds to the input values, while the vertical axis corresponds to the output values. Both axes span the entire range from black (0) to white or intense color (255).

The default calibration curve is a straight line at a 45° angle, which means that the printing device will receive the exact values contained in the image. Wherever the slope of the curve increases, PhotoStyler will print the image values brighter; wherever the slope of the curve decreases, PhotoStyler will print the image values darker.

You can edit the calibration curve in one of three ways:

- Click anywhere on the calibration curve and then drag the mouse to a new location.
- Apply one or more of the commands in the Calibration Curve menu.

- Combine the use of Calibration Curve menu commands with manual editing techniques.

Input and Output Indicators These indicators help you compare the original image values with output values at any point along the curve.

Color Channel Radio Buttons If you're editing the calibration curve for a True Color image, you can edit the curve for each RGB channel as well as for the integrated image.

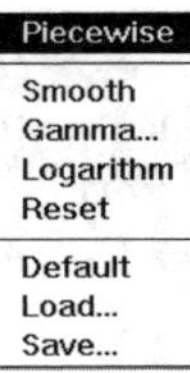

Calibration Curve Menu Commands The toolbox icon in the Calibration Curve dialog box conceals a menu that pops up when you click. Each of the commands in this menu alters the current or default calibration curve (see Figure 15–6) in a specific way.

- *Piecewise* breaks the curve down into five straight-line segments. Dragging the control points of one or more of these segments changes the input/output relationship sharply for a whole range of values (Figure 15–7, top left).
- *Smooth* removes the jagged edges of a calibration curve that you've edited manually. The resulting printout will show smoother transitions between colors or gray values (Figure 15–7, top right).
- *Gamma* changes the relationship between the midtone values of the image document and the midtone values in the printed image (Figure 15–7, bottom left). You specify the degree of variance in a dialog box that appears when you select this command. The acceptable range of values is from 0.01 to 7.99: Gamma values below 1.00 will darken the printed midtones, while gamma values above 1.00 will lighten them. This option may be useful for minimizing dot gain in images that contain a high percentage of midrange values.
- *Logarithm* (Figure 15–7, bottom right) alters the calibration curve in a way that will brighten values throughout the image during printing. This command is useful for printing images that will appear on coarse paper where dot gain is likely to be a problem.
- *Reset* returns the calibration curve to a straight line at a 45° angle.
- *Default* loads the default calibration curve for the currently active printing device. If your output device has no special curve, the calibration curve will revert to a straight line at a 45° angle.
- *Load* lets you load a previously saved calibration curve using the Load Map Curve dialog box in Figure 15–8 (left). You can either apply this curve as is to the next image you print or continue to edit the curve.

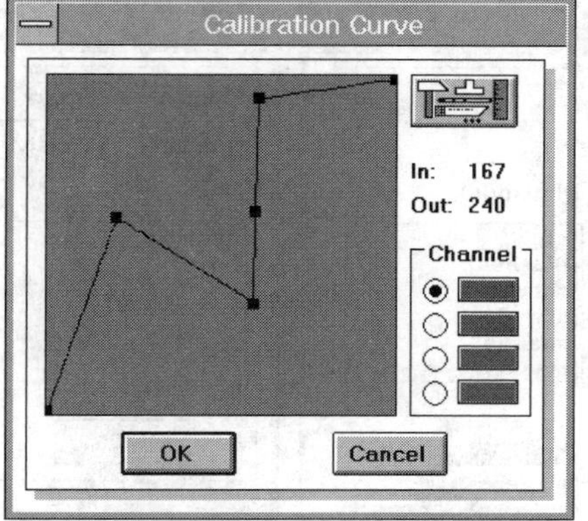

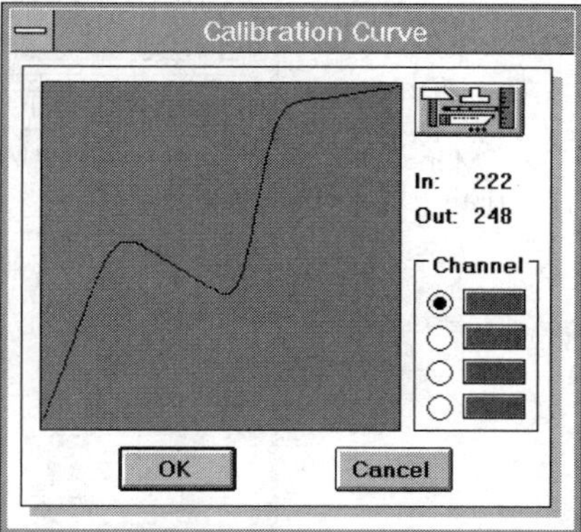

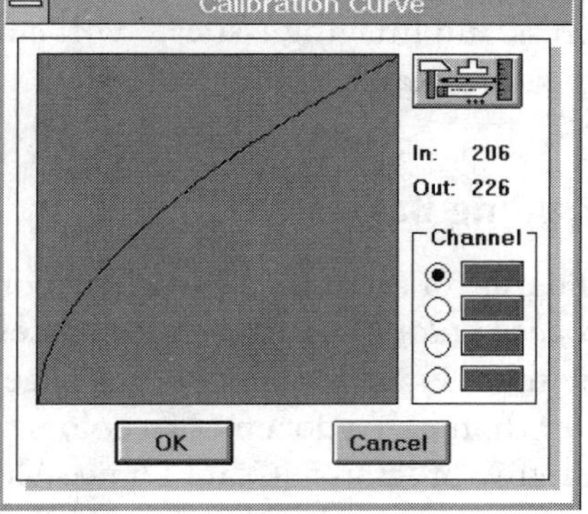

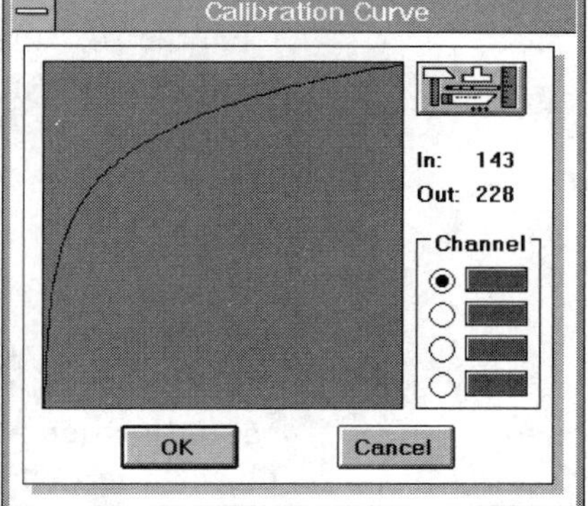

Figure 15-7. Altering the calibration curve with calibration curve menu commands:

l-r: piecewise, smooth

l-r: gamma, logarithm

- *Save* lets you save the current calibration curve to a file using the Save Map Curve dialog box in Figure 15–8 (right). All calibration curves have the file extension .GMP. You can then reload this curve later and apply it to the printing of other images.

Setting Up Color Separation Parameters

Before you print color separations to a color laser printer or split a color image to CMYK channels for output to a Monochrome printer or image-setter, it's essential to first define color separation parameters through the Separation Setup command in the File menu. This command lets you adjust the way PhotoStyler distributes color values among the cyan, magenta, yellow, and black channels of a True Color image.

We discussed Separation Setup in the context of image channels in Chapter 14. In this chapter, we'll introduce some background information about the relationship between process color printing and the four CMYK documents you generate when you output color separations.

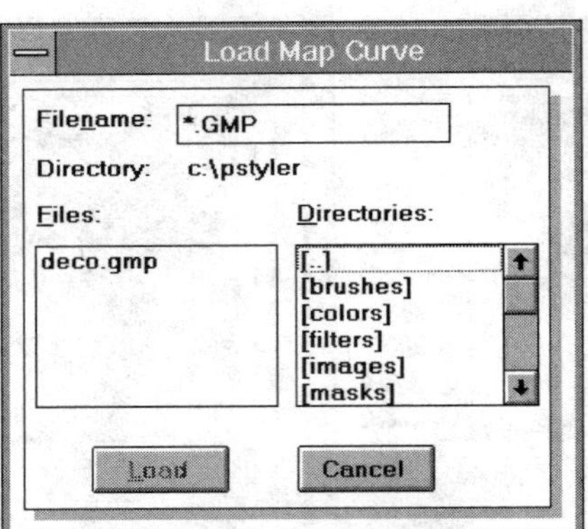

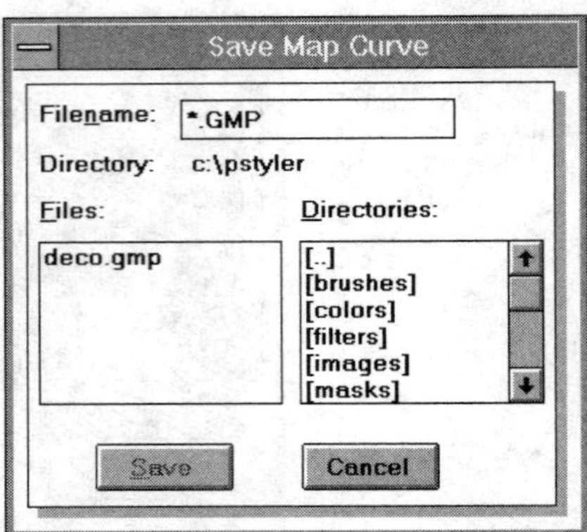

Figure 15-8.

The Load Map Curve and Save Map Curve dialog boxes

Chapter 16, "Prepress and Imaging Issues," will address color separation concerns in greater detail.

Process Color Printing Basics

There are two standards for color in the world of commercial printing: *spot color* and *process color*. The spot color system assigns discrete inks to different elements in a drawing or on a page, and it's economical only when fewer than half a dozen or so colors are involved. Many object-oriented drawing programs (Corel Draw, Aldus Freehand, Arts & Letters) support spot color, which makes sense since digital drawings consist of discrete objects that are easy to separate from one another mathematically. Until recently, spot color was the only kind of color supported by most PC-based page layout packages, too.

When continuous-tone images come into play, however, spot color just isn't practical or cost-effective to implement. There are simply too many colors in a True Color image, and they'd have to be separated on a pixel-by-pixel basis.

To make the printing of many subtle gradations of color economical, commercial print vendors have devised a system known as *process color*. In the process color system, only four colors of ink—cyan, magenta, yellow, and black—are printed, one at a time and in varying percentages. The variable percentages and the juxtaposition of different ink colors fool the eye into seeing many more colors.

The first three CMYK colors—cyan, magenta, and yellow—are often called the *subtractive primaries* because they're complementary to the light-emitting *additive primaries*—red, green, and blue—that computer monitors generate. If you mix equal amounts of the red, green, and blue values that appear on your monitor, you get white. In theory, you should be able to mix equal amounts of inks in their complementary colors—cyan, magenta, and yellow—to get black. In practice, however, equal amounts of CMY inks produce a muddy brown on the printing press due to imperfections in pigments. So, to compensate for this gap between theory and reality, commercial printers add black ink (the K in CMYK) to reproduce continuous-tone images.

Gray Component Replacement and the Separation Setup Command

Exercise care in determining how much black to add to an image. Add too much black, and colors will appear dirty or dark on paper. Add too little black, and colors won't be saturated enough. The controls in the Separation Setup dialog box (Figure 15–9), which appears when you choose the Separation Setup command in the File menu, let you determine just how to balance black with cyan, magenta, and yellow.

This art of redistributing color values to balance ink density and saturation is known as *gray component replacement* (GCR). The term has its origins in the observation that when three ink colors overprint on the printing press, the first two colors determine the hue, while the third color determines the level of saturation (the gray component). When you add black to an image, the black layer in effect becomes the third color, replacing equivalent amounts of the other colors and increasing color saturation levels.

Click the Default command button in the Saturation Setup dialog box to see the values that Aldus has found empirically to be effective in many cases:

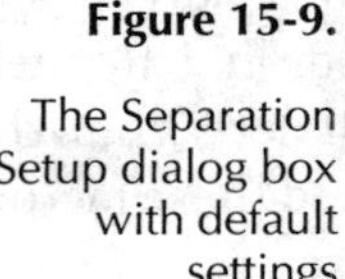

Figure 15-9.

The Separation Setup dialog box with default settings

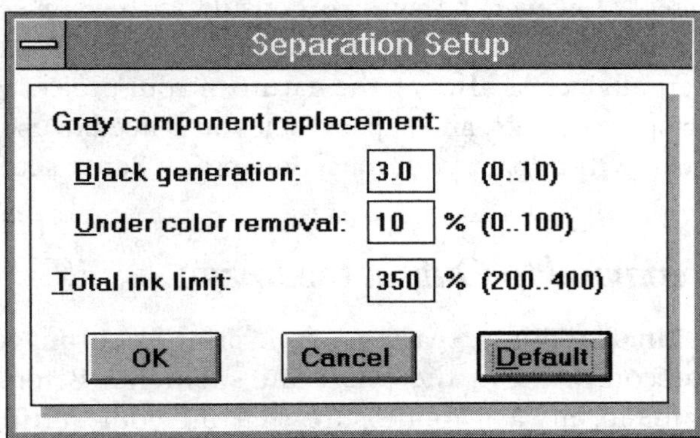

- The Black generation value determines the maximum amount of black the image can contain. This setting influences the range of Grayscale contrast in the black image channel. At the default setting of 3.0, no more than 30% of the total inks applied to a pixel can be black. Lighter areas of the image will contain much less than the maximum.

Note *If you set Black generation to zero, the image will print as a pure CMY image, and the K image channel will be blank.*

- The Under color removal (UCR) value determines how PhotoStyler will adjust gray values in the cyan, magenta, and yellow image channels to compensate for the black added. The UCR process saves on ink within the limits you specify through the Total ink limit option. At the default setting of 10%, PhotoStyler will reduce combined cyan, magenta, and yellow values by 10% in pixels that contain black. The UCR setting has the greatest impact in darker areas of an image, where black is most predominant.
- The Total ink limit value specifies the total amount of CMYK inks that can cover any pixel. Factors that should influence this setting include the type of press that will print your images, the absorbency of the paper stock that your print vendor will use, and the speed at which the inks normally dry. The default setting of 350% is appropriate for slower sheet-fed presses, coated paper stocks with low absorbency, and quick-drying inks. For jobs that use high-speed web presses, uncoated paper stocks, and inks that tend to spread, a lower value (typically 260-300%) is often preferable. Consult with your print vendor about the setting that will ensure the best balance of color saturation and color clarity for your project.

These default values should yield good results for many True Color images. However, be sure to consult with your service bureau and print vendor in advance, and make adjustments according to their expert advice. As always, the nature of your project will determine the type of press, inks, and paper stock you'll need to use, and these factors in turn will impact your ideal Separation Setup settings.

Using the Print Command to Output the Image

Print... Ctrl+P
Page Setup...
Printer Setup...

The final step in preparing a draft print or output file is to select the Print command in the File/Print submenu. Before you choose this command, always make sure that all your settings in the Printer

Setup, Page Setup, Halftone Screen, Calibration Curve, and (optionally) Separation Setup dialog boxes are correct. Review the checklist that applies to you in the sections that follow.

After reviewing all your settings, choose the Print command to access the Print dialog box shown in Figure 15–10. The options in this dialog box let you print one or multiple copies, scale the image to fit the page size, and center the image horizontally and/or vertically. We recommend that you don't scale an image to fit the page once you're ready for final output. If you do, you'll degrade the image by making it larger or smaller than your application requires. If you don't choose to center the image, it will print at the upper left corner of the page or of the film.

When you click the OK command button after choosing your Print settings, PhotoStyler will begin to "preprocess" the image. This may take only a few seconds or several minutes, depending on whether the image is Grayscale or Color and on whether you're sending the output directly to a laser printer or to a file for a high-resolution output device. After preprocessing the image, PhotoStyler will send the output through the Windows Print Manager.

Checklist: Printing a Halftone of a Grayscale Image

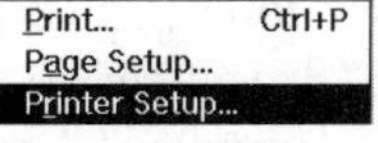

1. Printer: Is the printer that's actually connected to your computer listed in the Printer Setup dialog box? Is it selected as the currently active printer?

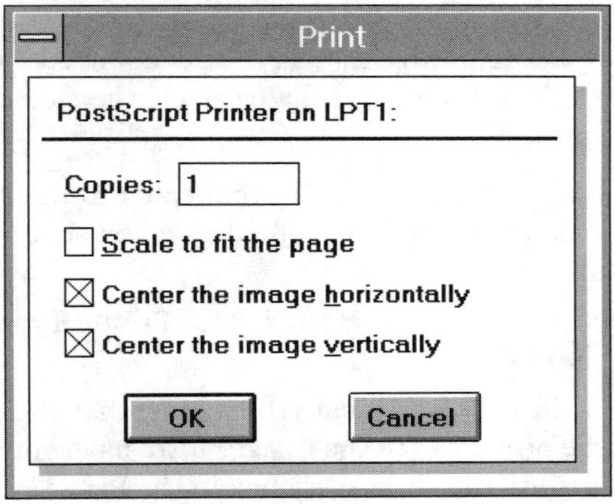

Figure 15-10. The Print dialog box with default settings

2. Port: Is your printer currently connected to the port shown in the Printer Setup dialog box? (The dialog box should list a port, not a Filename.)
3. Monochrome output: Is Monochrome selected as the Printer Type in the Page Setup dialog box?
4. Image title: Do you want anything other than the name of the image file to be printed with the image? If so, have you typed the desired message into the Title entry box in the Page Setup dialog box?
5. Crop marks, calibration bar: Are the Include crop marks (printer marks) and Include calibration bar options selected in the Page Setup dialog box?

Halftone Screen...

6. Halftone screen shape: Have you set Shape to Round (or a different shape, if you're aiming for special effects) in the Halftone Screen dialog box (Halftone Screen command button, Page Setup dialog box)?
7. Halftone screen frequency: Have you set Frequency in the Halftone Screen dialog box to a number that will give you the sharpest output possible within the limits of your printer resolution?
8. Halftone screen angle: Have you set Angle in the Halftone Screen dialog box to 45?

Calibration Curve...

9. Calibration Curve: Do you want to alter the way your printer reproduces the brightness and contrast values in the image? If so, have you created or loaded the desired calibration curve in the Calibration Curve dialog box (Calibration Curve command button, Page Setup dialog box)?

Checklist: Printing a Color Comp to a Color Laser Printer

Print... Ctrl+P
Page Setup...
Printer Setup...

1. Printer: Is the printer that's actually connected to your computer listed in the Printer Setup dialog box? Is it selected as the currently active printer?
2. Port: Is your printer actually connected to the port shown in the Printer Setup dialog box? (The dialog box should list a port, not a Filename.)
3. Color output: Is Color selected as the Printer Type in the Page Setup dialog box?
4. Image title: Do you want anything other than the name of the image file to be printed with the image? If so, have you typed the desired message into the Title entry box in the Page Setup dialog box?

5. Crop marks, calibration bar: Are the Include crop marks (printer marks) and Include calibration bar options selected in the Page Setup dialog box?

Halftone Screen...

6. Halftone screen shape: Have you selected Elliptical (or a different shape, if you're aiming for special effects) as the halftone screen Shape in the Halftone Screen dialog box (Halftone Screen command button, Page Setup dialog box)?
7. Halftone screen frequency: Have you set all four channels to the same screen frequency in the Halftone Screen dialog box? Is the screen frequency low enough to give you good output on a low-resolution printer?
8. Halftone screen angle: Have you set screen angles to cyan 105°, magenta 70°, yellow 90°, and black 45° in the Halftone Screen dialog box (Halftone Screen command button, Page Setup dialog box)?

Calibration Curve...

9. Calibration Curve: Do you want to alter the way your printer reproduces the brightness and contrast values in the image? If so, have you created or loaded the desired calibration curve in the Calibration Curve dialog box (Calibration Curve command button, Page Setup dialog box)?

Checklist: Printing Draft Color Separations to a Color Laser Printer

1. Separation Setup: Have you selected the desired Black generation, Under color removal, and Total ink limit settings in the Separation Setup dialog box (Separation Setup command, File menu)? If you plan to let your printer generate the separations, you don't need to be concerned about this step.

Print... Ctrl+P
Page Setup...
Printer Setup...

2. Printer: Is the printer that's actually connected to your computer listed in the Printer Setup dialog box? Is it selected as the currently active printer?
3. Port: Is your printer actually connected to the port shown in the Printer Setup dialog box? (The dialog box should list a port, not a Filename.)
4. Color output: Is Color selected as the Printer Type in the Page Setup dialog box?
5. Image title: Do you want anything other than the name of the image file to be printed with the image? If so, have you typed the desired message into the Title entry box in the Page Setup dialog box?

6. Crop marks, calibration bar: Are the Include crop marks (printer marks) and Include calibration bar options selected in the Page Setup dialog box?
7. Separation enabled: Have you selected the Separation by printer and Use printer's default separation options in the Page Setup dialog box? If not, review step 1.

Halftone Screen...

8. Halftone screen shape: Have you selected Elliptical (or a different shape, if you're aiming for special effects) as the halftone screen Shape in the Halftone Screen dialog box (Halftone Screen command button, Page Setup dialog box)?
9. Halftone screen frequency: Have you set all four channels to the same screen frequency in the Halftone Screen dialog box? Does the screen frequency match the capabilities of your printer?
10. Halftone screen angle: Have you set screen angles to cyan 105°, magenta 70°, yellow 90°, and black 45° in the Halftone Screen dialog box (Halftone Screen command button, Page Setup dialog box)?

Calibration Curve...

11. Calibration Curve: Do you want to alter the way your printer reproduces the brightness and contrast values in the image? If so, have you created or loaded the desired calibration curve in the Calibration Curve dialog box (Calibration Curve command button, Page Setup dialog box)?

Checklist: Printing CMYK Channel Documents as Separations

This checklist applies if you need to print draft color separations from a black-and-white laser printer that can't print separations directly from PhotoStyler. You can also use it to print image channel documents from a color printer.

1. Separation Setup: Have you selected the desired Black generation, Under color removal, and Total ink limit settings in the Separation Setup dialog box (Separation Setup command, File menu)?

RGB Channels
HSB Channels
HLS Channels
CMYK Channels

2. Separate image channels: Did you split the True Color image into separate CMYK Grayscale documents using the Split RGB True Color to command in the Image menu? Did you also save the separate documents as files?

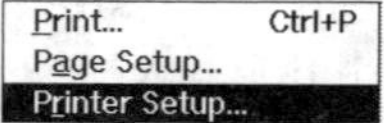

3. Printer: Is the printer that's actually connected to your computer listed in the Printer Setup dialog box? Is it selected as the currently active printer?

4. Port: Is your printer actually connected to the port shown in the Printer Setup dialog box? (The dialog box should list a port, not a Filename.)
5. Monochrome output: Is Monochrome selected as the Printer Type in the Page Setup dialog box?
6. Image titles: Do you want to print a title with each channel document that shows explicitly which color separation it represents? If so, are you typing the desired title for each document into the Title entry box in the Page Setup dialog box?
7. Crop marks, calibration bar: Are the Include crop marks (printer marks) and Include calibration bar options selected in the Page Setup dialog box?

Halftone Screen...

8. Halftone screen shape: For each of the four Grayscale CMYK documents, have you selected Elliptical as the halftone screen Shape in the Halftone Screen dialog box (Halftone Screen command button, Page Setup dialog box)?
9. Halftone screen frequency: Have you set all four Grayscale CMYK documents to the same screen frequency in the Halftone Screen dialog box? Is the screen frequency low enough to give you good output on a low-resolution printer?
10. Halftone screen angle: Have you set the screen angle for each Grayscale document as though it were a color separation generated automatically (cyan 105°, magenta 70°, yellow 90°, and black 45°)?

Calibration Curve...

11. Calibration Curve: Do you want to alter the way your printer reproduces the brightness and contrast values in the four images? If so, have you created or loaded the desired calibration curve in the Calibration Curve dialog box (Calibration Curve command button, Page Setup dialog box)?

Checklist: Generating an Output File for a Grayscale Image

When it's time to output a Grayscale image to a high-resolution imagesetter, use the checklist that follows.

1. Resolution and print width: Check the Information command in the View menu. Does the Image Information box show that the current image resolution and width (in inches) match the requirements of the printed document? If not, use the Resample command in the Transform menu to adjust image size and/or resolution.

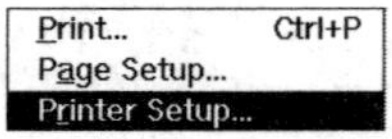

2. Active Printer: Does the Printer Setup dialog box (Printer Setup command, File/Print submenu) show PostScript, Filename as the currently active printer?
3. Imagesetter choice: When you click the Setup command in the Printer Setup dialog box, does the Printer option in the PostScript Printer on Filename dialog box show the correct imagesetter or family of imagesetters? If not, use the Printer drop-down list box to select the correct output device.
4. Image title: Do you want anything other than the name of the image file to be printed with the image? If so, have you typed the desired message into the Title entry box in the Page Setup dialog box?
5. Crop marks, calibration bar: Are the Include crop marks (printer marks) and Include calibration bar options selected in the Page Setup dialog box? 
6. Halftone screen shape: Have you set Shape to Round (or a different shape, if you're aiming for special effects) in the Halftone Screen dialog box (Halftone Screen command button, Page Setup dialog box)?
7. Halftone screen frequency: Have you set Frequency in the Halftone Screen dialog box to the number recommended by your client, company, or service bureau?
8. Halftone screen angle: Have you set Angle in the Halftone Screen dialog box to 45°? 
9. Calibration Curve: Changing the calibration curve for an imagesetter that is not your own is not recommended unless your service bureau is familiar with PhotoStyler and has agreed in advance to use its calibration controls.

Checklist: Generating Output Files for Color Separations from a True Color Image

Use this checklist when you're ready to output final color separations to film using an imagesetter at your service bureau. If you're going to output to a continuous-tone color printer or dedicated color prepress system, you may be able to present your service bureau with an ordinary RGB .TIF or .EPS image file; check with your service bureau to find out the requirements of their system.

1. Resolution and print width: Choose the Information command in the View menu. Does the Image Information box show that the

current image resolution and width (in inches) match the requirements of the printed document? If not, use the Resample command in the Transform menu to adjust image size and/or resolution.

2. Separation Setup: Have you selected the desired Black generation, Under color removal, and Total ink limit settings in the Separation Setup dialog box (Separation Setup command, File menu)? Are these the settings that your service bureau and print vendor recommend for your job?

RGB Channels
HSB Channels
HLS Channels
CMYK Channels

3. Separate image documents: Did you split the CMYK image into its component channels using the Split to CMYK channels command in the Image menu? Did you also save each channel document as a separate file, giving it a name that would help you recognize the color it represents?

4. Correction for negative output: If your print vendor wants you to output the separations as negatives (for example, right-reading, emulsion down), have you applied the Tune: Invert command (Image menu) and Flip Horizontal command (Transform menu) to each channel document? Or can the service bureau handle this part of the job for you?

Print... Ctrl+P
Page Setup...
Printer Setup...

5. Active Printer: Does the Printer Setup dialog box (Printer Setup command, File/Print submenu) show PostScript, Filename as the currently active printer?

6. Imagesetter choice: When you click the Setup command in the Printer Setup dialog box, does the Printer option in the PostScript Printer on Filename dialog box show the correct imagesetter or family of imagesetters? If not, use the Printer drop-down list box to select the correct output device.

7. Image title: Do you want anything other than the name of the image file to be printed with the separations? If so, have you typed the desired message into the Title entry box in the Page Setup dialog box?

8. Crop marks, calibration bar: Are the Include crop marks (printer marks) and Include calibration bar options selected in the Page Setup dialog box?

Halftone Screen...

9. Halftone screen shape: Have you selected Elliptical (or the shape recommended by your company or client) as the halftone screen Shape in the Halftone Screen dialog box (Halftone Screen command button, Page Setup dialog box)?

10. Halftone screen frequency: Have you set all four channels to the same screen frequency in the Halftone Screen dialog box? Is this

the frequency recommended by your client, company, or service bureau for this application?

11. Halftone screen angle: Have you set screen angles as recommended by your service bureau? If no recommendations are available, have you set angles to cyan 105°, magenta 70°, yellow 90°, and black 45° in the Halftone Screen dialog box (Halftone Screen command button, Page Setup dialog box)?

Calibration Curve...

12. Calibration Curve: Changing the calibration curve for an imagesetter that's not your own isn't recommended, unless your service bureau is familiar with PhotoStyler and has agreed in advance to use its calibration controls.

In this chapter, we've concentrated on basic issues related to output and to an explanation of PhotoStyler's commands and controls for printing. The next chapter takes you an extra step further into real-world output issues: working with service bureaus, quality control for color image printing, and outputting your images to slide or silk-screen format. If you're involved in any of these activities, Chapter 16 is for you.

16

Prepress and Imaging Issues

The mechanics of printing with PhotoStyler discussed in Chapter 15 are only part of the output story. Equally important for successful output are the "real-world" concerns you must tackle: choosing and working with service bureaus and print vendors, transferring image files, deciding upon the best output device, and ensuring quality control for grayscale and color image publishing. If you're planning to output your images to other media, such as silk-screen prints (for fine art) or 35 mm slides, you'll have a completely different set of concerns.

Our goal in this chapter is to introduce the major issues involved in producing color and grayscale images for commercial print applications, silk-screen prints, and slide media. We'll provide general guidelines intended to enrich your experience of and expertise with PhotoStyler. If you're seeking a truly encyclopedic (and literate!) treatment of color publishing applications, may we suggest Michael Kieran's *Desktop Publishing in Color* (Bantam ITC, 1991).

PhotoStyler Prepress Basics

After you create a masterpiece of PhotoStyler artwork, it has to undergo a number of processes before it's ready to be handed over to a commercial printing house. These processes are known collectively as *prepress* or, in the case of color images, as *color prepress*. Some prepress processes, such as sizing images correctly and determining the proper output resolution, are an integral part of composing the original image. Other processes, including setting up color separation parameters and taking steps to avoid moirés and minimize dot gain, are best undertaken in consultation with your other partners in output—service bureaus and print vendors. Still other processes are sheer matters of production logistics.

Producing True Color and Grayscale images for commercial print applications is no casual game for the unwary. That's especially the case with True Color output. Successful prepress production requires that you concern yourself with many issues you may never have considered before. If you fail to take even one of these issues into account, the final printed image could end up with unsightly dot patterns, unexpected color shifts, muddy inks, gaps between colors, and other unpleasant surprises.

In the pages that follow, we'll take a close look at major prepress issues you'll encounter when preparing images for commercial print applications. Still, don't take our advice as the final word. Find a good service bureau or color prepress house that has experience in color image production, and make it your trusted partner along every step of the prepress path. Consult with your print vendor early on in the project, too. The more closely you and your outside vendors work together, the greater the likelihood that your images will reach their final destination to everyone's satisfaction.

Tip

Whenever your project includes True Color images, have your service bureau produce a color proof of a test image file well before deadline. Based on the proof, you may find that you'll need to make color corrections or other adjustments in order to finalize your images for printing, and the opportunity to do so is well worth the added expense.

Image Sizing and Resolution Issues

In order to produce high-quality print images with adequate detail and a good balance among highlights, midtones, and shadows, PostScript-based imagesetters ideally require about two pixels per halftone dot. This means, for example, that an image you plan to output at a screen frequency of 133 lpi should have an *image resolution* of 266 dpi. Some color professionals feel that one and a half pixels per halftone dot (or 200 dpi for 133 lpi output) ensures adequate color quality. Your application, client demands, budget, available system memory, and storage space will determine how much image resolution is important for a given job.

If an image lacks the necessary resolution for the required print width, you can enlarge it using the Resample command in the Transform menu. However, do this as a last resort. If you enlarge it by more than a few percentage points, the image is sure to look blurry, "pixelized," or too obviously bitmapped. Your best insurance against grainy, jagged color or Grayscale images is to obtain enough pixels through the initial scan, before you even begin editing the image. When in doubt about the eventual print width of an image, err on the safe side—scan it in larger than you could possibly need it. Resampling an image downward at output time is less risky than resizing it upward! Review Chapter 4 if you need more information on matching input resolution to output needs.

File Storage and Transfer Issues

You already know that continuous-tone True Color image files can gobble up many megabytes of hard drive space. Even Grayscale image files can occupy more space than you ever imagined, especially if your project includes a large number of them. Depending on the print width and halftone screen frequency required by your application, a typical color image file generated by a flatbed or slide scanner can easily range anywhere from 4 to 20 Mb. Images scanned by a high-end drum scanner can be several times that large.

As if that weren't torture enough, PostScript files that you generate for imagesetter output tend to be even larger than the original image file. How do you transport such large files from your computer to the service bureau of your choice? Options for PC users have been limited until recently, but the technology in this area is undergoing a rapid metamorphosis.

Removable Hard Drives

Most service bureaus support Syquest removable drive cartridges for customers' file transfers. Syquest drive subsystems and compatible cartridges (see Figure 16–1) are available in either a 44- or an 88 Mb format. Trouble is, Macintosh applications have dominated the color publishing field until very recently, so some service bureaus don't yet support SyDOS (the PC branch of Syquest) links for PC-based customers. If your service bureau falls into this category, don't despair; you have other options.

Figure 16-1.

A SyDOS removable hard drive mechanism for the PC

Rewritable Optical Drives

Rewritable optical drives are newcomers on the storage media scene. IBM, Sony, Panasonic, MOST (see Figure 16–2), and other vendors manufacture models that let you store 128 or 256 Mb of image data on a single cartridge. The optical disks used with these drives are small and portable, very similar in appearance to 5.25" or 3.5" floppy disks.

Figure 16-2.

The MOST rewritable optical drive system: fast data transfer rate, up to 256 Mb storage

They're fully erasable like floppies, too, which is another big advantage. Rewritable optical drive systems are only beginning to catch on among service bureaus, but you can expect them to proliferate quickly. Again, make certain that the service bureau you choose supports optical storage media for the PC as well as the Mac.

Using File Compression and File-Splitting Utilities

If you don't use rewritable optical drives or Syquest removable media (or if your service bureau doesn't support them), consider compressing your image files down to a size that will fit on a single floppy. Several popular shareware compression utilities for the PC are available, with LHARC and PKZIP being the most venerable. Although these utilities can compress Grayscale images by as much as 20:1 ratios, they don't perform nearly as well with color images. On the plus side, they don't result in any loss of image data, either.

A new generation of software utilities and hardware solutions is springing up to fill the color compression gap. For light compression with no data loss, you can save your PhotoStyler image files in the LZW compressed TIFF format. The compression ratio with LZW compression increases with file size but rarely exceeds 5:1.

If greater compression is necessary (and if you have PhotoStyler version 1.1a or later), you can use one of the newer hardware- or software-based compression utilities that conform to the emerging JPEG (Joint Photographic Experts Group) standard. JPEG compression is a type of "lossy" compression, meaning that the initial compression process may result in slight data loss. As long as you keep compression ratios lower than about 14:1, you probably won't be able to detect any loss of image quality with the naked eye. Opinion in the industry is divided as to how much degradation is acceptable, though, so be cautious about using lossy compression on color images that are intended for high-end advertising markets.

Note *If you use a hardware-based solution for image compression purposes, make sure your service bureau supports the same hardware setup.*

What if the service bureaus in your area don't support any type of removable media for PC's and your image file is so large that even a compressed version won't fit on a single floppy disk? Investigate one of several shareware utilities for backing up large files onto multiple floppy disks. Available through on-line services and shareware catalogs, these utilities —such as the SPLIT.EXE and COMBINE.EXE utilities long known to TARGA users—also allow you to recombine files later. Be sure to provide a copy of the utility to the service bureau operator when you choose this method. You should also bear in mind that some service bureaus charge for the time required to decompress and recombine image files.

Transferring Files through the Macintosh

If the service bureaus and color houses in your area accept files from Macintosh customers only, you might arrange to transfer PhotoStyler image files to the Macintosh over a network or through a file-sharing utility such as DaynaViz' MacLink Plus. This approach is also useful if your service bureau supports removable storage media for the Mac but not for the PC. You can transfer files in one of two ways, depending on the requirements of your service bureau or color house:

- Save PhotoStyler image files in Mac TIFF or Binary EPS format, open and save them in Adobe PhotoShop, and (optionally) generate output files from the Mac, or
- Generate CMYK output files directly from PhotoStyler, then transfer them to the Macintosh and from there to a Syquest removable drive cartridge.

Consult with the service bureau you'll be using for output to see what kind of Macintosh file format they prefer. PostScript-based imagesetters will require PostScript output files. Some dedicated high-end color systems, such as the Scitex Raystar, support and translate files from most major Macintosh-based graphics applications.

The High Road or the Low Road: Dedicated Color Systems vs. PostScript Imagesetters

One of the issues you'll confront during your PhotoStyler color image publishing career is whether to use a PostScript-based imagesetter or a high-end dedicated color prepress system for final film output. A year or two ago, the decision would have been a clear-cut one: Only dedicated color prepress systems, such as those manufactured by Scitex, Crosfield, or Linotype-Hell, could provide the speedy output, high screen frequencies, exact screen angles, perfect registration, and clean trapping that process color prepress required. Of course, high-end color output was many times more expensive, but if you wanted quality, it was the only way to go.

Thanks to tremendous strides made by the PostScript-based imagesetting community and various color prepress software products, the issue isn't so clear-cut anymore. Several advances have combined to make imagesetters a viable color prepress output choice for all but the most demanding high-end advertising applications. Among them:

Improvements in Imagesetter Design

Until recently, an important advantage of using high-end color prepress systems for final output was the *rotary drum* mechanical design upon which the high-end film plotters are based. Rotary drum technologies ensure exact registration and alignment of halftone dots among the four color separations. Earlier generations of imagesetters, on the other hand, used a flatbed mechanism to generate film. There was greater room for misalignment of halftone dots from one color separation to the next, which resulted in poor ink registration and visible moiré patterns on the printing press. Anathema!

The latest generation of imagesetters is emulating its high-end counterparts by incorporating rotary drum mechanics into their laser imagers. The Agfa SelectSet 5000 imagesetter (Figure 16–3), the Linotronic 630, and new models by other manufacturers feature this type of design, geared specifically toward high-quality color separations. Even imagesetters that don't

Figure 16-3. The Agfa SelectSet 5000 imagesetter is based on a rotary drum mechanism and can handle large-format color output

Figure 16-4.

The Agfa 9800 imagesetter featuring balanced screen angles

use rotary drum technology are now introducing new film transport mechanisms that greatly improve critical accuracy in the placement of halftone dots. The Agfa 9800 imagesetter, for example (Figure 16–4), features a mechanism that greatly reduces movement and shifting of RC paper or film during exposure to the laser beams.

Improvements in Imagesetter Speed

When you output Grayscale images to an imagesetter, only one sheet of RC paper or one piece of film comes out. When you output color separations, on the other hand, the imagesetter has to produce four sheets of film for every image. That's why speed is critical for color image output.

High-end color systems used to run circles around imagesetters when it came to output speed. They're still faster, but the speed gap is narrowing. The advent of faster raster image processors (RIPS), added processor RAM, and faster hard drives have given imagesetters the speed necessary for continuous-tone color image output.

Improvements in Imagesetter Resolution

You may recall from Chapter 15 that the resolution of an output device limits the maximum screen frequency at which you can output images. Color images destined for trade magazines, glossy catalogs, and other medium- or high-budget commercial applications typically require output screen frequencies of 133, 150, or even 200 lpi. Most imagesetters now support output resolutions of at least 2540 dpi, sufficient for 150-line screens. The Linotronic 330 and Agfa SelectSet 5000 have maximum output resolutions of more than 3200 dpi and are capable of handling even the 200 lpi screens that Fortune 500 corporate advertising and fine art reproductions often require. These high-frequency applications used to be the private preserve of the dedicated color prepress systems, but now the imagesetters are starting to catch up.

Screen Angle Breakthroughs

The current trend toward improved screen angle technologies and innovations in PostScript Level 2 are perhaps the most important developments in making imagesetters fit for color separation work. You can now use imagesetter output and still avoid unsightly interference patterns (called *moirés*), something that was unthinkable just a year or so ago.

It used to be that dedicated color prepress systems had a clear advantage over imagesetters when it came to halftone screen angles. Earlier generations of PostScript imagesetters used *rational* screen angles, which refers to the PostScript limitation of having to use only whole pixels and fixed dot shapes when defining a halftone dot. In practice, rational screen angle technology meant that an imagesetter would output screen frequencies that differed from the ones requested by software applications. This was disastrous for color separations, since variations of as little as 0.01 in requested halftone screen angles result in visible color *moiré* (interference) patterns in print. Older imagesetters simply couldn't do better; there were inherent mathematical limitations on the screen frequencies that PostScript could translate into repeating halftone dot patterns.

High-end color prepress systems, on the other hand, don't suffer from those limitations because they don't have to use whole pixels when defining halftone dots; they use proprietary *irrational* screening algorithms, most of them licensed from Hell (now Linotype-Hell). Irrational screening technology is flexible, allowing the formation of elaborate halftone dot shapes to deliver the visual equivalent of what your software asks for. Expensive color prepress systems used to be considered the only "safe" output device for color images because imagesetter results could be so unpredictable.

Then, late in 1990, Hell merged with Linotype, the manufacturer of the famous line of Linotronic imagesetters. "Linos" that use RIP version 30 or later now sport High Quality Screens (HQS) that claim to be every bit as exact as their high-end cousins. Other imagesetter manufacturers, including Agfa Corporation, Scitex, and Optronix, have followed suit by introducing new imagesetters with their own or Adobe's Accurate Screen proprietary algorithms for irrational screen angles. Another obstacle to the output of accurate color separations on imagesetters has thus been removed.

PostScript Level 2 is also contributing to the improvement of screen angle technologies for imagesetters. Adobe's Accurate Screen algorithms (sometimes called "Balanced Screens" are built into Level 2 drivers for the latest crop of imagesetters. Ask your service bureau whether they are using the new Level 2 drivers with their imagesetters.

Trapping: Still a High-End Advantage?

High-end color prepress systems still retain an advantage over imagesetters when it comes to *trapping*—smoothing the differences between adjacent pixels that vary substantially in their color values. Trapping is important whenever an image contains areas of solid color that abuts areas of dissimilar colors. Generally speaking, trapping is less of a problem for continuous-tone images than for object-oriented graphics, because the colors of adjacent pixels tend to vary subtly. Still, if a PhotoStyler image contains even one or two areas where abrupt color shifts occur, accurate trapping should be a concern. Without trapping, a slight misregistration of ink colors on the printing press could result in visible blank gaps or thin lines of "ghost" color in print. This is especially true of low- and medium-budget color jobs run on high-speed web presses; the slower sheet-fed presses used for high-end color printing are less likely to present registration problems.

Color trapping algorithms used by the proprietary high-end systems are extremely sophisticated and don't miss a single pixel. Imagesetters, on the other hand, provide no trapping controls at all. If your images will be printed on a sheet-fed press, you may not need to concern yourself with trapping. But if your PhotoStyler images will be reproduced on a web press, you can provide for trapping in one of several different ways:

- Create trap manually while editing the image in PhotoStyler. Although PhotoStyler has no automatic trapping controls, there are several things you can do to minimize possible misregistration problems. See the "Avoiding Registration Problems: Creating Trap" section later in this chapter for tips on using PhotoStyler software features to prevent possible trapping headaches. You may not need to trap all your images; the critical images are the ones that contain one or more areas in which abrupt color shifts occur.

- Let prepress professionals at your service bureau or color house control trapping through the use of third-party software. Several high-end color separation and color correction packages for the Macintosh and the PC can provide for trapping. Many service bureaus that specialize in color prepress work have employees skilled in the use of these sophisticated packages. Inquire about the availability and cost of such services at the color house with which you'll be working.
- Output color film separations through a dedicated color prepress system. If you don't feel sure of your PhotoStyler trapping skills, or if your service bureau can't provide trapping through Macintosh or PC software, you may wish to consider letting a high-end system output your color image files to film. Alternatively, you might choose to let your print vendor handle trapping by conventional (manual) methods. Both of these alternatives can be costly; let your budget and application be your guide.

Which to Choose?

So where do things stand now? There's not as much difference between the high road and the low road as there used to be. Imagesetters have overcome problems related to speed, registration, screen angles, and screen frequencies that used to stand in the way of their being taken seriously as color output devices. They clearly hold the advantage when cost is an issue.

On the other hand, dedicated color prepress systems are still somewhat faster than their PostScript-based counterparts. In some cases, the proprietary color systems aren't even that much more expensive to use: you can sometimes group several pieces or pages of artwork on a single sheet of film, with no extra charge for the added run time. Imagesetter cost, on the other hand, is closely linked to the time required to run your files. At high screen frequencies, that can get quite expensive.

As always, your choice of an output device for color images boils down to a careful consideration of your application and its needs. Here are two checklists that should help you make that important decision.

Checklist: Imagesetter Output

If you can answer "yes" to all or most of the following questions, you can obtain reliable, high-quality output for your color images from a PostScript-based imagesetter. You'd be wasting your money or your company's money to use a dedicated color system for final output.

- Do the imagesetter operators have experience with continuous-tone images? With 24-bit color output?
- Is the imagesetter at your service bureau one of the newer models that features a faster RIP, more RAM, and irrational screen angle technologies?
- Are you producing low- or medium-budget color or Grayscale work rather than images for high-end advertising?
- Are you submitting either a large number of small- to moderate-sized color image files (4-7 Mb or smaller) or a small number of larger images?
- Have you paid close attention during your prepress work to avoiding PhotoStyler settings that might result in dot gain, moirés, or poor saturation?
- Has your print vendor communicated the information you need to specify the best possible Separation Setup options in PhotoStyler?
- Do your images require minimal trapping? If you need to do a fair amount of trapping, do you (or does a color separator colleague) feel confident about handling the trapping controls that PhotoStyler provides? If you don't feel comfortable, can your service bureau provide trapping services through the use of sophisticated color separation software?

Checklist: Proprietary Color System Output

Wondering whether you should go the high-end color route? Ask yourself the following questions. If you answer "yes" to all or most of them, you may want to play it safe and seek output from a proprietary system—at least until you're more familiar with PhotoStyler and color publishing requirements.

- Are you producing multiple color images with very large file sizes that might require long run times on an imagesetter?
- Do your images contain areas of abrupt color shifts and therefore require careful trapping? If so, is your service bureau unable to provide trapping services through the use of high-end Macintosh- or PC-based software?

- Are you ill at ease about specifying color separation parameters through PhotoStyler's Separation Setup dialog box?

The Output Media Issue

The final output medium that you present to your commercial print vendor influences the level of print quality you can expect to obtain. Possible media include plain paper, RC (resin-coated) paper, and film. As always, your application should be the final arbiter in your choice of output medium.

Note *If you're producing images for short-run, in-house projects, you may be able to use a continuous-tone color printer instead of an imagesetter as your final output device.*

Plain Paper Output

Plain paper output is never acceptable for color images, and only rarely is it satisfactory for Grayscale images. One reason is that commercial printers can't make printing plates directly from paper; they must first create a negative from your paper output. Adding this intermediate step degrades image quality to some extent.

A second reason why plain paper output is usually unacceptable has to do with the interaction between paper and laser printer toner. Toner tends to spread, even on papers with special finishes. If you output images from a plain-paper typesetter at a screen frequency above newspaper quality (see Table 15–2 in Chapter 15), halftone dots will be spaced too close together. Halftone dots laid down by the toner will blur—and so will the image.

As we mentioned in Chapter 15, there is one exception to this rule. If you're producing Grayscale images for documents (such as newspapers) that require only a low halftone screen frequency, then plain-paper output just might do. With halftone dots spaced further apart, a little ink spreading (also known as dot gain) won't devastate the image.

RC Paper Output

Imagesetters can output your PhotoStyler images to either light-sensitive RC paper or film. For Grayscale images output at halftone screen frequencies of 100 lpi or less, RC paper can serve as acceptable final output. It's less absorbent than papers used by high-resolution laser printers, so your screen frequency can be a little higher than newspaper quality without causing noticeable dot gain. Check with your service bureau and print vendor to see what they recommend as the maximum screen frequency to use with RC output.

As with plain paper, however, RC paper output requires that your print vendor generate an intermediate negative before creating printing plates. Distortion caused by this process may not be noticeable with Grayscale images, but errors are much more likely to occur with color images. After all, color separations produce four originals, not one, and even a minuscule misalignment of negatives could result in moiré patterns on the printing press. For this reason, film is *always* the output medium of choice for color images.

Film Output

The best output medium for both color images and high-budget Grayscale images is film, for two reasons. First, both types of images require high halftone screen frequencies (120 lpi or higher), and only film can accept such closely spaced halftone dots without generating too much dot gain. Second, your print vendor can generate plates directly from film output, so there's no danger that second-generation images will compromise print quality. Although the cost of film output may seem high when compared with RC paper output, you can save on stripping charges at the printer's.

Outputting to film doesn't solve all your production problems, of course. Your settings in the Separation Setup dialog box, the halftone screen angles you specify, and your choice of paper stocks can still trip you up if you're not aware of the pitfalls. There are plenty of variables under the control of the print vendor, too. But you stand a better chance of producing sharp, high-quality print images if you output directly to film.

Quality Control Issues

Many variables influence the eventual print quality of your images during the prepress and print production processes. Sometimes, software settings within PhotoStyler can avert problems; at other times, decisions you make concerning service bureau and print vendor options influence image output quality. Still other variables are controllable by the service bureau and print vendor themselves. Let's review some of the ways *you* can help ensure quality control when outputting your PhotoStyler images to print media.

Avoiding Dot Gain

Dot gain is a condition in which halftone dots print larger than they should, resulting in a darker image, a muddying of ink colors, and reduced image contrast. Some dot gain always occurs in printing, but the object is to minimize it or at least to compensate for it in advance. There are several junctures at which your prepress decisions can avoid dot gain or intensify it:

- when you specify a halftone screen frequency and angle for output
- when you specify Total ink limit, Under color removal, and black generation values using the Separation Setup command in the File menu
- when you specify an output medium at the service bureau
- when you specify press type, paper stocks, and inks in consultation with your print vendor

It's essential that you coordinate all of these aspects of your print job when making each decision. They're closely interrelated.

Note *Not all of the variables that influence dot gain are under your personal control. Dot gain can also occur during exposure of the film at the service bureau or on the printing press.*

Halftone Screen...

Dot Gain and Halftone Screen Settings

As we mentioned earlier in this chapter, images output at a low halftone screen frequency (under 85 for plain-paper output, under 100 for RC paper output) can tolerate a little dot gain without seriously degrading the print quality of the image. If you output images at a screen frequency higher than 100 lpi, film should be your output medium. You should also make certain that color images output at 100 lpi and above are printed on glossy paper stocks. Glossy papers are less absorbent than other stocks and will minimize dot gain.

Whenever possible, use the services of a recent-model imagesetter for your output. Many of the newer models feature extremely narrow laser beams, which can produce crisper halftone dots than earlier generations of imagesetters. Sharper halftone dots mean less dot gain at the prepress stage.

Dot Gain and Output Medium

Of the three output media available, plain paper tends toward the highest degree of dot gain. RC paper output yields less dot gain, unless you output images at a screen frequency higher than 100 lpi. Film output tends toward the smallest possible dot gain at any output screen frequency. Of course, you need to coordinate your choice of paper stocks so that it matches your output medium.

Dot Gain and Separation Setup Values

You should match your color separation parameters (Separation Setup command, File menu) to the press type, inks, and paper stocks that your print vendor will use to produce your images. Failure to do so may result in blotchy color from excessive dot gain.

The most crucial option in the Separation Setup dialog box is Total ink limit. In general, a Total ink limit value of 240-260% is best for web-press print jobs, porous or highly absorbent uncoated paper stocks, and water-based or slow-drying inks. A Total ink limit of 280-330%, on the other hand, is better for sheet-fed press jobs, coated paper stocks with low absorbency, and non-water-based or quick-drying inks. These are only general guidelines; get specific advice from your print vendor before you generate camera-ready output. Never assume that PhotoStyler's default Separation Setup values are right for all jobs.

Within the Total ink limit you've specified, the use of Under color removal can help minimize dot gain, too. Under color removal reduces the amount of CMY inks used wherever black appears and can result in sharper detail as well as better color saturation. Find out whether your print vendor uses the Under color removal technique and how much Under color removal is recommended for your job.

Dot Gain, Image Brightness, and Gamma

Monitors and display adapters differ from one another in the way they distribute brightness values across the visible color spectrum. In general, though, most images look lighter (and brighter) on your monitor than they will eventually print. This phenomenon is due in part to the differences between inks and computer display technology; dot gain is another factor.

If an image looks lighter on your monitor than you think it should—especially in the critical midtones—it will probably print with a good tonal range. Beware of images that display brilliantly saturated colors on your monitor, though: dot gain may do its evil work, leaving the printed image too dark and with too little detail in the midtones. For such images, it may be a good idea to increase the overall gamma using the Gray/Color Correction command in PhotoStyler's Image: Tune submenu (see Chapter 9). Globally lightening the midtones can help prevent excessive ink buildup on the printing press. Get the advice of your service bureau and print vendor before you apply a specific gamma setting to an image.

Dot Gain, Paper Stocks, and Inks

Dot gain is most problematic with newsprint and other low-grade uncoated paper stocks, which are highly porous and absorbent. When using such paper stocks, be sure to keep your halftone screen frequency at 85 lpi or lower.

For Grayscale images output at screen frequencies of 100 lpi or higher, use better-quality uncoated paper stocks, which are both less absorbent and more expensive than newsprint. Avoid papers with textured finishes, as these tend to break up continuous-tone images and smear ink unevenly. When possible, try to obtain paper with a smooth finish. Consult with your print vendor to find out which paper stocks are usually used with your type of application.

True Color images should usually be printed on coated paper stocks. It's possible to print True Color images on uncoated stocks, too, but you'll need to compensate for dot gain by reducing halftone screen frequency, lowering the Total ink limit, and perhaps increasing image gamma.

Avoiding Moirés

Color images on a printed page consist of cyan, magenta, yellow, and black halftone dots. The screen angle of each color separation is different, causing the dots to overlap in inconspicuous patterns and simulate realistic color. If the printed screen angles are incorrect or even slightly out of register, *moirés* result—visible patterns of color dots that draw attention to themselves instead of to the image.

Theoretically, color separations generated at the traditional industry-standard angles (cyan, 105°; magenta, 75°; yellow, 90°; and black,

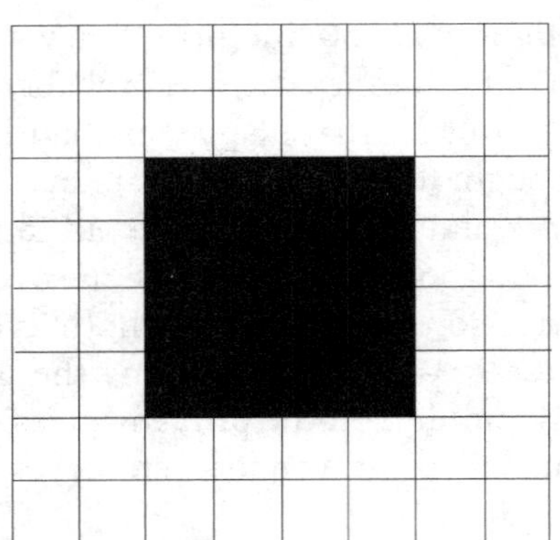
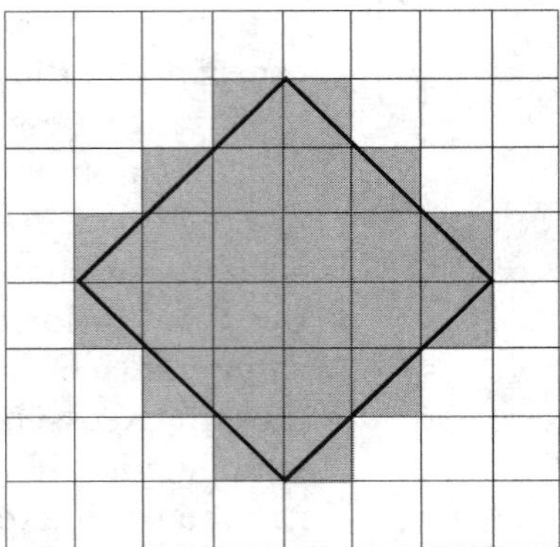

Figure 16-5. PostScript halftone dots use whole pixels, making traditional screen angles (here, 45°) difficult to achieve

45°) should be completely free of moirés. However, inherent mathematical problems in the way early versions of PostScript use whole pixels to generate halftone dots often cause moiré patterns to develop in desktop-separated color images (see Figure 16–5).

There's good news, though. As you've already seen earlier in this chapter, hardware and software improvements to imagesetters are converging to eliminate or reduce moiré patterns in color separation output. Your best insurance against moirés is to make certain that the imagesetter that generates your output is new enough to feature some kind of irrational screen angle technology. Also ask your service bureau about the film transport mechanism of their imagesetters and whether their imagesetters are based on rotary drum mechanisms.

Note *Poor plate registration on the printing press can cause moiré patterns in printed images, too. Sheet-fed presses generally foster tighter registration than do web presses.*

Avoiding Poor Saturation and Muddy Colors

The controls in PhotoStyler's Separation Setup dialog box are your best bet for improving color saturation while avoiding the muddy colors that can result when too much ink is applied on the printing press. Specifically, the Total ink limit option controls the maximum amount of ink that can be used, while Under color removal lets you substitute black for CMY to improve color saturation in shadow areas without increasing ink densities. Check with your service bureau and print vendor to make certain that your Separation Setup parameters match the characteristics of your chosen output medium, paper stocks, and inks. You may find that in many cases, PhotoStyler's default Total ink limit of 350% is too high for many color print applications.

Avoiding Registration Problems: Creating Trap

Perfect alignment or registration of CMYK printing plates is an ideal that's not always mechanically possible to achieve. Even the best printing presses must allow a small margin for registration error. Unfortunately, a "small" error—say, .002 of an inch—can result in thin blank gaps or "ghost color" lines appearing between areas of dissimilar color in a printed image.

The type of printing press used to run your color images is an important factor in determining how much registration error is likely to occur. Slow sheet-fed presses, used for the most critical high-end color jobs, have the smallest margin of error. The speedy web presses used for most magazines and brochures are more likely to evidence registration problems.

Frankly, this kind of color problem is less likely to occur with PhotoStyler images than with artwork created from an object-oriented drawing program. Color transitions in many continuous-tone images tend to be gradual, after all. But if any of your images contain areas of solid color that abut areas of dissimilar color, "ghosting" and color gaps could still be a problem. You might want to consider creating *trap* as insurance against possible registration errors.

Trap involves blending colors gradually in areas where there's an abrupt change in component color values. At present, PhotoStyler provides no automatic trapping controls. However, you can work around this limitation and create trap for your images manually using any or all of the techniques described in the following sections.

Tip

The amount of trapping required for a given color image depends on the halftone screen frequency at which it will be output and the pixel resolution of the image. As a rule of thumb, trapping increments should equal approximately three-quarters of the size of one halftone dot. As long as your images contain two pixels per halftone dot (for example, 300 dpi for an output screen frequency of 150 lpi), this translates to about 1.5 pixels as a minimum trapping increment. Of course, you can only blend colors across whole pixels, so using a soft edge or a brush shape of 1 or 2 pixels should be sufficient for images that will be printed on sheet-fed presses. Images that will be printed on web presses may require a little more trapping than this.

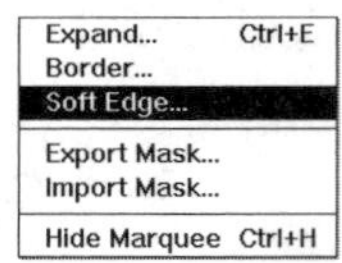

Adding a Soft Edge to a Selection Area or Mask

Many images contain abrupt color transitions between foreground and background or between adjacent objects. To avert potential trapping problems when retouching these images, try this technique:

1. Select an area of the image that contrasts sharply in color with adjacent pixels (see the Grayscale example in Figure 16–6). If the area is difficult or time-consuming to select, you should probably generate a mask from it by using the Export Mask command in the Select Palette menu. Save the mask file in case you need to reselect the same area later.
2. Add a soft edge to the selection area using the Soft Edge command in the Select Palette menu. (To add a soft edge to a mask, select the white areas with the Magic Wand tool and then use the Soft Edge command.) Factors such as paper stock, inks, and press registration tolerances have a bearing on how thick a soft edge you should define. In most cases, a soft edge of 1 to 3 pixels should be sufficient, but consult your print vendor for recommendations.
3. If you've added a soft edge to a mask document, import the mask to the True Color image using the Import Mask command in the Select Palette menu.
4. Paint in and retouch the selection area normally. Whenever you apply color to the edges of the selection area, the soft edge will create a buffer that will blend the color gradually with the colors of the surrounding pixels.

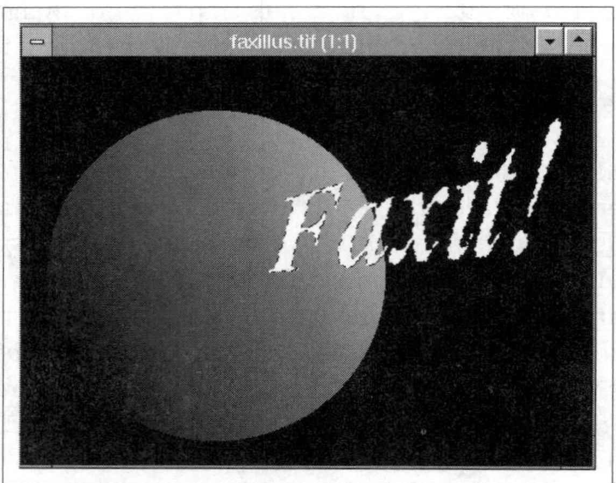

Figure 16-6.

Selecting an area that contrasts sharply with adjacent color values

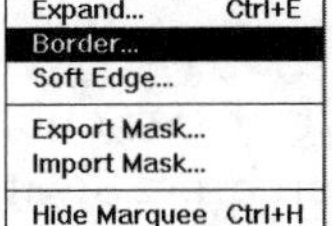

Selecting and Retouching Border Areas

Another way to trap colors in a PhotoStyler image is to define a border around a selection area, and then apply the Blur, Smudge, Lighten, or Darken tools to the border area. Here's a brief summary of the technique:

1. Select an area that differs visibly in color from the area that immediately surrounds it.
2. Choose the Border command from the Select Palette menu and define a narrow border area 1-3 pixels wide (let your press type and paper stock be your guide). You won't want an edited border area to be visible with the naked eye, so define the border width according to the print width and resolution of your image.
3. Activate the retouching tool of your choice and apply it to the border area, magnifying the image if necessary.

If you use the Lighten or Darken tool, change pixel values by only a few percentage points. If you use the Smudge tool, set Effect in the Smudge Options dialog box to a low value and drag in the direction that you want color smudging to occur. If you use the Blur tool, choose a Light or Medium Effect setting.

Matching Screen Colors to Print Colors

What you see on your monitor is never exactly what you'll get from the printing press. Printers' inks can't reproduce as many colors as RGB phosphors can, and the ones they do reproduce tend to look darker on paper than they do on your screen due to dot gain and inherent limitations of the ink pigments. How can you bridge the gap between what you think you're painting or editing and what your audience will actually see on paper?

There are several things you can do to gain a clearer idea of how a printed image will actually look. While you're editing, you can use a process-color swatch book. In the prepress phase, you can obtain a high-quality color proof from the new generation of continuous-tone printing devices. And if you output color separations to film, you can request a one-piece color proof from your service bureau that your print vendor can use for color matching on the press.

Using a Process-Color Swatch Book

Service bureaus and commercial print houses usually have one or more process-color swatch books on hand for color matching. Swatch books are printed samples of a wide variety of process colors specified according to their CMYK percentages. They're usually available on your choice of coated or uncoated paper stocks—the paper you use affects how colors look in print.

Pantone, Inc. and Trumatch manufacture the swatch books most frequently accepted as standards by service bureaus in the U.S. If you plan to output True Color images regularly, you should obtain a swatch book for one or both types of paper stocks according to your needs. Check with your service bureau and print vendor to see which swatch book(s) they recommend. If you work with the same vendors regularly, it's a good idea to use the same standard they do.

To use a swatch book effectively, you'll need to select and specify colors according to the CMYK model as you edit an image. Here's a suggestion for how to proceed:

1. First, choose the Separation Setup command in the File menu. Adjust the Black generation, Under color removal, and Total ink limit settings as your application requires. These settings must be the same ones you'll use when it's time to generate color separations. Otherwise, there will be a color mismatch.

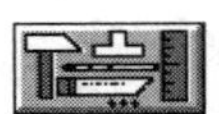

2. Display the Color Palette by pressing Ctrl-8. Then, click on the toolbox icon and choose the CMYK command from the Color Palette menu.
3. To display the color component scroll bars that let you specify color precisely, click on the toolbox icon of the Color Palette menu and choose the Scroll bar command (see Figure 16–7).
4. Choose a color from your printed swatch book, and then use the color component scroll bars to specify that color in PhotoStyler. If the printed and screen colors differ significantly, keep in mind that the printed color (not the monitor color) is the standard.

Continuous-Tone Print Proofs

It used to be that the only time you saw a color proof was after you already had output your artwork to film. At that point, changes to an image cost a fortune. The advent of low-resolution color laser printers a few years ago made it possible to obtain an inexpensive color comp

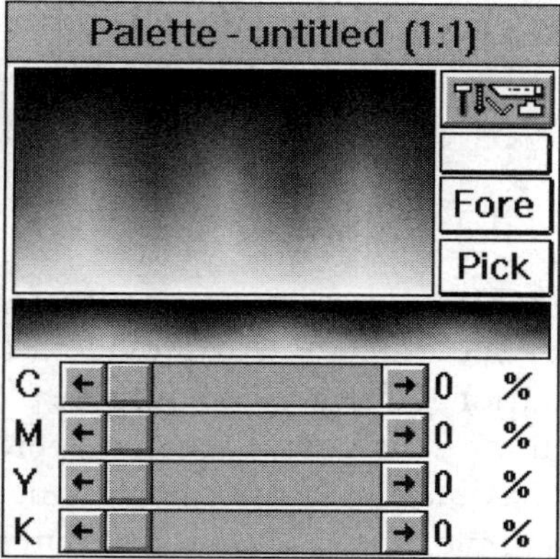

Figure 16-7. Displaying CMYK scroll bars on the Color Palette in preparation for specifying colors from a swatchbook

very early in the editing process. But, as we've already seen in Chapter 15, the low resolution of these printers and the wax-based inks they use limit their usefulness as realistic proofing devices.

The good news is that a new generation of continuous-tone color printers sporting near-photographic output quality is now turning up at an increasing number of service bureaus. You can obtain True Color output from these devices at a cost that's comparable to or only a little higher than the cost of a comp from a color laser printer. Although their nominal resolutions are often low (in the neighborhood of 200-400 dpi), they attain apparent resolutions of 1200-2000 dpi. At last, you can have the reassurance of knowing what an image will look like before you even think about sending output files to an imagesetter.

The photo-realistic success of these devices lies largely with the ink technologies on which they are based. Unlike color laser printers, which use wax-based inks that don't resemble printers' inks all that closely, the new continuous-tone printers use either inkjet or thermal dye technologies. In either case, the inks bear a close resemblance to press inks and spread smoothly onto the glossy or matte paper or transparency, simulating continuous tones with ease.

Some continuous-tone devices, such as the Iris line of drum-based inkjet printers, can output multiple images on a single sheet of glossy or matte paper or transparency for no extra cost. Among thermal dye transfer printers, leading manufacturers include Eastman Kodak, Fuji, and Tektronix. (PhotoStyler includes a driver for the Kodak XL7700 continuous-tone printer.) Many service bureau professionals feel that today's continuous-tone output devices reproduce color within 5-10% of accuracy of the final printed piece.

Find out from your service bureau what kinds of continuous-tone output options they offer and how you need to present your PhotoStyler image files for output. You may find it well worth the small investment to know (almost) exactly what colors you can expect on the eventual printed page.

Color Proofs from Film Output

When you output your True Color images to film, many color prepress houses and larger service bureaus will provide a one- or four-piece color proof for an additional charge. The purpose of this type of proof is twofold: to let you (or your client) see and approve the quality of color you'll actually be obtaining from the printing press, and to give the print vendor a sample to use as a color matching guide during printing. Typical color proof systems include DuPont's Cromalin, 3M's Matchprint, and Enco's PressMatch.

Film-based proofs are always advisable for color images, especially for critical jobs (such as advertising) where a client or company is staking large amounts of money on the quality of your work. In fact, for these critical jobs you should have your service bureau create proofs for one or more test images *before* your output deadline. It's important to check a color proof under standardized lighting conditions, too (5000 Kelvin). Be wary of any service bureau that offers color proofs without also offering you the chance to review them under these standard conditions.

Caution

Even the most perfect continuous-tone or one-piece color proof won't necessarily reproduce the moirés or registration problems that might show up on the printing press. Your best strategy for preventing such problems is to take the prepress precautions described throughout this chapter.

A Service Bureau Checklist

Choosing the right service bureau for your PhotoStyler image production needs is one of the most important steps in image production. Pricing is one consideration, but it shouldn't be the only one. Here's a set of questions you may want to review and field to any service bureau or color prepress house to determine which one can best meet your needs.

- Are service bureau personnel familiar with PhotoStyler? If not, do they have experience in the output of continuous-tone images from other PC- or Macintosh-based image editing packages?

- What kind of imagesetter(s) does the service bureau use? Does it feature irrational screen angle technology? What mechanical design features of the imagesetter promote accurate color separations? Is a proprietary color prepress system available?
- Does the film processor component of the imagesetter feature deep-bath technology? (If the answer is no, don't expect consistently high-quality output for continuous-tone images.)
- If you plan to output to film, does the service bureau use software controls and a densitometer to control the density of the film? What does the service bureau consider to be an acceptable level of deviation? How often does calibration take place?
- Is the service bureau willing to provide you with an initial consultation? Will they advise you on screen frequency, screen angles, output medium, and other issues based on your project requirements?
- Can the service bureau provide you with detailed written instructions on how to prepare your files for output? If there are no written instructions, are personnel willing to hold your hand until you're familiar with their way of working?
- Does the service bureau charge you if you need extra assistance in preparing your files? If so, at what rate?
- Does the service bureau support PC applications as well as Macintosh applications? If not, what provisions are there for file transfer to the Macintosh?
- Does the service bureau support removable storage media for its PC customers? If not, how are you expected to provide files? Will they recommend compression? What type?
- What image file formats will the service bureau accept (TIFF, PostScript, etc.)?
- Are costs based on job run time? If so, can you get an estimate for output of image files based on file size?
- Does the service bureau support any kind of color proofing system? Which kind(s)—low-resolution laser printer, continuous-tone printer, press match?
- Can the service bureau recommend specific print vendors who can handle your Grayscale or color image publishing job with high-quality results? More important, is the service bureau willing to talk to and coordinate efforts with the print vendor you choose?

A Print Vendor Checklist

As you've seen throughout this chapter and Chapter 15, your choices regarding printing presses, paper stocks, and inks are just as important to output quality as is anything you do in PhotoStyler or at the service bureau. For this reason, you should pick out a print vendor early in the image editing process and work closely with that vendor throughout the project. In fact, you should initiate a three-way line of communication between your project team, the service bureau, and the print vendor early on. If your service bureau and print vendor don't want to work together, it may be advisable to change one or both partners. The printing of continuous-tone images, especially color images, is a sensitive process that requires attention from all parties involved.

Here's a checklist of questions that can help you choose a print vendor who will be able to handle your job professionally and with no unpleasant surprises.

- Does the print vendor have experience with color publishing or with the publishing of continuous-tone images? Can the vendor show samples of projects similar to yours?
- More specifically, does the vendor have experience with continuous-tone images produced electronically on the desktop? Vendors who have such experience are more likely to be familiar with the special problems that PostScript output present.
- If you're outputting to film, should the film be right-reading or wrong-reading, positive (emulsion up) or negative (emulsion down)?
- What type of press does the print vendor recommend for printing images for your project? Web-fed? Sheet-fed? How will the press type affect your Under color removal and Total ink limit settings in PhotoStyler's Separation Setup dialog box?
- How accurate is the plate registration for the print vendor's press equipment? What's the tolerance for registration error?
- Does the print vendor have advice on avoiding moirés based on your particular job requirements?
- What types of paper stocks does the vendor recommend? Coated? Uncoated? What weight is best? What degree of porosity is permissible?
- Is the vendor willing or able to advise you on how best to coordinate halftone screen shape, angle, and frequency for your images according to the paper stock you've chosen?

- Can the vendor advise you on the best inks to use in order to minimize dot gain?
- Does the vendor want you to compensate for dot gain in advance, through PhotoStyler's halftone screen and Separation Setup settings and by reducing film density? Or should you leave these settings alone and let your service bureau separate your .RGB TIFF files with the help of high-end software?
- What method of color proofing does the vendor use or recommend? Does the vendor's recommendations match those of your service bureau?
- Is the print vendor willing to provide you with an initial consultation? How does the vendor charge for additional consultations later?
- What can the printer tell you about potential in-line problems or "ghosting" problems?
- Is the vendor willing to work together with your chosen service bureau to coordinate activities? Can the vendor recommend service bureaus with which they've developed good working relationships in the past?

Once you find a service bureau and printer combination you trust, always stick with them for similar color jobs. In the field of image publishing, quality control is a valuable commodity!

Tips for Slide and Transparency Output

Not everyone who creates or edits artwork with PhotoStyler will output their images to print media. There are several occasions when you might choose slide or transparency output as your preferred medium instead. For example, you might be creating artwork for clients who prefer to have images separated traditionally and then stripped into their publications. You might be producing images for your own print media, but you don't have the time or expertise to generate color separations directly through PhotoStyler. Or, you could be editing images for in-house corporate presentations. Let your application be the final arbiter for your output decisions.

Slides and transparencies have certain advantages over printers' inks when it comes to color. Film recorders, like computer monitors, generate color through light-emitting technology, so the colors on a slide will probably match your screen colors very closely. On the downside, you'll need to generate very large image files if you require high-resolution slide output (4000-8000 lines). See the "Lines and Pixels: Slides and Image Resolution" section for details.

Slides and Print Media for the Fainthearted

If your images will appear in print, but you're unsure of your color separation skills, you may prefer to generate slides and let an experienced color separation house or print vendor generate color separations. These days, most color separation houses are using electronic separation methods rather than manual ones. Still, if you don't have the time or the will to devote to the nitty-gritty details of quality color output, slides may be the way to go.

Ask your client and your print or color vendor what format they'll accept. Some will take 35 mm slide format, but high-end advertising applications usually require 4" x 5" transparencies for quality output. Once you know your format, turn to the "Lines and Pixels: Slides and Image Resolution" section to find out more about the file size, storage, and pixel width issues you'll need to grapple with.

Tip

Some color prepress professionals actually prefer to generate color separations from slides rather than from your image files. The high-resolution rotary drum scanners many color houses use to scan your slides will generate large files with tremendous color fidelity and brilliance, and their dedicated output systems can generate near-perfect film separations. Let your budget and the requirements of your project guide you when deciding whether to output from slides or directly from your PhotoStyler image files.

Slides as an Intermediate Output Medium

There may be times when you create artwork in PhotoStyler, then hand it over to a third party for printing and prepress. These clients may request your artwork in slide format. The rules for image resolution will be much different for you than for image editors who will be outputting directly to RC or film. Before you ever scan in or create a new image, find out the size and format of the transparency you'll need to provide. This information will determine your input resolution and the size of your image file.

Slides for Presentations

If you're planning to create PhotoStyler artwork for corporate presentations, you may be able to get away with smaller file sizes than your colleagues whose slides will be stripped for print media. You'll also have more output choices at your disposal. For example, many of the continuous-tone printers now coming onto the market can output to large 8 1/2" x 11" transparencies at near-photographic quality (2048 x 2048 pixels or higher). In some cases, continuous-tone printer transparencies may be more cost-effective than large-format slides.

Lines and Pixels: Slides and Image Resolution

Forget all you've learned about matching scanning resolution to print width. When you output to slides or transparencies, a different set of rules applies—and a different terminology, too. If you want the sharpest possible output, your PhotoStyler images will have to contain much more information than is required for most print media.

Film recorders image slides in terms of horizontal lines, with 2000, 4000, or 8000 lines (2 K, 4 K, or 8 K, respectively) being the standard 35 mm imaging widths. These "lines" have nothing to do with the lines per inch of halftone screen frequencies used in the printing industry. Instead, they translate directly into the amount of information—the raw number of pixels—contained in the width of a digital image.

If you recall that horizontal-format 35 mm slides have a fixed width-to-height aspect ratio of 3:2, you can quickly figure out how many pixels your image should contain to yield sharp images at a given film recorder resolution. For example, a slide recorded at a 2 K output resolution will look sharpest if your image contains 2000 pixels x 1333 lines. Similarly, a slide recorded at a resolution of 4 K will look sharpest with an image size of 4000 pixels x 2666 lines, and a slide recorded at 8 K will look sharpest if the image contains 8000 pixels x 5333 lines.

As you might imagine, file sizes can get quickly out of hand at such high pixel resolutions, especially for color images:

True Color file size = (No. of pixels horizontally) x (No. of lines vertically) x 3

Thus, an image file containing enough information for a sharp 2000-line slide would fill up 8 Mb of storage space, a file destined for 4000-line output would take up 31 Mb, and a file intended for sharp 8000-line output could eat up 127 Mb.

Don't let these figures discourage you. While it may be true that perfect high-resolution slide output isn't practical for most graphic designers or desktop publishers at this point in time, it's still possible to image smaller-than-ideal files at 4000-line resolution. Film recorders won't make your image sharper than it actually is, but the better film recording equipment will use cameras that make an image look better than the raw file size would lead you to believe. In our experience, you can image a 4-20 Mb file at 4000 lines and still obtain output that's stunning enough for your portfolio or for second-generation color separations. It all depends on the quality of the equipment a slide service bureau uses and on the expertise of bureau personnel.

Which brings us to the subject of choosing a slide service bureau. Maybe you're lucky enough to have access to your own or a corporation's film recorder. Recent-model slide film recorders, such as the Polaroid CI-5000 (Figure 16–8), have addressable output resolutions of 4 K (4000 lines), run under Windows, and are available at street prices of well under $4,000. If you don't have personal access to a film recorder, you'll need to depend on slide service bureaus for output. The next section includes a checklist of questions you can ask potential slide vendors that will match their expertise to your PhotoStyler project needs.

Checklist: Slide Service Bureaus

In the color publishing world, PostScript sets the standards. The standards in the world of film recording are multiple and fragmented. PostScript drivers are becoming increasingly popular, but there are

Figure 16-8.

The Polaroid CI-5000 desktop film recorder

also SCODL, Targa-based drivers, and proprietary imaging software. Each combination of hardware and software has its own limitations and set of capabilities, and you should obtain written file preparation guidelines from each service bureau you query. To help you, here are a few questions you can put to potential vendors:

- What type of equipment does the slide vendor use for imaging? What is the maximum addressable output resolution of the equipment? What is the maximum color resolution in bits per pixel? (8 to 11 bits per pixel is best.) What software drives the equipment?
- Does the slide vendor accept files from PCs as well as Macs? Does the vendor have plenty of experience generating slides from Windows-based applications?
- Does the vendor support removable storage media for the PC (Syquest drives, rewritable magneto-optical disks)? If not, how are you expected to store and present your image files? What file compression utilities will the vendor work with? Does the vendor charge extra for the time spent in decompressing and/or recombining files?

Tip *If you have access to a Macintosh, you can often reduce the size of a 24-bit color image file by transferring it to the Mac and then saving it in PICT format.*

- What imaging resolutions does the vendor support? What's the pricing schedule for each? Which resolution is suitable for your file size and project type? (A 2000-line resolution is usually adequate for in-house corporate presentations. Four thousand lines may give you sharper-looking results for fine art or portfolio work, even if your image files are smaller than what's required for 2000-line output.)
- Are larger transparency formats (4" x 5", 8" x 10") also available? What are the recommended file sizes for these?
- If you're creating transparencies from PhotoStyler images, does the vendor have a continuous-tone color printer that will output to transparency material? (You may need to go to a desktop publishing service bureau for this type of output.)
- What file format(s) does the slide vendor accept? If they accept multiple formats, which is recommended for the best color fidelity? Which yields shorter imaging times? What are the limitations of each format?
- What happens if the aspect ratio of your image file doesn't fit the standard 3:2 ratio? Does the film recorder software automatically

resize the image or interpolate pixels (and thereby risk degrading image quality)? Or does the software simply leave transparent or blank film space?

- If your image dimensions don't fit the 3:2 aspect ratio, will the imaging software center the image on the film automatically? Or must you provide explicit written instructions?
- If your image is in vertical rather than horizontal format, will the imaging software "sense" the correct aspect ratio and rotate the camera automatically? Or do you need to provide instructions, perhaps rotating the image file yourself?
- Does the slide bureau charge by the file or according to imaging time? If the former, which file types are more expensive? If the latter, can the vendor provide estimated imaging costs for each file based on file size?
- Does the slide bureau charge extra for special services such as troubleshooting, rotating vertical-format images, or centering images on the film?

With slide film recording as with printing, there are always a million questions that arise from the unique requirements of your project. As you gain experience with PhotoStyler, you'll find out how to eliminate potentially troublesome loopholes by asking the right questions in advance.

PhotoStyler, Silk-Screening, and Fine Art

Although most PhotoStyler users will generate images for print or slide media, some of you will be alert to other opportunities. Silk-screening applications, for example, can encompass both commercial products—T-shirts, promotional mugs, and so forth—and fine art of the Andy Warhol variety.

To prepare a PhotoStyler image for silk-screening, you must first generate spot color separations through an imagesetter or laser printer. Although PhotoStyler doesn't support spot color, there's a workaround, as you'll see in the "Preparing a PhotoStyler image for Silk-screening" section. After you generate the separations, a service bureau or silk-screening house will make stats from the separations and then expose each stat to a separate screen or stencil. Finally, the silk-screen artist will apply paint or ink through the screens onto the paper or canvas, taking care to ensure exact registration for each color used.

Silk-screening can be an economical way to reproduce your PhotoStyler artwork if you're aware of both the advantages and the limitations of this medium.

Silk-Screening Advantages

From the standpoints of system requirements, processing power, and economy, silk-screening applications have certain advantages over images reproduced by offset printing. A primary advantage is that file sizes need not be overwhelming. The reason for this has to do with the common use of coarse screens in the production of commercial silk-screened products and some fine art reproductions. Coarse screens require lower halftone screen frequencies, making smaller image files possible in PhotoStyler.

Let's assume, for example, that you want to generate a limited fine art edition of one of your PhotoStyler masterpieces, and that the output size of your hypothetical posters will be 12" by 16". If you were going to generate color separations at 200 lpi for offset lithography (the standard printing press method), your image would require a resolution of 400 dpi at 12" x 16". The size of your True Color image file would approach 92 Mb—enough to choke the processing speed of even a 486 PC with 32 Mb of system memory. On the other hand, a 12" x 16" image intended for silk-screen output at 55 lpi would require a resolution of only 110 dpi, resulting in a lowly image file size of 8.1 Mb (2.7 Mb for a Grayscale image). Quite a difference!

Note *Some fine art reproductions are silk-screened at high screen frequencies of 150-200 lpi, but this would be a higher-cost option.*

Another advantage of silk-screening is cost. Fine artists interested in generating limited editions of their work (say, 100 or fewer prints) will find silk-screening far more economical than offset lithography. If your artwork looks good with a small number of discrete colors (*not* the photographic look), silk-screen output might be the ideal medium for your PhotoStyler fine art pieces.

Silk-Screen Limitations

Silk-screening involves spot color, not process color as with offset printing, so you need to generate a separate halftone for *every* color you want to reproduce. The higher the number of discrete colors you want to reproduce, the more expensive the silk-screen production process will become. Consequently, you can forget about simulating 16.7 million colors—in fact, you'll probably find it uneconomical to reproduce more than about six to eight colors. If you're happy with a bold, Van Gogh-like piece, then silk-screening is for you. If you require subtle differentiations between many colors, stick with more expensive offset printing.

Another limitation of outputting your PhotoStyler images for silk-screening is the maximum output size you can obtain. If you generate separations on a laser printer, the paper sizes your printer can handle will determine the largest piece of artwork you can create —PhotoStyler doesn't give you the option of tiling oversized images at this time. Imagesetters, particularly some of the newer models, have much larger imaging areas than laser printers do, so you might benefit by outputting your separations to film or RC paper. On the other hand, the stats that a service bureau or silk-screen house makes from your halftones can be any size.

Preparing a PhotoStyler Image for Silk-Screening

Are you interested in reproducing your PhotoStyler artwork in the silk-screen medium? We've prepared a step-by-step road map to guide you through the process of designing images that will output well to this medium. The first method works best for images that will be silk-screened in multiple colors; the second is intended for images to be silk-screened in a single color.

Preparing an Image for Multiple-Color Silk-Screening

To prepare a PhotoStyler image for silk-screening in more than one color:

1. Scan in your source image at a resolution that will yield enough pixels for your final printed output at the screen frequency recommended by the silk-screen vendor. For example, given an 8" x 10" photograph as a source image, a final output size of 12" x 15", and a halftone screen frequency of 60 lpi, you'll want the scanned image to have a width of 1440 pixels (12" x 60 lpi x 2; see Chapter 4). Your optimum scanning resolution will be

   1440 pixels / 8" source image width = 180 dpi

   For images containing lots of detail, higher halftone resolutions and a silk-screen with a finer mesh will be necessary. Consequently, you'll also need to scan the image at a higher input resolution to obtain enough data.

2. Edit the image as you would normally. Enhance color or Grayscale values, paint, cut and paste, and apply filters.
3. When you've completed a final version, choose the Resample command in the Image menu. Resize the image to its final output size by changing the Resolution value only (see Chapter 13).
4. To avoid overwriting the original image, duplicate the image by pressing Ctrl-D.

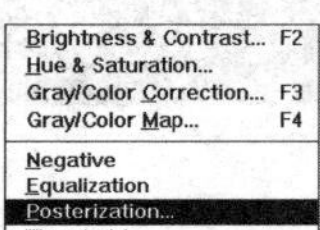

5. With the duplicate image active, choose the Tune/Posterization command from the Image menu. Set Levels per Channel to 2 and then select OK. This will reduce the total number of colors in the image substantially, in many cases to eight or fewer colors. This is a feasible number of colors for silk-screen work. Save the posterized image under a name that will help you recognize its purpose. Figure 16–9 shows a Grayscale version of an original image and one that has been posterized to 2 bits per channel.

6. To generate "pseudo" spot color separations, you'll need to select all the pixels that have the same color value and export a different mask document for each color. Begin this process by double-clicking the Magic Wand tool in the Select Palette and specifying a Color Similarity value of zero. Press Enter to exit the dialog box with this new setting.

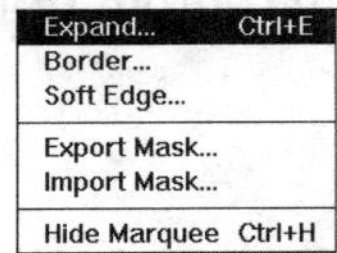

7. Click on a pixel of your choice of colors. If the Magic Wand fails to select all the pixels of that color, they are probably dispersed throughout the image. Choose the Expand command in the Select Palette menu, specify a Color Similarity value of zero, and make sure that Connected to Current Selection is *not* active. When you click OK, PhotoStyler will select all the remaining pixels of the chosen color.

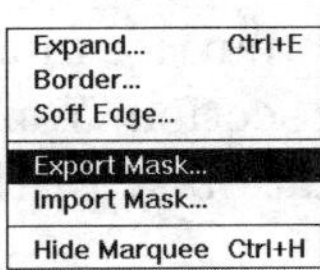

8. Choose the Export Mask command in the Select Palette menu to generate a high-contrast document that represents only pixels of the selected color.
9. Choose the Save As command in the File menu. Save the mask document under a name that will help you recognize the color you want the silk-screen vendor to apply.
10. Activate the posterized True Color image once more and repeat steps 6 through 9 for each color in the image document. Figure 16–10 shows individual mask documents for the six colors in the posterized image in Figure 16–9.

Figure 16-9.

Posterizing an image to 2 bits per channel in preparation for generating separations for silk-screening

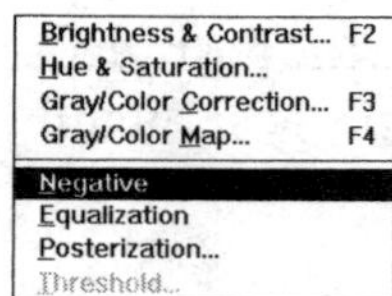

11. When you've saved all the mask files, use the Tune/Negative command in the Image menu to invert the black-and-white pixels of each mask document, as shown by the example in Figure 16–11. This step is necessary so that you'll receive your stats back from the vendor in positive format.
12. Output each inverted mask file at the screen frequency that your silk-screen vendor recommends.

Since screen frequencies for silk-screen work are often lower than for printed images, you may be able to generate acceptable output from a low- or high-resolution laser printer.

Preparing an Image for Single-Color Silk-Screening

For some art pieces or commercial products, you may find single-color silk-screening acceptable and economically more feasible. The techniques required to prepare an image for this kind of output are much less elaborate than the ones described in the foregoing section. You'll need only a Grayscale image and a little experimentation with the Threshold command in the Image/Tune submenu.

1. Scan in your source image at a resolution that will yield enough pixels for your final output size at the required halftone screen frequency. See the foregoing section for an example.
2. Edit the image as you would normally. Enhance color or Grayscale values, paint, cut and paste, and apply filters.

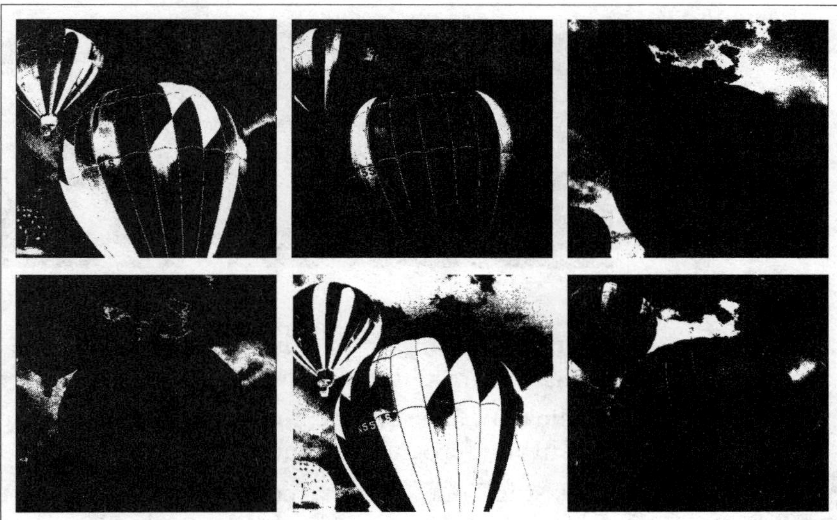

Figure 16-10. Masks representing the six colors in our posterized example image

l-r: red, yellow, blue

l-r: pink, black, white

3. When you've completed a final version, choose the Resample command in the Image menu. Resize the image to its final output size by changing the Resolution value only (see Chapter 13).

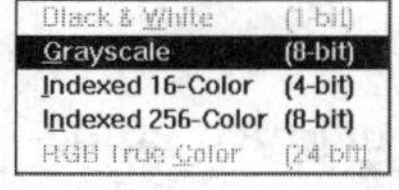

4. If the image is a True Color image, generate a Grayscale version by choosing the Convert to/Grayscale command in the Image menu. The newly generated Grayscale image will become the active document.

Brightness & Contrast... F2
Hue & Saturation...
Gray/Color Correction... F3
Gray/Color Map... F4
Negative
Equalization
Posterization...
Threshold...

5. With the Grayscale image active, choose the Tune/Threshold command from the Image menu. When the Threshold dialog box appears, experiment with various Threshold values until you find one that yields slightly more detail than you need in the white areas of the image. Acrylics and other paints used for silk-screening tend to spread, even with a fine-mesh screen, so you can count on some small detail areas getting clogged up. Figure 16–12 shows an original

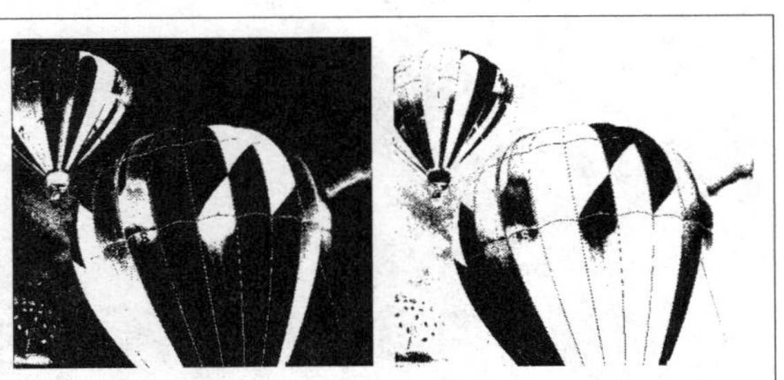

Figure 16-11. Inverting Grayscale values in the mask to generate a positive image

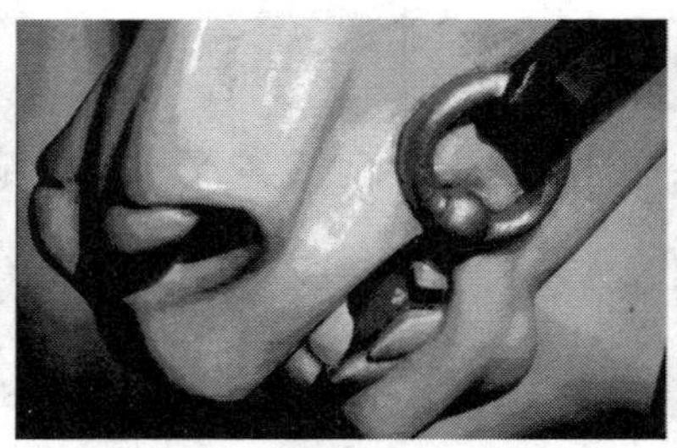

Figure 16-12. Using the Tune/Threshold command to prepare a Grayscale image for single-color silk-screening

Grayscale image, the Threshold level chosen, and the resulting high-contrast black-and-white image.

6. Click OK and save the high-contrast image under a name that will help you recognize its purpose.

Brightness & Contrast... F2
Hue & Saturation...
Gray/Color Correction... F3
Gray/Color Map... F4
Negative
Equalization
Posterization...
Threshold...

7. Use the Tune/Negative command in the Image menu to invert the black and white pixels of the thresholded image document. This step will create a positive image that the silk-screen artist can use to make a stat.
8. Finally, output the inverted image document at the halftone screen frequency that your silk-screen vendor recommends.

In this chapter, we've attempted to give you fairly detailed guidelines that will get you started in color publishing, imaging, and fine or commercial art silk-screening with PhotoStyler. The rest is learning by doing. Much success!

Part V:

PHOTOSTYLER AND THE WORLD

17

PhotoStyler Artists on Display

One consequence of the digital imaging revolution is that the boundaries between commercial art and fine art are beginning to blur more and more rapidly. Computers and PhotoStyler didn't start this transformation, of course. Visual people throughout the twentieth century have been struggling with the issue of how to integrate mass media with the creative spirit, and figures like Warhol and Rauschenberg brought attention to this phenomenon an entire generation ago. But computers have accelerated the trend, and PhotoStyler's powerful tools for manipulating light and color in existing images are bound to accelerate it even further.

In this chapter, we feature profiles of and selected images by several individuals who have used PhotoStyler as a vehicle for expressing themselves creatively. Our Gallery contributors (see the color PhotoStyler Gallery pages) come from a broad range of backgrounds and reflect a variety of interests: photography, traditional painting, animation, graphic design, and desktop publishing. Each one spotlights a different set of techniques for creating and enhancing images with PhotoStyler, from montaging to exploiting color to simulating motion and three-dimensional depth. We hope you'll enjoy the selection and find inspiration for your own creativity in these pages.

Emil Ihrig: from Found Art to Fine Art

Co-author and digital artist Emil Ihrig has been a "traditional" editorial photographer for twenty years, providing images for numerous regional and national magazines. In recent years, his digital artwork has appeared in *Verbum, Step by Step Electronic Design* magazine, and *Ventura Professional!*

"Photography has always been unjustly regarded as 'found art,'" Emil states. "People often don't realize that the eye behind the camera chooses, composes, and arranges what others will see. As I perceive it, PhotoStyler lets you transform so-called found art into something that's more readily recognizable as fine art."

Emil uses his own photographic images as the raw material for his PhotoStyler artwork, scanning them from slide transparencies. He maintains that PhotoStyler has strong advantages over the darkroom when the goal is to stylize photographs: "Editing images on the computer is often faster than in the darkroom. You have more leeway to play and experiment with an image, without worrying about wasting expensive materials. And the digital process is certainly kinder to the environment."

Although he often uses montaging and merging techniques, Emil's creative emphasis lies in special color effects. "I prefer compositions that are spare, not busy. My photographs tend to have a single focus of attention, and I like to streamline my PhotoStyler images in the same way." He finds PhotoStyler's filters, masking controls, and color channel-related features especially fascinating because of the way they extend the user's control over color. Even the Merge Control command attracts him for its color-related possibilities. The images we've chosen for the PhotoStyler Gallery reflect this fascination with color effects.

Dizzying Color

The three images on pages 2 and 3 of the PhotoStyler Gallery obtain their special color effects in three different ways. "Sky Race" came about through the use of the Composite option in the Image Compute dialog box; "Vertigo" resulted through a merge of a Grayscale and a True Color image as refined by the Merge Control command; and the finely etched color contrasts in "Homage to Andy" were achieved by splitting the original True Color image into RGB channels and editing each channel in a different way.

Brightness & Contrast... F2
Hue & Saturation...
Gray/Color Correction... F3
Gray/Color Map... F4
Negative
Equalization
Posterization...
Threshold...

We documented the techniques that produced the "Sky Race" image (page 2 of the PhotoStyler Gallery) in Chapter 14, but we'll review the process here briefly. Emil's starting point was a scanned color transparency of a hot-air balloon race, from which he generated a Grayscale equivalent using the Convert to Grayscale command in the Image menu. He also duplicated the original True Color image document and edited the two color versions in different ways: posterizing one image to 5 bits per channel and applying the Trace Contour filter to the other with a Threshold value of 75. To blend the color effects from these two versions evenly, he chose the Compute command in the Image menu, selected the Composite option, and designated the Grayscale version of the image as a mask to "mediate" between the two edited color images. See the "Creating Composite Channels or Images" section of Chapter 14 if you'd like to see some of the intermediate images on their way to the final version.

Edge Enhancement
Find Edge
Find Edge & Invert
Sharpen
Sharpen More
Sharpen Heavily
Trace Contour...

"Vertigo," so named because of the dizzying color swirls and distortion near the center of the image, resulted from a stylized montage of two photographs. Emil pasted a cropped Grayscale image of a plaster cat onto the lower right corner of the background photo of a paved walkway splashed with varicolored paint. At this point, the cat and its dark gray background were simply superimposed on the multicolored background photo. To blend the cat itself into the colored pavement, bring out color highlights, and remove the rectangular contours of the cat image's dark background, Emil applied special settings in the Merge Control dialog box. For the Use Floating Image setting, he chose Brightness Only, which brought forward some of the red and magenta from the sidewalk photo and spattered it across the cat's face. He then used the Floating Range slider to remove gray values between zero and 35 from the floating cat image. Not only did the gray background melt away—several of the paint splashes came to the foreground, giving the impression that the cat was hiding behind them.

If Darker
If Lighter
Always
Hue only
Color only
Brightness only
Additive
Subtractive

Range>>

After deselecting the floating image and merging it with the sidewalk image, Emil smoothed the areas where the contours of the cat met the background by applying the Eraser tool in Last Saved mode. He finalized the image by applying the 3-D Pinch filter to distort the cat's head and neighboring paint streaks. The distorted smears of paint seem to splash outward from the image and toward the viewer.

Edge Enhancement
Find Edge
Find Edge & Invert
Sharpen
Sharpen More
Sharpen Heavily
Trace Contour...

"Homage to Andy" refers to—who else?—Andy Warhol, of whom Emil has been a long-time fan. Beginning with a True Color scan of a close-up shot of a rose, Emil split the image into component RGB channels using the Split RGB True Color by command in the Image menu. To the Red channel, he applied the Trace Contour filter at a

Threshold value of 75; this was responsible for the red "etching" around the edges of the final image. He applied the Edge Enhancement filter to the Green channel to produce a sharp, high-contrast, textured effect. For the Blue channel, he chose the Tune/Posterize command in the Image menu and specified 8 bits per channel. Even though Gray-scale images such as channels contain 8 bits per channel anyway, explicitly specifying this number greatly increased the contrast and sharpness of the channel image.

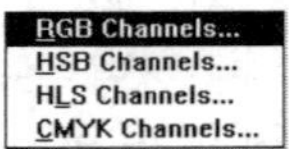

Once all the channels had been edited, Emil chose the Combine RGB True Color by RGB Channels command in the Image menu to build a new True Color image. The background of the recombined image was a dark olive green; to change it to the velvety-textured near-black you see in the final image, Emil increased contrast by choosing the Gray/Color Correction command in the Image/Tune submenu and using the left Input slider to remap color values between zero and 55 to black.

Man and Nature, Man and Mall

We chose to display the "Universe man" and "Mall sphinx" images together on page 4 of the PhotoStyler Gallery because of the source image and thematic concerns they share. Whereas the monochromatic "Universe man" suggests contemplation of humankind's relationship to the natural world, "Mall sphinx" shows man as a monolith, trapped within a self-created world of artifacts. "Golden idols" on page 5 of the Gallery is one more variation on this theme: commercial notions of beauty transform the human form into a glittering object of worship caged behind glass.

The abstract face used for both the "Universe man" and "Mall sphinx" images was originally part of a plaster of Paris head photographed in a department store window display. "The head would have lost its symbolic value if I had used it in its entirety," Emil maintains. "It would have been just too *personal*-looking." To reduce the head to its essentials, he traced around the desired areas with the Lasso tool, inverted the selection area, and filled the inverted area with a solid color. He then saved this intermediate image as a separate file.

The next step was to copy the simplified human face to the clipboard and then paste it into the photo of clouds that forms the backdrop for "Universe man." Selecting the abstract human face in the intermediate image was easy: Emil simply selected the solid-color background with the Magic Wand tool and then inverted selected and unselected areas.

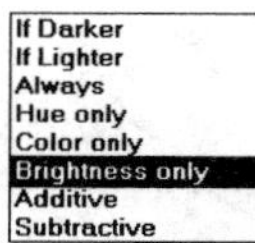

After pasting the abstract face into the cloud backdrop, Emil left it selected, repositioned it, and then set about achieving the goal of making it partially transparent. He chose the Merge Control command and set Use Floating Image to Brightness Only, which transformed the face into the monochromatic blue in harmony with the rest of the tones in the backdrop. This same setting also ensured that the clouds would show through the abstract face.

Brightness & Contrast... F2
Hue & Saturation...
Gray/Color Correction... F3
Gray/Color Map... F4
Negative
Equalization
Posterization...
Threshold...

However, the face didn't stand out sufficiently against the cloud backdrop. Leaving it selected, Emil remedied this situation by choosing the Gray/Color Correction command in the Image/Tune submenu and increasing contrast at the lower end of the Input spectrum. To complete the image, he chose the Soft Edge command in the Select Palette menu and applied a 3-pixel soft edge to the human mask so that it would blend in seamlessly with the background. Applying the Soft Edge automatically deselected the floating selection area, merging it with the underlying image.

If Darker
If Lighter
Always
Hue only
Color only
Brightness only
Additive
Subtractive

Emil's techniques for completing the "Mall sphinx" image were similar. After pasting the abstract face from the clipboard and repositioning it in the shadowy area along the mall walkway, he accessed the Merge Control dialog box and chose the Use Floating Image Always setting. He wanted the human face to emerge more subtly from the shadows in this image, so he set Floating Opacity to 40%. After deselecting the floating selection area, he finalized the image by refining contrast and brightness values in the Gray/Color Correction dialog box.

"It's difficult to reduce these two images to a simple 'statement,'" Emil says. "I wanted to evoke a different atmosphere with each image: meditative with the 'Universe man,' subliminally ominous with 'Mall sphinx'—and the tonal range of each image plays a large part in achieving that."

Tonal range plays an even larger part in the "Golden idols" image on page 5 of the PhotoStyler Gallery. This image originated from a single photograph of a mannikin taken at an upscale shopping center. Emil's goals were twofold: to intensify the golden highlights suggested by the mannikin's jewelry and by the reflections in the store window, and to evoke a sense of glittering artificiality.

Add Noise...
Emboss...
Maximum...
Median...
Minimum...
Motion Blur...
Mosaic...

Emil first heightened the overall glitter in the image by applying the Sharpen filter two times. He next used the Mosaic filter with a 5 x 5 pixel mosaic square to intensify this effect even further. Finally, he applied the Edge Enhancement filter, which enhanced the golden tones throughout the image and created the stylized look he sought.

Michael Johnson: Avoiding "Toolness"

"Throughout history, new art movements have developed because the tools of art have changed," asserts Michael Johnson, whose PhotoStyler efforts grace the cover of this book as well as page 5 of our PhotoStyler Gallery. "The invention of the photograph in the nineteenth century is a perfect example. The photograph captured 'reality,' freeing artists to move away from a literal approach to the visual world. Impressionism, Expressionism, Abstract Art—all of these movements would have been unthinkable if photography had never been introduced.

"Image editing software is today's new 'tool,'" says Michael, an Associate Professor of Fine Art at Cypress College in Orange County, California. "In the past, painters *represented* light and photographers captured it. Now, we have the opportunity to *paint* with light, to manipulate light itself. The new breed of artist is a synthesis of photographer and painter."

Michael, who holds a Master's degree in Painting and Fine Art from the California State University at Fullerton, founded the Computer Lab at Cypress College and teaches courses in computer-based graphic design, desktop publishing, and illustration. His "digital paintings" in PhotoStyler and TARGA-based applications have been exhibited in the U.S., Japan, and Europe.

Asked if he has a "philosophy" of image editing that he tries to pass on to his students, he replies, "Definitely—avoid *toolness,* the temptation to exploit technique at the expense of concept. We're constantly bombarded with new technological advances, and there's an ever-present danger that we might forget about ideas and become obsessed with the tools themselves."

Michael's own digital paintings in PhotoStyler reflect a balanced concern for both concept and technique. Readers of *Personal Publishing* magazine may recall his cover image from the September 1991 issue, which featured a high-tech parody of Grant Wood's *American Gothic.* U-Lead Systems, the original developers of PhotoStyler, also engaged Michael to create images for their initial advertising campaigns.

The image that appears on page 5 of our PhotoStyler Gallery reflects Michael Johnson's lifelong fascination with basic symbols. It also makes for an interesting study in the use of PhotoStyler tools and techniques to represent planes and perspective in two-dimensional media.

"Untitled" from study3.tga

"The Cubists," Michael Johnson maintains, "experimented with planes to create the impression that you were looking at an object from several different angles at once. We're in a position to do something similar when we montage parts of several images. Perspective and lighting and composition in some of my images are unrealistic, not because I'm struggling with technique, but because I want the viewer to *see* things in a different way."

The fire in the untitled image on page 5 of the PhotoStyler Gallery is one such unrealistic compositional element. The juxtaposition of fire and water is a recurrent theme in Michael's electronic artwork. Fire, which represents passion, consumes itself and its surroundings, but is trapped, left unfulfilled, by the repressing and self-repressing force of water.

The elements of this piece originated from several source images: a watery background, two separate photos of lily pads, the water lilies themselves, the flame, and a koi fish. Michael began with the background water, then worked forward. After pasting the background lily pads on top of the water, Michael created the impression that they were floating underwater by applying the Eraser tool with a degree of transparency in Last Saved mode. His experimentation with planes is evident here—the lily pads at the extreme background appear to be deep underwater, while the ones closer to the middle foreground seem to be rising from shallower depths.

The white flower in the middle foreground of the image, which seems to be rising above the surface of the water, serves to establish a horizontal plane and draw the eye from the dead fish to the fire. As for the fire itself, the source image included firewood underneath, but Michael erased that after pasting. In the final image, the fire seems to be feeding on itself, with no source of nourishment.

"Every PhotoStyler user has favorite tools," Michael points out. "Preferences are idiosyncratic, based on the way a person works. The kind of montaging I do calls for one- or two-pixel brush sizes for precise work and intensive use of the Smudge and Eraser tools."

Michael Uriss: Life Outside the Goldfish Bowl

PhotoStyler doesn't exist in a vacuum. For many users, an image in PhotoStyler is on its way to or from some other software package in which they're also proficient. We chose Michael Uriss' "Still Life with surfboards and goldfish bowl" for the PhotoStyler Gallery (page 6) because it 's a perfect example of how one can combine PhotoStyler creatively with other applications. Mike's technique also provides PhotoStyler users with a workable tip on how to edit large True Color images efficiently in spite of limited system memory.

Marilyn's Stilled Life

A native of the Midwest, Mike brings a sense of irony to his experience of Southern California, where he's lived since the mid-1980s. That irony is everywhere in evidence in "Still Life with surfboards and goldfish bowl." The pink sky, magic carpet sand dunes, flying surfboards, and fish frantically trying to escape into goldfish bowls that are on the verge of shattering all draw the eye toward the Marilyn Monroe surfboard. "I've always seen Marilyn as a victim of the Hollywood mythmaking machine," Mike states. 'Nuff said.

Mike, a graphics animator and designer specializing in interactive television broadcast applications, rendered the objects shown in "Still Life" in the wire-frame mode of AutoDesk's 3D Studio, and then imported the image as a TIFF file into PhotoStyler. "I started the image in 3D Studio because it's object-oriented and has specialized tools for applying surface textures and specifying lighting," he explains. "But PhotoStyler gave me the opportunity to add 'painterly' special effects I couldn't achieve with my other application."

His first problem after importing the image into PhotoStyler was a dearth of system memory. Converted to a TIFF file, "Still Life" consumed 2.5 Mb—for starters—in a system that had only 4 Mb of RAM at its disposal. "I knew that if I did all my editing in this image, Windows would be consuming virtual memory on the hard drive almost instantly," Mike says. "I'd be spending most of my time tapping my fingers instead of getting work done."

As Selection Shift+Ins
Inside Selection
Outside Selection
As New Document

Mike's solution to the problem of his memory limitations was an ingenious one. For each area that he wanted to edit, he traced a selection area with the Lasso tool, copied the selection to the clipboard, and then used the Paste As New Document command in the Edit menu to paste the clipboard image into its own document window. "I did all my editing in the separate window, then copied and pasted the edited image data back into the original document window, where it fit exactly into place because the original selection area was still active," Mike explains. "Applying filters and paint tools took less time this way—much less than if I'd tried to negotiate a 2.5 Mb file for every edit."

The twisted brown surfboard to the far right of the image looks as though it were being hurtled through the air with a wake of wind behind it. To create this effect, Mike selected the entire edge of the surfboard along with part of the background, and then applied the 2-D Ripple filter twice (Frequency Low, Amplitude 70). For the finishing touches, he also applied the Motion Blur filter with a length of 30 pixels and an angle of -180.

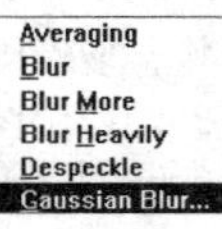

To create contrast between the two Marilyn Monroe portrait tiles on the far left surfboard, Mike applied a different set of filters and different image enhancements to each. He obtained the vivid, saturated colors in the upper tile by reducing gamma and increasing contrast for each image channel separately in the Gray/Color Correction dialog box. The lower Marilyn tile has the milky quality of a reflection in water, thanks to the Gaussian Blur and Mosaic filters and to enhancements made to the RGB blue channel in the Gray/Color Map dialog box.

One center of visual attention in the image is the trio of blue surfboard fins metamorphosed into "goldfish" springing off the surfboard of the same color and diving into the tipping fishbowl. Mike first generated this trailing edge effect by a happy accident when the action of the Smudge tool didn't quite catch up to his hand movements. Keep those happy accidents coming, Mike.

Paul Serrano: Adding an "Extra Dimension" to Reality

"I'm not an artist; I'm a working print media consultant with regular clients who need images in their publications," says Paul Serrano, head of The Serrano Company in Washington, D.C. "With PhotoStyler, I can montage existing photographs and illustrations intuitively to give them a more creative look. A composite image really *is* greater than the sum of its parts; it adds an 'extra dimension' to reality."

One of Paul's regular clients is a nonprofit research and education foundation that publishes the quarterly *Electric Railway Journal* for light rail professionals and fans worldwide. Using illustrations from past issues of the journal and photographs by Associate Publisher William S. Lind, Paul composed the "Electric Railway Journal Promotional Flyer" image featured on page 6 of our PhotoStyler Gallery.

Composition in Progress

Paul's goal in designing the promotional flyer image was to communicate the vitality of the "light rail renaissance" in the U.S. today. The scanned component images consisted of an illustration of the Houston monorail, a streetcar ticket voucher and stub, a light rail neon sign, and photos of colorful streetcars and streetcar scenes. As the centerpiece of his design, Paul chose the monorail illustration, which draws the other elements of the image together through its clean diagonal line and sets the tone for the other diagonals in the finished composite.

As Selection Shift+Ins
Inside Selection
Outside Selection
As New Document

Working from foreground to background, Paul first positioned the monorail in the master image and made two masks for it, one to protect each side from the other images that he planned to paste in. "My greatest ally in the montaging process was the Paste Outside Selection command in the Edit menu," he explains. "It gave me an intuitive way to place component images 'behind' the monorail or another component image to simulate depth." He assigned one- or two-pixel soft edges to many of the component images to help them blend more smoothly into the master image.

Bringing together images from so many different sources presented special problems. The source images were of different sizes and image resolutions and had dissimilar color compositions. To homogenize the component images, Paul corrected the gamma and color channels on each one (using the Gray/Color Correction command in the Image/Tune submenu) before pasting it into the master image. Some images were also sharpened to heighten contrast. In the case of the street scene behind the two human figures, he had to posterize and recolor the component image in order to make it seem to recede into the background and contrast with the surrounding images. To further the three-dimensional perspective in the composite image, he selected the "South Shore Line" neon sign and applied the 3-D Punch filter to it.

After pasting in all the enhanced components, Paul finalized the composite by creating type in a separate image document, adding drop shadows, and pasting the text into place in the master image. The result is an illustration emphasizing movement, color, and vitality—the "emerging second era" of light rail transportation.

Sybil Ihrig: Unmasking the Mask

Co-author Sybil Ihrig finds PhotoStyler's handling of masks one of the most fascinating aspects of the software. "Unlike most other image editing packages, PhotoStyler lets me open a mask file as a separate image document. Just being able to visualize a mask as an image in its own right stimulates all kinds of ideas about possible ways to edit the source image," she says.

"Magic Touch," Sybil's contribution to the PhotoStyler Gallery (page 7), reflects her interest in manipulating selection areas and masks. The only photo-realistic part of the image is the human hand, "because the reality we see around us is one we've created ourselves, out of our collective minds. If something looks 'unrealistic' to us today, it's only because we haven't *agreed* to see it in the way it's being presented to us. Tomorrow, that presentation may represent the new consensus and become the new reality."

Edge Enhancement
Find Edge
Find Edge & Invert
Sharpen
Sharpen More
Sharpen Heavily
Trace Contour...

Sybil's image originated as—you guessed it—Emil Ihrig's photo of the carousel horse you've been seeing intermittently throughout the example images in this book. To begin the transformation, Sybil used the Lasso tool to trace a selection area that included only the body of the horse and then exported it as a mask for later recall. She applied the Trace Contour filter with a default Threshold value of 127 to the selection area, metamorphosing the horse into a flat black surface filled with brightly colored outlines.

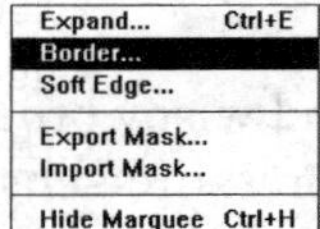

Next, Sybil chose the Border command in the Select Palette menu and generated a border selection area 9 pixels wide. To this new selection area, she added a Soft Edge of 3 pixels using the Soft Edge command in the Select Palette menu. She then filled the border area with a vibrant magenta chosen from one of the outline colors present in the horse. The positioning of the border outlines creates the impression of a glowing energy field surrounding both the horse and the human hand.

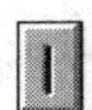

To complete the transformation, Sybil re-imported the mask that she had saved, added the hand and arm to the selection area, and then inverted selected and unselected areas of the image so that only the backdrop was selected. Finally, she applied a Bucket fill of black to the backdrop area; the fill "leaked" into the soft edge of the outline around the horse. As a result, the magenta "energy field" around the hand remains more intense than the outline around the horse itself.

"The power to alter reality brings an enormous responsibility with it," says Sybil. "We're not tweaking pixels here; we're tweaking perceptions."

Russ DeVerniero: Traditional Painting, Modern Media

"What's *that* doing here?" you might ask after a cursory look at the "Sumi" image on page 7 of our PhotoStyler Gallery. The delicate nature painting couldn't possibly have been created with anything other than a handful of traditional oriental brushes. Or could it? Ask Russ DeVerniero, who painted it pixel by pixel using only PhotoStyler and a mouse.

We've placed so much emphasis on PhotoStyler as a tool for enhancing and transforming photographs that you've probably forgotten about its *painting* capabilities. Yet, it's possible to execute an entire image without scanning so much as a single pixel. Russ, who's a graphics specialist in the Technical Support department at Aldus Corporation, has been a devotee of traditional Chinese brush painting for twenty years. He set himself the task of reproducing the themes, the styles, and the strokes of this ancient genre in a modern electronic medium.

Russ began by opening a new image, defining a circular selection area within it, and filling the circular area with a soft yellow. "Chinese brush painting follows strict conventions concerning the subjects, the manner of execution, and the symbols used," he explains. "A circular design like the one used here symbolizes wholeness and unity." During the entire project, he left the circular area selected to prevent "paint" from spreading into the black background area.

A major challenge was to reproduce the soft focus and wispy brush strokes of the genre using only a mouse instead of a pressure-sensitive pen. To meet the challenge, Russ worked at high magnification, used one- or two-pixel brush shapes, and made extensive use of the Transparency setting for the Airbrush, Paintbrush, and Pencil tools, the Rate of Flow setting for the Airbrush and Paintbrush, and the Spread Distance setting for the Paintbrush. "Chinese brush painting convention requires the artist to work from foreground to background, rather than from background to foreground as in the Western tradition," he adds. "Varying the transparency let me paint in layers—the trees appearing 'behind' the mist, for example." By maintaining a low Rate of Flow setting for the Airbrush and Paintbrush and a low Spread distance setting for the Paintbrush, he was able to "thin out" the paint at the ends of pine branches or other strokes. He also used the Blur and Smudge tools to soften the edges of strokes and to add texture.

Russ does look forward to a day when PhotoStyler might support the use of a pressure-sensitive pen. Though he was able to achieve some amazing effects with a mouse, he confesses that inherent limitations of the mouse allowed him to simulate only traditional Japanese brush strokes, not the more stringently stylized Chinese ones. Stay tuned for an update and future oriental masterpieces.

Marta Lyall: Mind over Matter

Marta Lyall's "Mind over Matter," which appears on page 8 of our PhotoStyler Gallery, is a variant of the cover illustration she designed for the September/October 1991 issue of *Aldus Magazine*. Her assignment for the magazine was to create an image that reflected the issue's "Education" theme. What started out as a depiction of compartmentalized academic disciplines—a globe for geography, a dissected frog representing the sciences, a classical column for history—took on surrealistic Magritte-like overtones as Marta and PhotoStyler began their partnership.

An Assistant Art Director for *Aldus Magazine* since 1989, Marta has had plenty of opportunities to work creatively with a host of new design, video, and illustration products. What did she find most interesting about PhotoStyler? "Merge Control," she says simply. "The Range sliders in the dialog box let you choose precisely which parts of the 'floating' image will show through and where the background image will dominate. It's a really flexible tool for image composition."

Marta, who holds an M.F.A. from the School of the Art Institute of Chicago, numbers the *Wall Street Journal*, Montgomery Ward, and the *Encyclopedia Britannica* among her graphic design and illustration clients. Currently, she's designing visuals for a company that makes educational video discs for schools.

Anatomy of a Transformation

To create "Mind Over Matter," Marta began by scanning images of various three-dimensional objects. The abdomen of the abstract frog, for example, originated from a plug-in rubber bulb. The "wooden" panels that serve as a backdrop to the other objects started as a single open box, which Marta filled with a custom woodgrain texture and then "cloned" five times. The white glove and the text that weaves through it were two separate images originally. And the cosmic swirls in the upper left compartment came from a scanned image of a world globe.

Ripple...
Whirlpool...

After completing the initial scans, Marta set about editing the source images. First, she selected each scanned bitmap, made it into a floating selection area, resized it as necessary, and manipulated it by applying various commands (Skew, Rotate, and Flip) from the Transform menu. The Whirlpool filter in the Image/2-D Spatial Effects submenu helped her achieve the twists and curves that give a "sleight of hand" look to the glove. The same filter transformed the North American continent of the globe into swirling cosmic clouds.

To composite the source images with the background panels or with each other, Marta made extensive use of the Merge Control command in the Edit menu. The Floating Range sliders in the Merge Control dialog box, for example, allowed her to make the darker areas of the glove, column, and globe transparent. As a result, the glove seems to be vanishing magically into the panel behind it, and the column emerges surrealistically from the shadows.

Merge Control also helped Marta combine the glove seamlessly with text that she had scanned in separately. "For me, the glove symbolizes the way people customize learning to fit their individual needs," Marta explains.

After merging the edited source images with their background, Marta painted the articulated legs of the "frog" from scratch using a variety of tools. She then finalized the image by selecting and refining the coloring of the background area, panels, and component objects. The illustration's effective use of the Merge Control command creates an impression of continual movement in and out of the shadows —not surprising when you consider that Marta has an extensive background in video arts and production.

Encore, Encore . . .

We'd like to hear from all PhotoStyler users who have developed editing techniques and images they'd like to share with others. If you'd like to submit your images or tips for possible inclusion in further editions of this book, please feel free to contact Sybil Ihrig at her CompuServe address of 72730,1153.

Appendix A

Enhancing PhotoStyler's Performance

Image editing can be a system- and memory-intensive process, especially if you work with True Color image files. What's the use of knowing how to swashbuckle your way through every special-effects technique, if you can't obtain peak *performance* from PhotoStyler along the way? There are three things you can do to avoid bottlenecks:

- Match your system components to the requirements of your most typical PhotoStyler applications
- Configure both MS-Windows and PhotoStyler for maximum speed
- Develop working habits that minimize potential drain on memory and system resources.

We'll explore each of these topics in this appendix.

Matching Your System to Your Applications

To maximize PhotoStyler's potential, you need a properly integrated system in which every component meets the needs of your applications. You should consider not only the speed of the CPU, but also the amount (and chip speed) of system memory, the graphics adapter and monitor, the input devices that will digitize your source images, and the output or printing devices that will help you proof your work. Not every PhotoStyler user requires a high-speed computer with tons of RAM and an octopus-like set of expensive peripherals. On the other hand, if you lack the components you need for your everyday assignments, you may experience a serious performance bottleneck and become frustrated.

The hardware setup that will give you adequate performance depends on the kinds of images you produce with PhotoStyler: high-end color, medium-budget color and Grayscale, or Grayscale only. In Table A–1, we've compiled a few suggestions for configuring your system to match your applications.

Note *You may not need to own the input and output devices listed under your category. In some cases, it will be more convenient to use the services of a color prepress house, desktop publishing service bureau, or slide service bureau.*

High-End Color Applications

Current technological advances in the desktop color field are starting to blur the distinctions between "high-end" and "low-end" color publishing. There are still a few imaging applications that remain the domain of the high end, however. These include fashion advertising, corporate advertising in prestigious publications, exclusive glossy catalogs, and annual reports for major corporations. Images destined for these and similar uses demand the very highest quality in input and output—a level of quality that desktop color peripherals haven't quite reached. For these applications, you'll be working with huge (30-40 Mb) color image files that require superior processing power, computing speed, system memory, and color fidelity. As Table A–1 shows, more powerful system components and peripherals will be necessary to aid you in achieving absolute visual perfection. You'll need to work regularly with a color prepress house, too, perhaps using their services for input as well as output.

Medium-Budget Color and Grayscale Publishing and Presentations

PhotoStyler and a new generation of lower-cost color-related peripherals and output devices are increasing the quality of desktop-produced

The PhotoStyler Gallery

Emil Ihrig

Sky race

Emil Ihrig
Vertigo

Emil Ihrig
Homage to Andy

Emil Ihrig
Universe man

Emil Ihrig
Mall sphinx

Michael Johnson
Untitled

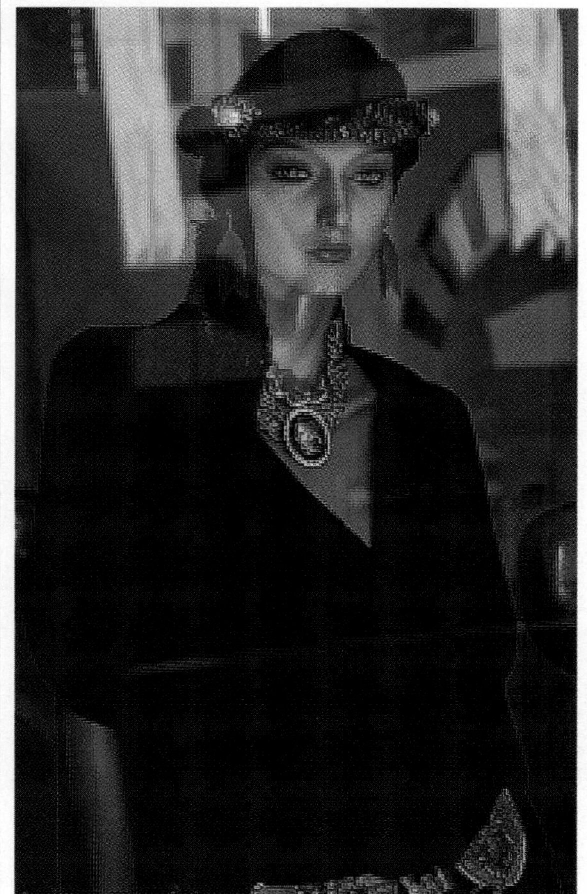

Emil Ihrig
Golden idols

Michael Uriss

Still life with surfboards and goldfish bowl

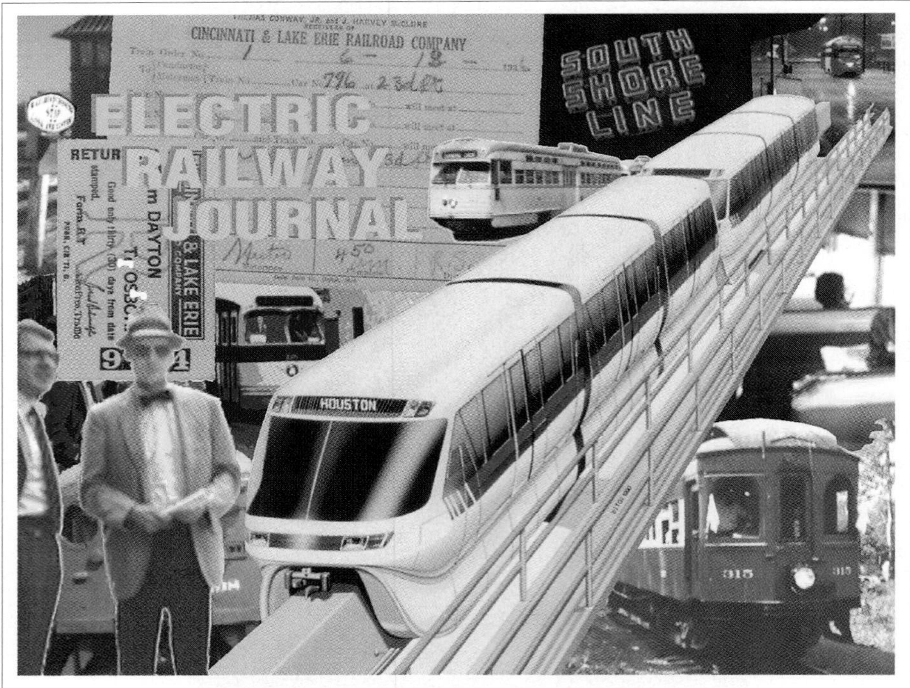

Paul Serrano

The Electric Railway Journal promotional flyer (from photographs by William S. Lind)

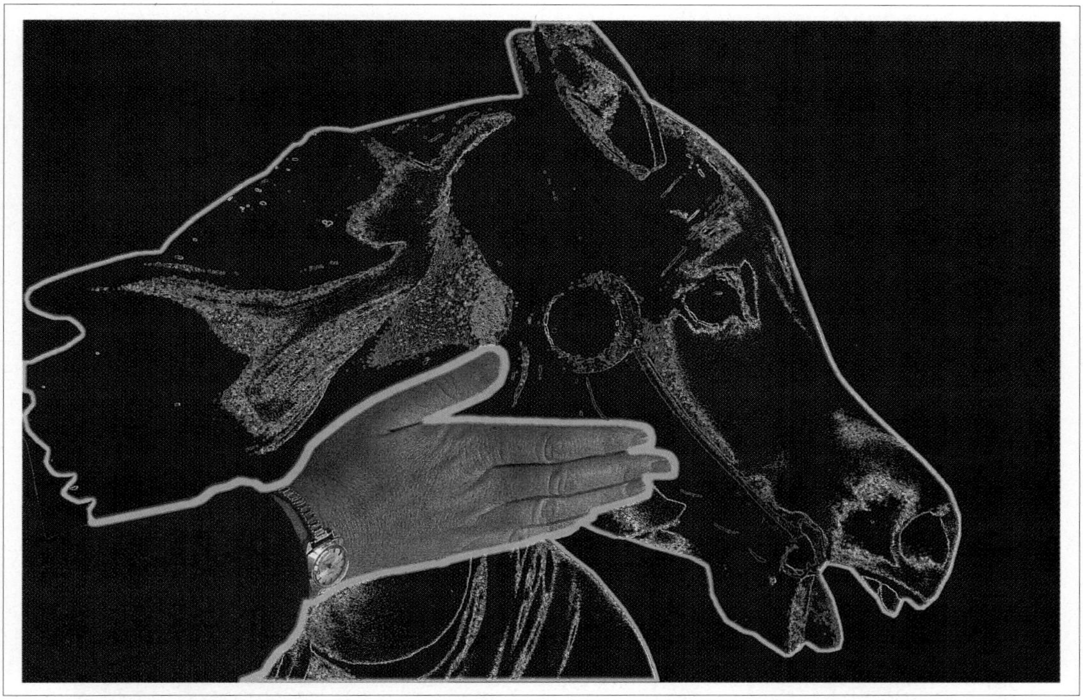

Sybil Ihrig
Magic touch

Russ DeVerniero
Sumi

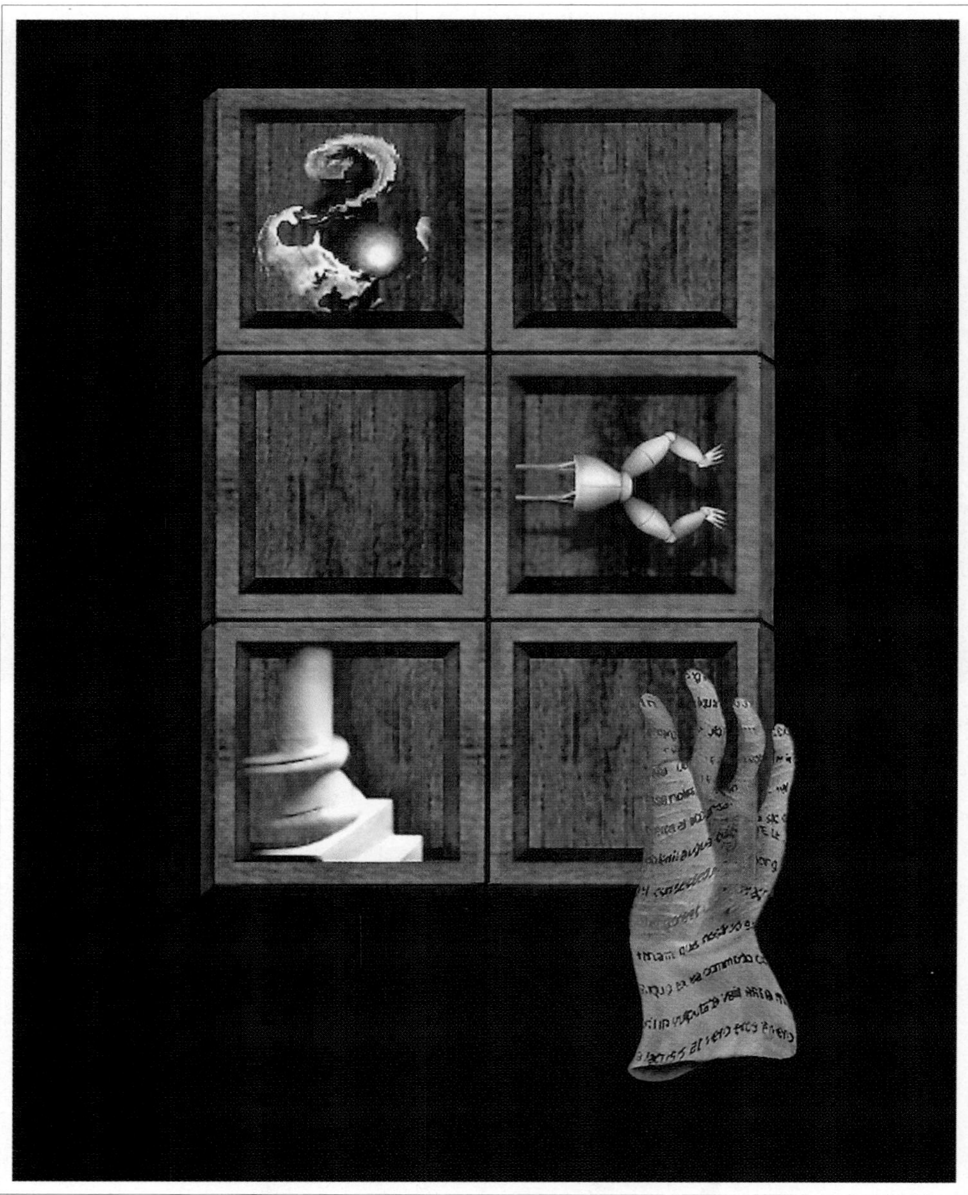

Marta Lyall

Mind over matter

Table A–1. Recommended System Configurations for Specific PhotoStyler Applications

Components	High-end color applications	Medium-budget color and Grayscale images	Grayscale images only
CPU	486-33 MHz or higher, or EISA	386-25 MHz or higher	386SX-16 MHz or higher
System memory (RAM)	16-32 Mb	8 Mb or more (4 Mb will perform slowly with True Color)	4 Mb or more
Hard drive	300+ Mb, fast access	120-200 Mb fast-access IDE	80-120 Mb fast-access
Graphics adapter	24-bit color (16 million colors)	15- or 16-bit color (32,000-64,000 colors)	256-color, high-resolution
Monitor	2-page color	17" or 1-page color	14"-17" with fine dot pitch
Image sources/ Input devices	Initial scans from a dedicated high-end drum scanner or high-resolution 24-bit slide scanner	24-bit flatbed scanner, medium-resolution slide scanner, or 24-bit color hand scanner for small images	Grayscale flatbed or hand scanner
Backup storage	Syquest for service bureaus; rewritable optical disk drives	Syquest for DTP and slide service bureaus, large-capacity tape drives	Tape drives
Output devices (proofing)	One-piece film proof from service bureau; thermal wax or thermal dye color printer	Grayscale or high-resolution b/wlaser printer; 300 dpi color printer; low-end film recorder for in-house presentations	600- or 300-dpi b/w laser printer
Output devices (final)	Dedicated color prepress system or imagesetter with irrational screen angles; film recorder at 8000 lines resolution	Imagesetter with irrational screen angles	High-resolution laser printer or imagesetter with irrational screen angles

color even as they reduce its cost. As a result, it's now possible to tackle medium-budget color and Grayscale image publishing and presentations successfully on the desktop. Typical desktop color imaging projects include corporate collateral and marketing materials, advertisements in standard trade publications, commercial magazines, medium-budget color catalogs, and in-house slide presentations. The system and peripheral requirements aren't quite as stiff as for the high-end applications, but you'll still need a fair amount of processing power so you won't be tapping your fingers waiting for PhotoStyler to complete each edit. Reasonable color fidelity is important, too. See Table A–1 for system recommendations.

The Low End: Grayscale Image Publishing

If you, your company, or your clients prefer to use PhotoStyler for Grayscale applications only, you can obtain adequate input, output, and editing performance with a less high-powered system. Even Grayscale image files can be large, though, so make certain you have at least the amount of memory and hard drive space recommended in Table A–1.

Optimizing Software Performance

Having a fast system doesn't automatically guarantee optimum PhotoStyler performance, though it helps. Performance bottlenecks can still occur unless you optimize software settings for both MS-Windows and PhotoStyler. The sections that follow offer suggestions for customizing MS-Windows and PhotoStyler to obtain peak image editing speed. First, though, let's take a look at the way PhotoStyler uses memory to manipulate and store images.

Note *Versions 1.1a and later versions of PhotoStyler feature a substantial increase in performance of filters, image display, and clipboard use. Be sure to upgrade your software to take full advantage of this increased speed.*

How PhotoStyler Uses Memory

For each image file that you open and edit, PhotoStyler uses anywhere from two to four times the amount of memory that the image file itself requires. For example, PhotoStyler may need 8-16 Mb to manipulate a single 4 Mb image file. The actual amount of memory consumed depends on how often you save the image, whether you use the Undo command in the Edit menu, and other factors that we'll detail later. As you can imagine, the amount of memory required can mount quickly if several images are open at the same time.

Where does all this memory come from? PhotoStyler uses both *system memory* (RAM) and *virtual memory* (hard drive space) to manipulate and store images. When you first open an image and begin editing it, PhotoStyler stores the image and your changes in system memory or RAM. If you run out of RAM, PhotoStyler will begin storing your edits in temporary files on the hard drive. RAM is always faster than a hard drive, so you'll more than likely notice a reduction in program speed when PhotoStyler begins storing to disk. If the hard drive in which Windows is installed runs out of space, a pop-up dialog box will appear asking you to specify additional drives (such as a network drive) for temporary storage.

MS-Windows and PhotoStyler share control of the way PhotoStyler uses system and virtual memory. Begin by optimizing Windows for use with large image files, and you'll have come a long way towards making PhotoStyler run faster.

Enhancing Windows Performance to Benefit PhotoStyler

The way you configure your MS-Windows software can impact the efficiency with which PhotoStyler runs. There are a number of things you can do to enhance your Windows performance in a way that will benefit PhotoStyler, too.

Using a Large Permanent Swap File

Unless you have an infinite amount of RAM, chances are that Photo-Styler will occasionally need to store some of your edits temporarily on the hard drive. The form that temporary storage will take depends on the mode in which you run MS-Windows. When running in real or standard mode, Windows creates a temporary swap file on the hard drive for each application (such as PhotoStyler) that you run. You don't have a great deal of control over how Windows uses these temporary swap files. But if you run Windows in 386 enhanced mode, you can choose between an expandable temporary swap file and a faster, permanent swap file.

By default, Windows creates a temporary swap file each time you run Windows in 386 enhanced mode. This swap file expands automatically as needed and vanishes when you exit Windows. A permanent swap file, on the other hand, remains on the hard drive even when Windows isn't running, and the area it occupies is always unavailable for use by non-Windows applications. This is a minor drawback when you consider the advantage of speed that a permanent swap file offers. A permanent swap file is faster than a temporary one because it occupies a *contiguous* area of space on your hard drive. Transferring data back and forth between the permanent swap file and RAM occurs more quickly because Windows doesn't have to pluck data from many separate, fragmented areas of the drive.

A permanent swap file is a good idea if you run Windows in 386 enhanced mode, have a fast hard drive (19 nanoseconds access time or less), and edit images whose average file size is 25% or more of the total amount of RAM in your system. To create a permanent swap file that will optimize the speed of virtual memory, follow these steps:

1. Erase any unneeded files from your hard drive. The more sizable the images you edit in PhotoStyler, the more space you'll want to reserve for the swap file.
2. Defragment your hard drive using a disk optimization utility such as the Speed Disk utility packaged with Norton Utilities. The size of a permanent swap file is limited by the size of the largest unfragmented segment of your hard drive.
3. Run Windows in real mode by typing **win /r** at the DOS prompt.
4. Close any applications that you normally load or run automatically upon starting Windows.
5. Choose the Run command from the File menu. When the Run dialog box appears, type **swapfile** and press Enter to access the Swapfile dialog box.
6. Adjust the size of the swap file as desired, using the Recommended swap file size list box in the Swapfile dialog box. Let the amount of RAM in your system and the average sizes of your image files guide you. Allot more space to a permanent swap file if you have less system memory than Table A–1 recommends or if you work regularly with large image files.
7. Click the Create command button to create a permanent swap file of the designated size.

Should you one day need the space occupied by the permanent swap file, you can delete the swap file from your hard drive. Just run Windows in real mode once more, run Swapfile again, and choose the delete the current swap file radio button in the Swapfile dialog box.

Caution *You can create a permanent swap file only on a local hard drive, never on a network drive. If you run Windows on a diskless workstation, you won't be able to use a permanent swap file.*

LESS = Optimizing Your Hard Drive Frequently
Whether or not you use a permanent swap file, make a habit of optimizing your hard drive often. Windows tends to fragment files much more than DOS-based applications, with the result that PhotoStyler's temporary files have to distribute themselves all over your hard drive. If you use PhotoStyler on a daily basis, optimize your hard drive at least once a week. You'll probably notice a definite improvement in PhotoStyler's speed, especially when saving files, applying filters, or filling selected areas.

Managing Disk Caches: SMARTDRV.SYS or Other Memory Managers

A large number of operations in PhotoStyler require that your system access the hard drive to look for information. If you perform the same set of operations frequently, repeated hard drive access can slow down software performance unnecessarily. Use of a *disk cache,* such as Windows's own SMARTDrive, can speed system performance by reducing the number of times that Windows and PhotoStyler must read from and write to the hard drive.

A disk cache works by setting aside an area in system memory and temporarily storing information there. If PhotoStyler requires the same information again, it pulls it out of the cache instead of off the hard drive. The same holds true if PhotoStyler needs to *write* the same information repeatedly to disk. Since system memory is faster than most hard drives, a disk cache can subtly increase the speed at which software operates.

When you installed Windows, you also installed SMARTDRV.SYS automatically. Your CONFIG.SYS file contains a statement such as:

```
device=c:\windows\smartdrv.sys 2048 512
```

However, the default configuration for SMARTDrive may not make the most of system memory for PhotoStyler's purposes. We suggest tailoring SMARTDrive in the following way:

Install SMARTDrive in Extended Memory if You Have It If you run Windows in standard or 386 enhanced mode, SMARTDrive will resize itself as needed—but only if you've installed it in extended memory. If you installed SMARTDrive in expanded memory, SMARTDrive will take up the maximum allowable space as defined in the CONFIG.SYS file. Assign SMARTDrive to extended memory and save much-needed RAM for manipulating those PhotoStyler image files.

Use a Maximum Cache Size of 1024K and a Minimum of 256K By default, Windows installs SMARTDrive with a maximum cache size of 2048K (assuming you have that much RAM available) and a minimum cache size of 512K. However, SMARTDrive becomes less efficient than fast RAM at cache sizes above 1024K. You're better off reducing maximum cache to 1024K and reserving system memory for other uses. For the same reason, a minimum cache size of 256K is preferable to the default minimum of 512K. Edit your CONFIG.SYS file and revise the SMARTDRV.SYS device line to fit these parameters.

Caution *Don't reduce the minimum cache size below 256K, or the cache may not be effective.*

Use a More Efficient Disk Caching Utility SMARTDrive is not necessarily the fastest or most efficient disk caching utility available. Several more efficient third-party disk-caching utilities are making the shareware rounds, some of them claiming 100% compatibility with MS-Windows. HyperWare's HyperDisk, for example, has received much favorable media attention as a disk-caching utility that's faster than SMARTDrive and is available for evaluation through shareware channels. Investigate for yourself to see if another utility will speed system performance with PhotoStyler. If it does, you'll probably be able to increase the maximum size of the cache to several megabytes.

Running Few Applications Concurrently

You may be an avid multitasker if you run Windows in standard or 386 enhanced mode. Every application you run, however, must be swapped out to system or virtual memory when it's not in the foreground. If you work with large image files in PhotoStyler, it's to your advantage to avoid running more than a few applications simultaneously. That way, more system and virtual memory will remain free for your edits.

Conserving System Memory and System Resources with a Program Manager Replacement

The MS-Windows Program Manager is notorious for consuming both system memory and *system resources*—the icons, menus, buttons, and other interface elements that make Windows applications so graphical. No matter how many megabytes of system memory your computer has, the amount of memory for system resources remains fixed at 128K. The greater the number of icons in your open Program Manager group windows, the smaller the share of system resources that remains for all the icons, buttons, and document windows in PhotoStyler and other applications. If you don't run many applications under Windows, this may not be a problem. But if you're a power Windows user and your desktop is cluttered with program groups and icons, you should think seriously about conserving system resources.

One easy way to conserve system resources is to minimize as many group windows as possible on your Windows desktop. This method will work for you only if you don't need to access many group windows during a Windows session. If you normally use applications from several different group windows, try combining their icons in a single group window and minimizing all the other group windows.

A more efficient way to conserve system resources is to use one of several commercially available utilities that replace the Windows Program Manager. The most well-known utility of this type is the Norton Desktop for Windows, but shareware catalogs and on-line services have additional offerings.

Enhancing PhotoStyler Performance

Within PhotoStyler itself, there are several things you can do to enhance software performance. Changing software defaults and adopting timesaving image editing habits can make a significant difference in the speed at which PhotoStyler helps you get your work done.

Using a Display Adapter with a Graphics Coprocessor and On-board Memory

Display adapters with graphics coprocessors are available for 8-bit (256 colors), 16-bit, and 24- or 32-bit color display. If your system configuration includes such a display adapter, images will take less time to redraw after every editing operation because the coprocessor will share the burden of redisplaying all those pixels. (The investment will pay off in terms of reduced wear and tear on your swap file and hard drive, too.) Display adapters with several megabytes of on-board memory will further speed image editing performance.

Disabling the Undo Command Temporarily

The status of the Undo command in the Edit menu has a strong impact on PhotoStyler's speed. By default, the Undo command is enabled through the Enable Undo option in the Preferences dialog box. Every time you alter an image document with the Undo command enabled, PhotoStyler must temporarily store the previous image data in system or virtual memory in case you change your mind. The size of this temporary file depends on the data type of the image, on the size of the original image file, and on the size of the image area that you altered. If you have several large image files open at once and are editing them all, you can deplete both system and virtual memory quickly.

Being able to change your mind about an edit is important. But if your system memory indicators in PhotoStyler's status bar take a serious dip and performance starts to slow down drastically, choose the Preferences command in the File menu and deselect the Enable Undo command temporarily. PhotoStyler's speed will improve immediately.

Once you disable the Undo command, available system and virtual memory will remain constant as you edit an image. You just won't have the chance to change your mind! You can re-enable the Undo command as soon as you once again have enough system memory to spare.

Saving Files Frequently

If you want to leave the Undo command in the Edit menu enabled, your next best option is to save image files frequently, after every edit if possible. This good work habit will preserve system and virtual memory from being consumed by unsaved edits. Save multiple versions of a file under different names if you wish, so you won't overwrite the original image file until you're sure of your changes.

Clearing the Clipboard Frequently

Although the PhotoStyler private clipboard stores cut or copied images temporarily to disk, it can slow performance if the images you store there are large or in 24-bit color. If you suspect that your PhotoStyler clipboard is clogged, choose the Clipboard command in the Edit menu and then click the Clear command button to clear the contents of the clipboard. The improvement in speed will be subtle, but noticeable if you have a limited amount of system memory.

Enabling the Don't Care about Background Quality Option

The Don't care about background quality option in the Preferences dialog box controls the speed with which PhotoStyler redraws all open images other than the active image document. When this option is disabled, PhotoStyler will redraw each inactive image perfectly, which can slow performance if more than one image document is open and not minimized. When Don't care about background quality is enabled, PhotoStyler will redraw all inactive image documents quickly, introducing color shifts. Leave this option enabled unless you need to compare two images that are open.

Limiting the Number of Open Image Documents

This is an obvious one. The higher the number of image files open at one time, the less system and virtual memory will be available. If you're running Windows in standard mode, minimizing inactive image documents to icons will save some memory. You'll save more, though, if you close all image documents that you're not using at the moment.

Speeding Creativity with Small "Preliminary" Images

Imagine yourself working on a True Color image for a large-format book cover or advertisement. Your image file is likely to occupy many megabytes of hard drive space and system memory. Even if you have 16 or more Mb of RAM and a substantial swap file, most PhotoStyler operations will take quite some time to process because of the sheer number of pixels in the image. How can you be spontaneous and creative when you'll be spending so much time waiting?

One solution is to create initial comps of your design using low-resolution scans or resampled-down versions of component images. The use of a small "preliminary" image file lets you experiment playfully with your artwork and try out a variety of techniques, unhampered by too much consciousness of the technology and its limitations. Save intermediate versions of your initial comps and keep a detailed journal of the techniques you use. Then, when you're ready to substitute a multi-megabyte scan or image file, you can reproduce the final composition without wasting time. If you have less memory or processing power than you'd like, this method of working will free you to be creative and save you time and money as well.

Using the Paste As New Document Command to Speed Editing of Limited Selection Areas

Mike Uriss, one of our contributing artists (see page 6 of the PhotoStyler Gallery), passed on a tip about a way to edit huge True Color image files speedily even when you have only a few megabytes of system memory. First, select the area you want to edit using any combination of Select Palette tools. Copy the selected area to the clipboard, and then use the Paste As New Document command in the Edit menu to paste the selected area from the clipboard into its own document window. Edit the selected area in this smaller, separate document window to conserve memory and speed the action of filters and paint tools. When you're done, copy the edited image data back to the clipboard and from there back into the original image document. If you haven't deselected the original selection area, the edited data will fit into place perfectly. No muss, no fuss.

If you have additional hints for maximizing PhotoStyler's performance, we'd like to hear about them for future editions of this book. Please contact us at Sybil Ihrig's CompuServe address: 72730,1153.

Appendix B:

How This Book Was Produced

This book was written and produced on two IBM-compatible computers. We used Microsoft Word 5.0 and Word for Windows version 2.0 to generate the text.

All artwork was created or captured on a 486/33 MHz EISA system outfitted with the Diamond Speed Star Hi-color 15-bit display adapter. We used Tiffany Plus to generate the screen captures and created line art with Corel Draw 2.0. Photographic images by Emil Ihrig were scanned using the Microtek ScanMaker 1850 and the Nikon 3500 slide scanners. We used Aldus PhotoStyler to edit both the photographic images and the screen captures.

To lay out the main body of the manuscript, we used a 386/33 MHz system running Ventura Publisher 3.0 for Windows. Fonts were the Optima and Trump Medieval families, courtesy of Linotype-Hell. Pages were output from Ventura Publisher to film with the help of an Agfa 9800 imagesetter at STATS of San Diego.

To produce the Color Section and the PhotoStyler Gallery, we imported our PhotoStyler images into Aldus PageMaker version 4.2 for the Macintosh with the help of DaynaViz' MacLinkPlus. Captions were also generated in PageMaker. Spring Accurate Color Imaging of San Diego used Aldus PrePrint to output color separations to film on an Agfa 5000 SelectSet imagesetter.

Index

A

B

C

D

G

H

I

J

K

L

M

P

R

S

T

U

V

W

Z